T0261648

The Economics of Communication and Information

The International Library of Critical Writings in Economics

Series Editor: Mark Blaug

Professor Emeritus, University of London
Professor Emeritus, University of Buckingham
Visiting Professor, University of Exeter

This series is an essential reference source for students, researchers and lecturers in economics. It presents by theme an authoritative selection of the most important articles across the entire spectrum of economics. Each volume has been prepared by a leading specialist who has written an authoritative introduction to the literature included.

A full list of published and future titles in this series is printed at the end of this volume.

The Economics of Communication and Information

Edited by

Donald M. Lamberton

Visiting Fellow
Urban Research Program
Australian National University, Canberra

THE INTERNATIONAL LIBRARY OF CRITICAL WRITINGS IN ECONOMICS

An Elgar Reference Collection
Cheltenham, UK • Brookfield, US

Published by
Edward Elgar Publishing Limited
8 Lansdown Place
Cheltenham
Glos GL50 2HU
UK

Edward Elgar Publishing Company
Old Post Road
Brookfield
Vermont 05036
US

A catalogue record for this book
is available from the British Library

Library of Congress Cataloging in Publication Data
The economics of communication and information / edited by Donald M.
  Lamberton.
    (International library of critical writings in economics : 70)
    Includes bibliographical references and index.
      1. Telecommunication—Economic aspects. 2. Information technology.
  3. Information services. I. Lamberton. D. M. (Donald McLean),
  1927–   . II. Series.
  HE7631.E354   1996
  384'.04—dc20   96–25695
                                                               CIP

ISBN 1 85898 294 4

Printed in Great Britain by Galliard (Printers) Ltd, Great Yarmouth

Contents

Acknowledgements

The editor and publishers wish to thank the authors and the following publishers who have kindly given permission for the use of copyright material.

American Economic Association for articles: Kenneth E. Boulding (1966), 'The Economics of Knowledge and the Knowledge of Economics', *American Economic Review*, **LVI** (2), May, 1–13; Jacob Marschak (1968), 'Economics of Inquiring, Communicating, Deciding', *American Economic Review*, **LVIII** (2), May, 1–18; Clifford Geertz (1978), 'The Bazaar Economy: Information and Search in Peasant Marketing', *American Economic Review*, **68** (2), May, 28–32; Kenneth J. Arrow (1985), 'Informational Structure of the Firm', *American Economic Review*, **75** (2), May, 303–7; Paul Milgrom and John Roberts (1990), 'The Economics of Modern Manufacturing: Technology, Strategy, and Organization', *American Economic Review*, **LXXX** (3), June, 511–28.

Basil Blackwell Ltd for articles: Friedrich August von Hayek (1975), 'The Pretence of Knowledge', *Swedish Journal of Economics*, **77** (4), 433–42; Eliakim Katz and Adrian Ziderman (1990), 'Investment in General Training: The Role of Information and Labour Mobility', *Economic Journal*, **100**, December, 1147–58.

Behavioral Science for article: Jacob Marschak (1965), 'Economics of Language', *Behavioral Science*, **10** (2), April, 135–40; reprinted (1974) in *Economic Information, Decision and Prediction: Selected Essays, Volume II*, Dordrecht: D. Reidel, 183–92.

Cambridge University Press for excerpt: Robert R. Alford and Edgar L. Feige (1989), 'Information Distortions in Social Systems: The Underground Economy and Other Observer–Subject–Policymaker Feedbacks', in Edgar L. Feige (ed.), *The Underground Economies: Tax Evasion and Information Distortions*, 57–79 and references.

Elsevier Science B.V. for articles: Donald M. Lamberton (1984), 'The Economics of Information and Organization', *Annual Review of Information Science and Technology*, **19**, 3–30; Stanley M. Besen (1986), 'Private Copying, Reproduction Costs, and the Supply of Intellectual Property', *Information Economics and Policy*, **2**, 5–22; Beth Krevitt Eres (1989), 'International Information Issues', *Annual Review of Information Science and Technology*, **24**, 3–32; Gunnar Eliasson (1990), 'The Firm as a Competent Team', *Journal of Economic Behavior and Organization*, **13** (3), 275–98.

Elsevier Science Ltd for articles: Donald A. Dunn (1982), 'Developing Information Policy', *Telecommunications Policy*, **6** (1), March, 21–38; Sandra Braman (1989), 'Defining Information: An Approach for Policymakers', *Telecommunications Policy*, **13** (3), September, 233–42.

International Science Journal for article: Axel Leijonhufvud (1989), 'Information Costs and the Division of Labour', *International Social Science Journal*, **120**, May, 165–76.

Johns Hopkins University Press for excerpt: Herbert A. Simon (1971), 'Designing Organizations for an Information-Rich World', in Martin Greenberger (ed.), *Computers, Communications, and the Public Interest*, 37–52.

Don Lamberton, Stuart Macdonald and Tom Mandeville for excerpt: Lawrence S. Welch (1983), 'The Technology Transfer Process in Foreign Licensing Arrangements', in Stuart Macdonald, D. McL. Lamberton and Thomas Mandeville (eds), *The Trouble with Technology: Explorations in the Process of Technological Change*, 155–68.

Lloyds Bank Plc. for article: Aubrey Silberston (1967), 'The Patent System', *Lloyds Bank Review*, **84**, January, 32–44.

Minerva for article: Stuart Macdonald (1986), 'Controlling the Flow of High-Technology Information from the United States to the Soviet Union: A Labour of Sisyphus?', *Minerva*, **XXIV** (1), Spring, 39–73.

National Academy of Sciences and the National Academy Press for excerpt: Stephen S. Roach (1986), 'Macrorealities of the Information Economy', in Ralph Landau and Nathan Rosenberg (eds), *The Positive Sum Strategy: Harnessing Technology for Economic Growth*, 93–103.

National Bureau of Economic Research Inc. for excerpt: Kenneth J. Arrow (1962), 'Economic Welfare and the Allocation of Resources for Invention', *The Rate and Direction of Inventive Activity: Economic and Social Factors*, 609–26.

Oxford University Press for article: Margaret Bray (1985), 'Rational Expectations, Information and Asset Markets: An Introduction', *Oxford Economic Papers*, **37**, 161–95.

Oxford University Press Inc. for excerpt: Reiner Stäglin (1989), 'Toward an Input–Output Subsystem for the Information Sector', in Ronald E. Miller, Karen R. Polenske and Adam Z. Rose (eds), *Frontiers of Input–Output Analysis*, 65–78.

Plenum Publishing Corporation for article: T.A. Marschak (1980), 'The Best Use of "Information Budgets" in Purposive Organizations: A Finite Approach', *International Journal of Policy Analysis and Information Systems*, **4** (1), March, 37–46.

RAND for article: Richard R. Nelson (1981), 'Assessing Private Enterprise: An Exegesis of Tangled Doctrine', *Bell Journal of Economics*, **12** (1), Spring, 93–111.

Reed Publishing and Patricia Glass Schuman for article: Patricia Glass Schuman (1982), 'Information Justice', *Library Journal*, **107** (11), 1 June, 1060–66.

Gerhard Rosegger for his own article: (1991), 'Advances in Information Technology and the Innovation Strategies of Firms', *Prometheus*, **9** (1), June, 5–20.

University of Chicago Press for articles: Nathaniel H. Leff (1984), 'Externalities, Information Costs, and Social Benefit-Cost Analysis for Economic Development: An Example from Telecommunications', *Economic Development and Cultural Change*, **32** (2), January, 255–76; Robert M. Townsend (1989), 'Currency and Credit in a Private Information Economy', *Journal of Political Economy*, **97** (6), 1323–44.

Robert Wright, Senior Editor at the New Republic in Washington, for his own article: (1986), 'The Information Age: Phantom of the Factory', *The Sciences*, **26** (4), July/August, 11–14.

Every effort has been made to trace all the copyright holders but if any have been inadvertently overlooked the publishers will be pleased to make the necessary arrangement at the first opportunity.

In addition the publishers wish to thank the Library of the London School of Economics and Political Science, the Photographic Unit of the University of London Library, and the Marshall Library, Cambridge University, for their assistance in obtaining these articles.

Introduction: 'Threatened Wreckage' or New Paradigm?

Donald M. Lamberton

Reflections

It is not often that an editor has the opportunity to update, expand and give new direction to a volume of readings now 25 years old, so I am grateful to Mark Blaug as Series Editor and Edward Elgar as publisher for allowing me to do just this. I suspect my 1971 Penguin Books modern economics readings, *Economics of Information and Knowledge*, was the first anthology in this field; or perhaps I should say, as the first anthology, it was an attempt to stake out a new territory which has now largely been appropriated by the mainstream, but which has also been extended to embrace, first, the process of communication and, latterly, computation.

In the event, this is a very different volume. Only four of the original articles survive; each can be regarded as a classic and one as testimony to the enduring nature of one of the oldest economic policy instruments – the patent system.

There are, I believe, good reasons for this turnover. First, while economists have always conceded that information and knowledge are important, in modern times information has become, as James Boyle argues, 'the problem case in which the internal tensions of the discipline come to the surface' (1992, 1444, n.73; for bibliography, see Part IX of this volume, pp. 535ff). Just why this has been the case will no doubt be clarified by historians in due course but, for the present, we might say, with the *New York Times*, that the 1980s was the decade of information acceleration. There was a sense of unusually rapid change in the interrelated technologies of communication, information and computation; a shifting of investment and consumption expenditure to these new outputs, as well as growing interdependence between nations that conjured up the popular but imprecise terms 'globalization' and 'the global village'.

These changes stemmed in part from the continuing advance of scientific and technological knowledge, but also from the dawning realization that organizational change was a necessary accompaniment and also (to an as yet unknown extent) amenable to economic analysis. Further impetus was given by the great expectations being generated: hopes that the new technologies would boost economic growth, redress inequities – and yield enormous profits.

A second reason for the turnover of articles is that the selection has tended to take on an historical character, reflecting my own learning progress and shifting interests. While this may have made the contents somewhat idiosyncratic, it should be to the advantage of readers that the great bulk of the material is drawn from the 1980s and 1990s. Furthermore, in the course of that learning, I have been increasingly persuaded that interdisciplinary effort is needed in tackling the role of information. Accordingly, the selection of these readings, which are intended primarily for those interested in economics, has endeavoured to provide linkages between economics and such 'disciplines of information' (Machlup and Mansfield 1983) as information science, communication studies, organizational science and even psychology and cognitive science. Only limited success can be hoped for, both because the boundaries between economics tribes and related social science disciplines are so numerous and because their occupants are so entrenched behind their barricades.

In all this, it will of course seem to the reader that reality is distorted and everything made into 'information'. A defence of emphasizing 'the new', was offered by the composer Stockhausen, who argued that 'the old' must not be allowed ascendancy:

> So you should give much less of what is known, in proportion to what is new, in a given context in order to create a balance between the two: let's say two or three seconds of a well-known motif or theme is enough to balance forty, fifty, or even more of unfamiliar, new sound formulas. And the new sound formulas must also be very sharp, not only background or sustained notes and chords or clusters. You see, a cluster is a very imprecise thing, it's just a band of sound. And if from within a cluster, you bring out a precise melody, it will stick in your mind forever because the cluster isn't strong, it's just a background (quoted in Cott 1974, 34).

The precise melody in our case is to be provided by information-theoretic considerations.

The title of this Introduction is intended to imply that the shift of focus to communication and information has profound implications for economics. Should we foresee 'threatened wreckage ... of the greater part of economic theory', as Hicks feared if the assumption of perfect competition were abandoned (1939, 83–5)? Hicks thought the 'getaway' of assuming that for the most part markets did not differ greatly from perfectly competitive markets was 'worth trying'. Following his lead, economists have succeeded in making competition a very flexible concept, culminating in the recent argument that there can not only be competition *in* markets but competition *for* markets – even if that creates a monopoly.

Or should we seek to modernize the neoclassical edifice? Should we look to the alternative of a new Information Age economics paradigm? Shackle argued that when 'economic theory elects to bring in imperfect competition and to recognize uncertainty, there is an end to the meaning of general equilibrium. Economics thereafter is the description, piece by piece, of a collection of fragments. These fragments fit together into a brilliant, arrestingly suggestive mosaic, but they do not compose a pattern of unique, inevitable order. One vital aspect of the process of theoretical innovation is its destructive aspect' (1967, 294–5). If this is correct, the introduction of informational considerations in the new economics will open the way for theorizing about change, growth and institutions. Heavy emphasis on the communication process, with all its non-static features, will be needed if 'precise melodies' are to be heard above the familiar sounds trying to ensure that new developments simply serve the purposes of traditional static theory.

I believe that the realization of the full potential of information economics is timely in societies facing major, continuing problems of adjustment to new technologies, new industries, new trading relationships, new forms of organization and even new forms of work. On a piecemeal basis, much can be done with seeming precision. However, the precision and determinateness of more aggregative and dynamic models will be found to be another matter; a price must be paid for such enrichment. The structural and behavioural changes conveyed by the term Information Age require the economist to leave the shelter of his Ouspenskian 'perpetual now'. The economics that survives will no doubt be less amenable to mathematical precision, and its policy counterpart will need to be more tolerant of the role of judgement.

This innovation process continues. Perhaps the final paper in this volume points up the threatening consequences, but at the same time probes into the furthest corners and deepest foundations of economic and social organization. The 1965 paper by Jacob Marschak, 'Economics of Language', may seem oddly placed in the final section headed 'New Directions', but little has been done to follow his lead. In a world in which it is difficult to escape globalization hype, the dominant economic consideration remains coordination. Economic integration has shifted attention to communication and information technologies, to the standardization of messages and protocols, and there is renewed interest in and successful pressures for strengthened intellectual property rights. In these circumstances, language illustrates very well the bind in which national cultures are placed. Language is an integral part of that amalgam of community of interests, creativity and communication processes that allow the society and economy to function – it is organizational capital. On the other hand, from a wider perspective, language separates, adds to costs, and so contributes to communication failure and conflict with asymmetries and inequities.

A 1971 Perspective

To the best of my knowledge, the first bibliography of information economics was that compiled by Harold Olsen, School of Library and Information Services, University of Maryland, and published in January 1971. For him the topic was of growing interest to the information community and to economists: the term 'information economics' meant the concepts and tools of economics as they apply to information activities. Over 300 items were included. The coverage began with theory and then turned to market and non-market organizational configurations of economic activity. Then followed decision processes as in budgeting and management; sector studies; innovation, entrepreneurship and incentives; planning; forecasting; social and psychological aspects; documentation and administration; information science and library research; copyright; user studies; evaluation; and development and automation.

My anthology entitled *Economics of Information and Knowledge* was published in the same year. While I consider myself an economist, I am currently located in an interdisciplinary Urban Research Program which, in a recent annual report, states that I have been working on information systems. To me there is no inconsistency between these labels; from a market economy perspective, I agree with Fritz Machlup – a pioneer to whom we are all much indebted – that the market mechanism is 'the largest and most effective information system in existence' (1979, 113). If I turn to non-market forms of organization, I find that information as a resource, the need for coordination and the adoption of new information technologies (such as electronic data interchange) confirm that these organizations too qualify as information systems.

For my 1971 readings I selected papers around several themes: economic organization; information and efficiency; policy; international dimensions; business planning; and, as a final essay, Shubik's 'Information, Rationality, and Free Choice in a Future Democratic Society' which seems even more relevant today. I was attempting to redress the neglect of information in economics, but at the same time I pointed to its destructive consequences for central ideas like optimality and equilibrium. Then, as now, I did not think it possible to abandon the traditions of economic thought as some of my more radically-minded colleagues wish to do. Rather I thought in terms of trying to see how far we could modify and extend economics to accommodate the role of information, a task I do not think we have finished largely because the work has taken us over many boundaries into other disciplines. We began by using results from other disciplines and moved on to joint ventures. We are possibly well on the way to the next stage of creating a new discipline of information science which accommodates economic interactions.

Rubinstein (1990, xi) has described the 1970s as the era of economics of information. His judgement, probably reflecting a game theory interpretation of the scope of developments, prompts two lines of thought: first, while the economics of information may have come of age and gained a measure of recognition in the 1970s, there was an earlier stage of development. In the very passage in which Adam Smith refers to the 'invisible hand', he touches on such informational phenomena as risk aversion and imperfect risk markets. There were also significant contributions from many precursors including – in alphabetical order – Arrow, Boulding, Kochen, Marschak, Shackle and Stigler.

Secondly, the 1970s dating leads to my belief that this component of the economics discipline has a future. Only a pessimist would predict its early demise in view of the progress of the last three decades: from 'a slum dwelling in the town of economics' (Stigler 1961, 61) to become the 'general framework ... for formulating any problems about the efficient allocation of resources' (Weizsäcker 1984, 1085), 'a fundamental and lasting contribution to economic analysis' (Stiglitz 1985, 21–2) and 'a remarkable achievement in economic theory' (Green 1985, 178), with 'issues of information now occupy[ing] centre stage' (Shin 1989, 864–5) instead of being banished to footnotes. Most recently there has even been a claim that 'information economics has transformed economic theory' (Morduch 1993, 931).

Make no mistake about the clarity of the vision and the extent of agreement. Machlup was at pains to show the diversity of beliefs, their wide scope and popular misconceptions. He listed the following definitions of the economics of information:

i.   It deals with the optimization of a communication system; it provides a benefit-and-cost analysis for alternative organizations.
ii. It is a merger of decision theory, operations research, and team theory, all concerned with management of large organizations of business and government.
iii. It analyzes the problem of the decentralized use of widely dispersed information, its possible centralization for application in central planning; it compares the results of free markets with those of centralized decision-making.
iv. It deals with the creation and utilization of new technology; the incentives for research, development, invention, innovation, diffusion, and utilization of new knowledge.
v.   It analyzes the consequences of variable uncertainty and asymmetrically distributed information for prices, quantities, and qualities of products and services in various markets.

vi. It provides a statistical analysis of the allocation of resources to the creation and dissemination of knowledge and information and, in particular, measures the size of the 'information' sector relative to the gross national product (1984, 6, n.2).

Quite rightly, he added that all these were aspects of the whole, although none could claim to be the sole concern.

Have we really made progress? Perhaps it is a tribute to the tolerance of the economics profession that the diversity remains. To many the economics of information deals with informational asymmetry. Others would identify it with game theory which has taught us about 'the infinite subtleties of rational behaviour' (Blaug 1994, 128) and the 'informational structure and learning process on which equilibrium outcomes do in fact depend' (Bianchi and Moulin 1991, 194). Others would point to information sector studies, rather traditional analyses of information industries, and the information policy initiative; yet others would show that they have assimilated the economics of information into traditional cost analysis or various subdisciplines like regional or health economics.

In the end, a judgement about progress depends on one's methodological position. How important is theoretical as opposed to empirical progress – 'a deeper grasp of the inner springs of economic behaviour and hence of the operations of the economic system' (Blaug 1994, 116–17)? Some will then put forward the symmetry thesis: that explanation is simply prediction written backwards. I confess to being ill at ease with the extremes of reliance on prediction. However, we should note that the most fully articulated economic models of perfect competition with perfect knowledge would seem to predict a zero allocation of resources to information activities, which I think we would all agree is far from reality.

To ask why the 1970s was the occasion for the emergence of new thinking about the role of information is to elaborate upon my earlier remarks. We might distinguish three features of the situation. First, think of the picture of the world we see through our viewing window. Major technological and social changes have added to the distortions. Second, our disciplinary spectacles filter out quite a lot of what is actually out there to be seen. Third, changes internal to our particular disciplines are also taking place. As Boyle's argument implies, the reason for the earlier marginalization of information can be traced back to the treatment of interest and profit in the history of economic thought. When ideas about the one have seemed firm and rigorous, those about the other have assumed vague proportions. Both concepts are intimately linked with information. Furthermore, in recent times the major controversies and critiques of mainstream economics have revolved around the role of information and strategic behaviour. I expect these three features will remain with us and so our deliberations, research, management and policy efforts will have to make allowance for such distorted views.

What have been the major thrusts in our efforts to gain a deeper grasp of the role of information? I shall now comment on several of these developments.

Informational Asymmetry

I mentioned earlier the implicit informational structure and learning process involved when a market situation adapts to change and reaches an equilibrium state, as when there is a bumper crop or a Barings' financial crisis. We can contrast several scenarios. First, everyone knows everything. This is perhaps a strange assumption to make and yet it occurs in textbooks and sometimes in day-to-day activities. Second, we can assume that there is limited information but no asymmetries: we are all equally ignorant. Third, we can go further and assume both limited information and unequal distribution of that information. We have then moved through these stages to an approximation of the real world of strategies. Variations on these models are endless.

I do not intend to look at each of these models; rather I wish to pose questions about what is omitted even when the door to asymmetry is opened. History matters or, in the jargon of this generation (thanks, I suppose, to Paul David), events are said to be path-dependent. So we should ask how did the asymmetry come about? What business strategies, for example, does it prompt? There are many possibilities: industrial espionage, R&D, merger, lobbying for government subsidies, strategic alliances, creation of a business intelligence department, or administrative efforts to ensure that information generated internally and that obtained from external sources blend together instead of remaining like water and oil.

Then we also need to take account of the costs of information. Not only is all information costly, but the cost of producing information is independent of the scale on which it is used. As a consequence, the role of information leads to pervasive economies of scale. Information-intensity seems to favour a large rather than a small scale. Each uncertain strategy comes up against the limits of affordability. It is no surprise, therefore, that firms and individuals tend to hedge their bets and adopt a mixture of strategies.

In relation to asymmetry, I ask you to fix firmly in mind that we have neglected the capability of *using* information. It is for this reason that the economics of information must be inextricably tied to the economics of communication. In the jargon of the mid-1990s, it might be said that those who cannot 'surf on the Net' will be left behind in the technological and economic race.

Information and Growth

The second major development concerns the contribution of information or knowledge to economic growth and development. Few seem to question the importance of this role. As Lionel Robbins once observed:

> In the last analysis the difference between the economic potential of the Stone Age and the twentieth century is a difference of range of relevant techniques and information (1969, 83).

In recent years this view has been rediscovered, encouraging us to think that the mystery of economic growth has been solved; a new orthodoxy is discernible. To the neoclassical theory's labour and capital has been added another factor of production: information or knowledge. This raises the return on investment, and the surplus so created can meet the costs involved and also fund further investment in information.

This rediscovery hardly does justice to earlier thinkers. Let me take just one illustration. Alfred Marshall wrote a century ago that ideas,

> whether those of art or science, or those embodied in practical appliances, are the most 'real' of the gifts that each generation receives from its predecessors. The world's material wealth would

be replaced quickly if it were destroyed, but the ideas by which it was made retained. If however the ideas were lost, but not the material wealth, then that would dwindle and the world would go back to poverty (Marshall 1890, 780).

It is interesting that a century later, Romer was echoing Marshall's thoughts:

> To see how important our ideas are compared with our more familiar tangible goods, imagine that all man-made objects other than books were about to be destroyed. Ask yourself how long would it take people to recover their current standard of living. Now compare this with a thought experiment in which our objects are preserved, but all books are destroyed and all the knowledge stored on our computers and our brains is wiped out – even fundamental ideas like the alphabet or the place system for recording numbers. In this second case we would still have useful objects such as houses, but our economic prospects would be grim (1993, 67).

Those who read this book should not need reminding of the crucial importance of communication and information. We might however infer from the 100-year gap between Marshall and Romer that persuading other audiences to this view of economic growth has been a slow process.

Where does this leave the economic growth mystery? Need we simply add a further factor of production to the old analytical framework? I think not. A role for information is not new. What have been missing are the links, the interactions, between information and economic activity. The information must be operative; there must be a capability of using information in purposeful ways. The Information Age demands that we have the means to utilize information through machines, through organizations and through our thinking and actions. We must therefore give attention to the design of organizations, which means allocating resources to that activity. We grant patents to new methods of manufacture but not to new ways of organizing, yet both are necessary to innovation. Current law and economics controversies about property rights in software may well mark a transition phase, with a blurring of the boundaries of both software and organization.

Organizational Capital

The third development I wish to consider is organizational capital: the mix of institutional arrangements, behavioural patterns and accumulated information that enables us to make use of information. The old view was that profit was the reward for uncertainty borne by the entrepreneur; the new view of profit is of organizational capital, a variable in the process. It is created by investment, even if not recognized as such in accounting practices of either the business world or national income statisticians. Differences in organizational capital can explain the comparative advantage of individual firms and, perhaps, of nations. In some countries we are accustomed to hearing that, in spite of good science, their industries fail to innovate. This failure could be a consequence of inappropriately designed organizations.

This design task has been left very largely to management specialists. I am inclined to think that this is a mistake. If we need an R&D industry to create the knowledge of science and technology, should we not also apply that approach to the design of organization? Here, as in other developments, I suggest that more attention be given to the role of communication and information. How might this be tackled?

The term information infrastructure has been popularized of late, in part by the US National II (information infrastructure) agenda and its extension to the 'global' stage. I propose to analyse information and infrastructure separately and then try to bring the pieces together and identify what is implied for the economics of communication and information.

A Taxonomy of Information

In the Information Age we should extend our thinking beyond information about other production and consumption to emphasize information about communication and information. I believe this calls for a new approach to a taxonomy of information.

Recent study of work-related and social telephone calls finds that they differ in importance and have different elasticities of demand. This illustrates a neglected direction for empirical research in the economics of information. Earlier GNP-style sector studies served a purpose by focusing on the aggregate of information activities. They were built upon an all-purpose definition of information as that which reduces uncertainty. This tended to translate into 'information as lubricating oil'. All decisions were thought to be wiser; the economy could be fine-tuned and adapted more closely to what consumers demanded. Eventually the elimination of what was called organizational slack would win the approval of both 'just-in-time' practitioners and economists alike.

This simple approach to information stands in sharp contrast to the way we have recorded the activities of business and government in our industrial or even our agricultural economies. Think, for example, of the rich detail available in terms of labour, prices, outputs and trade.

This disaggregation was not fostered by information sector efforts in the Machlup, Porat and OECD tradition which was based on national accounting and input/output (I/O) statistics. Occupations were grouped as information producers, information processors, information distributors and information infrastructure workers (e.g., in telecommunications). The categories adopted for information goods and services were hard to reconcile with occupational data. A consultant might produce many different kinds of information, just as a clerical worker might process a similar range; moreover, telecommunications facilities transmit almost without regard to content.

Some potentially important dichotomies have emerged, such as work-related vs social information mentioned above. Mainstream economics would suggest a distinction between investment in information and expenditures on current use, either as an input in production or for consumption purposes. The cost of information will depend upon the frequency of observation, its static or dynamic nature and the frequency with which it has to be updated, the degree of accuracy required, the promptness with which the information has to be made available and the universality of its distribution.

One dichotomy deserves special attention. I refer to the distinction between codifiable information and tacit knowledge. What is codifiable may seem fairly straightforward, e.g., who is to occupy which seat on a 747 flight, or the meter reading for electricity consumption or the details of a banking transaction. Modern electronic systems cope well with such information. We must be careful, however. A complex research question can be stated clearly, translated into a foreign language and despatched to the other side of the world. At that destination, research might be undertaken and the results sent back, understood and used. The success of the operation is possible only because of additional features of the system – e.g., the language, established and shared research traditions, possibly personal contacts, a stock of information – many things which together make up the infrastructure. Also we should perhaps look back to earlier stages of the research process, back to the inquiring period when interest in the problem was formed and action taken to shape the research question. Could all those steps have been taken with a depersonalized system, detached from a work context?

I have thus come closer to an attempted definition of tacit knowledge: knowledge that requires personal contacts and is gained only through participation in ongoing activities. Its absence is manifest in innumerable cases of failure in technology transfer: the 'message' is received but the meaning is missed because there is no appreciation of the context. This may be where the path-dependency of many phenomena can best be detected.

I have mentioned the I/O approach which held out promise but failed to deliver. It would have been fascinating to develop an information version of the transactions tables, with coordinates of the points between which information flows took place in the I/O matrix of the economy. As it is, we are pretty much limited to a few descriptions of the regional patterns of telecommunications. How much better had we been able to study where intellectual property is generated and where applied; where political campaign information is created and disseminated; even where advertising originates and later appears. And understanding the communication processes involved in those information flows and their implications for resource allocation would have been equally exciting.

But to go a few steps further with the 'characteristics' approach to information, look at Harry Goldwin's 1950s list of the fundamental elements of an information system which was resurrected a few years ago (Penniman 1989). His ideal system was intended to enable the user to

- receive the desired information
- at the time required
- in the briefest form
- in order of importance
- with any necessary auxiliary information
- with reliability indicated (which implied critical analysis)
- with the source identified
- automatically (little effort)
- without undesired or untimely information, and with the
- assurance that no response meant it doesn't exist.

I should like to pay tribute to the Canadian IDRC (International Development Research Centre) programme which has challenged us to go back to fundamentals in our attempts to grasp the profound transformations being precipitated by the events of the information revolution. Instead of once again asserting that information plays a very important role, the IDRC project has posed questions about how information contributes to the development process. It too has examined the characteristics of information and made use of an I/O framework (Menou 1993).

In her Foreword to Michel Menou's book, *Measuring the Impact of Information on Development*, which reports on the IDRC work, Martha Stone points out that evaluation of the various interventions that have sought to strengthen the capability to manage and exploit information resources has usually been related to short-term outputs. To do better than this, we have to cast the net more widely and that requires investigating the other 'I', namely infrastructure.

Infrastructure

This is a nebulous and overworked construct. Recent economic research has focused on a narrow public sector ownership version, including such things as transportation facilities, water and sewage lines and communication systems. I suspect that this limited scope is preferred very largely because of the measurement problems encountered if we try to include human capital, R&D capital and the like, which are found in both public and private sectors.

Policy debate and popular discussion have taken the same track. Infrastructure has become a powerful metaphor, with images of roads and bridges; dams and power stations; ports, airports and teleports; tall and smart buildings; and now information superhighways. It is not a very helpful construct. Consider a recent advertisement for battery-powered, desktop-sized UHF digital multiplex radiotelephone systems. The equipment was shown being dropped by a colourful parachute in 'the middle of nowhere', a green valley with snow-capped mountains in the background. The advert was labelled 'Instant Infrastructure'. It could be a useful exercise to number the elements of infrastructure necessary to make the parachute drop possible and productive. Perhaps the word infrastructure has been so widely adopted because it tends to generate daydreams of handsome profits and has served as a rallying point for lobbyists pursuing substantial public funds.

Let me juxtapose the parachute drop of a UHF system and another element of infrastructure, namely property rights. Property rights are necessary for the functioning of the economy. But if they become our definition of infrastructure, why stop with property rights? Why not include all the other economic, political and cultural institutions which are also necessary to the functioning of the economy?

In the case of telecommunications, customers with regional requirements are usually presented with a patchwork of interconnected, but not fully operable, transmission networks which are referred to as the telecommunications infrastructure. To this is added an alternative infrastructure that could be available from utility companies and cable television operators if regulatory barriers to these potential entrants to the telecommunications industry were removed. This is a far cry from the infrastructure envisaged in such futurist documents as the US National Telecommunications and Information Administration's *Agenda for Action*. It chose an expansive meaning which encompassed physical components, the information itself, applications and software, network standards and transmission codes, as well as people both as operators and educators. Note that while the NTIA stopped short of listing institutions like property rights, developments in the World Trade Organization and GII Commission have clearly indicated the dominant role of the market and related institutions.

It appears that the main elements omitted from most discussions of infrastructure are (i) information stocks and flows, (ii) human capital, and (iii) organizational capital. Information has long been recognized as capital, with expenditures on it being expected to generate future flows of income (Lamberton 1965). Both as elements of capital and an essential part of the infrastructure, we need to think more carefully about the different kinds of information that exist. Hence, the key role of a taxonomy of information.

If society is to have the capability of information-handling in all its complexity, organizational capital must be the necessary complement of human capital. Already information-handling is the dominant claim on resources: it is this circumstance that justifies the Information Age terminology.

The trouble is that the mix of organizational capital (which exists in both public and private sectors) and human capital has not only been omitted from discussions of infrastructure; it has also been omitted from economic theory. This goes back to the point about 'destructive consequences' made earlier. As Teece *et al.* point out: 'To admit that organizational/economic competence may be scarce undermines a very large body of neoclassical economic theory' (1994, n.17, 19). That body of doctrine has been resistant to this challenge. It was pointed out over 30 years ago that inputs of organization and information were variable but that firms lacked knowledge of their optimum combination (Lamberton 1965, Ch.II).

If infrastructure is capital, we ought to ponder the words of Schumpeter who said that the stock of capital

> is neither homogeneous nor an amorphous heap. Its various parts complement each other in a way that we readily understand as soon as we hear of buildings, equipment, raw materials and consumers' goods. Some of these parts must be available before we can operate others; and various sequences or lags between economic actions impose themselves and further restrict our choices; and they do this in ways that differ greatly according to the composition of the stock we have to work on (1953, 631).

Schumpeter wisely went on to decry the notion of 'a unitary or all-purpose concept of capital' (632). I agree wholeheartedly. I wish to include an information-handling capability and information itself as kinds of capital, and in particular I caution against a 'unitary and all-purpose concept' of information. When we hear of electronic books and journals, databases, satellites, fibre and World-Wide Web, can we say that we understand their complementary relationships? Can we appraise the various sequences and lags imposed by modern information technology? The answer must be a resounding NO. The 'technology push' has been so powerful that we have not been probing in the way that the IDRC is now attempting.

It is therefore difficult to give precise meaning to the words 'optimum utilization of information'. Machlup concluded that '[i]nstead of asking for the *optimum optimorum*, the very best of all possible alternative actions, social and private, we may, more modestly, resolve that in all actions that we decide to take, we try to act intelligently, with full consideration of the pertinent knowledge at hand and of the pertinent knowledge available at reasonable cost' (1982, 10). Depending upon one's inclinations, this might be seen as supporting, even embracing, theories of rational expectations, satisficing behaviour or a conjunction of the economics of information and evolutionary modes of analysis.

Is Information a Public Good?

This discussion of capital holds the key to the vexed question: Is information a public good? The answer will depend on whether we are dealing with 'all-purpose' information or are being more practical, recognizing that there are many kinds of information.

Many things have been proffered as public goods: the financial structure; income transfers from rich to poor; the prevention of the sale of poor quality goods or worthless stocks and shares; American Express, nationalism, sociability and ignorance all come to mind. Mentioned more often than anything else has been information. The librarian argues for free, publicly available libraries; the scientist expects access to books, journals and the Net and advocates the free flow of scientific knowledge nationally and internationally.

There are problems even in the library case. One test of a public good is that if the benefit goes to one person, does it go to all? If a good is sold, people who do not buy it should nevertheless be able to consume it. There is also a critical mass aspect: as the size of a network increases, costs go down as use extends. But there are assumptions tucked away relating to both capacity and externalities. There is a great deal of difference between a large well-equipped reading room and a small, inadequately-equipped, crowded space.

Information has traditionally been regarded as a public good. If it is made available to one, others can use it. Additional users will average down costs. It is an indivisible commodity. Since the costs of transmitting and of copying are low, it is difficult to appropriate the benefits. In the discussion of public goods, equal supply for all consumers has always been emphasized. I feel that inequality of demand has been given insufficient attention. This kind of inequality links directly with the capability of using information. Arrow once remarked that '[i]nformation exchange is costly not so much because it is hard to transmit but because it is difficult to receive' (1975, 18). These matters lead us back to questions about capability, infrastructure and different kinds of information.

And there is a closely related matter: externalities are mentioned so often, we might assume that the boundaries which determine whether an effect is inside or outside are brightly painted, high fences. But no: 'The externality of external costs derives neither from the fundamentals of economics nor from the nature of the business nor from technology. It derives from the legal system' (Katz 1986, 171) which should be categorized under infrastructure.

This being so, our thinking about the roles of communication and information is very much intertwined with some big questions. We must ask about the interactions, the innumerable intersecting forces, which give rise to the historical event, and about the other elements that Engels said (475–7) had to be allowed to come into their rights. We must ask about individualism and collective behaviour; questions that a market-based economics does its best to avoid. We have made some progress by developing an economics of information that explores both market phenomena and internal organization. We have to go further in terms of communication and information. Kenneth Arrow has declared his concern with the question of information-gathering in both private and collective spheres (1987, 242). My hope is that, by focusing on a taxonomy of information and relating it to infrastructure, we can make further progress.

The expectations and hopes I expressed in 1971 would appear to have stood up to the test of time rather well. The book has made its presence felt in relation to some of the topics named: consumer theory, welfare economics, economic development and oligopoly.

I speculated then that it might be an important means of bridging the gap between micro and macroeconomics, but here the ongoing conflict is revealed. On the one hand, evolutionary economics is working towards that goal while, on the other, rational expectations theorists have turned the clock back to the days of perfect information dominance, with the decision-maker being a 'superior statistician' and a 'superior econometrician' to boot.

Taking a broad view, I emphasized that information and knowledge problems were embedded within the corpus of economic analysis itself, whereas new subjects like health and defence economics were applications of the tools of economic analysis to a particular area of interest. The 1971 papers reflected 'an attempt to see what extent the customary conceptual framework of economics permits an adequate treatment of the role of information and knowledge in economic activity. The conclusion might be drawn that the traditional equilibrium mode of thought is not well-suited to the analysis of the processes by which information and knowledge are created, diffused, stored and used' (12).

The Articles in this Volume

It would be quite unnecessary to catalogue the contents of the 31 papers reprinted in this volume. Part I, entitled 'Overview', opens with Sandra Braman who offers definitions of information as a resource, a commodity, a perception of pattern and a constitutive force in society. She draws attention to the lack of reliable data about what kinds of returns can be expected from investment in information infrastructure. In so doing, she raises the essential difficulty with the notion of the optimum utilization of information. This lies in the absence of specification concerning who is utilizing it, for whom, for what, for how much, and (most critically) what is the nature of the information under discussion. Axel Leijonhufvud next argues that the costs of processing, transmitting and storing information have taken over the role that transportation played in economic development for so long. Robert Wright then critiques the control revolution thesis advanced by sociologist James Beniger, for whom artificial intelligence, the proliferation of microcomputers and the latest telecommunications are but additional phases in that revolution.

Part II, 'Information, Organization and Efficiency', begins with Lamberton who traces the emergence of information economics: the theoretical contributions; the shift of focus from information as a market additive to information and the information-handling capability as organizational resources; information sector studies; trade aspects, and information policy. In Chapter 5, Richard Nelson attacks the twin theorems of welfare economics as an insubstantial basis for the faith of many economists in private enterprise as a good way of organizing production. The enterprise form of organization is not guaranteed to provide administrative parsimony, responsiveness and innovativeness. Social anthropologist Clifford Geertz follows on by emphasizing the importance of information in peasant marketing where the means to knowledge already available in industrial and centralized economics is lacking: 'information is poor, scarce, maldistributed, inefficiently communicated, and intensely valued'. Stanley Besen concludes the section by exploring the impact of technological advances that have reduced copying costs and thereby generated claims of severe harm to owners of intellectual property, concluding that those claims may have been overstated.

In Part III, 'Macrorealities', four papers introduce some aspects of the information economy from a broader perspective. Stephen Roach begins by examining the trends of the US information economy and its high technology spending. He identifies 1983 as the point at which the stock of high-tech capital per information worker reached relative parity with its basic industrial counterpart. He poses questions about the dark side of the information economy: the extent to which improvements in living standards might turn out to be built on a foundation of foreign-produced and foreign-owned capital. In Chapter 9, Reiner Stäglin takes up the task of providing an input/output subsystem for the primary information sector, i.e., 'goods and services which intrinsically convey information (such as books) or which are directly useful in its production, processing, or distribution (such as computers) ... transacted on established markets'.

Robert Townsend next analyses a situation with private information, spatial separation and limited communication, in which both a currency-like object and more standard named credits are used. The credits require that agents have known trading histories, whereas the currency-object can be used among relative strangers. In Chapter 11, Margaret Bray provides an introduction to the role of information in asset markets by drawing on the rational expectations hypothesis. She contends that all recent progress in the economics of information has been built on that hypothesis.

Part IV, 'Management and Technology', begins with Herbert Simon's delightful, optimistic discussion of the problems of how to design organizations effectively for an information-rich world. Gunnar Eliasson then presents a theory of the firm as a competent team. A tacit organizational competence enhances the productiveness of all other factors through selecting and allocating competent people and can earn a monopoly rent in the capital market. In Chapter 14, Kenneth Arrow interprets invention broadly as the production of knowledge, with the corollary that 'an economic analysis of, for example, R&D activities, must inevitably rest upon recognition of the peculiar characteristics of information viewed as an economic commodity' (Dasgupta and David 1987, 520). Gerhard Rosegger expects that the development of highly efficient information networks will transform the strategic responses of firms to changing market conditions, especially in terms of the changing role of property rights to firm-specific technical and market knowledge.

The selections in Part V, 'International Aspects', illustrate very clearly the application of the Stockhausen proposition: that enormous masses of literature have not been allowed to blot out information-theoretic elements. Beth Krevitt Eres follows a common thread – information as a commodity in international trade – to find a path through the diverse literatures. That information is mobile fosters trade, but also makes countries fear the loss of national security and sovereignty as well as economic prosperity. These fears lead to non-tariff barriers.

In Chapter 17, Lawrence Welch takes up the neglected topic of the technology transfer process in foreign licensing arrangements. Transfer is a highly demanding exchange process, especially when companies are unrelated and whose only point of contact is a licensing arrangement.

Stuart Macdonald then records in detail the operation of a classic attempt to control the flow of high-technology information – from the United States to the Soviet Union through the US Export Control Act of 1949 and the CoCom network of nations that thereby became embroiled. He concludes that such controls 'operate with all the finesse and subtlety that might be expected from an apprentice butcher, and high technology is likely to bear not only the scars of such inept intervention, but also to suffer long-term damage from the obstacles which are being proposed or actually being erected against the free circulation of information'.

The papers in the previous sections have raised many policy issues, some of which are dealt with in Part VI, 'Information Policy'. Donald Dunn first discusses some of the policy issues that arise with the creation of new information. He contends that there would be social advantages in taking a broader integrative view of national information policy. Alford and Feige then focus on one element of the national system: social science information systems. These are highly vulnerable to the distorting effects of observer–subject–policymaker feedback. Accordingly, information must be treated as an endogenous variable whenever there are behavioural incentives and mechanisms to manipulate the information system. The underground economy is one of many examples. Whenever social indicators are used as triggers for policy, they cease to function as objective measures of system activity and become easily corrupted.

In Chapter 21, Aubrey Silberston provides a basic exposition of the working of the patent system; this remains the model of diverse efforts both to strengthen old forms and to create new forms of property rights in information.

Patricia Glass Schuman's paper reviews the US National Commission on Libraries and Information Science Report to show the need for continuing debate among the various stakeholders if a just distribution of information is to be guaranteed. Her discussion underlines the limitations of market solutions – and is a reminder that the trumpet calls of recent NII pronouncements have been heard before.

Part VII, 'Selected Classics', includes two papers from the 1971 readings – by Kenneth Boulding and Jacob Marschak. Here above all, the exhortation is simply to read for yourself. To these has been added von Hayek's 1974 Nobel Memorial Lecture entitled 'The Pretence of Knowledge' in which he attacked the propensity of economists to imitate as closely as possible the procedures of the physical sciences. He contended that 'We are only beginning to understand on how subtle a communication system the functioning of an advanced industrial society is based – a communication system which we call the market and which turns out to be a more efficient mechanism for digesting dispersed information than any that man has deliberately designed'. There are, he argued, insuperable limits to knowledge and hence to the ability to control.

Part VIII, 'New Directions', indicates six of many potential directions for research. Arrow provides a theoretical basis for exploring the interchange of information among the component parts of a firm. Marschak adopts a new approach to the assessment of the benefits and costs of alternative organizational schemes. Milgrom and Roberts give us a less restrictive optimizing model of the firm, emphasizing quality and speedy response to changing market conditions, while utilizing technologically advanced equipment and new forms of organization. Katz and Ziderman show that an information-theoretic approach can be usefully applied to labour mobility.

In Chapter 30, Leff takes up the example of telecommunications in the analytics of achieving a socially optimal allocation of investment resources in economic development. Taking account of externalities and using some results from the economics of information are both required for this task. And, as mentioned earlier, the final paper, Marschak's 'Economics of Language', addresses a neglected but important topic with considerable research potential.

Bibliography (Part IX)

An exhaustive bibliography of the economics of communication and information would currently take in a very large slice of the writings in economics in general and, with appropriate interpretation, would call for another volume. So here again, personal experience has been my guide. Items included are those which, for me, have advanced lines of thought, taken development into new territory, and provided linkages between tribes of economists and with other 'disciplines of information'. In many cases items have been included because, in the course of research supervision, graduate students have found them useful.

I have not attempted to include the full contents of relevant specialist journals or journals giving prominence to information topics, nor to other major collections of papers. In the first category there are, e.g., *Information Economics and Policy*, *Telecommunications Policy*, *Rand Journal of Economics*, *Journal of Economic Behavior & Organization*, *Journal of Financial Intermediation*, *Journal of Evolutionary Economics*, and *Economics of Innovation and New Technology*. From other disciplines, *Journal of the American Society for Information Science* must be listed, along with that Society's *Annual Review of Information Science and Technology*.

A list of major collections would begin with the Papers and Proceedings of the Seventy-eighth Annual Meeting of the American Economic Association (*American Economic Review*, **56**, May 1966). As President-elect for the conference, Fritz Machlup indicated his ambition 'to arrange a set of sessions displaying thematic unity without exception and without undue strain'. The chosen theme was 'Knowledge Production and Innovation'. Two other collections are Machlup and Mansfield (eds), *The Study of Information: Interdisciplinary Messages* and the companion volumes in this series by D.K. Levine and S.A. Lippman (eds), *The Economics of Information, Volumes I–II*.

Editor's Acknowledgements

My indebtedness to others, either through their tolerance and active support or by virtue of their opposition, is great. The pursuit of the underlying theme of the economic importance of communication and information went against the grain in the 1950s and, to a considerable extent, still does so. I acknowledge with deep thanks my teachers, colleagues and students throughout this venture, including Philip Andrews, Elizabeth Brunner, G.L.S. Shackle, Bela Gold, Manfred Kochen, Stuart Macdonald, Lawrence Welch, John Beggs, Joshua Gans, Peter Earl and David Allen.

Institutional support has come from many sources so I must again be selective. The short stay that the Rockefeller Foundation made possible at its Bellagio Centre in Italy had a special character. Patrick Troy made me welcome in his Urban Research Program, where I have had every assistance from the staff and a fine working environment.

Part I
Overview

[1]

Defining information

An approach for policymakers

Sandra Braman

Single-definition and pluralistic approaches to defining 'information' are politically problematic. All decision-making concerns can be incorporated in, and the definitional dilemma resolved with, a hierarchy of four categories of definitions that increase in scope and complexity of the social structure to which they are applied as well as the amount of power granted information. These categories of information are as a resource, commodity, perception of pattern, and constitutive force in society. The first, deepest and standard-setting analysis of any issue must be made defining information as a constitutive force in society. Other definitions may be used at the second and subsequent stages of analysis as appropriate.

Dr Sandra Braman is Research Assistant Professor in the Institute of Communications Research, University of Illinois, 222B Armory Building, 505 East Armory Avenue, Urbana-Champaign, IL 61820, USA (Tel: 217-333 1549).

[1]Lewis Hyde, The Gift: Imagination and the Erotic Life of Property, Vintage, New York, 1983.
[2]Mustapha Masmoudi, 'A new world information order for better human understanding', paper presented at Annual Conference of the International Institute of Communication, Ottawa, Canada, 1980; Mustapha Masmoudi, 'The new world information order', in Jim Richstad and Michael H. Anderson, eds, Crisis in International News: Policies and Prospects, Columbia University Press, New York, 1981, pp 77–96.
[3]Geza Feketekuty, 'Trade in professional services: an overview', paper presented at the University of Chicago Legal Forum,
continued on p 234

The abundance and diversity of definitions of information bewilder. Where some see the object and subject of religious acts[1] others see political force,[2] or a commodity on the order of boots and bullets.[3] After identifying more than 40 academic fields that deal with information, Machlup and Mansfield voice a common frustration over this confusion: 'Evidently, there should be *something* that all the things called information have in common [but] it surely is not easy to find out whether it is much more than the name.'[4] A recent survey reported that more than 100 definitions of the type of information processing called 'communications' alone are currently in use for international regulatory purposes.[5]

Theoretical pluralism[6] seems an appropriate way to think about phenomena that occur and processes that unfold in different ways at different levels of a highly articulated social structure.[7] Events throughout the social structure are, of course, interrelated; to Blau,[8] successive and ever more encompassing levels of the social structure nest, while for Wallace[9] the relationship among levels is one of expanding inclusiveness, with increasing complexities of pattern and rhythm. Descriptions of complex societies must thus account for each level and the interactions within and among them to be adequate.[10]

Because modes of information creation, processing, flows and use are shaped by socioeconomic and political class divisions and in turn reproduce them, policy-making, too, must take into account qualitative differences in phenomena at different levels of the social structure. A definitional hierarchy and sequencing in choice of definitions for use in particular situations are thus suggested here.

Technological determinism, too, may take more than one shape: sometimes society shapes technological development, and sometimes it is the reverse, depending on the particular historical conjuncture. Included among the factors that establish causal direction at any moment, however, is what might be called the social will – the will of a community, as expressed in its policy-making and policy implementation – to deliberately attempt to determine directions of change. Policy-making and analysis should be conducted *as if* social decisions can influence technological development in desired directions, even

0308-5961/89/030233-10$3.00 © 1989 Butterworth & Co (Publishers) Ltd

Defining information

continued from p 233
Chicago, IL, 1986; Geza Feketekuty and
Jonathan David Aronson, 'Restrictions on
trade in communication and information
services', *The Information Society*, Vol 2,
No 3–4, 1984, pp 217–48.
[4]Fritz Machlup and Ute Mansfield, eds,
*The Study of Information: Interdisciplinary
Messages*, Wiley, New York, 1983.
[5]Edward W. Ploman, *International Law
Governing Communications and Information*, Greenwood, Westport, CT, 1982.
[6]See for example, Bruce Ackerman, *Re-
constructing American Law*, Harvard University Press, Cambridge, 1984; Peter M.
Blau, 'Introduction: diverse views of social
structure and their common denominator',
in Peter M. Blau and Robert K. Merton,
eds, *Continuities in Structural Inquiry*,
Sage, Beverly Hills, 1981, pp 1–23; Felix
S. Cohen, 'Field theory and judicial logic',
Yale Law Journal, Vol 59, 1950, pp 238–
72; Chin Chuan Lee, 'Where are we in
understanding international communication research? A methodological perspective', paper presented at International
Communications Association, Honolulu,
Hawaii, 1985; Robert K. Merton, 'Fore-
ward: remarks on theoretical pluralism', in
Peter M. Blau and Robert K. Merton, *op cit*,
Ref 6, pp i–viii; Theda Skocpol, 'Bringing
the state back in: strategies of analysis in
current research', in Peter B. Evans, Diet-
rich Rueschmeyer, and Theda Skocpol,
eds, *Bringing the State Back In*, Cambridge University Press, New York, 1985,
pp 3–37.
[7]Charles K. Warriner, 'Levels in the study
of social structure', in Peter M. Blau and
Robert K. Merton, *op cit*, Ref 6, pp 179–90.
[8]Peter M. Blau, *op cit*, Ref 6.
[9]Walter L. Wallace, 'Hierarchic structure in
social phenomena,' in Peter M. Blau and
Robert K. Merton, *op cit*, Ref 6, pp 191–
234.
[10]Immanuel Wallerstein provides a model
of such a multilevel analysis in his historical work. His descriptions of medieval market transactions, for example, make clear
the ways in which the same piece of
information about the sale of a cow means
radically different things to the peasant and
to the global trader. Distinctions in
socioeconomic class and political position
enable each to understand, use – and
receive the benefits of – information differently, with the advantage always
accruing to those who take the longer and
broader view. See Immanuel Wallerstein,
The Capitalist World-economy, Cambridge
University Press, New York, 1979; Immanuel Wallerstein, *The Politics of the
World-economy: The States, the Movements, and the Civilizations*, Cambridge
University Press, New York, 1984.
[11]Richard Straus, ed, *Communications
and International Trade: A Symposium*,
International Institute of Communication,
Washington, DC, 1982.
[12]Joan Edelman Spero, 'Information: the
policy void', *Foreign Policy*, Vol 48, 1982,
continued on p 235

while the debate over the relationship between technology and society
continues.

Because it is a commonplace that information policy is characterized
by an extraordinary number of decision-making arenas and players, and
becoming a commonplace that many of the same issues, from network
design to data privacy, crop up across arenas from the international to
the local, the term 'information policy' is used here in a very general
sense.

As a last caveat, any typification is of course an over-simplification.
Individual approaches to defining information will fit into categories to
which they have been assigned to greater or lesser degrees. It is the
framework itself that, it is hoped, will be of assistance to the working
policymaker.

Approaches to the definitional dilemma

Disagreement over which definition of information should serve as the
basis of negotiations lies at the heart of many of today's information
policy debates. As Straus[11] notes, information policy issues seen in one
country as cultural are understood in another as economic. US
policymakers, both private sector[12] and public,[13] argue in favour of
using the trade perspective to discuss international information flow
specifically because it provides a way of distinguishing social from
economic issues, permitting policymakers to exclude social, political or
cultural concerns when dealing with what they prefer to see as purely
economic matters. Ambassador Diana Lady Dougan, head of the State
Department's Bureau of International Communication and Information
Policy, says directly:

We cannot accept such broad generalizations as the 'protection of cultural
integrity' to be a sufficient justification for information control, particularly as
these are too often only a guise for economic protectionism or censorship of the
press.[14]

The argument over how to define information is critical because that
definition is central to the just emerging information policy regime. A
regime is a normative and regulatory international framework or
'meta-agreement'[15] that is less rigid and formal than a legal system but
nonetheless serves to bind all parties involved. In the words of an
information policy analyst, a regime is 'an organizing device which
focuses on converging expectations regarding principles, norms, rules
and procedures in particular issue-areas'.[16] Regimes vary in degree of
formality, with the General Agreement on Tariffs and Trade (GATT)
often cited as the classic model.[17]

The entire issue area[18] of information is characterized by the recency
of its emergence. Battles over the nature of the regime to dominate are
still being fought, with the conflict over operational definitions a key
battleground.

Thus what would seem the most logical, and in many respects the
easiest, way out of this definitional dilemma – to choose one operational
definition of information for use in all situations – is unfortunately to
take a political stance that will at best polarize the policy discussion and
at worst exclude certain discussants from participation. These political
ramifications are both far-reaching and immediate.

Still, the pragmatic problem remains. A second approach starts from
the position that information is multifaceted, so that multiple definitions

continued from p 234
pp 139–56.
[13]Kenneth Leeson in Straus, *op cit*, Ref 11,
p 187.
[14]Diana Lady Dougan, *Promoting the Free Flow of Information*, Current Policy No 531, US Department of State, Washington, DC, 30 November 1983.
[15]Robert O. Keohane and Joseph Nye, *Power and Interdependence: World Politics in Transition*, Little and Brown, Boston, 1977.
[16]Stephen McDowell, *Building Consensus in the OECD: The Case of Transborder Data Flows*, presented to the Canadian Political Science Association, Hamilton, 1987.
[17]Karl J. Holsti, 'A new international politics? Diplomacy in complex interdependence', *International Organization*, Vol 32, No 2, 1978, pp 513–30; Charles W. Kegley, Jr, 'Decision regimes and foreign policy behavior', presented to the Conference on New Directions in the Comparative Study of Foreign Policy, Ohio State University, Columbus, Ohio, 1985; Robert O. Keohane, 'The theory of hegemonic stability and changes in international economic regimes, 1967–1977', in Ole Holsti, Randolph M. Siverson and Alexander L. George, eds, *Change in the International System*, Westview, Boulder, 1980, pp 131–62; Robert O. Keohane, 'The demand for international regimes', *International Organization*, Vol 36, No 2, 1982, pp 325–55; Stephen D. Krasner, 'Regimes and the limits of realism: regimes as autonous variables', *International Organization*, Vol 36, No 2, 1982, pp 497–510; Stephen D. Krasner, 'Structural causes and regime consequences: regimes as intervening variables', *International Organization*, Vol 36, No 2, 1982, pp 185–205; Stephen D. Krasner, ed, *International Regimes*, Cornell University Press, Ithaca, 1983; James Rosenau, 'A pre-theory revisited: world politics in an era of cascading interdependence', *International Studies Quarterly*, Vol 28, No 3, 1984, pp 245–306.
[18]William C. Potter, 'Issue area and foreign policy analysis', *International Organization*, Vol 34, No 3, 1980, pp 405–27; Jerel Rosati, 'Developing a systematic decision making framework', *World Politics*, Vol 33, No 2, 1981, pp 234–52; Martin Sampson, *Issues in International Policy Coordination*, University of Denver Monograph Series, Denver, 1982; Avild Underdal, 'Issues determine politics determine policies', unpublished manuscript, 1981; William Zimmerman, 'Issue area and foreign policy-process: a research note in search of a general theory', *The American Political Science Review*, Vol 67, 1973, pp 1204–12.
[19]James W. Carey and Norman Sims, 'The telegraph and the news report', unpublished manuscript, 1976.
[20]Herbert S. Dordick, Helen G. Bradley and Burt Nanus, *The New Network Marketplace*, Ablex, Norwood, NJ, 1981.
continued on p 236

apply concurrently. In the early 20th century formulation that influenced John Dewey and Robert Park, Franklin Ford argued that information appears differently when perceived by the individual, the class and the whole.[19] Contemporary commentators Dordick, Bradley and Nanus[20] emphasize the heterogeneous nature of information, which varies according to infinitely variable conjunctions of supplier, processor, user and channel of communication. Economist Schmoranz[21] identifies three distinct trade roles for information (as input and output of research and development, as transferable knowledge, and as a resource). To IBM, information operates simultaneously as an asset, a resource and a commodity.[22] US policymakers[23] have similarly used pluralistic approaches to defining information.

This pluralistic approach is flexible and open to the entire range of values that informs policy-making in many decision-making cultures. It does not, however, offer any concrete guidance in choosing from the many a single operational definition for use in analysing specific fact situations or issues, each one arising within a particular decision-making arena characterized by its own constraints and motivations.

A third approach, therefore, is offered here. With the introduction of a hierarchy into the pluralism described above, a decision-making rule can be articulated. This hierarchy is based on differences in level of scope (how broad a range of social phenomena is incorporated into the concept) and complexity (how finely and variously articulated is the social organization that appears through the lens of a particular definition). They also differ in the amount of power granted to information and its creation, flows and use, from very little or none at all to a great deal. Distinguished along these dimensions, definitions of information in common use in the policy-making process fall into four broad groups: information as a resource, as a commodity, as perception of pattern, and as a constitutive force in society. The general characteristics, strengths and weaknesses of each of these types of definition are discussed below, concluding with an exploration of the implications of this definitional hierarchy for the working policymaker. (It was, of course, impossible to incorporate into this discussion every definition of information that has appeared. The selection discussed emphasizes those definitions that have emerged in policy discussions.)

Information as a resource

Definitions of information as a resource are popular, appearing in several bodies of literature. Economists such as Jonscher[24] and Madec[25] provide models for measuring information, its flows and its value that emulate those developed for physical resources. Much of mass communication theory, beginning with Lazarsfeld, Berelson and Gaudet's[26] work on the two-step flow and including the multitude of diffusion studies, treats information as a resource.[27] The New World Information Order debate is built upon[28] and rife with[29] discussions of the political impact of international flows of information as a resource.

It is characteristic of definitions of this kind to be general in nature. Machlup, for example, defines the basic informational unit as 'anything that is known by somebody';[30] for Oettinger, 'the generic concept of information resources encompasses any information content represented in any way, embodied in any format and handled by any physical processor.'[31]

Defining information

continued from p 235
[21]I. Schmoranz, 'Macroeconomic sectors of the information economy', in Hans Peter Gassmann, ed, *Information, Computer and Communication Policies for the 80's*, OECD, Amsterdam, pp 75–82.
[22]Harry De Maio in Straus, *op cit*, Ref 11.
[23]Arthur A. Bushkin and Jane H. Yurow, *The Foundations of United States Information Policy*, OECD, Paris, 1980; Kenneth W. Leeson, *International Communications: Blueprint for Policy*, North–Holland, Amsterdam, 1984.
[24]Charles Jonscher, 'The economic causes of information growth', *InterMedia*, Vol 10, No 6, 1982, pp 34–7.
[25]Alain Madec, 'The political economy of information flows', *InterMedia*, Vol 9, No 2, pp 29–32.
[26]Paul F. Lazarsfeld, Bernard Berelson and Helen Gaudet, *The People's Choice: How the Voter Makes Up His Mind in a Presidential Campaign*, Columbia University Press, New York, 1984.
[27]For example, J. Oliver Boyd–Barrett, 'Cultural dependency and the mass media', in Michael Gurevitch, Tony Bennett, James Curran and Janet Woollacott, eds, *Culture, Society and the Media*, Methuen, New York, 1982, pp 174–95; Peter Golding, 'Media role in national development: critique of a theoretical orthodoxy', *Journal of Communication*, Vol 24, No 3, 1974, pp 39–53; Lucian W. Pye, 'Communication operation in non-Western societies', *Public Opinion Quarterly*, Vol 20, 1956, pp 249–57; Lucian W. Pye, 'Communication, institution building and the reach of authority', in Daniel Lerner and Wilbur Schramm, eds, *Communication and Change in the Developing Countries*, East–West Center, Honolulu, 1967, pp 35–55; Everett M. Rogers, *Modernization among Peasants: The Impact of Communication*, Holt, Rinehart and Winston, New York, 1969; Everett M. Rogers, 'Communication and development: the passing of the dominant paradigm', *Communication Research*, Vol 3, 1976, pp 213–40.
[28]Al Hester, 'The news from Latin America via a world news agency', *Gazette*, Vol 20, 1974, pp 82–98; Harold A. Innis, *The Bias of Communication*, The University of Toronto Press, Toronto, 1951; James W. Markham, 'Foreign news in the U.S. and South American press', *Public Opinion Quarterly*, Vol 25, 1961, pp 249–62; Fernando Reyes Matta, 'The Latin American concept of news', *Journal of Communication*, Vol 29, No 2, 1979, pp 164–71; Richard O'Mara, 'Latin America: the hole in the news', *Nation*, Vol 221, No 1, 1975, pp 16–18; Herbert I. Schiller, *Mass Communications and the American Empire*, Augustus M. Kelley, New York, 1969.
[29]Mustapha Masmoudi, 1980, *op cit*, Ref 2; Richstad and Anderson, *op cit*, Ref 2.
[30]Fritz Machlup, *Knowledge and Knowledge Production*, Princeton University Press, Princeton, 1980, p 7.
[31]Anthony G. Oettinger, 'Information re-
continued on p 237

It is among the strengths of definitions of information as a resource that they are relatively easy to comprehend. As a concept, the notion is easily grasped, widely applicable and open to extended applications in a number of different settings. As a metaphor, the definition of information as a resource has great power.

For Ravault,[32] it is an advantage of this type of definition that it emphasizes the uses people make of information rather than its effects upon people and society. This type of definition also has utility in the articulation of specific laws and regulations, finding its way variously into legal systems. In the USA, such a definition is implicit in the concept of the marketplace of ideas, a notion that is explicitly used to justify many information policy decisions.[33] In specific areas of the law, such as international trade,[34] information is directly treated as a resource. In another area, the federal government is increasingly choosing to treat its own informational resources, such as computerized census data and reports from federally funded research, as resources for selling.[35]

Problems are also encountered when defining information as a resource. As a result of their generality, discussions of information as a resource tend towards grand historical statements. A number of difficulties stem from the basic fact that, unlike physical matter, information is not composed of mass and energy and thus is not subject to physical laws, leading Braunstein[36] and others to argue that the combined effect of these characteristics is to make it impossible to adequately treat information like physical resources in economic terms.

From the perspective of information as a resource, information and its creators, processors and users are viewed as discrete and isolated entities. Information comes in pieces unrelated to bodies of knowledge or information flows into which it may be organized. The social structure as viewed this way is simple (there are two classes – haves and have-nots), and the scope of the phenomena covered is limited. Information is not seen to have any power in and of itself, though its role in sustenance of specific entities is acknowledged.

Definitions that treat information as a resource have implicit within them the notion that, also like physical resources, information can be processed. Those definitions that explicitly develop this aspect are sufficiently different qualitatively that they form their own group, definitions that treat information as a commodity.

Information as a commodity

One obvious characteristic of this category of definition is the profusion of terminology in use. 'Services', a term which itself has no consensual definition, is one example. Attempts to define services include *The Economist*'s 'Things which can be bought and sold but which you cannot drop on your foot',[37] Feketekuty's 'any exchanged product of economic activity that is not a good',[38] Cleevely and Cawdell's[39] taxonomy of applications, or, most often, simple listings of things to be included in this category.[40]

Another term often applied to information and its flows when treating them as commodities is transborder data flow (TDF). Though this label originally applied only to international information flows of computerized information, its use has come to include information of all types and to penetrate discussions in the domestic arena. As cases arise under

Defining information

continued from p 236

sources: knowledge and power in the 21st century', *Science*, Vol 209, 1980, p 194.
[32]Rene J. Ravault, 'Information flow: which way is the wrong way?' *Journal of Communication*, Vol 31, No 4, 1981, pp 129–34.
[33]Edwin Diamond, Norman Sandler and Milton Mueller, *Telecommunications in Crisis: The First Amendment, Technology, and Deregulation*, Cato Institute, Washington, DC, 1983; Harvey J. Levin, 'Foreign and domestic US policies: Spectrum reservations and media balance', *Telecommunications Policy*, Vol 6, No 2, June 1982, pp 123–35; Barbara Sweeney, 'The marketplace of ideas: an economic analogy for freedom of speech', paper presented to the Association for Education in Journalism and Mass Communication, Gainesville, FL, 1984.
[34]Sandra Braman, 'The GATT and services: shaping an information policy regime', paper presented to International Communications Association, Montreal, 1987.
[35]Mary M. Cheh, 'Government control of private ideas: striking a balance between scientific freedom and national security', *Jurimetrics Journal*, Vol 23, No 1, 1982, pp 1–32; Ruth L. Greenstein, 'Federal contractors and grantees: what are your First Amendment rights?', *Jurimetrics Journal*, Vol 24, No 3, 1984, pp 197–209.
[36]Yale M. Braunstein, 'The potential for increased competition in television broadcasting: can the market work?' in Timothy R. Haight, ed, *Telecommunications Policy and the Citizen*, Praeger, New York, 1979, pp 55–64.
[37]A GATT for services, *The Economist*, 12 October 1985, p 20.
[38]Feketekuty, *op cit*, Ref 3, p 3.
[39]David Cleevely and Richard Cawdell, 'A telecommunications taxonomy', *Telecommunications Policy*, Vol 10, No 2, June 1986, pp 107–19.
[40]See for example, *Exchange of information pursuant to the ministerial decision on services: Communication from the EEC to GATT*, Office of the US Trade Representative, Washington, DC, 1984; *Exchange of information pursuant to the ministerial decision on services: Communication from Japan to GATT*, Office of the US Trade Representative, Washington, DC, 1984.
[41]The US Supreme Court provides a venue for resolution of disputes involving information as it flows across state and municipal borders. Cases dealing with interstate issues during the 1980s include: *Edgar v Mite Corp.*, 457 US 624 (1981); *Keeton v Hustler Magazine*, 456 US 770 (1981); *Calder v Jones*, 465 US 783 (1983); *Capital Cities Cable v Crisp*, 467 US 691 (1983); *Dowling v US*, 473 US 207 (1984); *Louisiana Public Service Commission v FCC*, 476 US 355 (1986); *Posadas de Puerto Rico Associates v Tourism Company of Puerto Rico*, 478 US 328 (1986).

continued on p 238

interstate commerce in the USA, for example, TDF issues emerge when information encounters state,[41] and even municipal,[42] borders. McDowell[43] attributes this creeping presence to the fact that TDF actually refers not to a specific object or phenomenon, but to a perspective through which information policy matters can be viewed. Definitions of TDF include 'a point-to-point exchange of proprietary information based on contractual relationships',[44] 'international data transmissions over computer–communication systems',[45] and lists of items including broadcast programmes, remote satellite sensing, and computer data flow.[46] Branscomb[47] was able to identify seven variations on the theme.

The proliferation of terms referring to information as a commodity is but one indication of a second, and more important, characteristic of this type of definition – its increasing scope, penetration and domination. While information about supplies and prices has been considered a commodity for hundreds of years, it is only in the past few decades that both personal information and information about the public affairs of a community have come to be treated as commodities, a trend that has received philosophical treatment by Ellul,[48] Ong[49] and others.

The notion of information as a commodity requires as a complement a concept of an information production chain. The steps of such a chain, adapted from models suggested by Machlup[50] and Boulding[51], include information creation (creation, generation and collection), processing (cognitive and algorithmic), storage, transportation, distribution, destruction and seeking. Commoditized information gains in economic value as it passes through each stage of the chain.

Definitions of information that treat it as a commodity have heuristic and organizational value. A recent study of Supreme Court cases in the 1980s that dealt with information policy (operationally defined as those cases dealing with any stage of the information production chain) showed a Court that is extremely sensitive to distinctions among and relationships between stages of the chain.[52] Policymakers in other arenas, such as the international GATT or the US FCC, similarly reflect awareness – usually unconscious – of the notion of an information production chain in their thinking.

This type of definition also provides flexibility in response to the problem outlined by Hyde:

Gifts are a class of property whose value lies only in their use and which literally cease to exist as gifts if they are not constantly consumed. When gifts are sold, they change their nature as much as water changes when it freezes, and no rationalistic telling of the constant elemental structure can replace the feeling that is lost.[53]

Under a regime in which only one type of definition of information is permitted, economic value may well destroy other types of value inherent in social, cultural, religious and aesthetic information. The notion of an information production chain permits policymakers to *exclude* specific types of information, actors and actions at individual or several stages of the chain. It could be decided, for example, that religious information should never be treated as a commodity, even though other types of information are. Similarly, valuation of artistic information may operate under different rules from those that govern the economic treatment of, say, patents. Rather than commoditizing all information, the use of this type of definition of information as a commodity processed through an information production chain both

Defining information

continued from p 237
[42]US Supreme Court cases dealing with
disputes over information as it crossed
municipal borders during the 1980s include: *Metromedia v City of San Diego*,
453 US 490 (1980); *Community Communications Co. v Boulder*, 455 US 40
(1981); *Los Angeles v Taxpayers for Vincent*, 466 US 789 (1983); *Los Angeles v
Preferred Communications*, 476 US 488
(1986).
[43]McDowell, *op cit*, Ref 16.
[44]Meheroo Jussawalla and Chee–Wah
Cheah, 'Emerging economic constraints
on transborder data flows', *Telecommunications Policy*, Vol 7, No 4, December
1983, pp 185–96.
[45]United Nations Centre on Transnational
Corporations, *On the Effects of the Operations and Practices of Transnational Corporations*, New York, 1981, p 1.
[46]Allan Gotlieb, Charles Dalfen and Kenneth Katz, 'The transborder transfer of
information by communications and computer systems: issues and approaches to
guiding principles', *American Journal of
International Law*, Vol 68, 1974, pp 227–
57.
[47]Anne W. Branscomb, 'Global governance of global networks: a survey of
transborder data flow in transition', *Van-
derbilt Law Review*, Vol 36, 1983, pp
985–1043.
[48]Jacques Ellul, *The Technological Society* (J. Wilkinson, trans), Vintage, New York,
1964.
[49]Walter J. Ong, *Orality and Literacy: The
Technologizing of the Word*, Methuen,
New York, 1982.
[50]*Op cit*, Ref 30.
[51]Kenneth Boulding, 'The economics of
knowledge and the knowledge of economics', *American Economic Review*, Vol 56,
No 2, 1966, pp 1–13.
[52]Sandra Braman, *Information Policy and
the United States Supreme Court*, unpublished doctoral dissertation, University of
Minnesota, Minneapolis, 1988.
[53]*Op cit*, Ref 1, p 21.
[54]Fritz Machlup, 'The economics of information: a new classification', *InterMedia*, Vol 11, No 2, 1983, pp 28–37.
[55]F.A. Hayek, 'The use of knowledge in
society', *American Economic Review*, Vol
35, 1945, pp 519–30.
[56]Marc U. Porat, *The Information Economy*, doctoral dissertation, Stanford University, 1976.
[57]George Stigler, 'The economics of information', *Journal of Political Economy*,
Vol 69, No 3, 1961, pp 213–25.
[58]Gerhart Stadler, 'From technology to
law', *InterMedia*, Vol 9, No 1, 1981, pp
26–8.
[59]John Fiske, *Introduction to Communication Studies*, Methuen, New York, 1982;
David Ritchie, 'Shannon and Weaver: un-
ravelling the paradox of information', *Communication Research*, Vol 13, No 2, 1986,
pp 278–98; Claude E. Shannon, 'A mathematical theory of communication', *Bell*
continued on p 239

functions in the world of some concrete economic realities and offers a
means by which the commoditization process itself can be resisted.

The problems that arise from the non-materiality of information when
treating it as a resource are multiplied with the attempt to treat it as a
commodity. Economists find pragmatic difficulties in identifying those
areas that should be considered part of the economics of information
(Machlup[54] counts 17), and in accounting for information in economic
terms. Despite efforts going back at least to Hayek[55] or, in Porat's[56]
view, all the way back to Adam Smith, information, as Stigler says,
'occupies a slum dwelling in the town of economics'.[57] Stadler[58] suggests
that it may be failure to cope with these difficulties in the past that
accounts for the contemporary paucity of coherent policy dealing with
information.

Because of the *meta*-economic nature of information, another
problem with definitions of information that treat it as a commodity is
that they do not reach many of the critical phenomena in which
information is involved, or effects of information creation, flows,
processing and use. Still, the scope of the notion of information as a
commodity is wider than that of information as a resource, for it
incorporates the exchanges of information among people and related
activities as well as its use. The social structure, too, is more articulated
and therefore complex, comprising buyers, sellers and the organization
required in order to sustain a market, rather than simply entities
struggling individually for survival. With this type of definition,
information is granted at least economic power.

Information as perception of pattern

Definitions of information that treat it as perception of pattern broaden
the concept of information by adding context. Information from this
perspective has a past and a future, is affected by motive and other
environmental and causal factors, and itself has effects.

Definitions in this category range in complexity. The simplest
definitions focus on the capacity of information to reduce uncertainty.
In the classic statement by Shannon and Weaver, information is a
measure of the predictability of the signal, or the number of choices
open to the sender.[59] Entropy is thus equated with ignorance, and in
turn with less stable forms of organization, while stable social
formations are considered to have low entropy. Rogers describes
uncertainty as 'the degree to which a number of alternatives are
perceived with respect to the occurrence of an event and the relative
probabilities of these alternatives'.[60] Reduction of uncertainty is
important from the economist's point of view because it reduces the cost
of search and increases the 'productivity' of decision-making.[61] Mathematicians and engineers treat information flows as pathways which can
be valued by the degree to which uncertainty is reduced.[62]

More complex definitions of information as perception of pattern
centre on context. In semiotics, context is the codes, or systems of
meaning, within which any information exists.[63] Context has also been
important in understanding information within the policy-making
setting.[64] There is varying awareness of this perspective among
governmental and quasi-governmental agencies, however. While the
Nora/Minc report to the French government insists that, 'Information is
inseparable from its organization and its mode of storage',[65] the

Defining information

MacBride Commission report was specifically criticized for failing to emphasize the importance of the context.[66]

It is a strength of this type of definition that its exemplars come closer to tapping the real-world environment of information creation, processing, flows and use. Events during which information is treated as a resource or as a commodity inevitably occur during ongoing processes which are not incorporated into those simpler types of definition.

Another advantage of defining information as perception of pattern is that it provides a starting point for quantifying and valuing information, making this type of definition attractive from the engineers' and economists' point of view.

The primary disadvantage of this approach is that it is highly relativistic. Perception of pattern and context shift from observer to observer, so that any use of such a definition must make explicit the point of view from which it is being applied. The consequence is that while these definitions have intuitive appeal, they are difficult to use in a policy-making context.

Defining information in this way again broadens the scope of phenomena and processes covered, and such definitions are capable of application to a highly articulated social structure. For the first time in moving up this hierarchy of definitions, information is clearly granted power of its own, although its effects from this perspective are isolated in themselves – uncertainty, for example, is reduced as it regards a specific single question, without concern for trends or structural effects.

Clearly, there is a power differential weighted in favour of those perceiving information within the widest possible context. If knowledge is power, contextualized knowledge is greater power. It is not a far step from this point to the final category of definitions, those that treat information as a constitutive force in society.

Information as a constitutive force in society

Definitions in this category grant information an active role in *shaping* context. With definitions of information that treat it as a constitutive force in society, information is not just affected by its environment, but is itself an actor affecting other elements in the environment. Information is that which is not just embedded within a social structure, but creates that structure itself. In Krippendorff's words:

In the input–output table for an economy in which exchanges between and transformations within industries (categories of industries, sectors of an economy or geographical regions) are entered, information participates in the process by changing the table. It may change the transition function within one cell (eg, when information is geared toward a more efficient organization of the process), it may change the interaction between cells otherwise considered independent (eg, when industries, etc, become more informed about each other and coordinate their production and consumption) or it may add new cells, rows or columns (eg, when information introduces new technologies, communication technology for example, that cause structural changes in the economy). In such an analysis information is seen to be about or superordinate to the economy. It guides, controls and rearranges the economic activities and has, hence, the characteristic of a meta-economic quantity that cannot easily be built into a system of analysis that is essentially flat and provides no opportunity for self-reference.[67]

It is striking how much support the use of this type of definition of

continued from p 238
System Technical Journal, Vol 27, 1948, pp 379–423, 625–56; Claude E. Shannon and Warren Weaver, *The Mathematical Theory of Communication*, University of Illinois Press, Urbana, 1949.
[60]Everett M. Rogers, *Diffusion of Innovations*, 3rd edn, The Free Press, New York, 1983, p xviii.
[61]*Op cit*, Ref 57; *op cit*, Ref 45.
[62]Martin A. Rothblatt, 'The impact of international satellite communications law upon access to the geostationary orbit and the electromagnetic spectrum', *Texas International Law Journal*, Vol 16, 1981, pp 207–44; Shannon, *op cit*, Ref 59.
[63]Fiske, *op cit*, Ref 59.
[64]John P. Bennett, 'Data stories: learning about learning from the U.S. experience in Vietnam', in David Sylvan and Steve Chan, eds, *Foreign Policy Decision Making*, Praeger, New York, 1984, pp 227–29; Rob Kling, 'Value conflicts in computing developments: developed and developing countries', *Telecommunications Policy*, Vol 8, No 2, pp 127–47.
[65]Simon Nora and Alain Minc, *The Computerization of Society*, MIT Press, Cambridge, 1980.
[66]MacBride Commission Report, 1980; *op cit*, Ref 32.
[67]Klaus Krippendorff, 'Information, information society and some marxian propositions', paper presented at International Communications Association, San Francisco, 1984, pp 15–16.

Defining information

[68]Karl W. Deutsch, *Nationalism and Social Communication: An Inquiry into the Foundations of Nationality*, MIT Press, Cambridge, 1953; David M. MacKay, 'The wider scope of information theory', in Machlup and Mansfield, *op cit*, Ref 4, pp 485–92; Frederick Suppe, 'Toward an adequate information science', in L.B. Heilprin ed, *Toward Foundations of Information Science*, Knowledge Industry Publications, Inc, White Plains, NY, 1985, pp 7–27; Bruce H. Westley and Malcolm MacLean, 'A conceptual model for mass communication research', *Journalism Quarterly*, Vol 34, 1957, pp 31–8; Norbert Wiener, 'Some moral and technical consequences of automation', *Science*, 1960, pp 1355–8.
[69]Peter L. Berger and Thomas Luckmann, *The Social Construction of Reality*, Doubleday, New York, 1966; Thomas Luckmann, *Phenomenology and Sociology*, Penguin, New York, 1978; George Herbert Mead, *Mind, Self and Society*, University of Chicago Press, Chicago, 1934; C. Wright Mills, *The Sociological Imagination*, Oxford University Press, New York, 1959; Robert E. Park, 'Reflections on communication and culture', *American Journal of Sociology*, Vol 44, 1939, pp 191–205; Robert E. Park, 'News as a form of knowledge: a chapter in the sociology of knowledge', *American Journal of Sociology*, Vol 45, No 4, 1940, pp 669–86; Anselm Strauss, *George Herbert Mead on Social Psychology*, University of Chicago Press, Chicago, 1964.
[70]Gaye Tuchman, *Making News: A Study in the Construction of Reality*, The Free Press, New York, 1978.
[71]Todd Gitlin, 'Media sociology: the dominant paradigm', *Theory and Society*, Vol 6, 1978, pp 205–53.
[72]Bernard Berelson and Morris Janowitz, eds, *Reader in Public Communication*, Free Press, Glencoe, IL, 1966; Shearon Lowery and Melvin DeFleur, *Milestones in Mass Communication Research: Media Effects*, Longman, New York, 1983.
[73]Raymond Aron, *Main Currents in Sociological Thought*, Vol 1, Penguin, New York, 1965; Nicholas Garnham, 'Contribution to a political economy of mass communication', *Mass Communication Review Yearbook*, Vol 2, 1981, pp 123–46; Nicholas Garnham, 'Toward a theory of cultural materialism', *Journal of Communication*, Vol 33, No 3, 1983, pp 314–29; David Held, *Introduction to Critical Theory: Horkheimer to Habermas*, University of California Press, Berkeley, 1980; Osker Negt, 'Mass media: tools of domination or instruments of liberation? Aspects of the Frankfurt School's communications analysis', *New German Critique*, Vol 14, 1978, pp 61–80.
[74]Of course, such gross generalizations gloss over many distinctions among ways in which this general approach is developed. The body of critical theory, for *continued on p 241*

information receives from a variety of radically different theoretical and substantive approaches. In cybernetics and information theory, information flows shape systems and form the means by which they adapt to their environment and influence other systems.[68] To social psychologists, information creation and flows literally construct reality.[69] Sociologists such as Tuchman[70] and Gitlin[71] seek to operationalize these concepts as they play out in specific fact-creating situations. These and related ideas from social psychology and sociology have played a large role in the development of mass communication theory, both directly and indirectly.[72]

This approach provides the base for diverse political perspectives. The base/superstructure preoccupation of critical theorists[73] demonstrates a focus on the idea that information is a constitutive force in society.[74] Libertarian thinkers also see information as a constitutive force in society. The notion that the truth emerges not as a dictate from above but from discussion of facts among men and women, including those facts gathered by the men and women themselves, lies at the heart of work by thinkers such as Locke,[75] Mill[76] and others.

A second characteristic of this type of definition is that policy analyses that use it are necessarily teleological. Making any policy decision about information when defined as a constitutive force in society is making a decision about how society is to be structured – how classes are to be distinguished and how they may interact, the balance between the rights of the individual and those of the community, and the structure of communal decision-making processes. Every information policy decision supports a particular vision of how society should be. Because of this characteristic, a definition of information as a constitutive force in society should be used at the beginning of each decision-making process – and provide a standard for judgement during the policy evaluation process as well.

It is a strength of this type of definition that it is relatively friendly, enlarging the context in which users of other definitions work. Thus it is particularly easy to use this type of definition in the first step of a policy analysis that in subsequent stages chooses to use another or other operational definitions as appropriate.

It is difficult to quantify events and effects when dealing with information as a constitutive force in society, however. Thus, it is an area that does not invite empirical research. This itself has policy implications. International funding organizations such as the International Monetary Fund and the World Bank base their decisions to fund projects on projections of expected return in financial and development terms. A major reason there has been little funding by these organizations of projects to contribute to the building of information infrastructure throughout the Third World is that there are no reliable data about what kinds of returns can be expected. Results vary enormously from culture to culture, and the figures are astounding, sometimes in the order of 1:240 in financial return. Cultural, political and social impacts are even harder to quantify reliably and validly.

It seems on the surface also to be a problem that the use of definitions of information as a constitutive force in society invites ideological manipulation more directly than do other types of definition. This is, however, *only* a surface effect. Any definition of information can be used in the service of ideology. This is yet another reason to urge use of more than one definition in the course of a complete analytical process.

Definitions that treat information as a constitutive force in society are at the top of this definitional hierarchy – they apply to the entire range of phenomena and processes in which information is involved, can be applied to a social structure of any degree of articulation and complexity, and grant information, its flows and use an enormous power in constructing our social (and ultimately physical) reality.

Using definitions of information in policy-making

Each of these types of definition has its own use, determined by three closely related factors. The first is the perspective from which one views an information policy issue. The entity, whether individual, organization or state, that views itself as isolated and concerned only for its own survival will most naturally view information as a resource or, perhaps, a commodity. The policymaker, on the other hand, should be working from a perspective of concern about the shape of society as a whole, including all of its parts, and should therefore be drawn towards definitions that treat information as a constitutive force in society.

The second factor is the utility of a definition for a particular situation. Cohen, writing for lawyers, elaborates:

Among the difficulties that stand in the way of a comprehensive view of the legal order is the naive view of definitions as propositions which are true or false . . . . Once we recognize that a definition is, strictly speaking, neither true nor false but rather a resolution to use language in a certain way, we are able to pass the only judgment that ever needs to be passed on a definition, a judgment of utility or inutility.[77]

There are clearly times when it makes sense to treat information, or at least certain kinds of information, as commodities. It does not strengthen the argument of those concerned with civil liberties and other humanitarian values to deny the utility and appropriateness of such definitions for certain settings. For policymakers with responsibility for establishing the basic shape of society, however, definitions of information as a constitutive force in society should have the greatest utility for the first level of analysis and provide a standard against which decisions that treat information as a commodity or other entity should ultimately be judged.

The third factor is the relationship between a definition and the notions of power with which it is associated. The Lukes[78] distinction among types of power (instrumental, structural and consensual) have clear applicability to information, so often equated with power. Definitions of information as a resource or a commodity grant information, at most, instrumental power. With definitions of information as perception of pattern, the structural power of information is recognized. Definitions of information as a constitutive force in society incorporate not just instrumental and structural forms of power, but consensual power as well. Surely policy-making must take into account all of these types of power, so that according to this factor, too, policymakers should begin their work with a definition of information that treats it as a constitutive force in society.

Of course, at a fundamental level, any entity will continue to be concerned with the resource value of information even as it comes to view or treat it in other ways. Similarly, information can be treated as a commodity and as a constitutive force in society simultaneously. It should be possible for policymakers to use more than one definition of

continued from p 240
example, includes at least four distinct formulations of the relationship between information flows and society cast in terms of the base and superstructure.
[75]John Locke, *An Essay Concerning Human Understanding*, P.H. Nidditch, ed, Clarendon Press, Oxford, 1979.
[76]John Stuart Mill, *The Collected Works of John Stuart Mill*, University of Toronto Press, Toronto, 1963.
[77]Cohen, *op cit*, Ref 6, p 271.
[78]Steven Lukes, *Power: A Radical View*, Macmillan, London, 1974.

information in resolving a particular problem.

Often, the choice of which definition is used is political. Definitions of information that treat it as a commodity work to the advantage of those who win when the game is played on economic grounds, or for whom economic values are the only values. Definitions that treat information as perception of pattern begin to be sensitive to cultural, aesthetic or religious concerns. They can also be helpful in identifying ways of improving the efficiency of activities at specific stages of the information production chain, or identifying effects of information creation, processing, flows and use. It is definitions of information that treat it as a constitutive force in society, however, that incorporate all of the above concerns while acknowledging phenomena at all levels of the social structure.

Therefore, from this hierarchy the definitions that provide the deepest levels of analysis and should be used first are those that treat information as a constitutive force in society. The first decision that must be made is about the shape of the society that is desired. The next step is to determine what information policy principles are most likely to produce or support the desired society. Second or subsequent steps of analysis may choose to use other definitions of information as appropriate. Each such use, however, should bear in mind the fact that information so treated – as a commodity or as a resource – does so with effects that must be understood of information as a constitutive force in society. This definition provides the context, and ultimate analytical standard, of any decision made using other definitions of information.

In a way, the process of policy analysis, then, can be seen as pendulum-like, swinging back and forth between viewing decisions through the lens of information as a constitutive force in society and its other definitions. Policymakers may start, for example, with the notion of a marketplace-governed society in which information as a constitutive force in society serves critically as market governor. If at the same time information is then viewed as a commodity, a series of questions unravels. What happens when the governor of a process is potentially controlled by a subset of participants in the process? Are there different types of information, some of which can be treated as a commodity and some of which cannot? Should information critical to the governing of a process be held as a good common to all participants in that process? Should this be as true of a political governing process as of an economic one? What are the impacts on the ability of those affected by a process to participate in its unfolding when a particular type of information is treated as a commodity at each of the levels of the social structure?

Conclusion

To continue to battle over just what information is means encouraging the continuation of national and international policy-making that is characterized by conflict rather than cooperation, leaving open the door for evolution of an international information policy regime that is dominated by those most successful with brute force. Acceptance of a pluralistic and hierarchical approach to defining information, however, not only encourages cooperation but also focuses attention on what is actually going on here – information policymakers are making decisions about how society as a whole is to be shaped, not just simply to guide individual transactions. That society is intricate, multilevel and global in nature.

[2]

Information costs and the division of labour*

Axel Leijonhufvud

Introduction

Economic development, as opposed to 'mere' economic growth, is a process of system evolution towards more and more complex patterns of co-ordinated activities. It entails, in Adam Smith's language, 'increasing division of labour'.

What drives economic evolution in the direction of increasing division of labour are economies of scale. If we can sustain more complex forms of co-operation these scale economies will make us all richer. But to sustain increasingly complex economic structures requires us to maintain political and monetary stability as well as free trade – relatively free trade, at least – over large geographical areas.

'The Division of Labour depends on the Extent of the Market'. Product innovations create new markets and an almost infinite variety of cost-reducing process innovations extend the markets for particular commodities. For the entire system of interrelated markets, the lowering of transportation costs, extending markets over space, has been historically the main technical force tending to increase the division of labour.

It is reasonable to believe that the costs of processing, transmitting and storing information have by now taken over the role in economic

Axel Leijonhufvud is professor of economics at the Department of Economics, University of California at Los Angeles (UCLA). His address: 8857 Moorcroft Avenue, Canoga Park, CA 91304, USA.

development that transportation costs played for so long.

Economic development as the increasing complexity of economic systems[1]

Complexity, in ordinary discourse, is a vague notion. We have all heard complaints like 'modern life is so complicated' accompanied by contrasts drawn with a supposedly 'simpler' past. Often, it really is not clear whether this kind of statement has any content at all; if one tries to give it content, one discovers that it may just as easily be false as true.

Since the division of labour has been driven further today, people are apt to have a narrower range of productive skills so that, in this particular sense, their life is simpler, not more complicated. Most people would find life horribly difficult if they had to match Adam Smith's Scottish Highland farmer who was 'butcher, baker and brewer for his own family'. Claude Levi-Strauss found that people of a certain tribe had to recognize 4000 varieties of jungle plants and what, if anything, they were good (or bad) for. My own 'savage mind' contains a somewhat less extensive botanical knowledge. '[T]he intellectual advantage of civilization', observes Thomas Sowell, 'is not necessarily that each civilized man has more knowledge but that he *requires* far *less*' (Sowell, 1980, p. 7).

This kind of ambiguity is present, I suspect, because complex structures require simple building blocks. Just as one can build almost anything from toy blocks, complex 'modern' economic systems can be built using simple people almost all of whom do not know how to butcher, bake, brew – or fix their own car.

The notion of 'complexity', in any case, needs to be firmed up. To insist on a formula for quantifying complexity may be over-ambitious – a fake scalar measure may be worse than useless. But we need to make the concept concrete enough so that it is possible to speak meaningfully of greater or lesser complexity, even though a partial ordering is the best that can be hoped for. To that end, a concrete example may be the best way to begin.

In her charming book, *Medieval People*, the distinguished economic historian, Eileen Power (1963) describes the life of a serf of the Abbey of St. Germain-des-Près, by the name of Bodo.[2] We may suppose Bodo to have been a 'representative man' of the tenth century whom we could compare to some 'representative man' of twentieth-century Europe or North America in a variety of ways. Most obviously, Bodo had shorter life expectancy. His life was hard in various senses, one of which was that it was full of hard, physical labour. His nutrition was inadequate by modern standards. He was not a free man. He was poor.

Why was he poor? The answers take off in different directions depending upon the economic theory one happens to have in mind. One theory of economic development might direct our attention to innovations: chemical fertilizers, the internal combustion engine and the tractor had not yet been invented. Another might single out the capital labour ratio: Bodo had too little capital co-operating with him in production.

The aspect of the answer that I want to emphasize is that Bodo was poor because few people co-operated with him in producing his output and, similarly, few people co-operated in producing his real income, i.e. in producing for his consumption. The point is most easily made by focusing on the consumption side. Suppose, we could make an accurate value

added accounting of the consumption basket of the Bodo family. Far more than 50 per cent of it, surely, would be accounted for by the direct efforts of Bodo and family members. Almost all the rest would be due to other members of his village. Only a minute portion of it would be associated with an exchange transaction.

The point is made more vivid if we consider the spatial aspect. It is quite possible that Bodo spent his whole life within a radius of a few kilometers of St. Germain-des-Près. Perhaps he had never been out of sight of the place. Similarly, almost all of the value added contributions to his consumption basket would have been made by people within that same radius. Perhaps he used a little salt from the Atlantic coast – that would be about the extent of his participation in interregional trade.

There is a similar temporal aspect where we would consider, so to speak, the 'location in time, rather than in space, of the people having contributed to the representative individual's consumption. Bodo probably used some inherited tools. He tilled land that had been cleared by his forefathers. Modest as his house certainly was, it may nonetheless have been generations old. Still, in the poor society, production involves less use of durable capital goods. It is less 'roundabout' as Böhm-Bawerk would have put it.

Our rich twentieth-century representative man, then, occupies a node in a much larger network of co-operating individual agents than did poor Bodo. His network, moreover, is of very much larger spatial extent. The average distance from him of those who contribute to his consumption or make use of his productive contribution is longer. Similarly, his network also has greater temporal depth – the number of individuals who *t* periods into the past made a contribution to his present consumption is larger than in Bodo's case.

The debates around Böhm-Bawerk's 'roundaboutness' concept have left us with the lesson that a perfect index for it cannot be found. That conclusion is bound to carry over to the task of measuring the temporal complexity of production and thus to system complexity in general. Usable, though less than perfect, indices may however be constructed.

Looking at the division of labour in the way sketched above will suggest that tolerably good measures for the 'complexity' of an economy could be borrowed from the literature on industrial concentration. For instance, instead of looking at the proportion of industry output represented by the k biggest firms, we would look at the proportion of a representative family's consumption represented by the n largest individual value-added contributors. Or we might compute a Gini-coefficient on a similar basis. In principle, such measures could then be used to substantiate some (not all!) statements about the increase or decrease in the complexity of the division of labour between different points in time.

We need not linger over the problem of the best such measure. One reason for not bothering, clearly, is that none of the borrowed concentration measures might be operational at reasonable cost in the suggested application. The point is simply that the notion of 'complexity' is not inherently vague – at least not hopelessly so. When the dates of comparison are a thousand years apart, at least, the results will hardly be ambiguous!

There are, of course, a number of other candidates for the 'strategic factor' in economic development. I am not prepared to take inventory. After the first oil-shock, many writers looked back on Western economic development as characterized first and foremost by rising per capita use of inanimate energy. Old-style Eastern bloc planning adopted heavy industry, particularly steel, as the strategic factor. The heavy industry model, in turn, is perhaps no more than a special case of the 'industrial revolution' conception of economic development which makes the growth of manufacturing industries the key.[3] This conception rules our thinking, for instance, when we become alarmed that the trend of employment in manufacturing may begin to behave the way we like the trend in agriculture to behave.

All of these conceptions of what economic development is about have something to recommend them – a context in which they fit – and there is little purpose in trying to make a general case against them. For many purposes, however, I believe that it is better to conceive of economic development as the creation of increasingly more complex structures of the division of labour. The standard of living of the average person is thus seen to depend on our ability to maintain the conditions – 'the extent of the market' – that make these complex patterns of co-operation feasible.

The division of labour and increasing returns to scale

In standard economic analysis we usually work with models that will never generate the picture of economic development that I have just given. Neo-classical growth models, for instance, or Heckscher–Ohlin-based international trade models do not show this association between living standards and system complexity. Conventional economic wisdom has it that rich people demand more diversity in consumption and that economies of scale in production are commonplace, but conventional economic analysis usually assumes homothetic utility functions and constant returns to scale production functions. In economies that would conform to these assumptions, the division of labour in the system as a whole can be replicated in a system $1/n$-th as large. Following Martin Weitzman (1982) in happily taking the theory to its *in absurdum* limit, one might imagine an economy where each worker produces his tiny share of every commodity in GNP in his own backyard. The Smithian 'extent of the market' is completely irrelevant in such a model.

The same is true in conventional international trade theory. Comparative advantage based on spatially immobile resources dictate that autarky will be shunned and trade will take place, but the pattern of trade between two countries would be exactly the same if the two were $1/n$-th their actual size.[4]

The reason why economists retain the constant returns models so desperately is not only that the alternatives are more complicated to handle – that, after all, would just enlarge the employment opportunities for mathematical economists – but mainly that we lack a widely-accepted theory of pricing under increasing returns, lack a convincing model of how competition operates between firms with increasing returns, and lack also a micro-founded theory of income distribution for systems of this sort.[5] I will supply none of these missing theoretical pieces but will proceed as if we could nonetheless

Harvesting in the Middle Ages. The lack of spatial and temporal division of labour was one of the factors of the serfs' extreme poverty Rheinisches Landes Museum. Bonn. FRG

discern some of the main outlines of a theory for such an economy.

The starting-point is Adam Smith's famous pin-making example. The essentials of the case are familiar to all (Smith, 1776; Leijonhufvud, 1986). Suppose we have a number of pin-making artisans (say 10) each of whom carries out the entire process of making a pin, using a number of tools in succession. It is then possible, Smith maintained, to reorganize work so as to increase greatly the productivity of labour. The way to do it is to define the production process as an ordered sequence of (10) tasks and to have each artisan specialize in one of these tasks.

This reorganization of work will extract greater output from a given workforce. Each task will be performed more expertly and much faster than before. In part, this is due simply to specialization on routine tasks, in part to assignment of people to tasks so as to exploit the comparative advantages of a non-homogenous workforce. No time is lost switching from task to task, and so forth. In addition, the organization of work according to division of labour principles saves on human capital and perhaps also on tools. The original artisans can be replaced by factory workers with a much narrower range of skills.

Smith's example of the division of labour shows this organization to be more complex in the sense outlined previously: a greater number of people co-operate in the production of any given unit of output. I want to treat it, therefore, as my paradigmatic case.

The division of labour and the firm: scale economies

Smithian work-organization will generally show increasing returns to scale. The structure of such a system changes as it grows: 'The Division of Labour depends on the Extent of the Market'.

The sketch of the superior pin-making technology does not tell us whether the increased division of labour takes place altogether within one firm or, perhaps, between several. The intermediate good resulting from the completion of the i-th task might itself be a commodity with its own market. Since firm-boundaries are thus indeterminate (at this point of our story), we cannot tell whether the scale-economies realized

from increasing division of labour are to be classified as internal or external. That said, it will be convenient to proceed as if we had to deal simply with a single firm, operating a single plant.

The (minimum-cost) structure of the plant changes in a number of dimensions as the market grows. The sources of scale economies usually interact, so that the realization of economies in one dimension opens up new opportunities in the others (cf. Leijonhufvud, 1986, pp. 213–16).

(1) *Subdivision of labour*: As output expands, the firm will look for opportunities to subdivide the production process into a greater number of distinct tasks, realizing new Smithian economies.

(2) *Parallel lines economies*: At low levels of output, some factor stocks capable of yielding a continuous stream of input services will be idle much of the time. If, for example, one operative on an assembly line is idle half the time, then output can be doubled without doubling employment, by building a parallel line and have him work on both.

(3) *Mechanization*: The next step, often a short step, in the evolution that takes us from the handicraft of the skilled artisan to the chain of routine tasks of the factory hands is mechanization. The continued subdivision of labour results in operations so 'mechanical' that a machine can do them – and do them both faster and better. To keep such machines from being idle much of the time, however, will require a correspondingly wide 'extent of market', so mechanization normally entails a step-up at the most economical scale.

The exploitation of the economies that open up as the extent of the market grows produces increased functional differentiation of both capital equipment and labour. But the implications for capital and for labour are not symmetrical. The roles of capital and labour in firm governance are not symmetrical either – capital hires labour, not the other way around. This suggests the possibility of a theoretical account of the capitalist manufacturing firm based on the type of technology sketched above. When the division of labour is highly articulated within the firm, this technology would result in a pattern of work-organization well represented by Henry Ford's original assembly line. (It may be best, therefore, to think of our theoretical firm as located in time somewhere in the early part of this century.)

The technology enters the problem in the following ways:

inputs tend to be complementary to one another (e.g., the assembly line stops if one worker is missing or one machine breaks down);

the typical machine is highly specialized, 'dedicated' to particular tasks in the manufacture of a particular product. It may have no alternative uses, but is on the other hand not quickly or easily replaced: it has a thin market;

the typical factory worker works at a specialized task, but an unskilled one. There are lots of alternative jobs for which he could quickly and easily qualify, but on the other hand he is easily replaced: his market is a thick one;

because of the returns to scale the enterprise typically earns a monopoly rent and because inputs are complementary this is a joint rent.[6]

Naturally, this is a hard-drawn caricature. (I hope the apologies do not have to be spelled out at length!) Using these assumptions, I argue the nature of the manufacturing firm as follows: the joint rent creates a distributional problem which must be solved in order for the factors to exploit the returns to scale. Complementarities among inputs mean that marginal productivities are undefined and give no guidance to a 'fair' distribution. Division of the joint rent becomes a bargaining problem that is only partly determined by the co-operating inputs' alternative opportunities in outside markets.

Suppose the machines were owned by separate 'capitalists'. Each one of them can block any coalition of the others which tries to impose a particular distribution of income. In the extreme complementarity case, blocking is done by withdrawing one machine, reducing total output to zero. The core of this game is empty, therefore, which means very simply that this is not a stable social institution. Capitalists will not choose to freeze their wealth in the form of highly dedicated equipment unless a reliable institutional form is found.

To stabilize the co-operative arrangement required for the exploitation of the economies of scale, ideally no one should be in a position to threaten the withdrawal of a complement to other inputs. (In the end, of course, the best that can be done very often leaves us with management facing unionized labour in a bilateral bargain of this sort.) The firm, therefore, is created to control all machines that are complements and have thin outside markets.

In manufacturing, therefore, the normal solution to the organizational problem has been that 'capitalists unite' in a cartel called the 'firm', and hire labour. Labour will have strong incentives to unionize in this particular setting. 'Labour hiring capital' is not a feasible alternative to 'capital hiring labour' under the conditions assumed. To ensure the feasibility of worker-managed firms hiring capital equipment, either the capital inputs should not be highly complementary in the line of production in question or the market for such equipment should be thick enough for competition to guarantee reliable behaviour.

In the literature on vertical integration, the boundary between firm and market is analysed along very similar lines. High degrees of 'asset-specificity' (Williamson, 1975; 1986) threaten inter-firm contracts with post-contractual opportunism or 'hold-ups' (Klein, Crawford and Alchian, 1978) so that vertical integration within one firm becomes preferred.

Computers, robots, and the division of labour

How is computer-assisted manufacturing going to affect industrial firms of the type just described? It is a question to which answers will have to be frankly speculative, but it is at least possible to point out some of the dimensions which will require study.

Factory employment and service sector employment. In recent discussions, it has become fashionable to express alarm at 'deindustrialization' and the growth of the service sector. Is alarm the appropriate response to the decline in employment in certain manufacturing sectors?

Adam Smith and Karl Marx both believed that the division and subdivision of labour was fated to turn industrial work into simpler and simpler, more and more mindless tasks. They both feared that the eventual result would be a proletariat of mindless simpletons. (Remember

Charlie Chaplin working the assembly line in 'Modern Times'!) But the increasing mechanization, which they also saw as resulting from the division of labour, introduced an offsetting tendency. It has tended to replace workers with machines at precisely the most repetitive, mechanical tasks while at the same time creating a range of new jobs that require the exercise of skill and judgment in the operation, maintenance, repair, and refitting of machinery. During this century, this offsetting tendency has surely long since swamped the original one that so preoccupied Smith and Marx.

Computer-assisted manufacturing should complete this development, replacing virtually all routine production jobs with machines. Machine operators will tend to be replaced by a few production supervisors who may do their work at computer screens in a control booth. On-duty maintenance crews are also likely to be more skilled because of the nature of the new equipment.

The computerization of the traditional industries will create a range of new jobs in the repair, reprogramming and conversion of industrial robots. There do not seem to be strong reasons, however, why these jobs should be performed by employees of the manufacturing corporations. Many such jobs are likely to be done on contract by outside firms. Many of these might be quite small businesses, on the scale of a local plumber or electrical repair shop – firms whose prosperity and survival depend on the skills of a single owner.

If these conjectures turn out to be right, the 'old' jobs will disappear from the traditional manufacturing industries while many of the 'new' ones emerge outside. To the extent that the 'deindustrialization and growth of the service sector' is of this sort, it should be welcomed. If the former is due to foreign competition and the latter to the growth of government employment there is reason to be concerned. 'Deindustrialization' is a word with frightening connotations, because we are so acculturated to associate 'industrialization' with economic development. That association is probably becoming misleading. Suppose our old manufacturing industries go the way of Western agriculture: very few jobs and embarrassing output surpluses! Why not?

An end to batch economies? The economies of scale of the traditional 'factory system' were

associated with standardization of the product, i.e., they were economies turning out identical items in large volume. Large batch size will become less important with computerization. The automobiles coming off a Japanese assembly-line, for instance, are no longer identical. Computers keep track of the colour and various options required for each car and do so at very low cost.

Consumers, therefore, should be able to look to a future where they will not need to compromise as much as hitherto with the manufacturer's conception of the 'median taste'. This, of course, will be a clear gain – although the biggest gain will go to those with snobbish or otherwise idiosyncratic tastes.

This particular development should not be misunderstood. That smaller batches will become economical does *not* mean that the economies of large scale are weakened. It means, rather, that the economies of assembly-line production can be obtained even while turning out differentiated products. At present, what we see in Prato or Taipeh – and perhaps also in Canoga Park, California, where I live – is that these new possibilities to produce small batches economically, using industrial rather than artisanal methods, are being exploited most vigorously by relatively small newcomers. In lines of business where assembly-line economies remain important, however, the long-run effect may be that large producers will be able to invade the narrow 'ecological niches' where the absence of potential batch economies has previously protected the small ones.

The Italian garment firm Benetton is apparently an example of this. They colour their garments after they are sewn up, obtaining economies of scale by producing uniformly white garments, and are able to provide diversity of colours in small batches without suffering the diseconomies of the usual speciality shop.

Another possible example is single family housing. It has long been true that the quality of prefabricated housing can be controlled much better in various dimensions than is generally possible when houses are built, and not just assembled, on site. In Sweden, prefab housing has had a fairly extensive market; in the US it has not – presumably because of more diversity of preferences in the American market. If it becomes feasible to produce the elements of fabricated houses without standardizing the final output – by having computers keeping track of how the plumbing is connected and what lengths of pipe this requires where, etc. – then small construction contractors may find themselves driven out of business by larger corporations.

The reduction in the diseconomies of small batch size which is a likely consequence of the revolution in information processing will not create a general tendency towards decentralization and smaller units. But there are a number of other new trends to consider and some of them may be more promising for small business.

The all-purpose robot?   Suppose that someone eventually develops an all-purpose machine, a robot that with the proper software and optional attachments can do 'anything' (i.e. everything that any machine can do). Not a likely story, of course, but the unrealistic assumption allows us to discuss in general terms the consequences of capital that can be converted from one use to another – i.e. capital that is 'redeployable' in the terminology of Klein and Leffler (1981).

Smith, Babbage, Marx, and Mill thought the division of labour in pin-making was efficient because, if required to switch tasks all the time, the workmen tended to lose concentration and dexterity. Now the computer, supposedly, does not lose its concentration, but robots apparently do lose their 'dexterity' if asked to switch a lot. A workmen can go back and forth between using a drill and a screwdriver, let us say, with little loss of time. To use robots to best advantage, I gather, one should not ask them to do that. Some production planning principles learned in the organization of human work may, therefore, gain rather than lose in relevance once applied to robots rather than humans. In particular, the precise sequencing of tasks becomes a more rigid requirement. (Suppose, for instance, that a piece of sheet metal has to be cut to a certain shape, have a number of holes drilled, be heated and bent, and then be enamelled or otherwise surface treated. With robots, one wants to make sure that all the holes are drilled at the same stage and not at two different stages; with human workers on the assembly line, it might not matter much.)

The term 'assembly line' should be understood here, not concretely, but as a figure of speech to remind us that production is an ordered sequence of tasks. Now, the theory of the 'old' manufacturing firm sketched previously argued in effect that we should find these task-sequences to be vertically integrated whenever it would otherwise be the case that owners of embodied capital at one stage of the production-chain could be 'held to ransom' by those at one or more other stages. The conditions that set up a possible 'hold-up' situation include: (i) a high degree of complementarity beween capital inputs at various stages; (ii) specialized inputs, such as 'dedicated' machines, that cannot be converted to other uses at low cost; (iii) thin markets for the specialized capital which makes it time-consuming and otherwise costly either to replace a particular piece of equipment or to find alternative employment for it.[7]

The all-purpose robot, we may suppose, would eliminate conditions (ii) and (iii). It could be reprogrammed and refitted for some alternative use at relatively low cost. And the market for all-purpose machines should be pretty thick – although, admittedly, there may be problems with 'all-purpose failures'.

The consequences would be two-fold. First, the rationale for large, vertically integrated manufacturing firms is much weakened. Here, therefore, we find that tendency favouring small firms that we missed in considering batch economies. Second, the all-purpose robot might well have a rental market. This kind of convertible capital might, therefore, favour the development of firms that are 'non-capitalistic' in the sense that they rent, rather than own, most of their non-human capital.

Return of the putting-out system?   The putting-out system never disappeared altogether, of course. 'Jobbers' have been ever-present in the garment districts of the world. But as a mode of organizing industry they declined relatively to the factory system with the coming of the industrial revolution. The system did allow the organization of production along Smithian division of labour lines; its evolutionary disadvantages probably had most to do with the amount of capital tied up in inventories and in costs of keeping track of inventories, including the losses due to theft. If so, these are the types of costs that have been radically reduced by computerized inventory control and the like.

As just noted, malleable capital, in the guise

Measuring time Keystone

of our hypothetical all-purpose robot, would reduce or eliminate the difficulties of linking various stages of production by contract rather than by overarching ownership. If a production process involves several firms, however, a co-ordinating agent will still often be required.

'Putting-out' in the literal sense refers to a co-ordinating agent who owns the raw material or intermediate product that his subcontractors work on. No doubt this arrangement will survive here and there in the world where significant differences in the cost of capital prevail between the jobber and his subcontractors. But, in general, we should not expect a return of the practice in this particular form. In an industrial organization context where, as we have just argued, the co-ordinating agent might well choose not to own the capital equipment the reasons are also weak for him to own the goods in process.

Subcontracting of most or all stages of production by a centrally placed co-ordinating agent is likely, however, to assume increasing importance. The co-ordinating firm may even stay out of manufacturing more or less completely while specializing in trading and in final goods marketing.

Division of labour in the macroeconomy

Let us move the focus of discussion from the firm to the larger system. Picture a non-linear input–output system, representing a manufacturing sector where each firm produces under increasing returns to scale. Every firm, we will assume, also uses at least one intermediate product that represents a significant proportion of value added in the firm's output and is, of course, also produced under increasing returns by some other firm or firms.

New sources of comparative advantage?   A subsystem of interrelated firms of this sort will show increasing returns. That means, as before, that part of the total income of the system is in the nature of a joint rent and that the distribution of that rent, also as before, poses a problem. In the hypothetical system where, by assumption, the 'hold-up' problem is no longer present it should be possible to rely on contractual agreements, governed by competition, to provide a solution. But, in general, asset specificity will not be altogether eliminated, and the contracting difficulties and transactions costs might well be formidable.

In a recent interesting paper, Julia Bamford discusses the sociological aspects of the economic growth of 'Terza Italia' ('Third Italy'). Her paper yields, among other things, some interesting insights on this problem. Stable, relatively tightly-knit communities are seen to have, in effect, a comparative advantage in stabilizing patterns of co-operation among numerous firms that together earn joint rents. Such communities can bring shared cultural values to bear on the contracting parties so as to at least narrow the range of bilateral monopoly indeterminacies. They can also keep track of an individual entrepreneur's reputation for fair bargaining and post-contractual performance. By contrast, highly mobile, 'melting-pot' societies would have a comparative disadvantage in this setting.

Costs and benefits of integration.   Finally, some questions to which there are no easy answers: What are the costs and benefits of 'belonging to' such a structure? What are the alternatives? How will the costs and benefits change as a consequence of the new technologies?

The benefit, of course, is that the average standard of living will be higher the more thoroughly integrated the local economy is in the world-wide division of labour. This, at least, is true in long-run equilibrium.[*] But getting to the long run can be fatal, we have been told, and there are indeed serious risks in committing oneself to such integration. The necessary political conditions for a very high degree of international division of labour might fail and usher-in international financial disorder or protection-

ism. In addition, the local economy becomes more dependent upon international business cycle conditions which cannot be controlled by national stabilization policies.

The problem is that productive structures such as the one sketched above are incapable of proportional reduction in activities. Although there are other, more widely held explanations for it, I believe this is illustrated by Okun's Law, i.e. the rather robust empirical regularity that output varies with an amplitude roughly three times that of employment over the cycle.

For concreteness, think of a 'representative firm' that runs two parallel assembly lines with some machines and their operatives serving both lines. In recession, the firm shuts down one line, but it cannot lay off half the workforce. To cover the higher unit costs at the reduced output, the firm would require a higher relative price paid for its product. But its customer firms are in the same position. Consequently, everyone is making losses in the recession and most cannot avoid making losses by further output reductions at the margin. Furthermore, the individual worker who has been laid off cannot induce the firm to start up the idle assembly line by lowering his real supply price, nor can the individual firm induce an expansion in the entire input–output structure by reducing the supply price of its output.

To the extent that final demands for the net outputs of such a system are foreign, national monetary policies can do little to stimulate a real recovery from recession. It will be easy enough to inflate, but difficult to bring about expansion of the input–output structure. As the division of labour becomes increasingly complex and spreads across space with less and less regard for national boundaries, failures to co-ordinate macroeconomic policies become more costly.

Recessions in systems of this kind are more difficult to deal with, therefore, than macromodels with the usual constant returns production functions would suggest. Large movements in real exchange rates are similarly seen to cause serious problems for production systems of this kind. To shrink a system with built-in economies of scale that has been adapted to one vector of exchange rates in order to re-expand in a new direction can be a horribly difficult process quite different from the smooth adjustment along the production possibilities frontier suggested by models that abstract from indivisibilities, nonconvexities, and complementarities in production.

Conventional economics is not conducted with the kind of production theory discussed here. Past neglect of it means both that intuition is not trained to go very far with the analysis and that there is little formal theory to fall back on when intuition runs out. For very practical reasons – the European Common Market's integration in 1992! – we need more theoretical work in this area.

Notes

* An earlier version of this paper was given at the third annual PROTER Conference on the Post-Industrial Society, Spoleto, July 10–12, 1986, and published as 'Costi dell'informazione e divisione del lavoro', in *l'Industria*, VIII:1, gennaio-marzo, 1987.

1. The general view of economic development taken here has its *locus classicus* in Allyn Young (1928). After long neglect Young's ideas have become the object of promising formal development in Romer (1986; 1987). The present article, however, attempts to avoid entanglement in old and thorny questions of where the lines between external and internal economies of scale are to be drawn.

2. Basil Yamey tells me that Eileen Power was so fond of using Bodo in her teaching that her London School of Economics colleagues claimed she was inculcating 'bodolatry' in the students.

3. Note that the three ideas mentioned all fit comfortably into constant returns models of production. They tend to miss, therefore, the increasing returns–division of labour theme of this article.

4. It is, however, in particular, international trade theorists who have taken up the subject in recent years and made some progress with it. That international trade predominantly consists of cross-shipments of similar products between areas with similar factor endowments is the apparent motivating fact behind this effort. Cf. the excellent survey by Helpman (1984) and the book by Helpman and Krugman (1985).

5. For the possibility – doubted or denied by generations of theorists – of combining increasing returns with perfect competition, cf. Chipman (1965, sect. 2.8; 1970), Helpman (1984), and Romer (1986; 1987).

6. In exceptional cases, competition from producers of close substitutes might make profits non-positive. But the jointness problem would, of course, remain.

7. Again, 'machine' is a figure of speech. The argument applies also whenever there are costs to dissolving a particular organization of inputs and finding alternative employments for them.

8. There is a tradition of citing increasing returns as a reason for protectionism (the 'infant industry' argument). The hunch underlying the opinions voiced above is that the loss from the general decrease in the division of labour occasioned by protectionism will more than offset the gain in some more or less 'infant' sector. But this is not a demonstrated conclusion. Helpman and Krugman end their book with this assessment of the state of our knowledge on this issue: 'Our analysis . . . suggests an overall presumption that trade remains beneficial in a world characterized by economies of scale and imperfect competition. Indeed, the presumption is for extra gains, over and above the conventional gains from trade' (p. 265).

References

BAMFORD, J., forthcoming. 'The Family, Agriculture, and the Community'. In *The Development of the Small Firm Economy in Italy*.

CHIPMAN, J. S., 1965. 'A Survey of the Theory of International Trade: Part 2, The Neoclassical Theory'. *Econometrica*, October.

CHIPMAN, J. S., 1970. 'External Economies of Scale and Competitive Equilibrium'. *Quarterly Journal of Economics*, August.

HELPMAN, E., 1984. 'Increasing Returns, Imperfect Markets, and Trade Theory'. In R. W. Jones and P. B. Kenen (eds.), *Handbook of International Economics*. Amsterdam: North-Holland.

HELPMAN, E.; KRUGMAN, P. R., 1985. *Market Structure and Foreign Trade.* Cambridge, MA: MIT Press.

KLEIN, B.; LEFFLER, K. B., 1981. 'The Role of Market Forces in Assuring Contractual Performance'. *Journal of Political Economy*, August.

KLEIN, B.; CRAWFORD, R. G.; ALCHIAN, A., 1978. 'Vertical Integration, Appropriable Rents, and the Competitive Contracting Process'. *Journal of Law and Economics*, October.

LEIJONHUFVUD, A., 1986. 'Capitalism and the Factory System'. In R. Langlois (ed.), *Economics as a Process*. Cambridge: Cambridge University Press.

POWER, E., 1963. *Medieval People*, 10th edn. New York: Barnes & Noble.

ROMER, P. M., 1986. 'Increasing Returns, Specialization, and External Economies: Growth as Described by Allyn Young'. Rochester Center for Economic Research, Working Paper No. 64, December.

ROMER, P. M., 1987. 'Growth Based on Increasing Returns Due to Specialization'. *American Economic Review*, May.

WEITZMAN, M., 1982. 'Increasing Returns and the Foundation of Unemployment Theory'. *Economic Journal*, December.

WILLIAMSON, O. E., 1975. *Markets and Hierarchies*. New York: Free Press.

WILLIAMSON, O. E., 1986. 'The Economics of Governance: Framework and Implications'. In R. Langlois (ed.), *Economics as a Process*. Cambridge: Cambridge University Press.

YOUNG, A., 1928. 'Increasing Returns and Economic Progress'. *Economic Journal*, December.

[3]

THE INFORMATION AGE
Robert Wright

Phantom of the Factory

Some sportcasters can make a sloppy, one-sided baseball game seem like athletic history in the making. Some newspaper reporters can turn a town council meeting that climaxed during the pledge of allegiance into three hours of high political drama. Some trend watchers—journalists and academics alike—can spot harbingers of social and cultural transformation at a Daughters of the American Revolution tea. All of these professional observers are attuned to a fundamental truth: there is little money to be made by telling people that nothing special is going on.

Inflated rhetoric has its price, of course. On those occasions when something special *is* going on, trend watchers are pushed by past excess to the outer limits of language. Having called ripples "waves," they must call waves "tidal waves." Witness the names already given to the present period of flux: the micromillennium, the microelectronics revolution, the technetronic era, the telematic society, the wired society, the network nation. My favorite, on grounds of sheer cleverness, is the mediacracy. For convenience, I use the information age; it is no less melodramatic than the rest, perhaps, but it is straightforward, and most people have at least a vague idea of its meaning: the information age is a revolution in work and play resulting from innovations in electronic communication and the coming of the computer.

Or is it? Harvard University Press is about to publish a book by James Beniger, a sociologist at the University of Southern California's Annenberg School of Communication, that may puncture the popular conception of the information age. Not that Beniger sees the information age as unimportant; on the contrary, he argues that, when viewed as an economic, and not strictly a technological, phenomenon, it is a watershed in human history. It's just that he sees it as nothing new. After listing more than fifty labels that have been affixed to the present (including those above), he writes, "Unlike most of the other writers, I do not conclude that the crest of change is either recent, current, or imminent. Instead, I trace the causes of change back to the middle and late nineteenth century." There he sees the seeds of "the control revolution" (the title of his book). And the momentous developments we keep reading about—artificial intelligence, the proliferation of microcomputers, massive communication via satellite—Beniger sees as but additional chapters in that revolution.

I find this view of things a little threatening. If the information age is indeed old hat, then this column might just as topically be called Victorian Update—and might just as well be written by someone other than me. Nor am I alone in being professionally jeopardized by Beniger's book. As the number of catchy synonyms for the information age suggests, trend watchers have turned speculation about the earthshaking impact of information technology into a small but thriving industry. Surely they will agree with me that this book poses a clear and present danger to the material well-being of arm-chair theorists and self-styled sages everywhere. Surely they will applaud me when I declare that I, for one, am not going to take Beniger's thesis lying down.

Beniger likes to look at the big picture. He not only views the control revolution against the backdrop of human history but steps back further and evaluates its place in the history of life. This perspective succeeds in (among other things) illuminating the role information plays at different levels of organic organization: What does human language have in common with the genetic code, the messages moving along a jellyfish's neural net, and the chemical trails that bind an ant colony? One answer is that all affect the movement of life—and, more often than not, coordinate that movement. Just as the preacher's sermon, the quarterback's audible, the Stop sign, and the rules of Monopoly impose order on the behavior of people, so can simpler instructions, made of only a few molecules, induce a cell or an organism or a bunch of them to behave coherently. At all levels of life, information is influence, communication is control.

Before the control revolution, says Beniger, came the crisis of control, a product of the industrial revolution. The crisis lay in a suddenly energetic economy: During the nineteenth century, the "entire societal processing system, from extraction and production to distribution and consumption," was invigorated by steam power. By the second half of the nineteenth century, raw materials were being processed with startling facility. Petroleum flowed from refineries, and steel from mills, in unprecedented volume. This hardly sounds troublesome; if a nation in the midst of industrial revolution couldn't use lots of cheap steel and oil, who could?

But, Beniger says, the matter was not so simple. Metal, for example, was assuming more and more elaborate forms; the ingredients of a single sewing machine had to pass "from foundry through tumbling, annealing, japaning...drilling, turning, milling, grinding, polishing, ornamenting, varnishing, adjusting, and testing." The efficient control of such a process was no easy task, and, besides, there were questions of distribution: how to get sewing machines out of warehouses and into shops all across America. The problem wasn't one of transportation per se; trains existed, and train tracks went wherever there were plenty of people to carry. But the system lacked coordination. Freight traveled circuitously; boxcars sat idly. Henry Varnum Poor, editor of the *American Railroad Journal*, wrote in 1854 that "cars in perfect order have stood for months upon switches without being put to the least service, and without its being known where they were."

America in the second half of the nineteenth century, seen from Beniger's point of view, was like a man with immense muscles but an unformed nervous system. It was a bumbling giant of a nation, a mass of unrealized potential: Arnold Schwarzenegger without definition.

Help was on the way. A technology of coordination was budding. Beniger's list of key innovations in control between 1830 and 1939 holds a hundred and fifty items. It includes the obvious: the telegraph (invented in 1838 but only later used to centrally regulate a large train system, the Erie); the transatlantic cable (laid in 1866); the telephone (invented in 1876 and eventually used to lubricate almost every phase in production and distribution). But the list goes well beyond the obvious, too. Through Beniger's paradigm, many things not commonly considered information technology are seen to be instruments of economic coordination: the postage stamp (1852), paper money (1862), the wristwatch (1905).

Indeed, even innovations not normally thought of as *any* kind of technology made Beniger's list. One example is the "shop-order system of accounts," under which each inchoate sewing machine carried a slip of paper charting its path through the labyrinth of production. More pervasive and important was the idea of dividing the labor of processing information—bureaucracy. Though invented millennia ago, it enjoyed sudden growth and refinement during the nineteenth century, as is reflected in a number of information utensils then appearing in offices: blotting paper (1856), the pencil with eraser (1858), carbon paper (1872), and the modern typewriter (1873)—the one with the QWERTY keyboard.

Also part of the control revolution were the mail-order catalogue (1872), the full-page advertisement (1878), and the national publicity stunt (1889). Advertising, after all, is an instrument of control—not just in its insidious manipulation of individual tastes but, more innocently, in the aggregate, as well; by using it to boost and fine-tune the demand for goods, companies can enjoy the efficiencies of large-scale and predictable production.

In short, the industrial revolution created a crisis of control in production, distribution, and demand, and resolution came only with the control revolution: a series of innovations in the way information is passed among people. The revolution continues today. Television shapes demand more powerfully than the full-page advertisement. Department store catalogues are being supplemented in some towns by videotex, which makes mail order instantaneous. And microprocessors overseeing legions of robots orchestrate automated production. Thus does Beniger see the twentieth century's electronics and microelectronics revolutions to be of a piece with the advent of the postage stamp and the telegraph. All fit into a nationwide project—more than a hundred years old, now—to build a nervous system that can master modern industrial muscle.

A rguments like Beniger's are more easily made than backed up. Human history is a messy process, in which causes and effects merge and diffuse with blatant disregard for analytical convenience. Defining eras, and isolating their endpoints, is like trying to find faces in passing clouds. Vindicating those definitions is sometimes as difficult as convincing a psychiatrist that your reading of a Rorschach inkblot is "correct."

For the most part, Beniger supports his argument the way historical arguments are typically supported: he tells a story that renders his point plausible; he lists crisis after crisis, and then solution after solution, in production, distribution, and demand. His story is convincing in the way that such narratives can be convincing, but it must be accorded the skepticism they are always due; a skillful narrator can, by shining the spotlight on the right facts, make history jump through hoops. Fortunately (for Beniger, as least), he has found less suspect support, as well: nice, hard, cold numbers.

The context for Beniger's numbers was set forty-six years ago by the Australian economist Colin Clark, in his book *The Conditions of Economic Progress*. Clark was, like Beniger, a lover of the big picture; he looked for the broadest economic forces, the weightiest trends. One of the trends he saw is arguably the weightiest in all of economics. "A wide, simple and far-reaching generalisation in this field," he wrote, "is to the effect that, as time goes on and communities become more economically advanced, the numbers engaged in agriculture tend to decline relative to the numbers in manufacture, which in their turn decline relative to the numbers engaged in services." (Clark did not take sole credit for this observation but traced it back to 1691, when Sir William Petty, a British economist, wrote, "We may take notice that as Trade and Curious Arts increase; so the Trade of Husbandry will decrease.") Clark thus divided the economy into three sectors, each of which flowers in its turn.

As it turns out, Clark's services sector houses an important subdivision—between services that deal primarily with information and those that don't. For example, plumbers, aside from a greeting, a brief interrogation, and the crafting of an ample bill, don't spend much time handling information. But lawyers, actuaries, accountants, and teachers do. Even doctors spend about half their time as information processors—listening to patients, collecting additional data through direct inspection, scanning memories and books for diagnoses.

Thus, the rise of the services sector masks the rise of a fourth distinct sector: the information sector. The agriculture and manufacturing sectors also include workers who really belong in this sector. Even agricultural conglomerates and manufacturing firms have to handle information, after all. (That is one of Beniger's main points; as companies have grown and become more bureaucratic, they have handled more and more.) For purposes of analysis, paper shufflers of all stripes should also be transplanted into the information sector.

The function of this sector, broadly speaking, is to keep the other sectors running smoothly—to mediate the flow of information that controls the flow of matter and energy in the rest of the economy. If Beniger is right—if the latest information technology is but the tail end of a long, gradual growth of the economy's capacity for control—the information sector should have begun expanding toward the end of the industrial revolution and expanded steadily into the twentieth century, as the nation's industrial muscle found greater coordination.

That is exactly what happened. In 1830, the information sector accounted for less than one percent of the labor force, but in 1840 the figure was four percent. By the end of the century, it had risen to thirteen percent, and in 1930 fully one-fourth of American workers made their living by handling information. It was in 1960—well before the appearance of the phrase "information age"—that the American economy became indisputably an information economy: the information sector, with forty-two percent of the labor force, edged out the manufacturing sector, at thirty-five percent, to become the largest part of the work force.

Not only had the information economy grown considerably by 1960; it had also just about quit growing. Between 1950 and 1960, its share of the labor force rose from thirty-one to forty-two percent, yet during the next decade that figure climbed only four more points, and further slowing seems on the way. If the estimates for 1980 used by Beniger are correct (recent data of such fine definition are hard to come by), the number rose by less than half a percentage point during the past ten years. The only other time this century it has failed to muster even a one-point gain was between 1930 and 1940, when the economy wasn't changing much in any respect.

The upshot, apparently, is that everybody did indeed miss the boat: the information age didn't dawn on trend watchers until the economic ascent of information had almost ended. How embarrassing: all these books and magazine articles (and columns) are dwelling on news that is somewhere between thirty and one hundred and thirty years old.

But perhaps there's hope yet. It may be that the leveling off of the information sector's growth signals another revolution, in some sense part of the control revolution, and yet, in a way, utterly new. And it may be that it is the first faint stirring of the next revolution, not an echo of the last, that all the talk is really about.

Another information-age book will be coming off the presses this summer, shortly before Beniger's. It extends the work of the late Princeton economist Fritz Machlup, the first person to clearly discern the information economy. In 1962, Machlup's book *The Production and Distribution of Knowledge in the United States* revealed that the knowledge industry (Machlup chose this term over "the information industry" only after some deliberation) was big business. The mass media, the schools, such professions as law, such trades as typesetting—all told, they had accounted for twenty-nine percent of the gross national product in 1958. And it appeared, Machlup wrote, that the figure had been rising for some time. In the wake of Machlup's death (in 1983), two of his associates, Michael R. Rubin and Mary T. Huber, have taken data he was gathering for a multivolume series, updated it, and arrayed it in a book called *The Knowledge Industry in the United States:*

This article first appeared in the July/August 1986 issue of THE SCIENCES.

Individual subscriptions are:
$21.00 per year within the US
$28.00 outside the US

Please write to:

THE SCIENCES
2 East 63rd Street
New York
NY 10021

or call 1-800-THE NYAS

1960–1980. Their numbers suggest—if only tentatively—that something important is starting to happen.

These data, like Beniger's, show a slowing of growth in the information sector. But they also show the slowing to be uneven. As Rubin and Huber define the information sector, it is populated by four kinds of workers: managers and proprietors (the people who do the paperwork that keeps the McDonald's franchise running); sales workers (car dealers spend most of their time talking, after all, and even manning a cash register amounts to recording exchanges of assets); clerical workers (secretaries, court reporters); and professional and technical workers (doctors, lawyers, engineers, draftsmen, scientists, laboratory workers). As it turns out, the first two of these categories grew as a percentage of the labor force between 1970 and 1980, while the second two shrank. So the question is: What do clerical workers have in common with professional and technical workers? The answer is that both have good reason to fear computers.

Clerical workers face the more immediate threat. Machines long ago began to assume such tasks as numerical computation, but it was only in the late seventies that word processors invaded the office. The invasion has proceeded apace. (And, whereas it once victimized mainly secretaries whose bosses didn't mind typing letters into a word processor, its threat is spreading: IBM recently demonstrated a machine that takes dictation.)

In the professional and technical fields, too, some workers can feel computers breathing down their necks. CAD-CAM systems (the acronym stands for computer-aided design and computer-aided manufacturing) reduce the number of draftsmen, even engineers, required to see some projects through to completion. And if the demand for accountants, lawyers, and doctors has been largely unaffected by computers, it may not remain so for long. One of the more impressive examples of artificial intelligence is INTERNIST, a program that can diagnose some diseases about as surely as the average physician. As for accountants, software now gives in minutes the kind of guidance in financial planning and income tax preparation that once took hours. And for $39.95, you can slip a copy of DiskWILL into a disk drive and receive instant advice on composing your last will and testament. (And this program, unlike a lawyer, will not charge for five minutes of thought devoted to, while shaving Monday morning, to your impending death.)

Of course, none of this necessarily means that the sudden slowing of growth in information-sector employment is coming at the hands of computers. Per-

haps nothing more is at work here than the difficulty of collecting precisely comparable statistics from year to year. Nor is it certain that many white-collar workers stand in imminent danger of losing their jobs to machines; much of the promise of artificial intelligence remains unfulfilled. Nonetheless, notwithstanding the continuity that Beniger cogently attributes to the control revolution, an important line was crossed somewhere along the way, and it may turn out to be a great divide.

The line separates information transmission from information processing. During most of the control revolution, innovations in processing have not been technological in the strict sense of the word, but organizational—lying mainly in a rerouting of information flow among humans. To be sure, technology has played a role; the telephone has permitted executives separated by several floors or city blocks or cities to function as if they were standing next to each other on the information assembly line. But the telephone —and the telegraph, the radio, the television, and the satellite—are, by themselves, technologies of information *transmission.* Only in the second half of this century, with the coming of the computer, has the large-scale automation of information *processing* reached the workplace, and only in the 1970s, with the coming of the microcomputer, did it reach workplaces of meager means.

In short, until recently, new information technologies had allowed people to do things they couldn't previously do. But lately, technology has begun to do things people used to do. Or, in Beniger's terminology: during the first phase of the control revolution, humans acquired control of the energy and matter whose movement had been accelerated by machines; during the second, some of that control is being delegated to other machines.

Beniger, of course, is fully aware of the distinction between transmission and processing, and he knows that much of the latter is now being automated. But he believes that this, too, is old hat. The great divide, he insists, was crossed a hundred years ago, in the 1880s, when Herman Hollerith invented a machine that aggregated data recorded on punch cards. In the census of 1890, the machine proved its worth, cutting tabulation and analysis from nine years to less than seven. By the First World War, various automatic information processors were in use, aiding insurance actuaries and battleship gunnery officers, among others.

Beniger's point is well taken; the technological roots of the computer go back a long way (and so, for that matter, do technological roots in general). Nonetheless, it is not clear that automated information

processing had much *economic* impact until the Second World War—at least, not the most elemental kind of impact; machines may have been doing a limited amount of work that people could have done, but they weren't taking away and degrading lots of jobs that people already held. That encroachment had to await other developments: mass production of the programmable computer, and then of the microprocessor. The first gave us a machine that could, in principle, perform any intellectual task. The second provided so many of those machines that just about any curious person could spend his time trying to fuse that principle with practice. Hence, the hacker.

The resultant phase of experimentation is still young. (How many articles about artificial intelligence, or even the software industry, did you see before 1980?) But all around are eerie intimations of our expendability: not just INTERNIST and CAD-CAM and DiskWILL, but also electronic chessboards that can humiliate humans without breaking a sweat, and other ominous toys. This, I think, is what underlies the apprehensive excitement about the information age: for the first time, the man in the street has met the ghost in the machine.

In justifying his depiction of the control revolution as a unified and important phenomenon, Beniger invokes a historical parallel: "Just as the Industrial Revolution marked an historical discontinuity in the ability to harness energy, the Control Revolution marks a similarly dramatic leap in our ability to exploit information." True enough. But what was most important about the industrial revolution in practical terms—in human and political terms—was that, as energy was harnessed, machines began to eliminate some jobs and eviscerate others. So, if artificial intelligence lives up to its billing, it is the second part of the control revolution—an explosive growth in the *automation* of control and a likely displacement of white-collar workers—that will hold the more consequential parallel with the industrial revolution.

Coping with the fallout will be difficult. The tried and true palliatives for automated unemployment, such as a shorter work week, may be less easily applied to white-collar workers. And, even if they are effective, other challenges will arise: How many Americans, in this age of easy decadence, will make wise use of more leisure time? Blessed with questions such as this, political, economic, and social analysts of all stripes—including trend watchers—can rest assured that theirs (and maybe theirs alone) will be a growth industry. ●

ROBERT WRIGHT *is a senior editor of* THE SCIENCES.

Part II
Information, Organization and Efficiency

[4]

The Economics of
Information and
Organization

DONALD M. LAMBERTON
University of Queensland

INTRODUCTION

The *ARIST* basis of this survey is unevenly distributed over time. Not since SPENCE in 1974 has an *ARIST* author attempted a broad overview of developments in information economics. In the intervening decade a number of chapters have focused on economic dimensions of various aspects of the information society (e.g., HINDLE & RAPER on resource availability issues; MICK on information-system costing; GRIFFITHS on the value of information; ZIMMERMAN & BRIMMER and ROSENBERG on aspects of national policy). Other chapters have tended to furnish broad scenarios (e.g., KOCHEN). In so doing they reflected major developments in research and publication. Information economics was emerging as a response to the deficiencies of economic theory built on unrealistic assumptions about the richness and sureness of information available to decision makers, failures of government and business policies, and the spectacular advent of intelligent electronics with its greatly enhanced capacities for communication, computation, and control.

Milestones are plentiful. In 1976, the entry "Economics of Uncertainty and Information" was added as category 026 in the American Economic Association (AEA) Classification System for Articles and Abstracts; in 1982 that category was extended to include "Game Theory and Bargaining Theory." Theoretical and empirical pioneering contributions had been made to the economics of information from as early as 1921 but especially since the 1960s by Knight, Hayek, Marschak, Bell, Machlup, Shackle, Boulding, Kornai, Simon, Arrow, and others. More recently there have been bibliographies and surveys—e.g., HIRSHLEIFER & RILEY, LAMBERTON (1971; 1974; 1975; 1976; 1978; 1982), MIDDLETON & JUSSAWALLA, OLSEN,

Annual Review of Information Science and Technology (ARIST), Volume 19, 1984
Martha E. Williams, Editor
Published for the American Society for Information Science (ASIS)
by Knowledge Industry Publications, Inc.

4   DONALD M. LAMBERTON

SPENCE, and TOMASINI—as well as conferences and symposia organized
by a variety of institutions—e.g., AEA, Princeton University, the University
of Lund in Sweden, the University of Pennsylvania, the International
Economic Association, the U.S. National Science Foundation (NSF) (jointly
with the National Bureau of Economic Research), the City University of New
York, Unesco (United Nations Educational, Scientific, and Cultural Organization), and IBM. This flurry of activity generated a still-burgeoning literature
that has already reached every category in the entire AEA classification of
economic articles.

It is important to emphasize this diversity. Much of this literature—e.g.,
that by KING ET AL., MACKAAY, MCCALL, NELSON & WINTER,
PORAT & RUBIN, RUBIN, and SOWELL—goes far beyond the narrow con-
fines of AEA category 026. Behind this diversity and detail is an exciting but
untold story of a battle for recognition and respectability by the economics
of information. Because of the volume and technical complexity of the literature, this survey is highly selective and views recent developments in the
economics of information as part of what may well be, in the Kuhnian sense,
the emergence of a new paradigm that is transforming economics and probably other social sciences. More specifically, the theme developed here is that
information and organization, in their inextricably interwoven roles, are
demanding recognition of: 1) their fundamental character as economic resources; 2) their capacity—with its limitations—for initiating, responding to,
and controlling change; and 3) associated, profound policy implications at all
levels of decision making. Two recent titles epitomize this theme: *The
Economics of Organization* by HESS and *The New Science of Organizations:
A Reconceptualization of the Wealth of Nations* by RAMOS. To establish this
theme and to tell a small part of the story of the conflict between the old and
new paradigms in economics, it is helpful to consider briefly the work of two
distinguished pioneers of information economics.

Before doing this, however, it might be well to touch on the formal definitions of organization. ARROW (1974, p33) suggests that a definition is probably impossible:

> Rather the concept is really a primitive term in a system, its signi-
> ficance being revealed by assumptions and their consequences. . .
> the term, "organization" should be interpreted quite broadly.
> Formal organizations, firms, labor unions, universities, or govern-
> ment, are not the only kind. Ethical codes and the market system
> itself are to be interpreted as organizations; the market system,
> indeed, has elaborate methods for communication and joint
> decision-making. As this example makes clear, the participants in
> organizations may be themselves organizations as well as individ-
> uals. Furthermore, it is important to note that individuals typically
> belong to many organizations.

A TRIBUTE TO TWO PIONEERS

Both Jacob Marschak (1898–1977) and Fritz Machlup (1903–1983) were
economists whose interests and contributions ranged widely but included
major developments in information economics, and both appear to have

THE ECONOMICS OF INFORMATION AND ORGANIZATION   5

taken up information economics in an attempt to analyze more completely problems already defined in economics. Marschak was keenly interested in the revival of expected-utility theory, explorations of statistical decision theory, and the development of subjective probability theory. In bringing these to bear on the demand for money and other assets, he re-examined the concept of liquidity and the importance in economic behavior of anticipating information. This interest generated a series of papers beginning with "Towards an Economic Theory of Organization and Information" (1954) and including "Remarks on the Economics of Information" (1959) and "Economics of Inquiring, Communicating, Deciding" (1968). These papers are available in MARSCHAK.

While Marschak started from the basic idea that the value of information is governed by the benefits generated by its optimal use, he recognized the importance of communication and the factors limiting the transmission of information. This recognition led to the branch of game theory known as the theory of teams. "A team is an organization in which the members have different information and choose different actions. The problem is the choice of optimal decision rules, prescribing for each member his action as a function of his information" (ARROW, 1979a, p505).

Machlup likewise found it necessary to reconsider the way in which the role of information was conventionally treated. He analyzed the economics of the patent system, which is a policy instrument that creates property rights in information as an incentive to innovation. He sketched for the U.S. Senate a cost-benefit analysis but realized that the operation of the patent system was only part of the much bigger process of investment in education and research (U.S. CONGRESS. SENATE). He saw that the existing framework of national accounting had to be modified if this bigger process were to be analyzed. The outcome was *The Production and Distribution of Knowledge in the United States* (MACHLUP, 1962). This comprehensive work defined the knowledge "industry" and furnished the oft-quoted statistic that this industry accounted for approximately 29% of the U.S. gross national product (GNP) in 1958. This pioneering effort stimulated other studies of the knowledge industry or information sector of other industrialized countries and led to attempts to make comparisons with the structure of developing economies. From the late 1970s on, Machlup was working on "the most ambitious project of his career" (CHIPMAN, pp489–490): a second edition, in eight volumes, of *The Production and Distribution of Knowledge.* Volumes I (MACHLUP, 1980) and II (MACHLUP, 1982) were published before his death.[1] These massive and detailed empirical studies are a major contribution to an increased understanding of the most rapidly expanding part of the global economic system: the information sector. Machlup's contribution had profound implications for conventional economic theorizing. As Boulding had remarked, "the very concept of a knowledge industry contains enough dynamite to blast traditional economics into orbit" (BOULDING, p39).

---

[1] Volume III, *The Economics of Information and Human Capital,* and Volume IV, *The Study of Information: Interdisciplinary Messages,* were reported by KOCHEN to be in press. An NSF grant was made to economist William J. Baumol to complete Machlup's work in progress.

6   DONALD M. LAMBERTON

Together these two pioneers had done much to shape the pattern of development of information economics. Marschak initiated true theoretical work and established a link with the study of organization as an information-handling decision system. Machlup provided a detailed statistical account of information activities.

THEORETICAL CONTRIBUTION:
CONFLICT AND NEW DIRECTIONS

The innovations of Marschak and Machlup did not transform economics quickly. As recently as 1974, SPENCE reported that "the principal effort" of research on information economics was directed "toward finding ways to incorporate information flows and informational gaps into models of markets in order to rigorously assess the impact of information, or its absence, on market performance" (p58). He did not assign importance to the new thrusts. There are several reasons for the slowness of the transformation. First, straightforward traditional economic analysis had proved very valuable in the hands of Marschak's proteges, Sam Scherer and Herbert Simon, who showed that the expectations of technologists about the impact of atomic energy had no prospect of fulfillment and the economics profession appreciated the advantages of such competence. Further, as Machlup himself emphasized, the market mechanism was "the largest and most effective information system in existence" (MACHLUP, 1979, p113). More time was needed for a full appreciation of the dictum that "to build exclusively on price signals is not a thrifty but a miserly treatment of information" (KORNAI, p313).

A second element in the situation was a willingness to attempt to ignore the further implications of both Marschak's ideas about organization and the rich detail exposed meticulously by Machlup: to contend that traditional economics could do the job of analysis because information is just another commodity. Depending on the analytical task, this could be true, but much escaped this net—for example, the shaping of strategies to cope with the processes of structural adjustment in industry, decisions to invest in R&D and other information, responses to changing patterns of international trade, and many business and government policy dilemmas.

To some extent the economic theorists were engaged in sleight-of-hand. For example, SAMUELSON could argue that the existence of increasing returns is the prime case of deviations from the theorist's model of the perfectly competitive economy. He could also add that "Universal constant returns to scale (in everything, including the effective acquisition and communication of knowledge) is practically certain to convert laissez-faire or free enterprise into perfect competition" (p117), without being concerned with the failure of the economics profession to explore the acquisition and communication of knowledge. As recently as 1980, WELCH, following in Marschak's footsteps, pointed to the limited treatment of communication in the analysis of economic adjustment processes, which relied on two simplistic and fundamentally different concepts: vertical communication (i.e., two-way message flow between an agent such as a factory manager and the central planner) and horizontal communication (i.e., direct message exchange between agents).

THE ECONOMICS OF INFORMATION AND ORGANIZATION   7

In the last two decades, Arrow's research on uncertainty and information (e.g., ARROW, 1974; 1979b), which was recognized by the 1982 Nobel Prize in economics, had led him to the following observations:

> One of the most interesting economic characteristics of information is that its cost is independent of the scale on which it is used. A given piece of information costs the same to acquire, whether the decision to be based on it is large or small. Thus, the formula for a steel alloy has a given cost, though it may be used to make one ton or a hundred thousand tons. Therefore if by joining in an organization a number of individuals can acquire separate signals which can then be used by all of them, net benefits (benefits less costs of information) increase more than proportionately to the size of the organization.
>
> Specialization in information gathering is one instance, in my view the most important instance, of the economic benefits of organization. The basic gain in all such cases is that a group working together can produce more in total than the sum of their products working individually. This surplus cannot be achieved if all individuals perform the same tasks, for then they might as well be working separately. It is achieved only by specialization of function, by a suitable sharing of duties. This is precisely the division of labor among individuals whose importance was so much stressed by Adam Smith.
>
> Of all forms of division of labor, the division of information gathering is perhaps the most fundamental. Indeed the chief gain from other forms of specialization is that the individual worker can acquire the skills for a particular task more effectively if the range of the task is restricted: in other words, the efficiency gain is owing to the lower cost of information permitted by specialization (ARROW, 1979b, p310).

In effect, Arrow was saying that individuals organize for the effective acquisition and communication of information. Because such efforts pervade the entire economy and confer advantages on scale, it seems unlikely that the magical "universal constant returns to scale" will be available to lead the economy toward the perfectly competitive model, as was suggested by Samuelson. It is even harder to reconcile this emphasis on organization with comments of STIGLER in his 1982 Nobel lecture, "The Process and Progress of Economics." In that speech he asserted that the economics of information had been accepted without struggle. The critical role of information had been long established in some parts of economic analysis—e.g., in oligopoly theory, which analyzed behavior in industries with only a few firms. However, in that case and in many other areas "the amount of information possessed by individuals in the market was arbitrarily postulated rather than derived from economic principles" (STIGLER, p539). Stigler took credit for proposing the use of standard economic theory to study information activities. He observed that an extensive literature emerged quickly

8   DONALD M. LAMBERTON

after his initial efforts, and "more than a hundred articles a year are now
devoted to this subject." On his interpretation, diffusion of the new ideas was
not only rapid but was also characterized by an absence of controversy
because no established scientific theory was being challenged: "In fact, all I
was challenging was the neglect of a promising subject. Moreover, the
economics of information was susceptible to study by quite standard techniques of economic analysis. The theory immediately yielded results which
were intuitively or observationally plausible. Here was a Chicago theory that
didn't even annoy socialists!" (p539).

The battle lines remain drawn. Arrow's line of reasoning emphasizes a pervasive condition in the economy that is inherent in organizing the effective
use of information, one that strikes at the very basis of the traditional mode
of economic theorizing. To clarify the issues, the starting point must be an
appreciation of the fact that recognition of the importance of knowledge is
only a first step toward an information economics. Early writers do not
appear to have gone very far in the attempt to treat changes in knowledge as
endogenous, as arising from within the working of the economic system,
although the suggestion that this began with Machlup (WILLIAMS) must be
rejected. For example, KNIGHT had already given careful consideration to
methods of meeting uncertainty. He observed that "information was one of
the principal commodities" (p261), that "vast sums of public money" and
"Great investments of capital and elaborate organizations" were devoted to
information activities. Admittedly he thought that they called for discussion,
in the context of his book *Risk, Uncertainty, and Profit*, "only in so far as
they affect the general outline of the social economic structure" (p260). He
pointed to "the existence of highly specialized industry structures performing the functions of furnishing knowledge and guidance" (p260).

Before pursuing Knight's question about the way in which methods of
dealing with uncertainty affect "the general outline of the social economic
structure," some further consideration of definition is called for. SPENCE
contended that recent interest in, for example, computers and telecommunications had obscured both "the pervasive influence of information in many
other markets" and "the impact of the information sectors on the rest of the
economy" (p57). This overemphasis was being redressed by recent research
that focused, as noted earlier, "largely upon the informational structure of
markets" (p58). STIGLITZ, in his introductory remarks to a Stanford symposium, again emphasized the market context but took the view that imperfect information altered "the conventional notion of a market" (p389). He
contended that central statements from the economist's theory of competition became questionable: "The basic character of how we ought to view the
competitive economy is altered if we take seriously imperfections of information" (p389). All papers in the symposium related to "the problems arising
from costly information" (389).

HIRSHLEIFER & RILEY distinguished the economics of uncertainty in
which individuals are limited "to terminal actions, permitting them only to
adapt to uncertainty" from the economics of information, which examines
"the consequences of informational actions, which allow [individuals] to
overcome uncertainty" (p1393). Their survey captured a wide range of information activities: acquisition, dissemination, R&D, espionage and monitoring,

THE ECONOMICS OF INFORMATION AND ORGANIZATION   9

wagering and speculation, signaling, and education, ending with comments on rational expectations and informational efficiency. Institutional or organizational aspects barely rated a mention. There were "interesting complications ...when the informational decision process has multipersonal aspects" (p1397), but these were not pursued. They concluded: "Information generation is in large part a disequilibrium-creating process, and information dissemination a disequilibrium-repairing process" (p1414). Where does organizational change of the kind plainly envisaged by Knight allow individuals to *overcome* uncertainty?

ARROW (1974; 1979b) added this new dimension. The past three decades have been preoccupied with decision making under a given uncertainty. "The problems of the economics of information proper arise when the probability distribution of states of the world is a variable" (1979b, p308). This opens up more ways of improving decision making. First, the decision maker can take advantage of the existence of signals, of messages about the environment. Second, the choice of which signals to receive becomes a decision variable. Third, in sharp contrast to the individual decision maker who dominates the economics of information literature reviewed by HIRSHLEIFER & RILEY, a group or organization will normally be the real-world decision maker. This is because specialization in gathering information is the way of achieving important economic benefits. To the extent that choices about organizational structure and efficiency are not constrained fully by past events, organizational change becomes a third strategy for overcoming uncertainty by changing the perception of the environment and the capacity to learn. At the same time this change improves the prospects of the other two ways: larger resources allow fuller exploitation of signals while enhanced organizational capacity can widen the range of signals considered for reception. However, organizational structure may be inappropriate, and "[s]clerosis of organisations may be as dangerous to health as sclerosis of the arteries" (ARROW, 1979b, p310). Arrow argues "that the combination of uncertainty, indivisibility, and capital intensity associated with information channels and their use imply (a) that the actual structure and behavior of an organization may depend heavily upon random events, in other words on history, and (b) the very pursuit of efficiency may lead to rigidity and unresponsiveness to further change" (ARROW, 1974, p49). As NELSON (1981) pointed out, traditional economics had not recognized that "man's data processing capacity, his ability to understand complex or novel situations, and his ability to gain agreement" are bounded, with important consequences for administrative parsimony, responsiveness, and innovativeness (p95).

There seem to be major implications for economic theory. The conservative approach (HAYEK), which emphasized that the economy was an information system but held that there were important limitations on the availability of information, left the institutional structure intact, with the consequence (for the most part not mentioned) of probable advantage to those individuals and organizations "having access to better information, or a better position in the institutional structure" (STARRETT, p282). This is equally true of the original version of the rich and sure information model of the economy, the modernization of that Hayekian system by SOWELL, or the resurrection of perfect knowledge thinking by the rational (consistent) expectations approach now in vogue. This latter approach prompted the comment: "It would be ironic if the outcome of a decade and a half of concern with the economics of (imperfect) knowledge resulted in the renewed dominance of models incorporating perfect knowledge assumptions" (O'DRISCOLL, p157). The biggest loss might well prove to be the inhibiting of the attempt by economists to probe deeply into the organizational aspects of the economy. Even Bayesian analysis, with its systematic way of incorporating subjective beliefs and a role for additional information in the revision of an initial set of probability assignments, explicitly falls short of what is needed: it "can be useful in describing the process of normal science within a paradigm, but new paradigms are not related to old ones by a generalized Bayes formula" (POIRIER, p397).

Of course, it might be argued that in order to cope with the disorderly real world, economics is devoting more attention to how decisions are made. Various approaches to *how* decisions are made rather than *what* decisions are made—i.e., to procedural rationality—have been developed: operations research (OR) and management science, artificial intelligence (AI), computational complexity, and cognitive simulation (SIMON). These approaches seem to be concerned with "the distinction between the perceived environment and the environment" (HAHN, p40), or, as Simon put it, "Procedural rationality is the rationality of a person for whom computation is the scarce resource" (SIMON, p504). He argues that there is no theorem that proves that the decision process will converge to limit survival to those who have found the objective optimum: "It is much more likely, in a world with rapidly advancing human knowledge and technology, with an unpredictable shifting political situation, with recurrent and unforseen (if not always unforeseeable) impacts of demographic, environmental, and other changes, that the location of the objective optimum has little relevance for the decision-makers or the situations that their decisions create" (SIMON, p505).

Simon believes that there are several specific domains of economics that can benefit from the procedural rationality approach—e.g., that part of microeconomics concerned with how decisions should be made, the theory of business fluctuations, and the Marxian or Schumpeterian domain of the long-term dynamics of the capitalist system. This belief may be beyond challenge, but consider the long term, in which the contention is: "The search for new products or new marketing strategies surely resembles the search for a good chess move more than it resembles the search for a hilltop" (SIMON, p505). Even if this statement is correct, the decision strategy may bear little resemblance to the search for a good chess move once it is recognized that the strategy can take advantage of the existence of signals, that the choice of which signals to receive must be made, and that the organization itself is a variable.

THE ECONOMICS OF ORGANIZATION

The study of organizational change and organizational options should then be properly an activity for economics. Comments and efforts here are of various kinds. For example, in the context of industrial economics BRAD-

THE ECONOMICS OF INFORMATION AND ORGANIZATION 11

BURD & OVER (p51) treat an industry's monopoly price as a "collective good" that is achieved and sustained by organizing:

> The costs of the necessary organization can be divided into those incurred in the formation of the organization and those incurred in maintaining it. In order to establish the communication demands, signalling mechanisms, and other rules of behavior which govern the operation of an organized industry, and in order to determine initially how the costs and benefits of the collective good are to be apportioned, an industry must incur fixed formation costs. . . .Maintaining the organization to ensure adherence to the price and output policies agreed to when the organization was formed is also costly. Resources must be expended to maintain channels of communication and on other interfirm activities such as exchanging information and policing the industry agreement, as well as on all intrafirm communication that guides the marketing department in its efforts to compete vigorously without violating the industry agreement.

The existence of such organizational capital changes the significance of any given level of concentration. TEUBAL likewise assigns an important role to "intangibles accumulation or capability creation, of which knowledge from R&D is just one possibility" (p56). Both efforts are in the tradition of the pioneering work of ANDREWS, who distinguished technical from managerial costs and examined the effects of changing organization. The possibilities of using the distinction between production and organization, the latter being equated with a modified information sector, have been touched on by JONSCHER. Of course, it is easy to overlook the possibility that expenditures fail to achieve the objectives that led to their being incurred. Because the effects of new information technologies—e.g., copying machines, word processors, and videotex—are so difficult to evaluate, this form of failure has been labeled the Xerox effect (LAMBERTON ET AL.). The further possibility that activities that are included in the information sector may be unproductive is emphasized by BHAGWATI—e.g., lobbying for protection, competing for a share of licenses, and evading governmental regulations. However, these activities may draw on the same organizational capacities as those activities that are deemed to have social value in a dynamic context, such as innovation.

At the international level, supranational forms of organization have received too little attention from economists; one must turn to journals of international business and even anthropology (e.g., WOLFE). While studies on transborder data flow have tended to emphasize an underlying conflict between free trade and dependence, they also have begun to cast new light on specialization in and location of the activities of multinationals. Two intriguing aspects of current developments in communications technology are noteworthy. First, these developments challenge the new orthodoxy according to which "Technology. . .has never been so internationally mobile. It now seems that only labor is a geographically fixed factor" (STOUT, p165). Second, these international firms might be viewed as organizations for international cooperation, which means that they are within the scope of efforts to compare the economic efficiency of alternative forms of international organization (e.g., TINBERGEN).

These samples of recent research initiatives illustrate the potential importance of organizational change at different levels: the individual business firm, the industry, the nation, and the global economy. The terminology differs in these various attempts to develop an analysis of the role of organization: organizational capital, information stock, capability, intangibles. In each case the analysis seeks to include an investment in permanent organizational resources, an investment that allows for the influence of past events on present decisions.

How does organizational change come about? What is the role of information in that process? One response can be to proceed in the way that has too often been done with technology—i.e., to assume that there is a manual that describes various forms of organization and that an optimal choice of organizational form will be made from the many alternatives listed. However, this approach makes no more sense in choosing a type of organization than in choosing a technology (NELSON, 1980). In a real world the pages of such a manual are widely scattered, they are costly to locate and translate, and they have very limited application to the special circumstances of any existing organization, constrained as it is by its history and its organizational assets.

SCHOTTER attempted to provide an economic theory of social institutions, which may help to answer this question. He regards institutions as regulating factors (i.e., regularities) in the behavior of social agents such as households, business firms, and government agencies. These regularities, created by the agents themselves, are used as informational devices to supplement competitive price information. Although Schotter shares the interest in organizational forms, his analysis suffers from a limitation that has been noted in other contexts—it is basically concerned with dynamic adjustments to changes that are beyond the control of the decision maker (SLATER). Can analysis be widened to deal with situations in which the strategies and payoffs are shaped by the chosen form of organization?

CASSON should stimulate renewed interest in the concept of the entrepreneur. Noting that economic theory has long ceased to discuss the role of the entrepreneur, he adopts a functional approach and argues that the demand for entrepreneurship stems from the need to adjust to change while the supply is limited both by the scarcity of the requisite personal qualities and the difficulty of identifying them when they are available. Contract and conjecture about the future are the two mechanisms of coordination, the latter requiring very special circumstances. Conflict over the sharing of benefits must be resolved before the contract mechanism can operate. The entrepreneur accepts the conjecture role, and because information in a public good, the entrepreneur is subject to continuing competitive threat. The increasing cost of synthesizing information from different sources limits the scope of the entrepreneur's activities.

According to Casson the acquisition and processing of information play a crucial role in determining whether decisions will be left to a market mechanism or dealt with internally by the business organization. Such internalization is very important in reducing transaction costs, and the advantages seem

THE ECONOMICS OF INFORMATION AND ORGANIZATION 13

so great "that almost every facet of economic organization takes this internalization for granted" (CASSON, p218). Important issues of delegation, incentives, and control must be analyzed. These ideas have a direct bearing on the growth and dynamics of the firm. Casson's concluding chapter examines alternative theories of the entrepreneur, all of which assign an important role to information.

HOENACK gives a comprehensive economic analysis of the internal workings of all kinds of organizations: public and private, market and planned, profit-making and nonprofit, and legislatures. Recent developments in information economics are invoked to show that:

> ...information costs lead employers to delegate discretion over
> an organization's resource allocation to employees. Employees
> take advantage of this discretion by pursuing their own objectives
> at the expense of their employers' objectives. Employers can limit
> the costs of this behavior by imposing constraints on employees.
> The nature of these constraints depends on the costs of imposing
> them and how much they reduce employers' costs of employees'
> contributions to the organization's outputs. (HOENACK, p15)

WILDAVSKY addresses a problem posed by Marx when he declared bureaucracy's hierarchy to be "a *hierarchy of information*. The top entrusts the lower circles with an insight into details, while the lower circles entrust the top with an insight into what is universal, and thus they mutually deceive each other" (MARX, p69).[2] Wildavsky focuses on an important element that contributes to the Xerox effect: "More data are produced because it is possible. The quota of data enhancement is over-fulfilled. But the task of data reduction becomes harder. The chance that collectible data will be missed goes down; but the probability it will be lost or misinterpreted goes up" (WILDAVSKY, pp29-30). Problems of how to measure the productivity of information combine with the absence of user charges to ensure overproduction of data. "Bureaucracy, the division of labour, and MIS, the multiplication of data, cancel each other out" (WILDAVSKY, p36). The remedy, says Wildavsky, is organizational: internalize. This will lead individuals and organizational units to ascertain the costs of information. However, he fails to recognize that the basic problem of the value of information will remain.

HESS acknowledges the contributions of Marschak and Arrow and gives the most compact but technically demanding treatment of the economics of organization. He recognizes that the economist's focus on markets has been misplaced: "Markets and organizations are substitutes and the replacement of one by the other is a common event" (p1). Just as systems can be compared—e.g., capitalism and socialism—so the choice or design of components of those systems needs to be studied. Organizations have a comparative advantage over markets where uncertainty is great and informational difficulties exist, but the construction and operation of organizations are costly and depend strongly on a complicated communication system.

---

[2] See MCLENNAN, p14, for support of this translation.

In 1972, Arrow was reported as viewing information economics "as an effort to plug a hole" in the economist's theory of general equilibrium (*NEW YORK TIMES*). If no more than this is involved, his position represented a big advance on the view that information could be treated as just one more commodity. (Perhaps some of the inadequacies of this view can be probed by considering what is implied if a perfect holiday or a perfect transport system or perfect manufactured goods were assumed.) As noted earlier, Arrow's efforts have taken him far beyond plugging holes, and he has sought to develop a systematic treatment of the economic role of organization as an information mechanism. Likewise, SIMON has pointed out that there are "some standard techniques for avoiding a separate theory of procedural rationality—in particular, the proposal that we simply fold in the costs of computation with all of the other costs in the general optimization problem" (p506). He believed that this would leave "unanswered all of the fascinating and important questions of what constitutes an efficient decisionmaking procedure" (p506). The emphasis, echoing the title of the well-known paper by CHAMBERLIN, must be on "the organization as a variable." Economists have to draw on organizational science (RAMOS) and information science in this effort, but history (e.g., CHANDLER; CHANDLER & DAEMS; WILLIAM-SON) will be a needed companion discipline. Optimization within an organizational framework is only a beginning. Further stages will involve a thorough application of the idea of organizational innovation. In this connection, it is proving extraordinarily difficult to escape the notion that technological change is concerned only with machines. The reality is that the concept of useful ways of doing things embraces both machines and ways of organizing.

INFORMATION-SECTOR AND -INDUSTRY STUDIES

Studies on the information sector and the information industry range widely. The important point is the need to look beyond individual case studies of either an information supplier or a user to the broader analysis of the economy-wide input–output interdependence of economic activities. Individual case studies are illustrated by studies of technological developments in, for example, banking, electronic mail, and telecommunications generally; a broader analysis would tackle, for example, the extension of Machlup's "knowledge industry" or the information sector study.

An OECD (Organization for Economic Cooperation and Development) project on the international comparison of information sectors used the typology of Table 1 and yielded the statistics graphed in Figure 1 (ORGANIZATION FOR ECONOMIC COOPERATION AND DEVELOPMENT). Figure 1 confirms the similar trend in the several countries for which data were available. LAMBERTON (1977) and KARUNARATNE & CAMERON (1980) showed that the Australian experience also fits this picture. JUSSAWALLA & CHEAH and KARUNARATNE & CAMERON (1981) published the first studies that were extended to developing countries. In line with earlier research that had shown that the service sectors of developing countries were larger than had been generally assumed, these studies reported relatively large information sectors in Singapore, Papua New Guinea, Fiji, and New Zealand. Work being carried out jointly by the East–West Institute of Culture and

THE ECONOMICS OF INFORMATION AND ORGANIZATION 15

Table 1
Typology of Information Occupations

Information Producers:	Scientific and technical workers (components)
	Market search and coordination specialists
	Information gatherers
	Consultative services
Information Processors:	Administrative and managerial
	Process control and supervisory
	Clerical and related (components)
Information Distributors:	Educators
	Communication workers
Information Infrastructure Occupations:	Information machine workers
	Postal and telecommunications

Information Producers create new information or package existing information into a form appropriate to a particular recipient.

"Scientific and technical" workers are primarily engaged in research, development, and other inventive activities. "Information gatherers" includes a variety of occupations that by investigation and assessment are mainly concerned with creating new information. "Market search and coordination specialists" principally provide, via search activities, market information to buyers and sellers or (as in brokerage) both. "Consultative services" are primarily engaged in applying a pre-existing body of information to the particular needs of the "client" or "situation."

Information Processors are primarily concerned with receiving and responding to information input. The response may be to decide, to administer, or to perform some manipulative operation on the information received.

"Administrative and managerial" occupations receive information in the form of details about firm (or departmental) performance and environment, instructions from above, and so on, all of which are processed into some form of communication to those who are superior or subordinate to them. Their job is to decide, organize, plan, interpret, or execute policy, whether in private or public undertakings. "Process control and supervisory" occupations also coordinate and control but usually in the context of a specific technical process or by a body of subordinate workers engaged in such a process. "Clerical and related" occupations receive information as correspondence and data, verbal or recorded, and manipulate it into a form appropriate to the employer.

Information Distributors are primarily concerned with conveying information from the initiator to the recipient.

"Educators" mainly convey information that has already been produced, and "communication workers" include various occupations in the news and entertainment media. Both groups include elements of information "production" (as, respectively, with research activities of university teachers and investigative journalism), but their primary activity is considered "distributive."

Information Infrastructure occupations install, operate, and repair the machines and technologies used to support the aforementioned information activities.

Source: ORGANIZATION FOR ECONOMIC COOPERATION AND DEVELOPMENT, Vol. 1, p24.

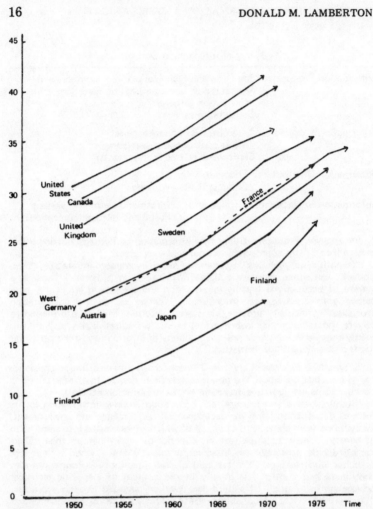

Figure 1. Information occupations as percent of economically active population. Data for Finland were derived from two separate sources (ORGANIZATION FOR ECONOMIC COOPERATION AND DEVELOPMENT, Vol. 1, p25).

Communication in Honolulu and the University of Queensland in Australia is extending the comparison to other Asian countries.

As mentioned, the pioneering work of Machlup was only partially updated before his death, and that task is now being completed under the direction of William J. Baumol. In recent years, Rubin has added to the database of Porat and Rubin (RUBIN; RUBIN & SAPP; RUBIN & TAYLOR). These supplementary U.S. studies explored the importance of the information sector in international trade, the relative importance of innovative vs. traditional infor-

THE ECONOMICS OF INFORMATION AND ORGANIZATION 17

mation activities, unemployment in information occupations, and inflation and the prices of information goods and services, as well as effected basic comparisons between the years 1967 and 1972.

COOPER has argued that projections of past U.S. rates of growth of the information sector are unwarranted and that a slower growth rate, with emphasis on products rather than services, is to be expected. However, world trade prospects and the increased marketability of information-sector products and services could have a significant bearing on such outcomes. Cooper also thinks that a restructuring of national accounts to reflect an information economy is unwarranted. This view seems to rest on the fact that old outputs have been regrouped into a new category, but this fact by itself does not invalidate a new accounting approach. Manufacturing activities existed before the Industrial Revolution, and agricultural activities continued afterward. Rather, interest focuses on the relative importance of the new and old components, the changing emphasis on specialization, and the perceived role of the new components in causing change and making it possible for society to cope with change (MACDONALD ET AL.). In this way, restructuring of national accounts may be warranted. This may well mean that the new data would be used in research first and in business and policy applications later. Certainly, a deeper analysis of the relationship between information use and productivity is needed (JONSCHER). It would be unwise to predict an increased demand for the services of libraries simply because society has entered an information age. Such a prediction would ignore the basic nature of technological change and structural adjustment in the economy.

Whether the "sector" concept to be used is as all-embracing as that of PORAT & RUBIN is an open question. An input–output study of the impact of technological change on the Austrian economy (AUSTRIAN ACADEMY OF SCIENCES) as of 1976 illustrates the merging of sector and industry studies. For example, the study distinguished traditional categories, such as food processing, textiles, chemicals, and the electrical industry, as well as such groupings as trade, information industry, and banks and insurance. Such analysis can contribute to an understanding of the process of technological change, provided the complexity of that process can be allowed for in the modeling. For example, economists have tended to assume that technological change is beneficial and is brought about by one kind of information production, R&D. Such a simplistic view inevitably leads to faulty analysis and unwise policy recommendations. In contrast, a more complex modeling of the information process is emerging (FREEMAN; KAY; NELSON & WINTER; SAHAL), with explicit attention to the role of information (STERN).

MANAGEMENT OF INFORMATION RESOURCES

Because this topic tends to have received coverage elsewhere in *ARIST* volumes, this section focuses on what is important in the contributions to managerial economics. The literature reveals two interesting developments of awareness. First, there is recognition of the need to account for the information function, which parallels the efforts of national income analysts to identify an information sector. Second, there is recognition of the link between information and organization, in particular, the fact that organization, information channels, and "capability" have the characteristics of capital in the economic sense. Here again the literature is massive, and only a few contributions can be mentioned. However, these contributions cross-reference much of the useful literature.

The book edited by KING ET AL. comes first because it is a collection of 24 papers from the years 1969-1982, but it has only one contribution from the 1980s. Its three main sections analyze the costs of information products and services, the pricing of information products and services, and the value of information when broad social effects are taken into account. Basic economic concepts are adequately explained, but the "key-papers" approach by King et al. requires the use of sequential papers in which new thinking was evolving. Consequently, although this volume is helpful in explaining recent history, it lacks the coherence of the volume edited by MASON & CREPS, which focuses on information-management problems. The characteristics of information as a commodity are explored, and the chapter by SASSONE examines market demand for services of information analysis centers. This chapter is significant because it is one of the few in which popular misunderstandings about "underutilization" of information resources are neatly challenged. Other papers address questions on innovation, including organizational innovation.

The two volumes edited by GOLDBERG & LORIN contain the papers from a symposium sponsored by IBM Systems Research Institute on the economics of information processing. Cost trends have fostered efforts to automate clerical paperwork and to provide relevant computer-based information to decision makers. The new technology has major implications for information processing. Here, too, the Xerox effect is acknowledged: "End users are programming, software packages are being utilized, and turnkey systems are being installed in profusion. This rush to 'get it onto the hardware' will undoubtedly result in a melange of uncoordinated, disconnected, noncommunicating systems in far too many organizations" (pv). The lack of "a relevant theory underlying the usage, structure, value, and cost of information in organizations" was also noted (pv). In an attempt to provide systematic coverage of these complex topics, the volumes cover: 1) organizations and data processing, 2) analysis of enterprise information requirements, 3) models of the information processing industry, 4) economic factors in justifying information systems, 5) economics of information processing management, 6) systems and applications development, and 7) quantification of software projects.

The economic models by DUNN & FRONISTAS of the information services market are the most significant. It is true that assumptions are made without empirical support—e.g., that the quantity of services demanded is a linear function of user cost and that total production costs are at most a quadratic function. These matters are far less important than the author's development of a user-cost concept. User cost is the determinant of a single user's use of information services and is given by "the sum of the service's market price and its unit monetary time cost to the user—the latter being the product of this user's value of time and the time it takes for him to use one unit of the considered service" (p143). To allow for the use of network telecommunications, a (distance-independent) unit transmission cost can be included. Values

THE ECONOMICS OF INFORMATION AND ORGANIZATION 19

of time and capabilities to use information may well differ among users and even among uses by the same user. Pricing policies may not be uniform, transaction costs may differ, and users may face different network access and communications conditions.

Although this treatment is still in the world of optimization rather than innovation, it is a major improvement on the usual producer/seller-oriented analyses. It can be adapted to both market and in-house activities and is a convenient basis for tackling studies of innovation and even organizational change. By highlighting all the factors that influence differential costs, it goes far in explaining differential cost/profits in industry and differential earnings among individuals. This equity aspect is of considerable importance, domestically and internationally, and has been emphasized by BACKHOUSE, BJØRN-ANDERSEN ET AL., SCHUMAN, and STARRETT.

Returning to the narrower view of managerial matters, even a brief review must mention the article by BAUMOL & BLACKMAN. This paper analyzes the cost impact of computerization in libraries. Because conventional library operations are labor intensive, there is a cumulative rise in cost per volume and/or student served relative to the general price level. The relative decline in computer hardware costs has led to computerization efforts. Baumol and Blackman show that because the decline in hardware prices has increased the proportion of software and other labor-intensive activities in the total budget, unit costs should not be expected to fall along with hardware costs as computerization takes place. Their findings may well have wide application, and it is to be hoped that their analysis will stimulate many careful investigations of other information activities. Those findings do, however, rest on a restricted view of the process of technological change involved. The various factors contributing to the Xerox effect will be operating, but they may be temporary. To the extent that they do operate, they add to unit costs. If there are learning effects, these additional costs may disappear later. They may also stimulate organizational innovation and so conceivably reduce costs. The finding of Baumol and Blackman assumed no such change, which was reasonable in a case where little radical change had taken place. BLACK & MARCHAND move in this same direction by seeking to expand the criteria for assessing the value of information. If this is not done, fascination with technology and its application will outstrip the social value of processing and using information.

TRADE IN INFORMATION GOODS AND SERVICES

DEUTSCH explored the propensity to engage in international transactions and began a study of the shifts in the balance of international communication flows. While this study was directed to political aspects of communication, it can be adapted to economic analysis. RUBIN & SAPP provided measures of U.S. information-sector imports and exports with breakdown by product. Broadly, this trade consisted in 1978 of exports of computers, computer services, and cameras and of imports of color television sets, cameras, and newspaper print. The trade balance favored exports, information exports having grown from 0.56% GNP in 1965 to 1.29% in 1978.

Analysis of trade patterns requires more detailed knowledge. One approach is to observe directly the communication flows between countries. SAITO ET

AL. analyzed information flow by means of mail, telegram, Telex, facsimile, and telephone and data communications for Japanese and U.S. domestic communications and for U.S.-Japan trans-Pacific communications. Domestic and international flows were closely related to gross domestic product and gross international trade, respectively. Factors influencing the flows were found to be technological innovation, service inauguration, and regulatory events. MANDEVILLE examined information flows between Australia and Japan. Movement of people was treated as a communication mechanism, and Australia-Japan business travel was found to be closely linked to direct foreign investment in Australia by Japan. Foreign language proficiency had an important bearing on the costs of this form of international information flow. Royalty and licensing payments were the only official statistics on technology flow but can give only a rough indication. Although Australia imports much more technology than it exports, its relationship with Japan was approximately in balance but was low—i.e., 3% of payments/receipts. In terms of goods, Australia exported bulk primary commodities and imported technologically sophisticated goods from Japan. Because patenting is linked to marketing, it is not surprising that Japan patents in Australia. Both Australia and Japan are below the OECD average in their use of international data communications. Both countries show stronger links with the United States and the United Kingdom than with each other in terms of international telephone traffic. These details are given because Mandeville attempted to work with a wider definition of communication activity than did SAITO ET AL. Taken together the work of these researchers has developed an approach that may cast a new light on trade and investment interdependence. Such understanding is needed both for busiess planning (SELIG) and economic development policy (LAMBERTON, 1983). Electronic colonialism (VAGIANOS) is a reality, and some countries seek to advance their own interests by increasing barriers to information flows, while others seek to break them down (JUSSAWALLA; SPERO).

INFORMATION POLICY

The debate on information policy is long established but has been inconclusive. In one sense information policy must be paramount. In contrast to science and technology policy, for example, which has aimed to coordinate given organizational units, information policy must seek optimally designed units because organizations are iniormation mechanisms. If researchers ignore the fact that the Frascati-type R&D definition (on which most national statistics are based) captures only a small part of the total innovation cost and if they interpret technology narrowly to exclude organizational matters, it may seem that science and technology policy can be clearly separated from information policy. If these assumptions are relaxed, major difficulties arise. The analytical difficulties are those posed by NELSON (1980), who challenges traditional notions of R&D policy and argues that even the economist's analytical distinction between movements along and movements of the production function is, in many cases, fuzzy. These matters assume importance because the coordination, issue-by-issue approach takes the institutional contraints as given. The design of those institutions, including business organizations, affects not only the coordination process but shapes the perceptions of the

THE ECONOMICS OF INFORMATION AND ORGANIZATION 21

environment and of the economic process itself. The solution may seem relatively straightforward—design optimal organizations. However, capital investment in organization absorbs resources, and: "the theoretical problems of design of organizations along these lines have barely begun to be analyzed" (ARROW, 1979b, p312). Achievement of optimal design presupposes a capacity to design such systems and an understanding of decision systems that seems elusive. It takes time to build organization and to construct physical assets, and there are likely to be time/cost tradeoffs. Further, there is the element of resistance because organizational change involves conflict of interest and redistribution of power and economic benefits. Once it is recognized that informational efficiency and organizational arrangements are not separable, mere coordination of given units can be seen as a makeshift measure rather than a genuine policy.

An emphasis on "basic science and hardware" may well inhibit research on the structural aspects of the information sector: the interrelationships among the primary and secondary sectors and noninformation activities (LAMBERTON, 1982). In economies in which as many as three out of four people work in the service sector, organizational aspects deserve more attention than they now receive. Those organizational aspects may have an important bearing on productivity trends. The production problem has given way to the organizational problem. The former have been well served by traditional science and technology, but the latter calls for major developments in information policy. If the wider view of the information sector were to replace the narrower emphasis on basic science, confidence in the identity of *the* driving forces behind the growth of the information sector might be undermined. If such a change of viewpoint yielded an improved knowledge of the structural aspects of the information sector, it could make possible the interpretation of "best-practice" science indicators or even create better science, technology, and innovation indicators.

The boundaries of the information sector extend beyond national borders. For example, satellite communications merge national and international currency markets. More generally, the growth of the information economy is reflected in the increasing importance of trade in services: shipping, airlines, telecommunications and transborder data flows, banking, tourism, motion pictures, engineering/construction, modeling, and franchising. There has been lobbying at OECD for a Data Declaration, comparable with the earlier Trade Declaration, which was designed to reduce trade barriers and generally to promote free trade. Resolution of these issues calls for empirical studies of international information flows in a broadly defined way. A precondition would be a rethinking of traditional trade theory (JUSSAWALLA & LAMBERTON; SHELP).

Recent calls for industrial policy and technology policy and the widespread debate about the creation of a microelectronics industry and the promotion of "high technology" pose the need for integrating policies on the economy, technology, and information. So far there has been little reason to expect that other countries will emulate Japan's Fifth Generation Computer project, an endeavor that has sent shivers down the spines of some trading competitors. This project is closer to Machlup's broad "knowledge industry" approach than a narrow scientific and technological information one. Information processing systems are expected to play the following roles: 1) to increase productivity in low-productivity areas; 2) to meet international competition and contribute toward international cooperation; 3) to assist in saving energy and resources; and 4) to cope with an aged society (FEIGENBAUM & MCCORDUCK). This formulation of goals raises questions about the scope of national information policy. DUNN (p38) advocates boundaries that include:

> . . .what we know as a people, what we are doing to learn more, and the tools that we use to conduct individual transactions and to communicate on a person-to-person basis. . . .There is a value in bringing together the ideas and issues involved in this set of national activities, because doing so calls to our attention the interrelatedness and importance in our lives. There are opportunities for improving the operation of the systems that provide information services. . . .Many of these opportunities will be enhanced by taking an integrated view of this area.

The book by RUBIN serves effectively as a substitute for the diffuse literature on U.S. information policy. Not only does this work update and add to information-sector statistics, it also reviews the information policy debate and provides extensive extracts from relevant documents. The coverage extends to transborder data flows, government participation in the marketplace, management of scientific and technological information, technological information as a source of market power, and personal privacy. JUSSAWALLA & LAMBERTON and O'BRIEN extend the debate to developing countries. The discussion by SAUNDERS ET AL. is the most comprehensive available of a particular but important aspect of the situation of the developing countries, telecommunications.

It is doubtful that the implications of the basic proposition that information is an economic resource have penetrated the debate on international economic relationships. There are conflicts of interests, and there are disparities of economic power. Bargaining leads to the formation of coalitions of varying degrees of permanence. Not surprisingly, for reasons outlined in this review, the uncertainties and informational problems favor resort to organizational solutions rather than simple market solutions. The effort by WOLFE is one of few to develop a systematic study of supranational organization.

CONCLUSION

During the period covered by this review, the literature of the economics of information has shown a sharpening focus on the role of organization. Initially, it seemed an important step when information was described as a resource. Slowly, the full implications of this statement were explored. The real resource has proved to be neither the information itself nor the hardware that is used to store and transmit it. Organization is the key resource that enables communication to be used effectively, and like stocks of information and the hardware, it possesses the essential attributes of capital as economists have used that concept—it can generate profit and income.

THE ECONOMICS OF INFORMATION AND ORGANIZATION 23

A presentation of the interwoven roles of information and organization and an exploration of their economic significance has been complicated by the conflicting attitudes among economists and by the lack of an agreed terminology that inevitably characterizes the emergence of a new vantage point or paradigm.

Research results enable a plausible case to be made for calling the modern economy an information economy. This creates a need for:

- Greater understanding of the ways in which organizational constraints affect the learning process;
- Progress in the design of optimal forms of organization;
- The treatment of information as a line item, with assessment of both its value and its cost;
- Modernization of educational practice to take account of the conditions of the information economy;
- Reassessment of research priorities to give greater attention to informational efficiency and organizational design;
- Rethinking of much economic theory in line with the idea that markets and organizations are substitutes for one another; and
- Reformulation of many policies of business and goverments that tend to ignore the economic character of organizational constraints.

BIBLIOGRAPHY

ANDREWS, P. W. S. 1949. Manufacturing Business. London, England: Macmillan; 1949. 308p.

ARROW, KENNETH J. 1974. The Limits of Organization. New York, NY: W. W. Norton; 1974. 86p. ISBN: 0-393-05507-8.

ARROW, KENNETH J. 1979a. Jacob Marschak. In: Sills, David L., ed. International Encyclopedia of the Social Sciences, Biographical Supplement: Volume 18. New York, NY: Free Press; 1979. 500–507. ISBN: 0-02-895510-2; LC: 68-10023.

ARROW, KENNETH J. 1979b. The Economics of Information. In: Dertouzos, Michael L.; Moses, Joel, eds. The Computer Age: A Twenty-Year View. Cambridge, MA: MIT Press; 1979. 306–317. ISBN: 0-262-04055-7.

AUSTRIAN ACADEMY OF SCIENCES; AUSTRIAN INSTITUTE FOR ECONOMIC RESEARCH. 1981. Mikroelektronik: Anwendungen, Verbreitung und Auswirkungen am Beispiel Österreichs. New York, NY: Springer-Verlag; 1981. 186p. ISBN: 3-211-81679-8.

BACKHOUSE, ROGER. 1982. Information Services for Trade Unionists. Buckden, England: Elm Publications; 1982. 36p. ISBN: 0-950-5828-40. (Information and Library Manager Occasional Papers no. 1. ISSN: 0262-9755).

BAUMOL, W. J.; BLACKMAN, S. A. BATEY. 1983. Electronics, the Cost Disease, and the Operation of Libraries. Journal of the American Society for Information Science. 1983 May; 34(3): 181–191. ISSN: 0002-8231.

BELL, DANIEL. 1976. The Coming of Post-Industrial Society: A Venture in Social Forecasting. Harmondsworth, England: Penguin Books; 1976. 507p. ISBN: 0-14-055115-8.

BHAGWATI, J. N. 1982. Directly Unproductive, Profit-Seeking (DUP) Activities. Journal of Political Economy. 1982 October; 90(5): 988-1002. ISSN: 0022-3808.

BJØRN-ANDERSEN, N.; EARL, M.; HOLST, O.; MUMFORD, E., eds. 1982. Information Society: For Richer, For Poorer. Amsterdam, The Netherlands: North-Holland; 1982. 320p. ISBN: 0-444-86426-1.

BLACK, SENA HOOSENALLY; MARCHAND, DONALD A. 1982. Assessing the Value of Information in Organizations: A Challenge for the 1980s. The Information Society Journal. 1982; 1(3): 191-225. ISSN: 0197-2243.

BOULDING, K. E. 1963. The Knowledge Industry. Review of Fritz Machlup, *The Production and Distribution of Knowledge in the United States.* Challenge. 1963 May; 11(8): 36-38. ISSN: 0577-5132.

BRADBURD, R. M.; OVER, A. MEAD, JR. 1982. Organizational Costs, "Sticky Equilibria", and Critical Levels of Concentration. Review of Economics and Statistics. 1982 February; 64: 50-58. ISSN: 0034-6535.

CASSON, MARK. 1982. The Entrepreneur: An Economic Theory. Totowa, NJ: Barnes & Noble; 1982. 418p. ISBN: 0-389-20328-9.

CHAMBERLIN, E. H. 1953. The Product as an Economic Variable. Quarterly Journal of Economics. 1953 February; 67: 1-29. ISSN: 0033-5533.

CHANDLER, A. D., JR. 1977. The Visible Hand: The Managerial Revolution in American Business. Cambridge, MA: Belknap Press of Harvard University Press; 1977. 608p. ISBN: 0-674-94051-2.

CHANDLER, A. D., JR.; DAEMS, H., eds. 1980. Managerial Hierarchies: Comparative Perspectives on the Rise of the Modern Industrial Enterprise. Cambridge, MA: Harvard University Press; 1980. 256p. ISBN: 0-674-54740-3.

CHIPMAN, JOHN S. 1979. Fritz Machlup. In: Sills, David L., ed. International Encyclopedia of the Social Sciences, Biographical Supplement: Volume 18. New York, NY: Free Press; 1979. 486-491. ISBN: 0-02-895510-2; LC: 68-10023.

COOPER, MICHAEL D. 1983. The Structure and Future of the Information Economy. Information Processing and Management. 1983; 19(1): 9-26. ISSN: 0306-4573.

DEUTSCH, KARL W. 1979. Tides Among Nations. New York, NY: Free Press; 1979. 342p. ISBN: 0-02-907300-6.

DUNN, DONALD A. 1982. Developing Information Policy. Telecommunications Policy. 1982 March; 6(1): 21-38. ISSN: 0308-5961.

DUNN, DONALD A.; FRONISTAS, ARISTIDES C. 1982. Economic Models of Information Services. In: Goldberg, Robert; Lorin, Harold, eds. The Economics of Information Processing; Volume 1. New York, NY: Wiley-Interscience; 1982. 238p. ISBN: 0-471-09206-1.

FEIGENBAUM, EDWARD A.; MCCORDUCK, PAMELA. 1983. The Fifth Generation. Artificial Intelligence and Japan's Computer Challenge to the World. London, England: Addison-Wesley; 1983. 275p. ISBN: 0-201-11519-0.

FREEMAN, CHRISTOPHER. 1982. The Economics of Industrial Innovation. 2nd edition. London, England: Frances Pinter; 1982. 250p. ISBN: 0-86187-211-8.

THE ECONOMICS OF INFORMATION AND ORGANIZATION 25

GOLDBERG, ROBERT; LORIN, HAROLD. 1982. The Economics of Information Processing. New York, NY: Wiley-Interscience; 1982. Volume 1: p238; Volume 2: p185. ISBN: 0-471-09206-1 (v.1); 0-471-09767-5 (v.2).

GRIFFITHS, JOSÉ-MARIE. 1982. The Value of Information and Related Systems, Products, and Services. In: Williams, Martha E., ed. Annual Review of Information Science and Technology: Volume 17. White Plains, NY: Knowledge Industry Publications for the American Society for Information Science; 1982. 269-284. ISBN: 0-86729-032-3; ISSN: 0066-4200; LC: 66-25096.

HAHN, F. H. 1973. On the Notion of Equilibrium in Economics. Cambridge, England: Cambridge University Press; 1973. 44p. ISBN: 0-521-20326-0.

HESS, JAMES D. 1983. The Economics of Organization. Amsterdam, The Netherlands: North-Holland; 1983. 284p. ISBN: 0444-86589-6.

HINDLE, ANTHONY; RAPER, DIANE. 1976. The Economics of Information. In: Williams, Martha E., ed. Annual Review of Information Science and Technology: Volume 11. Washington, DC: American Society for Information Science; 1976. 27-54. ISBN: 0-87715-212-8; ISSN: 0066-4200; LC: 66-25096.

HIRSHLEIFER, J.; RILEY, JOHN G. 1979. The Analytics of Uncertainty and Information: An Expository Survey. Journal of Economic Literature. 1979 December; 17(4): 1375-1421. ISSN: 0022-0515.

HOENACK, STEPHEN A. 1983. Economic Behavior within Organizations. Cambridge, England: Cambridge University Press; 1983. 290p. ISBN: 0-521-23993-1.

JONSCHER, CHARLES. 1983. Information Resources and Economic Productivity. Information Economics and Policy. 1983: 1(1): 13-35. ISSN: 0167-6245.

JUSSAWALLA, MEHEROO. 1983. International Trade and Welfare Implications of Transborder Data Flows. Prometheus. 1983 June; 1(1): 84-97. ISSN: 0810-9028.

JUSSAWALLA, MEHEROO; CHEAH, CHEE-WAH. 1983. Towards an Information Economy: A Case Study of Singapore. Information Economics and Policy. 1983; 1(2): 161-176. ISSN: 0167-6245.

JUSSAWALLA, MEHEROO; LAMBERTON, D. M., eds. 1982. Communication Economics and Development. Elmsford, NY: Pergamon Press; 1982. 345p. ISBN: 0-08-027520-6.

KARUNARATNE, N. D.; CAMERON, A. D. 1980. Input-Output Analysis of the Australian Information Economy. Information and Management. 1980; 3(5): 191-206. ISSN: 0378-7206.

KARUNARATNE, N. D.; CAMERON, A. D. 1981. A Comparative Analysis of the 'Information Economy' in Developed and Developing Countries. Journal of Information Science. 1981 July; 3(3): 113-127. ISSN: 0165-5515.

KAY, NEIL M. 1979. The Innovating Firm. London, England: Macmillan; 1979. 266p. ISBN: 0-333-23265-8.

KING, DONALD W.; RODERER, NANCY K.; OLSEN, HAROLD A., eds. 1983. Key Papers in the Economics of Information. White Plains, NJ: Knowledge Industry Publications for the American Society for Information Science; 1983. 372p. ISBN: 0-86729-040-4.

KNIGHT, FRANK H. 1921. Risk, Uncertainty, and Profit. (Reissued by London School of Economics and Political Science). Boston, MA: Houghton, Mifflin; 1921. 381p.

26   DONALD M. LAMBERTON

KOCHEN, MANFRED.   1983.   Information and Society.   In: Williams,
   Martha E., ed.   Annual Review of Information Science and Technology:
   Volume 18.   White Plains, NY: Knowledge Industry Publications for the
   American Society for Information Science; 1983.   277–304.   ISBN:
   0-86729-050-1; ISSN: 0066-4200; LC: 66-25096.
KORNAI, J.   1971.   Economic Systems Theory and General Equilibrium
   Theory.   Acta Oeconomica.   1971; 6(4): 297–317.
LAMBERTON, DONALD M., ed.   1971.   Economics of Information and
   Knowledge.   Harmondsworth, England: Penguin Books; 1971.   384p.
   ISBN: 0-1408-0248-7.
LAMBERTON, DONALD M., special ed.   1974.   The Information Revolu-
   tion.   Annals of the American Academy of Political and Social Science
   1974 March; 412: 162p.   LC: 73-89781.
LAMBERTON, DONALD M.   1975.   Who Owns the Unexpected? A Perspec-
   tive on the Nation's Information Industry.   St. Lucia, Australia: Univer-
   sity of Queensland Press; 1975.   32p.   ISBN: 0-7022-1294-6.
LAMBERTON, DONALD M.   1976.   National Policy for Economic Infor-
   mation.   International Social Science Journal.   1976; 28(3): 449–465.
   ISSN: 0020-8701.
LAMBERTON, DONALD M.   1977.   Structure and Growth of Communica-
   tions Services.   In: Tucker, K. A., ed.   The Economics of the Australian
   Service Sector.   London, England; Croom Helm; 1977.   143–166.
   ISBN: 0-85664-354-8.
LAMBERTON, DONALD M.   1978.   The Economics of Communication.
   In: Rahim, Syed A.; Lamberton, D. M.; Wedemeyer, D.; Holmstrom, J.;
   Middleton, J.; Hudson, B., eds.   Planning Methods, Models, and Organi-
   zation: A Review Study for Communication Policy Making and Planning.
   Honolulu, HI: East-West Center; 1978.   21–97.
LAMBERTON, DONALD M.   1982.   The Theoretical Implications of
   Measuring the Communication Sector.   In: Jussawalla, Meheroo; Lam-
   berton, D. M., eds.   Communication Economics and Development.   Elms-
   ford, NY: Pergamon Press; 1982.   36–59.   ISBN: 0-08-027520-6.
LAMBERTON, DONALD M.   1983.   Information, Organization, and Development Policy.   Information Society Journal.   1983; 2(1): 35–51.   ISSN:
   0197-2243.
LAMBERTON, DONALD M.; MACDONALD, S.; MANDEVILLE, T. D.
   1982.   Productivity and Technological Change.   Canberra Bulletin of
   Public Administration.   1982 Winter; 9(2): 23–30.   ISSN: 0811-6318.
MCCALL, JOHN J., ed.   1982.   The Economics of Information and Uncertainty.   Chicago, IL: University of Chicago Press; 1982.   324p.   ISBN:
   0-226-55559-3.
MACDONALD, STUART; LAMBERTON, DONALD M.; MANDEVILLE,
   T. D.   1983.   The Trouble with Technology: Explorations in the Process
   of Technological Change.   New York, NY: St. Martin's Press; 1983.
   224p.   ISBN: 0-86187-285-1.
MCLENNAN, DAVID.   1971.   The Thought of Karl Marx.   London, England: Macmillan; 1971.   237p.   ISBN: 0-333-117107.
MACHLUP, FRITZ.   1962.   The Production and Distribution of Knowledge
   in the United States.   Princeton, NJ: Princeton University Press; 1962.
   416p.   LC: 63-7072. (2nd edition, 1979, ISBN: 0-691-08608-7).
MACHLUP, FRITZ.   1979.   An Economist's Reflections on an Institute for
   the Advanced Study of Information Science.   Journal of the American
   Society for Information Science.   1979 March; 30(2): 111–113.   ISSN:
   0002-8231.

THE ECONOMICS OF INFORMATION AND ORGANIZATION 27

MACHLUP, FRITZ. 1980. Knowledge: Its Creation, Distribution and Economic Significance: Volume I, Knowledge and Knowledge Production. Princeton, NJ: Princeton University Press, 1980. 272p. ISBN: 0-691-04226-8.

MACHLUP, FRITZ. 1982. Knowledge: Its Creation, Distribution and Economic Significance: Volume II, The Branches of Learning. Princeton, NJ: Princeton University Press; 1982. 205p. ISBN: 0-691-04230-6.

MACKAAY, EJAN. 1982. Economics of Information and Law. Boston, MA: Kluwer Nijhoff; 1982. 293p. ISBN: 0-89838-100-2.

MANDEVILLE, T. D. 1983. Information Flows between Australia and Japan. Paper presented at: Eighth Pacific Regional Science Association Conference; 1983 August 17-19; Tokyo, Japan. 22p. Available from the author, Information Research Unit, University of Queensland, St. Lucia, Australia, 4067.

MARSCHAK, JACOB. 1974. Economic Information, Decision and Prediction Selected Essays: Volume II. Boston, MA: D. Reidel; 1974. 362p. ISBN: 90-277-0545-3.

MARX, KARL. 1971. Critique of Hegel's Philosophy of Right. In: McLennan, David, ed. Karl Marx Early Texts. Oxford, England: Basil Blackwell; 1971. 61-72. ISBN: 0-631-11630-2; LC: 73-129588.

MASON, ROBERT M.; CREPS, JOHN E., JR., eds. 1981. Information Services: Economics, Management, and Technology. Boulder, CO: Westview Press; 1981. 211p. ISBN: 0-89158-938-4.

MICK, COLIN K. 1979. Cost Analysis of Systems and Services. In: Williams, Martha E., ed. Annual Review of Information Science and Technology: Volume 14. White Plains, NY: Knowledge Industry Publications for American Society for Information Science; 1979. 37-64. ISBN: 0-914236-44-X; ISSN: 0066-4200; LC: 66-25096.

MIDDLETON, KAREN P.; JUSSAWALLA, MEHEROO. 1981. The Economics of Communication: A selected Bibliography with Abstracts. Elmsford, NY; Pergamon Press, 1981. 249p. ISBN: 0-08-026325-9.

NELSON, RICHARD R. 1980. Production Sets, Technological Knowledge, and R&D: Fragile and Overworked Constructs for Analysis of Productivity Growth? American Economic Review. 1980 May; 70(2): 62-67. ISSN: 0002-8282.

NELSON, RICHARD R. 1981. Assessing Private Enterprise: An Exegesis of Tangled Doctrine. Bell Journal of Economics. 1981 Spring; 12(1): ISSN: 0361-915X.

NELSON, RICHARD R.; WINTER, SIDNEY G. 1982. An Evolutionary Theory of Economic Change. Cambridge, MA: Belknap Press of Harvard University Press; 1982. 437p. ISBN: 0-674-27227-7.

NEW YORK TIMES. 1972. Nobel Winner Engrossed by Balancing Act. 1972 November 26: pF5.

O'BRIEN, RITA CRUISE, ed. 1983. Information, Economics and Power: The North-South Dimension. Boulder, CO: Westview Press; 1983. 156p. ISBN: 0-86531-604-X.

O'DRISCOLL, GERALD P., JR. 1979. Rational Expectations, Politics, and Stagflation. In: Rizzo, Mario J., ed. Time, Uncertainty, and Disequilibrium. Lexington, MA: Lexington Books; 1979. 153-176. ISBN: 0-669-02698-0.

OLSEN, HAROLD A. 1971. The Economics of Information: Bibliography and Commentary on the Literature. Washington, DC: American Society for Information Science; 1971. 30p. Available through ASIS.

28   DONALD M. LAMBERTON

ORGANIZATION FOR ECONOMIC COOPERATION AND DEVELOPMENT
(OECD). 1981. Information Activities, Electronics and Telecommuni-
cations Technologies: Impact on Employment, Growth and Trade. Paris,
France: OECD; 1981. 140p. ISBN: 92-64-12241-9.

POIRIER, DALE J. 1977. Econometric Methodology in Radical Economics.
American Economic Review. 1977 February; 67(1): 393–399. ISSN:
0002-8282.

PORAT, MARC U.; RUBIN, MICHAEL R. 1977. The Information Economy.
Washington, DC: U.S. Government Printing Office; 1977. 9 volumes.
(Office of Telecommunications Special Publication 77-12 (1-9)).

RAMOS, ALBERTO G. 1981. The New Science of Organizations: A Reconceptualization of the Wealth of Nations. Toronto, Canada: University
of Toronto Press; 1981. 210p. ISBN: 0-8020-5527-3.

ROSENBERG, VICTOR. 1982. National Information Policies. In: Williams,
Martha E., ed. Annual Review of Information Science and Technology:
Volume 17. White Plains, NY: Knowledge Industry Publications for the
American Society for Information Science; 1982. 3–32. ISBN: 0-86729-
032-3; ISSN: 0066-4200; LC: 66-25096.

RUBIN, MICHAEL R. 1983. Information Economics and Policy in the
United States. Littleton, CO: Libraries Unlimited; 1983. 340p. ISBN:
0-87287-378-1.

RUBIN, MICHAEL R.; SAPP, MARY E. 1981. Selected Roles of Information Goods and Services in the U.S. National Economy. Information
Processing and Management. 1981; 17(4): 195–213. ISSN: 0306-4573.

RUBIN, MICHAEL R.; TAYLOR, ELIZABETH. 1981. The Information
Sector and GNP: An Input-Output Study. Information Processing and
Management. 1981; 17(4): 163–194. ISSN: 0306-4573.

SAHAL, DEVENDRA. 1981. Patterns of Technological Innovation. London,
England: Addison-Wesley; 1981. 381p. ISBN: 0-201-06630-0.

SAITO, TADAO; INOSE, HIROSHI; SEI, KAGEYAMA. 1983. A Compara-
tive Study of the Mode of Domestic and Transborder Information Flows
Including Data. Information Economics and Policy. 1983; 1(1): 75–92.
ISSN: 0167-6245.

SAMUELSON, PAUL A. 1967. The Monopolistic Competition Revolution.
In: Kuenne, Robert E., ed. Monopolistic Competition Theory: Studies
in Impact. New York, NY: Wiley; 1967. 105–138. LC: 66-28747.

SASSONE, PETER G. 1981. A Theory of the Market Demand for Information Analysis Center Services. In: Mason, Robert M.; Creps, John E., Jr.,
eds. Information Services: Economics, Management, and Technology.
Boulder, CO: Westview Press; 1981. 23–38. ISBN: 0-89158-938-4.

SAUNDERS, ROBERT J.; WARFORD, JEREMY J.; WELLENIUS, BJØRN.
1983. Telecommunications and Economic Development. Baltimore,
MD: Johns Hopkins University Press; 1983. 395p. ISBN: 0-8018-2827-7.

SCHOTTER, ANDREW. 1981. The Economic Theory of Social Institutions. Cambridge, England: Cambridge University Press; 1981. 177p.
ISBN: 0-521-23044-6.

SCHUMAN, P. G. 1982. Information Justice. Library Journal. 1982
June; 107(11): 1060–1066. ISSN: 0363-0277.

SELIG, GAD J. 1982. A Framework for Multinational Information Systems
Planning. Information and Management. 1982; 5(2): 95–115. ISSN:
0378-7206.

SHACKLE, G. L. S. 1972. Epistemics and Economics: A Critique of
Economic Doctrines. Cambridge, England: Cambridge University
Press; 1972. 482p. ISBN: 0-521-08626-4.

THE ECONOMICS OF INFORMATION AND ORGANIZATION   29

SHELP, RONALD K.   1981.   Beyond Industrialization: Ascendancy of the
    Global Service Economy.   New York, NY: Praeger; 1981.   242p.   ISBN:
    0-03-059304-2.
SIMON, H. A.   1978.   On How to Decide What to Do.   Bell Journal of
    Economics.   1978 Autumn; 9(2): 494-507.   ISSN: 0361-915X.
SLATER, J. R.   1982.   Review of Schotter, *The Economic Theory of Social
    Institutions*.   Economic Journal.   1982 September; 92(367): 714-715.
    ISSN: 0013-0133.
SOWELL, THOMAS.   1980.   Knowledge and Decisions.   New York, NY:
    Basic Books; 1980.   422p.   ISBN: 0-465-03736-4.
SPENCE, A. MICHAEL.   1974.   An Economist's View of Information.   In:
    Cuadra, Carlos A.; Luke, A. W.; Harris, Jessica L., eds.   Annual Review
    of Information Science and Technology: Volume 9.   Washington, DC:
    American Society for Information Science; 1974.   57-78.   ISBN:
    0-87715-209-8; ISSN: 0066-4200; LC: 66-25096.
SPERO, JOAN EDELMAN.   1982.   Information: The Policy Void.   Foreign
    Policy.   1982 Fall; 48: 139-156.   ISSN: 0015-7228.
STARRETT, D.   1976.   Social Institutions, Imperfect Information, and the
    Distribution of Income.   Quarterly Journal of Economics.   1976 May;
    90(2): 261-284.   ISSN: 0033-5533.
STERN, BARRIE T.   1982.   Information and Innovation.   Amsterdam, The
    Netherlands: North-Holland; 1982.   191p.   ISBN: 0-444-86496-2.
STIGLER, GEORGE J.   1983.   Nobel Lecture: The Process and Progress of
    Economics.   Journal of Political Economy.   1983 August; 91(4): 529-
    545.   ISSN: 0022-3808.
STIGLITZ, J. E.   1977.   Symposium on Economics of Information: Intro-
    duction.   Review of Economic Studies.   1977; 44: 389-391.   ISSN:
    0034-6527.
STOUT, D. K.   1980.   The Impact of Technology on Economic Growth in
    the 1980s.   Daedalus.   1980 Winter: 159-167.   ISSN: 0011-5266; LC:
    12-30299.
TEUBAL, M.   1983.   The Accumulation of Intangibles by High-Technology
    Firms.   In: Macdonald, Stuart; Lamberton, D. M.; Mandeville, Thomas,
    eds.   The Trouble with Technology.   New York, NY: St. Martin's Press;
    1983.   56-74.   ISBN: 0-86187-285-1.
TINBERGEN, JAN.   1978.   Alternative Forms of International Co-Opera-
    tion: Comparing Their Efficiency.   International Social Science Journal.
    1978; 30(2): 223-237.   ISSN: 0304-3037.
TOMASINI, LUIGI M.   1974.   The Economics of Information: A Survey.
    Économie Appliquée.   1974; 27(2-3): 319-337.   ISSN: 0013-0494.
U.S. CONGRESS. SENATE.   1958.   An Economic Review of the Patent
    System: Study no. 15. Prepared by Fritz Machlup for the U.S. Senate
    Subcommittee on Patents, Trademarks and Copyrights, 85th Congress,
    2nd Session. Washington, DC: US Government Printing Office (GPO);
    1958.   89p.   Available from GPO.
VAGIANOS, LOUIS.   1983.   Electronic Colonialism.   Bulletin of the
    American Society for Information Science.   1983 April; 9(4): 28-29.
    ISSN: 0095-4403.
VON HAYEK, F. A.   1975.   The Pretence of Knowledge.   Swedish Journal
    of Economics.   1975; 77(4): 433-442.
WELCH, ROBERT L.   1980.   Vertical and Horizontal Communication in
    Economic Processes.   Review of Economic Studies.   1980; 47: 733-746.
    ISSN: 0034-6527.

30   DONALD M. LAMBERTON

WILDAVSKY, AARON.   1983.   Information as an Organizational Problem.
    Journal of Management Studies.   1983; 20(1): 29–40.   ISSN: 0022-
    2380.
WILLIAMS, B. R.   1964.   Review of Fritz Machlup, *The Production and
    Distribution of Knowledge in the United States.*   Economic Journal.
    1964 March; 74(293): 174–175.   ISSN: 0013-0133.
WILLIAMSON, O. E.   1981.   The Modern Corporation: Origins, Evolution,
    Attributes.   Journal of Economic Literature.   1981 December; 19(4):
    1537–1568.   ISSN: 0022-0515.
WOLFE, A. W.   1977.   The Supranational Organization of Production: An
    Evolutionary Perspective.   Current Anthropology.   1977 December;
    18(4): 615–635.   ISSN: 0011-3204.
ZIMMERMAN, EDWARD; BRIMMER, KARL.   1981.   National Planning
    for Data Communications.   In: Williams, Martha E., ed.   Annual Review
    of Information Science and Technology: Volume 16.   White Plains, NY:
    Knowledge Industry Publications for the American Society for Informa-
    tion Science; 1981.   3–49.   ISBN: 0-914236-90-3; ISSN: 0066-4200;
    LC: 66-25096.

[5]

Assessing private enterprise: an exegesis of tangled doctrine

Richard R. Nelson*

This paper proposes that the twin theorems of welfare economics provide an insubstantial basis for the faith of many economists that private enterprise is a good way of organizing production. Most economists implicitly recognize this. A reading of the literature in advocacy of private enterprise suggests that administrative parsimony, responsiveness, and innovativeness often are ascribed as virtues of the enterprise form of economic organization. The argument that private enterprise has these virtues has, however, no basis in orthodox microeconomic theory. This essay is concerned with considering arguments for those alleged virtues, and sketching some of the theoretical and empirical questions that are opened when these are scrutinized.

1. What are the real arguments?

■ The history of modern Western orthodox economic thought is inextricably connected with the articulation of the virtues of private enterprise. Adam Smith's classic statement clearly is the fount: "[H]e intends only his own gain, and he is in this, as in many other cases, led by an invisible hand to promote an end which was no part of his intention. Nor is it always the worse for the society that it was no part of it. By pursuing his own interest he frequently promotes that of the society more effectually than when he really intends to promote it." [1] While the major figures who have molded the evolution of orthodox doctrine since Adam Smith have not been blind to the limitations of private enterprise, support of the basic institution has been a hallmark of orthodoxy. Relatedly, from the early nineteenth century socialists, through Marx, through the collection of those who today advocate widespread nationalization or mechanisms of central planning, heterodoxy has been unified by little more than suspicion or denial of the efficacy of private enterprise.

The term private enterprise is herein used as shorthand for a system of organizing production of goods and services utilizing privately owned firms, presumed to be motivated by profit, connected to input supplies and product demands through market-like arrangements, with very little monitoring and

* Yale University.

The research leading to this paper was financed by the German Marshall Fund. The author is indebted to many individuals for comments on earlier drafts, but particularly to James Douglas, Michael Krashinsky, C.E. Lindblom, Susan Rose-Ackerman, Oliver Williamson, and Charles Wolf.

[1] Notice how cautious is this statement (1937, p. 423) compared with more modern articulations.

constraining from higher authorities. I shall reconsider this definition later. Here I simply want to signal that the focus is on the organization of production and not directly on such questions as what goods should be bought by households and what goods subsidized or financed by government, or how equitable the income distribution ought to be, although these questions are not unconnected.

Recent intellectual discussion of the economic organization question tends to proceed by using the concepts of modern welfare economics. Adam Smith's proposition is translated into the familiar twin theorems relating competitive equilibrium to a social optimum. However, if one carefully considers the older discussion, or looks with open mind at the various strands of the recent discussion, it seems dubious that the arguments addressed by contemporary welfare economics touch all, or even a large part, of the matters under analysis.

It is apparent that for many scholars the values at stake in the debate about economic organization transcend those that can be treated with conventional economic calculus. It can be argued that the most important issue is a kind of polity, society, and culture associated with different kinds of economic mechanism.

Even regarding more narrowly defined economic performance criteria, modern welfare economics does not provide very persuasive support for private enterprise. Recognize that the standard welfare economics arguments do not propose that private enterprise is better than any other organizational solution; only that if certain assumptions are met, "it can't be beat." But everyone realizes that the real conditions do not meet the assumptions needed to produce the twin theorems. And, indeed, few economists have in mind a "pure" private enterprise solution. Most private enterprise enthusiasts support some form of active antitrust activity, which reflects a tacit admission that there may be "tendencies" toward monopoly that need to be held off. Many who profess the basic creed support various kinds of regulation under certain conditions, justify certain kinds of subsidy, and even admit the need for direct governmental operation of certain activities. Contemporary welfare economics provides no argument that justifies a flawed, patched up private enterprise.

Many economists recognize this but espouse private enterprise nonetheless. The proprivate enterprise stance seems to rest on implicit beliefs that private enterprise performs well according to three related but separable criteria not treated by conventional welfare economics: (1) administrative parsimony, (2) responsiveness, and (3) innovativeness.

Recall that von Mises' criticism of the central planning alternative was not that private enterprise was optimal, but that prices were essential to rational economic calculation and that it would be administratively infeasible under central planning to achieve a sensible allocation of resources. Since that time, economists have backed off from the proposition that prices are strictly essential to economic calculation. But there appears to remain a belief that private enterprise is "administratively parsimonious," compared with central planning, in the sense that it is less cumbersome and costly to run. Lange responded to von Mises' criticism by proposing a Socialism that would make use of prices. Hayek rejoined that, in his analysis, Lange had misspecified the real economic problem by not recognizing that the difficulties of running the system stem from the fact that demand and supply conditions are always changing. He argued that, even with Lange's proposed mechanism, Socialism would be less "responsive" to change than private enterprise.[2] The responsiveness of private enterprise, in comparison with the sluggishness of more bureaucratic alternatives, is certainly part of the conventional wisdom of most Western economists. Schumpeter, and later Galbraith, stressed another aspect of economic change: the basic improvability of existing products and processes. They argued that a primary virtue of private enterprise is its "innovativeness." A good number of Western economists seem to agree.

The three propositions about private enterprise sketched above are not the same, but there is a strong common premise linking them, and separating them from the proposition of contemporary welfare economics. Contemporary welfare economics assumes no constraints on man's information gathering, processing, communicating, deciding, and agreeing capabilities. Man is infinitely rational: his economic problems stem from the fact that resources and technological possibilities are limited. The three propositions considered above presume explicitly or implicitly that man's data processing capacity, his ability to understand complex or novel situations, and his ability to gain agreement are bounded. I propose that serious analysis of the strengths and weaknesses of private enterprise must come to grips with this bounded rationality problem.[3] Arguments for private enterprise must take the form that, given man's limitations, patched up private enterprise is as good an organizational solution as can be devised.

Even this argument presumes, of course, some specification as to what free enterprise is and what are the alternatives. We are considering here not a pure private enterprise regime, but a complex patched up one, and presumably the comparison should not be with a completely stylized straw man alternative.[4] And there is also the problem that, once one recognizes the complex nature of actual private enterprise regimes, it is not easy to determine precisely when a regime stops being a form of private enterprise but must be labeled something else.

Unfortunately, it is fair to say that most economists have not come to grips with either the bounded rationality problem, or the problem of delineating alternatives and boundaries. The purpose of this essay is to relate some of the important questions to these aspects of the problem. The organizational design question is examined and the "administrative parsimony" concept is introduced in Section 2. Section 3 is concerned with "the responsiveness" proposition about private enterprise. "Innovativeness" is considered in Section 4. In the concluding section some strands will be pulled together and the discussion

---

[2] It is interesting that von Mises (1951) and Hayek (1969), the two advocates of private enterprise in this debate, pose their arguments in a form much more distant from that of contemporary welfare economics than does Lange (1936), the advocate of Socialism.

[3] The most forceful articulation of the meaning and significance of bounded rationality is, of course, that by Simon (1957). J. Marschak (1968) has stated a very similar point of view, but in terms more congenial with orthodox economic theory. Williamson (1970, 1975) and Lindblom (1977) both develop analysis of organizational alternatives in which bounded rationality is recognized centrally.

[4] The recent work by Montias (1976) is quite explicit about the complexity of different kinds of economic systems, and the blurry lines between different systems. See also Ward (1967) on comparative systems. Williamson's work on different ways to organize large multiproduct firms also is relevant to the discussion. Wolf's recent essay is an interesting attempt at comparing the two imperfect alternatives of private market and public provision.

focused on the organizational choices facing economies that profess a basic private enterprise creed; I shall propose that a central one among these is whether a "mixed" economy combines the best features of its purer ingredients, or the worst.

2. Organization design and organization costs

■ It seems useful at the outset to explore in what ways the economic problem poses problems of organization. Then we can go on to consider what might be meant by the private enterprise alternative, and its competitors.

□ **Crusoe's problem and the economic organization problem.** By economic organization economists clearly mean a structure that patterns interaction among individual economic units.[5] If I may fall back on the example oft used by classical economists, Robinson Crusoe had an economic problem, but (ignoring Friday) not one that posed issues of economic organization. He had access to certain resources, and there were a number of ways that he could employ these resources and his own time and effort to meet his varied wants. Were Crusoe God, he could and should pick the best possible use of resources and time, given his needs and preferences, and the conventional treatment poses his economic problem in that way. But given the limits on his perceptive and cognitive capacities, for Crusoe this was quite impossible. Moreover, at least some of this effort and time needed to be directed to gathering information and thinking.

It might be proposed that Crusoe's problem was somehow to find the optimum of a "super" problem that involves costs of information gathering, processing, and deciding. Another less stilted way of saying it is that Crusoe had to try to do the best he could, given his human as well as his resource limitations.

Society's problem would be a collection of disjoint Crusoe problems if each individual preserved economic autonomy, and met his or her own wants directly with his or her own resources and devices. However, the advantages of, or sometimes even the imperatives of, division of labor and cooperation call for coordinated interaction, not economic disjointedness, among individuals. In short, there is need for organization.

There are two related, but roughly separable, elements to the organization problem. First, some machinery must exist to determine whose and what wants have priority; I shall call this the priorities determination problem, and I will not consider it directly here. Second, some machinery must exist to allocate resources and guide production to meet demands. The focus here is on the organization of production.

In turn, the problem of organizing production can be broken down into three roughly separable subproblems. First, there must be procedures for assigning responsibility and authority for undertaking various broadly defined tasks: Crusoe never had to face the issue of determining division of labor. Second, information about what other units want and can make available must flow between economic units: Crusoe had no need to coordinate his actions with those of others. Third, the values and preferences of others (the priorities)

---

[5] Of the many general commentaries on "the problem of economic organization" I find Knight's old classic (1933) still among the most illuminating.

must somehow be made effective in guiding individual decision, given division of labor, and information. Crusoe may have been unthoughtful or lazy, but the work he had laid out before him was directly related to his own wants. I propose that it is useful, and quite general, to characterize a mode of organizing production in terms of how it treats these three related, overlapping, but still roughly distinguishable functions. The organization of production defines regimes of responsibility and authority, the nature of information flows relevant to coordination, and the incentives and controls determining how decisions are made and carried out.

In advanced economies most production is carried out by specialized organizations—call them firms. Firms provide goods and services to final demanders and other firms; they procure needed inputs from other firms, and other economic units (e.g., individuals for labor). The focus of this essay is how firms operate under different broad modes of organization of production. However, I shall simplify the analysis of these questions drastically by assuming away all complexities associated with the organization of firms, how decisions are arrived at within firms, and the mechanisms by which decisions get carried out. I assume a top decisionmaker whose orders are carried out. Thus I at once ignore a wide range of positive analytic issues; Williamson, for example, has argued persuasively that organization significantly influences firm behavior; and normative considerations of industrial democracy are completely repressed.

☐ **The private enterprise mode of organizing supply and the alternatives.** How would one characterize the pure "private enterprise" mode of organizing production? A broad reading of many commentaries leads me to propose the following:

First, regarding domains of responsibility and authority, firms have "property rights" in their machinery and inventory, and are free to use them in any way they like. Firms produce what they wish and sell to or buy needed inputs and labor from whom they wish. A consequence is the possibility of competitive sources of supply and demand.

Second, information relevant to coordination is generated largely in the course of transactions among economic units. There may be well-organized markets with well-advertised prices for certain goods and services. But there is no central information collecting or indicative planning mechanism. An important consequence is explicit decentralization of decisionmaking in the sense that there is no real formal mechanism to check on mutual consistency of planned actions, much less on the consonance of those actions with some sort of higher objective.

Third, regarding the way it is decided what firms do, given their capabilities and information, firms pursue their own interests as they see them; while profit is conventionally presumed to be the operative motive of standard firms, nothing in the private enterprise system legally compels this. Self-motivation is relied upon to guide and discipline actions of the economic units. There is no systematic overview and evaluation of the behavior of economic units from the top, and no central mechanism for giving orders.

What are the alternatives to pure private enterprise as a supply regime? One can consider radically different supply regimes, as for example that of the Soviet Union. The global contrast between an idealized central planning model and an idealized private enterprise model is sufficiently sharp in all dimensions

98 / THE BELL JOURNAL OF ECONOMICS

that one is tempted to propose that there is only one basic dimension, not three. In Williamson's (1975) terms, the polar extremes along that dimension are market (private enterprise) and hierarchy (central planning).

I propose that it is useful to distinguish among all three different dimensions. There are many examples of deviation from the pure private enterprise design in one of the dimensions, but not in the others. Consider, for example, mechanisms controlling entry or granting sole source rights in a field, as in licensing of physicians, or turnpike restaurant concessions. These generally involve role ascription, but little "central planning" or "monitoring from the top." Indicative planning is a mechanism that is concerned with coordination, but its articulated ideology involves little role ascription and is ambiguous regarding sanctions. Environmental and safety regulation involves higher order sanctions, but not much in the way of role ascription and only weak (at best) mechanisms for planning and coordination. In fact, what economists still call "private enterprise" economies are extremely variegated creatures, with very few sectors or activities organized according to the pure model, and considerable differences among sectors and activities in terms of how they deviate.

Later I shall argue that the real organizational questions facing Western economies reside exactly in what deviations are appropriate, or viable, where, and how much total deviation is possible before the design becomes unworkable. But for the present I want to repress deviation and diversity and talk as if relatively pure types do or could exist.

☐ **The issue of administrative parsimony.** Economic organization involves resources dedicated to administration. Of course, consideration of the administrative costs associated with different kinds of economic organizations cannot proceed fruitfully in the absence of a way of assessing economic performance more generally. Presumably, one can have very low administrative costs if one does not care about what the system does. In turn, assessment of economic performance depends on the criterion one uses.[6]

Let me cut through the criterion problem by blithely assuming away the Arrow problem, and presuming the existence of a well-behaved social welfare function that is invariant to organizational regime. These assumptions ought to make the reader uncomfortable; they discomfort me. On the one hand, I have obscured any equity-efficiency tradeoff issues. On the other hand, I have repressed what some consider to be the essence of the economic organization choice question—that preferences and values are endogenous to economic organization. I make these assumptions simply because I do not know how to proceed without them. If they are made then in principle at least, one can compare regimes in terms of how well they score on a common scale. Let me also normalize for total resources available and for technology commanded (at least initially). Then one regime can do better than another, because fewer resources are absorbed in administration, or because it allocates the remaining resources better, or both.

---

[6] Among the several studies which have attempted to compare alternative ways of organizing taking into account costs of "running the system," Marschak and Radner (1972) and Hurwicz (1973) are very interesting examples. I already have remarked on the comparative organizational theorizing of Montias and Williamson. And, of course, transaction costs have been a central concern of Coase.

Analysis of administrative requirements to achieve a given quality of resource allocation of course depends on how one views the economic problem. Here I would argue, along with Hayek and Schumpeter, that it involves responding to unforeseen changes in demand and supply conditions, and the challenge and opportunity of innovation.

Indeed absent these aspects, and they are assumed away in most treatises on welfare economics, the administrative problem would appear relatively trivial, and easy to resolve parsimoniously through any of a variety of means. Consider an economy operating under steady, unchanging conditions. Put aside for the moment the question of how an economy gets to any equilibrium. This is the responsiveness question in disguise and, besides, over a long enough interval the initial costs of "getting there" become small relative to the costs of continuing to be there. If there are no differences between organizational regimes in terms of the places they can get to (and we are assuming resources and technology are the same) the comparative organization question boils down to the question of what equilibria can be sustained at what administrative costs.[7]

But under steady-state conditions, almost any achievable equilibrium would appear easy and cheap to sustain. Once any equilibrium is established, all that is required is that what is done today be repeated tomorrow, or, if that is impossible (a worker gets sick or dies or a machine breaks down), that replacement be available and that there be some buffering (a stock of inventory) to tide over in the interim period. Even under a tight centrally planned system with rigid prices, a bit of job searching on the part of new entrants to the work force, small stocks of inventory, and a bit of *blat* ("graft") ought to suffice to take care of such disturbances.

Many of the articles that propose that the administrative resources involved in a centrally planned regime are large compared with those of a private enterprise system put forth the picture of a set of costly communications channels which run from the firms to the center and back again under a centrally planned regime, and mention the high expense (perhaps even the infeasibility) of computing a consistent economic plan, much less a welfare maximizing one. But, under steady-state conditions, resources are already basically allocated, and there is not much information flowing in the system to suggest that resource allocation needs to be changed. Big computational machinery is not needed, and the communication channels can be rather thin.

How much variation in economic activity is required before the information problem becomes a difficult one for a hierarchical system to handle? That is an interesting question. I would put forth the proposition that a considerable amount of the variation can be handled by a nominally centrally planned system in a routine way, provided that variation is roughly predictable. Under these circumstances, firms can be "preprogrammed" to respond to the predicted variation in a coordinated way. My impression (shared by many other students of organization) is that under roughly predictable conditions hierarchical systems tend to rely on preprogramming, not much information flows to and from the center, and not much real decisionmaking goes on in the center.

Thus far the focus has been on the job assignment and information network

---

[7] I am not alone in this presumption. Hayek (1945), of course, stated it forcefully. So has Williamson (1976).

aspects of organization. However, when one examines the third requirement of organization—motivation and enforcement of decisions—some differences between private enterprise and a centrally planned system come into view. Under a private enterprise regime it is not merely that the firm manager does not need to ask higher authority what to do. It is that the motivation and control flow not from hierarchical checking of whether instructions or pre-programmed policies have been fulfilled, but from self interest. Under strict steady-state conditions my argument is that a centralized regime can avoid most of the asking and telling by preprogramming. But the control system involves checking on whether the program has in fact been fulfilled. And it is here, with respect to the control system, that the argument for administrative parsimony of private enterprise may become more persuasive, even assuming steady-state conditions.

If one puts forth as a theoretical proposition that the more complex the decision rule to be followed, the more costly the monitoring of whether it is in fact being followed, one can identify the classic tradeoff issue of (bureaucratic) administrative theory. Under the general principle that reward is tied to the extent of order or decision-rule fulfillment, one can have very simple rules that do not take into account many differences or nuances in situations, but which are relatively cheap to monitor, or one can have more complex and subtle decision rules, but with higher monitoring expense.

Of course, in counter to the proposition that a stylized central planning regime would be forced to work with rather crude decision rules, or have high administrative costs, one can argue that a stylized private enterprise system faces the same tradeoff regarding the values that are reflected in prices. While Western economists have, until recently, been at least partially blind to the costs of running a private enterprise system, recent recognition of transaction costs, and decision costs, is beginning to permit serious consideration of organizational alternatives. Markets and transactions that ignore all but a few dimensions of benefits and costs are cheap compared with those that consider many. In a free enterprise regime the tradeoff is between leaving externalities and imposing a more costly market-transactional structure.

One wonders, however, how serious these "tradeoff" problems would be for either regime, under steady-state conditions, or if variation were limited and relatively predictable. It is unpredicted change that opens the question of what one (a firm) should do, thus complicating the question of what are the appropriate rules and monitoring systems, and generating new externalities in old markets. And with unpredicted change, the questions of who should do what, and of how we should coordinate our actions, no longer are trivial. This brings us to the responsiveness problem.

3. The responsiveness issue

■ The context of Hayek's criticism of the Lange proposal for a Socialist supply regime emphatically was not the steady state: "It is, perhaps, worth stressing that economic problems arise always and only in consequence of change. So long as things continue as before, or at least as they were expected to, there arise no new problems requiring a decision, no need to form a new plan." I suspect that organizational problems in a steady state are not completely trivial, but it is apparent that these problems are vastly compounded by not fully foreseen change.[8]

☐ **Tracking a moving target—the liabilities of a centralized system.** In examining the responsiveness argument resources and preferences cannot be assumed constant nor their movements closely predictable. As they change, so should resource allocation, patterns of production, and consumption. While God, knowing all from the beginning, and having no bounds on his rationality may "know" the changing optimal configurations, man cannot. In general, the appropriate overall system's response will not be known, nor will it be known what the individual responses should be and how they should be meshed together. Whereas under the steady-state assumptions, the informational and calculational requirements of deciding what to do were trivial, even degenerate, the heart of the dynamic problem is that the individual economic units have to figure out what to do at any time with no assurance that what they were doing last time is the appropriate thing this time. While in this section firms have to decide from period to period what inputs to use and what outputs to produce, I assume here that they know all input/output relationships. The additional issues which are raised if the full set of technological possibilities is not known will be considered in the following section.

If we preserve here the assumptions that the time paths of resources and preferences, and the social welfare function, are independent of the organizational regime, the organizational problem can be defined in terms of tracking as closely as possible a moving optimum that is knowable and achievable only by God. All of the issues discussed in the preceding section are relevant here, but in addition there is the enormously complicating problem that the target is moving unpredictably. The focus here will be on the implications of that complication. The responsiveness proposition can be interpreted as that the private enterprise system tracks well with limited administrative overhead, and that departures from private enterprise design add to administrative cost or make for worse tracking or both.

Even if one abstracts from the control problem, the argument that centralization imposes high information and calculation costs carries considerable weight in a dynamic context. Let me put forth the theoretical proposition that complex decision rules are costly to calculate and employ, as well as being difficult to monitor. Then if significant and unpredictable change is expected, a regime cannot rely fully on preprogrammed rules but must involve a central coordinator who controls actions through monitoring adherence to orders and rules. Since costs require that established decision rules be kept relatively simple, events will inevitably occur for which there is no sensible preprogrammed response. Information and requests for instructions then must flow from the firms to the center, and orders from the center to the firms.

Hayek's implicit argument was that in an environment of rapid change,

---

[8] The quotation is from Hayek, page 25 (Bornstein). I am not aware of very many efforts to formulate and explore the proposition that private enterprise adapts to change more effectively than does a more centrally structured system. But for one interesting attempt see T. Marschak (1968). Powell has presented a fascinating analysis of how the Soviet economy adjusts to unexpected change.

even if very considerable administrative resources were involved, the need for flow of information from firms to the center and back again would result in decisions that are less sensitive to change and differences in conditions than decisions firms would make themselves were they properly motivated. To me at least, this sounds plausible.

The control problems of a centralized regime also would seem to be significantly increased by the need to respond to changing resource supplies and preferences. The costs of both employing and monitoring complex decision rules require that these be kept relatively simple. In a dynamic context there is a much wider range of circumstances where the rules do not provide clear guidance and enterprises should send information and questions to the center. Enterprises thus need to be monitored not only in terms of how well they follow the rules they were told to follow; they also need to be evaluated in terms of the extent to which they provide the center with the information it needs to intervene in determining what the enterprises are to do. In general, it is easier to judge whether somebody followed a rule he was told to than it is to judge that one should have been sent certain information that one never received, or whether the information that one did receive was irresponsibly edited or biased.

It is apparent that a private enterprise supply regime operates in a way so as to avoid many of these problems. Since returns to firms are directly related to their own performance, while at any time firms will be compelled to work with relatively simple decision rules, they have motivation to modify the rules as they go along so as better to deal with changing circumstances. This bypasses the need for information exchange with the center to guide rule modification. Prices can be changed by firms on the basis of the information that they have and without consultation with or having to reach agreement with the center. The case is similar for the input and output decisions of firms and choices of trading partners.

The argument that in a dynamic context firms in a private enterprise system are lighter on their feet than firms in a centralized system rests basically on the self-motivation and market connection aspects of free enterprise, less directly on the freedom of entry or pluralism aspect. This latter provides a stick of potential competition to spur rapid response, and provides for diversity of response (the potential value of which I shall examine later).

☐ **Private enterprises responsiveness—fast but poorly guided?** Fast response is one thing. Well-directed response is something else again.

Virtually all formal theory is concerned with equilibrium conditions. Very little of formal theorizing has been concerned with the questions of how a private enterprise system gets to equilibrium, or how it would stay there in the face of perturbations. Even in the context of partial equilibrium models of private enterprise, the question of dynamic response to a shift in a demand curve or factor supply conditions can involve some complications, particularly if responses are discrete—think of the corn-hog cobweb cycle. In a general equilibrium context, where changes in output in response to changes in demand influence factor prices and personal incomes which in turn may feed back to further change demands, the question of stability is even more complicated. To someone who proposes that private enterprise responds accurately to changed market conditions, the failure of general equilibrium theorists to prove stability, save under very stringent conditions, should be a severe embarrassment. To my knowledge, we have no well-worked-out generally accepted formalism which explains how a decentralized market system tracks a moving target at all, much less how it tracks it "better than another system would."

It should be noted that economies whose supply is organized through central planning face the same stability problems as a private enterprise system, if income distribution is sensitive to plans, consumer sovereignty guides production plans, and planners use something analogous to gradient methods in adjusting to disequilibrium. On the other hand, if "planners' preferences" determine production targets, and planners employ something like a gradient method to adjust production to the planners' optimum, then under standard assumptions equilibrium is stable. Also, if income distribution is insensitive to product demands, a private enterprise regime is stable under the same assumptions. Let us make these assumptions and let slide the issue of stability. Only then can we proceed with a discussion of responsiveness.

Even assuming the overall response of private enterprise ultimately converges to the new equilibrium, and that that new equilibrium is close to the social optimum, it is not at all obvious that the path to equilibrium is direct or smooth. Certainly the fact that private enterprise entails many competitive firms (a requirement for the equilibrium to have nice social properties) complicates the responsiveness problem. Even were it well understood by the firms in the industry how much the industry's overall capacity should and ultimately will expand or contract, the fact that there is a multitude of firms and these are prohibited to collude would seem a situation prone to chaotic response absent a central mechanism to direct firms as to how to divide up the increment or decrement to overall capacity. Of course, if plants were perfectly divisible, there were no economies of scale, and everybody responded gradually and proportionately to excess profitability, the system could smoothly converge. But add a little bit of lumpiness, or attempts at advance planning by firms; then companies cannot decide what to do unless they know what other firms in the industry are going to do. Such a system may overshoot, cycle, or adjust smoothly but slowly. It is hard to pull out any strong case for rapid smooth adjustment.[9]

Similarly, under conditions of lumpiness and attempts by firms to plan their investment, private enterprise systems without a central overview mechanism would not appear to be able to solve the interindustry coordination problem very well. An expansion of the demand for automobiles calls for greater automobile output, and for more steel production to be used to produce more automobiles. How fast automobile capacity ought to expand is a function of how fast steel capacity will expand, and *vice versa*. This problem is much discussed in the literature on the "dynamic externalities" involved in investment scheduling in less developed countries. And the problem has provided much of the theoretical justification for various mechanisms of "indicative planning" in more developed countries.[10]

Not only do market-guided responses to changed conditions lack the advantages of central coordination, but, under disequilibrium conditions, the "market-failure" problems associated with profit-guided actions are greatly

---

[9] Richardson (1960) provides a good discussion of this.
[10] See Chenery (1953), for example.

extended from what they would be under equilibrium conditions. A variety of costs are inflicted by processes of change that are not reflected in profitability calculations. Shortages are generated for goods in excess demand. Slack and unemployment are associated with goods in excess supply. These dynamic adjustment externalities of private enterprise systems are intimately associated with income redistribution consequences of market adjustments.

It is no wonder that many countries that have expressed strong general adherence to private enterprise have established mechanisms to try to make industry responses to changed conditions proceed in a more orderly and coordinated fashion, and to guide those processes so as to reduce the extent of income losses and individual hardships. While often the acknowledgement of the potential advantage of a planning structure to complement or supplant a market structure has been couched as "providing a substitute for nonexisting future markets," and while often the specific proposals tend to be for an extended dialogue among firms regarding their plans guided by a set of industry predictions (a framework of indicative planning), these proposals explicitly acknowledge a serious weakness in the responsiveness of private enterprise, at least as private enterprise customarily has been characterized. Similarly, government programs to restrain firms from leaving depressed areas, and to encourage firms to invest where unemployment is high, implicitly recognize both externality and equity issues involved in the dynamic response of private enterprise to changed market conditions.

Put briefly, the argument that private enterprise is quick to respond and sensitive to changes is persuasive, to me at least. But once one explores the direction and quality of response, the case for private enterprise supply is less than overwhelming.

4. Private enterprise as an engine of progress

■ From Smith on, economists have recognized that discovery or invention of new ways of doing things and new things to be doing was the driving force of economic progress. And private enterprise has been advocated as the system best able to generate and make socially fruitful that driving force. The "marginal this equals marginal that" arguments in advocacy of private enterprise seem puny in comparison with this claim. The question, of course, involves how, in fact, private enterprise generates and incorporates innovation, and how alternative systems would do the task.

□ **Characteristics of innovative activity.** To explore this question it is important to make some explicit assumptions about the nature of the processes generating innovations. I propose that a fruitful model of innovation involves the following elements.[11] First, just as in regards to analysis of the economic problem of responding to changed demand and supply conditions, in analysis of the innovation problem limits on man's information-acquiring and cognitive processes should be recognized right from the start. While the "responsiveness" problem involved man's limited abilities to deduce from data in disequi-

---

[11] The model presented here is closely akin to one presented in Nelson and Winter (1980), and also resembles the model put forth by Evenson and Kislev (1976), and Marschak, Glennan, and Summers (1967).

librium what a new equilibrium would be and how to get there smoothly, the innovation problem stems from man's understanding that the current ways of doing things that he knows certainly do not include all conceivable ways, and that there almost certainly are better ways to be doing things that he does not know. There are better product designs, better processes, better decision procedures, better ways of organizing things, that are there to be found or invented. And with effort, cleverness, and a bit of luck, some of them can be.

Second, the innovation process can be modeled as a "search" over a perhaps dimly perceived set of alternative possibilities. Man knows something about the characteristics of a number of elements in this set, and can make some crude probabilistic inferences about what their true economic characteristics might be. However, this knowledge is far from certain. He can engage in various kinds of activities to find out more. I shall call all of the search-related activity R&D.

Third, this period's round of R&D activities yields two kinds of advances. Better techniques, or practices are found and can be implemented. But knowledge has been enhanced as well in a more general sense. Today's discoveries and dry holes provide clues as where to look and where not to look tomorrow.

Fourth, people disagree about the most promising alternatives to explore, and about the promising strategies for proceeding with the exploration. To some extent discussion can resolve these differences, but given bounds on man's rational capacities, it is highly unlikely that differences can be fully resolved. Further, if man is able to resolve them, it is extremely unlikely that his choice would be God's choice.

Were it not for this last complication, the innovation problem might be modeled as a huge dynamic programming problem, involving uncertainty. In principle at least, optimal R&D strategies could be deduced from such a model. These strategies almost certainly would involve employment at any time of resources exploring several different alternatives even in circumstances where ultimately at most one of these would be actually employed in practice, and exploitation of what is learned at one stage in the process to guide allocation in the next stage.

Given the imperatives of division of labor, it is organizationally inevitable that this vast search strategy would have to be divided into "projects" with different smaller scale organizations concerned with operating one, or at most a small number of, projects at any time. In this sense the "allocation" problem would pose an organizational problem. As with the problem of resource allocation more generally, some mechanisms must be established to determine who is responsible for what, to channel information flow, and to motivate and control the actions of the individual economic units doing R&D.

☐ **The liabilities of a centralized system and the virtues of private enterprise.** For a wide variety of reasons, the idea of organizing the innovation system as a stylized hierarchial regime is extremely unattractive. The difficulties are essentially those stressed by Hayek in the "responsiveness" discussion, but are magnified. A considerable amount of the important information is specific to a particular project (Hayek's specificity of information regarding time and place). Only at the project level is the information immediately available regarding what happened in the last round of effort. To channel this information back to a center would be enormously time consuming, and, given limitations on coding, certainly much information would be lost in so doing.

Central computation facilities would be overwhelmed by the mass of data coming in from all the projects, and much of the potential advantages of centralization would be lost by a requirement to divide the information receiving and processing task.

A centralized system could respond by delegating responsibility, simplifying the requirements for information flow to and from the center, limiting the range of items that must be decided at the center, and establishing mechanisms to monitor the performance of the suborganizational units. But the problems of this strategy would be vastly greater than they would be in governing routine behavior in the steady state. Where creativity and daring need to be encouraged and rewarded, it is hard to see how they could be on a systematic basis under such an administrative regime. This is particularly so in a context where different individuals disagree *ex ante* as to what should be done, and therefore are likely to disagree *ex post* on what should have been done, and on whether an unfortunate outcome was the result of bad luck or bad judgment, or a good outcome the result of genius or chance.

In view of this problem it is easy enough to see arguments for pluralism, real decentralization, and self-motivation in the system that engages in R&D. But notice that (again) as it has been developed thus far, the arguments are negative ones about the liabilities of centralized systems in the innovation business. What happens to the theoretical case for private enterprise when the allocation of resources to R&D it generates is evaluated against some notions of a social ideal?

☐ **The anatomy of market failure in the generation of innovation.** It is certain that a private enterprise system cannot behave optimally regarding both innovation and more routine economic activities. The problem, put simply, is this. Innovation takes R&D resources and involves risks. To motivate the effort under private enterprise requires that the innovator (or those who finance him) can make a profit. Under the ground rules of private enterprise, the only way that this can be done is by having at least a temporary period where the innovating firm and not its competitors can produce the new product or use the new process, or receive compensation from other firms that do. This implies either secrecy, or property rights (patent protection), or a degree of market power to hold off rivals and potential rivals from competition.

Most contemporary writers, and I include Schumpeter of *Capitalism, Socialism and Democracy* in this list, as well as Galbraith, have stressed the latter mechanism—market power. Welfare loss triangles are admitted and downplayed: "[I]n capitalist reality as distinguished from its text book picture, it is not that kind of competition which counts but the competition from the new commodity, the new technology, the new source of supply. . . . This kind of competition is as much more effective than the other as a bombardment is in comparison with forcing a door, and so much more important that it becomes a matter of comparative indifference whether competition in the ordinary sense functions more or less promptly" (Schumpeter, 1942, pp. 84–85).[12]

As with the responsiveness argument it is easy to see the flexibility and

---

[12] For contemporary analyses of competition in the sense of Schumpeter, see Klein (1977) and Nelson and Winter (1980).

vigor of private enterprise. But how about the quality of the effort? Regarding the allocation of resources to R&D, it is easy enough to identify several kinds of discrepancies between investments that are privately profitable and those that are socially valuable.[13]

Consider an industry consisting of a large number of competing firms, each doing its own R&D. Each firm and its R&D effort are small enough so that there is no major bureaucratic control problem. Given that there are many firms, there is the potential for a wide variety of alternatives to be explored. Then the basic problems of a centralized regime are averted.

But there are several different kinds of "market failure" that need to be recognized. First, if firms have less than perfect ability to exclude other firms from using their technology, there is the well-known "template externality" that stems from the chances of imitation by other firms of the technology that is found (created) by one. If patents prevent direct mimicking, but there is a "neighborhood" illuminated by the invention that is not foreclosed to other firms by patents, the externality problem is there in modified form. Second, and less well recognized in the literature, there is a problem akin to that of multiple independent tappers of an "oil field"; individual companies can make money from projects which would not be worthwhile had they access to the best technologies developed by others, projects which yield little social value. There are incentives for a firm to duplicate the prevailing best technology patented by another firm in a way that does not infringe on patents. More generally, there are incentives for a firm to develop a technology even if it is worse than the current best one, if it is better than the one it has and the best is blocked by patents. The first problem tends to repress total R&D spending to a level below a social optimum. The second may spur R&D spending, but towards an allocation of effort that is socially inefficient. If patent rights are stronger, the second problem rises in importance, and the first diminishes.

Nor is there any guarantee that a competitive regime in fact would explore a variety of opportunities. In the competitive situation there would appear to be a syndrome regarding R&D allocation similar to that described by Hotelling in the case of location decisions. Where the returns to a firm from a technical advance must be assessed against the technology it currently is using, rather than against the best technology in the industry, and where the rough location of the best available technology is known and the neighborhood looks both promising and unprotected by patents, there are incentives placed in the system for everybody to cluster around the same broad opportunity. If one considers how technology will evolve over a long time horizon, too much attention is focused on particular parts of the landscape and not enough real diversification of effort is achieved. Using the externality language, the knowledge externality created by one firm pulls other firms to be doing roughly the same thing. If a firm explores new terrain, it is less likely to come up with something. And if it does, it knows that other firms will soon cluster around.

It should be noticed that most of the problems with private enterprise allocations of R&D described above have to do with the pluralism or free entry

---

[13] The literature on externalities in R&D is quite scattered. While the earlier work by economists on this topic tended to stress "underinvestment" in R&D, more contemporary work has recognized that misallocation, or poor timing, may be more important aspects. See, for example, Barzel (1968), Kamien and Schwartz (1975), or Dasgupta and Stiglitz (1980).

aspects. Monopolize the industry; now both the template externality and the incentive for doing R&D which would not be profitable if one had access to the best technology go away. And the knowledge externalities that come from successful exploration of uncharted regions of the set now are internalized. What are the debits of concentrated structure to be charged against these credits? Traditional theory would argue that the size of output in the industry would be lower. This causes the traditional triangle loss. It also feeds back to R&D incentives by reducing the size of the output to which R&D supplies. It is hard to say whether there would be more or less R&D undertaken in the monopolized case than in the competitive case. The greater degree of internalization and the smaller scale of output pull in different directions. Also, it should be considered that there will be less incentive in the monopolized case to do R&D that is profitable in the competitive case only because someone else has a patent. While this is another factor that acts to pull down the R&D level in the monopolized case relative to the competitive case, it suggests that the most important difference in the two regimes is the efficiency of R&D allocation. If the monopolist can be assumed to be a profit maximizer and if the consequences of choosing any R&D projects are more or less obvious, there are strong arguments that monopoly would generate a better portfolio of R&D projects than a regime of competition.

However, introduce again the facts that different people see alternatives in different ways and that a large organization has difficulty in simultaneously encouraging creativity and monitoring performance. Then private monopoly looks less attractive in terms of the portfolio of projects it would be likely to carry for many of the same reasons that a state centralized system of R&D management looks unattractive. Note that the argument against monopoly and for competition here is not the standard one of textbook economic theory. It does not derive from the logic of maximizing choices or from arguments that have a family relationship to the proposition that it is socially desirable to set the level of output where marginal cost equals price. Rather, the argument is that differences in perception as to what are the best bets will have a greater chance to surface and be made effective in terms of diversity of R&D projects in a competitive regime than in a monopolized one. Any regime of competitive R&D is bound to involve some waste and duplication. The costs and dangers of monopoly are principally those of reliance on a single mind for the exploration of technological alternatives, and those involved in trying to control a multifaceted R&D allocation from the center through bureaucratic controls.

One is tempted to look to a regime of oligopoly—involving neither the R&D incentive problems of a multitude of small producers, nor the pricing and single source reliance problem of a true monopoly—as a happy compromise. Many prominent economists, from Schumpeter to Galbraith, are associated with this position. But oligopolistic structure has the potential of combining the worst aspects of competition and monopoly. In many oligopolistic industries a considerable amount of R&D done by firms seems to be "defensive" and aims to assure that a firm has available a product similar to that developed by a competitor, rather than aiming to come up with something significantly different. Small numbers may yield considerable R&D duplication without any real R&D diversity.

It is clear enough that were man omniscient and omnipotent, he would not choose to organize his R&D activities through private enterprise. The case for private enterprise as an engine of progress must be posed in recognition of bounded rationality, and it must be made in terms of comparison of organizational alternatives. To my knowledge, this kind of case has not been powerfully made.

And, of course, most economies that profess a basic private enterprise faith do not rely totally on private enterprise to support and guide R&D. In most of these countries basic research is largely funded by governments and undertaken in universities. For public goods, like defense, governments not only fund the lion's share of R&D, but guide it quite closely. Government funding and guidance have played a very major role in R&D relating to agriculture and medicine. The European countries have flirted with a major governmental role in the funding and guidance of industrial R&D more generally. And the question of the appropriate role of industry and government in industrial R&D is a live topic not only in Europe but increasingly in the United States and Japan.

5. Where are we in the discussion?

■ This essay has had several purposes. I wanted, first, to hammer as hard as I know how on the point that the analysis contained in contemporary welfare economics provides an extremely shaky intellectual basis for the favorable views that most Western-trained economists apparently have about private enterprise. I wanted, second, to make explicit the kinds of arguments in favor of private enterprise that many economists seem to believe, but which have in general tended to lurk behind the scenes—being forced from the center stage, as it were, by the more formal arguments of welfare economics. The third purpose was to begin to explore these arguments—their possible explicit articulation, their strengths, their weaknesses, and the kinds of questions that naturally arise when they are pursued. In the course of this examination I hoped to make clear that although these arguments, unlike the arguments of contemporary welfare economics, could not be dismissed out of hand as irrelevant, they rested on very soft analytic footings. Finally, I wanted to try to identify what to me at least are among the most salient issues for further exploration.

If my points are accepted, they suggest that much of the traditional arguments for private enterprise espoused by economists should be regarded as prejudices and not soundly based on any analytic structure. Like many human prejudices, these may reflect informal generalization from empirical observation. In fact, the empirical work on economies which rely heavily on central planning mechanisms, and on those parts of free enterprise economies which are heavily monitored by higher authorities, often tend to show high administration cost, inflexibility, and difficulty in exploring and sensibly screening technological alternatives. But there are some examples to the contrary. And there are plenty of examples of relatively unfettered private enterprise that do not seem to be working well. My reading of the empirical literature does not suggest an overwhelming case for private enterprise solutions, or against selectively monitoring entry, establishing mechanisms to make possible more *ex ante* coordination than is possible through market mechanisms alone, and for governmental regulation or overview to constrain or supplement profit incentives.

In my view, perhaps the most pernicious aspect of contemporary theoriz-

110 / THE BELL JOURNAL OF ECONOMICS

ing about the virtues and vices of private enterprise and alternative supply regimes is that somehow it has led economists not to see what should have been plain: The current supply regimes of economies that profess a broad private enterprise faith are very variegated, and differ significantly from sector to sector; further they almost never are "pure" private enterprise, but involve various degrees of ascription, central coordination, and higher level monitoring.

While the analysis in the preceding three sections has, by and large, proceeded as if the most relevant comparisons were between globally different systems designs, I believe that for the economies of North America, Western Europe, and Japan, the short- and medium-term questions are about where to supplement or supplant the institutions of private enterprise with others which involve more ascription of roles, more centralized information channels, and more higher-order monitoring and regulation. In part, the discussion is about the appropriate mix within particular sectors; for example, in the United States there currently is considerable disagreement about how to organize or reorganize the evolving energy sectors. The voucher proposal is about the organization of education. For many urban public services an important and live question is whether they should be provided through public agencies, or through regulated private concession. In part the discussion is about such cross-cutting issues as how to assure appropriate standards of safety across all job classifications, or how to protect environmental values. The questions here also involve what policies should be undertaken to guide industrial investment and to shelter individual workers in circumstances where one kind of industry is declining and another is expanding. As remarked earlier, R&D policy and the mix between public and private funding is a very live issue.

But over the longer run, it may be important to begin to explore the question of how much supplementary machinery can be loaded on to a basic private enterprise design, before one ends up with a system that preserves a few of the advantages of private enterprise and many of the disadvantages. In the 1950s scholars like Crosland believed that through Keynesian macro-economic policies, a variety of redistribution schemes, and the public provision of certain basic goods and services, one could have welfare state socialism along with the (apparently believed by him) parsimony, responsiveness, and innovativeness advantages of private enterprise. But there are serious questions as to how far access to consumer goods can be decoupled from wages and profits before the incentive aspects of private enterprise dry out. Many scholars recently have been asking similar questions about the expanded regulatory systems which now permeate free enterprise economies. I raise these questions here not because I have any strong notions about the answers, but because I believe that ultimately these are the kinds of questions that will arise as the economies that profess a basic private enterprise style become more and more mixed. And these kinds of questions increasingly are being posed by those who doubt that the welfare state private enterprise that is evolving will be a long-run viable solution.

Unfortunately, even if the economics profession decided seriously to join in the discussion, at the present time we might not have much to contribute. Our well worked out theoretical ideas are not particularly relevant, and the ideas that may have some relevance are at a most rudimentary stage of development. We have collected some empirical information which bears on the issues, but not very much. It is time to get on with the task.

References

BARZEL, Y. "Optimum Timing of Innovation." *Review of Economics and Statistics* (August 1968).

CHENERY, H. "The Application of Investment Criteria." *Quarterly Journal of Economics* (Febuary 1953).

COASE, R. "The Problem of Social Cost." *Journal of Law and Economics* (October 1966).

DASGUPTA, P. AND STIGLITZ, J. "Market Structure and the Nature of Inventive Activity." *Bell Journal of Economics* (Spring 1980).

EVENSON, R. AND KISLEV, Y. "A Stochastic Model of Applied R&D." *Journal of Political Economy* (April 1976).

GALBRAITH, J.K. *American Capitalism*. Boston: Houghton Mifflin Co., 1952.

HAYEK, F.A. "The Use of Knowledge in a Society." *American Economic Review* (1945). Reprinted in M. Bornstein, ed., *Comparative Economic Systems*, Homewood, Ill.: Richard R. Irwin, 1969.

HURWICZ, L. "The Design of Mechanisms for Resource Allocation." *American Economic Review* (May 1973).

KAMIEN, M. AND SCHWARTZ, N. "Market Structure and Innovation." *Journal of Economic Literature* (March 1975).

KLEIN, B. *Dynamic Competition*. Cambridge: Harvard University Press, 1977.

KNIGHT, F. *The Economic Organization*. New York: Harper and Row, 1933.

LANGE, O. "On the Economic Theory of Socialism." *Review of Economic Studies* (1936).

LINDBLOM, C.E. *Politics and Markets*. New York: Basic Books, 1977.

MARCH, J. AND SIMON, H.A. *Organizations*. New York: John Wiley and Sons, 1958.

MARSCHAK, J. "The Economics of Enquiring, Communicating, Deciding." *American Economic Review* (May 1968).

—— AND RADNER, R. *Economic Theory of Teams*. Yale University Press, 1972.

MARSCHAK, T. "Centralized versus Decentralized Resource Allocation: The Yugoslav Laboratory." *Quarterly Journal of Economics* (November 1968).

——, GLENNAN, T., AND SUMMERS, R. *Strategy of R&D*. New York: Springer Verlag, 1967.

MONTIAS, J.M. *The Structure of Economic Systems*. New Haven: Yale University Press, 1976.

NELSON, R.R. AND WINTER, S.G. *The Schumpeterian Tradeoffs Revisited*. Mimeograph, Yale University, 1980.

POWELL, R. "Plan Execution and the Workability of Soviet Planning." *Journal of Comparative Economics* (1977).

RICHARDSON, G.B. *Information and Investment*. Oxford: Oxford University Press, 1960.

ROSS, S. "The Economic Theory of Agency: The Principal's Problem." *American Economic Review* (May 1973).

SCHUMPETER, J. *Capitalism, Socialism, and Democracy*. New York: Harper & Brothers, 1942.

SIMON, H.A. *Models of Man*. New York: John Wiley & Sons, Inc., 1957.

——. "Rationality as Process and as Product of Thought." *American Economic Review* (May 1978).

SMITH, A. *An Inquiry into the Nature and Causes of the Wealth of Nations*. New York: Random House, 1937.

VON MISES, L. *Socialism: An Economic and Sociological Analysis*. New Haven: Yale University Press, 1951.

WARD, B. *The Socialist Economy*. Berkeley: University of California Press, 1967.

WILLIAMSON, O. *Corporate Control and Business Behavior*. Englewood Cliffs: Prentice Hall, 1970.

——. "Franchise Bidding for Natural Monopolies—In General and with Respect to CATV." *Bell Journal of Economics* (Spring, 1976).

——. *Markets and Hierarchies: Analysis and Antitrust Considerations*. New York: Free Press, 1975.

WOLF, C. "A Theory of Nonmarket Failure." *Journal of Law and Economics* (April 1979).

[6]

The Bazaar Economy: Information and Search in Peasant Marketing

By CLIFFORD GEERTZ*

There have been a number of points at which anthropology and economics have come to confront one another over the last several decades—development theory; preindustrial history; colonial domination. Here I want to discuss another where the interchange between the two disciplines may grow even more intimate; one where they may come actually to contribute to each other rather than, as has often been the case, skimming off the other's more generalized ideas and misapplying them. This is the study of peasant market systems, or what I will call bazaar economies.

There has been by now a long tradition of peasant market studies in anthropology. Much of it has been merely descriptive—inductivism gone berserk. That part which has had analytical interests has tended to divide itself into two approaches. Either the bazaar is seen as the nearest real world institution to the purely competitive market of neoclassical economics—"penny capitalism"; or it is regarded as an institution so embedded in its sociocultural context as to escape the reach of modern economic analysis altogether. These contrasting approaches have formed the poles of an extended debate between economic anthropologists designated "formalists" and those designated "substantivists," a debate that has now rather staled for all but the most persevering.

Some recent developments in economic theory having to do with the role of information, communication, and knowledge in exchange processes (see Michael Spence; George Stigler; Kenneth Arrow; George Akerlof; Albert Rees) promise to mute this formalism-substantivism contrast. Not only do they provide us with an analytic framework more suitable to

*The Institute for Advanced Study.

understanding how bazaars work than do models of pure competition; they also allow the incorporation of sociocultural factors into the body of discussion rather than relegating them to the status of boundary matters. In addition, their actual use on empirical cases outside the modern "developed" context may serve to demonstrate that they have more serious implications for standard economic theory and are less easily assimilable to received paradigms than at least some of their proponents might imagine. If this is so, then the interaction of anthropology and economics may come for once to be more than an exchange of exotic facts for parochial concepts and develop into a reciprocally seditious endeavor useful to both.

I

The bazaar economy upon which my discussion is based is that of a town and countryside region at the foot of the Middle Atlas in Morocco I have been studying since the mid-1960's. (During the 1950's, I studied similar economies in Indonesia. See the author, 1963.) Walled, ethnically heterogeneous, and quite traditional, the town is called Sefrou, as is the region, and it has been there for a millenium. Once an important caravan stop on the route south from Fez to the Sahara, it has been, for about a century, a thriving market center of 15,000–30,000 people.

There are two sorts of bazaar there: 1) a permanent one, consisting of the trading quarters of the old town; 2) a periodic one, which meets at various spots—here for rugs, there for grain—outside the walls on Thursdays, as part of a very complex regional cycle involving various other market places and the other days of the week. The two sorts of bazaar are distinct but their boundaries are quite permeable, so that in-

VOL. 68 NO. 2 ECONOMICS AND ANTHROPOLOGY 29

dividuals move freely between them, and they operate on broadly the same principles. The empirical situation is extremely complex—there are more than 600 shops representing about forty distinct commercial trades and nearly 300 workshops representing about thirty crafts—and on Thursdays the town population probably doubles. That the bazaar is an important local institution is beyond doubt: two-thirds of the town's labor force is employed there.

Empirical detail aside (a full-scale study by the author is in press), the bazaar is more than another demonstration of the truth that, under whatever skies, men prefer to buy cheap and sell dear. It is a distinctive system of social relationships centering around the production and consumption of goods and services—that is, a particular kind of economy, and it deserves analysis as such. Like an "industrial economy" or a "primitive economy," from both of which it markedly differs, a "bazaar economy" manifests its general processes in particular forms, and in so doing reveals aspects of those processes which alter our conception of their nature. Bazaar, that Persian word of uncertain origin which has come to stand in English for the oriental market, becomes, like the word market itself, as much an analytic idea as the name of an institution, and the study of it, like that of the market, as much a theoretical as a descriptive enterprise.

II

Considered as a variety of economic system, the bazaar shows a number of distinctive characteristics. Its distinction lies less in the processes which operate and more in the way those processes are shaped into a coherent form. The usual maxims apply here as elsewhere: sellers seek maximum profit, consumers maximum utility; price relates supply and demand; factor proportions reflect factor costs. However, the principles governing the organization of commercial life are less derivative from such truisms than one might imagine from reading standard economic textbooks, where the passage from axioms to actualities tends to be rather nonchalantly traversed. It is those principles—matters less of utility balances than of information flows—that give the bazaar its particular character and general interest.

To start with a dictum: in the bazaar information is poor, scarce, maldistributed, inefficiently communicated, and intensely valued. Neither the rich concreteness or reliable knowledge that the ritualized character of nonmarket economies makes possible, nor the elaborate mechanisms for information generation and transfer upon which industrial ones depend, are found in the bazaar: neither ceremonial distribution nor advertising; neither prescribed exchange partners nor product standardization. The level of ignorance about everything from product quality and going prices to market possibilities and production costs is very high, and much of the way in which the bazaar functions can be interpreted as an attempt to reduce such ignorance for someone, increase it for someone, or defend someone against it.

III

These ignorances mentioned above are *known* ignorances, not simply matters concerning which information is lacking. Bazaar participants realize the difficulty in knowing if a cow is sound or its price right, and they realize also that it is impossible to prosper without knowing. The search for information one lacks and the protection of information one has is the name of the game. Capital, skill, and industriousness play, along with luck and privilege, as important a role in the bazaar as they do in any economic system. They do so less by increasing efficiency or improving products than by securing for their possessor an advantaged place in an enormously complicated, poorly articulated, and extremely noisy communication network.

The institutional peculiarities of the bazaar thus seem less like mere accidents of custom and more like connected elements of a system. An extreme division of labor and localization of markets, heterogeneity of products and intensive price bargaining, fractionalization of transactions and stable clientship ties between buyers and sellers, itinerant trading and extensive traditionalization of occupation in ascriptive terms—these things do not just co-occur, they imply one another.

The search for information—laborious, uncertain, complex, and irregular—is the central experience of life in the bazaar. Every aspect of the bazaar economy reflects the fact that the primary problem facing its participants (that is, "bazaaris") is not balancing options but finding out what they are.

IV

Information search, thus, is the really advanced art in the bazaar, a matter upon which everything turns. The main energies of the bazaari are directed toward combing the bazaar for usable signs, clues as to how particular matters at the immediate moment specifically stand. The matters explored may comprise everything from the industriousness of a prospective coworker to the supply situation in agricultural products. But the most persistent concerns are with price and quality of goods. The centrality of exchange skills (rather than production or managerial ones) puts a tremendous emphasis on knowing what particular things are actually selling for and what sorts of things they precisely are.

The elements of bazaar institutional structure can be seen in terms of the degree to which they either render search a difficult and costly enterprise, or facilitate it and bring its costs within practical limits. Not that all those elements line up neatly on one or another side of the ledger. The bulk have effects in both directions, for bazaaris are as interested in making search fruitless for others as they are in making it effectual for themselves. The desire to know what is really occurring is matched with the desire to deal with people who don't but imagine that they do. The structures enabling search and those casting obstructions in its path are thoroughly intertwined.

Let me turn, then, to the two most important search procedures as such: clientelization and bargaining.

V

Clientelization is the tendency, marked in Sefrou, for repetitive purchasers of particular goods and services to establish continuing relationships with particular purveyors of them, rather than search widely through the market at each occasion of need. The apparent Brownian motion of randomly colliding bazaaris conceals a resilient pattern of informal personal connections. Whether or not "buyers and sellers, blindfolded by a lack of knowledge simply grop[ing] about until they bump into one another" (S. Cohen, quoted in Rees, p. 110), is, as has been proposed, a reasonable description of modern labor markets, it certainly is not of the bazaar. Its buyers and sellers, moving along the grooved channels clientelization lays down, find their way again and again to the same adversaries.

"Adversaries" is the word, for clientship relations are not dependency relations, but competitive ones. Clientship is symmetrical, egalitarian, and oppositional. There are no "patrons" in the master and man sense here. Whatever the relative power, wealth, knowledge, skill, or status of the participants—and it can be markedly uneven—clientship is a reciprocal matter, and the butcher or wool seller is tied to his regular customer in the same terms as he to them. By partitioning the bazaar crowd into those who are genuine candidates for his attention and those who are merely theoretically such, clientelization reduces search to manageable proportions and transforms a diffuse mob into a stable collection of familiar antagonists. The use of repetitive exchange between acquainted partners to limit the costs of search is a practical consequence of the overall institutional structure of the bazaar and an element within that structure.

First, there is a high degree of spatial localization and "ethnic" specialization of trade in the bazaar which simplifies the process of finding clients considerably and stabilizes its achievements. If one wants a kaftan or a mule pack made, one knows where, how, and for what sort of person to look. And, since individuals do not move easily from one line of work or one place to another, once you have found a particular bazaari in whom you have faith and who has faith in you, he is going to be there for awhile. One is not constantly faced with the necessity to seek out new clients. Search is made accumulative.

Second, clientelization itself lends form to the bazaar for it further partitions it, and does so in directly informational terms, dividing it into overlapping subpopulations within which more rational estimates of the quality of information, and thus of the appropriate amount and type of search, can be made. Bazaaris are not projected, as for example tourists are, into foreign settings where everything from the degree of price dispersion and the provenance of goods to the stature of participants and the etiquette of contact are unknown. They operate in settings where they are very much at home.

Clientalization represents an actor-level attempt to counteract, and profit from, the system-level deficiencies of the bazaar as a communication network—its structural intricacy and irregularity, the absence of certain sorts of signaling systems and the undeveloped state of others, and the imprecision, scattering, and uneven distribution of knowledge concerning economic matters of fact—by improving the richness and reliability of information carried over elementary links within it.

VI

The rationality of this effort, rendering the clientship relation dependable as a communication channel while its functional context remains unimproved, rests in turn on the presence within that relation of the sort of effective mechanism for information transfer that seems so lacking elsewhere. And as that relation is adversary, so is the mechanism: multidimensional intensive bargaining. The central paradox of bazaar exchange is that advantage stems from surrounding oneself with relatively superior communication links, links themselves forged in sharply antagonistic interaction in which information imbalances are the driving force and their exploitation the end.

Bazaar bargaining is an understudied topic (but see Ralph Cassady), a fact to which the undeveloped state of bargaining theory in economics contributes. Here I touch briefly on two points: the multidimensionality of such bargaining and its intensive nature.

First, multidimensionality: Though price setting is the most conspicuous aspect of bargaining, the bargaining spirit penetrates the whole of the confrontation. Quantity and/or quality may be manipulated while money price is held constant, credit arrangements can be adjusted, bulking or bulk breaking may conceal adjustments, and so on, to an astonishing range and level of detail. In a system where little is packaged or regulated, and everything is approximative, the possibilities for bargaining along non-monetary dimensions are enormous.

Second, intensiveness: I use "intensive" in the way introduced by Rees, where it signifies the exploration in depth of an offer already received, a search along the intensive margin, as contrasted to seeking additional offers, a search along the extensive. Rees describes the used car market as one in which intensive search is prominent as a result of the high heterogeneity of products (cars driven by little old ladies vs. taxicabs, etc.) as against the new car market, where products are considered homogeneous, and extensive search (getting new quotations from other dealers) predominates.

The prominence of intensive bargaining in the bazaar is thus a measure of the degree to which it is more like a used car market than a new car one: one in which the important information problems have to do with determining the realities of the particular case rather than the general distribution of comparable cases. Further, it is an expression of the fact that such a market rewards a "clinical" form of search (one which focuses on the diverging interests of concrete economic actors) more than it does a "survey" form (one which focuses on the general interplay of functionally defined economic categories). Search is primarily intensive because the sort of information one needs most cannot be acquired by asking a handful of index questions of a large number of people, but only by asking a large number of diagnostic questions of a handful of people. It is this kind of questioning, exploring nuances rather than canvassing populations, that bazaar bargaining represents.

This is not to say that extensive search plays no role in the bazaar; merely that it is ancillary to intensive. Sefrou bazaaris make a terminological distinction between bargaining to test the waters and bargaining to conclude an exchange, and tend to conduct the two in different places: the first with people with whom they have weak clientship ties, the second with people with whom they have firm ones. Extensive search tends to be desultory and to be considered an activity not worth large investments of time. (Fred Khuri reports that in the Rabat bazaar, bazaaris with shops located at the edge of the bazaar complain that such shops are "rich in bargaining but poor in selling," i.e. people survey as they pass, but do their real bargaining elsewhere.) From the point of view of search, the productive type of bargaining is that of the firmly clientelized buyer and seller exploring the dimensions of a particular, likely to be consummated transaction. Here, as elsewhere in the bazaar, everything rests finally on a personal confrontation between intimate antagonists.

The whole structure of bargaining is determined by this fact: that it is a communication channel evolved to serve the needs of men at once coupled and opposed. The rules governing it are a response to a situation in which two persons on opposite sides of some exchange possibility are struggling both to make that possibility actual and to gain a slight advantage within it. Most bazaar "price negotiation" takes place to the right of the decimal point. But it is no less keen for that.

REFERENCES

G. A. Akerlof, "The Market for 'Lemons': Quality, Uncertainty and the Market Mechanism," *Quart. J. Econ.*, Aug. 1970, *84*, 488–500.

Kenneth J. Arrow, *The Limits of Organization*, New York 1974.

R. Cassady, Jr., "Negotiated Price Making in Mexican Traditional Markets," *Amer. Indigena*, 1968, *38*, 51–79.

Clifford Geertz, *Peddlers and Princes*, Chicago 1963.

———, "Suq: The Bazaar Economy in Sefrou," in Lawrence Rosen et al., eds., *Meaning and Order in Contemporary Morocco: Three Essays in Cultural Analysis*, New York forthcoming.

F. Khuri, "The Etiquette of Bargaining in the Middle East," *Amer. Anthropologist*, July 1968, *70*, 698–706.

A. Rees, "Information Networks in Labor Markets," in David M. Lamberton, ed., *Economics of Information and Knowledge*, Hammondsworth 1971, 109–18.

M. Spence, "Time and Communication in Economic and Social Interaction," *Quart. J. Econ.*, Nov. 1973, *87*, 651–60.

G. Stigler, "The Economics of Information," in David M. Lamberton, ed., *Economics of Information and Knowledge*, Hammondsworth 1971, 61–82.

[7]

Information Economics and Policy 2 (1986) 5–22. North-Holland 5

PRIVATE COPYING, REPRODUCTION COSTS, AND THE SUPPLY OF INTELLECTUAL PROPERTY

Stanley M. BESEN*

The Rand Corporation, Washington, DC 20037-1270, USA

Recent technological advances that have substantially reduced the cost of private copying of intellectual property, and led to widespread copying, have produced claims of severe harm to producers. This paper develops a model to analyze the effect of private copying on the profits of producers and the welfare of consumers. When originals and copies are perfect substitutes and all originals are copied the same number of times, a necessary and sufficient condition for both profits and consumer welfare to decrease is that copying is less efficient than producing originals. However, when some originals are copied and others are not, producer profits may decline even when copying is efficient, and some consumers may benefit from inefficient copying. The analysis suggests that published estimates of the harm to producers resulting from private copying may be seriously in error.

Keywords: Copyright, intellectual property, private copying.

1. Introduction

Private copying of intellectual property, once a laborious undertaking, has been made commonplace by recent technological advances – exemplified by the personal computer and the videocassette recorder. Because private copying is not easily detected and, additionally, is sometimes held to be fair use, and thus not a copyright infringement, producers of intellectual property often cannot protect their rights through legal actions against copiers. This has led copyright holders to claim that private copying imposes large losses on them. For example, an estimate prepared for the Recording Industry Association of America [Greenspan (1983)] indicates that home taping of audio materials, records, and cassettes displaced sales by more than $1 billion in 1982.[1] Many producers are now seeking to have royalties placed on recording devices and media to replace the revenues that are claimed to be lost as a result of private copying. Four countries – Austria, the Federal Republic of Germany, the Congo, and Hungary – have adopted royalty arrangements, and others are considering similar measures. [Unesco and WIPO (1984).]

Producers of intellectual property can respond to the prevalence of wide-

---

*I appreciate helpful comments from David W. Grissmer, M. Susan Marquis, Peter H. Reuter and an anonymous referee, and from participants in seminars at the Massachusetts Institute of Technology, the Office of the Register of Copyrights, and Rice University. Special thanks go to Herman Quirmbach for an exceptionally thorough and careful review of the Rand report on which this paper is based and to Sheila N. Kirby for many useful discussions and for her efforts in preparing the paper for publication. This paper is based upon work supported by the National Science Foundation under Grant no. IST-8216474.

[1]There are, however, reasons to be skeptical of this and other estimates.

spread private copying in a number of ways. They can accelerate the marketing of their products in order to make the acquisition of an original more convenient than copying. They can embody originals in technologies that make copying more difficult. A third possibility, which is explored in this paper, is that producers can change the price they charge for originals. The implications of this behavior for producer profits and consumer welfare depends on whether copying is efficient or inefficient, and on whether producers raise prices in an effort to appropriate the 'resale' value of the original or set a 'limit price' for originals to discourage copying.

The economics of copying is analytically similar to the economics of new and used goods markets. The central issue revolves around the effect of the existence of secondary markets on producer profits and consumer welfare. Benjamin and Kormendi (1974), analyzing new and used durable goods markets, concluded that both competitive and monopolistic producers of primary goods would sometimes be better off banning or restricting the secondary market, a conclusion that derived from their assumption that used and new goods are not perfect substitutes for one another.

Liebowitz (1981, n.d.) used a variant of the Benjamin–Kormendi model to analyze copyright issues specifically. He pointed out that the purchase price consumers are willing to pay for intellectual property is the sum of their own valuation plus the resale (or loan) value of the good, thus allowing for the possibility of indirect appropriability by primary producers of the value of copies. The effect of copying on producer profits was shown to depend importantly on the relative sizes of the markets for originals and copies, the degree to which originals and copies are considered substitutes in consumption, the number of copies made from each original, and the costs of operating the market for copies and originals. Liebowitz concluded that total welfare would always increase as a result of copying provided there were no costs associated with the functioning of such markets.

Novos and Waldman (1984) examined the effects of increased copyright protection on social welfare by analyzing a model in which consumers do not vary in their valuation of the intellectual property, but differ in their costs of obtaining a copy. In their model, in contrast to that of Liebowitz, copiers bear only the costs of copying and do not share in the cost of purchasing originals. Their analysis provides some support for the claim that an increase in copyright protection may decrease the social welfare loss associated with underproduction of goods that are only partially non-excludable. Moreover, by explicitly recognizing that copying may involve a higher social marginal cost than does the production of originals, Novos and Waldman raised the possibility that an increase in copyright protection may increase social welfare as individuals shift from the secondary to the primary market.

Johnson (1985), in a related paper, allowed both variation in consumer preferences and in copying technologies and identified both short-run and long-run effects. Johnson assumed, as do Novos and Waldman, that copiers do not contribute to the cost of purchasing originals. He concluded that the effect of unlimited copying on social welfare in the long run is ambiguous, depending on the elasticity of supply and the value consumers place on product variety. In the short run, however, society may be better off by restricting copying because of the higher social marginal cost associated with it.

The present paper adopts the same approach as does Liebowitz, in that we assume that the demand for originals reflects the demand for the copies that are made from them. However, as the number of copies that are made from an original increases, this assumption becomes increasingly less tenable because 'free rider' behavior becomes more likely the larger is the group that 'shares' an original. The approach taken here, therefore, seems more appropriate where copying occurs in small groups whose membership can be restricted to those who share in the costs of originals.

There are two ways in which the present paper can be distinguished from previous work. One is to regard the analysis as an extension of the new good-used good models where it is natural to assume that there are no costs of converting a new good into a used one. Only the passage of time is required. By contrast, the production of copies from originals involves real resource costs, and it is these costs that are the focus of our analysis. We show below that the introduction of copying costs importantly effects the results that are obtained.

An alternative interpretation is that the present paper is based on models of optimal product durability. In these models, it is generally assumed that producers determine the amount of durability to build into their products [Hirshleifer (1971)]. In the present paper, by contrast, consumers determine whether or not copies will be made, which is analogous to consumers choosing how durable a product will be by investing in maintenance activities. As will be evident from our analysis, it makes a great deal of difference to the conclusions reached regarding the effects of copying on social welfare that it is consumers, rather than producers, who actually make this choice.

Our results lend support to the general conclusion that copying need not necessarily be harmful to producers. The introduction of copying will increase consumer welfare and producer profits in the short run if copying technologies are efficient and if producers can appropriate the use-valuation of copiers by increasing the price that is charged for originals. At the same time, the model shows that the introduction of copying can, in the short run at least, reduce consumer welfare.

The paper focuses on copying of materials that have initially been sold directly to consumers and thus is relevant to the copying of books and journals, computer software, and pre-recorded audio and videocassettes. Issues involved in off-air taping are not considered. Although no attempt is made here to measure the losses in profits, if any, that result from private copying, the approach taken provides a framework within which to make such estimates. It also indicates why previous estimates of harm may be in serious error. Finally, the analysis may be useful in establishing appropriate royalty fees, if such an arrangement is adopted.

2. The basic model

The approach taken here is based on Benjamin and Kormendi's analysis of the market for durable goods. The basic model involves a number of simplifying assumptions, some of which are relaxed in subsequent sections. We assume that consumers regard originals and copies as perfect substitutes. The demand curve for a given intellectual property is downward sloping, reflecting the fact that products of different publishers are imperfect substitutes. The publisher's costs for originals consist of the cost of producing the 'first copy' plus a constant marginal cost for each original produced.[2] We assume that first copy costs have already been incurred, so that the analysis is concerned only with the short run. Publishers are assumed to be unable to prevent copying through legal action, either because they cannot detect copying, or because copying is considered to be fair use. As a first approximation, we assume that the marginal cost of making a copy is constant and independent of the number of copies made from each original; that publishers cannot alter the production process to make copying more costly; and that, if copying occurs, a fixed number of copies is made from each original. Later sections relax some of these assumptions. A more general analysis, that would treat both copying costs and number of copies as endogenous, is beyond the scope of the current paper.

We begin by assuming that private copying does not exist and that a technology is invented that permits copies to be made from each original. Since originals and copies are perfect substitutes, the price of *using* either will be the same. One can think of this as involving either (i) a set of users agreeing to purchase an original and divide its price and the cost of copying equally among them, or (ii) purchasers of originals competing to sell copies to other users. In (ii), the price of a copy would equal the price of an original *plus* the cost of making copies *minus* the revenues from the sale of the copies, which is the cost of using an original. If the price of a copy is less than this amount, some would-be purchasers of originals would buy copies and the effect would be to equalize the cost of using an original and the price of a copy. For similar reasons, the price of a copy cannot exceed the cost of using an original. Where Novos and Waldman, and Johnson assume implicitly that purchasers of originals make them freely available to copiers, in our model copiers must purchase the right to copy and, therefore, must pay more than copying costs to use a good.

The effect of introducing copying is to increase the demand for originals, either because their costs can be shared or copies can be sold, but the increase in demand will be less than proportional to the number of copies made. To be more precise, if without copying the demand for originals is $P = a - bQ$, when n copies are made from each original and the cost of a copy is r (where r includes both reproduction costs and transaction costs, if any) the demand curve becomes

[2]According to Berg (1971, p. 799), first copy costs of journals 'include the costs of screening articles, operating an organization, and manufacturing the first copy of the maunuscript.' Keon (1982, p. 11) identifies the 'fixed costs' of producing a sound recording as the cost of recording and mixing the initial master tape, plus 'the promotion and advertising expense incurred in marketing ... and the costs of preparing a pressing or manufacturing run and the cover design.' To the extent that a publisher receives revenues in the form of page charges to authors, direct grants, the sale of advertising, or submission fees, the amount that must be recovered from users is reduced. For some publications, this source of support is substantial. For example, almost 40 percent of the income of six journals published by the American Institute of Physics is obtained from publication charges [Marks (1982)].

$P = (1 + n)a - ((1 + n)^2 bQ) - nr$ for values of $P > r$.[3] The demand curve is unchanged below r since, at such prices, originals are cheaper than copies. Note that the rotation of the demand curve requires only the assumption that originals and copies are perfect substitutes. The demand curve has a higher intercept because, at high prices, the price is divided among several users. The demand curve is steeper than the initial demand curve because the market is saturated at a smaller number of originals. The greater is the number of copies per original, the steeper is the new demand curve.

The demand for originals is also affected by copying costs. That is, the effect of copying on the demand for originals not only reflects the fact that the value of originals has increased, because their costs can be shared, but also that there are costs incurred in making copies.

We assume that producers attempt to maximize profits. Although this is clearly plausible for commercial firms, it may be objected that non-profit producers have other objectives. However, if, as seems likely, entry is relatively free, even non-profit firms will be forced to set journal prices so as to maximize profits if they are to survive unless they receive substantial revenues from other sources, e.g., page charges.

If c is the producer's marginal cost, before copying the price charged for an original, P^*, is $(a + c)/2$ and the quantity sold, Q^*, is $(a - c)/b$. If n copies are made per original the price of an original, P^{**}, is $((a + c)/2) + (n(a - r)/2)$ and the quantity sold, Q^{**}, is $(a(1 + n) - c - nr)/(2b(1 + n)^2)$. Copying raises the price of originals, since a must exceed r.[4] If c and r are both equal to zero the price of an original increases to $(1 + n)$ times the price in the absence of copying. In general, however, the price of an original rises by less than that proportion, since $(a + c)$ exceeds $(a - r)$. That the price of originals will rise in the presence of copying follows from the assumption that only a limited number of copies can be made from each original.[5]

If there is copying, the cost of using an original is, of course, less than the price of an original since the price, and the associated copying costs, are shared among users. Under the assumption that originals and copies are perfect substitutes, we

[3]See Hirshleifer (1971). The significance of the assumption that the demand for originals fully reflects the value of the copies that can be made from them less the cost of reproduction should not be underestimated. The purchaser of an original will be unwilling to pay the value of the copies that will be made if he is unable to capture these amounts from other users.

[4]If $r > (a + c)/2$, copying does not occur because it is less expensive to purchase an original than to copy.

[5]Keon (1982, p. 15) argues otherwise claiming that 'the introduction of home taping equipment and the subsequent increased incidence of home taping will curtail record companies' ability to increase price ... in the face of increased competition from this source. Therefore, while home taping may cause lost sales, it also prevents recording companies from compensating for any lost sales by raising the prices of pre-recorded tapes and records.' However, so long as the number of copies made from each original is limited, producers will be able to raise the prices of originals when copying occurs. In a more general analysis, the limitation will be produced by rising marginal costs as the size of the sharing group is expanded [Buchanan (1965)]. In the more general case, group size will be finite only if these costs rise more rapidly than the associated increase in the price of originals. But, since the cost of copying affects the demand for originals, this condition will almost certainly be met.

can determine the cost of a 'use' by dividing the price of an original and copying costs by $(1 + n)$. The result is

$$(((a(1 + n) + c - nr)/2 + nr)/(1 + n) = ((a + c)/2) + ((r - c)n/2(1 + n)).$$

Whether this is greater than or less than $(a + c)/2$, the price of an original if there is no copying, depends entirely on the relationship between c and r, the respective costs of producing originals and copies. If $c > r$, so that producing copies is less expensive than producing originals, the cost of a use is reduced when copying is introduced.[6] If $c < r$, copying raises the price of a use. Where $c = r$, the cost of a use equals the price that would have been charged for an original had there been copying, $(a + c)/2$. Thus, whether consumers benefit or lose when copying is introduced depends on whether copying is more efficient than producing originals. Perhaps surprisingly, consumers are worse off when copying is introduced if copying is inefficient.

There are two other ways to measure the effect of copying that are equivalent to examining the cost of a use. One is to compare the number of originals sold without copying to the number of originals *plus* copies after copying is introduced. If $c > r$, i.e., if copying is efficient, the latter exceeds the former. Alternatively, one can measure consumer surplus directly. If copying is efficient, consumer surplus rises.

Without copying, publisher profits, in the short run are:

$$((a - c)(a - c))/4b, \text{ while after copying they are}$$

$$((a(1 + n) - c - nr)(a(1 + n) - c - nr))/4b(1 + n)(1 + n)$$
$$= (a - c + X)^2/4b,$$

where $X + (n(c - r))/(1 + n)$.

As in the case of consumer welfare, the effect of copying on publisher profits depends entirely on the relationship between r and c. If $r > c$, i.e., if copying is inefficient, copying reduces producer profits. However, if $r < c$, profits are increased when copying is introduced. This occurs because the publisher is able to substitute efficient private copying for his own production of originals.[7]

''/here the cost of copying is less than the cost of producing originals, total welfare and the welfare of both consumers and publishers are increased by the introduction of copying. Because copying is more efficient than producing originals, there is a gain even if the number of uses, originals plus copies, remains unchanged, since fewer resources are employed. Moreover, there will generally be an increase in the number of uses as their price decreases, leading to further increases in consumer welfare and publisher profits. Finally, larger

---

[6]If the same copying 'technology' is available to the publisher as to consumers, this situation cannot occur. However, some costs, e.g., distribution, may be lower for consumers, yet the publisher cannot adopt the lower cost technology.

[7]Hirshleifer (1971) obtains this result when he analyzes whether a monopolist will increase the durability of his product if he can do so costlessly.

publisher profits are likely to lead to an increase in the number of first copies that are produced. Here, both publisher and consumers are made better off as a result of copying.

Where reproduction cost exceeds the cost of originals but is lower than the price of originals, output is produced at more than minimum cost because, by assumption, marginal costs are lower for originals than for copies. Thus, even if here were no effect on total output, so that the number of originals plus copies just equals the number of originals that were made before copying was possible, a welfare increase would result because producing originals is more efficient than making copies.

Second, where copying is inefficient, the number of originals plus copies is smaller than output before copying unless demand is completely inelastic. In general, the higher price of a use reduces the number of uses. There is thus a deadweight loss that results from the failure of output to be supplied that is valued at more than its cost of production.[8]

In this case, it may be in the interest of *both* consumers and publishers to ban copying. Since the cost of copying is higher than the marginal cost of originals, but lower than the price of originals when there is no copying, consumers will copy even though it would be more efficient to have additional originals produced by the publisher.[9] But, if copying is permitted, the resulting increase in the price of originals reduces consumer surplus below the level obtained when copying is banned. Here, overall welfare, as well as the welfare of consumers, may be increased by banning copying.

It is important to observe that copying will continue to occur even where it makes consumers worse off. Since, by assumption, copying cannot be detected, consumers cannot enter into enforceable agreements not to copy. For the same reason, publishers must assume that copying will occur, and, thus, they will raise the price of originals. If agreements not to copy were enforceable, and if copying were inefficient, consumers would enter into such agreements, and the price of originals would fall. Publisher profits would, as a result, increase, and consumers would benefit from the decline in the cost of a use.

We have thus far not explored the possibility that the publisher could set a 'limit price' for originals to discourage copying. Since copies will be made only if the price of an original exceeds the cost of a copy, by reducing the price of originals to just below the cost of copying, r, the publisher can discourage copying.[10] The quantity sold under the limit pricing strategy Q_L, is equal to $(a - r)/b$. Under certain circumstances, such a strategy will produce greater profits than if the publisher accepted the existence of copying and raised its prices. A necessary condition is that the marginal cost of reproduction exceeds that of making an original, but that is not sufficient.[11] In general, the limit pricing

[8]This is in addition to any deadweight loss that existed before the introduction of copying.

[9]A more general model would permit n to vary depending on the relationship between r and c. If the assumption that originals and copies are perfect substitutes is retained, one way to limit n is to assume that r is an increasing function of n. But, in such a model, copying will occur to the point where r equals the price of an original, so that inefficient copying may occur.

[10]Since $P^* = (a + c)/2$, we need consider only cases in which $r < (a + c)/2$.

[11]The condition is that $(r - c)(a - r)(1 + n)^2 > (a(1 + n) - c - nr)^2/4$.

strategy is more likely to be profitable the larger is the gap between the marginal costs of originals and copies.

Several things should be noted about the equilibrium under limit pricing. First, production costs are minimized, since it is inefficient for copies to be made when copying costs exceed the cost of producing originals. Second, consumer surplus is higher than before copying was possible, since originals now sell at the lower limit price. Third, profits fall because publishers are forced to charge less than the profit-maximizing price. Finally, the sum of publisher profits and consumer surplus increases because limit pricing reduces the deadweight loss that results from monopoly pricing; this ignores the effect of lower producer profits on the supply of first copies.

Thus, faced with copying, there are two types of responses available to the publisher: raising prices of originals or adopting a limit pricing strategy. Breyer (1970, p. 301), argues that 'as long as prices for low volume texts and tradebooks do not rise far above the costs of the original publisher, it seems unlikely that a [copying] competitor will enter the market' and (p. 335) that 'In many cases photocopying will not seriously interfere with journal revenues ... because publishers can make up for a decline in the number of subscriptions by raising their prices.' Clearly, however, these are *alternative* strategies, not ones that can be adopted simultaneously.

To summarize the argument thus far, we have examined the case in which reproduction is costly and the number of copies per original is fixed. The principal results of the analysis are as follows:

(1) There will be no incentive to copy, and therefore no need to forbid it, if the cost of copying exceeds the price that maximizes producer profits in the absence of copying.

(2) If the publisher's marginal cost of producing originals is greater than the marginal cost of copying, producers make greater profits and consumers are also better off if copying is permitted.

(3) If the cost of copying is less than the price that maximizes producer profit without copying, but exceeds the cost of originals, and if producers raise the price of originals when the private copying is introduced, copying will occur if it is permitted but both producer profits and consumer surplus will fall. Here, consumers are better off if copying is banned, yet each consumer has an incentive to copy.

(4) If introducing copying causes publishers to adopt a limit pricing strategy, although publishers are worse off than if there were no copying, consumers are better off. Moreover, total welfare, profits plus consumers surplus, rises even where reproduction costs are greater than the costs of producing originals. Of course, such an outcome requires that profits be greater when the limit pricing strategy is pursued than where the publisher accepts the existence of copying.[12]

---

[12]An interesting example of limit pricing concerns the recent reduction in the sales price of videocassettes [Wall Street Journal (1983)]. It is reported that 'the studios are cutting prices, trying to lure consumers to buy instead of rent'.

3. Some illustrative examples

In order to illustrate the effect of copying on the welfare of consumers and the profits of publishers consider the following examples:

Demand curve without copying $P + a - bQ$.

Demand curve with copying, one copy per original $P = 2a - 4bQ - r$.

Marginal cost of reproduction c.

Suppose that $a = 10$, $b = 1$, and $c = 1$, then the price of originals without copying is 5.5, 4.5 originals are sold, 'profits' (ignoring 'first copy' costs) are 20.25, and consumer surplus is 10.13, as shown in table 1. If copying is permitted and $r = 3$, the profit maximizing price for an original rises to 9, two originals are sold, the number of uses, originals plus copies, falls to 4, profits decline to 16, and consumer surplus is reduced to 8. Because copying is inefficient, i.e., because $r > c$, both consumer surplus and producer profits are reduced by the introduction of copying.

If $r = 0.5$, however, so that $r < c$, both publisher and consumers are made better off by copying. With copying, the price of originals rises to 10.25, 2.31 originals are sold, the number of uses increases to 4.62, profits rise to 21.39, and consumer surplus increases to 10.70. Since copying is efficient, both consumers and the publisher are better off.

Table 1
The effects of copying where all originals are copied.

	Price of originals	Number of originals sold	Number of uses	Consumer surplus	Publisher 'profits'
No copying	5.5	4.5	4.5	10.13	20.25
Copying ($r = 3$)	9.0	2.0	4.0	8.0	16.0
Copying ($r = 0.5$)	10.25	2.31	4.62	10.70	21.39

4. The measurement of harm from copying

Several groups of copyright owners have attempted to measure the losses purportedly arising from private copying. For example, as noted previously, a report prepared for the Recording Industry Association of America estimates that lost sales of records and audio cassettes amounted to more than $1 billion in 1982. Davies (1983) reports the results of a 1979 United Kingdom survey that indicate that lost sales of records and audio tapes amounted to over $600 million, which was the equivalent of 70 percent of the value of retail sales in that year. Keon (1982) reports that a study of the impact of home audio taping in the British market performed for the British Phonographic Industry Copyright Association concluded that a conservative estimate of lost sales in 1977 was over

$100 million.[13] Kennedy (1985) reports on a study conducted by Future Computing that estimates that producers of business software for computers lost revenues of $1.3 billion between 1981–1984 and projected losses of $800 for 1985.

These studies have been criticized on a number of grounds. For example, Keon notes that lost profits will be smaller than lost sales because, to the extent that fewer originals are sold as a result of copying, production costs are also reduced. Moreover, he observes that the methods employed to estimate the number of copies that replace the purchase of originals are often questionable. Estimates of the amount of copying that is occurring do not appear to be reliable.[14] From our perspective, however, the most glaring shortcoming involves the implicit assumption that the price of originals is unaffected by the existence of copying. Most studies estimate the number of copies made in lieu of purchasing originals and multiply this by the existing price of originals to determine lost sales. Where the price of originals is increased, these methods obviously overstate the losses to producers.[15] If limit pricing is employed, these approaches understate the harm that is done to producers, but also ignore the increase in efficiency.

In the one study in which recognition is taken of the fact that copying may affect the price of originals, Greenspan (1983, pp. 7–8) argues that copying has depressed prices of originals by at least 5 percent. This estimate appears to be based entirely on a comparison of changes in the prices of prerecorded tapes and movements in the general price level, attributing the difference to private copying. However, as our model makes clear, estimating the effect of copying on the price of originals requires information about the amount of copying, the cost of producing originals, and the cost of copying, none of which is taken into account in deriving Greenspan's estimate.

These methods may also overstate the increase in producer revenues that would result from imposing a royalty on recording media. Because the royalty would increase the cost of copying, it will reduce the demand for originals, and, hence, the revenues from the sale of originals. This decline must be offset against the royalties that are collected.[16]

[13]Actual estimates were between $90 and $210 million, depending on the method used to estimate the number of copies that represent foregone purchases of originals.

[14]Among the estimates of computer software copying are that (i) MicroPro is paid for 'about one out of five copies of WordStar in the U.S., and about one out of ten in Europe'. [Regulation (1983, p. 13)]; (ii) 'for every copy of a VisiCorp product sold there is at least one pirate copy.' *Id.*; and (iii) 'illegal copies account for from two to nine times the number of programs sold legally.' [Washington Post (1984, p. 15)]. The sources of these estimates are not provided.

[15]Where the number of copies per original is endogenous, one effect of raising the price of originals is to increase the number of copies per original. In such cases, although producers may mitigate some of the effects of copying by raising the price of originals, this will be partially offset by the decrease in the number of originals that are sold. As a result, estimating the harm from copying becomes even more complex.

[16]Even where the number of copies per original is endogenous, where the cost of copying increases by the amount of the royalty, the optimum size of the sharing group is unaffected. Nevertheless, the royalty reduces the demand for originals since it increases the cost of a use. Where the imposition of a royalty affects the number of copies per original, it is even more difficult to determine the effect of the royalty on producer revenues. This situation will be examined in later work.

S.M. Besen / Private copying, reproduction costs, and the supply of intellectual property   15

5. Variable number of copies per original

We have thus far assumed that, if copying occurs, the same number of copies is made from each original. Admittedly, this is an oversimplification. In reality, the number of copies that are made from each original is likely to vary depending on transactions costs, preferences of consumers, copying costs, etc. In order to get an intuitive sense of how allowing the number of copies to vary per original would alter our basic results, we treat a very simple case in which the number of copies per original is allowed to take on one of two values: 0 or n. We can then divide consumers into two groups: (a) for one group, copying is uneconomic because r is greater than the price of originals. For example, one could think of these consumers as being widely scattered or in remote locations, where there are few, if any, users with whom they can 'share'; (b) for the second group, r is less than the price of originals and the size of the sharing group is n. It is, of course, possible that $r > c$ for this group.

Further, we assume that the producer cannot charge different prices for originals to the two groups of users. This occurs either because producers cannot distinguish among members of two groups or because of a legal barrier to price discrimination. The 'first sale' doctrine, which prevents motion picture producers from charging different prices for pre-recorded videocassettes to owners of video rental stores than to 'final' consumers, is an example of the latter. It is also assumed implicitly that consumers cannot move between the two groups.

Assume that in the absence of copying the demand curves for both potential copiers and those who will not copy are $P = a - bQ$, so that their horizontal sum is $P = a - (b/2)Q$. With copying, above a, the demand curve for originals is, as before, $P = a(1 + n) - (1 + n)^2 bQ - nr$. Below a, but above r, it is $P = a + ((an - nr)/(1 + (1 + n)^2)) - ((b(1 + n)^2)/(1 + (1 + n)^2))Q$. Below r it is $P = a - (b/2)Q$. Since the demand curve is convex, the discontinuity in marginal revenue creates the possibility that marginal cost will intersect marginal revenue twice.

There are two possible types of equilibria. In the first, the price of originals is so high that purchases are made only by members of the group that engages in copying. Here, copiers are better off if $r < c$, for the same reason as above, and non-copiers are necessarily worse off, because they choose not to purchase any originals at the higher price, even if $r < c$ for copiers.

In the second type of equilibrium, some non-copiers continue to purchase originals. However, the price of originals becomes $((a + c)/2) + (n(a - r)/(2(1 + (1 + n)^2)))$. Since this must be higher than the price where there is no copying, those users who are unable to share are necessarily made worse off by the introduction of copying. However copiers may be better off even if $r > c$. Indeed, if n is very large, i.e., if there is a large number of copies per original, the price of originals will be unchanged when copying occurs. If this occurs, copiers will be better off. However, it does not seem likely that this result will generalize to groups of any size since we know that if there are only sharers they are made better off when copying is introduced only if $r < c$. Recall that where all originals vere shared equally we had only to consider in detail the case where $r > c$ since if $r < c$ for all groups both producers and consumers benefit from copying if the value of all subsequent users can be captured in the sale of originals. Here, even if $r < c$ for copiers, by assumption $r > c$ for non-copiers.

It should also be noted that producer profits are necessarily reduced by the introduction of copying where $r > c$. This can be shown by observing that, in the absence of copying, the price for each of the groups was the same as in the non-copying case analyzed above, $(a + c)/2$. We know, however, that in the present case the price charged to each of the groups rises when copying is introduced. But the demand curve for the group not engaged in copying has not changed so the profit-maximizing price for that group is unchanged. Raising price thus reduces profits from serving that group. And, from the previous analysis, we know that profits from the copying group fall where $r > c$. Where $r < c$ for the copying group, the effect on profits is more complex since profits from serving this group rise while profits from serving the other group decline.

Next, it should be observed that even where producer profits and the welfare of non-copiers is reduced, total welfare may actually increase since copiers may be better off. Moreover, in the presence of non-copiers, copiers may be better off even if $r > c$ since the same price is charged to both groups. This assumes that it is more profitable to continue to serve non-copiers than to raise the price of originals sufficiently to exclude them. Where the profit maximizing price does not change, copiers are better off if $r < P^*$. This result is an artifact of the assumptions that the two groups are of equal size and have the same demand for originals. Total welfare is more likely to increase the smaller is r.

Next, we can observe that where $r < c$, producer profits may increase when copying is introduced. However, this condition does not guarantee an increase in profits as it did above because here there are non-copiers for whom, by definition, $r > c$.

This model can also be used to analyze the effect of 'organized' copying. Suppose that some originals are acquired by 'pirates' who distribute $(1 + n)$ units for each original they purchase. Assume, further, that the producer cannot distinguish between pirates and other purchasers nor can he detect sales made by the pirates. In this case, the price paid by purchasers of 'true' originals will exceed the price paid for pirated copies, but all consumers may be worse off than if piracy were eliminated. Similarly, the model can be applied to the simultaneous sale and rental of products like videocassettes. In the presence of the 'first sale doctrine' the same price will be charged both for cassettes that are purchased by final consumers and those purchased for the purpose of rentals. The existence of the rental market may, for the reasons discussed here, make purchasers worse off and even renters may benefit from the elimination of the 'doctrine'. Another possibility is that the existence of the rental market may benefit renters while harming other consumers.

Finally, we note that non-copiers can be made better off when copying is introduced if and only if limit pricing maximizes producer profits. Here, of course, although profits decline, both copiers and non-copiers are better off. This outcome is more likely the higher is r.

6. Some illustrative examples

In order to illustrate the workings of the model where the number of copies per original varies, assume that the demand curves for non-copiers and potential copiers are both $P = 10 - Q$ and that $n = 5$. Before copying, the situation is illustrated in the first column of table 2.

The cases in table 2 are designed to illustrate a range of possible outcomes when some originals are copied and others are not. Consider the case in which $c = 2$ and $r = 0$. Copying is clearly efficient, and copiers lose when copying is introduced. Profits decline because of the inability of publishers to price discriminate, i.e., to charge higher prices for those originals that will be copied. Unlike the case in which all originals are copied to the same extent, and where publishers benefitted from efficient copying, here they do not, because only some of their customers copy. Non-copiers lose because they must pay a higher price for originals but have no one with whom to share the cost. In this example, the increase in the benefits to copiers is so great that the surplus, 67.49, is greater than the surplus without copying.

If we turn to the case in which $c = 2$ and $r = 3$, so that copying is inefficient, i.e., $r > c$, another interesting result emerges. Here, as before, publisher profits decline and non-copiers are harmed because the introduction of copying leads to a rise in the price of originals. However, copiers are better off *even though copying is inefficient*. The reason is that the increase in the price of originals that

Table 2

The effects of copying where only some originals are copied.

$P = 10 - Q$	Copying	$n = 5$
$c = 2, r = 0$		
Profit	32	22.47
Non-copier surplus	8	5.53
Copier surplus	8	39.49
Total	48	67.49
$c = 2, r = 3$		
Profit	32	20.56
Non-copier surplus	8	6.22
Copier surplus	8	20.62
Total	48	47.40
$c = 2, r = 4$		
Profit	32	24
Non-copier surplus	8	18
Copier surplus	8	18
Total	48	60
$c = 9, r = 0$		
Profit	0.50	18.06
Non-copier surplus	0.25	–
Copier surplus	0.25	9.03
Total	1.00	27.09

results when copying is introduced is limited by the presence of non-copiers, so that the price of a use to copiers actually falls.[17]

Next, consider the case where $c = 2$ and $r = 4$. Here, profit maximization involves setting a limit price. In this case, profits fall to 24, below their value without copying, but above the value of 19.95 that results if the price of originals is increased. Here, non-copiers as well as copiers are made better off by the introduction of an inefficient copying technology.

Finally, where $c = 9$ and $r = 0$ and copying is introduced, profits increase from 0.50 to 18.06, the surplus of copiers increases, and non-copiers are excluded from the market.[18] Although total welfare increases, non-copiers are made worse off even though copying is efficient.

7. Partial copying

To this point we have assumed that copiers desire to purchase an entire original. Although this may be an appropriate assumption for intellectual property such as computer programs, for property such as scientific and professional journals it seems less apt. In order to explore the effect of the existence of 'partial' copying, we consider a simple model.

We assume that there exists one class of buyers who want complete 'editions' and another who desire to use only selected portions of originals but who would, in the absence of the ability to copy, consider the purchase of an entire edition and that there is a single partial copier for each purchaser of an original.[19] Moreover, we assume that the demand of the would-be copiers for originals is the same as that of purchasers of originals reduced in proportion to the amount of copying that will be done. In particular, if the demand by the purchasers of originals is $P = a - bQ$, the demand for originals by those who wish only to copy $1/q$ of an original is $P = (a/q) - (b/q)Q$. In the absence of copying, the market demand curve for prices above a/q is $P = a - bQ$ while for prices at or below a/q it is $P = a(1/q + ((1 - (1/q))/(1 + q))) - (1/(1 + q)bQ)$.[20] With the introduction of copying, and assuming that purchasers of originals can capture from copiers the value of partial copying, the market demand curve becomes $P = a(1 + (1/q) - ((1 + 1/q)bQ - (r/q))$, where r/q is the cost of a (partial) copy. In a sense, we have already examined the case in which $1/q$ is close to one, i.e., where a complete copy is desired. There, purchasers of originals and copies, as well as producers of originals benefit if $r < c$, i.e., if copying is less expensive

---

[17]It does not pay the publisher to serve only copiers, since profits from serving this group were only 16 when there was no copying, and they will necessarily be lower where copying is inefficient.

[18]Only by setting the price of originals below 10 will non-copiers continue to purchase, but this results in smaller profits than if only copiers are served.

[19]Because purchasers of originals and copies do not regard the two as equivalent it is necessary here, as it was not in the perfect substitutes case, to separate consumers into groups at the start of the analysis.

[20]Note that the 'intercept' of the demand curve below a/q is simply the extension to the vertical axis of the section of the demand curve with slope $b(1 + (1 + q))$.

than producing additional originals. Moreover, all groups are worse off if $r > c$, unless limit pricing prevails.

At the other extreme are cases in which $1/q$ is small, i.e., copiers wish to obtain a small proportion of an original, where the existence of partial copying affects neither the number of originals produced nor their prices. Here, the introduction of copying makes neither producers nor the purchasers of originals worse off and makes partial copiers better off.[21]

8. Price discrimination

Using the previous analysis, it is straightforward to analyze the case in which different prices are charged to different users, depending upon whether copies will be made from the originals that they purchase. Although it is common for the price of journals to be higher for libraries than for individuals,[22] more refined forms of discrimination based on frequency of copying appear not to be practiced.[23] Nevertheless, it is possible to analyze the effect of introducing a simple form of discrimination in which different prices are charged to copiers and non-copiers.

Price discrimination permits the decoupling of the interests of copiers and non-copiers. The price charged to non-copiers is neither raised or lowered when copying is practiced so that their welfare is independent of copying. Similarly, whether copiers are better or worse off when copying is introduced does not depend on the behavior of non-copiers. Unlike the case in which both groups of users pay the same price, where a higher price can be charged to copiers they benefit from copying only if $r < c$.

9. Comments on the long run

The analysis in this paper is confined to the short run, where the number of

[21] This reflects the assumption that the value that copiers place on an original is proportional to the amount copied.

[22] Dyl (1983, p.163) reports that for 76 academic economics journals, the mean library price was 148 percent of the mean individual price. When this is broken down by publisher type, the figures are 126 percent, 136 percent, and 191 percent for professional associations, universities, and private publishers, respectively. Moreover, where 80 percent of the private publishers discriminated, less than half of the professional associations and only about 58 percent of the universities did so. When only discriminators are considered, private publishers charged libraries 224 percent of the individual price with the figures for professional associations and universities being 161 and 156 percent respectively. The author reports, however, that 'the difference is statistically meaningful only for private publishers.' Spilhaus (1982, p. 25) reports that 'In publications issued by societies . . . the member receives journals at a rate near the production costs and libraries pay from 2 to 10 times more to make up the difference between actual page charge collections and the first-copy costs.'

[23] Many publishers have, however, sought an arrangement under which they would receive royalties based on the number of copies made. Weinberg (1975) provides a discussion of these efforts. Under the present copyright law, permission of the publisher is required for certain types of copying, but others are considered fair use or non-infringing. Moreover, it is clear that permission is not obtained for all infringing uses.

first copies is fixed. However, to the extent that producer profits are affected by the existence of private copying, the incentive to produce first copies will also be affected. If the introduction of private copying reduces profits in the short run, in the long run it is likely to reduce the incentive both to create and distribute intellectual property. If copying leads to higher profits, in the long run more first copies will be produced.

Assessing the effects of these developments is far from straightforward. It has long been recognized that a trade-off may exist between having efficient incentives for creating intellectual property and promoting its efficient use [Plant (1934)]. Where private copying promotes more widespread use, it may increase total welfare even if fewer first copies are produced. Moreover, it has been noted more recently that an excessive amount of resources may be devoted to the creation of intellectual property where such property has complete protection [Hirshleifer and Riley (1979)]. Here, copying, by reducing the incentives for creation may actually increase welfare. Whether private copying, in fact, leads to increased welfare when it reduces the return to producing first copies is, of course, an empirical question, the answer to which is likely to vary among different types of intellectual property.

10. Conclusions

In the models employed in this paper, several significant conclusions emerge about the effect of copying on the supply of intellectual property:

(1) The introduction of copying will increase consumer welfare and producer profits in the short run if (a) private reproduction costs are lower than the production costs of the producer, and (b) the price of originals can be raised to reflect the value of the copies that are made from them.
(2) Copying may reduce both consumer welfare and producer profits even when it is in the private interest of consumers to copy. This occurs where the cost of private reproduction exceeds the production costs of the producer but are less than the price of originals, and profits are maximized by raising the price of originals. These inefficiencies result from the inability of consumers to enter enforceable agreements that prohibit copying.
(3) The introduction of copying may cause producers to reduce their prices in order to discourage copying if private reproduction cost is close to the price of originals before copying is introduced. The result is to make consumers better off and producers worse off than before the introduction of copying.
(4) Where some originals are copied but others are not, where the price of originals is raised when copying becomes possible, and where the same price is charged to all consumers, purchasers of originals that are not copied are necessarily made worse off than if there were no copying. At one extreme, the price of originals is set so high that only originals that will be copied are purchased. At the other, the price of originals does not change as a result of copying but copiers contribute little or nothing to the cost of first copies.

However, although non-copiers are necessarily worse off, profits and total consumer welfare may rise.

(5) The introduction of copying may cause producers to reduce the price of originals even where only some originals are copied. Here, all consumers are better off and producers are necessarily worse off.

(6) Where copiers demand the use of only a small portion of an original and where there are users who demand an entire original for their own use, the existence of copiers makes neither the purchasers of originals nor producer worse off and makes copiers better off. However, the greater the proportion to be copied, i.e., the more that copying is a substitute for the purchase of an original, the more questionable becomes this conclusion. If almost an entire original is to be copied, the effect of copying on producers and other consumers will depend on the relationship between private reproduction costs and the production costs of the producer.

(7) The long-run effect of private copying on consumer welfare cannot be determined *a priori* even if copying reduces consumer welfare and profits in the short run. This is because inefficient copying, by reducing the number of 'first copies' produced, may reduce 'excessive' product variety.

Application of the model developed in this paper to the question of whether to subject copying to copyright liability is clearly a long way away. Nonetheless, the results reported here indicate that such applications must focus on the extent of copying, the incremental costs of publishing, and the costs of copying, among other factors. Moreover, we are confident that such an inquiry will confirm Breyer's (1970, p. 351) assertion that '. . . the desirability of copyright protection will vary from one type of "writing" to another. One must know facts about the particular industry involved before one can weigh the various costs and benefits associated with copyright protection.'

References

Benjamin, Daniel K. and Roger C. Kormendi, 1974, The interrelationship between markets for new and used durable goods, Journal of Law and Economics 17, 381–401.

Berg, Sanford V., 1971, Increasing the efficiency of the economics journal market, Journal of Economic Literature 9, 798–813.

Breyer, Stephen, 1970, The uneasy case for copyright: A study of copyright in books, photocopies and computer programs, Harvard Law Review 84, 281–351.

Buchanan, James M., 1965, An economic theory of clubs, Economica 32, 1–14.

Davies, Gillian, 1983, The private copying of sound and audio-visual recordings, A Study Requested by the Commission of the European Communities.

Dyl, Edward A., 1983, A note on price discrimination by academic journals, Library Quarterly 53, 161–168.

Greenspan, Alan, 1983, Statement Re S. 31 before the Subcommittee on Patents, Copyrights, and Trademarks, Senate Committee on the Judiciary, Oct. 25.

Hirshleifer, Jack, 1971, Suppression of inventions, Journal of Political Economy 79, 382–383.

Hirshleifer, Jack and John G. Riley, 1979, The analytics of uncertainty and information – An expository survey, Journal of Economic Literature 17, 1375–1421.

Johnson, William R., 1985, The economics of copying, Journal of Political Economy 93, 158–174.

Kennedy, Don, 1985, Software ripoff, PC Magazine, March 19, 34.

22   *S.M. Besen / Private copying, reproduction costs, and the supply of intellectual property*

Keon, Jim, 1982, Audio and video home taping: Impact on copyright payments (Consumer and Corporate Affairs Canada, Ottawa).

Liebowitz, S.J., 1981, The impact of reprography on the copyright system (Consumer and Corporate Affairs Canada, Ottawa).

Liebowitz, S.J., n.d., Copying and indirect appropriability: Photocopying of journals, Journal of Political Economy, forthcoming.

Marks, Robert H., 1982, Journal income: A multipublisher's view, Ad Hoc Committee on Economics of Publication (ed.), Economics of Scientific Journals (Council of Biology Editors, Bethesda, MD).

Novos, Ian E. and Michael Waldman, 1984, The effects of increased copyright protection: An analytical approach, Journal of Political Economy 92, 236–246.

Plant, Arnold, 1934, The economics of copyright in books, Economica (NS) 1, 167–195.

Regulation, 1983, Software piracy and the law, Regulation 7, 12–13.

Spilhaus, A.F., Jr., 1982, Page charges, Ad Hoc Committee on Economics of Publication (ed.), Economics of Scientific Journals (Council of Biology Editors, Bethesda, MD).

United Nations Educational, Social, and Cultural Organization (Unesco) and World Intellectual Property Organization (WIPO), 1984, Unauthorized reproduction for private purposes of sound and audiovisual recordings, broadcasts, and printed matter, April 16.

Wall Street Journal, 1983, Movie studios' cuts in videocassette prices stir battle with retailers on video rental, Sept. 23, 57.

Washington Post, 1984, Maryland firm agrees to pay in computer software piracy suit, Washington Business, March 19, 15.

Weinberg, Louise, 1975, The photocopying revolution and the copyright crisis, The Public Interest 38, 99–118.

Part III
Macrorealities

[8]

Macrorealities of the Information Economy

STEPHEN S. ROACH

The information economy and the associated surge in high technology spending may well offer promise of renewed productivity growth in the United States, but at current exchange rates the resulting improvements in living standards could well turn out to be built on a foundation of foreign-produced and foreign-owned capital.

Technology has taken on a new role as a conditioner of economic change in the United States. Historically, economists have been preoccupied with technological change in the narrow or microeconomic sense—focusing mainly on the process of innovation, its diffusion, and potential linkages to productivity. A shortcoming of this approach is that it fails to consider the role of technology in the context of dramatic shifts that have occurred in the macrostructure of the economy. Indeed, it can now be demonstrated that high technology holds the key to the evolution of what can be called "the information economy"—a core of activities that increasingly has become a dominant source of economic progress in the United States.

This discussion of the macrodimensions of the information economy draws, in large part, on work we have previously published at Morgan Stanley.[1] The findings of that work can be summarized in a relatively straightforward way. First, the process of structural change in the U.S. economy began in earnest in the 1960s and started with a shift of output and earnings away

---

[1]See The industrialization of the information economy, Morgan Stanley *Economic Perspectives*, June 15, 1984; and S. S. Roach, The information economy comes of age, *Information Management Review*, 1985 (1):9–18.

from traditional manufacturing activities and toward industries engaged predominantly in the creation, manipulation, and distribution of information. An important by-product of such trends was that job growth shifted dramatically away from employment on the factory assembly line and toward the white-collar work force. Such workers had labored for years at a distinct disadvantage because they had relatively limited productive capital at their disposal. With the explosion in high technology spending in the late 1970s, however, that all began to change, and by 1983 U.S. capital endowment per worker had shifted dramatically away from the factory sector and into the information economy. Therein lies the potential for a resumption of improved longer-term performance of the U.S. economy: the industrialization of the information economy.

SHIFTS IN OUTPUT AND EARNINGS

Information has become a reality for most industries—whether they are in the factory or the so-called service sector. The information intensity of a firm's output is highest in such areas as communications, finance, and insurance, as well as in some of the more traditional service areas, such as those provided by business consultants and professionals. In such information-intensive industries, companies usually do not produce physical products, but instead combine the flow of information with their skilled labor force and high technology capital to generate a knowledge-based "commodity." Even in manufacturing the growing use of robotics, computer-aided design/computer-aided manufacturing (CAD/CAM), and management information systems (MIS)-based control underscores the potential applications that information technologies can have on the traditional factory assembly line.

Figure 1 lays out the broad boundaries of the information economy. Shown in the upper panel of the figure is a decomposition of private nonfarm output into two broad groupings of industries. Defined in this context, the "information sector" includes not only traditional services but also finance, insurance, real estate, trade, transportation, communications, and public utilities. The "goods sector" is what is left over: manufacturing, mining, and construction. The share of output going to the goods sector has declined steadily since the mid-1960s from about 45 percent to about 37 percent in 1984. By contrast, the output share of the information sector has risen to over 60 percent, and our Morgan Stanley projections suggest that this group of industries will generate close to two out of every three dollars of national output by the end of 1985.

As the lower panel of Figure 1 indicates, similar shifts can be observed in the composition of corporate profits. In 1984 the information sector accounted for essentially half the volume of total corporate profits in the United

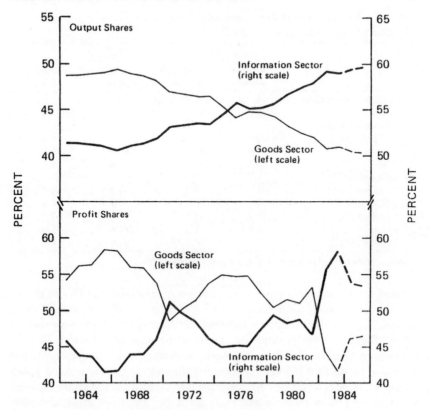

FIGURE 1 The emergence of the information economy.
NOTE: Dashed lines indicate Morgan Stanley economics projections.
SOURCE: Morgan Stanley *Economic Perspectives*, June 15, 1984.

States—increasing its earnings share almost 25 percent over the past decade. Moreover, on a per unit basis, the rise in profitability for information-intensive industries exceeded the growth in output over the past 10 years—a clear sign of an advantageous shift in earnings leverage that is another important by-product of an emerging information economy.

INFORMATION WORKERS AND THE INVESTMENT RESPONSE

Table 1 illustrates one of the most important characteristics of the information sector—the employment of a relatively large share of what traditionally has been referred to as the economy's "white-collar" occupations. These workers, hereafter referred to as the information work force, are

TABLE 1 Growing Information-Intensity of the Work Force
(share of private nonfarm work force)

	Average: 1962 to 1972		1983	
	Information Workers	Production Workers	Information Workers	Production Workers
Private nonfarm work force	49.2%	50.8%	56.2%	43.8%
Information sector	62.3	37.7	65.7	34.3
Finance, insurance, and real estate	92.9	7.1	92.4	7.6
Services	61.9	38.1	66.6	33.4
Trade	62.5	37.5	61.6	38.4
Transportation and public utilities	40.8	59.2	49.7	50.3
Goods sector	28.7	71.3	33.6	66.4
Manufacturing	30.4	69.6	36.8	63.2
Mining	28.8	71.2	44.4	55.6
Construction	21.9	78.1	21.4	78.6

SOURCE: Bureau of Labor Statistics Occupational-Industry Matrix.

defined to include executives, administrators, managers, professional specialists, technicians, salesworkers, and the support staffs of each of these groups. As the table indicates, the concentration of information workers is clearly highest in the information sector of the economy. Indeed, in 1983 information-intensive industries employed, on average, two information workers for every production worker; in contrast, the ratio is reversed in the goods sector. Thus, we can tentatively conclude that the information sector includes not only the fastest-growing and most profitable industries of the economy but, as expected, a highly disproportionate share of the information work force.

If shifts in the mix of output, earnings, and employment persist long enough, it is only natural to expect a complementary response in the composition of the remaining factor of production—the capital stock. It took more than 10 years for such a shift to occur, but when it did it came with a vengeance! Figure 2 overlays compositional shifts in capital spending with the trends in the mix of the work force just described. The upper panel highlights the essence of an emerging information economy: a rising share of the information work force together with an explosion of the high technology portion of business capital spending. From the mid-1960s through 1984, high-tech spending—defined as computers, office machines, communications equipment, instruments, industrial control and measuring devices, and miscellaneous electrical components and machinery—almost tripled as a portion of total business fixed investment, rising from about 12 percent to over 35 percent. Similarly, during the same period, the employment share of information workers climbed an estimated 10 percentage points to about 55 percent of the nonfarm work force.

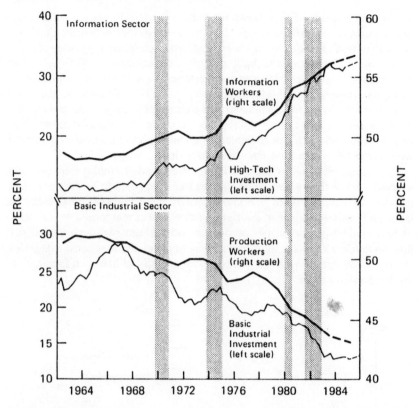

FIGURE 2   Structural change and the information economy (investment and employment shares).

NOTE: Shaded areas indicate recessionary periods as designated by the National Bureau of Economic Research. Dashed lines indicate Morgan Stanley economics projections.

SOURCE: Morgan Stanley *Economic Perspectives*, June 15, 1984.

A COMMON THREAD

The shifts in the composition of employment and capital accumulation turn out to be far more than a mere coincidence. Indeed, it is increasingly important to view the extraordinary acceleration of spending on high technology as the complementary investment response to the rapid expansion of the information work force. This conclusion is based on the fact that high technology capital turns out to be the mainstay of "production" in the information segment of our economy.

This assertion can be verified by examining the interindustry flows of shipments for a large number of high technology items. Figure 3 shows the sectoral allocations of such flows for 1982—the latest year for which there are reliable benchmark statistics. It is no surprise that industries that have been identified as being among the most information-intensive in the economy were also recipients of the bulk of high-tech equipment. Indeed, almost 85 percent of computers, other office machinery, and communications equipment was shipped to the information sector in 1982. To be sure, the share was somewhat lower for instruments and photographic equipment, and clearly, most measuring and control devices are purchased by manufacturing companies. Nonetheless, about 70 percent of all purchases of high-tech equipment were made by information-intensive industries.

Thus, high-tech investment and information-worker employment go hand in hand—more than a decade of parallel trends appears to be far more than just happenstance. Figure 4 brings together these compositional shifts in labor and capital. Shown in the figure are ratios (in real terms) of the stock of basic industrial capital per production worker and high-tech capital per information worker—the most logical way to match the functional categories of productive capital with the workers who actually utilize such facilities in the production process.

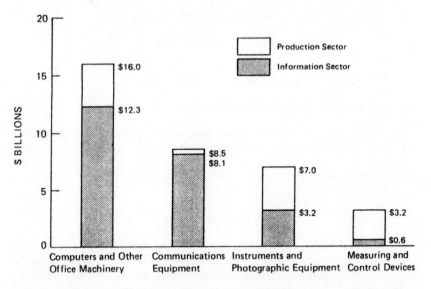

FIGURE 3   Who uses high-tech equipment? (Allocation of private domestic final shipments in 1982.)
SOURCE: Morgan Stanley economics estimates based on input-output industry distribution tables provided by the Interindustry Service of Data Resources, Inc.

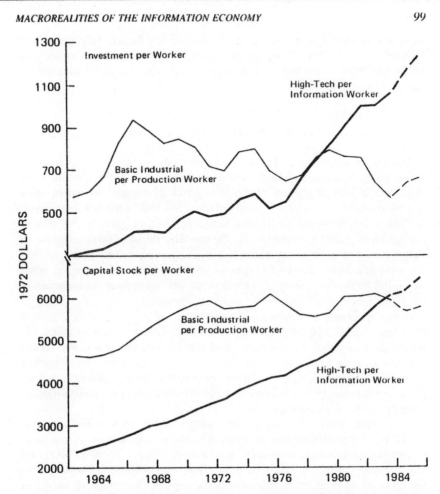

FIGURE 4   Investment and capital stock per worker: high-tech versus basic industrial.
NOTE: Investment and capital stock are expressed in constant 1972 dollars. Dashed lines
indicate Morgan Stanley economics projections.
SOURCE: Morgan Stanley *Economics Projections*, June 15, 1984.

Figure 4 reveals a dramatic convergence between these two components
of the economy's overall capital:labor ratio. Over a span of 20 years, the
stock of high-tech capital per information worker moved from about half the
size of its basic industrial counterpart to a position of relative parity in 1983.
This trend, perhaps more than anything else, brings the information sector
to the forefront of economic change in the United States; its workers are now

as richly endowed with capital as are typical production workers on the factory assembly line. What has occurred is essentially a new process of industrialization—one that should dispel any doubts about the potential vitality of the information economy.

PRODUCTIVITY IMPLICATIONS

During the long sweep of U.S. economic history, trends in capital:labor ratios and productivity change have tended to move together. While many point to the slower growth of the total stock of capital per worker as a key element in this nation's productivity shortfall, what has been overlooked is the dramatic shifts that have been taking place in the mix of capital endowment across sectors. Potentially, these relative movements may have even more to say about this nation's productivity potential than do summary ratios that lump together and weigh the many diverse types of capital against a variety of widely disparate occupational categories of the work force.

A key question, of course, is whether the rapidly rising endowment of high-tech capital embodies efficiencies that ultimately could generate improvements in information-worker productivity. On that count, the verdict is still out. Some believe that there has been unnecessary and indiscriminate spending on new technologies. Others believe that the productivity payback of the information economy cannot be accomplished without major improvements in technology management.

Over time, however, productivity change in the information economy should be less conditioned by managerial behavior and become more a function of the extraordinary revolution in microprocessing. Critical in this regard are the steady miniaturization of the "chip" and increasing economies in the costs of its production. Moreover, the rapidly changing technology of hardware is likely to be increasingly augmented by concomitant breakthroughs in operating systems or software—trends that ultimately hold the potential for the introduction of efficiencies in the workplace that are well beyond the realm of present-day comprehension. Just as economies on the assembly line once were the engine of productivity growth in "smokestack America," high technology also has the potential to spark even greater efficiencies in the information economy.

Of special note in this regard is the "leverage factor"—the fact that information workers currently account for about 60 percent of all hours worked in the economy. That implies, most critically, that improvements in information-worker productivity should add about 50 percent more to overall productivity change than would comparable increments for production workers. Thus, like it or not, productivity change in the aggregate is now increasingly in the hands of improved efficiencies in the information economy.

A DARK SIDE

Despite this constructive turn of events, the emergence of the information economy has a dark side. Unfortunately, it turns out that a strong dollar and an ever-widening foreign trade deficit have taken an unusually heavy toll on U.S. high technology producers. Indeed, in a recent report we at Morgan Stanley estimate that imports of high-tech equipment have risen to over twice the level prevailing in late 1982—producing a 60 percent increase in the market share of foreign-produced technology items (Table 2).[2]

In the context of the steadily growing technological requirements of an expanding information economy, not only does such a development hint at a potentially chronic dimension of the U.S. trade deficit, but it also underscores the risk that American capital-goods producers could be squeezed out of participating in the most dramatic structural transformation of the U.S. economy since the Industrial Revolution. The information economy may well offer a promise of renewed productivity growth, but at current exchange rates, the resulting improvements in living standards could well turn out to be built on a foundation of foreign-produced and foreign-owned capital.

Such a problem underscores the notion that no matter how powerful the forces of transformation are, the dynamics of a technology-based information economy are vulnerable to the same problems that have plagued Washington over the past two decades. Quite simply, an expansive fiscal policy in the context of monetary discipline and flexible exchange rates will continue to cause currency strains and heightened import penetration. And as recent trends strongly hint, the high technology sector in the United States could find itself as the new victim of this untenable imbalance in the mix of public policy.

REALITIES OR VISIONS?

Despite the caution flag raised by import penetration, the U.S. economy is clearly passing through a critical milestone in its postindustrial history. Much has been written about the productivity shortfall of the past decade. Little attention has been given, however, to the possibility that such an occurrence might well be the by-product of an economy making a rather orderly transition from a basic industrial society to one that emphasizes

---

[2]See Trading away the capital spending recovery, Morgan Stanley *Economic Perspectives*, February 6, 1985.

TABLE 2   Functional Breakdown of Capital Goods Imports
(billions of current dollars)

	1982 Quarter 4	1983 Quarter 4	1984 Quarter 1	1984 Quarter 2	1984 Quarter 3	Cumulative Change Over 7 Quarters
Total capital goods imports (excluding motor vehicles)	$34.2	$45.5	$57.5	$55.9	$68.7	$34.5
High technology imports	19.7	29.9	36.8	35.8	42.9	23.2
Computers and office machinery	6.3	10.4	13.8	12.7	15.7	9.4
Communication equipment and electronic components	10.1	15.1	18.1	18.1	21.0	10.9
Instruments	3.3	4.4	4.9	4.9	6.1	2.8
Basic industrial imports	9.8	10.9	14.5	14.9	18.5	8.7
Construction and specialized machinery	3.5	4.2	5.3	5.8	7.0	3.5
Other industrial machinery	6.3	6.8	9.2	9.1	11.4	5.1
Other imports	4.7	4.7	6.3	5.3	7.3	2.6
Memo items:						
Import share of						
High technology	26.6%	33.9%	40.7%	37.8%	43.0%	n.a.
Basic industrial	16.4	16.9	21.2	20.5	24.6	n.a.

SOURCE: Census-based tabulation of U.S. international transactions.

information-intensive activities. The dramatic improvements that have recently occurred in the high-tech capital endowment of the information work force suggest that this transitional interlude may be coming to an end. Instead, around the corner could very well lurk the long-awaited revival of productivity growth in the United States—the seeds of which were sown through the industrialization of the information economy.

There is no assurance, of course, that technology is *the* answer to productivity. One thing is certain, however. The structure of the U.S. economy in the mid-1980s bears little resemblance to that of the past. The eroding market share of manufacturing output and the related loss of assembly-line jobs have forced business managers headlong into the Information Age. For a long time the steps were tentative, but in the last 7 years or so the steps have become more purposeful: a conscious effort has been made to build an infrastructure of productive capital in the information economy. Without that development corporate America would have found itself caught in something of a time warp—outgrowing its industrial heritage but unwilling to look to the future. That hesitation has passed, and economic performance over the next several decades now appears to depend critically on the new realities of the information economy.

[9]

Toward an Input–Output Subsystem for the Information Sector

REINER STÄGLIN

Over the last decade increasing attention has been given to the information sector or the information economy, particularly with regard to the "information revolution" as an argument for structural changes in advanced economies. Two different research lines have been followed. Analysts have concentrated, on the one hand, on the impact of new information technology on employment and economic development, and on the other hand, on the relevance of information activities and information occupations and their collection in the so-called fourth sector or information sector.

Numerous publications and research papers were produced in the debate on the consequences of microelectronic technology (Bundesministerium für Wissenschaft und Forschung, 1981; Ernst, 1982; Kaplinsky, 1985; Rathenau, 1980), new generations of computers (OTA, 1984; Peitchinis, 1984), robotics and word processors (Hunt and Hunt, 1983; OECD 1982), computer-controlled machine tools (Leontief and Duchin, 1986; Roessner, 1984), and revolutionary advances in communications technology (Eliasson, 1982; Soete, 1985; Zeman, 1979). An excellent synopsis of many of these works is given by Freeman and Soete (1985) in their assessment on information technology and employment.

There are not many publications that emphasize information activities. The origins of this research can be traced to the pioneering books by Machlup (1962) on *Production and Distribution of Knowledge in The United States* and by Bell (1973) on *The Coming of Post-Industrial Society*. Over the past 10 years, some sociologists and economists, such as Masuda (1980), Stornier (1984), and Wallace (1986), took this information route and emphasized the trend toward the information society by stressing the growth of information-related occupations in every industry. Many analysts refer to this approach to the information sector. Some of them describe the economies of information (Arrow, 1980), the computerization of society (Nora and Minc, 1980), and the fourth economic sector (DIW, 1986, Ch. 4; Gassmann, 1981); others deal with the new service economy (Gershuny and Miles, 1983), the postindustrial economy (Stornier, 1984), or the information economy itself (Karunaratne, 1984; Porat and Rubin, 1977). Studies are also available that depict the information market (DIW and IFO, 1986), and the production of knowledge (Machlup, 1980), but in all information studies, the methodology for measuring the volume of information activities is not dealt with in detail.

To understand the methodology, we refer to the efforts of the Organisation for Economic Co-operation and Development (OECD) in the field of Information, Computer, and Communications Policy (ICCP), particularly to the questionnaire for updating the information-related data base (OECD, 1981, 1982, 1986), and to the connected DIW Information Report (1984). Additionally, the contributions of Karunaratne (1986) and Lamberton (1982) have to be taken into account.

The OECD staff have proposed standardized concepts and catalogues of "informational" and "noninformational" activities (goods, services, and occupations) to ensure intercountry comparisons with regard to the size of the information sector as a percentage of gross domestic product (GDP) at factor cost. The correspondingly collected data for the Federal Republic of Germany by the German Institute for Economic Research (DIW Information Report, 1984) have shown that a classification of goods and services as "informational" and "noninformational" according to the guidelines of the OECD causes some confusion. This can be overcome by using the input–output framework. An input–output table reveals the interdependencies between intermediate and final outputs and allows for the distinction between informational and noninformational activities if an input–output subsystem for the information sector can be developed (see also Karunaratne, 1986). Such an informational subsystem corresponds to the extension of the traditional input–output framework to account for interindustry energy flows and for environmental issues (Miller and Blair, 1985, Chs. 6 and 7).

DEFINITION OF THE INFORMATION SECTOR

The OECD (1981) analysis in the field of Information, Computer, and Communications distinguishes three separate, yet related, types of information activities:

- the primary information sector,
- the secondary information sector, and
- the information occupations.

The primary information sector includes "goods and services which intrinsically convey information (such as books) or which are directly useful in its production, processing, or distribution (such as computers). Further, these goods and services must be transacted on established markets" (OECD, 1981, p. 21). The secondary information sector records the value added by information activities used in producing noninformation goods and services, which mainly include employee compensation of information workers and depreciation on information capital. The information occupations, measured as a proportion of the total labor force employed, include those employees who produce information (scientific and technical, consultative services, etc.), process information (administrative and managerial, clerical and related, etc.), and distribute information (educators, communication workers, etc.) as well as persons employed in the information infrastructure (information machine workers, postal and telecommunications workers, etc.).

We will concentrate on the primary information sector for which the OECD staff have proposed a rather voluminous inventory of goods and services that are assumed to be informational, comprising final products as well as intermediate goods. This inventory is based on the International Standard Industrial Classification (ISIC) of all economic activities (United Nations, 1971).

Although this OECD catalogue of primary information sector components offers a base for estimating the value-added contribution of the production of information goods and services, methodological problems arise with regard to intermediate products: The glass curved for clocks and watches is included in the inventory, but the parts of iron and steel for clockworks, for instance, are not. The same is true for chips produced in electrical engineering. They are classified as noninformational, although automatic switching devices, which include various kinds of chips, are listed with the ISIC category. These problems and some corresponding classification difficulties with respect to double-counting and omissions can be shown only on the basis of an input–output table, which divides total production into intermediate and final output and allows an analyst to assess the indirect production needs of the information sector. Though the input–output idea has not yet been adopted by the OECD, the DIW (1984) has made a first attempt following these lines when updating and improving the data base on information activities for the Federal Republic of Germany as presented in the ICCP Report No. 6. This first step has to be followed by other investigations to provide an improved approach, probably that of an informational input–output subsystem as presented in this chapter.

AN INPUT–OUTPUT SUBSYSTEM FOR THE PRIMARY INFORMATION SECTOR

The use of an input–output framework is helpful in collecting and arranging data on information goods and services according to the categories of gross production and intermediate and final demand, because it ensures consistency with macroeconomic variables. In addition, the possibility of disaggregating intermediate demand according to production sectors enables the evaluation of interdependencies between the primary information sector and other parts of the economy. In an informational input–output subsystem, therefore, the definitions and classifications should correspond to those of an available input–output table.

Framework of an Informational Input–Output Subsystem

The idea of an input–output subsystem for the primary information sector is given in Figure 6-1, in which the different matrices of this system are defined.[1] Matrix A reflects the starting point. It shows the traditional input–output table extended by breaking down each of the n production sectors into an informational part, I, and a noninformational part, NI. The theoretical (hypothetical) framework of matrix A includes three separate tables on information activities: an informational output table, a corresponding input table, and an informational input and output table. In these tables, three issues of the primary information sector are represented: the output pattern of information goods and services to noninformational parts of the various sectors and to final demand components (matrix B), the input pattern of information goods and services from noninformational suppliers and from primary inputs (matrix C), and the output and input pattern within the informational parts of the different sectors 1 to n (matrix D).

1. A first definition of these informational matrices was presented at the Sixth Starnberger Kolloquium zur Weiterentwicklung der Volkswirtschaftlichen Gesamtrechnungen (Sixth Colloquium in Starnberg on further development on national accounts) (Stäglin, 1988).

Alternative Accounting Frameworks

FIGURE 6-1 Matrices of an informational input–output subsystem. (A) Input–output table with an informational (*I*) and noninformational (*NI*) breakdown. (B) Informational output table. (C) Informational input table. (D) Informational input and output table.

The three informational matrices form the input–output subsystem for the primary information sector. This can also be seen from Figure 6-2 with the final input–output table (matrix *E*), in which the information sector is shown as sector $n + 1$. The different hatching of rows and columns shows the coincidence among the three informational matrices *B*, *C*, and *D*, the theoretical basis of matrix *A*, and the final input–output matrix *E*. If the detailed listing of the primary information sector components in matrix *E* (Figure 6-2) is disregarded, the output pattern and the input pattern of the information sector $n + 1$ as a whole ($\sum I$) can be taken from the matrices *B*, *C*, and *D* (Figure 6-1). The column totals of the informational output table yield the row distribution of the primary information sector in the final input–output matrix E, the row totals of the input table result in the column distribution, and the overall total of the intrasectoral informational input and output table adds the intrasectoral cell $^I x^I$. These interconnections can be confirmed by the specified elements in the different matrices.

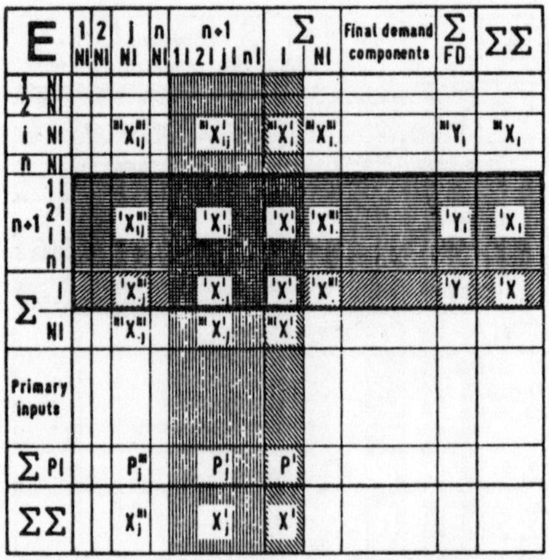

FIGURE 6-2   Input–output table with a separate primary information sector.

It should be emphasized that the informational input–output system developed so far is limited to the primary information sector, that is, it excludes the secondary information sector.[2] Additionally, the primary information sector is not completely recorded: imported information goods and services are not yet taken into account explicitly. They also can be divided into intermediate inputs and final goods. The intermediate imports are used for producing information goods and services, but also for noninformation outputs.

Partial Implementation of an Informational Input–Output Subsystem

Although the input–output subsystem for the primary information sector is still incomplete, it has been partially implemented by the DIW in the process of data collection on information activities for the Federal Republic of Germany. Figures 6-1 and 6-2 indicate the kind of data collected on information goods and services and their arrangement according to the input–output subsystem. This can be seen as well from parts of the matrices B, D, and E. It concerns all rows of the informational output table and all elements of the informational input and output table. Thus, the output distribution of the separate primary information sector can be shown (matrix E). By eliminating the informational parts I from matrix A, we can also derive the noninformational parts NI, summarized in matrix E.

The procedure of compiling the output pattern of the primary information sector

2. The secondary information sector is included in the input-output approach followed by Karunaratne (1986, pp. 18–21). He does not start with the empirical disaggregation of an input-output table, but he makes use of the input–output method by introducing "information intensity coefficients." These coefficients are also used to generate the primary information economy on the basis of the industry technology assumption. This implies that information intensity of intermediate inputs is proportional to the informational intensity prevailing in the total sectoral output, which is not the case in the DIW input–output approach.

is described in detail in the DIW Information Report (1984). In the following sections we present a summary, concentrating on the needs of an informational input–output subsystem.

Output data for the primary information sector in 1980

The starting point of the data collection was given with the institutionally based input–output table for 1980 compiled by the DIW. This table contains 60 sectors of production, 6 components of final demand, and 7 components of primary inputs and was published as a wall-chart in cooperation with Spektrum der Wissenschaft (1985). For our purpose the table was aggregated into 12 production sectors. A detailed description of the classification is available from the author.

The input–output table was used twice: first, as a classification scheme for allocating the ISIC items of informational goods and services to branches and, second, as a basis for estimating the output pattern of the different information products according to the detailed input–output categories of intermediate and final demand. The figures on 1980 production of information goods and services were mainly collected from statistics of the Federal Statistical Office on manufacturing, on taxable turnover, on foreign trade, and from national accounts. Compilation problems arise because of scarce statistical data and missing counterparts of ISIC items in the official German nomenclature.

Table 6-1 shows the aggregated information for the 1980 production value of informational ISIC items listed in the OECD inventory and the distribution of these items to total intermediate and final demand. Furthermore, the noninformation goods and services belonging to the 12 sectors of origin are shown. The addition of the data for informational and noninformational activities results in the totals. Hence, it is possible to calculate the informational goods and services as a percentage of the total (informational and noninformational) deliveries.

Informational output table and informational input and output table for 1980

The implementation of the informational output table (matrix B) and of the informational input and output table (matrix D) enables us to calculate all output elements of the primary information sector in matrix E. The informational output table in Table 6-2 shows the deliveries of the information goods and services according to their sectors of origin and destination. The purchasing sectors are divided into noninformational sectors and final demand components. It can be seen from Table 6-2 that the noninformational part of the service sector (11) purchases most information goods and services, followed by the trade and transport sector (10). Within the final demand components, private and government consumption covers most of the informational output. The intersectoral flows between the informational part and the noninformational part of the 12 production sectors reflect the different importance of information activities.

The same is true for the transaction values in Table 6-3 although they reflect informational flows only. In this informational input and output table, the rows and columns represent the informational part of the production sectors, that is, Table 6-3 shows the intrasectoral transactions within the primary information sector expressed by $n + 1$ in matrix E of Figure 6-2. Analyzing the results, we see that the service sector

TABLE 6-1   Intermediate Demand, Final Demand, and Gross Production for Informational and Noninformational Goods and Services in the Federal Republic of Germany, 1980[a] (Million DM[b] and Percent)

Sector		(1-12) Intermediate Demand	(13-17) Final Demand	(1-17) Gross Production
1. Agriculture	Informational	5	—	5
	Noninformational	48,709	15,926	64,635
	Inform. (% of total)	0.01	—	0.01
2. Energy, Mining	Informational	530	240	770
	Noninformational	98,347	36,923	135,270
	Inform. (% of total)	0.54	0.65	0.57
3. Chemical	Informational	1,927	3,136	5,063
	Noninformational	195,210	138,611	333,821
	Inform. (% of total)	0.98	2.21	1.49
4. Metals	Informational	—	—	—
	Noninformational	77,617	39,710	117,327
	Inform. (% of total)	—	—	—
5. Mach, Veh	Informational	5,395	19,139	24,534
	Noninformational	74,371	225,564	299,935
	Inform. (% of total)	6.76	7.82	7.56
6. Electric	Informational	9.975	36,614	46,589
	Noninformational	59,827	85,122	144.949
	Inform. (% of total)	14.29	30.08	24.32
7. Timb, Tex	Informational	21,166	10,071	31,237
	Noninformational	52,102	82,945	135,047
	Inform. (% of total)	28.89	10.83	18.79
8. Food, Bev	Informational	—	—	—
	Noninformational	67,455	119,293	186.748
	Inform. (% of total)	—	—	—
9. Construc	Informational	—	13,504	13,504
	Noninformational	23,446	158,724	182,170
	Inform. (% of total)	—	7.84	6.90
10. Trade, Tr	Informational	27,471	30,458	57,929
	Noninformational	157,553	177,547	335,100
	Inform. (% of total)	14.85	14.64	14.74
11. Services	Informational	155,524	85,452	240,976
	Noninformational	75,749	182,538	258,287
	Inform. (% of total)	67.25	31.89	48.27
12. Pub, Priv	Informational	6,616	76,469	83,085
	Noninformational	7,070	120,425	127,495
	Inform. (% of total)	48.34	38.84	39.46
(1-12)	Informational	228,609	275,083	503,692
	Noninformational	937,456	1,383,328	2,320,784
	Inform. (% of total)	19.61	16.59	17.83

Source: New calculations on the basis of the DIN information report (1984) and input output accounting.
[a]Sector definitions are available from the authors. Inform., Informational.
[b]DM, Deutsche Mark.

TABLE 6–2   Informational Output Table for the Federal Republic of Germany, 1980[a] (Million DM[b] at Current Prices)

Sector	1 Agricult	2 Energy, M	3 Chemical	4 Metals	5 Mach, Veh	6 Electric	7 Timb, Tex	8 Food, Bev	9 Construc
1. Agricult	5	—	—	—	—	—	—	—	—
2. Energy, M	—	530	47	13	58	36	21	27	27
3. Chemical	4	6	—	—	—	—	—	—	—
4. Metals	12	77	518	223	644	488	281	226	307
5. Mach, Veh	3	16	116	50	2,705	2,581	68	36	74
6. Electric	11	369	1,239	371	982	811	1,699	1,053	703
7. Timb, Tex	—	—	—	—	—	—	—	—	—
8. Food, Bev	—	—	—	—	—	—	—	—	—
9. Construc	202	403	2,030	433	2,135	2,108	1,138	979	861
10. Trade, Tr	6,227	2,577	6,991	3,873	9,088	4,435	4,436	5,237	6,082
11. Services	176	148	541	212	647	338	280	440	338
12. Pub, Priv									
(1–12)	6,640	4,126	11,482	5,175	16,259	10,797	7,923	7,998	8,392

Continued overleaf

72

TABLE 6–2 (cont.)

Sector	10 Trade, Tr	11 Services	12 Pub, Priv	(1–12) Intern Demand	13+14 Pr + Gov Consump	15+16 Cap. Form +Stocks	17 Exports	(13–17) Final Demand	(1–17) Gross Product
1. Agricult	—	—	—	5	—	—	—	—	5
2. Energy, M	—	—	—	530	—	—	240	240	770
3. Chemical	209	119	40	607	462	56	2,618	3,136	3,743
4. Metals	—	—	—	—	—	—	—	—	—
5. Mach, Veh	466	497	58	3,797	962	7,128	11,049	19,139	22,936
6. Electric	152	186	13	6,000	7,685	6,599	22,330	36,614	42,614
7. Timb, Tex	1,352	1,482	120	10,192	4,664	1,376	4,031	10,071	20,263
8. Food, Bev	—	—	—	—	—	—	—	—	—
9. Construc	—	—	—	—	—	13,504	—	13,504	13,504
10. Trade, Tr	6,059	3,551	490	20,389	26,132	2,867	1,459	30,458	50,847
11. Services	20,675	25,906	2,624	98,151	76,249	4,295	4,908	85,452	183,603
12. Pub, Priv	843	2,132	164	6,259	76,254	63	152	76,469	82,728
(1–12)	29,756	33,873	3,509	145,930	192,408	35,888	46,787	275,083	421,013

Source: New calculations on the basis of the DIN information report (1984) and input–output accounting.

*Sector definitions are available from the author.

*DM. Deutsche Mark.

TABLE 6–3 Informational Input and Output Table for the Federal Republic of Germany, 1980[a] (Million DM[b] at Current Prices)

Sector	1 Agricult	2 Energy, N	3 Chemical	4 Metals	5 Mach. Veh	6 Electric	7 Timb, Tex
1. Agricult	—	—	—	—	—	—	—
2. Energy, M	—	—	—	—	—	—	809
3. Chemical	—	—	—	—	2	322	—
4. Metals	—	—	—	—	—	—	—
5. Mach, Veh	—	1	10	—	83	104	89
6. Electric	—	1	14	—	385	2,901	46
7. Timb, Tex	—	—	62	—	149	464	2,482
8. Food, Bev	—	—	—	—	—	—	—
9. Construc	—	—	26	—	268	282	490
10. Trade, Tr	—	3	54	—	371	402	1,278
11. Services	—	—	—	—	16	—	36
12. Pub, Priv	—	—	—	—	—	—	—
(1–12)	—	5	166	—	1,274	4,475	5,230

Continued overleaf

74

TABLE 6–3 (cont.)

Sector	8 Food, Bev	9 Construc	10 Trade, TR	11 Services	12 Pub, Priv	(1–12)
1. Agricult	—	—	—	—	—	—
2. Energy, M	—	—	—	—	—	1,320
3. Chemical	—	—	17	170	—	—
4. Metals	—	—	—	—	—	1,598
5. Mach, Veh	—	5	48	1,253	6	3,975
6. Electric	—	1	395	229	3	10,974
7. Timb, Tex	—	221	342	7,239	14	—
8. Food, Bev	—	—	—	—	—	—
9. Construc	—	35	457	5,484	40	7,082
10. Trade, Tr	—	168	1.776	53,245	76	57,373
11. Services	—	—	9	296	—	357
12. Pub, Priv	—	430	3.044	67,916	139	82,679
(1–12)						

Source: New calculations on the basis of the DIM information report (1984) and input–output accounting.
ªSector definitions are available from the author.
ᵇDM. Deutsche Mark.

75

(11) appears as the most important branch on the output side as well as on the input side. Only 52 of the 144 cells of the estimated informational input and output table contain figures.

USE AND FURTHER DEVELOPMENT

The definition of an input–output subsystem for the information sector as well as the compilation of the two informational matrices have shown that it is beneficial to express the primary information sector as a subsystem of an input–output table. The matrices of this informational input–output subsystem can be used for empirically oriented structural analysis as they depict the composition of the fourth sector. They reflect the importance of information activities in the different sectors of production. An intertemporal analysis of these matrices for several years would show the internal versus the external development of information goods and services.

The input–output subsystem for the information sector (matrix E in Figure 6-2) can also be used for measuring the direct and indirect information content of final demand. This approach includes the Leontief inverse, multipliers, and linkages (Karunaratne, 1986). In addition, many of the evaluations that are feasible for energy and environmental input–output analysis (Miller and Blair, 1985, Chs. 6 and 7) can be performed for the primary information sector, too. By integrating the occupation-by-sector matrices, that is, one component of the secondary information sector, we also can compute the information-induced employment effects. Further development of the informational input–output subsystem can contribute to an extension of the statistics on services, one of the important issues for structural analysis of the "services society."

One aspect has priority for future explorations: the estimation of input patterns of the primary information sector including a disaggregation in accordance with the informational parts of the different production sectors (matrix C). Independent from this proceeding, the OECD inventory on information goods and services should be improved by covering the conceptional understanding of the input–output framework. Finally, the secondary information sector has to be included in the input–output subsystem to estimate the size of all information activities in the Federal Republic of Germany.

ACKNOWLEDGMENT

I would like to express thanks to my colleague Mrs. Ingrid Ludwig for contributing to this chapter.

REFERENCES

Arrow, K. J. 1980. "The Economies of Information." In *The Computer Age: A Twenty-Year View*, edited by M. L. Dertonzos and J. Moses. Cambridge, MA: MIT Press.

Bell, D. 1973. *The Coming of Post-Industrial Society: A Venture in Social Forecasting*. New York: Basic Books.

Bundesministerium für Wissenschaft und Forschung. 1981. *Mikroelektronik, Anwendungen, Verbreitung und Auswirkungen am Beispiel Österreichs* (Micro-electronics: Use, Diffusion, and Repercussions Shown for Austria as Example). Vienna.

DIW/Deutsches Institut für Wirtschaftsforschung. 1984. "Information Activities: Updating and Improving the Data Base for the Federal Republic of Germany," ICCP (Information, Computer, and Communications Policy) Report No. 6, By R. Filip-Köhn, G. Neckermann, and R. Stäglin (DIW) in cooperation with W. Dostal (IAB) and J. Seetzen (Heinrich-Hertz Institute). Forschungsprojekt im Auftrag des Bundesministers für Forschung und Technologie. (Research project for the Federal Ministry of Research and Technology) (December). Berlin.

DIW/Deutsches Institut für Wirtschaftsforschung. 1986. "Die Nutzung von grenzüberschreitendem Datenfluss (GDF) in der Bundesrepublik Deutschland und ihre gesamtwirtschaftliche Bedeutung." Gutachten im Auftrag des Bundesministers für Wirtschaft. (The Use of Intercountry Data Flows in the Federal Republic of Germany and Their Economic Importance). (Report for the Federal Ministry of Economic Affairs) (January). Berlin.

DIW and IFO/Deutsches Institut für Wirtschaftsforschung und IFO-Institut für Wirtschaftsforschung. 1986. "Wirtschaftsinformation in der Bundesrepublik Deutschland— Schwachstellen und Verbesserungsmöglichkeiten." Teil I: "Zusammenfassung und Schlussfolgerungen." Gutachten im Auftrag des Bundesministers für Wirtschaft. (Economic Information in the Federal Republic of Germany—Weak Points and Possibilities to Improve. Part I: Summary and Conclusions). (Report for the Federal Ministry of Economic Affairs) (August). München.

Eliasson, G. 1982. "Electronics, Economic Growth and Employment—Revolution or Evolution." IVI. Booklet No. 131. Stockholm.

Ernst, D. 1982. *The Global Race in Micro-Electronics: Innovation and Corporate Strategies in a Period of Crisis.* Frankfurt: Campus.

Freeman, C., and L. Soete. 1985. "Information Technology and Employment: An Assessment." Science Policy Research Unit (April). Brighton, England: University of Sussex.

Gassmann, H. P. 1981. "Is There a Fourth Economic Sector?" *OECD Observer* (November), Paris.

Gershuny, I., and I. Miles, 1983. *The New Service Economy—the Transformation of Employment in Industrial Society.* New York: Praeger.

Hunt, H. A., and T. L. Hunt. 1983. *The Human Resource Implications of Robotics.* Kalamazoo, Michigan: Upjohn Institute for Employment Research.

Kaplinsky, R. 1985. *Micro-electronics and Employment.* Geneva: International Labour Organization.

Karunaratne, N. D. 1984. "Planning for the Australian Information Economy." *Information Economics and Policy.* Vol. 1, pp. 365–367.

Karunaratne, N. D. 1986. "Empirics of the Information Economy." Paper presented at the Eighth International Conference on Input–Output Techniques, 28 July–2 August, Sapporo, Japan.

Lamberton, D. 1982. "The Theoretical Implications of Measuring the Communication Sector." In *Communication Economics and Development,* edited by M. Jussawalla and D. Lamberton. New York: Pergamon Press.

Leontief, W. and F. Duchin. 1986. *The Future Impact of Automation on Workers.* New York: Oxford University Press.

Machlup, F. 1962. *The Production and Distribution of Knowledge in the United States.* Princeton, NJ: Princeton University Press.

Machlup, F. 1980. *Knowledge and Knowledge Production.* Princeton, NJ: Princeton University Press.

Masuda, Y. 1980. *The Information Society.* Tokyo: Institute for the Information Society.

Miller, R. E., and P. D. Blair. 1985. *Input–Output Analysis: Foundations and Extensions.* Englewood Cliffs, NJ: Prentice-Hall, pp. 200–265.

Nora, S., and A. Minc. 1980. *The Computerization Society: A Report to the President of France.* Cambridge, MA: MIT Press.

78   *Alternative Accounting Frameworks*

OECD [Organisation for Economic Co-operation and Development]. 1981. "Information Activities, Electronics and Telecommunications Technologies. Impact on Employment, Growth and Trade." ICCP Report No. 6. Vol. 1. Paris: OECD, pp. 34–38.

OECD. 1982. "Micro-electronics, Robotics, and Jobs." Paris: OECD, Committee for Information, Computer and Communications Policy.

OECD. 1986. "Trends in the Information Economy." ICCP. Paris: OECD.

OTA. 1984. "Computerized Manufacturing Automation: Employment, Education and the Workplace." Washington, D.C.: Office of Technology Assessment. Congress of the United States. OTA-CIT 235 (April).

Peitchinis, S. 1984. *Computer Technology and Employment: Retrospect and Prospect.* London: St. Martin's Press.

Porat, M. U., and M. R. Rubin, 1977. *The Information Economy.* OTC. Washington D.C.: Government Printing Office.

Rathenau, W. 1980. "The Social Impact of Microelectronics" (The Rathenau Report). The Hague: Government Publishing Office.

Roessner, D. S. 1984. "Impact of Office Automation on Office Workers." Vol. 2. Atlanta, GA: Georgia Institute of Technology (April).

Soete, L. 1985. *Technological Trends and Employment: 3, Electronics and Communications.* London: Gower Press.

Spektrum der Wissenschaft in Zusammenarbeit mit dem DIW. 1985. Input/Output-Struktur für die Wirtschaft der Bundesrepublik Deutschland. Input/Output-Wandtafel. (Input–Output Structure for the Economy of the Federal Republic of Germany. Input–Output Wall-Chart). Heidelberg and Berlin.

Stäglin, R. 1988. "Der Informationssektor als Satellitensystem der Input–Output-Rechnung". (The Information Sector as Satellite System of Input–Output Accounting). In Schriftenreihe Forum der Bundesstatistik. Band 5. Edited by Statistisches Bundesamt. Stuttgart and Mainz.

Stornier, T. 1984. *The Wealth of Information. A Profile of the Post-Industrial Economy.* London: Thomas Methuen.

United Nations. 1971. *ISIC.* Series M. No. 4. Revision 2. Add. 1. New York: United Nations.

Wallace, D. 1986. "Introduction to Information Society. Text/Workbook with "Hands-On" Microcomputer Exercises." Philadelphia, PA: Institute for Information Studies (July).

Zeman, P. 1979. "The Impact of Computer/Communications on Employment in Canada: Overview of Current OECD Debates." Montreal: Institute for Research on Public Policy.

[10]

Currency and Credit in a Private Information Economy

Robert M. Townsend

University of Chicago

In an environment with private information, spatial separation, and limited communication, a currency-like object and more standard named credits can be distinguished. The credit objects can be used among agents in an enduring relationship, that is, among agents with known trading histories, whereas the currency-like object must be used among relative strangers. In this environment, collectively determined Pareto-optimal rules make the level of the currency-like object and the mix of currency to named credits responsive to individual needs and to economywide states. Total indebtedness is determined by the number of lenders, that is, by preference or demand shocks, and the mix of currency to credits is determined by transaction patterns among the agents.

I. Introduction

Can we find a physical environment in which currency-like objects play an essential role in implementing efficient allocations? Would these objects coexist with more ordinary, named credits? Can we do this without further ad hoc decentralization of the economy, without insisting as an extra condition not coming from the physical environ-

I gratefully acknowledge helpful comments from the participants of the Money and Banking Workshop at the University of Chicago, the National Bureau working group on Financial Structure and Economic Activity, the Northwestern University Summer Workshop in Capital Theory and Monetary Economics, and seminars at the University of Iowa and the University of Rochester; from the participants of courses at Carnegie-Mellon University and the University of Chicago and from the referees; computational assistance from Christopher Phelan; and financial support from the National Science Foundation under grant SES-8708242.

[*Journal of Political Economy*, 1989, vol. 97, no. 6]

ment that allocations be achieved in competitive markets? Put differently, if agents in the environment can precommit at an initial date to
arbitrary tax and transfer schemes over time, over all the commodities
of the environment up to the technology of storage and communication available to them, would they choose to distribute some currency-
like object at the initial date, choose what in other models are exogenous initial conditions? Would this currency-like object coexist with
named commitments by some agents to other agents to give up commodities now for commodities later on? And, if we looked at a cross
section of otherwise identical economies that vary by the configuration of "demand" and "transaction" shocks, would the amount of the
currency-like object issued vary in absolute amount and vary relative
to the use of named credits?

The model of this paper answers all these questions in the affirma-
tive by drawing sharp distinctions among various communication,
record-keeping technologies. The currency-like object of the model
plays a role in allowing exchanges among relative strangers, agents
whose histories are otherwise not known to one another. The more
standard credit objects of the model are used among agents who
know their past histories and can keep track of past commitments to
one another. Both classes of objects coexist. Indeed, the model of the
paper allows cross-sectional variations in the magnitudes of each of
these and in the magnitude of one relative to the other.

It is important to be clear also about what the model does not do,
especially since the terms "currency" and "credit" mean different
things to different people, dependent perhaps on observations of
various economies over various dates and dependent also on prior
monetary theories that are used to interpret observations. In the
model of this paper, agents precommit in the planning period to all
institutions and resource allocation rules to the extent that the information structure allows. Thus there is no government in the model,
apart from these plans, and no distinction between private and public.
So if agents in the model agree, as they do, to the use of currency to
intertemporally reallocate consumption, it may well be said that currency is a form of private credit. Conversely, all debts may be said to
be public. But that is not to say that the ordinary credit and the
currency of the model are not different. They do differ in their
communication and record-keeping aspects. Thus the hope is that the
stylized model of the paper may allow one to see an aspect of reality
that otherwise might not have been as apparent.

Formally, the paper proceeds as follows. Section II describes the
basic physical environment. Section III sets out a programming problem for the determination of full communication, private information
Pareto-optimal allocations. Section IV does the same for the environ-

ment with no cross-location communication. This motivates the introduction in Section V of tokens as a communication device. This is the currency-like object. To deliver a price system and hence measurable currency, Section VI weakens the planning problem, allowing unobserved cross-household exchange. Section VII then extends the environment somewhat and displays an example of optimal variations in currency relative to total indebtedness and relative to the indebtedness of nonmovers, that is, to named credits. Section VIII touches on the costs of the various record-keeping systems.

II. The Physical Environment

Consider an economy with one underlying consumption good, three dates, N locations, and N^2 agents (essentially N per location). At the first date, that is, at $t = 0$, all agents get together to decide on Pareto-optimal rules, to be described in this essay. Thus there is full commitment to the arrangement, that is, perfect costless enforcement of it. At the beginning of the second date, $t = 1$, agents are dispersed to locations, N agents to each location. Finally, at the beginning of date $t = 2$, a fraction λ of the population of each location stays put in its initial location assignment, and a fraction $(1 - \lambda)$ of the population of each location is shifted to new locations in such a way that each "shifter" encounters no agents he has known previously at date $t = 1$. Thus λN agents of each location stay in residence for two periods and $(1 - \lambda)N$ agents of each location are dispersed in some way to the other $N - 1$ locations.[1] For much of the analysis, N will be taken to be arbitrarily large; that is, the mathematics assumes $N = \infty$. The $N = \infty$ economy is envisioned as the limit of finite N economies as $N \to \infty$, but this limit is never taken explicitly.

After settling in the location assignment of date $t = 1$, every agent receives *one* unit of the single consumption good of the model. This good can never be transferred across locations. The consumption good may be eaten by someone at date $t = 1$, at the endowment location, or alternatively it may be stored at that location for consumption at that location at date $t = 2$. The gross return on storage is some parameter $R \geq 1$, so that one unit of the consumption good

---

[1] For example, let $N = 4$ and let λ take on values $j/N, j = 1, 2, \ldots, N - 1$. If $\lambda = \frac{1}{4}$, let one agent remain at each location and let the three departing agents move to the other three locations, one to each of the three nearest location neighbors to the right, moving clockwise around a circle. If $\lambda = \frac{2}{4}$, let two agents remain at each location and let the two departing agents move to the two nearest location neighbors to the right, one to each, and so on for $\lambda = \frac{3}{4}$. Here, of course, λ is such that λN is an integer, and this is assumed to be true generally. Similar integer assumptions are made throughout the text. Of course when $N = \infty$, only fractions of the population need be specified.

stored at the end of date $t = 1$ yields R units of the consumption good at the beginning of date $t = 2$.

Whatever might be his location, each agent has preferences over units of consumption c_1 and c_2 in periods 1 and 2, respectively, as represented by a utility function $U(c_1, \tau) + V(c_2, \tau)$. Here τ is a shock to preferences, a "demand" shock, which among other things determines an agent's rate of intertemporal substitution. For simplicity, shock τ can take on one of a finite number of values, that is $\tau \in \{1, 2, \ldots, n\}$. For each τ, the function $U(\cdot, \tau)$ is strictly concave, is continuously differentiable, and satisfies the Inada conditions $U'(0, \tau) = \infty$ and $U'(\infty, \tau) = 0$; similarly for $V(\cdot, \tau)$.

It is supposed that at each location at date $t = 1$, a fraction $\omega(\tau)$ of agents in the population receive shock τ. Of course these fractions must add to unity, that is, $\Sigma_\tau \, \omega(\tau) = 1$. In the absence of any other information, each agent in the planning period $t = 0$ naturally views his own shock τ as determined in a random way, that shock τ will occur with probability $\omega(\tau)$.

At the same time at date $t = 1$ that the distribution of shocks τ is determined, date $t = 2$ location assignments are also determined and revealed (but not executed).[2] Similarly, with fraction $1 - \lambda$ of the agents of each location to be shifted at the beginning of date $t = 2$, each agent in the planning period views his probability of being shifted as determined in a random way. If we let θ denote the "location" or "transaction" shock, which takes on two values (i.e., $\theta = 1$ for "staying" and $\theta = 2$ for "moving"), each agent views $\theta = 1$ as being drawn with probability λ and $\theta = 2$ as being drawn with probability $1 - \lambda$. For simplicity of notation, let $\lambda(\theta)$ denote the fraction of agents who receive shock θ, so that here, for example, $\lambda(\theta = 1) = \lambda$ and $\lambda(\theta = 2) = 1 - \lambda$.

Finally, it will be supposed initially that the distribution of the population by preference shocks τ is independent of the distribution of the population by location movements θ, so that from an individual's point of view the random variables τ and θ are also independent. Economywide, the fraction of agents who receive shocks τ and $\theta = 2$ is $\omega(\tau)(1 - \lambda)$, and so on.

It is supposed in what follows that preference shocks τ received at the beginning of date $t = 1$ are privately observed by the individual but that future location assignments θ received at the beginning of date $t = 1$ are fully observed. Further, though the *population fractions*

---

[2] Here and below several alternative environments will suggest themselves. Here an alternative would be for agents to see preference shocks prior to seeing location assignments. Such alternatives suggest interesting paths to pursue in subsequent efforts. The effort here is to produce a simple, albeit dramatic, example economy.

ω and λ may be determined at random at the beginning of date $t = 1$ with probabilities prob(ω) and prob(λ), respectively, for each of a finite number of possible values of ω and λ, the actual draws of ω and λ are presumed to be public information as well.

As is evident, the environment under consideration in this paper is essentially the one considered by Diamond and Dybvig (1983), but here with a slightly more general preference specification and enlarged to accommodate distinct locations. The key idea is that the model determines the consumption paths of the individual agent types and hence determines the amount of the consumption-investment good that is invested at date $t = 1$ and claimed by the agent types at date $t = 2$. The latter amount is a natural measure of aggregate lending or indebtedness.

III. The Optimal Credit Arrangement with Full Cross-Location Communication

In the context of the environment described above, we may index the consumption of each agent by the individual-specific shocks τ and θ, at least with the imposition of certain incentive-compatibility constraints described below, so that announcements of preference shocks coincide with actual realizations. Consumption may be indexed by economywide fractions ω and λ as well. Thus the number of units of consumption at date t of the "representative agent" is denoted $c_t(\tau, \theta, \omega, \lambda)$. As is evident, then, no effort is made to distinguish agents by name or by their initial date $t = 1$ location assignment. Consumption at date $t = 1$ for an agent at one location is supposed to be the same as the consumption at date $t = 1$ for an agent at any other location *if* their shocks τ and θ coincide.[3] Similarly, the issue at date $t = 2$ for an individual is what announced (and actual) preference shocks were at date $t = 1$ and whether or not an agent moved. Thus the key assumption *in this section* is that announced preference shocks at date $t = 1$ are public at date $t = 2$ even in a location distinct from the location in which shocks were announced. In this sense full cross-location communication is assumed, histories are common knowledge, and so formally there are no strangers.

The objective in what follows, then, is to characterize an allocation

---

[3] Also, the assumption is that only the individual state (τ, θ) and the aggregate state (ω, λ) matter. For finite N economies, one ought to list the entire vector of states across individuals, but for $N = \infty$ with nameless individuals, that vector is captured by aggregate state (ω, λ). The $N = \infty$ case also ensures that an individual mover can infer nothing at date $t = 2$ about the preference shocks of others in a set of new arrivals. Otherwise, e.g., with $N = 4$, $\lambda = \frac{3}{4}$, $n = 2$, $\omega(\tau = 1) = \frac{1}{2}$, and $\omega(\tau = 2) = \frac{1}{2}$, a newly arrived agent with $\tau = 1$ would know for sure that the only other new arrival is a $\tau = 2$.

of the consumption good that is Pareto optimal from the point of view of the representative agent in the planning period, at date $t = 0$. This is done by consideration of the following problem.

PROGRAMMING PROBLEM 1. Maximize by choice of the consumptions $c_i(\tau, \theta, \omega, \lambda)$ the objective function

$$\sum_\omega \text{prob}(\omega) \sum_\lambda \text{prob}(\lambda) \sum_\theta \lambda(\theta) \sum_\tau \omega(\tau)$$
$$\cdot \{U[c_1(\tau, \theta, \omega, \lambda), \tau] + V[c_2(\tau, \theta, \omega, \lambda), \tau]\} \tag{1}$$

subject to the resource constraints, for every state (ω, λ),

$$\sum_\tau \sum_\theta \omega(\tau)\lambda(\theta)c_1(\tau, \theta, \omega, \lambda) \le W(\omega, \lambda) \tag{2}$$

and

$$\sum_\tau \sum_\theta \omega(\tau)\lambda(\theta)c_2(\tau, \theta, \omega, \lambda) \le [1 - W(\omega, \lambda)]R \tag{3}$$

and subject to incentive-compatibility constraints, for all $\theta = 1, 2$, for all $\tau', \tau = 1, 2, \ldots, n$, and for each (ω, λ),

$$U[c_1(\tau, \theta, \omega, \lambda), \tau] + V[c_2(\tau, \theta, \omega, \lambda), \tau]$$
$$\ge U[c_1(\tau', \theta, \omega, \lambda), \tau] + V[c_2(\tau', \theta, \omega, \lambda), \tau]. \tag{4}$$

Here again the objective function is the expected utility of the representative agent from the point of view of date $t = 0$, with expectations over individual shocks τ and θ and over population fractions ω and λ. Constraint (2) is a resource constraint for date $t = 1$, applicable for all locations, where $W(\omega, \lambda)$ stands for per capita "withdrawals" of consumption from possible investment at date $t = 1$, conditioned on ω and λ. Constraint (3) is a resource constraint for date $t = 2$, again applicable for all locations. Constraints (2) and (3) are both written in per capita terms and hold for the $N = \infty$ economy. The class of constraints (4) is a class of incentive-compatibility constraints; it ensures that for given and fully observed location shock θ and population fractions ω and λ, an individual would prefer at date $t = 1$ to announce the actual observed preference shock τ and receive consumption stream $\{c_1(\tau, \theta, \omega, \lambda), c_2(\tau, \theta, \omega, \lambda)\}$ rather than announce counterfactual preference shock τ' and receive consumption stream $\{c_1(\tau', \theta, \omega, \lambda), c_2(\tau', \theta, \omega, \lambda)\}$. It is the imposition of these constraints that allows one to refer to announcements of τ values and actual τ values synonymously. That these constraints may be imposed without loss of generality is implied by the work of Dasgupta, Hammond, and Maskin (1979), Myerson (1979), Harris and Townsend (1981), and

Townsend (1982). Otherwise it is supposed that there is full commitment to the consumption allocations $c_t(\tau, \theta, \omega, \lambda)$; reneging and default are precluded from consideration as if enforcement were perfect and costless.

Solutions to program 1 sometimes can be characterized easily.[4] For example, it is clear that location movement per se should not matter in an optimum, and so index θ can be dropped from the notation. For purposes here, however, it suffices to concentrate on movers and to note that first- and second-period consumptions can be ordered by τ values in a nontrivial way. That is, there exists *some* (re)ordering of τ values such that, for fixed ω and λ, $c_1(\tau, \theta = 2, \omega, \lambda)$ is strictly monotone increasing in τ over some range. Further, if $c_1(\tau, \theta = 2, \omega, \lambda) > c_1(\tau', \theta = 2, \omega, \lambda)$, then $c_2(\tau, \theta = 2, \omega, \lambda) < c_2(\tau', \theta = 2, \omega, \lambda)$, for otherwise the incentive constraints at the realized value of τ would be violated, since naming value τ would be strictly preferred to naming value τ'.

IV. The Optimal Credit Arrangement with No Cross-Location Communication

Now suppose that preference shock announcements of an individual agent at date $t = 1$ are *not* public information at date $t = 2$ *if* that agent shifts locations between dates 1 and 2. Thus the history of a "shifter" or "mover" would be private information, and a shifter may be said to encounter relative strangers. Otherwise, the structure of the model remains unchanged. That is, agents are still presumed to commit themselves in the planning period to some social arrangement, that is, to some economywide credit arrangement, that specifies consumptions and hence transfers to agents conditioned on the economywide state (ω, λ), on the individual-specific but publicly observed location shocks θ, and possibly on individual announcements of the individual-specific and privately observed preference shocks τ. Now, however, these latter announcements may have less content. For suppose that agents who move are to reannounce preference shocks at date $t = 2$ since there is no one present who knows the date $t = 1$ announcement. On his arrival at his new location at date $t = 2$, any mover has a choice in the family of consumptions $\{c_2(\tau, \theta = 2, \omega, \lambda)\}$, indexed by τ, and thus it is clear that any such mover would *always* name the τ value that achieves the highest level of consumption, inde-

---

[4] Technically, program 1 can be converted to a linear program by consideration of lotteries over consumptions, not deterministic allocations. Often, however, these lotteries do not appear in solutions, and they are ignored here altogether for simplicity of exposition and computation. For a more extended discussion of lotteries and the pitfalls of proceeding without them, see Townsend (1988a).

pendent of the realized τ value. In fact, with the imposition of sequential incentive compatibility, as in Townsend (1982), we must have

$$V[c_2(\tau, \theta = 2, \omega, \lambda), \tau] \geq V[c_2(\tau', \theta = 2, \omega, \lambda), \tau] \quad \text{for all } \tau, \tau' \text{ values,} \tag{5}$$

and so it is apparent that $c_2(\tau, \theta = 2, \omega, \lambda)$ must be some constant, independent of preference shocks τ, denoted $\bar{c}_2(\theta = 2, \omega, \lambda)$.

By the same logic, then, as we roll the dynamic program back to date $t = 1$, incentive-compatibility conditions (4) at $\theta = 2$ with $c_2(\tau, \theta = 2, \omega, \lambda) = \bar{c}_2(\theta = 2, \omega, \lambda)$, for all τ, imply that $c_1(\tau, \theta = 2, \omega, \lambda)$ must be some constant, independent of preference shocks τ, denoted $\bar{c}_1(\theta = 2, \omega, \lambda)$. Of course, no problem of this kind emerges for agents who do not move; with past histories fully observed by at least two agents present in each location, past histories can be made public to all agents present, as in Harris and Townsend (1981). With the assumption of full commitment, then, intertemporal tie-ins can still be used to distinguish agents by preference shocks τ in a beneficial way. That is, those who stay at a location with their cohorts can enter into more effective agreements than those who must deal in the future with relative strangers. But overall, from the point of view of the planning period, all agents are made worse off by the absence of cross-location communication. Consumption is now dependent on whether or not an agent is a mover and a mover's consumption path is independent of shocks τ.

V. Tokens as a Communication Device

Now suppose that there is some object in the environment that is intrinsically useless, that can be carried about and concealed by the agents, and that otherwise is subject to strict societal control. That is, the object can be manufactured and distributed to agents only under agreed-on rules.

Such tokens in our private information, limited communication environment can be enormously beneficial. In fact, for the environment considered in this paper, one can recover the solution to the original, full communication programming problem. Consider the following scheme. At date $t = 1$, all agents are again to announce preference shocks τ. Let those who are designated movers and who declare themselves to have a particular τ value consume the date 1, $c_1(\tau, \theta = 2, \omega, \lambda)$ solution to the original full communication programming problem. Further, let those who were to consume more in the second period under the $c_2(\tau, \theta = 2, \omega, \lambda)$ solution receive more tokens in the first period in a monotone fashion, under some allocation rule $m(\tau, \omega, \lambda)$. That is, if $c_2(\tau, \theta = 2, \omega, \lambda) < c_2(\tau', \theta = 2, \omega, \lambda)$, let

$m(\tau, \omega, \lambda) < m(\tau', \omega, \lambda)$. Thus higher levels of tokens are to entitle movers to higher levels of second-period consumption. In fact, at date $t = 2$, let movers declare one of the possible values of these privately observed token holdings, some value of $m(\tau, \omega, \lambda)$ for a possible value of τ. As more is preferred to less, agents will never declare fewer tokens than they actually hold, and the target consumption bundles $c_2(\tau, \theta = 2, \omega, \lambda)$ are achieved. As is apparent, then, movers face the same menu of consumption streams as in the solution to the original programming problem, so that solution can be implemented here in an incentive-compatible way.

Of course the key to achieving this result is the alteration, with the introduction of tokens, of the second-period incentive-compatibility constraints themselves. Conditions (5) are now replaced with the following. Let $m(\tau, \omega, \lambda)$ denote actual, beginning-of-second-period token holdings of a mover conditioned on having announced shock τ at date $t = 1$ and conditioned on the economywide state (ω, λ). Also let $f(m, \omega, \lambda)$ denote the date $t = 2$ deposit or payment of tokens conditioned on an announcement of m units of tokens, on being a mover, and on the economywide state (ω, λ). Finally, let $c_2(m, \theta = 2, \omega, \lambda)$ denote the proposed consumption bundle under these latter conditions. Now suppose that an individual enters date $t = 2$ with $m(\tau, \omega, \lambda)$ units of tokens, so that he is a mover and had announced shock τ at date $t = 1$. Then, in contemplating a counterfactual announcement of $m = m(\tau', \omega, \lambda)$, either

$$m(\tau, \omega, \lambda) < f[m(\tau', \omega, \lambda), \omega, \lambda], \tag{6}$$

so that the counterfactual announcement is not feasible, or

$$V\{c_2[m(\tau, \omega, \lambda), \theta = 2, \omega, \lambda], \tau\}$$
$$\geq V\{c_2[m(\tau', \omega, \lambda), \theta = 2, \omega, \lambda], \tau\}, \tag{7}$$

so that "honest" announcements of tokens are incentive compatible. The point, of course, is that with the kind of societal control assumed in this paper, tokens are reliable records of past actions even among relative strangers. Equations (6) and (7) allow more effective indexation on unobserved first-period announcements than (5) does.

VI. Unobserved Trades and the Emergence of an Exchange Rate

Thus far tokens allow agents with different histories to be distinguished in the obvious way: those entitled to higher second-period consumptions carry a greater number of tokens. But there is no natural value for tokens per se. They serve as badges or stamps, as if a receipt for some past action or transfer. For three actions to be distinguished, say actions 1, 2, and 3, it is enough that the three actions entitle one to a different number of tokens, say low, medium, and high. Relative differences, such as between low-medium and medium-high, do not matter.

As tokens would seem in many circumstances to be more than a badge or stamp, in fact to have some value or price in terms of consumption goods, and as our interest here is in the number of tokens in the economy as a function of the state of the economy, something must be done to alter the model. The idea here is to weaken ex ante beneficial restrictions on trade by supposing additional private information, that strangers carrying tokens can make deals with one another on the side, unobserved and anonymously, both before and after they appear before the local distribution center of their new location.

It should be noted that, despite this modification, the full commitment postulate remains in place. Agents agree in the planning period to show up at the distribution center of their second-period location assignment and are restricted there to making announcements in some prespecified message space and to engaging in prespecified trades as a function of messages. This they still do. But now consumption cannot take place at the distribution center of the second period. Rather, movers are assigned, both before and after they appear at the distribution center, to a foggy location where they can make unobserved deals with one another. In fact, just prior to their arrival at the center of their new location, movers can commit in the foggy location to trades in consumption and tokens, and again, as with the $t = 0$ initial agreement, these side exchanges are honored. In short, what is weakened in the new environment is the amount of public information, not the amount of commitment.

It is important also not to weaken or, better put, to strengthen the communication technology at the same time. If agents were to carry tokens with their names on them and agents were identified by name at exchange windows of the second location, then this side exchange could be precluded. But to explore the communication and record-keeping idea of the paper, we must somehow take seriously that cross-location communication can be limited a priori, either exogenously, as here, with uniform tokens or endogenously, as in Section VIII, where it is costly to make distinctions.

To motivate the formal description of the unobserved side exchanges that now are possible, it is useful to consider first two proposed second-period allocation rules, functions that map announced (and actual) token holdings into second-period consumption. The first proposed allocation rule appears in figure 1. Under it, house-

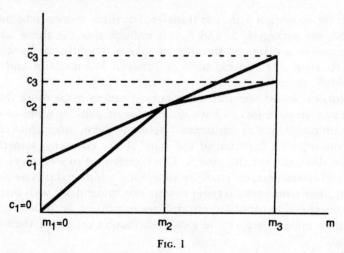

FIG. 1

holds announcing token level m_j are to get second-period consumption allocation c_j, $j = 1, 2, 3$, and it is supposed that there is a nontrivial fraction of agents who would announce each of these m's if this rule were to prevail. But now consider some linear schedule that pivots on the intermediate point (m_2, c_2) and is otherwise above the old schedule. The claim is that if agents of types m_1 and m_3 pool tokens ex ante and pool consumption ex post, then points $\tilde{c}_1$ and $\tilde{c}_3$ can be obtained for these types, respectively, so that types m_1 and m_3 are strictly better off.

Suppose that number n_3 agents are carrying m_3 units of tokens and give up $(m_3 - m_2)$ units of tokens, and number n_1 agents acquire $(m_2 - m_1)$ units of tokens. Then if

$$n_1(m_2 - m_1) = n_3(m_3 - m_2), \tag{8}$$

this redistribution of tokens is feasible, with all agents carrying m_2 units of tokens to the distribution center and acquiring c_2 there. Further, multiplying (8) by the slope s of the linear pivot schedule of figure 1 yields as a feasible redistribution $(c_2 - \tilde{c}_1)$ "taxed" from agents initially carrying m_1 and $(\tilde{c}_3 - c_2)$ given to agents initially carrying m_3. Finally, the numbers n_1 and n_2 are not critical for this analysis; only their ratio,

$$\frac{n_1}{n_3} = \frac{m_3 - m_2}{m_2 - m_1} \equiv m^*, \tag{9}$$

matters. Thus all that is required is that a group of finite size N be divided into a fraction $\rho = m^*/(1 + m^*)$ of agents initially carrying m_1 and a fraction $(1 - \rho)$ of agents carrying m_3. (Since the rational num-

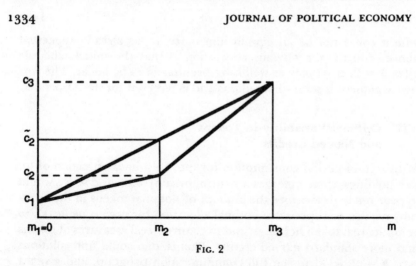

FIG. 2

bers are dense in the real line, the argument is easily modified, for ρ is not rational. On the other hand, note that the argument still holds even if values of m are restricted to integers, as if there were an indivisibility.)

The second proposed allocation rule appears in figure 2. Under it, let a group of agents of number N each initially carrying m_2 units of tokens get together; let a fraction ρ agree to acquire $(m_3 - m_2)$ units of tokens and let a fraction $(1 - \rho)$ surrender $(m_2 - m_1)$ units. If

$$\rho N(m_3 - m_2) = (1 - \rho)N(m_2 - m_1), \tag{10}$$

this redistribution of tokens is feasible. Further, multiplying (10) by the slope s of the linear schedule connecting the endpoints in figure 2 yields agents who pretend to be type m_3 surrendering $(c_3 - \tilde{c}_2)$ units of consumption and agents who pretend to be type m_1 acquiring $(\tilde{c}_2 - c_1)$ units of consumption as a feasible redistribution of the consumption good. Thus each pretender ends up with $\tilde{c}_2$. Of course, $\tilde{c}_2 > c_2$, and so each of the N agents is made better off by this scheme.

Only linear schedules escape the kind of manipulations described in figures 1 and 2. The slope of any linear schedule is the obvious price of tokens in terms of the consumption good, the inverse of the nominal price of consumption. The intercept of the linear schedule is interpreted as a guaranteed minimal consumption.

To proceed more formally, it is supposed first that some *arbitrary* schedule $c_2(m, \theta = 2, \omega, \lambda)$ is proposed for movers announcing m given state (ω, λ). Second, following Townsend (1978, 1983), a game that allows side payments yet preserves anonymity among movers is defined. Third, a symmetric outcome of the game is described, inducing some de facto consumption schedule $\tilde{c}_2(m, \theta = 2, \omega, \lambda)$. In particular, it is argued that the de facto schedule must be linear, for otherwise it could not be an equilibrium outcome, as already suggested above. Fourth, the obvious conclusion is that the initial schedule $c_2(m, \theta = 2, \omega, \lambda)$ may as well have been taken to be linear. The formal argument is somewhat tedious and is reserved for the Appendix.

VII. Optimal Variability in Tokens and Named Credits

With second-period consumption for movers a linear function of token holdings, there emerges a natural price system, and so we would appear ready to measure the amount of nominal tokens in the economy needed to support an optimal allocation for each state (ω, λ), to compute real token holdings, and to compare real measures of tokens and more standard named credits. That is, one could find solutions $c_2(\tau, \theta = 2, \omega, \lambda)$ to the full communication program, and given a price $p(\omega, \lambda)$ of consumption for tokens, holdings $m_2(\tau, \omega, \lambda)$ would be easily determined, as in figure 3, allowing a nonzero intercept. Given price $p(\omega, \lambda)$, relative differences among tokens now matter. Relative differences in consumption must be supported by relative differences in tokens. In this sense tokens are no longer just a badge or stamp.

Still, a residual problem remains for the model under consideration: the exchange rate $p(\omega, \lambda)$ need not be pinned down until *after* state (ω, λ) is realized. To put this another way, different lines in figure 3 imply different amounts of tokens in the system, and since any line will do for each state (ω, λ), there is no legitimate way to compare nominal magnitudes across states. In fact, this is a familiar "problem" for the model as it stands: the scale or nominal magnitude on the entire stochastic process for tokens is arbitrary. Yet we shall want to compare nominal magnitudes cross-sectionally over economies that have experienced different, realized shocks.

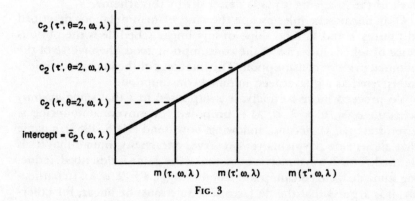

FIG. 3

Two further modifications to the model will thus be considered. The second, to be considered in the next section, allows the issue of tokens to be costly. Here, in this section, tokens are still virtually costless, but one allows some initial conditions to be predetermined and, below, constant across economies (to allow across comparisons relative to realized shocks). This is accomplished formally as follows.

Suppose that in each location at the first date there are two rounds of departures of movers, with nonmovers in the population as the residual. The fraction of first-round movers is λ_1, and a fraction $\omega_1(\tau)$ *of these movers* experience preference shock τ. For the purpose of an example, let λ_1 and $\omega_1(\tau)$ be deterministic, so that there is no uncertainty about these fractions, and notation for these fractions in consumptions can be suppressed. Consumption by first-round movers takes place in the first period prior to departure. *After* first-round movers have left, the fraction of second-round movers is determined. The fraction of second-round movers is λ_2, and a fraction $\omega_2(\tau)$ *of these movers* experience preference shock τ. The fractions λ_2 and $\omega_2(\tau)$ are drawn randomly with probabilities prob(λ_2, ω_2), and their realizations are known to everyone. However, as noted, consumptions of first-round movers are already determined, and so these cannot be indexed by the state (λ_2, ω_2). After second-round movers have departed, a fraction $\lambda_3 = 1 - \lambda_1 - \lambda_2$ of agents in the population are in the residual category, and a fraction $\omega_3(\tau)$ *of these nonmovers* experience preference shock τ. For the purpose of an example, let $\omega_3(\tau)$ be deterministic. Of course, λ_3 is determined as a residual given λ_2. Thus notation for fractions λ_3 and ω_3 is suppressed from consumptions.

Thus let $c_1(\tau, \theta = 1)$ denote consumption at date 1 for first-round movers, $\theta = 1$, as a function of announced (and actual) preference shocks τ, and let them receive tokens in the amount $m(\tau, \theta = 1)$. As will be noted, token levels $m(\tau, \theta = 1)$ must be somewhat arbitrary. Let $c_1(\tau, \theta = 2, \omega_2, \lambda_2)$ and $m(\tau, \theta = 2, \omega_2, \lambda_2)$ denote first-period consumption and token amounts to second-round movers, $\theta = 2$, as functions of announced (and actual) preference shocks τ and state (ω_2, λ_2). As will be noted, token amounts $m(\tau, \theta = 2, \omega_2, \lambda_2)$ will be determinate given the $m(\tau, \theta = 1)$ levels. Let $c_1(\tau, \theta = 3, \omega_2, \lambda_2)$ denote first-period consumption for nonmovers. Let $p(\omega_2, \lambda_2)$ denote the price of tokens in terms of consumption at date 2, the inverse of the nominal price level, and let $\bar{c}(\omega_2, \lambda_2)$ denote the intercept of the linear consumption-token schedule. Finally, let $c_2(\tau, \theta, \omega_2, \lambda_2)$ denote second-period consumption for $\theta = 1, 2, 3$ agents as a function of preference shocks τ and state (ω_2, λ_2). Note that these consumptions are endogenous for movers, $\theta = 1, 2$ agents, in the sense that they are determined by $p(\omega_2, \lambda_2)$, $\bar{c}(\omega_2, \lambda_2)$, and the specification of tokens.

That is, for each (ω_2, λ_2) state,

$$c_2(\tau, \theta = 1, \omega_2, \lambda_2) = \bar{c}(\omega_2, \lambda_2) + m(\tau, \theta = 1)p(\omega_2, \lambda_2), \quad (11)$$

$$c_2(\tau, \theta = 2, \omega_2, \lambda_2) = \bar{c}(\omega_2, \lambda_2)$$
$$+ m(\tau, \theta = 2, \omega_2, \lambda_2)p(\omega_2, \lambda_2). \quad (12)$$

With this notation and with $\bar{e}$ denoting the per capita endowment of the consumption good at date 1, now possibly different from unity, the program for the determination of Pareto-optimal consumptions and tokens follows.

PROGRAMMING PROBLEM 2. Maximize by choice of $c_1(\tau, \theta = 1)$, $m(\tau, \theta = 1)$, $c_1(\tau, \theta = 2, \omega_2, \lambda_2)$, $m(\tau, \theta = 2, \omega_2, \lambda_2)$, $c_1(\tau, \theta = 3, \omega_2, \lambda_2)$, $\bar{c}(\omega_2, \lambda_2)$, $p(\omega_2, \lambda_2)$, and $c_2(\tau, \theta, \omega_2, \lambda_2)$, $\theta = 1, 2, 3$, the objective function

$$\sum_{\omega_2, \lambda_2} \text{prob}(\omega_2, \lambda_2) \Big(\lambda_1 \sum_{\tau} \omega_1(\tau)\{U[c_1(\tau, \theta = 1), \tau]$$

$$+ V[c_2(\tau, \theta = 1, \omega_2, \lambda_2), \tau]\}$$

$$+ \lambda_2 \sum_{\tau} \omega_2(\tau)\{U[c_1(\tau, \theta = 2, \omega_2, \lambda_2), \tau]$$

$$+ V[c_2(\tau, \theta = 2, \omega_2, \lambda_2), \tau]\}$$

$$+ \lambda_3 \sum_{\tau} \omega_3(\tau)\{U[c_1(\tau, \theta = 3, \omega_2, \lambda_2), \tau]$$

$$+ V[c_2(\tau, \theta = 3, \omega_2, \lambda_2), \tau]\} \Big)$$

$$(13)$$

subject to resource constraints, for each (ω_2, λ_2) configuration,

$$\lambda_1 \sum_{\tau} \omega_1(\tau)c_1(\tau, \theta = 1) + \lambda_2 \sum_{\tau} \omega_2(\tau)c_1(\tau, \theta = 2, \omega_2, \lambda_2)$$

$$+ \lambda_3 \sum_{\tau} \omega_3(\tau)c_1(\tau, \theta = 3, \omega_2, \lambda_2) = W(\omega_2, \lambda_2), \quad (14)$$

$$\lambda_1 \sum_{\tau} \omega_1(\tau)c_2(\tau, \theta = 1, \omega_2, \lambda_2) + \lambda_2 \sum_{\tau} \omega_2(\tau)c_2(\tau, \theta = 2, \omega_2, \lambda_2)$$

$$+ \lambda_3 \sum_{\tau} \omega_3(\tau)c_2(\tau, \theta = 3, \omega_2, \lambda_2) = [\bar{e} - W(\omega_2, \lambda_2)]R \quad (15)$$

subject to the incentive constraints, for $\theta = 1$ movers and possible values of τ and τ',

$$U[c_1(\tau, \theta = 1), \tau] + \sum_{\omega_2, \lambda_2} \text{prob}(\omega_2, \lambda_2) V[c_2(\tau, \theta = 1, \omega_2, \lambda_2), \tau]$$

$$\tag{16}$$

$$\geq U[c_1(\tau', \theta = 1), \tau] + \sum_{\omega_2, \lambda_2} \text{prob}(\omega_2, \lambda_2) V[c_2(\tau', \theta = 1, \omega_2, \lambda_2), \tau],$$

for $\theta = 2, 3$, for each (ω_2, λ_2) configuration, and for all τ and τ' values,

$$U[c_1(\tau, \theta, \omega_2, \lambda_2), \tau] + V[c_2(\tau, \theta, \omega_2, \lambda_2), \tau]$$

$$\tag{17}$$

$$\geq U[c_1(\tau', \theta, \omega_2, \lambda_2), \tau] + V[c_2(\tau', \theta, \omega_2, \lambda_2), \tau],$$

and subject to constraints (11) and (12) above.

For the purpose of a numerical example, let first- and second-period utility functions be

$$U(c, \tau) = \frac{c^\tau - 1}{\tau}, \quad V(c, \tau) = \frac{c^{(1-\tau)} - 1}{1 - \tau},$$

with $0 < \tau < 1$, so that high τ values make a household relatively urgent to consume in the first period. For first-round movers, let fraction $\lambda_1 = \frac{1}{4}$ for sure and possible τ values be .35 and .6, with fractions $\omega_1(\tau = .35) = \frac{1}{2}$ and $\omega_1(\tau = .6) = \frac{1}{2}$ for sure. For second-round movers, let possible values for λ_2 be $\frac{1}{4}$ and $\frac{1}{2}$, each drawn with probability $\frac{1}{2}$, and let the possible τ values be .35 and .6 again, with fractions $\omega_2 = [\omega_2(\tau = .35), \omega_2(\tau = .6)]$ either $[\frac{2}{3}, \frac{1}{3}]$ or $[\frac{1}{3}, \frac{2}{3}]$, each possibility drawn with probability $\frac{1}{2}$, independent of the λ_2 draw. For nonmovers, $\lambda_3 = 1 - \lambda_1 - \lambda_2$, and the possible τ value is degenerate at $\tau = .5$ so that $\omega_3(\tau = .5) = 1$ for sure. Also let the storage return $R = 1$ and let the per capita endowment $\bar{e} = 10$. Finally, for first-round movers, let $m(\tau = .35, \theta = 1) = 10$ and let $m(\tau = .6, \theta = 1) = 0$ as a somewhat arbitrary initial condition. Naturally, though, patient first-round movers, that is, low-τ agents, receive more tokens than first-round movers who are urgent to consume.

A solution to program 2 with this specification of the environment has been computed by a numerical maximum procedure.[5] Some properties can be noted.[6] First the obvious: urgent consumers eat

[5] Technically, the search for solutions is facilitated by the observation that consumptions can be found directly as a solution to a concave programming problem, and values for tokens, prices, and intercepts can be filled afterward as solutions to eqq. (11) and (12). Also, values of τ were deliberately chosen in such a way as to make the incentive constraints nonbinding. In practice this was done by computing solutions for given τ values, ignoring the incentive constraints, and then checking to see if the incentive constraints were satisfied. In principle, solutions with binding incentive constraints can be found, but the search procedure would be more time intensive.

[6] A complete tabulation appears in table 1 of my working paper (Townsend 1988b).

more in the first period than in the second period, uniformly over states (ω_2, λ_2). Of course, first-round movers must eat the same in the first period over all states since the state is not yet revealed, whereas second-round $\theta = 2$ movers do not. Nevertheless, there is no need to distinguish from one another the second-period consumptions of first- and second-round movers, and the optimal solution does not do so. As a consequence, the computed token holdings of second-round movers mimic the preset (arbitrary) token holdings of first-round movers and are either 10 or zero depending on whether the mover is patient or urgent. This in turn makes the per capita token balances in the population a strictly monotone increasing function of the final number of patient movers. In this sense, nominal token balances vary with the state of the economy and do so in the obvious way. Curiously, the price level term $p(\omega_2, \lambda_2)$ and intercept term $\bar{c}(\omega_2, \lambda_2)$ move over states (ω_2, λ_2) in an effort to support the configuration of consumptions of patient and urgent movers, and this configuration does change over states. These can move over states in which the number of patient movers is the same because the distribution of τ shocks in the population changes over such states. The associated price movement over these states makes real token holdings different from nominal token holdings, and thus there is more state dependence in real token holdings than in nominal holdings.

One might take as a measure of real named debt in this economy the amount of second-period consumption claimed by nonmovers, namely $\lambda_3 c_2(\tau = .5, \theta = 3, \omega, \lambda)$ since this is achieved by cohort-specific accounts with the identity of first-period agents intact. This measure of debt also moves with the state. So also does total second-period consumption, as a measure of total indebtedness. Finally, the ratio of real tokens to total indebtedness also moves with the state (and this is true as well when intercepts are added to the purchasing power of tokens), as does the ratio of real tokens to named debts.[7]

VIII. On the Costs of Tokens and Named Credit Systems

Part, but not all, of the analysis thus far hinges on some implicit assumptions about the costs of various technologies that should now be brought out more fully. First, throughout the analysis, the cost of setting up, maintaining, and using any within-location accounting system is presumed to be zero. Second, from the analysis of Section IV

---

[7] There are no indications that this example is exceptional in any way. Various parameter configurations have also yielded similar qualitative properties over states. Tokens and named credits are distinguished and vary optimally with the state.

onward, the cost of direct communication across locations is presumed to be infinity (whereas in Sec. III it is zero). Third, in order to remove indeterminacy as between the use of tokens and within-location accounts, the cost of tokens is nonzero but essentially negligible. This last assumption requires some elaboration.

A problem that emerges if tokens are completely costless is that tokens can be used by nonmovers. That is, within-location accounts would not be needed, and one could get by with just one asset. In this case, measures of tokens would be pinned down and would still move around, at least on the assumption that initial movers must carry some tokens with them. But one could not compare tokens to credit in such a model.

The obvious remedy is to make the issue of tokens costly. Thus suppose that there is some minimal size token, say one unit, and each unit issued at date 1 after the revelation of shocks costs ψ units of the consumption-investment good at date 1. With this cost it is clear that nonmovers should always use within-location accounts. Movers, on the other hand, do not have fruitful access to within-location accounts and should use either a minimal size configuration of tokens or nothing. The implicit assumption of the analysis is that for every draw of state (ω_2, λ_2), tokens dominate in this choice since they allow consumptions to be indexed by preference shocks τ, even though their issue is costly. This can be delivered formally for *sufficiently low cost* ψ by a continuity argument.

Two further points should be noted in passing. First, the determination of optimal token issue for any positive finite cost ψ would be nontrivial. With the minimal size or indivisibility assumption on tokens, integer amounts of them must be assigned to support planned consumption levels. Still, the token-consumption points must all lie on a linear schedule (from the earlier analysis). A sufficient, but not necessary, condition for this is that planned consumptions be rational numbers, so that one can find among them a least common denominator. But one can get arbitrarily close to any arbitrary consumption array *if* one is willing (and able) to issue the requisite number of tokens. Second, with costly token issue, the nominal issue of tokens would be pinned down for all economywide states even if schedules are determined ex post. The complaint at the beginning of Section VII motivating two rounds of movers is now moot. But examples seem difficult to compute. Again, the solution described earlier is an example in the limit for virtually negligible costs.

Another possibility to ensure the use of both within-location accounts and tokens would be to make tokens work less well when they are used. In particular, one could increase the number of underlying commodities and add second-period shocks to second-period preferences. Then with only one instrument to index second-period consumptions, it is possible that agents might wish to understate token holdings.[8] Since understatement cannot be precluded but is not incentive compatible, the effect would be to mitigate the ability to index second-period consumptions. Thus within-location accounts might dominate. Distinguishing tokens from internal accounts in this manner begs the question, however, of multiple-token issue. In particular, multiple-token issue would give moving agents a complete communication system and, in the absence of costs, could be complete for nonmovers also. Similarly, multiple tokens would allow the early movers in the solution described earlier to be distinguished from late movers, and so again in the absence of costs, there would arise an indeterminacy. Thus it seems that one is driven again to an explicit consideration of costly token issue and the idea that a one-token system might dominate a two-token system if there were differential setup costs. But like the earlier discussion of costs, this takes us beyond the analysis of the present paper.

Appendix

Derivation of de Facto Linear Schedules

The first step is to start with an arbitrary schedule $c_2(m, \theta = 2, \omega, \lambda)$ with the sole restrictions that it be monotone increasing in m (for incentive compatibility) and that m range over a finite number of values. However, if agents are to be allowed to collude in arbitrary ways, then this schedule must specify what is to happen for *arbitrary* fractions $f(m)$ of agents reporting m at the distribution center. That is, some feasible outcome must be specified no matter what agents report. Denote this modified schedule by $c_2[m, \theta = 2, \omega, \lambda, \mathbf{F}]$, where $\mathbf{F}$ denotes the vector of fractions $f(m)$, $m \in M$, and suppose for feasibility that

$$\lambda \sum_\tau \omega(\tau) c_2[\tau, \theta = 1, \lambda, \omega, \mathbf{F}] + (1 - \lambda) \sum_m f(m) c_2[m, \theta = 2, \lambda, \omega, \mathbf{F}]$$

$$\leq R \left[1 - \lambda \sum_\tau \omega(\tau) c_1(\tau, \theta = 1, \lambda, \omega) - (1 - \lambda) \sum_\tau \omega(\tau) c_1(\tau, \theta = 2, \lambda, \omega) \right].$$

$$(A1)$$

Note that this specification would allow for group penalties for "collusion" *if* this could be detected. "Deviation" by a finite number of players carries no weight, however, that is, does not influence averages. Also note that agents are still restricted at the distribution centers to announcing values of tokens m. Crucial in this is that they do not know whom they have dealt with in the foggy location, for otherwise their collusion could be detected by a more elaborate scheme. Also, despite the possibility of agreed-on side exchanges,

---

[8] Townsend (1987) provides an example of limited single-token systems and beneficial multiple-token systems.

tokens m on hand are still the only relevant state variable, and so announcements can be restricted to it.

The game to be played by movers against schedule $c_2[\tau, \theta = 2, \lambda, \omega, F]$ given beginning-of-second-period conditions, M, the finite set of possible values for m under date 1 handouts $m(\tau, \omega, \lambda)$, and $h(m)$ the actual fraction of movers holding balances m, $m \in M$, is described as follows. First, moving agents arriving at a particular location are assigned names in an anonymous fashion, taking numbers one at a time and unobserved by others. The set of names can be taken to be the set of positive integers, and we may refer to a generic agent named i, $i = 1, 2, \ldots$.

Second, each of these agents announces a strategy under which he is willing to be an anonymous go-between, naming a local location for trades but not revealing his identity. More specifically, let $\Delta_m^i(m, +)$ denote the number of pieces of paper (hence the m subscript) proposer i is willing to give out to anyone in the set of movers if m is named (hence the first argument in parentheses) and a plus sign (for handout) is indicated (hence the second argument in parentheses), let $\Delta_m^i(m, -)$ denote the number of pieces of paper required to be handed in to proposer i if m is named and a minus sign is indicated, and let $\Delta_c^i(m, +)$ and $\Delta_c^i(m, -)$ denote handouts and take-ins of the consumption good if m is named and a plus or minus is indicated, respectively. Here it is understood that if an agent goes to proposer i and names m and a plus for paper, he *must* choose a minus for consumption and vice versa. Also, he cannot claim both a plus and a minus for paper at the same m. Of course, an agent could choose to do nothing with a particular proposer i, effectively setting $\Delta_m^i(\cdot, \cdot)$ and $\Delta_c^i(\cdot, \cdot)$ to zero, and the proposer can specify that some of these components be zero as well. For example, motivated by figure 1, some agents of type m_3 might want proposer i to name $\Delta_m^i(m_3, -) = m_3 - m_2$ and agents of type m_1 want $\Delta_m^i(m_1, +) = m_2 - m_1$, with $\Delta_c^i(m_3, +) = s\Delta_m^i(m_3, -)$ and $\Delta_c^i(m_1, -) = s\Delta_m^i(m_1, +)$. Alternatively, motivated by figure 2, some agents of type m_2 might want proposer i to name $\Delta_m^i(m_2, +) = m_3 - m_2$ and $\Delta_m^i(m_2, -) = m_2 - m_1$, with $\Delta_c^i(m_2, -) = s\Delta_m^i(m_2, +)$ and $\Delta_c^i(m_2, +) = s\Delta_m^i(m_2, -)$. A further component of the strategy of proposer i is specification of a maximal *finite* number $\bar{g}^i(m, +)$ of households that can come to him and announce m and a plus for paper, and similarly $\bar{g}^i(m, -)$ for announcement of m and a minus. Let S_i denote the strategy of agent i.

The third event of the game is that moving agents go in turn to the locations of the proposers and choose actions $(m, \pm)$, where here and below the plus/minus notation indicates that either a plus or a minus must be filled in. Thus $(m_{ji}, \pm)$ denotes the action taken by player j with proposer i. Whatever nontrivial action $(m_{ji}, \pm)$ is taken by player j with proposer i, it is registered on proposer i's computer. Further, proposer i himself may choose to take an action with himself, and if done this is also registered on his computer. The strategy that player j adopts with proposer i is a function of balances m carried in from his initial location as well as whether or not the quotas $\bar{g}^i(\tilde{m}, \pm)$, $\tilde{m} \in M$, are filled or not by the time it is player j's turn, something that is observable at the location of proposer i (though the identity and specific moves of previous players with proposer i are concealed from player j). Thus let $g_j^i(\tilde{m}, \pm)$ denote the number of players who have come to proposer i and indicated $(\tilde{m}, \pm)$ prior to the arrival of j, and let quota *indicator* $I_j(\cdot, \cdot)$ be

$$
I_j^i(\tilde{m}, \pm) = \begin{cases} 1 & \text{if } g_j^i(\tilde{m}, \pm) = \bar{g}^i(\tilde{m}, \pm) \\ 0 & \text{if } g_j^i(\tilde{m}, \pm) < \bar{g}^i(\tilde{m}, \pm). \end{cases}
$$

PRIVATE INFORMATION ECONOMY   1343

The strategy of player j with proposer i is denoted $\sigma_{ji}(m, \{l_j^k(\bar{m}, \pm)\})$, where it is understood that k ranges over proposers $\{1, 2, \ldots\}$, and for each k, $\bar{m}$ ranges over M. A player j can deal with more than one proposer i. But each player j is fully committed (somehow) to carry out his action with any proposer i, that is, eventually to arrive with currency balances if necessary prior to participation at the distribution center and to arrive with the consumption good if necessary afterward. We do not ask how this commitment is enforced but take it as given that some commitment among agents is necessary for the initial allocaton rule $c_2(\cdot)$ to be weakened.

Of course, each agent j knows the actual distribution of type m movers in the population. Thus given a specification of strategies $\sigma_l^*(\cdot, \cdot)$ of each of the other players l, $l = 1, 2, \ldots, l \neq i$, each player i has well-defined expectations over the eventual outcome, in particular over the induced $\mathbf{F}$. Thus in a *Nash equilibrium* of the second stage of the game, given individual balances m for player j and quota indicators $\{l_j^k(\bar{m}, \pm)\}$ over proposers k, strategy $\sigma_{ji}^*(m, \{l_j^k(\bar{m}, \pm)\})$, $i = 1, 2, \ldots$, for agent j solves the following problem: Maximize by choice of the $(m_{ji}, \pm)$ the objective function

$$
EU\left\{c_2\left[m + \sum_{i=1}^{\infty} \Delta_m^i(m_{ji}, +) - \sum_{i=1}^{\infty} \Delta_m^i(m_{ji}, -), \theta = 2, \omega, \lambda, \mathbf{F}\right]\right.
$$
$$
\left. + \sum_{i=1}^{\infty} \Delta_c^i(m_{ji}, +) - \sum_{i=1}^{\infty} \Delta_c^i(m_{ji}, -)\right\}.
$$
(A2)

Here, of course, currency balances are adjusted before announcements are made at the distribution center and consumption levels are adjusted afterward.

Given a specification of Nash equilibrium decision rules $\sigma_l^*(\cdot, \cdot)$ at the second stage over all players l, each agent i chooses an initial intermediation strategy $S_i = S_i^*$ to be maximal among all feasible strategies given the strategies S_k^* of other players k. Feasibility means that i believes that he is able to abide by the strategy he announces for all possible realizations of random variables, that he can honor his commitments to hand out tokens and consumption.

A complete specification of a *Nash equilibrium* for a game is a specification of Nash strategies S_k^* at the first stage of the game and Nash equilibrium decision rules $\sigma_i^*(\cdot, \cdot)$ at the second.

Attention will be restricted in what follows to equilibrium outcomes of a game that are the same for any moving agent of type m, regardless of the numbered turn a type m agent is assigned. It will be supposed similarly that the numbering of players is immaterial to the outcome of a game. Then, for any proposed schedule $c_2(m, \theta = 2, \lambda, \omega, \mathbf{F})$, there emerges a de facto schedule $\bar{c}_2(m, \theta = 2, \lambda, \omega)$ defined in the obvious, more concise notation than (A2), for any player j of type m:

$$
\bar{c}_2(m, \theta = 2, \lambda, \omega) = c_2\left[m + \sum_{i=1}^{\infty} \Delta_m^{i*}(m_{ji}, \pm), \theta = 2, \lambda, \omega, \mathbf{F}^*\right] + \sum_{i=1}^{\infty} \Delta_c^{i*}(m_{ji}, \pm),
$$
(A3)

where here $\Delta_m^{i*}(\cdot, \cdot)$ and $\Delta_c^{i*}(\cdot, \cdot)$ denote part of the Nash equilibrium strategy S_i^* of proposer i, where the $(m_{ji}, \pm)$ are determined under the Nash equilibrium decisions $\sigma_{ji}^*(m, \cdot)$, and where $\mathbf{F}^*$ is the distribution of types at the distribution point induced by the Nash equilibrium strategies.

It should now become apparent that the effective schedule $\tilde{c}_2(m, \theta = 2, \lambda, \omega)$ must be linear in m. For suppose otherwise. In fact suppose that the de facto schedule appears as in figure 1. We may suppose that second-period strategies are maximal given a configuration of first-period proposals, consistent with the definition of equilibrium and the definition of a de facto schedule. But the specification of proposals itself could not be maximal. One agent type m_1 or m_3 could propose some preplay redistribution of m and postplay redistribution of c for some *finite* coalition of these types, as described above. All such types would voluntarily come to such a proposer making themselves strictly better off, and since they have zero mass in the aggregate, F^* would be unaltered by these actions. Further, even if the proposer himself changed from an earlier strategy, this cannot alter F^* since the proposer was able to deal only with a finite number of agents. That is, virtually all agents must have achieved the earlier supposed equilibrium outcome without going through the proposer, and so agents who had gone through the proposer originally still have the same distribution of the outcomes available to them, doing now what others had done after them originally, and so on. Thus the original specification could not have been a Nash equilibrium. Similarly, the de facto schedule depicted in figure 2 cannot be associated with a Nash equilibrium. And since this argument applies for *any* three specifications of m, regardless of the dimensionality of M, linearity must hold over all $m \in M$.

References

Dasgupta, Partha S.; Hammond, Peter J.; and Maskin, Eric S. "The Implementation of Social Choice Rules: Some General Results on Incentive Compatibility." *Rev. Econ. Studies* 46 (April 1979): 185–216.

Diamond, Douglas W., and Dybvig, Philip H. "Bank Runs, Deposit Insurance, and Liquidity." *J.P.E.* 91 (June 1983): 401–19.

Harris, Milton, and Townsend, Robert M. "Resource Allocation under Asymmetric Information." *Econometrica* 49 (January 1981): 33–64.

Myerson, Roger B. "Incentive Compatibility and the Bargaining Problem." *Econometrica* 47 (January 1979): 61–73.

Townsend, Robert M. "Intermediation with Costly Bilateral Exchange." *Rev. Econ. Studies* 45 (October 1978): 417–25.

———. "Optimal Multiperiod Contracts and the Gain from Enduring Relationships under Private Information." *J.P.E.* 90 (December 1982): 1166–86.

———. "Theories of Intermediated Structures." *Carnegie-Rochester Conf. Ser. Public Policy* 18 (Spring 1983): 221–72.

———. "Economic Organization with Limited Communication." *A.E.R.* 77 (December 1987): 954–71.

———. "Information Constrained Insurance: The Revelation Principle Extended." *J. Monetary Econ.* 21 (March/May 1988): 411–50. (a)

———. "Optimal Activist Currency Rules." Manuscript. Chicago: Univ. Chicago, Dept. Econ., March 1988. (b)

[11]

Oxford Economic Papers 37 (1985), 161–195

RATIONAL EXPECTATIONS, INFORMATION AND ASSET MARKETS: AN INTRODUCTION

By MARGARET BRAY[1]

1. Introduction

FINANCIAL markets are a subject of perpetual fascination to economists and others. There are very large sums of money to be gained and lost on them. They are obviously crucially important not only to the people and institutions who invest directly, but also to the many others who invest indirectly through holding unit trusts (mutual funds), pension or life assurance policies. Moreover the financial markets do not operate in isolation; they affect and are affected by the rest of the economy.

One important economic function of such markets is the spreading and sharing of risk. An entrepreneur can reduce the risks which he carries by selling shares in his firm. Investors may be willing to carry some of the risk because they are less risk averse than the entrepreneur. They may also be willing to invest even if they are more risk averse because the market allows them to hold a diversified portfolio which reduces risk. Investing £10,000 in ten different firms whose profits are imperfectly correlated is very much less risky than investing £10,000 in one of the firms. The view that such markets perform a socially important function in spreading risk reasonably well is widely held, (see Arrow (1964) and Diamond (1967) for theoretical models). But there are distinguished dissidents; in Chapter 12 of the General Theory, Keynes argues forcefully that the markets increasingly provide a casino for speculators, rather than a guide for investors, and may be socially useless or even positively dangerous.

Recent theoretical work on asset markets, based on the rational expectations hypothesis, has argued that they may have an additional informational role. Traders have information which affects their evaluation of the value of assets, the demand for the assets, and thus prices. Other traders may attempt to infer the information from prices. The major achievement of recent work has been to develop a coherent description of this phenomenon, and use it to ask how well the markets transmit and aggregate the information.

Much of this literature is highly technical, and inaccessible without a considerable mathematical apparatus. Yet the basic issues can be understood with much less background, as this paper seeks to demonstrate. It is written as an introduction to recent work on information in asset markets, assuming intermediate microeconomics, enough calculus to differentiate a quadratic, a little manipulation of linear equations, and enough probability theory to know about means, variances, and conditional distributions. I use

[1] I am grateful to Craig Alexander, Jeremy Edwards, Anna Lemessany, Peter Sinclair, and Martin Weale for comments on an earlier version of this paper.

162   RATIONAL EXPECTATIONS, INFORMATION AND ASSET MARKETS

expected utility theory, but anyone who does not know the theory, and is willing to take on trust my assertion that it is a sensible way to model choice under uncertainty, should be able to follow the argument.

Much of the paper is concerned with elaborating a simple model. The model introduced in Section 2 is the standard deterministic partial equilibrium model of supply and demand in a spot market, modified by the assumption that production decisions must be made before the market operates on the basis of price expectations. I use this model to introduce a perfect foresight equilibrium; the deterministic version of a rational expectations equilibrium. In Section 3 I introduce a futures market, operating at the date when production decisions are made. A futures contract is a financial asset, whose gross return is the spot price. I argue that arbitrage implies that in this deterministic model, if expectations are held with certainty, the futures price must be equal to the present discounted value of the expected spot price. Section 4 introduces briefly the expected utility theory of choice under uncertainty. Section 5 applies this theory to a stochastic version of the model on the assumption that dealers are risk neutral, using an arbitrage argument to establish that the futures price is equal to the present discounted value of the expected spot price. Section 6 shows how the simple arbitrage argument breaks down when risk neutral dealers have diverse information, introducing the informational role of asset prices. The formal definition of a rational expectations equilibrium in an asset market with asymmetric information is introduced in Section 7. Section 8 introduces risk aversion, simplifying matters mathematically by working with exponential utility functions, and normal random variables. The joint equilibrium of the spot and futures market when dealers are risk averse is calculated, on the assumption that no-one has any private information about the spot price when trading on the futures market. Information is introduced in Section 9, firstly on the assumption that all dealers have the same information, secondly on the assumption that there are informed and uniformed traders, but the informed traders all have the same information, and thirdly on the assumption that dealers have diverse information. In this model the futures market is remarkably informationally efficient; it aggregates information perfectly. Section 10 is concerned with the implications and robustness of the informational efficiency result in this and related models. In the models which I use calculating the rational expectations equilibrium is relatively straightforward, but in Section 11 I introduce a version of the spot and futures market model which has no rational expectations equilibrium. I discuss the nature and significance of the problems associated with the existence of rational expectations equilibrium, and the literature on the subject. Section 12 attempts an evaluation of the models, discussing the assumptions, concentrating largely on the rational expectations assumption, and referring briefly to the empirical and experimental evidence. Section 13 discusses some open questions prompted by these models.

The results which I establish have no claims to originality, the first model which I develop has its origins in the cobweb model (Kaldor 1934), and in Muth's paper on rational expectations (1961). The futures market model is based on Danthine (1978), and related to Grossman (1976 and 1977) and Bray (1981). The non-existence example in Section 11 is new in detail, but is similar to that of Kreps (1977). I give references to other, related literature, where appropriate. A more technical introduction to this and many other topics can be found in Radner's (1982) survey of 'Equilibrium Under Uncertainty' and in the symposium issue (April 1982) of the Journal of Economic Theory on 'Rational Expectations in Microeconomic models', in particular the introduction by Jordan and Radner. Stiglitz (1982) discusses a range of issues concerned with information and capital markets.

2. Supply and demand with a production lag: perfect foresight equilibrium

In the standard model of supply and demand, production and consumption decisions are taken simultaneously, based on the price. If production takes time, production decisions have to be based on the expected price. For example a farmer plants a crop in January which will be harvested and sold in June. To begin with assume that there is no uncertainty, an assumption which will be relaxed in Section 4. Demand $D(p_s)$ is a deterministic function of p_s, the spot price of wheat in June. Supply $S[p_s^e]$ is a deterministic function of p_s^e, the farmers' point expectation belief in January about what the spot price will be in June. For now, assume that all farmers are subjectively certain about what the price will be, and all have the same beliefs. If the market in June clears, supply equals demand. $D[p_s] = S[p_s^e]$. The expected price determines production which in turn determines the actual price. In fact the price p_s, is a function of the expected price.

In Fig. 1 when the price is p_s^e, $Q = S[p_s^e]$ is produced. When Q is put on

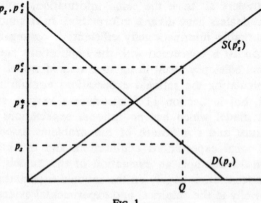

FIG. 1

the spot market in June the price is p_s. If $p_s \neq p_s^e$ the farmers, despite their subjective certainty, are wrong. Beliefs are wrong unless $p_s^e = p_s^*$, the price at which the supply and demand curves intersect so $S[p_s^*] = D[p_s^*]$. This could well be described as a self-fulfilling belief. However the standard terminology is a perfect foresight equilibrium or more recently (following Muth (1961)) a rational expectations equilibrium.

A rational expectations equilibrium can be defined as a situation in which people do not make systematic mistakes in forecasting. In this case where beliefs are point expectations held with certainty, rational expectations equilibrium requires that beliefs be correct, i.e. that people have perfect foresight. The rational expectations assumption is now used very widely, but remains controversial. The assumption avoids many of the difficult dynamic problems apparently associated with expectation formation, making it possible to proceed with other questions. For the time being I will simply assume rational expectations without further discussion, returning to the matter in Section 12.

3. Financing production: futures markets and arbitrage

The revenue from selling the crop arrives some time after most of the production costs are incurred. This leaves a farmer with the problem of finding funds to cover the investment in planting the crop. He may have sufficient wealth to finance this from his own resources. If not he will have to borrow.

Assume that everyone knows that the price in June will be p_s. There are perfect capital markets, that is the farmer can borrow or lend as much as he wishes at the same interest rate. £1 borrowed in January must be repaid with £$(1+r)$ in June. Suppose that a farmer has wealth W_0 in January, and incurs the costs of producing output y, which have a present discounted value in January of $C(y)$. He invests the remainder of his wealth $W_0 - C(y)$ at interest rate r until June. His wealth in June is the sum of his revenue from output $p_s y$ and the return on his other investment

$$W = p_s y + (W_0 - C(y))(1+r) = p_s y - C(y)(1+r) + W_0(1+r)$$

The value of profits from production in June is $p_s y - C(y)(1+r)$. Note that $W_0 - C(y)$ may be negative, in which case the farmer is borrowing to cover some of his costs. The farmer maximises his June wealth by maximizing profits. If C is a convex function of y and $p_s > C'(0)(1+r)$, this is done by setting $p_s = C'(y)(1+r)$. The value of y is independent of his initial wealth, which simply determines how much, if anything he has to borrow.

The farmer may also finance his production by selling on the futures market. A futures market is an institution on which money is exchanged for promises to deliver goods in the future. For example a farmer may sell wheat in January for delivery in June. As before suppose the farmer has wealth W_0 in January, produces y, incurring costs $C(y)$, and sells z on the futures market at price p_f. This leaves him $W_0 - C(y) + p_f z$ to invest at interest r. In June he sells the remainder of his output $y - z$ on the spot market. His wealth in June is

$$W = p_s(y - z) + (W_0 - C(y) + p_f z)(1 + r)$$
$$= p_s y - C(y)(1 + r) + (p_f(1 + r) - p_s)z + W_0(1 + r). \qquad (3.1)$$

The farmer maximises his wealth, as before by choosing output y so $p_s = C'(y)(1 + r)$. If $p_f > p_s/(1 + r)$, so that the futures price exceeds the present discounted value of the spot price, he can make arbitrarily large profits by selling on the futures market. He will increase z indefinitely, and will wish to set $z > y$, selling more on the futures market than he produces, meeting the shortfall $z - y$ by buying on the spot market. However he is unlikely to find a willing buyer at this price. There are two possible classes of buyers, consumers and speculators. Consumers (e.g. food manufacturers and wholesalers) may choose to buy futures in January rather than wanting to buy on the spot market in June, thus hedging against uncertainty about the June spot price. For the sake of simplicity I will assume that consumers do not participate in the futures market; if they did it would complicate the models without substantially affecting the conclusions. Speculators buy futures contracts, which they sell on the spot market, never actually taking delivery of the goods, in the hope of making a profit on the difference between the futures price and the present value of the spot price. Suppose a speculator with wealth W_0 in January buys x futures contracts in January, sells x on the spot market in June, and invests the rest of his wealth in the safe asset paying interest r. His wealth will be

$$W = p_s x + (W_0 - p_f x)(1 + r)$$
$$= (p_s - p_f(1 + r))x + W_0(1 + r). \qquad (3.2)$$

If $p_f > p_s/(1 + r)$ both speculators and farmers will wish to sell futures. With no willing buyers the market cannot clear. If $p_f < p_s/(1 + r)$ both speculators and farmers will want to buy futures. Thus the only price at which the futures market can clear is when $p_f = p_s/(1 + r)$. This is an example of an arbitrage argument—these arguments are based on the premise that in equilibrium it cannot be possible for anyone to make arbitrarily large certain profits. If the market is perfectly arbitraged $p_s = p_f(1 + r)$. The wealth in June of farmers and speculators does not depend on the size of their future trades. In this deterministic model with perfect foresight, a futures contract is a safe asset paying interest r. There is no reason for anyone to use the futures market in preference to borrowing or lending at rate r elsewhere. If the futures market ceased to exist no-one would be any better or worse off.

In fact under certainty there seems little reason for the futures market to exist. Any understanding of futures markets, and other asset markets such as the stock market, depends upon introducing uncertainty.

4. Choice under uncertainty

The farmer faces risks in both the quantity and price of output. A futures market allows the farmer to shift the price risks to speculators. If his output y is certain he can completely eliminate the risk by setting $z = y$, selling his entire output on the futures market. But why will the speculator be willing to assume the risk, and at what price? The currently available answers to this, and many other questions about economics under uncertainty, are derived from a widely accepted model of choice under uncertainty: the theory of expected utility. An introduction to the theory can be found in among other places Deaton and Muellbauer (1980), in a survey by Schoemaker (1982) or, in a valuable collection of readings, Diamond and Rothschild (1978).

Assume that an investor has decided to invest a certain amount W_0 for a period. He has a number of different assets to choose between, and a definite set of beliefs about the joint probability distribution of the returns on the different assets. He cares only about the probability distribution of his wealth $\tilde{W}$ at the end of the period, which depends upon the way he allocates his initial wealth W_0 between the different assets. The theory of expected utility shows that if his preferences over the probability distribution of $\tilde{W}$ satisfy some plausible assumptions he will choose a portfolio which maximises the mathematical expectation $EU(\tilde{W})$ of a function $U(\tilde{W})$ given his beliefs about the probabilities. For a discrete probability distribution $EU(\tilde{W}) = \sum_i U(W_i)p_i$ where W_i is wealth in state i and p_i the probability of state i. For a continuous probability distribution

$$EU(\tilde{W}) = \int_{-\infty}^{\infty} U(W)f(W)\,dW$$

where f is the probability density function. In both cases the probability distribution depends upon the investors beliefs, and his choice of portfolio.

The theory has two essential elements, the utility function, and the probability distribution which determines the mathematical expectation. The functional form of the utility function U describes attitudes to risk. U is increasing provided investors prefer more to less wealth. If $U(\tilde{W}) = \tilde{W}$ the investor is risk neutral, caring only about expected wealth, and not at all about its riskiness. If $U(\tilde{W})$ is strictly concave the investor is risk averse, strictly preferring investments yielding the expectation of $\tilde{W}$ for sure, to random $\tilde{W}$. Risk aversion in investment choices for an individual seems highly plausible, and is often assumed.

The assumption that uncertainty can be described in terms of probability distributions is widely made today, but historically has not commanded universal acceptance. Keynes was a notable dissenter. There is very little controversy about applying the mathematical theory of probability to assess the probabilities associated with a series of similar events, where after a time there is enough data to construct probabilities from frequency distributions, (for example weather or life expectancy data), situations described by Knight (1921) as risk. The argument is rather whether meaningful probabilities can be assigned to unique events, where there is no objective frequency data to rely on, situations described by Knight as uncertainty. The subjectivist or Bayesian viewpoint on probability is that Knight's distinction is invalid. It is always possible to elicit probabilities by forcing people to make bets. (See Raiffa (1968)). There is however no guarantee in subjectivist theory that different people will form the same probability distributions, unless there is frequency data to base them on, which brings us back to Knight's risk. For some purposes it is enough to assume that people act as if they had subjective beliefs expressible as probability distributions. However many models postulate that people have the same correct beliefs about probability distributions, (rational expectations). These models do not seem to be applicable to situations which Knight would describe as uncertain.

I am now in a position to use the theory of expected utility to extend the theory of asset pricing under certainty to uncertainty. Initially I will assume risk neutrality, and then proceed to consider risk aversion.

5. Risk neutrality: arbitrage again

Returning to the futures market example suppose that once farmers have chosen their level of inputs their output y is certain. The June spot price is uncertain because spot demand is uncertain. A risk neutral farmer will choose his output y and futures sales z to maximise the expected value of his wealth, from (3.1) this is

$$E\tilde{W} = E\tilde{p}_s y - C(y)(1+r) + (p_f(1+r) - E\tilde{p}_s)z + W_0(1+r).$$

(Throughout this paper a tilde $\tilde{}$ above a variable indicates that it is random.) A speculator will choose his futures purchases x to maximise the expected value of his wealth, from (3.2) this is

$$E\tilde{W} = (E\tilde{p}_s - p_f(1+r))x + W_0(1+r).$$

Decisions depend upon the mathematical expectation $E\tilde{p}_s$ of $\tilde{p}_s$, its average value. The risk neutral dealers do not care about any other characteristics of the probability distribution. $E\tilde{p}_s$ is not a point expectation held with certainty, the dealers are aware that there is uncertainty and would expect to observe that usually $E\tilde{p}_s \neq \tilde{p}_s$.

Precisely the same arbitrage argument as before implies that unless $p_f = E\tilde{p}_s/(1+r)$ there are unlimited positive expected profits to be made and the market cannot clear. The argument is less compelling than under certainty. Although a speculator may wish to exploit opportunities for making positive expected profits he may not be able to do so. Suppose that $E\bar{p}_s > p_f(1+r)$, so buying futures contracts generates a positive expected return. A risk neutral speculator will choose to spend his entire wealth on futures contracts, he will also wish to borrow without limit to exploit further the opportunity for profit. There is a chance that the spot price will be so low that he cannot repay his debts; lending to the speculator becomes risky. Speculators may face either a higher interest rate than r, or limits on credit, limiting their ability to arbitrage the market.

6. Diverse information

The simple arbitrage argument also breaks down if different dealers (farmers and speculators) have different beliefs about the expected spot price. This is not incompatible with the dealers having rational expectations, if they have access to different information. Suppose for example that $\bar{p}_s = \tilde{I} + \tilde{e}$ where $\tilde{I}$ and $\tilde{e}$ are independent random variables, $E\tilde{e} = 0$, and so $E\bar{p}_s = E\tilde{I}$. There are two types of dealers. The informed dealers observe $\tilde{I}$ before the futures market opens; their expectation of $\bar{p}_s$ is conditional upon $\tilde{I}$, $E[\bar{p}_s \mid \tilde{I}] = \tilde{I}$. The uninformed dealers observe nothing, their expectation of $\bar{p}_s$ is $E\bar{p}_s = E\tilde{I}$. If both types of dealers are risk neutral, face no borrowing constraints, and stick to their beliefs, the informed will want to buy or sell an unlimited amount unless $p_f = E[\bar{p}_s \mid \tilde{I}]/(1+r) = \tilde{I}/(1+r)$, and the uninformed dealers will want to buy or sell an unlimited amount unless $\bar{p}_f = E\bar{p}_s/(1+r)$. Unless by coincidence $E[\bar{p}_s \mid \tilde{I}] = E\bar{p}_s$ (i.e. if $\tilde{I} = E\tilde{I}$) the market apparently cannot clear.

It is however most unlikely that the uninformed dealers will stick to their beliefs. Knowing that there are informed dealers in the market whose trading affects the futures price they will try to make inferences from the futures price about the spot price. They are using the price of a financial asset, a futures contract, to make judgements about its quality. Judging quality from price is not confined to financial markets. Consumers may also do so, assuming that cheap goods are also cheap and nasty. One of the major successes of recent economic theory has been the development of models which take this into account.

In these models prices have two roles, their conventional role in determining budget sets for consumers and profit opportunities for firms, and an additional role in transmitting information. Hayek (1945) in a discussion of decentralisation and planning argues that the conventional role of prices must also be understood as an informational one. In standard Walrasian competitive equilibrium models once households and firms know current prices they have no use for any further information about the plans, characteristics and opportunities of others in the economy, they need make no attempt to infer this information from prices. As Grossman (1981) argues recent models of asymmetric information move beyond this, some agents want some information held by others, in this case information about the spot price in the future. They try to infer as much information as they can from current prices. In some cases the price system may be entirely efficient at transmitting information, prices are so informative that there is no additional information currently known to anyone in the economy which would be helpful. In other cases prices may be less informationally efficient, conveying some information, but still leaving a frustrated desire to see the current contents of someone else's mind, or computer file. In either case agents are trying to look beyond prices, to solve an inference problem, which is unnecessary in standard Walrasian models. The central question addressed by the models which I am about to discuss is how informationally efficient are prices? These models make use of the idea of a rational expectations equilibrium. I will now show how this equilibrium is defined, and explain how it yields an equilibrium price for this example.

7. Rational expectations equilibrium and risk neutrality

The definition of a rational expectations equilibrium for the spot and futures markets has four parts. A very similar definition can be formulated for any asset market model. The first part describes how dealers form their beliefs.

Part 1. Each dealer (farmer or speculator) observes some private information $\bar{I}_i$ and the futures price $\bar{p}_f$. Given this information he has beliefs about the spot price $\bar{p}_s$ which can be expressed as a conditional probability distribution.

For example dealer i might believe that given the futures price $\bar{p}_f$ and private information, $\bar{I}_i$, the conditional distribution of $\bar{p}_s$ was normal with mean $E[\bar{p}_s \mid \bar{p}_f, \bar{I}_i] = \frac{1}{2}\bar{p}_f + \frac{1}{4}\bar{I}_i$ and variance $\frac{1}{8}$. At this stage I have not required that the beliefs be correct, only that they exist.

The second part of the definition states that given their beliefs dealers choose their portfolio in accordance with expected utility theory.

Part 2. Each dealer chooses the holding of futures contracts, and for farmers, output, which maximises his expected utility given his beliefs about the spot price, conditional upon his private information and the futures price.

Parts 1 and 2 of the definition give the supply and demand for futures. Note that supply and demand are affected by both the numerical value of the futures price and information, and by beliefs. If a risk neutral dealer believes that $E[\bar{p}_s \mid \bar{p}_f, \bar{I}_i] = \frac{1}{2}\bar{p}_f + \frac{1}{4}\bar{I}_i$, he will buy or sell an unlimited amount depending on whether $\bar{p}_f - [\frac{1}{2}\bar{p}_f + \frac{1}{4}\bar{I}_i]/(1+r)$ is positive or negative. To emphasize this point I will write $d_i[\bar{p}_f, \bar{I}_i; B_i]$ for dealer i's demand for futures, where B_i is shorthand for beliefs.

170 RATIONAL EXPECTATIONS, INFORMATION AND ASSET MARKETS

The next part of the definition is

Part 3. The spot and futures prices are at levels where both markets clear.

In different years the information will be different, so if the markets are to clear prices must be a function of the information. Demand and the market clearing prices also depend upon beliefs, so I will write

$$\bar{p}_f = f[\bar{I}_1, \bar{I}_2,..., \bar{I}_n; B_1, B_2 ... B_n]$$
$$\bar{p}_s = g[\bar{I}_1, \bar{I}_2,..., \bar{I}_n; B_1, B_2 ... B_n].$$

An omniscient economist could calculate the function f. Knowing the joint distribution of $[\bar{I}_1, \bar{I}_2 ... \bar{I}_n]$ the economist could then calculate the joint distribution of $[\bar{p}_f, \bar{p}_s, \bar{I}_1, \bar{I}_2 ... \bar{I}_n]$, and so the conditional distribution of $\bar{p}_s$ given $\bar{p}_f$ and $\bar{I}_i$ for each i. This would tell the economist what the correct beliefs for each dealer would be, call them $\hat{B}_i$. As the joint distributions depend upon the original beliefs, $[B_1, B_2 ... B_n]$, the correct beliefs $[\hat{B}_1, \hat{B}_2 ... \hat{B}_n]$ also depend upon the original beliefs. A more formal way of saying the same thing is that $[\hat{B}_1, \hat{B}_2 ... \hat{B}_n]$ is a function of $[B_1, B_2 ... B_n]$.

The last part of the definition is

Part 4. Each agent has rational expectations. They have correct beliefs about the joint probability distribution of the futures price, spot price and private information, so

$$B_i = \hat{B}_i \qquad i = 1, 2 ... n.$$

Note that this states that beliefs about the entire conditional probability distribution are correct. Much of the macroeconomic literature works with models where only the conditional mean is relevant, but the rational expectations hypothesis is not confined to such models.

This definition may appear unnecessarily long winded. Stating that the beliefs are correct in Part 1 would make for greater brevity, but stating the definition in this way gives more insight. It is helpful in calculating the rational expectations equilibrium in simple models, where making a guess about the functional form of beliefs, calculating supply and demand, and then checking to see if there is indeed a set of beliefs which generates rational expectations often works. This approach is also very helpful in understanding issues associated with the existence and stability of rational expectations equilibrium.

I have stated the definition in terms of a spot and futures market, but very similar definitions can be formulated for any set of financial asset markets. I have not been specific about the information $\bar{I}_i$. All that is required is that it be a random variable, but it may be continuous or discrete, a scalar or a vector. It may always take the same value, $\bar{I}_i = 0$, in which case it is effectively no information.

I will now calculate the rational expectations equilibrium for the futures market example with risk neutral dealers. Here the informed agents observe $\tilde{I}$ and the uninformed agents observe nothing. Recall that $\tilde{p}_s = \tilde{I} + \tilde{e}$, $\tilde{I}$ and $\tilde{e}$ are independent and $E\tilde{e} = 0$. In accordance with Part 1 of the definition, suppose that the informed dealers believe that $E[\tilde{p}_s \mid \tilde{I}, \tilde{p}_f] = \tilde{I}$, and the uninformed dealers believe that $E[\tilde{p}_s \mid \tilde{p}_f] = \lambda\tilde{p}_f$ where λ is a constant. Utility maximisation (Part 2 of the definition) for risk neutral dealers implies that the informed dealers will want to buy or sell an unlimited amount unless $E[\tilde{p}_s \mid \tilde{I}, \tilde{p}_f] = \tilde{p}_f(1 + r)$, and the uninformed dealers will want to buy or sell an unlimited amount unless $E[\tilde{p}_s \mid \tilde{p}_f] = \tilde{p}_f(1 + r)$. Thus market clearing (Part 3 of the definition) implies that

$$E[\tilde{p}_s \mid \tilde{I}, \tilde{p}_f] = \tilde{I} = \tilde{p}_f(1 + r)$$

and

$$E[\tilde{p}_s \mid \tilde{p}_f] = \lambda\tilde{p}_f = \tilde{p}_f(1 + r).$$

This is impossible unless $\lambda = 1 + r$, and $\tilde{p}_f = \tilde{I}/(1 + r)$. It remains to check that Part 4 of the definition holds. If $\tilde{p}_f = \tilde{I}/(1 + r)$ knowing $\tilde{p}_f$ tells the informed dealers nothing about $\tilde{I}$ and $\tilde{p}_s$ which they did not know already from observing $\tilde{I}$ directly. As $\tilde{p}_s = \tilde{I} + \tilde{e}$, the correct conditional expectation for the informed dealers is $E[\tilde{p}_s \mid \tilde{I}] = E[\tilde{p}_s \mid \tilde{I}, \tilde{p}_f] = \tilde{I}$. The uninformed dealers observe $\tilde{p}_f = \tilde{I}/(1 + r)$, so can infer $\tilde{I}$ from $\tilde{p}_f$, knowing that $E[\tilde{p}_s \mid \tilde{I}] = \tilde{I}$, their correct conditional expectation is $E[\tilde{p}_s \mid \tilde{I}] = E[\tilde{p}_s \mid \tilde{p}_f] = \tilde{I} = (1 + r)\tilde{p}_f$, which is the form assumed with $\lambda = 1 + r$. This is a rational expectations equilibrium.

This is a very striking result, indicating that the market is completely efficient as a transmitter of information from the informed to the uninformed. Much of the recent theoretical work on asset markets has been concerned with investigating the circumstances under which a rational expectations equilibrium exists, and is informationally efficient.

This example has a number of peculiar features. The assumption of risk neutrality is special, and I have argued that even with risk neutrality the market may not be perfectly arbitraged. In equilibrium neither farmers nor speculators have any reason to trade futures. The expected profits from trade are always zero. It seems possible that the futures market will die away. But without a futures market the informational differences will persist, so there will be a motive for trade. These peculiarities stem from the risk neutrality assumption.

8. Rational expectations equilibrium under risk aversion

I will now introduce risk aversion into the model. This can generate considerable mathematical complexities, which I will minimise by assuming

172   RATIONAL EXPECTATIONS, INFORMATION AND ASSET MARKETS

that both farmers and speculators have utility functions of the form

$$U_i(\tilde{W}) = -e^{-k_i\tilde{W}} \equiv -\exp(-k_i\tilde{W})$$

where k_i is a positive constant. I will use the second form of notation, which avoids the need for superscripts. Remember that 'exp' is an abbreviation for 'exponential' and not for 'expectation'.

This utility function is widely used and has some attractive properties. Its first derivative is positive ($U' > 0$) implying that utility is increasing in wealth. The second derivative is negative ($U'' < 0$) implying risk aversion. The constant $k_i = -U''/U'$ is the coefficient of absolute risk aversion, higher values of k_i imply greater risk aversion. Above all there is the very useful result that if $\tilde{W}$ is normal with mean $E\tilde{W}$ and variance var $\tilde{W}$

$$E\{-\exp(-k\tilde{W})\} = -\exp(-k[E\tilde{W} - \tfrac{1}{2}k \text{ var } \tilde{W}]). \tag{8.1}$$

This result implies that the expected utility maximising portfolio is one that maximises $E\tilde{W} - \tfrac{1}{2}k$ var $\tilde{W}$. As I will demonstrate this makes for a very tractable model of asset demand, which is linear in expected asset return and prices. The major unattractive feature of the utility function, which I will also demonstrate is that asset demand is independent of wealth.[2]

I will now use (8.1) to result to analyse the behaviour of the spot and futures market model under risk aversion. The first step in defining and calculating the rational expectations equilibrium is a description of the information and beliefs. The first case I will look at is where dealers have no private information, each farmer and speculator has the same belief that

$$\tilde{p}_s \sim N(\mu, \sigma^2). \tag{8.2}$$

Later I will look at a version of the model where each agent has the same piece of information, and then at versions with diverse private information. Once the mathematics has been done for the first case the others follow very simply.

Equation (8.2) gives the beliefs described in Part 1 of the definitions of a rational expectations equilibrium. I will use this to derive the utility maximising speculators' demand for futures, and the farmers' demand for futures and spot supply (Part 2 of the definition). I will then make an assumption about spot demand which enables me to write down market clearing conditions for the spot and futures markets (Part 3 of the definition). These conditions will generate a 'correct distribution' for the spot price which will depend upon the parameters of the model, including μ and σ^2. I will show that there are values of μ and σ^2 which generate correct beliefs, (Part 4 of the definition), thus deriving the rational expectations equilibrium.

---

[2] $E(\exp(-k\tilde{W})$ is the moment generating function of the random variable $\tilde{W}$, an object which mathematicians find interesting. The result is proved in most texts on probability, e.g. Meyer (1970).

There are n dealers, m farmers and $n-m$ speculators. Farmers are indexed by $i = 1, 2 \ldots m$, and speculators by $i = m + 1, \ldots n$.

Speculators

Speculator i has a utility function $-\exp[-k_i \tilde{W}_i]$. If he buys x_i futures at price p_f, sells them on the spot market at price $\tilde{p}_s$, gets interest r on a safe asset, and has initial wealth W_{i0}, his final wealth $\tilde{W}_i$ is from (3.2) a random variable

$$\tilde{W}_i = (\tilde{p}_s - p_f(1+r))x_i + W_{i0}(1+r).$$

As speculators believe that $\tilde{p}_s \sim N(\mu, \sigma^2)$, they believe that $\tilde{W}_i$ is normal, and

$$E\tilde{W}_i = (\mu - p_f(1+r))x_i + W_{i0}(1+r)$$
$$\text{var } \tilde{W}_i = \sigma^2 x_i^2.$$

From (8.1) the speculator will choose x_i to maximise

$$E\tilde{W}_i - \tfrac{1}{2}k_i \text{ var } \tilde{W}_i = (\mu - p_f(1+r))x_i + W_{i0}(1+r) - \tfrac{1}{2}k_i\sigma^2 x_i^2.$$

Thus

$$x_i = \frac{1}{k_i\sigma^2}(\mu - p_f(1+r)) \qquad (i = 1,\ldots n). \tag{8.3}$$

The speculator buys futures if $\mu > p_f(1+r)$, there is a positive expected profit to be made on holding futures, and sells futures if $\mu < p_f(1+r)$, there is an expected loss to be made on holding futures. His trades are inversely proportional to σ^2, the variance of the spot price, and to k_i, which measures risk aversion. Note that x_i does not depend on initial wealth W_{i0}, due to the special utility function for which the coefficient of absolute risk aversion $k_i = -U''/U'$ does not depend on wealth.

Farmers

The speculators choose to take on risk by entering the futures market. If the farmers' output is certain they can entirely avoid risk by hedging; selling their entire output on the futures market. If they sell more or less than this they are assuming risk which they could avoid, in pursuit of profits, effectively acting as speculators. If y_i is farmer i's output, and z_i his future sales, $x_i = y_i - z_i$ can be thought of as speculative purchases of futures. The farmer's wealth is from (3.1) a random variable

$$\tilde{W}_i = (p_f y_i - C(y_i))(1+r) + (\tilde{p}_s - p_f(1+r))x_i + W_{i0}(1+r).$$

The first term is profits from production if all output is sold on the futures market. The second term is profits from speculation. The third term is the future value of initial wealth. As he believes that $\tilde{p}_s \sim N(\mu, \sigma)$ he believes

174   RATIONAL EXPECTATIONS, INFORMATION AND ASSET MARKETS

that $\tilde{W}_i$ is normal, with mean and variance

$$E\tilde{W}_i = (p_f y_i - C(y_i))(1+r) + (\mu - p_f(1+r))x_i + W_{i0}(1+r)$$
$$\text{var } \tilde{W}_i = \sigma^2 x_i^2.$$

If the farmer has a utility function $-\exp(-k_i\tilde{W}_i)$ from (8.1) he chooses (x_i, y_i) to maximise

$$E\tilde{W}_i - \tfrac{1}{2}k_i \text{ var } \tilde{W}_i = (p_f y_i - C(y_i))(1+r) + (\mu - p_f(1+r))x_i + W_{i0}(1+r)$$
$$- \tfrac{1}{2}\sigma_i^2 x_i^2.$$

I will assume that the farmer's costs are

$$C(y_i) = \tfrac{1}{2}cy_i^2$$

where c is a positive constant. Thus the farmer will maximise

$$(p_f y_i - \tfrac{1}{2}cy_i^2)(1+r) + (\mu - p_f(1+r))x_i + W_{i0}(1+r) - \tfrac{1}{2}\sigma_i^2 x_i^2.$$

The first order condition for y_i implies that $p_f = cy_i$. The futures price determines the level of output, which is set so that the futures price is equal to the marginal cost of production. This result is valid for arbitrary utility functions. In this case it implies that

$$y_i = c^{-1}p_f \qquad (i = 1,\dots m). \tag{8.4}$$

The first order condition for x_i implies that

$$x_i = \frac{1}{k_i\sigma^2}(\mu - p_f(1+r)) \qquad (i = 1, \dots m). \tag{8.5}$$

The farmer's speculative demand for futures is precisely the same as if he were a pure speculator. This result is not valid if output is uncertain, but is convenient. (See Bray (1981).)

The futures market

The futures market clearing condition is

$$\sum_{i=1}^{n} x_i = \sum_{i=1}^{m} y_i. \tag{8.6}$$

The sum of speculative demand for futures from farmers and speculators is equal to farmers' output, sold forward to hedge against uncertainty. Using the expressions for x_i, and y_i, (8.3)–(8.5)

$$\sum_{i=1}^{n} \frac{1}{k_i\sigma^2}(\mu - p_f(1+r)) = \sum_{i=1}^{m} c^{-1}p_f = mc^{-1}p_f. \tag{8.7}$$

Thus the futures price depends upon the distribution of the spot price μ and σ^2. However the spot price depends upon the physical quantity produced, $\sum_{i=1}^{m} y_i$, which in turn depends upon the futures price. The equilibria of the spot and futures markets have to be considered simultaneously.

The spot market

    Assumption: Spot demand is

$$D(\bar{p}_s) = \bar{a} - b\bar{p}_s$$

where $\bar{a}$ is a normal random variable with mean $E\bar{a}$ and variance var $\bar{a}$, and b a positive constant.

Thus spot demand is subject to random variation as $\bar{a}$ varies. Spot supply comes from two sources. Farmers sell any output which they have not already sold on the futures market, so farmer i sells spot $x_i = y_i - z_i$. Speculator i sells spot everything which he bought on the futures market from farmers, x_i. Total spot sales $\sum_{i=1}^{n} x_i$ are thus equal to farmers' total output $\sum_{i=1}^{m} y_i$. (This is implied by the futures market clearing condition (8.6)). As (8.4) implies that $\sum_{i=1}^{m} y_i = mc^{-1}p_f$ the spot market clears when

$$\bar{a} - b\bar{p}_s = mc^{-1}p_f. \tag{8.8}$$

Rational expectations equilibrium

    Eliminating p_f from the market clearing conditions (8.7) and (8.8) implies that

$$\bar{p}_s = b^{-1}\bar{a} - b^{-1}mc^{-1}\phi^{-1}\mu \tag{8.9}$$

where

$$\phi = 1 + r + mc^{-1}\sigma^2 \left[\sum_{i=1}^{n} k_i^{-1} \right]^{-1}. \tag{8.10}$$

As $\bar{a}$ is normal and all the other terms on the right hand side of (8.9) are constants $\bar{p}_s$ is normal. The dealers' beliefs about the form of the distribution of $\bar{p}_s$ is correct. From (8.2) they believe that $\bar{p}_s \sim N(\mu, \sigma^2)$. Equation (8.9) implies that

$$E\bar{p}_s = b^{-1}E\bar{a} - b^{-1}mc^{-1}\phi^{-1}\mu \tag{8.11}$$

and

$$\text{var } \bar{p}_s = b^{-2} \text{ var } \bar{a}. \tag{8.12}$$

Beliefs about the mean and variance are correct if $E\bar{p}_s = \mu$ and var $\bar{p}_s = \sigma^2$. In this case (8.11) and (8.12) imply that the beliefs are correct if and only

$$\sigma^2 = b^{-2} \text{ var } \bar{a} \tag{8.13}$$

$$E\bar{p}_s = \theta^{-1}\phi E\bar{a} \tag{8.14}$$

where substituting for σ^2 in (8.10)

$$\phi = 1 + r + mc^{-1}b^{-2} \text{ var } \bar{a} \left[\sum_{i=1}^{n} k_i^{-1} \right]^{-1} \tag{8.15}$$

176   RATIONAL EXPECTATIONS, INFORMATION AND ASSET MARKETS

and

$$\theta = b\phi + mc^{-1}. \tag{8.16}$$

Thus from (8.9), (8.14) and (8.16) as $\mu = E\bar{p}_s$

$$\bar{p}_s = \theta^{-1}\phi E\bar{a} + b^{-1}(\bar{a} - E\bar{a}) \tag{8.17}$$

and from (8.8) and (8.17)

$$p_f = \theta^{-1}E\bar{a}. \tag{8.18}$$

If the futures price is given by (8.18) and dealers' beliefs about the expected spot price by (8.13)–(8.16) the futures market clears. The futures price determines output. Output determines the distribution of the spot price. At this futures price, and this expected spot price, dealers' beliefs about the distribution of the spot price are correct. This is a rational expectations equilibrium.

Introducing risk aversion changes the model in several respects. If all dealers are risk neutral arbitrage implies that $(1+r)p_f = E\bar{p}_s$: the expected return on risky futures is the same as the return on the safe asset. Dealers are indifferent about how many futures they hold, and have no positive reason to trade on the futures market. In this model with risk aversion (8.14) and (8.18) imply that $\phi p_f = E\bar{p}_s$, and from (8.15) $\phi > 1 + r$. The risk premium $\phi - (1 + r)$ is an increasing function of the variance of the spot price b^{-2} var $\bar{a}$, and each dealer's risk aversion parameter k_i. Speculators are willing to take on some of the farmer's risk in order to earn a positive expected return. This model in fact overemphasizes the riskiness of speculative portfolios, because it considers only a single risky asset. In practice speculators can diminish, but not eliminate risk by holding a portfolio of several risky assets whose returns are imperfectly correlated.

Both speculators and farmers wish to hold definite amounts of futures, and the market will trade actively. As $\mu = E\bar{p}_s > p_f(1+r)$ (8.3) and (8.5) imply that demand from speculators, and the speculative element of farmer's demand will be strictly positive in equilibrium. Farmers as a whole must be net sellers of futures, to meet the demand from speculators. But an unusually risk tolerant farmer might be a net purchaser.

9. Rational expectations equilibrium and information

In the model which I have just analysed the spot price is stochastic and differs from year to year, but the futures price is a constant, a function of the parameters of the model, including the mean and variance of $\bar{a}$, the stochastic intercept in the spot demand function, which is by assumption the source of all the uncertainty.

I am now going to modify the model by assuming that dealers have information about $\bar{a}$ in January when the futures market operates. I will look at three different information structures of increasing complexity, asking in each case how well the futures price reflects the information.

Example 1. Symmetric Information
  Assume that

$$\tilde{a} = \tilde{I} + \tilde{e} \tag{9.1}$$

$\tilde{I}$ and $\tilde{e}$ are independent scalar normal random variables, $E\tilde{I} = E\tilde{a}$, and $E\tilde{e} = 0$. As the sum of normal variables is normal $\tilde{a}$ is still normal, var $\tilde{a} =$ var $\tilde{I} +$ var $\tilde{e}$. Assume also that all dealers, farmers and speculators observe $\tilde{I}$ each January. Conditional upon the information $\tilde{I}$ each dealer believes correctly that $\tilde{a}$ is a normal random variable whose mean $E(\tilde{a} \mid \tilde{I}) = \tilde{I}$ is random, whereas var $(\tilde{a} \mid \tilde{I}) =$ var $\tilde{e}$ is not random. The model is unchanged, apart from the fact that beliefs about the mean of $\tilde{a}$ change from year to year. The rational expectations equilibrium can be calculated as before. Paralleling (8.12) and (8.14)–(8.18)

$$\text{var}\,[\tilde{p}_s \mid \tilde{I}] = b^{-2}\,\text{var}\,[\tilde{a} \mid \tilde{I}] = b^{-2}\,\text{var}\,\tilde{e} \tag{9.2}$$

$$E[\tilde{p}_s \mid \tilde{I}] = \theta^{*-1}\phi^* E(\tilde{a} \mid \tilde{I}) = \theta^{*-1}\phi^*\tilde{I} \tag{9.3}$$

where

$$\phi^* = 1 + r + mc^{-1}b^{-2}\,\text{var}\,[\tilde{a} \mid \tilde{I}]\left[\sum_{i=1}^{n} k_i^{-1}\right]^{-1} \tag{9.4}$$

$$\theta^* = b\phi^* + mc^{-1} \tag{9.5}$$

$$\tilde{p}_s = \theta^{*-1}\phi^* E(\tilde{a} \mid \tilde{I}) + b^{-1}[\tilde{a} - E(\tilde{a} \mid \tilde{I})] = \theta^{*-1}\phi^*\tilde{I} + b^{-1}\tilde{e} \tag{9.6}$$

and

$$\tilde{p}_f = \theta^{*-1} E(\tilde{a} \mid \tilde{I}) = \theta^{*-1}\tilde{I}. \tag{9.7}$$

These equations differ from (8.12) and (8.14)–(8.18) in two ways. Firstly the terms relating to the unconditional distribution of $\tilde{a}$, $E\tilde{a}$ and var $\tilde{a}$ in the previous equations, have been replaced by the corresponding terms for the distribution conditional upon the information $E(\tilde{a} \mid \tilde{I})$ and var $(\tilde{a} \mid \tilde{I})$. Secondly the futures price $\tilde{p}_f$ is now a random variable rather than a constant.

The expressions θ^* and ϕ^* are not random because var $(\tilde{a} \mid \tilde{I})$ is not random. Thus provided the numerical values of θ^* and ϕ^* are known it is possible to infer $\tilde{I}$, and $E[\tilde{p}_s \mid \tilde{I}]$ from $\tilde{p}_f$.

$$E[\tilde{p}_s \mid \tilde{I}] = \theta^{*-1}\phi^*\tilde{I} = \phi^*\tilde{p}_f$$

and so the conditional distribution of $\tilde{p}_s$ given $\tilde{p}_f$ is normal

$$E[\tilde{p}_s \mid \tilde{p}_f] = E[\tilde{p}_s \mid \tilde{I}] = \phi^*\tilde{p}_f \tag{9.8}$$

and

$$\text{var}\,[\tilde{p}_s \mid \tilde{p}_f] = \text{var}\,[\tilde{p}_s \mid \tilde{I}] = b^{-2}\,\text{var}\,(\tilde{a} \mid \tilde{I}) = b^{-2}\,\text{var}\,\tilde{e}. \tag{9.9}$$

178 RATIONAL EXPECTATIONS, INFORMATION AND ASSET MARKETS

Anyone knowing the numerical value of ϕ^* would form the same conditional expectation of the spot price $\bar{p}_s$ from the futures price $\bar{p}_f$, as if he knew the information $\bar{I}$. This observation is perhaps not very interesting in the context of this example, in which, by assumption all the dealers know $\bar{I}$, but it is helpful in analysing the next two examples.

Example 2

As in the previous example

$$\bar{a} = \bar{I} + \bar{e}$$

$\bar{I}$ and $\bar{e}$ are independent, and normal. $E\bar{a} = E\bar{I}$, and $E\bar{e} = 0$. However now only some of the dealers observe $\bar{I}$. The others have no private information. In the rational expectations equilibrium the uninformed dealers will infer what information they can about the spot price from the futures price. If the futures price is completely efficient as an information transmitter the uninformed traders will trade as if they had the information.

This observation suggested to Radner (1979) and Grossman (1978) that models with asymmetric information could be analysed by considering the corresponding model in which the information is pooled and made available to all dealers, (called a full communications equilibrium by Radner, an artificial economy by Grossman). If the futures price is a perfect transmitter of information in the rational expectations equilibrium of the original model, dealers' beliefs about the distribution of the spot price given the futures price in the original model will be the same as if they had the information available to them in the full communications equilibrium. Thus supply, demand and prices, will be the same in the full communications equilibrium as in the rational expectations equilibrium of the original model.

Observing this point Radner and Grossman argued that the first step in analyzing this type of model should be to examine the full communications equilibrium. This is much easier than looking at the rational expectations equilibrium with asymmetric information directly, because if dealers know all the information which could possibly be reflected in prices already they have no motive for using prices as information, so prices do not affect beliefs in the full communications equilibrium. Having characterised prices in the full communications equilibrium ask what dealers' correct beliefs would be conditional on the full communications equilibrium prices. In particular ask whether the beliefs are the same as they would be if dealers know all the information. If they are it has been established that a rational expectations equilibrium exists in which beliefs, prices, supply and demand are the same as in the full communications equilibrium.

Consider the four part definition of a rational expectations equilibrium in an asset market with asymmetric information. The first part refers to beliefs, the second to utility maximisation given beliefs, the third to market clearing, and the fourth to correct beliefs. If the full communications equilibrium prices allow dealers to form precisely the same beliefs as if they had all the information, utility maximisation leads to the same trades as in the full communications equilibrium. As the trades are the same the market clears at the same prices. The beliefs generating the trades are correct. This is a rational expectations equilibrium. This argument breaks down if beliefs given the full communications equilibrium prices are not the same as beliefs given all the information. In this case if a rational expectations equilibrium exists prices transmit some, but not all information.

In this example the full communications equilibrium is one in which all dealers observe $\tilde{I}$. This is precisely example 1 where I have already argued that conditioning on the futures price alone leads dealers to the same beliefs as if they knew the information $\tilde{I}$. Thus the full communications equilibrium prices of example 1 are also rational expectations equilibrium prices for example 2. In this rational expectations equilibrium the futures price transmits all the information from the informed to the uninformed dealers.

Example 3. Diverse Information

I now generalise the information structure considerably. Suppose that each dealer observes a random information variable $\tilde{I}_i$. This may be a scalar or a vector, it may be constant, in which case it is effectively no information. The only restriction is that $(\tilde{a}, \tilde{I}_1, \tilde{I}_2 \dots \tilde{I}_n)$ has a joint normal distribution. It seems an impossible task to ask a single price to aggregate all this diverse information, so that in the rational expectations equilibrium, dealers can trade as if they had all the information. Yet this is in fact so, owing to the following properties of normal random variables.

Lemma: Conditional distributions of normal random variables

If $[\tilde{a}, \tilde{I}_1, \tilde{I}_2 \dots \tilde{I}_n]$ has a joint normal distribution,

$$\tilde{I} = E[\tilde{a} \mid \tilde{I}_1, \tilde{I}_2 \dots \tilde{I}_n]$$

and

$$\tilde{e} = \tilde{a} - \tilde{I}$$

then $\tilde{I}$ and $\tilde{e}$ are independent normal random variables, $E\tilde{a} = E\tilde{I}$, $E\tilde{e} = 0$ var $\tilde{a} =$ var $\tilde{I} +$ var $\tilde{e}$. The conditional distribution of $\tilde{a}$ given $\tilde{I}$ is the same as the conditional distribution of $\tilde{a}$ given $\tilde{I}_1, \tilde{I}_2 \dots \tilde{I}_n$. Both conditional distributions are normal, with mean

$$E(\tilde{a} \mid \tilde{I}) = E[\tilde{a} \mid \tilde{I}_1, \tilde{I}_2 \dots \tilde{I}_n] = \tilde{I}$$

and variance

$$\text{var}\,(\tilde{a} \mid \tilde{I}) = \text{var}\,[\tilde{a} \mid \tilde{I}_1, \tilde{I}_2 \dots \tilde{I}_n] = \text{var}\,\tilde{a} - \text{var}\,\tilde{I} = \text{var}\,\tilde{e}.$$

Proof: See appendix.

This result shows that for the purposes of forming beliefs about $\tilde{a}$ knowing $\tilde{I} = E[\tilde{a} \mid \tilde{I}_1, \tilde{I}_2 \dots \tilde{I}_n]$ gives the same information as knowing $\tilde{I}_1, \tilde{I}_2 \dots \tilde{I}_n$. The conditional mean $\tilde{I}$, a single number, aggregates perfectly all the diverse information. (It is a sufficient statistic for the information.)

This result can be used to compare two full communications equilibria, for the spot and futures market model. In the first equilibrium dealers observe the vector of random variables $\tilde{I}_1, \tilde{I}_2 \dots \tilde{I}_n$. In the second they observe $\tilde{I} = E[\tilde{a} \mid \tilde{I}_1, \tilde{I}_2 \dots \tilde{I}_n]$. In both equilibria the conditional distribution of $\tilde{a}$ is normal, with the same mean and variance. Thus the equilibrium prices are the same. The equilibrium in which all dealers observe $\tilde{I}$ is the equilibrium of the first model studied in this section. The prices in both equilibria are given by (9.2)–(9.7). In these equilibria, from (9.7)

$$\tilde{p}_f = \theta^{*-1}\tilde{I} = \theta^{*-1}E[\tilde{a} \mid \tilde{I}_1, \tilde{I}_2 \dots \tilde{I}_n] \tag{9.10}$$

and from (9.2) and (9.3)

$$\text{var}\,[\tilde{p}_s \mid \tilde{p}_f] = \text{var}\,[\tilde{p}_s \mid \tilde{I}] = \text{var}\,[\tilde{p}_s \mid \tilde{I}_1, \tilde{I}_2 \dots \tilde{I}_n] = b^{-2}\,\text{var}\,\tilde{e} \tag{9.11}$$

$$E[\tilde{p}_s \mid \tilde{p}_f] = E[\tilde{p}_s \mid \tilde{I}] = E[\tilde{p}_s \mid \tilde{I}_1, \tilde{I}_2 \dots \tilde{I}_n] = \theta^{*-1}\phi^*\tilde{I} = \phi^*\tilde{p}_f \tag{9.12}$$

and

$$\tilde{p}_f = \theta^{*-1}\tilde{I} = \theta^{*-1}E[\tilde{a} \mid \tilde{I}_1, \tilde{I}_2 \dots \tilde{I}_n]. \tag{9.13}$$

Conditioning only on the futures price dealers form the same beliefs about the spot price as they would if they know either $\tilde{I} = E[\tilde{a} \mid \tilde{I}_1, \tilde{I}_2 \dots \tilde{I}_n]$, or the entire information vector $\tilde{I}_1, \tilde{I}_2 \dots \tilde{I}_n$. By the same argument as before these must also be rational expectations equilibrium prices for the model in which dealer i observes information $\tilde{I}_i$.

This is a much stronger result than before. It argues that a market price can not only transmit a single piece of information from one set of dealers to another, but also aggregate a large and diverse set of information perfectly.

10. The robustness of the informational efficiency result

In the previous Section I showed that in a simple futures market model the market price can aggregate diverse information so efficiently that each dealer's beliefs about the return on holding an asset (the spot price) given only its price are the same as if he had access to all the information to the market. He finds his own private information completely redundant.

This surprising result is not limited to futures markets. From a speculator's point of view a futures contract is one of many financial assets, others include shares and bonds issued by firms, and government securities. The original version of this model (Grossman 1976) considered a stock market. The stock lasts for one period, and pays a random gross return $\tilde{R}$. An investor with wealth W_{i0} who buys x_i units of the stock at price p and invests $W_{i0} - px_i$ in a safe asset paying interest r, has final wealth

$$\tilde{W}_i = (\tilde{R} - p(1+r))x_i + W_{i0}(1+r).$$

The gross return $\tilde{R}$ pays a role precisely analogous to the spot price in the futures market. If $\tilde{R}$ is normally distributed and the investor has an exponential utility function $-\exp\,[-k_i\tilde{W}_i]$ the argument used to derive the speculators demand for futures yields the investors demand for the stock

$$x_i = \frac{1}{k_i \, \text{var} \, \tilde{R}} (E\tilde{R} - p(1+r)).$$ (10.1)

If there are n investors and a fixed supply of the stock S, market clearing requires that

$$\sum_{i=1}^{n} \frac{1}{k_i \, \text{var} \, \tilde{R}} (E\tilde{R} - p(1+r)) = S.$$ (10.2)

The stock and futures markets models are mathematically very similar, apart from the fact that the supply of the asset in the stock market is taken as exogenous.

Now suppose the investors have diverse information, $\tilde{I}_1, \tilde{I}_2 \ldots \tilde{I}_n$, and $[\tilde{R}, \tilde{I}_1, \tilde{I}_2 \ldots \tilde{I}_n]$ is joint normal. Experience with the futures market model suggests looking at the full communications equilibria, in which market clearing implies that

$$\sum_{i=1}^{n} \frac{1}{k_i \sigma^2} [E[\tilde{R} \mid \tilde{I}_1, \tilde{I}_2 \ldots \tilde{I}_n] - (1+r)\bar{p}] = S$$

where $\sigma^2 = \text{var}\,[\tilde{R} \mid \tilde{I}_1, \tilde{I}_2 \ldots \tilde{I}_n]$ so

$$E[\tilde{R} \mid \tilde{I}_1, \tilde{I}_2 \ldots \tilde{I}_n] = \sigma^2 \left[\sum_{i=1}^{n} k_i^{-1} \right]^{-1} S + (1+r)\bar{p}.$$ (10.3)

Anyone knowing the numerical value of $\sigma^2 \left[\sum_{i=1}^{n} k_i^{-1} \right]^{-1} S$ and $(1+r)$ could infer $E[\tilde{R} \mid \tilde{I}_1, \tilde{I}_2 \ldots \tilde{I}_n]$ from the price $\bar{p}$, and would form the same beliefs about $\tilde{R}$ as if he knew $\tilde{I}_1, \tilde{I}_2 \ldots \tilde{I}_n$. By a now familiar argument this implies that the full communications equilibrium is also a rational expectations equilibrium; the rational expectations equilibrium price aggregates the information perfectly.

Grossman wrote the paper embodying this result before he had the idea of using an artificial economy, or full communications equilibrium, to analyse the model. He had to use more complex arguments and was not able to prove such a general result. The paper was important firstly because if was the first satisfactory asset market model embracing risk aversion and asymmetric information, and secondly because Grossman pointed out a most important paradox. In Grossman's model, just as in the spot and futures market model, knowing the asset price renders dealers private information redundant. If this information is costly no dealer has any incentive to gather the information, particularly if he knows that another dealer is using the same information. Yet if no-one gathers the information it cannot be reflected in the price, which generates incentives to gather the information.

Grossman and Stiglitz (1980) resolve this paradox by modifying the model

182   RATIONAL EXPECTATIONS, INFORMATION AND ASSET MARKETS

slightly. Suppose now that the asset supply is a normal random variable $\tilde{S}$. The relationship between the full communications equilibrium price $\tilde{p}$, $E[\tilde{R} \mid \tilde{I}_1, \tilde{I}_2 \dots \tilde{I}_n]$ and $\tilde{S}$ is given by (10.3), modified only by replacing the constant S by random $\tilde{S}$

$$E[\tilde{R} \mid \tilde{I}_1, \tilde{I}_2 \dots \tilde{I}_n] = \sigma^2 \left[\sum_{i=1}^{n} k_i^{-1} \right]^{-1} \tilde{S} + (1+r)\tilde{p}. \qquad (10.4)$$

Even if the numerical values of $\sigma^2 \left[\sum_{i=1}^{n} k_i^{-1} \right]^{-1}$ and $(1+r)$ are known it is impossible to infer $E[\tilde{R} \mid \tilde{I}_1, \tilde{I}_2 \dots \tilde{I}_n]$ from $\tilde{p}$ because $\tilde{S}$ is different each time the market operates. Conditioning on $\tilde{p}$ does not yield the same information as conditioning on $\tilde{I}_1, \tilde{I}_2 \dots \tilde{I}_n$. The full communications equilibrium is not a rational expectations equilibrium. (This is also true in the spot and futures market model, if farmers' output is uncertain, and dealers have information about both spot demand and output (Bray, 1981).)

Grossman and Stiglitz calculate the rational expectations equilibrium for a version of the stock market model in which there are two groups of dealers. The informed dealers all observe the same information, on which they base their expectations. The uninformed dealers form their expectations on the basis of the price. The informativeness of the price increases as the proportion of informed dealers increases. In the absence of information costs the informed dealers have higher expected utility than the uninformed, because they are less uncertain of the asset return (its conditional variance is lower for the informed than the uninformed). If information is costly informed dealers may be better or worse off. If the proportion of informed dealers is large and the price conveys much of the information to the uninformed dealers they are likely to be worse off. If the proportion of informed dealers is small and the price conveys little information to the uninformed they are likely to be better off. Grossman and Stiglitz show that for each level of information costs there is an equilibrium proportion of informed dealers, so that the benefits of the information just balance the costs, and dealers are indifferent between being informed and uninformed. They derive a variety of interesting comparative static results from this model.

11. Existence of rational expectations equilibrium

Expectations play a crucial role in all the models which I have presented, as in many others. Whenever I have needed to close models by specifying expectations I have followed standard practice in postulating rational expectations. In each case I have been able to show that a rational expectations equilibrium exists by solving explicitly for the equilibrium. This is not always possible. Indeed in some examples, such as the one which follows it can be shown that there is no set of prices and beliefs which satisfy Parts 3 and 4 of the definition. There is no rational expectations equilibrium.

The example is similar in form to that of Kreps (1977). It is a somewhat modified version of the spot and futures market model. For mathematical simplicity assume that there is one farmer and one speculator. Each maximises the expectation of a utility function $-\exp(-\tilde{W})$. The speculator believes the spot price $\tilde{p}_s \sim N(\mu, \sigma^2)$. The interest rate $r = 0$. Arguing as before the speculators' excess demand for futures is

$$x_s = \frac{1}{\sigma^2}(\mu - p_f). \tag{11.1}$$

The farmer has a cost function for output $C(y) = sy + \frac{1}{2}y^2$. He also believes that $\tilde{p}_s \sim N(\mu, \sigma^2)$. Utility maximisation for the farmer implies that he sets output so $C'(y) = p_f$ or

$$y = p_f - s. \tag{11.2}$$

He hedges by selling y on the futures market, and in addition speculates by buying futures

$$x_f = \frac{1}{\sigma^2}(\mu - p_f). \tag{11.3}$$

Futures market clearing implies that $x_s + x_f = y$, or from (11.1)–(11.3)

$$\frac{2}{\sigma^2}(\mu - p_f) = p_f - s. \tag{11.4}$$

Spot demand is

$$D(p_s) = \tilde{a} - \tilde{p}_s$$

where $\tilde{a}$ is a normal random variable, and var $\tilde{a} = 1$. Spot market clearing implies that $D(\tilde{p}_s) = y$, that is

$$\tilde{a} - \tilde{p}_s = p_f - s. \tag{11.5}$$

Equation (11.5) implies that

$$E\tilde{p}_s = E\tilde{a} - p_f + s \tag{11.6}$$

and

$$\text{var } \tilde{p}_s = \text{var } \tilde{a} = 1. \tag{11.7}$$

If the farmer and speculator are to form rational expectations $\mu = E\tilde{p}_s = E\tilde{a} - p_f + s$, and $\sigma^2 = \text{var } \tilde{p}_s = 1$. The futures market clearing condition (11.4) becomes

$$2(E\tilde{a} - p_f + s - p_f] = p_f - s$$

so

$$p_f = \tfrac{1}{5}(2E\tilde{a} + 3s). \tag{11.8}$$

Spot market clearing and rational expectations imply (11.6), which with

184   RATIONAL EXPECTATIONS, INFORMATION AND ASSET MARKETS

(11.8) implies that

$$E\bar{p}_s = \tfrac{1}{5}(3E\bar{a} + 2s).\qquad(11.9)$$

So far I have had no difficulty in calculating the rational expectations equilibrium, but introducing asymmetric information can cause complications. Suppose that there are only two sorts of weather, good and bad. The farmer observes the weather; the speculator does not. If the weather is good $E\bar{a} = \tfrac{5}{4}$ and $s = \tfrac{1}{6}$. If it is bad $E\bar{a} = 1$ and $s = \tfrac{1}{3}$.

There are only two possibilities, either the futures price is different in different weather or it is not. If the futures price is different the speculator can infer the weather from the price. Trades and prices will be the same as if both farmer and speculator knew the weather. In this case in good weather $E\bar{a} = \tfrac{5}{4}$, $s = \tfrac{1}{6}$, from (11.8) $p_f = \tfrac{2}{3}$ and from (11.9) $E\bar{p}_s = \tfrac{49}{60}$. In bad weather $E\bar{a} = 1$, $s = \tfrac{1}{3}$, from (11.8) $p_f = \tfrac{2}{3}$, and from (11.9) $E\bar{p}_s = \tfrac{44}{60}$. Thus the futures price is the same in both weathers, contradicting the supposition that it was different.

The alternative supposition is that the futures price is the same whatever the weather, in which case the speculator's demand will be the same. If the farmer has rational expectations his excess demand for futures will be using (11.2), (11.3) and (11.6), and recalling that $\sigma^2 = 1$ and $\mu = E\bar{p}_s$,

$$x_f - y = (E\bar{p}_s - p_f) - (p_f - s) = E\bar{p}_s + s - 2p_f$$
$$= E\bar{a} + 2s - 3p_f.$$

In good weather $E\bar{a} + 2s = \tfrac{19}{12}$, in bad weather $E\bar{a} + 2s = \tfrac{5}{3}$. If p_f is independent of the weather the speculator's demand for futures is independent of the weather, but the farmer's is not. The futures market cannot clear at the same price in both weathers. This exhausts the possibilities. In this example the assumptions of market clearing and rational expectations are logically inconsistent. There is no rational expectations equilibrium.

In defining a rational expectations equilibrium for an asset market model in Section 3 I argued that the market clearing condition induces a mapping from the beliefs people hold to the correct beliefs. This is an almost universal feature of models with expectations, it crops up for example in equation (8.11) which gives the correct expected spot price $E\bar{p}_s$, as a function of the subjectively held expectation μ. A rational expectations equilibrium is a fixed point of this mapping. Fixed point theorems give conditions under which mappings have fixed points; notably continuity. The non-existence problems for rational expectations models with asymmetric information stem from discontinuities in the mapping, where a small change in prices can induce a large change in the information which can be inferred from them. In the example, if prices are identical in both weathers, the speculator cannot infer the weather, but if they are very slightly different he can.

Checking that an equilibrium exists is an essential preliminary to using a model; assuming that an equilibrium exists and arguing from there, can yield no valid conclusions if in fact no equilibrium exists. Knowing the circumstances under which a model has an equilibrium puts logical limits on the range of applicability.

Existence problems are attacked from two directions, existence theorems and non-existence examples. Existence theorems establish that under certain conditions, typically conditions on preferences, technology, and the structure of transactions and information, an equilibrium exists. For some special models equilibrium can be shown to exist by calculating the equilibrium, but in general the problem is attacked indirectly, often using fixed point theorems which establish that a set of equations has a solution, but not what the solution is. Non-existence examples show that in certain cases no equilibrium exists. These examples are helpful because they show certain conjectured general existence results cannot be valid; a claim that *all* models of a certain type have an equilibrium is wrong if a single such model has no equilibrium, just as a single black swan is enough to invalidate the claim that all swans are white.

The non-existence example which I demonstrated earlier is not robust; a small change in the parameters of the model would allow an equilibrium to exist, non-existence is a freak eventuality. Radner (1979) studies a much more general asset market model which shares two features with this example. In both models there are only a finite number of different possible information signals. In the example there are two, good weather or bad weather. In Radner's model there may be a large but finite number of different signals received by a finite number of individuals. The vector of joint signals can only take a finite number of different values. In Radner's model, as in my example, there may be no rational expectations equilibrium. Radner shows rigorously that equilibrium exists generically. Generic existence is defined precisely in the paper; the idea which it captures is that whilst equilibrium may fail to exist in some special cases, almost any perturbation of the model will restore existence. Radner's proof proceeds by considering the full communications equilibrium, in which dealers pool all their information signals before trading. The price vector in the full communications equilibrium $\bar{p}$ is a function of the joint signal $\bar{s}$, $\bar{p} = p(\bar{s})$. If the price vector is different whenever any element in the signal is different, the price reveals the signal, the full communications equilibrium is a rational expectations equilibrium, in which prices fully reveal the information.

The crucial question is whether the map from the signals into prices is invertible. There are a finite number, m, of signals, whereas prices can be any vector in R^{n+}, so there are an infinity (indeed a continuum) of different possible prices. Radner's result confirms the intuition that if the utility functions generating demand are reasonably well behaved, the map from signals to prices fails to be invertible only in special circumstances, in which case a small perturbation of the model restores invertibility.

The assumption that there are a finite number of different possible signals

186   RATIONAL EXPECTATIONS, INFORMATION AND ASSET MARKETS

plays a crucial role in this invertibility argument. If there are a continuum of different possible signals the argument may break down. Jordan and Radner (1982) devise an example with an informed and uninformed dealers and one relative price. The informed dealer observes a signal $\bar{s}$ in $[0, 1]$. Given the price, the informed dealer's demand changes with the signal, if there are two different signals $s_1 \neq s_2$, with $p(s_1) = p(s_2)$ the informed dealer's demand is different for the two signals, but the uninformed dealer who observes only the price has the same demand. The market cannot clear at the same price for both s_1 and s_2. On the other hand if the function is invertible the uninformed dealer can infer s from p, the prices are the same as in the full communications equilibrium. But Jordan and Radner show that the full communications equilibrium price function has the form shown in Fig. 2, and is not invertible. This is a robust example, changing the parameters of the model changes the price function a little, but does not make it invertible.

The importance of invertibility for the existence of rational expectations equilibria in which prices reveal all the information suggests that the relative dimensions of the signal space and the price space may be important. This is confirmed by Allen (1982) who shows that if the dimension of the signal space is less than the dimension of the price space a fully revealing rational expectations equilibrium exists generically. Jordan (1983) shows that if the dimension of the price space is higher than the dimension of the signal space rational expectations equilibrium exists, generically, but is not fully revealing.

The literature on fully revealing equilibria is concerned with equilibria in which dealers can infer the entire information signal from the prices. This is sufficient to enable them to form the same expectations as if they saw the signal. But it is not necessary; dealers want to know about a vector of asset returns $\tilde{R}$. If $\tilde{R}$ and the information $\tilde{I}$ are joint normal, knowing $E(\tilde{R} \mid \tilde{I})$ tells them as much as knowing $\tilde{I}$. The vector $E(\tilde{R} \mid \tilde{I})$ has the same

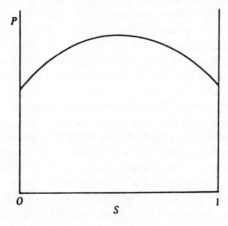

FIG. 2

dimension as $\bar{R}$, the number of risky assets. This may be much lower than the dimension of $\bar{I}$. Grossman (1978) uses this result to analyse a stock market model in which returns are normal, and dealers care only about the mean and variance of return. By applying the captial asset pricing model Grossman shows that provided the market portfolio is not a Giffen good dealers can infer $E(\bar{R} \mid \bar{I})$ from the information, and so a rational expectations equilibrium exists in which dealers trade as if they had all the information. Grossman also exploits the properties of normal random variables in his paper on futures markets (1977), showing how they can act to transmit information.

The existence of rational expectations equilibrium in asset markets is an attractive and challenging problem for mathematical economists. A more sophisticated discussion, and further references are in Radner (1982), which surveys the literature on 'Equilibrium Under Uncertainty', and by Jordan and Radner (1982) which introduces a symposium issue of the Journal of Economic Theory, on Rational Expectations in Microeconomic Models, which includes a number of related papers. More recent work on the matter includes Jordan (1982a, 1982b), Allen (1983), and Anderson and Sonnenschein (1985).

12. Evaluating the models

A model is a simplified, stylised description of certain aspects of the economy. It omits many details in order to concentrate on certain features and their interrelationships. One of the major objectives of modelling is often to show that the description is logically consistent by demonstrating that an equilibrium exists, an issue which I have discussed at some length. If a model is to be used as a basis for saying something about real economies logical consistency is essential; even grossly unrealistic models may be useful in establishing logical limits to rhetoric. But is is obviously desirable that a model be a correct, as well as a consistent, description.

Unfortunately there is no clear and universally applicable criterion for the correctness of models. Any model omits details, abstracts and simplifies. Reality is too complicated to be thought about in totality. Assumptions in economic models are most unlikely to be completely adequate descriptions of behaviour. The question to ask is whether they are plausible enough to generate implications which say something about the aspects of reality with which the model is concerned. This is inevitably a matter of judgement, and must often depend upon the use to which a model is being put.

The three major assumptions made in the financial market models which I described are that markets clear, that agents are price-takers and that they have rational expectations. These assumptions are very widely made; they are also central to the 'new-classical' macroeconomics (Begg 1982a). Market clearing and price-taking seem in general quite plausible for financial markets, where prices move readily, there is little evidence of sustained excess supply and demand, and a large number of traders.

188   RATIONAL EXPECTATIONS, INFORMATION AND ASSET MARKETS

The rational expectations hypothesis can be stated loosely, that people do not make systematic mistakes in forecasting; more precisely, people's subjective beliefs about probability distributions correspond to the objective probability distributions. Employing the rational expectations hypothesis imposes two logical requirements, that objective probability distributions exist, and that a rational expectations equilibrium exists. In constructing a model an economist creates the objective probability distributions, but these models can only be applied to situations where the distributions could in principle at least be derived from data. This requires that the structure and parameters of the economy are in some way constant through time. Rational expectations models describe long run stationary equilibria.

One important criticism of the rational expectations hypothesis is that it assumes that agents know too much. Consider the spot and futures market model with asymmetric information. In rational equilibrium the uninformed dealers believe correctly that the conditional distribution of the spot price given the futures price is normal, has conditional mean given by (9.8) $E[\bar{p}_s \mid \bar{p}_f] = \phi^* \bar{p}_f$ and a constant conditional variance. All they need to know is the fact of normality, and the numerical value of ϕ^* and var $[\bar{p}_s \mid \bar{p}_f]$. The uninformed dealers do not have to know the structure of the model, just two parameters of the reduced form. Further by observing the markets operating in rational expectations equilibrium for a number of years the numbers ϕ^* and var $[\bar{p}_s \mid \bar{p}_f]$ could be estimated by standard statistical techniques. Apparently it is quite easy to learn how to form rational expectations.

In financial markets there are very large amounts of money at stake; and there is every incentive to apply the considerable abilities and resources of professional investors to make the best possible forecasts. However the argument that it is easy or even possible to learn how to form rational expectations by applying standard statistical techniques is misleading. Economists are interested in expectations because they believe that expectations affect what happens. This belief is reflected in the models, if agents in these models do not have rational expectations the model behaves differently from the rational expectations equilibrium. In Section 7 I defined a rational expectations equilibrium as a fixed point of the mapping from subjectively held beliefs into 'correct beliefs' induced by the market clearing condition. Outside rational expectations equilibrium subjective beliefs differ from both correct beliefs, and the rational expectations equilibrium beliefs. For example in the spot and futures market model in rational expectations equilibrium dealers believe that $E[\bar{p}_s \mid \bar{p}_f] = \phi^* \bar{p}_f$. If dealers believe that $E[\bar{p}_s \mid \bar{p}_f] = \phi \bar{p}_f$ where $\phi \neq \phi^*$, the correct conditional expectation will be of the form $E[\bar{p}_s \mid \bar{p}_f] = \hat{\phi} \bar{p}_f$ where $\hat{\phi} \neq \phi$, the expectation is incorrect, and $\hat{\phi} \neq \phi^*$, the correct expectation is not the same as in the rational expectations equilibrium. Changing to the 'correct' expectation formation rule $E[\bar{p}_s \mid \bar{p}_f] = \hat{\phi} \bar{p}_f$, changes the behaviour of the model, and this rule becomes incorrect. The obvious question to ask is whether repeated changes of the expectation formation rule ultimately lead to a rational expectations equilibrium. Is it possible to describe a plausible learning process which ultimately yields rational expectations? The answer depends upon how 'plausible' is understood. One possibility is to insist that agents learn using correctly specified Bayesian models. David Kreps and I argue elsewhere (Bray and Kreps, 1986) that is is in fact not plausible, because it in effect assumes a more elaborate and informationally demanding form of rational expectations equilibrium. However if agents do learn in this way and if the model has suitable continuity properties, expectations eventually become rational in the conventional sense.

Another possible way to model learning is to assume that agents estimate the model as if it were in rational expectations equilibrium, for example in the spot and futures market model they regress $\tilde{p}_s$ on $\tilde{p}_f$ using ordinary least squares, and use the estimated regression coefficients in forecasting $\tilde{p}_s$ from $\tilde{p}_f$. In Bray (1982) I studied this procedure for the model of example 2 where there are uninformed dealers, and informed dealers all of whom have the same information. I found that provided the uninformed dealers did not form too large a proportion of the market, the model would eventually converge to its rational expectations equilibrium. Bray (1983)[3] and Bray and Savin (1984) study similar econometric learning processes for a simple macroeconomic model and a version of the cobweb model. In both these models if the parameters of the supply and demand functions have the usual signs agents eventually learn how to form rational expectations. In all these examples agents are estimating misspecified economic models, so convergence to rational expectations equilibrium is not based on standard theorems on the asymptotic properties of estimators, is somewhat surprising, and hard to prove. Convergence to rational expectations equilibrium may be slow, and takes place only if the parameters of the model lies in a certain range. Although many of the examples which have been studied converge in economically plausible circumstances there is no general theory which establishes that convergence will always take place.

Expectations are important for economics; they crop up unavoidably in considering a vast range of issues. The enormous virtue of the rational expectations hypothesis is that it gives a simple, general and plausible way of handling expectations. It makes it possible to formulate and answer questions, for example, on the efficiency of markets as transmitters as information, which would otherwise be utterly intractable. All recent progress on the economics of information is built on the rational expectations hypothesis.

Consider for a moment the alternative hypotheses. One possibility is that

---

[3] Bray (1983) is much the shortest and simplest of these papers on learning, and the best introduction to the issues as I see them. Bray and Savin (1984) contains computer simulations which shed light on the rates of convergence and divergence, and discusses the relationship between this work, and time-varying parameter models in econometrics. Related literature is surveyed briefly in Blume, Bray and Easley (1982). Bray and Savin (1984) contains more recent references.

agents use a simple forecasting rule which generates systematic mistakes. In any application it is necessary to specify the rule, for example adaptive expectations. If there is good evidence that people do forecast in this way this is attractive, but it seems implausible that in the long run in a stable environment they will fail to notice their mistakes and modify the rule. Another alternative is to try to model the dynamics of the learning process. At present this seems to make for models which are too complicated and mathematically difficult to use for addressing most questions. Rational expectations equilibrium is a way of avoiding many difficult dynamic issue; if an issue is intractable in the current state of knowledge circumventing it is probably the most fruitful research stragegy.

Another alternative is to rely on survey data for expectations. Where possible this may be valuable in empirical work, if not very helpful for theorists.

A further alternative is to follow Keynes and argue that expectations cannot be described as probability distributions, they are volatile, and not susceptible to formal description. This makes it impossible to incorporate expectations explicitly into formal models, except by treating them as exogenous. Begg (1982b) argues that this is Keynes' strategy in the General Theory and is followed in traditional text-book treatments of Keynesian theory. In some cases I think this is an entirely defensible, indeed attractive strategy for modelling short-term events. The danger is that if expectations are unobservable, inexplicable, exogenous and volatile it leaves the model with no predictive and very little explanatory power as anything can be attributed to a shift in expectations. The rational expectations hypothesis also postulates unobservable expectations, but otherwise in total opposition to Keynes treats expectations as explicable, exogenous, and stable (unless the underlying model changes in which case expectations change appropriately). In medium to long term models the extreme rational expectations hypothesis is more attractive than the extreme exogenous expectations hypothesis. There is currently no generally acceptable intermediate hypothesis. Note that although Keynes himself would probably shudder if he knew there is no reason why rational expectations should not be incorporated into 'Keynesian' models, which would have quite different properties from the 'new-classical' rational expectations models. (See Begg 1982b.)

The rational expectations hypothesis seems at present much the most satisfactory generally applicable hypothesis on expectations formation. But it must be remembered that rational expectations models describe long run equilibria, on the assumption that the dynamics induced by learning eventually converge to rational expectations equilibrium. We have no good reason to believe that this assumption is always, or even often, valid.

I have discussed the assumptions of the financial market models at some length. The other criteria for the correctness of the models as descriptions is to look at implications of the models, and compare them with data. There are two sources of data, experimental data from laboratory situations, and empirical data from real markets. Ultimately the objective is to understand real markets, but laboratory data generated by setting up a market with groups of students, enables the experimenter to control and design the experiment, eliminating the host of extraneous factors which affect real market data.

Plott and Sunder (1982) set up a series of asset markets with informed and uninformed traders. The return on the asset depended on which of two or three states of the world occurs. The informed traders all had the same piece of information, in most cases telling them which state of the world had occurred. Plott and Sunder calculated two prices for each market, firstly the rational expectations equilibrium price in which the uninformed dealers inferred the as much as possible from the price, secondly the prior information price in which the uninformed dealers traded only on the basis of their prior information. Although the rational expectations model was not a perfect fit, prices did show a tendency to move towards their rational expectations equilibrium level. Plott and Sunder interpret the data as supporting the rational expectations rather than the prior information model.

Real market data has been used to test the efficient markets hypothesis, that using information in addition to the current price of an asset does not make for better predictions, the market price efficiently aggregates all the information. Three different forms of the hypothesis have been considered, the weak form, considering the information in past prices, the semi-strong form, considering more general publically available information, and the strong form, considering private information. The empirical literature is vast; Brealey (1983) provides a very readable introduction, and numerous references. Broadly the literature supports the weak and semi-strong forms of the efficient markets hypothesis, but private information does seem to give some advantage. The efforts of numerous academic investigators have failed to uncover a rule for forecasting market prices in order to manage a portfolio which does significantly better than holding a fixed well diversified portfolio. These results are consistent with the theoretical models which I have been describing and can be taken as support for the application of the rational expectations hypothesis to financial markets.

13. Further questions

These models answer some questions, but provoke others. Many of the models consider asset markets in isolation, taking the return generated by the asset as exogenous. (The spot and futures market model is an exception.) But financial markets are part of a larger system. One of their major functions is to enable enterprises to spread, and share risk, with consequences for output, investment and employment. It now appears that the markets may also have a role as transmitters of information. The ramifications of this role are not understood, but may be investigated using techniques similar to those which I have described.

192   RATIONAL EXPECTATIONS, INFORMATION AND ASSET MARKETS

Another set of open questions concern the mechanism of price formation. In these models price is a function of information, for example in the spot and futures market model where dealers have diverse information the futures price $\bar{p}_f = \theta^{*-1}E[\bar{a} \mid \bar{I}_1, \bar{I}_2, \ldots \bar{I}_n]$, (9.10), where θ^* is a parameter, and $\bar{I}_i$ agent i's information, a normal random variable. As the information varies from year to year the price varies. If the dealers have diverse information no individual dealer can check that the price is at the correct level given all the information. If a dealer thinks that the futures price is high or low given his private information, he can only conclude that other dealers have different information which leads them to expect a high or low spot price. Any numerical value of $\bar{p}_f$ can clear the market, it is far from clear what pushes $\bar{p}_f$ to its correct value. (This point is originally due to Beja, (1976)).

Universal price-taking is of course a convenient fiction. People set prices, unilaterally, by auction procedures, or by haggling. If there is a very limited range of prices at which goods can be sold price-taking is a good approximation. It may be necessary to consider the detailed mechanics of price making, the activities of brokers, jobbers, and market makers, to understand some aspects of the determination of prices in asset markets. In discussing their experimental results Plott and Sunder suggest that some of the information is transmitted by the oral auction process which they use, including unaccepted bids and offers. If this is so it provides an additional reason for looking at the institutional details of market structure.

The models which I have a very stark, simple, time structure, things happen at only two dates. In practice many financial markets operate repeatedly, the same asset is traded at a large number of dates, indeed trade may best be modelled as a continuous time process. There is a literature on continuous time models of financial markets (e.g. Black and Scholes (1973), and Merton (1973)), but this literature takes no account of informational asymmetries. Continuous time models with asymmetric information are attractive means of investigating the rate at which markets disseminate information, although they may pose formidable technical difficulties. There is certainly a case for looking at a richer temporal structure than has been considered up to now.

Faculty of Economics and Politics, Cambridge

APPENDIX

Proof of Lemma. Conditional distributions of normal random variables
    Anderson (1958) shows that

$$\bar{I} = E[\bar{a} \mid \bar{I}_1, \bar{I}_2 \ldots \bar{I}_n] = E\bar{a} + \Sigma_{ay} \Sigma_{yy}^{-1} (\bar{y} - E\bar{y}) \tag{A.1}$$

where $\bar{y}$ is notation for the vector $[\bar{I}_1, \bar{I}_2 \ldots \bar{I}_n]$, $\Sigma_{ay} = \text{cov}(\bar{a}, \bar{y})$, $\Sigma_{yy} = \text{var}(\bar{y})$. Equation (A.1) implies that $\bar{I}$ is a linear function of $[\bar{I}_1, \bar{I}_2 \ldots \bar{I}_n]$. As linear functions of normal random variables are normal, $\tilde{I}$ and $\tilde{e} = \tilde{a} - \tilde{I}$ are normal.

$$\text{cov}\,(\tilde{e}, \tilde{y}) = \text{cov}\,[\tilde{a} - E\tilde{a} - \Sigma_{ay}\,\Sigma_{yy}^{-1}\,(\tilde{y} - E\tilde{y}), \tilde{y}]$$
$$= \Sigma_{ay} - \Sigma_{ay}\,\Sigma_{yy}^{-1}\,\Sigma_{yy} = 0.$$

Thus $\tilde{e}$ and $\tilde{y}$ are uncorrelated, and as they are normal independent. Since $\tilde{I}$ is a linear function of $\tilde{y}$, $\tilde{I}$ and $\tilde{e}$ are uncorrelated, that is

$$\text{cov}\,(\tilde{I}, \tilde{e}) = \text{cov}\,(\tilde{I}, \tilde{a} - \tilde{I}) = 0 \qquad (A.2)$$

and so $\tilde{I}$ and $\tilde{e}$ are independent.

From (A.1)

$$E\tilde{a} = E\tilde{I} \qquad (A.3)$$

and so $E\tilde{e} = E\tilde{a} - E\tilde{I} = 0$. As $\tilde{I}$ and $\tilde{e}$ are independent

$$\text{var}\,\tilde{a} = \text{var}\,(\tilde{I} + \tilde{e}) = \text{var}\,\tilde{I} + \text{var}\,\tilde{e}.$$

As $\tilde{I}$ is a function of $\tilde{I}_1, \ldots \tilde{I}_n$ and $\tilde{e}$ is independent of $\tilde{I}_1, \tilde{I}_2 \ldots \tilde{I}_n$ the conditional distribution of $\tilde{a} = \tilde{I} + \tilde{e}$ given $\tilde{I}_1, \tilde{I}_2 \ldots \tilde{I}_n$ is normal (as $\tilde{e}$ is normal), with mean

$$E[\tilde{a} \mid \tilde{I}_1, \tilde{I}_2 \ldots \tilde{I}_n] = E[\tilde{I} \mid \tilde{I}_1, \tilde{I}_2 \ldots \tilde{I}_n] + E[\tilde{e} \mid \tilde{I}_1, \tilde{I}_2 \ldots \tilde{I}_n]$$
$$= \tilde{I} + E\tilde{e} = \tilde{I} = E(\tilde{a} \mid \tilde{I})$$

and

$$\text{var}\,[\tilde{a} \mid \tilde{I}_1, \tilde{I}_2 \ldots \tilde{I}_n] = \text{var}\,[\tilde{e} \mid \tilde{I}_1, \tilde{I}_2 \ldots \tilde{I}_n] = \text{var}\,\tilde{e} = \text{var}\,(\tilde{a} \mid \tilde{I}).$$

It can be shown that the conditional expectation of $\tilde{a}$ given $\tilde{I}_1, \tilde{I}_2 \ldots \tilde{I}_n$ is the unique linear function of $\tilde{I}$ of $\tilde{I}_1, \tilde{I}_2 \ldots \tilde{I}_n$ satisfying (A.2) and (A.3). These equations characterise the conditional expectation of one normal random variable given another. (See Bray (1981) for an application of this fact.)

REFERENCES

ALLEN, B. (1982), "Strict Rational Expectations Equilibria with Diffuseness" *Journal of Economic Theory*, 27, 20–46.

ALLEN, B. (1983), "Expectations Equilibria with Dispersed Information: Existence with Approximate Rationality in a Model with a Continuum of Agents and Finitely Many States of the World" *Review of Economic Studies*, 50 267–85.

ANDERSON, T. W., (1958), *An Introduction to Multivariate Statistical Analysis*, Wiley, New York.

ANDERSON, R. M. and SONNENSCHEIN, H., (1985), "Rational Expectations with Econometric Models", forthcoming, *Review of Economic Studies*.

ARROW, K. (1964), "The Role of Securities in the Optimal Allocation of Risk-Bearing", *Review of Economic Studies*, 31, 91–96.

BEGG, D. K. H. (1982a), *The Rational Expectations Revolution in Macroeconomics*, Philip Allan, Oxford.

BEGG, D. K. H. (1982b), "Rational Expectations, Wage Rigidity and Involuntary Unemployment: A Particular Theory", *Oxford Economic Papers*, 34, 23–47.

BEJA, A. (1976), "The Limited Information Efficiency of Market Processes", Research Program in Finance Working Paper No. 43, University of California, Berkeley.

BLACK, F. and SCHOLES, M. (1973), "The Pricing of Options and Corporate Liabilities", *Journal of Political Economy*, 81, 637–659.

194   RATIONAL EXPECTATIONS, INFORMATION AND ASSET MARKETS

BLUME, L., BRAY, M. M. and EASLEY, D. (1982), "Introduction to the Stability of Rational Expectations Equilibrium", *Journal of Economic Theory*, 26, 313–317.

BRAY, M. M. (1981), "Futures Trading, Rational Expectations, and the Efficient Markets Hypothesis", *Econometrica*, 49, 575–596.

BRAY, M. M. (1982), "Learning, Estimation, and the Stability of Rational Expectations", *Journal of Economic Theory*, 26, 318–339.

BRAY, M. M. (1983), "Convergence to Rational Expectations Equilibrium" in *Individual Forecasting and Aggregate Outcomes*, ed. R. Frydman and E. S. Phelps, Cambridge: Cambridge University Press.

BRAY, M. M. and KREPS, D. M. (1986), "Rational Learning and Rational Expectations", forthcoming in 'Essays in Honor of K. J. Arrow', edited by W. Heller, D. Starrett and R. Starr.

BRAY, M. M. and SAVIN, N. E. (1984), "Rational Expectations Equilibria, Learning and Model Specification", Economic Theory Discussion Paper No. 79, Department of Applied Economics, Cambridge.

BREALEY, R. (1983), *An Introduction to Risk and Return* Second Edition, Blackwell, Oxford.

DANTHINE, J. P. (1978), "Information, Futures Prices and Stabilising Speculation", *Journal of Economic Theory*, 17, 79–98.

DEATON, A. and MUELLBAUER, J. (1980), *Economics and Consumer Behaviour*, Cambridge University Press, Cambridge.

DIAMOND, P. A. (1967), "The Role of a Stock Market in a General Equilibrium Model with Technolgoical Uncertainty", *American Economic Review*, 57, 759–773.

DIAMOND, P. A. and ROTHSCHILD, M. (1978), *Uncertainty in Economics*, Academic Press, New York.

GROSSMAN, S. J. (1976), "On the Efficiency of Competitive Stock Markets Where Traders Have Diverse Information", *Journal of Finance*, 31, 573–585.

GROSSMAN, S. J. (1977), "The Existence of Futures Markets, Noisy Rational Expectations and Informational Externalities", *Review of Economic Studies*, 44, 431–449.

GROSSMAN, S. J. (1978), "Further Results On the Informational Efficiency of Competitive Stock Markets", *Journal of Economic Theory*, 18, 81–101.

GROSSMAN, S. J. (1981), "An Introduction to the Theory of Rational Expectations Under Asymmetric Information", *Review of Economic Studies*, 48, 541–560.

GROSSMAN, S. J., and STIGLITZ, J. E. (1980), "On the Impossibility of Informationally Efficient Markets", *American Economic Review*, 70, 393–408.

HAYEK, F. A. (1945), "The Use of Knowledge in Society", *American Economic Review*, 35, 519–530.

JORDAN, J. S. (1982a), "Admissable Market Data Structures: A Complete Characterisation, *Journal of Economic Theory*, 28(1), 19–31.

JORDAN, J. S. (1982b), "A Dynamic Model of Expectations Equilibrium", *Journal of Economic Theory*, 28(2), 235–54.

JORDAN, J. S. (1983), "On the Efficient Markets Hypothesis", *Econometrica*, 51, 1325–1343.

JORDAN, J. S. and RADNER, R. (1982), "Rational Expectations in Microeconomic Models: an Overview", *Journal of Economic Theory*, 26, 201–223.

KALDOR, N. (1934), "A Classificatory Note on the Determinateness of Equilibrium", *Review of Economic Studies*, 1, 122–136.

KEYNES, J. M. (1936), *The General Theory of Employment, Interest and Money*, Macmillan, London.

KNIGHT, F. H. (1921), *Risk, Uncertainty and Profit*, Houghton Mifflin, New York.

KREPS, D. (1977), "A Note on Fulfilled Expectations Equilibria", *Journal of Economic Theory*, 14, 32–43.

MERTON, M. (1973), "An Intertemporal Capital Asset Pricing Model", *Econometrica*, 41, 867–888.

MEYER, P. L. (1970), *Introductory Probability and Statistical Applications* Second Edition, Addison Wesley, Reading, Massachusetts.

MUTH, J. F. (1961), "Rational Expectations and the Theory of Price Movements", *Econometrica*, 29, 315–335.

PLOTT, C. R. and SUNDER, S. (1982), "Efficiency of Experimental Security Markets With Insider Information: An Application of Rational Expectations Models", *Journal of Political Economy*, 90, 663–98.

RADNER, R. (1979), "Rational Expectations Equilibrium Generic Existence and the Information Revealed by Prices", *Econometrica*, 47, 655–678.

RADNER, R. (1982), "Equilibrium Under Uncertainty" in *Handbook of Mathematical Economics, Vol. II*, Editors K. J. Arrow and M. D. Intriligator, Amsterdam, North-Holland.

RAIFFA, H. (1968), *Decision Analysis: Introductory Lectures on Choice Under Uncertainty*, Addison Wesley, Reading, Massachusetts.

SCHOEMAKER, P. S. H. (1982), "The Expected Utility Model: Its Variants, Purposes, Evidence and Limitations", *Journal of Economic Literature*, 20, 529–563.

STIGLITZ, J. E. (1982), "Information and Capital Markets", in *Financial Economics: Essays in Honor of Paul Cootner*, Editors W. F. Sharpe and C. M. Cootner, Prentice-Hall.

Part IV
Management and Technology

[12]

DESIGNING ORGANIZATIONS
FOR AN
INFORMATION-RICH WORLD

Speaker   HERBERT A. SIMON

*Richard King Mellon Professor of
Computer Science and Psychology
Carnegie-Mellon University*

Discussants   KARL W. DEUTSCH

*Professor of Government
Harvard University*

MARTIN SHUBIK

*Professor of the Economics of Organization
Yale University*

Moderator   EMILIO Q. DADDARIO

*Chairman of Subcommittee
    on Science, Research, and Development
U.S. House of Representatives*

38

DADDARIO. I was attracted to participate in this series by the appropriateness of the theme, *Computers, Communications, and the Public Interest.* Perhaps the title of the present session should be "Designing Organizations for an Information-Rich, *Communications-Poor, Problem-Overwhelmed* World." If anything characterizes the current age, it is the complex problems of our technological civilization and the unpleasant physical and mental trauma they induce. John W. Gardner and other social critics warn us that a nation can perish from internal strains: indifference, unwillingness to face problems, incapacity to respond to human suffering, failure to adapt to new conditions, and the waning energy of old age. Gardner speaks of the "waxwork of anachronisms" in government and the "impenetrable web of vested interests" in unions, professions, universities, and corporations. He argues for "a society (and institutions) capable of continuous change, continuous renewal, and continuous responsiveness."[1]

I see no room for complacency by the growing community devoted to communications and information processing in the face of the obvious needs of our society. Today we exchange a growing proportion of knowledge in new ways: via magnetic tapes, remote consoles wired to computers, national and international information networks, and large data banks. Expansion is so rapid, it is hard to document what is happening.

What concerns many of us is what I expect our speaker and discussants will be addressing in part. The creation of powerful computerized information systems, unless we take precautionary steps, may spawn new systems in Parkinsonian abandon, leading to quality-poor scientific and technical information. Furthermore, science can only flourish when it is untrammeled and open-ended. We must be careful not to institutionalize our information systems in such a way that they inhibit or interfere with this necessary freedom.

Herbert Simon is a member of the distinguished Panel on Technology Assessment of the National Academy of Sciences. I owe the panel a personal debt of gratitude for an outstanding report it recently completed on technology assessment.[2]

SIMON. If men do not pour new wine into old bottles, they do something almost as bad: they invest old words with new meanings. "Work" and "energy" are venerable English words, but since the Industrial and Scientific Revolutions they have acquired entirely new definitions. They have become more abstract and divorced from directly sensed qualities of human activity; and they have become more precise, finding expression in quantitative units of measurement (foot-pound, erg) and exact scientific laws (Conservation of Energy). The word "energy" uttered in a contemporary setting may represent quite different concepts and thought processes from the word "energy" uttered in the eighteenth century.

Old word meanings do not disappear; they tend to persist alongside the new. This is perhaps the most insidious part of what C. P. Snow has dubbed the problem of the two cultures. To know what a speaker means by "energy" it is not enough to know what century he is speaking in, but also whether his talk belongs to the common culture or the scientific culture. If the former, his words should not be credited with the quantitative precision that belongs to the latter; and if the latter, his words should not be interpreted vaguely or metaphorically.

Old Words in New Meanings

All of this is preliminary to raising a difficulty I must hurdle to communicate. I intend to use familiar words like "information," "thinking," and "organization," but not with the meanings that the common culture has attached to them over the centuries. During the past twenty-five years these words have begun to acquire new, increasingly precise and quantitative meanings. Words associated with the generation and conversion of information are today undergoing a change of meaning as drastic as that experienced by words associated with the generation and conversion of energy in the eighteenth and nineteenth centuries.

Within the common culture, one cannot carry on a twentieth-century conversation about energy with a physicist or engineer. Similarly, it is increasingly difficult to carry on a twentieth-century conversation about information with a social scientist who belongs to the humanistic rather than scientific subculture of his discipline. The difficulty does not stem from jargon but from a complete disparity of meanings hidden behind a superficially common language.

What do I mean when I say: "Machines think"? The word "machine" seems obvious enough: a modern electronic digital computer. But "machine" has all sorts of unintended humanistic overlays. A machine, in the common culture, moves repetitively and monotonously. It requires direction from outside. It is inflexible. With the slightest component failure or mismanagement it degenerates into senseless or random behavior.

A computer may exhibit none of these mechanical properties. While retaining the word "machine" in the scientific culture as a label for a computer, I have revised drastically the associations stored with the word in my memory. When I say "Machines think," I am *not* referring to devices that behave repetitively and inflexibly, require outside guidance, and often become random.

The word "think" itself is even more troublesome. In the common culture it denotes an unanalyzed, partly intuitive, partly subconscious and unconscious, sometimes creative set of mental processes that sometimes allows humans to solve problems, make decisions, or design something. What do these mental processes have in common with the processes computers follow when they execute their programs?

40

The common culture finds almost nothing in common between them. One reason is that human thinking has never been described, only labeled. Certain contemporary psychological research, however, has been producing computer programs that duplicate the human information processing called thinking in considerable detail.[3] When a psychologist who has been steeped in this new scientific culture says "Machines think," he has in mind the behavior of computers governed by such programs. He means something quite definite and precise that has no satisfactory translation into the language of the common culture. If you wish to converse with him (which you well may not!) you will have to follow him into the scientific culture.

As the science of information processing continues to develop, it will not be as easy to sequester it from the main stream of managerial activity (or human social activity) as it was to isolate the physical sciences and their associated technologies. Information processing is at the heart of executive activity, indeed at the heart of all social interaction. More and more we are finding occasion to use terms like "information," "thinking," "memory," and "decision making" with twentieth-century scientific precision. The language of the scientific culture occupies more and more of the domain previously reserved to the common culture.

Make no mistake about the significance of this change in language. It is a change in thought and concepts. It is a change of the most fundamental kind in man's thinking about his own processes—about himself.

The Scarcity of Attention

My title speaks of "an information-rich world." How long has the world been rich in information? What are the consequences of its prosperity, if that is what it is?

Last Easter, my neighbors bought their daughter a pair of rabbits. Whether by intent or accident, one was male, one female, and we now live in a rabbit-rich world. Persons less fond than I am of rabbits might even describe it as a rabbit-overpopulated world. Whether a world is rich or poor in rabbits is a relative matter. Since food is essential for biological populations, we might judge the world as rabbit-rich or rabbit-poor by relating the number of rabbits to the amount of lettuce and grass (and garden flowers) available for rabbits to eat. A rabbit-rich world is a lettuce-poor world, and vice versa.

The obverse of a population problem is a scarcity problem, hence a resource-allocation problem. There is only so much lettuce to go around, and it will have to be allocated somehow among the rabbits. Similarly, in an information-rich world, the wealth of information means a dearth of something else: a scarcity of whatever it is that information consumes. What information consumes is rather obvious: it consumes the attention of its recipients. Hence a wealth of information creates a poverty of attention and a need to allocate that attention efficiently among the overabundance of information sources that might consume it.

To formulate an allocation problem properly, ways must be found to measure the quantities of the scarce resource; and these quantities must not be expandable at will. By now, all of us have heard of the *bit*, a unit of information introduced by Shannon in connection with problems in the design of communication systems.[4] Can we use the bit as a measure of an information-processing system's capacity for attention?

Unfortunately, it is not the right unit. Roughly, the trouble is that the bit capacity of any device (or person) for receiving information depends entirely upon how the information is encoded. Bit capacity is not an invariant, hence is an unsuitable measure of the scarcity of attention.

A relatively straightforward way of measuring how much scarce resource a message consumes is by noting how much time the recipient spends on it. Human beings, like contemporary computers, are essentially serial devices. They can attend to only one thing at a time. This is just another way of saying that attention is scarce. Even the modern time-sharing systems which John Kemeny described are really only doing one thing at a time, although they seem able to attend to one hundred things at once.[5] They achieve this illusion by sharing their time and attention among these hundred things. The attention-capacity measure I am proposing for human beings applies as well to time-sharing systems and also to an organization employing many people, which can be viewed as a time-sharing system.

Scarcity of attention in an information-rich world can be measured in terms of a human executive's time. If we wish to be precise, we can define a standard executive (IQ of 120, bachelor's degree, and so on) and ask Director Lewis Branscomb to embalm him at the National Bureau of Standards. Further, we can work out a rough conversion between the attention units of human executives and various kinds of computers.

In an information-rich world, most of the cost of information is the cost incurred by the recipient. It is not enough to know how much it costs to produce and transmit information; we must also know how much it costs, in terms of scarce attention, to receive it. I have tried bringing this argument home to my friends by suggesting that they recalculate how much the *New York Times* (or *Washington Post*) costs them, including the cost of reading it. Making the calculation usually causes them some alarm, but not enough for them to cancel their subscriptions. Perhaps the benefits still outweigh the costs.

Having explained what I mean by an information-rich world, I am now ready to tackle the main question. How can we design organizations, business firms, and government agencies to operate effectively in such a world? How can we arrange to conserve and effectively allocate their scarce attention?

I shall proceed with the help of three examples, each illustrating a

42

major aspect of the problem of organizational design. I make no attempt
to cover all significant problem areas, and any fancied resemblance of my
hypothetical organizations to real organizations, living or dead, in the city
of Washington, are illusory, fortuitous, and the product of the purest
happenstance.

Information Overload

Many proposals for eliminating *information overload* (another
phrase to describe life in an information-rich world) call for a new computing system. There is good precedent for this. The Hollerith punched
card is a creative product of the Census Bureau's first bout with information overload, and a series of crises in the central exchanges of the phone
company led to the invention of automatic switching systems.

Today, some argue that the postal service is doomed to collapse from
information overload unless means are found to automate the sorting
operations. This cannot be so. There is no reason why mail-sorting costs
should increase more than proportionally with the volume of mail, nor
why unit costs should rise with volume. A major cause of the problem is
that certain information-processing services are almost free, resulting in an
explosive demand for them. The Post Office is not really prepared to
provide this implicit subsidy and reneges by performing the services badly,
with insufficient resources. The crisis in the Post Office does not call for
computers; it calls for a thoroughgoing application of price and market
mechanisms.

This is not to argue that any particular manual Post Office operation,
such as sorting, cannot be made more economical by computer. This kind
of technical question is settled by cost-benefit analysis within reasonable
limits of error and debate. But there is no magic in automation that allows
it to resolve dilemmas posed by an organization's unwillingness or inability
to allocate and price scarce information-processing resources, whether the
resources are sorting clerks or electronic devices. Free or underpriced
resources are always in desperately short supply. What is sometimes alleged to be technological lag in the Post Office is really failure of nerve.

A computer is an information-processing system of quite general
capability. It can receive information, store it, operate on it in a variety of
ways, and transmit it to other systems. Whether a computer will contribute
to the solution of an information-overload problem, or instead compound
it, depends on the distribution of its own attention among four classes of
activities: listening, storing, thinking, and speaking. A general design principle can be put as follows:

*An information-processing subsystem (a computer or new organiza-
tion unit) will reduce the net demand on the rest of the organization's
attention only if it absorbs more information previously received by others
than it produces—that is, if it listens and thinks more than it speaks.*

To be an attention conserver for an organization, an information-processing system (abbreviated IPS) must be an information condenser. It is conventional to begin designing an IPS by considering the information it will *supply*. In an information-rich world, however, this is doing things backwards. The crucial question is how much information it will allow to be *withheld* from the attention of other parts of the system.

Basically, an IPS can perform an attention-conserving function in two ways: (1) it can receive and store information that would otherwise have to be received by other systems, and (2) it can transform or *filter* input information into output that demands fewer hours of attention than the input.

To illustrate these two modes of attention conservation, let me talk about some of the information needs of a nation's Foreign Office. (Since the United States has a State Department and not a Foreign Office, I am obviously talking about some other country.) The bulk of information that enters a system from the environment is irrelevant to action at the time of entry. Much of it will never be relevant, but we cannot be sure in advance which part this is.

One way to conserve Foreign Office attention is to interpose an IPS (human, automated, or both) between environment and organization to index and store information on receipt. A second way is to have an IPS analyze, draw inferences from, and summarize the information received, then index and store the products of its analyses for use by the rest of the system.

This proposal has a familiar ring about it. I have simply described in unconventional language the conventional functions of a conventional intelligence unit. Moreover, I have solved the information-overload problem simply by adding information processors. I eliminated scarcity by increasing the supply of scarce resources. Any fool with money can do that.

But the very banality of my solution carries an important lesson. The functional design an IPS must have to conserve attention is largely independent of specific hardware, automated or human. Hardware becomes a concern only later in economic considerations.

My proposal, however, is actually far less conventional than it sounds. If the IPS is to be even partly automated, we must provide precise descriptions (in the language of the scientific culture) of the processes denoted by vague terms like "analyze" and "summarize." Even if we do *not* intend to automate the process, the new information-processing technology still will permit us to formulate the programs of human analysts and summarizers with precision so that we can predict reliably the relation between inputs and outputs. Looking more closely at the structure and operation of the IPS, we see it really will not resemble a traditional intelligence unit very closely at all. (My thinking on this problem has benefited greatly from acquaintance with the analyses that have been made over the past several years of information-processing requirements in the U.S. State Department.

44

These planning activities have been laudably free from premature obsession with automated hardware.)

The purpose of the intelligence IPS I have proposed is not to *supply* the Foreign Office with information but to *buffer* it from the overrich environment of information in which it swims. Information does not have to be attended to (*now*) just because it exists in the environment. Designing an intelligence system means deciding: when to gather information (much of it will be preserved indefinitely in the environment if we do not want to harvest it now); where and in what form to store it; how to rework and condense it; how to index and give access to it; and when and on whose initiative to communicate it to others.

The design principle that attention is scarce and must be preserved is very different from a principle of "the more information the better." The aforementioned Foreign Office thought it had a communications crisis a few years ago. When events in the world were lively, the teletypes carrying incoming dispatches frequently fell behind. The solution: replace the teletypes with line printers of much greater capacity. No one apparently asked whether the IPS's (including the Foreign Minister) that received and processed messages from the teletypes would be ready, willing, and able to process the much larger volume of messages from the line printers.

Everything I have said about intelligence systems in particular applies to management information systems in general. The proper aim of a management information system is not to bring the manager all the information he needs, but to reorganize the manager's environment of information so as to reduce the amount of time he must devote to receiving it. Restating the problem this way leads to a very different system design.

The Need to Know

That brings me to the question of *the need to know*. How do we go about deciding where information should be stored in an information-rich world and who should learn about it?

Those of us who were raised during the Great Depression sometimes do not find it easy to adapt to an affluent society. When we ate potatoes, we always ate the peel (which my mother insisted was the best part of the potato). Nonreturnable containers seem to us symbols of intolerable waste.

Our attitudes toward information reflect the culture of poverty. We were brought up on Abe Lincoln walking miles to borrow (and return!) a book and reading it by firelight. Most of us are constitutionally unable to throw a bound volume into the wastebasket. We have trouble enough disposing of magazines and newspapers. Some of us are so obsessed with the need to know that we feel compelled to read everything that falls into our hands, although the burgeoning of the mails is helping to cure us of this obsession.

If these attitudes were highly functional in the world of clay tablets, scribes, and human memory; if they were at least tolerable in the world of the printing press and the cable; they are completely maladapted to the world of broadcast systems and Xerox machines.

The change in information-processing technology demands a fundamental change in the meaning attached to the familiar verb "to know." In the common culture, "to know" meant to have stored in one's memory in a way that facilitates recall when appropriate. By metaphoric extension, "knowing" might include having access to a file or book containing information, with the skill necessary for using it.

In the scientific culture, the whole emphasis in "knowing" shifts from the storage or actual physical possession of information to the process of using or having access to it. It is possible to have information stored without having access to it (the name on the tip of the tongue, the lost letter in the file, the unindexed book, the uncatalogued library); and it is possible to have access to information without having it stored (a computer program for calculating values of the sine function, a thermometer for taking a patient's temperature).

If a library holds two copies of the same book, one of them can be destroyed or exchanged without the system's losing information. In the language of Shannon's information theory, multiple copies make the library *redundant*. But copies are only one of three important forms of redundancy in information. Even if a library has only one copy of each book, it still has a high degree of informational overlap. If half the titles in the Library of Congress were destroyed at random, little of the world's knowledge would disappear.

The most important and subtle form of redundancy derives from the world's being highly lawful. Facts are random if no part of them can be predicted from any other part—that is, if they are independent of each other. Facts are lawful if certain of them *can* be predicted from certain others. We need store only the fraction needed to predict the rest.

This is exactly what science is: the process of replacing unordered masses of brute fact with tidy statements of orderly relations from which these facts can be inferred. The progress of science, far from cluttering up the world with new information, enormously increases the redundancy of libraries by discovering the orderliness of the information already stored. With each important advance in scientific theory, we can reduce the volume of explicitly stored knowledge without losing any information whatsoever. That we make so little use of this opportunity does not deny that the opportunity exists.

Let me recite an anecdote that illustrates the point very well. We are all aware that there is a DDT problem. DDT is one of technology's mixed blessings. It is very lethal to noxious insects, but uncomfortably persistent and cumulatively harmful to eagles, game fish, and possibly ourselves. The

46

practical problem is how to enjoy the agricultural and medical benefits afforded by the toxicity of DDT without suffering the consequences of its persistence.

A distinguished chemist of my acquaintance, who is a specialist neither in insecticides nor biochemistry, asked himself this question. He was able to write down the approximate chemical structure of DDT by decoding its name. He could recognize from general theoretical principles the component radicals in the structural formula that account for its toxicity. The formula also told him on theoretical grounds why the substance is persistent and why the molecule does not decompose readily or rapidly. He asked, again on theoretical grounds, what compound would have the toxicity of DDT but decompose readily. He was able to write down its formula and saw no theoretical reason why it could not easily be produced. (All of this took ten minutes.)

A phone call to an expert in the field confirmed all his conjectures. The new compound he had "invented" was a well-known insecticide, which had been available commercially before DDT. It is not as lethal as DDT over as broad a band of organisms but is nearly so, and it decomposes fairly readily. I do not know if the new-old chemical "solves" the DDT problem. The durability of DDT was intended by its inventors to avoid frequent respraying and reduce the costs of treatment. There may be other economic issues, and even chemical and biological ones.

What the story illustrates is that good problem-solving capacities combined with powerful (but compact) theories (and an occasional telephone call) may take the place of shelves of reference books. It may often be more efficient to leave information in the library of nature, to be extracted by experiment or observation when needed, than to mine and stockpile it in man's libraries, where retrieval costs may be as high as the costs of recreating information from new experiments or deriving it from theory.

These considerations temper my enthusiasm for using new technology to store and retrieve larger and larger bodies of data. I do not mean to express a blanket disapproval of all proposals to improve the world's stores of information. But I do believe we must design IPS's with data-analysis capabilities able to keep up with our propensities to store vast bodies of data.

Today's computers are moronic robots, and they will continue to be so as long as programming remains in its present primitive state. Moronic robots can sop up, store, and spew out vast quantities of information. They do not and cannot exercise due respect for the scarce attention of the recipients of this information. Computers must be taught to behave at a higher level of intelligence. This will take a large, vigorous research and development effort.

In a knowledge-rich world, progress does not lie in the direction of reading and writing information faster or storing more of it. Progress lies in the direction of extracting and exploiting the patterns of the world so that far less information needs to be read, written, or stored. Progress depends on our ability to devise better and more powerful thinking programs for man and machine.

Technology Assessment

Attention is *generally* scarce in organizations, *particularly* scarce at the tops, and *desperately* scarce at the top of the organization called the United States Government. There is only one President. Although he is assisted by the Budget Bureau, the Office of Science and Technology, and other elements of the Executive Office, a frightening array of matters converges on this single, serial, human information-processing system.

There is only one Congress of the United States. It can operate in parallel through committees, but every important matter must occupy the attention of many Congressmen. Highly important matters may claim the time and attention of all.

There is only one body of citizens in the United States. Large public problems such as the Vietnam War, civil rights, student unrest, the cities, and environmental quality (to mention five near the top of the current agenda) periodically require a synchrony of public attention. This is more than enough to crowd the agenda to the point of unworkability or inaction.

Congressman Daddario has devoted a great deal of thought in recent years to improving the procedures in society and government for dealing with the new technology we produce so prodigiously. At the request of his House Subcommittee on Science, Research, and Development, a panel of the National Academy of Sciences on which I served recently prepared the report on technology assessment to which he referred.

Technology assessment is not just a matter of determining the likely good and bad effects of new technological developments. Even less is it a matter of making sure, before new technology is licensed, that it will have no undesirable effects. The dream of thinking everything out before we act, of making certain we have all the facts and know all the consequences, is a sick Hamlet's dream. It is the dream of someone with no appreciation of the seamless web of causation, the limits of human thinking, or the scarcity of human attention.

The world outside is itself the greatest storehouse of knowledge. Human reason, drawing upon the pattern and redundancy of nature, can predict some of the consequences of human action. But the world will always remain the largest laboratory, the largest information store, from which we will learn the outcomes, good and bad, of what we have done. Of course it is costly to learn from experience; but it is also costly, and frequently much less reliable, to try through research and analysis to anticipate experience.

48

Technology assessment is an intelligence function. If it operated perfectly, which it is certain not to, it would do two things for us. First, it would warn us before our taking action of the really dangerous (especially the irreversibly dangerous) consequences possible from proposed innovations. Second, it would give us early warning of unanticipated consequences of innovations as they became visible, before major irreversible damage had been done. In performing both of these functions, technology assessment would be mindful of the precious scarcity of attention. It would put on the agenda only items needing attention and action (including the action of gathering information to evaluate the need for further attention).

A phrase like "technology assessment" conjures up a picture of scientific competence and objectivity, deliberateness and thoughtfulness, concern for the long run, and a systems view that considers all aspects and consequences. But these desirable qualities of a decision-making system cannot be imposed without considering the organizational and political environment of the system.

As our scientific and engineering knowledge grows, so does the power of our actions. They have consequences ramifying over vast reaches of space and time. The growth of knowledge allows us to recognize consequences we would have been ignorant of or ignored before. We are able to make bigger waves and at the same time have more sensitive instruments to detect the rocking of the boat. Today we sterilize and quarantine everything that travels between earth and moon. Less than five hundred years ago we diffused tuberculosis, smallpox, and syphilis throughout the Americas in happy ignorance.

The injunction to take account of *all* effects conjures up the picture of an integral stretching out through space and time without ever converging. We must assume, as mankind has always assumed, that a reasonable allocation of our limited attention and powers of thought will solve the crucial problems facing us at least as fast as new ones arise. If that assumption is wrong, there is no help for us. If it is right, then technology assessment becomes part and parcel of the task of setting an agenda for society and government.

To bring the notion of technology assessment out of the realm of abstraction, let me go back to the example of DDT. Although I have not researched the history of DDT, I believe it was introduced on a large scale without thorough (or at least adequate) study of its potential cumulative danger in the atmosphere and in organisms (especially predators). It was hailed for its agricultural and medical benefits as one of technology's miracles. Now, some decades later, we learn that the miracle has a flaw.

The possible adverse effects of DDT have been known to specialists for some time. They were probably even known, but ignored, at the time DDT was introduced. If so, this would underscore my fundamental theme of the scarcity of attention.

DESIGNING ORGANIZATIONS FOR AN INFORMATION-RICH WORLD   49

Suppose the dangers of DDT were not known beforehand but were discovered only in the laboratory of nature. Then, with apologies to eagle lovers, I am not sure that we (or even the eagles) have suffered unconscionable or irreversible loss by letting actual use tell us about DDT rather than trying to anticipate this experience in advance. Technology assessment has been (and is being) made by the environment. We are getting signals from the environment calling attention to some of its findings, and these signals are strong enough to deserve and get our attention. The DDT issue has been claiming attention intermittently for some months, with the loudest environmental signal being the detection of DDT in Great Lakes game fish. The issue is now high enough on the agenda of newspapers, courts, and committees to bring action.

I know this sounds complacent, and I really do not feel complacent. But it serves no useful social purpose to treat with anguish and hand-wringing every public problem which by hindsight might have been avoided if we had been able to afford the luxury of more foresight. Now that we *know* the problems, we should address them rather than hold inquests about who should have seen the problems earlier.

Our information about the effects of DDT and of long-continued diffuse contamination is in many respects unsatisfactory. (So is our information about almost any issue of public policy.) But this does not mean we could improve the situation by massive collection of data. On the contrary, we mainly need carefully aimed, high-quality biological investigations of the cause and effect mechanisms underlying the diffusion and metabolism of DDT. After we understand better the chemistry and biology of the problem we might make sense of masses of data, but then we probably would not need as much.

First-rate biologists and chemists capable of doing the required research are in as short supply as most other high-quality information-processing systems. Their attention is an exceedingly scarce commodity, and we are unlikely to capture much of it soon. The practical question, as always, is how to deal with the situation given the scrappy, inadequate data we now have.

We begin to ask questions like these: Assuming the worst possible case for the harmful effects of DDT, what is the magnitude of the effects in human, economic, and ecological terms, and to what extent are these effects irreversible? In the same terms, what would it cost us to do without DDT? What is the next best alternative?

These are common-sense questions. We do not have to know anything about the technology to ask them, although we might learn something about it from the answers. The most effective IPS for getting answers consists of a telephone, a Xerox machine (to copy documents the telephone correspondents suggest), and some very bright professionals (not necessarily specialists) who do know something about the technology. With this retrieval

50

system, just about anything in the world now known on the problem can be extracted in a few man-weeks of work. (The time required goes up considerably if hearings and briefings are held or a research project is organized.)

There are numerous locations inside and outside the federal government where the questions may be asked. They may be asked by the Office of Science and Technology, the National Academy of Sciences, the National Academy of Engineering, the RAND Corporation, Resources for the Future, or a Congressional committee. (An excellent example of the last is the recent series of reports on steam-powered automobiles.)

The location of the investigating group is significant from only one standpoint, which may be crucial. The location of the group can determine the attention it commands and the legitimacy accorded its findings. These are interdependent but by no means identical matters.

Legitimacy may sometimes be achieved (and even attention secured) by the usual credentials of science: the right degrees, professional posts, and reputations. But many an impeccable report is ignored, and many a report without proper credentials gains a high place on the agenda. The Ralph Naders of the world demonstrate that writing and speaking forcefully, understanding the mass media, and being usually right about the facts can compensate for missing union cards and lack of access to organizational channels. Rachel Carson showed that even literary excellence is sometimes enough to turn the trick.

I agree with Congressman Daddario that we can and should strengthen and make more effective the processes of technology assessment in our country. We shall still need the world itself as a major laboratory, but we may be able to substitute foresight for hindsight to a modest extent. Did we have to wait until all Los Angeles wept before doing anything about automobile exhausts? Well-financed institutions for technology assessment should be spending a hundred million dollars a year instead of ten million to find out whether the steam automobile offers a long-term solution to the smog problem. Our current measures are temporary expedients at best.

Strengthening technology assessment means improving our procedures for setting the public agenda. It does not mean pressing more information and problems on an already burdened President, Congress, and public. In an information-rich world, there is no special virtue in prematurely early warnings. Let the world store information for us until we can focus attention and thought on it.

Assessing Information-Processing Technology

The final issue I should like to address is itself a problem in technology assessment. The science and technology of information processing is only a quarter-century old, and we have merely the faintest glimmerings of what it will be like after another quarter-century. How shall we assess it and make sure it develops in socially beneficial ways?

DESIGNING ORGANIZATIONS FOR AN INFORMATION-RICH WORLD 51

The most visible and superficially spectacular part of the technology is its hardware: computers, typewriter consoles, cathode-ray tubes, and associated gadgets. These devices give us powerful new ways for recording, storing, processing, and writing information to improve and replace the human IPS's with which we had to make do throughout man's history.

By itself, the hardware does not solve any organizational problems, including the problems of attention scarcity. The hardware boxes will begin to make inroads on these problems only as we begin to understand information-processing systems well enough to conceive sophisticated programs for them—programs that will permit them to think at least as well as man does.

Each step we take toward increasing our sophistication and scientific knowledge about the automated IPS also increases our sophistication and scientific knowledge about the human IPS, about man's thought processes. What we are acquiring with the new technology is something of deep significance—a science of human thinking and organization.[6]

The armchair is no more effective a scientific instrument for understanding this new technology than it was for previous technologies. If we are to understand information processing, we must study it in the laboratory of nature. We must construct, program, and operate many kinds of information-processing systems to see what they do and how they perform.

Our first systems have performed and will perform in all sorts of unexpected ways (most of them stupid), and by hindsight they seem incredibly crude. They will never pass a cost-effectiveness test on their operating performance, and we shall have to write them off as research and development efforts. From their behavior, we may learn that the new technology contains dangers as well as promises. There already is considerable concern about threats to privacy that the new technology might create. Such concerns will be mere armchair speculations until they are tested against a broad base of experience.

Very early in the computer era, I advised several business firms not to acquire computers until they knew exactly how to use them and pay for them. I soon realized this was bad advice. Computers initially pay their way by educating large numbers of people about computers. They are the principal forces for replacement of the vague, inadequate common-culture meanings of words in the information-processing vocabulary by the sharp, rich, scientific meanings these words must have in the future.

I think this points to a clear public policy for understanding and assessing the new technology. We need greatly increased public support for research and development efforts of as varied a nature as possible. They should certainly include network experiments of the sort John Kemeny envisages. They should include data-bank experiments. Above all, they should include experiments in robotry, large-scale memory organization, and artificial intelligence, leading to a basic foundation for a science of information processing.

52

Past experience suggests that a program pursued in the experimental spirit I have indicated will have valuable by-products. List processing is an esoteric development of computer-programming languages that was motivated initially about fifteen years ago by pure research interests in artificial intelligence. Today, its concepts are deeply imbedded in the design of large programming and operating systems regularly used in accounting and engineering computation.

The exploration of the moon is a great adventure. After the moon, there are objects still farther out in space. But man's inner space, his mind, is less well known than the space of the planets. It is time we establish a national policy to explore this inner space systematically, with goals, timetables, and budgets. Will you think me whimsical or impractical if I propose that one of these goals be a world-champion chess-playing computer program by 1975; and another, an order-of-magnitude increase by 1980 in the speed with which a human being can learn a difficult school subject, such as a foreign language or arithmetic?

If we are willing to dedicate ourselves to national goals of this kind (if you do not like my two, substitute your own), set deadlines for them, and commit resources to them (as we have committed resources to exploration of outer space), I think we soon shall have an understanding of both the information processors we call computers and those we call man. This understanding will enable us to build organizations far more effectively in the future than has ever been possible before.

REFERENCES

1. John W. Gardner, "What Kind of Society Do We Want?", *Reader's Digest*, September 1969.
2. National Academy of Sciences, *Technology: Processes of Assessment and Choice*, Report to the Committee on Science and Astronautics, U.S. House of Representatives, Government Printing Office, July 1969.
3. Edward A. Feigenbaum and Julian Feldman, *Computers and Thought*, McGraw-Hill, 1963.
4. Claude Shannon, *Mathematical Theory of Communication*, University of Illinois Press, 1949.
5. John G. Kemeny, "Large Time-Sharing Networks," this volume.
6. National Academy of Sciences, *Technology*; Herbert A. Simon, *The Shape of Automation*, Harper & Row, 1965; Herbert A. Simon, *The Sciences of the Artificial*, MIT Press, 1969.
7. John Platt, "What We Must Do," *Science*, 166 (1969), 1115–1121.
8. Anthony G. Oettinger, "Compunications in the National Decision-Making Process," this volume.
9. Joel Moses, "Symbolic Integration," MAC-TR 47 (thesis), Project MAC, Massachusetts Institute of Technology, AD662666, December 1967.
10. Nicholas Johnson, "The Silent Screen," *TV Guide*, July 5, 1969, pp. 6–13.

[13]

Journal of Economic Behavior and Organization 13 (1990) 275-298. North-Holland

THE FIRM AS A COMPETENT TEAM*

Gunnar ELIASSON

Industrial Institute for Economic and Social Research (IUI), S-114 53, Stockholm, Sweden

Received June 1989; final version received February 1989

Results from empirical studies of firm behavior are synthesized into *a theory of the firm as a competent team*. I demonstrate the existence of a tacit organizational competence exercising a leverage on the productivities of all other factors through selecting and allocating competent people, thus earning a monopoly rent in the capital market. The competence identified can only be fairly compensated through sharing in firm value growth in the equity market, exhibiting undervaluation of prime assets. Policies aimed at firm efficiency should improve the market measurement function, including stimulating insiders to exhibit information through trades.

1. Introduction

From a series of depth interviews with the managers and detailed surveys describing the cost and financial structure of Swedish firms [Eliasson (1976, 1984b, 1989b)], a profile of modern business has emerged that is only partially recognized in economic theory but whose salient features must play an important role if we are to understand the forces currently shaping the world economy. In this paper I describe this profile and suggest its implications. In particular, I argue that insider trading and corporate takeovers are necessary for the effective working of capital markets.

Three basic concepts are central to my argument; those of (i) the *business opportunity space*, (ii) *tacit knowlege*, (iii) the *experimental nature of competition*. Before proceeding we need to understand what they are about.

Management assesses its business potential from the point of view of its particular, but limited, capacity to orient itself successfully in a largely unknown *business opportunity space* that includes nature and the accumulated knowledge of all agents in the economy. So do all its competitors, and the business opportunity space depends on what they all plan to do on the basis of their perceptions of one another, and how all their plans are realized. The opportunity space is so large, compared with local (and

*The final version of this paper has benefited significantly from comments by Pontus Braunerhjelm, Richard Day, Bengt Holmström, Harald Lang, Erik Mellander, Sten Nyberg, Pavel Pelikan, Frank Stafford, Clas Wihlborg and Bengt-Christer Ysander, and three anonymous referees, one of whom read the manuscript very carefully.

heterogeneous) information processing capacity of firms, as to prevent all but a 'fractional' penetration and understanding of each firm. Its content cannot be catalogued.

There is a *top competent team* of the firm, that will be more precisely defined below. The firm is organized such that this team exercises a top down 'leverage' or scale effect on the productivities of the entire business organization.

The concept of tacit knowledge [see Polanyi (1967), Nelson and Winter (1982), Murnane and Nelson (1984) and Pelikan (1989)] is subtle. I will define it in terms of *'limited communicability' of knowledge*. It is an asset that is embodied in individuals or teams of individuals and can be traded only in the markets for management. Direct communicability is limited by the codability of the content of the knowledge base, the transferability of the code and the competence of receivers to read the code and to apply the so acquired competence to their own situation.[1] Tacit knowledge defies the notion of full information and optimization behavior. With it, economic filtering and experimental economic behavior enter.

In their pursuit of profits modern business firms operate in more or less free and experimentally organized markets, ranging from the international financial markets to markets with restricted competitive access, as in the Eastern planned economies, and the public sectors of the Western nations. By experimentally organized I mean that agents are free to enter markets in competition with incumbent producers. Engaging in competition is synonymous with testing a hypothesis about ones own competence through setting up an experiment in the market. Very frequently the hypothesis is rejected [Eliasson (1987a)].

The 'leverage' or scale effect on the productivities of all factors of the tacit knowledge 'T' of the top competent team can be expressed [Romer (1986, p. 1015)] by the production function,

$$Q = F(T, x), \tag{1}$$

assumed to be concave in *measured* factor inputs x for any fixed value of T. Romer demonstrates that F exhibits increasing returns to scale in T. For Romer T is the exogenous, aggregate level of knowledge available to all firms. I assume, however, that T is 'tacit', or unique and incommunicable. Romer's results for the economy then hold for the individual firm. It is the

---

[1]Codability in this sense has an exact meaning in computer science, which is a useful reference for illustration. In my context the limits of codable, communicable competence are necessarily vague, and impossible to establish empirically. That is the meaning of tacitness. Each of us knows that we don't know *how* to walk, even though we do it. When the competitor sees that it can be done, but cannot acquire the instruction manual in the market, he has to start learning by experimenting. The knowledge is tacit.

factor T that receives the residual profit when all other factors have been paid.

Tacit knowledge means that $T(I)$ of one firm cannot be transferred into competitor $T(II)$. Such a transfer requires that the code in which $T(I)$ is stored can be made explicit or communicable and that firm II can interpret the same code. The competence to interpret the code must also reside in $T(II)$. The assumption about an intractable opportunity space above can now be exactly reformulated as large enough to include at least one firm that is not able to interpret $T(I)$. This lack of receiver competence is sufficient for the existence of tacit T.

The more heterogeneous the local knowledge base, the larger the 'tacit' element of the total knowledge base of the economy. Limited local receiver competence poses limits to the communication of information. The outcome of economic activity cannot be ascertained before it has been tried in the market. This establishes the experimental nature of economic activity. As a consequence, the state of full information is at each point in time unattainable, leaving individual agents, at each point in time partially and differentially informed. This also establishes the experimental allocation of organizational competence as the rationale for the firm.[2]

Section 2 accounts for the organization of management and decision making in the firm. This account is complemented in section 3 with accounting data, showing the extent of knowledge based information use in manufacturing. Section 4 returns to the competence of the firm and the organizational techniques of reproducing and upgrading it through the selection (filtering) and on-the-job-learning of people through careers. Finally, section 5 considers the instrument that measures top level business competence and the nature of its compensation, and discusses the reliability and precision of that instrument, namely the equity market. The incentive and compensation schemes that emerge must influence both the supply and allocation of competence.

2. Organization of management and decision making

The top team embodies the organizational competence in measurable managerial categories. The exercising of top organizational competence is best illustrated when a badly managed firm is taken over by new owners and its top executive group replaced. The team at the top decides on the

[2]Even though this formulation breaks away from mainstream tradition, I have of course borrowed ideas not only from Simon (1955, bounded rationality) but also from Marschak and Radner (1972, 'teams') and Alchian and Demsetz (1972). The notion of a team in the disequilibrium firm growth model of Penrose (1959) incorporates certain features of my firm model. I am grateful for the anonymous referee who reminded me of Penrose's book. Even though I once read it I missed that association.

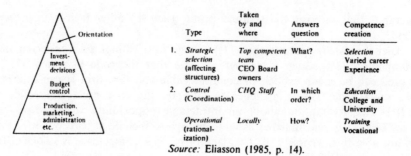

Type	Taken by and where	Answers question	Competence creation
1. *Strategic selection* (affecting structures)	*Top competent team* CEO Board owners	What?	*Selection* Varied career Experience
2. *Control* (Coordination)	*CHQ Staff*	In which order?	*Education* College and University
Operational (rationalization)	*Locally*	How?	*Training* Vocational

Source: Eliasson (1985, p. 14).

Fig. 1. Levels of decision making within a business organization.

orientation of business, on its *organization* and on the hiring of (lower level) talent. This top competent team is responsible for the creation of residual profits, when all other factors have been compensated. (The top competent team, hence, as mentioned exercises the leverage effect associated with *T*). It can only be adequately compensated through sharing in the residual profits.

The top competent team is best identified through its authority to exercise control. It is not well defined in organizational language. In Sweden it is made up of the dominant owners on the Board of Directors and the top corporate officers. The relative influence of outside directors and corporate officers varies between firms and over time. Certain national characteristics can be observed that are based on tradition and legal rules. The point is that the team is self-organized and cannot easily be described by legal positions, titles or organization charts. Nonetheless, it exercises the control function that links the internal financial accounts with the external capital market. Rate of return targets are confronted with the market interest rate, and used to coordinate all local decisions.

Schumpeter (1942, p. 123) called the invention of double entry accounting in medieval Italy a major technological innovation that made rational profit and cost calculation possible. He observed that it has become the central instrument for organizing, building and coordinating today's large business organizations. This calculating device – a financial control function – makes it possible for the firm to integrate profitably the financial and real dimensions of economic activity at the central level.

Decisions related to the entire firm are typically separately organized (very much as shown in fig. 1); the *strategic level* in charge of orientation, reorganization and the hiring of talent, the *control level coordinating* existing unit (divisional) activities and the *local rationalization level* in charge of performance upgrading of existing activities. Each draws on different bodies of tacit knowledge.

At the rationalization level decisions are local, delegated, well structured and carefully prepared by experts. Observation is relatively easy. Most business administration literature is concerned with well defined problems at this level. Previously, such decisions focused on new machine investments (e.g. robotization in workshops). Today we find that rationalization decisions in manufacturing firms in a large measure involve information activities such as accounting, accounts receivable, software development, etc.

Existing, well structured activities of the entire firm are coordinated into an orderly, fast flow. 'Budgeting' is designed to monitor and coordinate divisions of the entire business entity. Central coordinators deal with well defined elements in that flow process, relying on the language of targeting, budgeting, reporting and control to achieve flow efficiency. Middle management enters as communicators between the top executive level and the shop floor [Eliasson (1976, p. 219, 1989b)]. Also marketing and distribution belong here, connecting the production system with ultimate demand.

The situation is dramatically different at the top corporate (*strategic*) *level* where decisions are made by the competent team that affect the structure of the hierarchy or the choice of control technique. At this level decisions are concerned with innovative organizational activities, the *choice of decision model*, the frame of reference, the direction and the business problem of the organization as a whole. These are not analytical activities, but a dialectical process among groups of competent people, bringing (often) inconsistent approaches together into a synthesis [Mason (1969), Mitroff (1971), Eliasson (1976, p. 87)]. The *top competent team* resides here.

Balancing the top level innovative and organizational decisions with the middle level coordination task of running production efficiently embodies a major organizing problem in large business firms. It involves applying competence vertically through the layers of management (the pyramid in fig. 1). With tacit knowledge being the dominant input, individuals who aspire to be members of the top competent team must engage in on the job learning at all levels, eventually to be filtered to the top (see right column in fig. 1). The organization of these careers is also experimental. Hence the competent team currently in charge will be dependent on the preceding team, and so on, each firm being a separate path dependent entity, with an organizational memory.[3]

This means that a large number of different organizational forms have been tried and are currently practiced. Sometimes the innovative mode dominates, sometimes the conservative mode. It depends, which one happens

---

[3]Historic studies [see e.g., Eliasson (1980) and Jagrén (1986, 1988a)] show the critical trade-off between dynamic (Schumpeterian) efficiency [see Eliasson (1985, p. 15 and p. 330)] associated with innovative reorganizations of firms, and the (static) flow efficiency, achieved through middle level coordination of existing activities; or the minimization of internal slack or waste. While innovative reorganizations decide the long-term survival of firms, coordination efficiency can generate superior performance for years.

to be regarded as most efficient. The tightly controlled U.S. conglomerate organizations differ clearly from the tightly, but differently controlled 'banking groups' in West Germany and even more so from the more loosely structured Wallenberg Group of companies in Sweden.[4] The objectives of the top competent team, the dominant owners and/or the capital market agents that rule the firm ultimately have to be geared to the value that 'the market' sets on the firm. At each point in time this value determines the liquidity of the tradable assets of the firm and the spot market value of the competent team. It also determines part of the team's compensation. The analysis of this market valuation is taken up below.

3. The technology of economic information processing and communication

The outcome of competition, and the nature of the local market environments of each firm depend on how the total economic system is organized to coordinate individual action. Co-ordination takes place within firms, through administrative procedures and between firms in markets, through prices that are determined by the ongoing, combined actions of all agents.

The firm exists on the basis of its management's competence to internalize the co-ordination of activities and to earn a positive return on assets over the market interest rate. The 'asset' that accomplishes that coordination is the local knowledge base that we have called T. Its character – and thus the firm – is revealed when the *control system* of the firm has been defined. It relates the objectives of the top competent team to real operations via administrative technique. Since the knowledge base is locally embodied in individuals or teams and largely incommunicable, the firm can be viewed as a hierarchy of ordered teams of people embodying the human competence needed to coordinate resources (machines, raw materials, labor, etc.) to generate economic value or profits. Managerial technique becomes the art of organizing competent people, such that maximum economic value is created. Obviously this has something to do with incentives. Long-run survival of each firm as a successful generator of economic value requires that team competence be constantly upgraded, and new knowledge effectively diffused through the organization.

The knowledge intensive information activities in which the firm beats competitors in the market are of four different kinds; *innovation* (or knowledge creation), *knowledge transfer* (learning), *knowledge allocation* (filtering) and *co-ordination*. Such internal information processing in firms is a dominant resource-using activity. Its efficiency determines the productivity of

---

[4]See Dahmén (1988) and Glete (1989). Dahmén's observation that the banks, the financial markets and the firms perform basically similar functions is interesting in this context. A broadly defined firm, the *industrial bank* can sometimes be organized to beat both the firm and the market in general in earning a systematically higher return to assets than the interest rate.

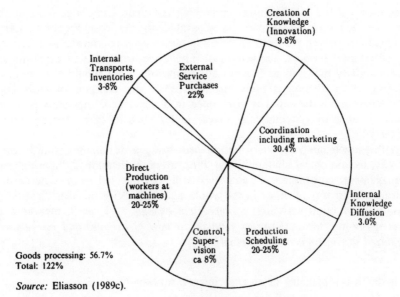

Fig. 2. Distribution of labor costs
– Large Swedish firms
– Global operations
– Percent.

the economic system and the relative size distribution of firms. 'Knowledge creation' associated with product improvement, product specification, technology, co-ordination, and marketing requires investment as much as, or more than all funds spent on machines and buildings in the large Swedish corporations [Eliasson (1987a, p. 12 and 58)]. We do not have good cost data on the transfer of knowledge within the firm, but evidence tells that some 'advanced' firms devote resources not much less than resources spent on R&D on formal, 'measurable', internal education programs. We know that the competence accumulated through these activities in a firm is learned through participation in market competition, or direct purchasing in the markets. Until the competence has been diffused in the market it is a 'tacit' or 'unique' competitive advantage of the firm.

Not much more than 30 percent of internal labor costs in large Swedish firms can be characterized as direct production (see fig. 2). Some 8 percent is devoted to innovation, and some 3 percent to measured internal education.[5] Altogether some 60 percent or more of total labor input is devoted to co-ordination, filtering and the creation and diffusion of knowledge. Part of this

---

[5]This is a minimum figure, i.e., what has been recorded in firm cost accounts as 'education'. See Fölster (1988).

goes into 'on the job learning', enhancing the tacit knowledge base of the firm, an activity that cannot be separated in the cost accounts. Large resources moreover are devoted to attempts to acquire knowledge (purchasing of external services, acquisition of innovative firms etc.) an experimental search activity that now and then leads to mistakes that should also count as learning costs. Strong diminishing returns in the creation of such tacit knowledge guarantees that a firm, once in a superior competence position, won't be able to systematically invest in learning to take over the entire industry.[6]

With knowledge-based information processing a dominant resource-using activity, technological change in the 'innovative', 'educational', 'filtering' and 'management co-ordination' activities will be the efficiency determining characteristics of the firm or of the whole economy. With this classification of various production activities *'technological change'* as I see it, measured in macroeconomic terms, is *directly linked to how hierarchies and markets are organized to control economic activity.*

4. Is the firm a planning or an experimental machine?

Competition depends on the number, financial strength, aggressiveness and orientation of participating agents. With many competitors with different competence, behavior will be largely experimental, outcomes uncertain and the monopoly rent created by each Schumpeterian innovation temporary. The business positions may be suddenly upset by unexpected success of competing innovators. Firms that behave as analytical planning machines, carefully gathering relevant information needed for fully informed business decisions may do worse on average than daring firms that act prematurely on a prior *sense of direction.*

Because critical elements of industrial know-how are tacit and not communicable there can be no corresponding markets for 'information'. Agents have to experiment in order to acquire it. A slow or overly 'academic' decision process gives time for competitors to come up with better ideas. Moreover, in markets with technological product competition the outcome of a new business idea will always be highly uncertain until it has been tried in the market. The more aggressive and competent competing firms, the larger the likelihood that 'someone else' will be the first to succeed. As a

---

[6]This is related to Schumpeter's (1942) worry about the economic power of routinized innovative activity. The nature of organizational learning in large firms and the diminishing returns associated with such activities are explored in Eliasson (1988d). Granstrand and Sjölander (1990) show that a broad internal technology base makes the firm more efficient in acquiring and implementing new complementary knowledge. One way of doing this is through the acquisition of new innovative firms. This in turn illustrates the importance for competence upgrading in large firms of viable markets for innovations, or of a supply of innovative firms [Eliasson (1986)].

consequence, decisions (including 'inaction') are often premature and mistakes frequent and expected. The long-run survival of firms will depend on willingness of the competent team to change course and its ability to identify and correct mistakes.

The competence endowment of a firm can now be summarized by the following six characteristics;

(1) *Sense of direction* (intuition)
(2) *Daring* (risk-willingness)
(3) *Efficiency in identifying* mistakes (analysis).
(4) *Effectiveness in correcting* mistakes (activity)
(5) *Effectiveness in managing* ('co-ordinating') successful experiments.
(6) *Effectiveness in feeding* acquired experience back onto (1).

The ability to *sense the direction* [item (1) in table] *better than the market at large* reduces the uncertainty that the firm is experiencing compared to outside market analysts, and allows it to act faster and more daringly. What the outsider may regard as non-calculable uncertainty, the executive team converts into an appreciable risk situation (a hypothesis, an experimental design) on which it acts. This conversion, however, is entirely subjective. Each actor imposes a simplified personal (subjective) theory on all the 'facts' to achieve *subjective order* out of an immensely complex business situation. Such boundedly rational behavior [Simon (1955) and Day (1971)] is necessary to be able to act, to carry out the experiment. 'Bounded rationality' hence incorporates *important management technology, namely the competence to choose the right 'theory' through which to filter the facts, to evaluate the business situation*. No outsider can make the same 'conversion' except by proxy, i.e., evaluating the team which has set up the business experiment. (Hence, outsiders will perceive risk neutral – or even risk averse – behavior on the part of the top executive team, as riskwilling).

The more competitive the market setting, the more critical the filter that selects the competent team at the top that can take early and fast action on a sense of direction that is relatively better than that of other teams. In this sense *the firm is setting up and enacting subjectively controlled experiments, based on hypotheses about opportunities in the market.*[7] Each agent (competitor or market analyst) is an outsider in this game. Each individual actor may nevertheless act *as if* he appreciates his environment as a learnable, estimable process by imposing his personal interpretation. Hence, the agents can optimize on their perceptions of their environment even if the economy is experimentally organized. Behaving as if the economic environment is

---

[7]The competent team so defined has all the characteristics of Alchian and Demsetz' (1972) jointness and the Marschak and Radner (1972) team. It is, however, not only the optimal design of incentives that matters, but the tacit competence of the top team to organize the firm so as to create a monopoly rent.

predictable in order to be able to optimize in a mathematical sense will, however, normally mean that you are making an error. Rational learners will, hence, eventually learn that they won't be right in expectation [Day (1975)].

Making the competence to transform 'uncertainty' into 'computable' or 'insurable risks' [Eliasson (1985, p. 315)] the rationale for the existence of the firm is most adequately credited to Knight (1921).[8] [In a parallel paper (1989c), I have shown in detail how these boundedly rational 'interpretation' systems are organized in firms, and how firms manage the trade-off between long-term innovation efficiency and short-term co-ordination efficiency]. In Knight (1921) computable risks could be handled in the insurance market. The entrepreneur is not concerned with insurance or risk taking [Schumpeter (1954, p. 556)] but with uncertainty, which by definition corresponds to a market failure [Le-Roy and Singell (1987)]. The entrepreneur enters with local 'tacit' competence to put the business on a rational, computable footing. He has chosen his 'view', his theory, and faces *uncertainty associated with choice of model, a 'subjectively computable risk'.*

[8] Even though I have found in discussions with colleagues, and from an anonymous referee that it is unclear whether Knight really argued this. It is still a good idea, however, to model the firm as an entity concerned with 'subjectively computable risks'.

Look at the probability distribution $P(x, \theta) = P(x \mid \theta) P(\theta)$. I am uncertain about which decision model θ to choose. Zellner (1983, p. 141 f.) argues that a rational decision maker first chooses θ as a drawing from a probability distribution $P(\theta)$. θ are 'boundedly rational models' or parameters, even though Zellner doesn't use that term. Following Bayes' (1763) decision model the total decision problem can then be defined as a drawing from a simultaneous probability distribution $[= P(x, \theta)]$ of observations (decisions) and parameters (decision models). I may view my choice of decision model as a drawing from a distribution of 'boundedly rational' models that I think I know. I can then integrate both into a simultaneous distribution of decisions and observations. The decision maker, however, is only interested in the expected utility of his decision. The probability distributions therefore cannot be integrated. The decisions become drawings from the conditional probability distribution $P(x \mid \theta)$, conditioned by the prior imposed by choice of model from $P(\theta)$. Subjective probability distributions, however, cannot simply be cumulated to single valued probability distributions [Hart (1942)] and be made to look like a 'regular risk situation'; not for outsiders, possibly for insiders.

A more general and Bayesian procedure is to weigh the distributions of 'utilities' together to be able to choose from the simultaneous distribution of utilities of having chosen the correct model and the distribution of utilities from the outcome of the chosen decision. This is the only way to take in relevant information in the order it becomes known to the decision maker, i.e., to handle risk aversion. This view is voiced in different ways by Hart (1942), Shipley (1975), Kahneman and Tversky (1979), Tversky and Kahneman (1981), de Bondt and Thaler (1985), Fishburn (1987) etc.

One should of course ask whether it is at all possible to represent tacit knowledge on measrable form. There is no good answer. You can use the assumption as a pedagogical device. You can also say that the ambition to decode the 'tacit memory' means assuming that it can be decoded, which is very much the assumption of artificial intelligence approaches to management decision making. However, new results on so-called 'neural networks' [Crick (1989), Maddox (1989)] have demonstrated mathematically how complex systems with synaptic interconnections develop controlling memories. The output of these memories allows the external observers neither to derive their logical origin, nor their organization such that their output can be predicted. Formally these structures are related to mathematical chaos.

Confidence in the decision model chosen and willingness to act (prematurely) on its predictions are conditioned by the ability of the competent team to cope with mistakes, early and reliable identification of mistakes and effective correction of mistakes [type (3) and (4) of the competences identified]. Firm management now faces a narrow and well defined analytical problem, that is more in line with the 'decision theory' one learns at school. This is the management activity most easily observed by outsiders. Hence, it is also fairly well described in literature, however, not from the point of view of the purpose presented here.[9] Finally, if the experiment has been checked and cleared, an entirely new information technology clicks in, designed for efficient flow operation [item (5) of the organization and increased preparedness for future innovative, experimental and possibly disastrous action, *learning* feedback, item (6)].

The long-term success of a large corporation (therefore) depends on its ability to organize its career system filter, to upgrade the tacit knowledge base of its top competent team. This team sets the direction of the firm, and mobilizes and directs lower level competence. The selection of this team is largely self-organized, but the dominant owners play a critical role, either as raiders in the market, if the corporate officers manage to form a closed shop – as is often the case in the U.S. – or through competence contributions via a varied, informal interaction with the CEO, which is more typical of Swedish groups.[10] Hence the knowledge of how to organize a firm is 'tacit'. It is no surprise that so little empirical literature on this exists. Those who know do not write articles. The design of this filter, however, means life or death for the firm in the long term.

The career has two functions; (1) to *allocate* people with competence on tasks and (2) to *educate* competent ('talented') people by giving them a varied job experience so as to accumulate competence for even more demanding

[9]A small digression may be illustrative at this point. Even though the analytical signal that the firm is going under may be crystal clear, corrective action is not as simple as it may sound, especially in the modern welfare state. The information system used for identifying a mistake is increasingly put to use to convince employees, media and politicians that corrective action is 'needed' [Eliasson (1976, 1984, 1989b)]. The difference between the profit making private firm and the state operated firm illustrates this. One cannot, on theoretical or empirical (scientific) grounds claim that the state, or the executive team selected by the state is less competent than a private business leader to sense the direction of markets and/or to identify mistakes early. *A politically controlled business will, however, always be handicapped when it comes to correcting mistakes.* The political platform and the political goals mean that state operated firms will be badly organized for the efficient corrective action that is so critical in the experimentally organized economy. I have argued elsewhere, that this organizational method of the capitalistically organized economy to override – in business decision making – the political value system is an important efficiency characteristic of the private market organization [Eliasson (1988c)].

[10]This insight turns the ways of thinking in strategic literature from the 60s upside down. It was then thought that a management system separted from the people could be designed. People could enter and exit the system. The system and the firm would be invariant to its people. For a review of this literature see Eliasson (1976, Ch. IV).

tasks. The organization problem is to design the *incentive* system so that these tasks are well performed. Since the best characteristics of a top executive person have no clear definition, the filter is designed experimentally to monitor people and eventually to determine that the track record of this person or this team makes him or it competent enough to be given higher authority and more responsibility.

Business opportunities arise stochastically, as you go on experimenting. Hence, competence includes both the ability to sense an opportunity, the willingness to grab it before somebody else does, and identify and brutally scrap it, if it turns out to be a mistake. The weathering of major mistakes is the universal 'criterion' of a large, old and successful business firm [Eliasson (1980)]. The organization has to allow mistakes to happen both to experience successes and to learn to identify and correct mistakes. The absence of a trail of mistaken decisions in an individual's career signals that the person has systematically avoided mistakes, or done nothing. He or she lacks experience in identifying and correcting mistakes.[11] Provided the notion of an experimentally organized economy is empirically relevant, such persons should never be promoted beyond the co-ordination level.

Even so, monitoring is always needed. Competence will never be completely ascertained, and the leverage exercised on the firm of top business officers makes for very serious consequences of bad business judgement, or misuse of trust. Outside financiers or the analysts in the market will never be able to evaluate the business situation, only to take an outsider position on insider's decisions. Hence, it is often demanded of the top corporate team, very much as in small professional groups [see e.g. Gilson and Mnookin (1984)], that the persons trusted with authority also chip in 'hostage' equity stakes. Hence, the team will gain handsomely if it lines up with the profit objectives of the owners of the firm and performs with competence, and lose significantly if not. Such 'hostage arrangements' make top corporate officers share or lose, together with the owners. With insiders as significant owners, they cannot unload bad assets much ahead of an efficient market (see below). With tacit competence and ownership merged at the top reorganizing the firm and changing its direction normally means changing the top executive team.

---

[11]Some would argue that the selection of competence in a firm cannot be explained but rather requires a stochastic explanation. This is, however, wrong if the efficiency of selecting competence is dependent on past successes in selecting competence (learning through experience), a very reasonable assumption I would say. The competence of the firm then becomes path dependent and the competent team of the firm is equipped with a tacit 'organizational memory'. The same memory of the entire industry depends on how the capital market responds to the clashing of all inconsistent plans in the market, affecting the structural reorganization of the economy, i.e. the market self-organization of the technological (organizational) memory of the entire economy. This is in essence the design of the Swedish micro to macro model [Eliasson (1977, 1985, 1989e)].

Tacit knowledge integrates the two operating dimensions of a business: the real and the financial. Separability of transactions into financial and real markets in a Fisherian (1907) sense cannot be maintained. The top executive team and the dominant owners not only carry the risks associated with equity but also contribute the non-tradable organizational know-how that exercises a scale effect on the performance of the entire firm. The size of this scale effect means that the competent team can never be fully compensated for its contribution – if positive – through regular salary arrangements. Neither can they be made effectively responsible for incompetence.

Compensation in the form of capital gains corresponding to the equity stake is the efficient incentive arrangement for such contributions of tacit knowledge. Hence, the only way for an executive to get properly compensated is through becoming a part owner of the firm; and vice versa, a top executive who dares not take on a (for him) significant equity position is signalling a lack of confidence in his own competence, that is in itself a form of incompetence.

Let ε be the addition to net worth of the firm. ε is just the residual profit earned by the owners of the firm, net of costs for measured inputs. [For an exact definition see Eliasson (1984a) eq. (3b)]. Compensation for risk and tacit knowledge contributes to the size of ε. The present value of all expected future ε should somehow relate to the size of T. ε is composed of a random component ex post, representing the outcome of risktaking, and a systematic component representing inputs of top level, uncompensated organizational competence.

The competence input by owners depends on a number of factors.

(1) genuine organizational competence,
(2) ability (sense of direction) to place the business in the right price environment (selection),
(3) ability to influence product and factor prices in one's favor.

Monopoly market power, including the ability to hire excellent managerial talent cheaply [item (3)] of course, is part of items (1) and (2) type performance. In fact, the salaries of an excellent top level executive team rarely comes close to their contributions to the flow of income (or ε). The only way for the team to be properly compensated is to hold equity in the firm. The less the equity stake of the competent team the more surplus value it generates for the 'other' owners.[12] Inputs of competence, hence, cannot be regarded as independent of access to ε (that is of *incentive* arrangements).

[12]There is a third ε-contribution that has to be mentioned, namely the excess ε flow resulting from badly functioning markets. This can be a natural resource rent, even though this would mean that the capital input ('the natural resource') has not been properly measured. It could also be the result of a too low interest rate, a common situation in postwar Europe with regulated capital markets.

Suppose that the only task of the dominant owner is to monitor the *external* management market and the *internal* market (the career organization) for management talent, a principal-agent task, so to speak. If competence accumulation is largely of the 'learning by managing' kind, the high performing manager will always be in a hostage relationship to the dominant principal, who knows more about him than any outsider. If the manager (the agent) is also risk averse, he is likely to be underpaid. He contributes (because of asymmetric information) surplus profits to the owner principal. The only way of recouping those returns is for the manager to take on an ownership stake.

The natural thing would then be to define the top competent team exactly as the recipients of ε, treating management with no equity stake as hired hands, the ultimate competence having been exercised by owners in succeeding to hire such competent management for salary compensation only. Actually, however, the distinction between management and owners is not that important. A large group of 'free riding owners' are not part of the competent team, and lower level executives within the firm do not belong to the competent group. But they could hold larger stakes than the members of the top team. My conclusions in this paper do not depend on an exact definition of a team the composition of which varies from firm to firm.

Given what has been said so far the only source of valuation of the top management team is valuation in the stock market. Let us turn to that subject now.

5. The firm's information system, insider trading and efficient markets

5.1. A capital measurement design

Human competence carries economic value. Human capital theory assumes human competence to be reflected in wages and salaries. So why cannot top team competence in firms be valued similarly? Obviously the quality of this method of measurement depends on what you assume about the efficiency of markets.

Much intangible capital in a business firm can be measured and capitalized along the same principles as for machines or buildings. The efficiency of the labor, the stock or the investment goods markets in evaluating these goods defines the quality of measurement. Similarly, as long as production costs to recreate information, software or a machine tool are known, or the item can be purchased in the market, replacement values can be established. Any critique on how to measure the capital value of an investment in an educational program, or in new software to keep track of accounts receivable can be leveled at the evaluation of a piece of machinery. A good reason for making these assets explicit is to force firm management to pay attention to the associated capital costs, and demand a return also from these assets.

A first requirement of an efficient market valuation of a firm is that known, and measurable intangible assets have been accounted for. The ultimate innovative, organizational competence of 'the top competent team', however, has no defined reproduction value. It is tacit and cannot be traded. It does, however, earn a rent (ε) and to the extent the top competent team can be associated with the equity contract that defines the firm, the value of that contract should be the present value of expected future rents.[13] Shares in that contract can be traded in the stock market.

Tables 1 and 2 list measured assets. The information needed to construct these measures is not proprietary and is available if analysts devote some effort to obtain it. An efficient or at least semi-efficient market should be aware of the non-tangible assets (3) through (6) even though they are rarely specified in the accounts. The residual (12) is the market estimate of the present value of extra future profits expected to be generated by the top competent team. That residual may very well be negative if incompetence is known to rule at the top. The firm should then be a potential take-over target. A negative value could also be the result of an uninformed or incompetent valuation, or of a systematic risk aversion of all agents in the market, or of other price distortions, like taxes.[14]

Using information from a variety of IUI data bases (including those used in fig. 2) we have compiled tables 1 and 2 for the ten largest Swedish multinationals. These ten firms[15] dominate Swedish industry employing directly and indirectly some 30 percent of the domestic manufacturing labor force and as many abroad. They are generally regarded as the flagships of

[13]Within the classical model with no risk and all markets, except the capital market, in equilibrium, the $\bar{\varepsilon}$ of an individual firm can now be seen as the imputed factor cost for inputs of knowledge that exhausts total value added, an observation made already by McKenzie (1959). This is the same as to say that if there are increasing returns to tacit knowledge (T) inputs and if other inputs are paid their marginal products, the capital market can never be in equilibrium.

[14]In a *tax free* world a q-value of 1 would mean that the negative risk factor exactly offsets the contribution of competence. The fact that the q-ratio between market and replacement valued assets in Swedish industry stayed consistently well below 1 from 1970 to 1984 can be attributed to three facts only; (1) incompetence of executives in running manufacturing firms, (2) incompetence of traders in the equity market in evaluating the firms or (3) excessive macro (political) risks associated with Government and Labor Union ambitions to expropriate private wealth. As far as can be seen, development since the early 80s eliminates the first explanation. The fact that the U.S. and U.K. stock exchanges exhibited a similar strong undervaluation during the same period apparently removes the political explanation, at least as the only one. The undervaluation in Sweden was much deeper. Could it be that traders in all three markets exhibit the same inability to assess fundamentals, and if so, why?

[15]They are Electrolux, SKF, Ericsson, ASEA, Volvo, Swedish Match, Sandvik, Atlas Copco, Alfa Laval, and AGA. For details of the data see Eliasson (1989a).

Table 1

Capital stock measurements of 10 Swedish corporations 1985–SEK billion.

	(1) Alt I[a]	(2) Alt II[a]	(3) Alt III[a]	(4)
	Replacement valuation		According to plan	According to the books
Tangible assets				
(1) Machines, buildings and inventories	149.5	149.5	120.0	105.3
(2) Financial assets	146.5[b]	146.5[b]	146.5[b]	140.6
Non tangible				
(3) Software investments	n.a.	n.a.	n.a.	0
(4) Technical know-how (Accumulated R&D)	46.2	25.5	16.3	0
(5) Market knowledge	54.6	20.1	12.9	0
(6) Educational, human embodied capital	27.3	8.1	5.2	0
(7) Total replacement valued (measured) capital [sum of (1) through (6)]	424.1	349.7	300.9	245.9
(8) –debt	152.2	152.2	152.2	152.2
(9) –concealed tax debt	44.8	44.8	36.4	29.0
(10) = Net worth [(7)–(8)–(9)]	227.1	152.7	120.3	64.7
(11) Corresponding asset values according to the market	84.0	84.0	84.0	84.0
(12) Residual value [(11)–(10)]	–143.1	–68.7	–36.3	+19.3
(13) Deduct for risks, including political risks	n.a.	n.a.	n.a.	n.a.
(14) Deduct for lack of information or incompetence of equity market specialists	n.a.	n.a.	n.a.	n.a.
(15) Residual value measuring executive and entrepreneurial competence	n.a.	n.a.	n.a.	n.a.
(16) Real rate of return on total assets [=(1)+(2)+(4)+(5)+(6)], percent, (N.B.!) 1986	6.9	9.7	11.0	–

[a]Alt I means depreciation 5.6 percent for all categories. Alt II means depreciation 5.6, 15, 25, 35 percent, respectively. Alt III means depreciation 5.6, 100, 100, 100 percent.

[b]Adjusted upwards with SEK 5.9 billion for undervalued shares and hydro-electrical property.

[c]An analogous computation using book values would no longer give a comparable real rate of return.

Swedish industry. When all the computations are done using reproduction values of measurable assets, we find a very large negative market valuation (before correcting for risks) of the contribution of the top competent team, an obviously absurd result for these 10 firms. Even with the highest estimate of assets in the denominator, the real rate of return (1986) of the group of

Table 2

The composition of investments[a] (INV) and capital (K)–The 10 largest Swedish multinationals–in percent.

	INV	K		
		Alt I[b]	Alt II[b]	Alt III[b]
(1) Machinery and buildings	39	39	61	100
(2) R&D	22	22	19	0
(3) Marketing	26	26	15	0
(4) Education	13	13	6	0
Total	100	100	100	100

[a]Investments have been assumed to grow at a rate of 5.5 percent in volume, i.e., at the rate recorded 1976/1986.

[b]Alt I: Depreciation: 5.6 percent for all categories. ALT II: Depreciation: 5.6, 15, 25, 35 percent, respectively. ALT III: Depreciation: 5.6, 100, 100, 100 percent.

ten of 6.9 percent is significantly above the real interest rate on industrial loans of 6.0 percent the same year. What is wrong with the capital market?[16]

One possible explanation would be in terms of a systematic *aversion to risk* on the part of all agents in the market. One would, however, expect an efficient market to filter out enough daring bidders to get the price right on the margin. The *second* explanation is more intriguing. With easily available data on book values of assets [column (4)] a positive residual valuation of about SEK 20 billions shows up. Not very much, but positive. Posit that this is all market analysts look at. As you retrieve more information from the databases of firms, hidden values appear, and all of a sudden a large negative residual value emerges, suggesting excessive incompetence in running these flagships of Swedish industry. But could this rather be a reflection of incompetence on the part of stock market analysts, commentators and traders to understand the proper value of the firm?

5.2. Access to the value growth and the selection of competent teams

The discounted value of future profits generated by the competent team is available today:

– in cash through dividends
– in the market through growth in the price of the firm (capital gains).

[16]It is no argument that the stock market evaluation may have increased relative to net worth since 1985 (year in the table). The valuation was wrong then and for years before, and the continued increase in the market valuation of equity, putting perhaps a positive value on the top competent team, is currently, generally interpreted as a warning, that the market may be too high.

The value to the owners of the contribution of the top competent team
depends on what market traders think of the earnings capacity of the firm,
i.e., on the competence of the market to evaluate future ε-flows. One would
expect a competent management to add value to the firm above the sum of
the reproduction value of its assets. The transfer of ownership entitlements
(without selling assets), hence, depends on the *competence of the capital
market* to assess the value of the firm. This valuation is critical for an
innovating firm that is selling its know-how to a larger firm which intends to
develop the innovation for industrial scale production. Without an efficient
market for innovations and with many competent competitors (insiders) the
innovators will not be adequately compensated [Eliasson (1986)].

The competence rents ε are competed away through the innovative
organizational knowledge creating new rents ε. The creation of rents affects
the growth of the economy, by improving economic performance of the
innovators, and eliminating (exit) low performers through increased competition. The first key to macroeconomic growth therefore is the incentive
system that drives innovative behavior. Second, path dependence (caused by
tacit knowledge as discussed in section 4) makes it impossible to estimate
from current observations the future path of the economy. But this would be
needed to transform the future distributions of rents onto a standard scale. It
follows that economic growth cannot be represented by an estimable
distribution function that is invariant of time. In experimentally organized
economies individual firm rents are unpredictable and because tacit knowledge grows partly through failure, past failures may be as good an indicator
of future success, as past successes. Markets in the experimentally organized
economy are not even weakly efficient, because the evolution of the economy
depends on how markets for corporate control are organized to stimulate
experimentation and enforce targets. Markets are dependent themselves on
the way the economy develops. Because they lack the requisite tacit
knowledge outside (market) analysts cannot fairly assess the value of firms or
industries. The efficiency of the market for corporate control will depend on
how effectively insider knowledge is transmitted to the market. With this
knowledge being largely tacit *it can only be diffused indirectly through direct
participation in the market of the competent teams.* Thus compensation both
for competence, and for the incentives to inform the market relate directly to
how informed is the valuation of shares.[17] The efficiency of the stock market
will critically affect the competence level of industry. But market analysts will
be unable to value the tacit competence capital through analytical methods.
Instead the efficiency of the capital market will depend on their ability to
identify insider trades effectively.

---

[17]Note the difference between having *access to valuable information* about the corporation and
contributing valuable competence to the corporation, and making it known to the market.

5.3. Insider trading and market efficiency

An important capital market function is to initiate change in fundamentals and in the composition of competent teams. While the efficiency of the market to value fundamentals hinges on its expertise in monitoring insider trading, the efficiency of the market to improve fundamentals, or upgrade the organizational memory requires competence of the same kind as that being evaluated. An efficient market therefore requires that a significant number of competent industrialists operate as insiders or 'raiders'.

There will also be an incentive for the top competent team – if having significant ownership stakes in the business – to influence the market valuation of the firm. While the efficiency of the market increases if it evaluates the competent team, rather than the entire business situation, this efficiency depends on how good and fast analysts are in identifying the trades of the insiders and their attempts to influence the market. The better they are the smaller the cost to other owners in the form of capital gains lost to the insiders. Getting asset prices right involves the 'reshuffling' of wealth among shareowners, benefiting the early insiders until trades take place at 'the right prices'. The influence on industrial structures of raider activity has been increasingly discussed in the business journals during the 80s. At the same time firms like Electrolux, expanding through acquisitions, have done the same thing for years. The 'synergistic effects' on the generation of ε of raiding activities by dominant owners [according to Bradley, Desai and Kim (1983)][18] appear to dominate over the wealth reshuffling effects.[19]

Assessing people is difficult. The top team (1) knows best and (2) exercises a leverage on the future orientation of the firm's activities. Hence, the financial risk taken on by the top team, defines the credibility of its signals to the market. The 'pilot ownership share' defines how much of future gains the top executive team will appropriate, or will lose from mismanagement. A competent team that is not entering a hostage relationship with the owners of the firm (taking on significant pilot ownership) not only does a disservice to themselves but also to other stock owners. Rules that do not allow members of the competent team to hold stock in their business, and thereby become rich in proportion to their ability to manage the corporation, in this view, prevents efficient allocation of competence in firms. At the same time a market that does not effectively identify and evaluate insiders as holders of competence is not an efficient market. Rather than prohibiting insider trades the legislators should be concerned about getting the information out quickly

[18]The 'synergy' vs. information effects of Bradley, Desai and Kim (1983) should correspond roughly to what Schleifer and Summers (1987) mean by 'efficiency' and 'wealth reshuffling' effects.

[19]Bradley, Desai and Kim (1983) are probably correct in that conclusion, even though Ravenscraft and Scherer (1987) doubt it. But all evidence rests on empirical analyses of models without the self-organizing property that is the essence of the synergies they discuss.

through reporting requirements etc. A reliable and identifiable market signaling system is needed. Three different forms of *signaling* are discussed in literature:

(1) through *dividends*,
(2) through *own stock repurchases*,
(3) through *pilot and concentrated ownership*.

The market evaluates the ability of the corporation to achieve a steady growth in dividends highly as a predictor of future dividends and of actual ε-generating capacity. Large and once profitable corporations, however, have an immense potential for fooling the market for a long time, while small or newly started firms are at a disadvantage. With uninformed analysts in the stock market, one would expect cautious, risk avese evaluations. Reliable signals would only come from trades of insiders. Stock repurchases are allowed in the U.S., not in Sweden. If the market does not understand, the firm can buy its shares back until 'the market understands' better. In general, stock repurchases have been profitable. Similarly, direct insider trades of corporate officers on personal account are reliable signals. The more efficient the market, the lower the costs of insider trading to other owners, and the faster all later transactions take place at the 'right price'. Without active insiders, the stock market would be dominated by uninformed analysts, and share important properties with the used car market, the bad cars 'the lemons', determining the price, and the quality assets going for bargain prices. This market would be a boon to skilled raiders, and its valuations, and the rewards to pilot owners, as unstable as we can observe.

With the exception of Demsetz and Lehn (1985), and Morck, Schleifer and Vishny (1986) there are few empirical studies about pilot ownership. Since new empirical information is critical for understanding the interaction of capital markets and the restructuring of economies I hope to see more evidence forthcoming, and especially evidence that distinguishes capital gains due to the transmission of insider information from capital gains due to (insider) contributions of competence.

Finally, a few words on the paradoxical finding that the contribution of the top competent teams of the best Swedish corporations may be negatively valued by the stock market. The market registers marginal transactions, and the competence we want to measure is an invisible 'stock'. In massive transactions it becomes visible, and allocated approximately to the right owner. Transactions in controlling blocks of stock normally command a premium, raising the value of stock to those who sell. Analogously, massive purchases by the 'competent team' signal a significant, upward shift in prices, and vice versa for sales. When the market afterwards returns to 'normal' and undervalues the competence contribution it serves the rational function of 'locking in' the competence in the firm, very much as a computer user can be locked into the system of a particular vendor by the massive investment in learning needed to use it. The absence of an informed market, thus reinforces the hostage arrangements.

References

Alchian, A.A. and H. Demsetz, 1972, Production, information costs and economic organization, American Economic Review, Dec., 777–795.

Arrow, K.J., 1962, The economic implications of learning by doing, Review of Economic Studies 29, June, 155–173.

Arrow, K.J., 1973a, Information and economic behavior (Federation of Swedish Industries, Stockholm).

Arrow, K.J., 1973b, Higher education as a filter, Journal of Public Economics 2, July, 193–216.

Arrow, K.J., 1974, The limits of organization (New York).

Arrow, K.J., 1982, Risk perception in psychology and economics, Economic Inquiry, Jan.

Bayes, T., 1763, An essay towards solving a problem in the doctrine of chances, The Philosophical Transactions 53, 370–411, Reprinted in Biometrica 1958, 45, 296–315.

Blume, T. and D. Easley, 1982, Learning to be rational, Journal of Economic Theory 26, 340–351.

Bradley, M., A. Desai and E.H. Kim, 1983, The rationale behind interfirm tender offers, Journal f Financial Economics 11, 183–406.

Bray, M., 1982, Learning, estimation and the stability of rational expectations, Journal of Economic Theory 26, 318–339.

Coase, R.H., 1937, The nature of the firm, Economica, New Series IV, Nov., 13–16.

Crick, F., 1989, The recent excitement about neural networks, Nature 337, Jan., 129–132.

Dahmén, E., 1988, Entrepreneurial activity, banking and finance. Historical aspects and theoretical suggestions, Paper to the IUI Conference on the markets for innovation, ownership and control (IUI, Stockholm).

Day, R.H., 1971, Rational choice and economic behavior, Theory and Decision 1 (D. Reidel Publishing Co., Dordrecht) 229–251.

Day, R.H., 1975, Adaptive processes and economic theory; in: Day–Groves, eds. 1975, Adaptive economic models (New York).

Day, R.H. and G. Eliasson, eds. 1986, The dynamics of market economies (IUI-North-Holland, Amsterdam).

De Bondt, W.F.M. and R. Thaler, 1985, Does the stock market overreact? Journal of Finance XL, no. 3, July, 793–808.

Demsetz, H. and K. Lehn, 1985, The structure of corporate ownership: Causes and consequences, Journal of Political Economy 93, no. 6, Dec., 1155–1177.

Eliasson, G., 1976, Business economic planning–Theory, practice and comparison (Wiley, New York).

Eliasson, G., 1977, Competition and market processes in a simulation model of the Swedish economy, American Economic Review 1.

Eliasson, G. ed. 1978, A micro-to-macro model of the Swedish economy, IUI Conference Reports 1978:1 (Stockholm).

Eliasson, G., 1980, Företag, marknader och ekonomisk utveckling–en teori och några exemplifieringar, The firm, markets and economic development–A theory and some illustrations; in: E. Dahmén and G. Eliasson, eds.

Eliasson, G., 1984a, Micro heterogeneity of firms and the stability of industrial growth, JEBO 5, nos. 3–4.

Eliasson, G., 1984b, Informations-och styrsystem i stora företag, Information and control systems in large business organizations; in: Eliasson, Fries, Jagrén, Oxelheim, eds., Hur styrs storföretag?–en studie av informationshantering och organisation, How are large business groups managed? A study of information handling and organization (IUI-Liber, Kristianstad).

Eliasson, G., 1985, The firm and financial markets in the Swedish micro to macro model– Theory, model and verification (IUI, Stockholm).

Eliasson, G., 1986, Innovative change, dynamic market allocation and long-term stability of economic growth; IUI Working paper, no. 156, to be published in: David and Dosi, eds., Innovation and the diffusion of technology. (Oxford University Press, Oxford) forthcoming.

Eliasson, G., 1987, Technological competition and trade in the experimentally organized economy, Research Report, no. 32 (IUI, Stockholm).

Eliasson, G., 1988a, Ägare, entreprenörer och kapitalmarknadens organisation–en teoretisk presentation och översikt; in: J. Örtengren, et al., eds., Expansion avveckling och företagsvärdering i svensk industri–en studie av ägarformens och finansmarknadernas betydelse för strukturomvandlingen (IUI, Stockholm).

Eliasson, G., 1988b, The knowledge base of an industrial economy, IUI Research report no. 33 (Stockholm).

Eliasson, G., 1988c, Schumpeterian innovation, market structure and the stability of industrial development; in: H. Hanusch, ed., Evolutionary economics, applications of Schumpeter's ideas (Cambridge University Press).

Eliasson, G., 1988d, The international firm: A vehicle for overcoming barriers to trade and a global intelligence organization diffusing the notion of a nation, Paper prepared for the Prins Bertil Symposium on corporate and industry strategies for Europe at Handelshögskolan, Stockholm, Nov. 9–11, 1988; IUI Working paper no. 201.

Eliasson, G., 1989a, The knowledge-based information economy; in: Eliasson, Fölster, Lindberg, Pousette (1989).

Eliasson, G., 1989b, The firm, its objectives, its controls and its organization–A study on the use of information in market and administrative processes, and the transfer of knowledge within the firm, Working paper (IUI, Stockholm) forthcoming.

Eliasson, G., 1989c, Bounded irrational behavior, dynamic market coordination and the limits of organization, IUI Working paper no. 207b (Stockholm).

Eliasson, G., 1989d, How industrial knowledge accumulation drives a path-dependent economic process, in: B. Carlson, ed., Industrial dynamics (Kluwer Academic Publishers, The Hague).

Eliasson, G., 1989e, Modeling long-term macroeconomic growth, IUI Working paper no. 220 (Stockholm).

Eliasson, G., S. Fölster, T. Lindberg and T. Pousette, 1989, The knowledge-based information economy, IUI working paper (Stockholm) forthcoming.

Fama, E.F., 1980, Agency problems and the theory of the firm, Journal of Political Economy 88, April, 288–307.

Fisher, I., 1907, The rate of interest–Its nature, determination and relation to economic phenomena (MacMillan, New York).

Fishburn, P.C., 1987, Reconsiderations in the foundations of decision under uncertainty, Economic Journal 93, no. 388, Dec., 825–841.

Frydman, R., 1982, Towards an understanding of market processes: Individual expectations, learning, and convergence to rational expectations equilibrium, American Economic Review 72, no. 4, 652–668.

Gibrat, R., 1930, Une loi des répartitions économiques: L'éffet proportionnel, Bulletin de la statistique général de la France, 469 ff.

Gilson, R.J. and R.H. Mnookin, 1984, Sharing among the human capitalists: An economic inquiry into the corporate law firm and how partners split profits, Working paper no. 16 (Law and Economics Program, Stanford Law School, Stanford, CA).

Glete, J., 1989, Long-term firm growth and ownership organization, Journal of Economic Behavior & Organization 12, no. 3, 329–351.

Granstrand, O. and S. Sjölander, 1990, The acquisition of technology and small firms by large firms, Journal of Economic Behavior and Organization.

Hanusch, H., ed., 1988, Evolutionary economics: Application of Schumpeter's ideas (Cambridge University Press, Cambridge).

Hart, A.G., 1942, Risk, uncertainty, and the unprofitability of compounding probabilities; in: Lange, McIntyre and Yntema, eds., Studies in: Mathematical economics and econometrics in memory of Henry Schultz (University of Chicago Press, Chicago).

Holmström, B., 1982, Moral hazard in teams, Bell Journal of Economics, Autumn.

Jagrén, L., 1986, Concentration, exit, entry and reconstruction of Swedish manufacturing; in: The economics of institutions and markets, IUI Yearbook 1986–1987 (IUI, Stockholm).

Jagrén, L., 1988a, Företagens tillväxt i ett historiskt perspektiv; in: J. Örtengren et al., eds., Expansion, avveckling och företagsvärdering i svensk industri (IUI, Stockholm).

Jagrén, L., 1988b, The combination, reorganization and productivity growth of a business organization–The case of Electrolux, internal IUI mimeo.

Kahneman, D. and A. Tversky, 1979, Prospect theory: Analysis of decision under risk, Econometrica 47, no. 3, March.

Keynes, J.M., 1936, The general theory of employment, interest and money (MacMillan, London).

Knight, F., 1921, Risk, uncertainty and profit (Houghton–Mifflin, Boston).

LeRoy, S., L.D. Singell, Jr., 1987, Knight on risk and uncertainty, Journal of Political Economy 95, no. 2, 394–406.

Maddox, J., 1989, More ways with neural networks, Nature 337, Feb. 2, 403.

Marshak, J. and R. Radner, 1972, Economic theory of teams (Cowles Foundation Monograph, Yale).

Mason, R.O., 1969, A dialectical approach to strategic planning. Management Science 11, no. 8, April.

McKenzie, L.W., 1959, On the existence of general equilibrium for a competitive market, Econometrica, 27, no. 1, June, 30–53.

Miller, M.H. and K. Rock, 1985, Dividend policy under asymmetric information, Journal of Finance XL, no. 4, 1031–1051.

Mitroff, J.J., 1971, A communication model of dialectical inquiring systems–A strategy for strategic planning, Management Science 17, no. 11, July.

Morck, R., A. Schleifer and R.W. Vishny, 1986, Management ownership and corporate performance: An empirical analysis, Working paper no. 2055, Oct. (NBER, Cambridge, MA).

Murnane, R.J. and R.R. Nelson, 1984, Production and innovation when techniques are tacit: The case of education, JEBO 5, nos. 3–4, Sept./Dec.

Myers, S.L. and N.S. Majluf, 1984, Corporate finance and investment decisions when firms have information that investors do not have, Journal of Financial Economics 13, 187–221.

Nelson, R.R. and S.G. Winter, 1982, An evolutionary theory of economic change (London and Cambridge, MA).

Pelikan, P. 1969, Language as a limiting factor for centralization, American Economic Review LIX, no. 4, Sept.

Pelikan, P., 1987, Why private enterprise? Towards a dynamic analysis of economic institutions and policies; in: The economics of institutions and markets, IUI Yearbook 1986-1987 (IUI, Stockholm).

Pelikan, P., 1989, Evolution, economic competence and the market for corporate control, JEBO 12, 279–303.

Penrose, E., 1959, The theory of the growth of the firm (Oxford).

Polanyi, M., 1967, The tacit dimension (Doubleday Anchor, Garden City, NY).

Ravenschaft, D.J. and F.M. Scherer, Mergers, sell-offs and economic efficiency (The Brookings Institution, Washington, DC).

Romer, P.M., 1986, Growth based on increasing returns and long-term growth, Journal of Political Economy 94, no. 5, Oct., 1002–1037.

Schleifer, A. and R.W. Vishny, 1986, Large shareholders and corporate control, Journal of Political Economy 94, no. 3, 461–489.

Schleifer, A. and L.H. Summers, 1987, Breach of trust in hostile takeovers, NBER Working paper no. 2342.

Schumpeter, J.A., 1942, Capitalism, socialism and democracy (Harper and Row, New York).

Schumpeter, J.A., 1954, History of economic analysis, Oxford University Press (1986; ed. Allen & Unwin, London).

Shipley, F.B., 1975, Convergence of adaptive decisions; in: Day–Groves, eds., Adaptive economic models (New York).

Simon, H.A., 1955a, A behavioral model of rational choice, Quarterly Journal of Economics 69, 99–118.

Simon, H.A., 1955b, On a class of skew distribution functions, Biometrika 42, Dec.,

Simon, H.A. and C.P. Bonini, 1958, The size distribution of business firms, American Economic Review 48, Sept., 607–617.

Tversky, A. and D. Kahneman, 1981, The framing of decisions and the psychology of choice, Science, Jan., 453–458.

Wicksell, K., 1898, Geldzins und güterpreise (Interest and prices), published: 1965 (AMK Bookseller, New York).

Wihlborg, C., 1990, The incentive to acquire information and financial market stability, IUI Working paper no. 218 (Stockholm).

Zellner, A., 1983, Statistical theory and econometrics, Ch. 2 in Griliches–Intriligator, eds., Handbook of economics 1, 1983 (North-Holland, Amsterdam).

Örtengren, J., T. Lindberg, L. Jagrén, G. Eliasson, P.O. Bjuggren and L. Björklund, 1987, Expansion, avveckling och företagsvärdering i svensk industri–en studie av ägarformens och finansmarknadernas betydelse för strukturomvandlingen (IUI, Stockholm).

[14]

Economic Welfare and the Allocation of Resources for Invention

KENNETH J. ARROW
THE RAND CORPORATION

INVENTION is here interpreted broadly as the production of knowledge. From the viewpoint of welfare economics, the determination of optimal resource allocation for invention will depend on the technological characteristics of the invention process and the nature of the market for knowledge.

The classic question of welfare economics will be asked here: to what extent does perfect competition lead to an optimal allocation of resources? We know from years of patient refinement that competition insures the achievement of a Pareto optimum under certain hypotheses. The model usually assumes among other things, that (1) the utility functions of consumers and the transformation functions of producers are well-defined functions of the commodities in the economic system, and (2) the transformation functions do not display indivisibilities (more strictly, the transformation sets are convex). The second condition needs no comment. The first seems to be innocuous but in fact conceals two basic assumptions of the usual models. It prohibits uncertainty in the production relations and in the utility functions, and it requires that all the commodities relevant either to production or to the welfare of individuals be traded on the market. This will not be the case when a commodity for one reason or another cannot be made into private property.

We have then three of the classical reasons for the possible failure of perfect competition to achieve optimality in resource allocation: indivisibilities, inappropriability, and uncertainty. The first problem has been much studied in the literature under the heading of marginal-cost pricing and the second under that of divergence between social and private benefit (or cost), but the theory of optimal allocation of resources under uncertainty has had much less attention. I will summarize what formal theory exists and then point to the critical notion of information, which arises only in the context of uncertainty. The

NOTE: I have benefited greatly from the comments of my colleague, William Capron. I am also indebted to Richard R. Nelson, Edward Phelps, and Sidney Winter of The RAND Corporation for their helpful discussion.

economic characteristics of information as a commodity and, in particular, of invention as a process for the production of information are next examined. It is shown that all three of the reasons given above for a failure of the competitive system to achieve an optimal resource allocation hold in the case of invention. On theoretical grounds a number of considerations are adduced as to the likely biases in the misallocation and the implications for economic organization.[1]

Resource Allocation under Uncertainty

The role of the competitive system in allocating uncertainty seems to have received little systematic attention.[2] I will first sketch an ideal economy in which the allocation problem can be solved by competition and then indicate some of the devices in the real world which approximate this solution.

Suppose for simplicity that uncertainty occurs only in production relations. Producers have to make a decision on inputs at the present moment, but the outputs are not completely predictable from the inputs. We may formally describe the outputs as determined by the inputs and a "state of nature" which is unknown to the producers. Let us define a "commodity-option" as a commodity in the ordinary sense labeled with a state of nature. This definition is analogous to the differentiation of a given physical commodity according to date in capital theory or according to place in location theory. The production of a given commodity under uncertainty can then be described as the production of a vector of commodity-options.

This description can be most easily exemplified by reference to agricultural production. The state of nature may be identified with the weather. Then, to any given set of inputs there corresponds a number of bushels of wheat if the rainfall is good and a different number if rainfall is bad. We can introduce intermediate conditions of rainfall

---

[1] For other analyses with similar points of view, see R. R. Nelson, "The Simple Economics of Basic Scientific Research," *Journal of Political Economy*, 1959, pp. 297–306; and C. J. Hitch, "The Character of Research and Development in a Competitive Economy," The RAND Corporation, p. 1297, May 1958.

[2] The first studies I am aware of are the papers of M. Allais and myself, both presented in 1952 to the Colloque International sur le Risque in Paris; see M. Allais, "Généralisation des théories de l'équilibre économique général et du rendement social au cas du risque," and K. J. Arrow, "Rôle des valeurs bousières pour la répartition la meilleure des risques," both in *Econométrie*, Colloques Internationaux du Centre National de la Recherche Scientifique, Vol. XL, Paris, Centre National de la Recherche Scientifique, 1953. Allais' paper has also appeared in *Econometrica*, 1953, pp. 269–290. The theory has received a very elegant generalization by G. Debreu in *Theory of Values*, New York, Wiley, 1959, Chap. VII.

ALLOCATION OF RESOURCES FOR INVENTION

in any number as alternative states of nature; we can increase the number of relevant variables which enter into the description of the state of nature, for example by adding temperature. By extension of this procedure, we can give a formal description of any kind of uncertainty in production.

Suppose—and this is the critical idealization of the economy—we have a market for all commodity-options. What is traded on each market are contracts in which the buyers pay an agreed sum and the sellers agree to deliver prescribed quantities of a given commodity *if* a certain state of nature prevails and nothing if that state of nature does not occur. For any given set of inputs, the firm knows its output under each state of nature and sells a corresponding quantity of commodity-options; its revenue is then completely determined. It may choose its inputs so as to maximize profits.

The income of consumers is derived from their sale of supplies, including labor, to firms and their receipt of profits, which are assumed completely distributed. They purchase commodity-options so as to maximize their expected utility given the budget restraint imposed by their incomes. An equilibrium is reached on all commodity-option markets, and this equilibrium has precisely the same Pareto-optimality properties as competitive equilibrium under certainty.

In particular, the markets for commodity-options in this ideal model serve the function of achieving an optimal allocation of risk bearing among the members of the economy. This allocation takes account of differences in both resources and tastes for risk bearing. Among other implications, risk bearing and production are separated economic functions. The use of inputs, including human talents, in their most productive mode is not inhibited by unwillingness or inability to bear risks by either firms or productive agents.

But the real economic system does not possess markets for commodity-options. To see what substitutes exist, let us first consider a model economy at the other extreme, in that no provisions for reallocating risk bearing exist. Each firm makes its input decisions; then outputs are produced as determined by the inputs and the state of nature. Prices are then set to clear the market. The prices that finally prevail will be a function of the state of nature.

The firm and its owners cannot relieve themselves of risk bearing in this model. Hence any unwillingness or inability to bear risks will give rise to a nonoptimal allocation of resources, in that there will be

WELFARE ECONOMICS AND INVENTIVE ACTIVITY

discrimination against risky enterprises as compared with the optimum. A preference for risk might give rise to misallocation in the opposite direction, but the limitations of financial resources are likely to make underinvestment in risky enterprises more likely than the opposite. The inability of individuals to buy protection against uncertainty similarly gives rise to a loss of welfare.

In fact, a number of institutional arrangements have arisen to mitigate the problem of assumption of risk. Suppose that each firm and individual in the economy could forecast perfectly what prices would be under each state of nature. Suppose further there were a lottery on the states of nature, so that before the state of nature is known any individual or firm may place bets. Then it can be seen that the effect from the viewpoint of any given individual or firm is the same as if there were markets for commodity-options of all types, since any commodity-option can be achieved by a combination of a bet on the appropriate state of nature and an intention to purchase or sell the commodity in question if the state of nature occurs.

References to lotteries and bets may smack of frivolity, but we need only think of insurance to appreciate that the shifting of risks through what are in effect bets on the state of nature is a highly significant phenomenon. If insurance were available against any conceivable event, it follows from the preceding discussion that optimal allocation would be achieved. Of course, insurance as customarily defined covers only a small range of events relevant to the economic world; much more important in shifting risks are securities, particularly common stocks and money. By shifting freely their proprietary interests among different firms, individuals can to a large extent bet on the different states of nature which favor firms differentially. This freedom to insure against many contingencies is enhanced by the alternatives of holding cash and going short.

Unfortunately, it is only too clear that the shifting of risks in the real world is incomplete. The great predominance of internal over external equity financing in industry is one illustration of the fact that securities do not completely fulfill their allocative role with respect to risks. There are a number of reasons why this should be so, but I will confine myself to one, of special significance with regard to invention. In insurance practice, reference is made to the moral factor as a limit to the possibilities of insurance. For example, a fire insurance policy cannot exceed in amount the value of the goods insured. From the purely actuarial standpoint, there is no reason for this limitation;

ALLOCATION OF RESOURCES FOR INVENTION

the reason for the limit is that the insurance policy changes the incentives of the insured, in this case, creating an incentive for arson or at the very least for carelessness. The general principle is the difficulty of distinguishing between a state of nature and a decision by the insured. As a result, any insurance policy and in general any device for shifting risks can have the effect of dulling incentives. A fire insurance policy, even when limited in amount to the value of the goods covered, weakens the motivation for fire prevention. Thus, steps which improve the efficiency of the economy with respect to risk bearing may decrease its technical efficiency.

One device for mitigating the adverse incentive effects of insurance is coinsurance; the insurance extends only to part of the amount at risk for the insured. This device is used, for example, in coverage of medical risks. It clearly represents a compromise between incentive effects and allocation of risk bearing, sacrificing something in both directions.

Two exemplifications of the moral factor are of special relevance in regard to highly risky business activities, including invention. Success in such activities depends on an inextricable tangle of objective uncertainties and decisions of the entrepreneurs and is certainly uninsurable. On the other hand, such activities should be undertaken if the expected return exceeds the market rate of return, no matter what the variance is.[3] The existence of common stocks would seem to solve the allocation problem; any individual stockholder can reduce his risk by buying only a small part of the stock and diversifying his portfolio to achieve his own preferred risk level. But then again the actual managers no longer receive the full reward of their decisions; the shifting of risks is again accompanied by a weakening of incentives to efficiency. Substitute motivations whether pecuniary, such as executive compensation and profit sharing, or nonpecuniary, such as prestige, may be found, but the dilemma of the moral factor can never be completely resolved.

A second example is the cost-plus contract in one of its various forms. When production costs on military items are highly uncertain, the military establishment will pay, not a fixed unit price, but the cost of production plus an amount which today is usually a fixed fee. Such a contract could be regarded as a combination of a fixed-price contract with an insurance against costs. The insurance premium could be

---

[3] The validity of this statement depends on some unstated assumptions, but the point to be made is unaffected by minor qualifications.

regarded as the difference between the fixed price the government would be willing to pay and the fixed fee.

Cost-plus contracts are necessitated by the inability or unwillingness of firms to bear the risks. The government has superior risk bearing ability and so the burden is shifted to it. It is then enabled to buy from firms on the basis of their productive efficiency rather than their risk bearing ability, which may be only imperfectly correlated. But cost-plus contracts notoriously have their adverse allocative effects.[4]

This somewhat lengthy digression on the theory of risk bearing seemed necessitated by the paucity of literature on the subject. The main conclusions to be drawn are the following: (1) the economic system has devices for shifting risks, but they are limited and imperfect; hence, one would expect an underinvestment in risky activities; (2) it is undoubtedly worthwhile to enlarge the variety of such devices, but the moral factor creates a limit to their potential.

Information as a Commodity

Uncertainty usually creates a still more subtle problem in resource allocation; information becomes a commodity. Suppose that in one part of the economic system an observation has been made whose outcome, if known, would affect anyone's estimates of the probabilities of the different states of nature. Such observations arise out of research but they also arise in the daily course of economic life as a by-product of other economic activities. An entrepreneur will automatically acquire a knowledge of demand and production conditions in his field which is available to others only with special effort. Information will frequently have an economic value, in the sense that anyone possessing the information can make greater profits than would otherwise be the case.

It might be expected that information will be traded in, and of course to a considerable extent this is the case, as is illustrated by the numerous economic institutions for transmission of information, such as newspapers. But in many instances, the problem of an optimal allocation is sharply raised. The cost of transmitting a given body of information is frequently very low. If it were zero, then optimal allocation would obviously call for unlimited distribution of the informa-

---

[4] These remarks are not intended as a complete evaluation of cost-plus contracts. In particular, there are, to a certain extent, other incentives which mitigate the adverse effects on efficiency.

ALLOCATION OF RESOURCES FOR INVENTION

tion without cost. In fact, a given piece of information is by definition an indivisible commodity, and the classical problems of allocation in the presence of indivisibilities appear here. The owner of the information should not extract the economic value which is there, if optimal allocation is to be achieved; but he is a monopolist, to some small extent and will seek to take advantage of this fact.

In the absence of special legal protection, the owner cannot, however, simply sell information on the open market. Any one purchaser can destroy the monopoly, since he can reproduce the information at little or no cost. Thus the only effective monopoly would be the use of the information by the original possessor. This, however, will not only be socially inefficient, but also may not be of much use to the owner of the information either, since he may not be able to exploit it as effectively as others.

With suitable legal measures, information may become an appropriable commodity. Then the monopoly power can indeed be exerted. However, no amount of legal protection can make a thoroughly appropriable commodity of something so intangible as information. The very use of the information in any productive way is bound to reveal it, at least in part. Mobility of personnel among firms provides a way of spreading information. Legally imposed property rights can provide only a partial barrier, since there are obviously enormous difficulties in defining in any sharp way an item of information and differentiating it from other similar sounding items.

The demand for information also has uncomfortable properties. In the first place, the use of information is certainly subject to indivisibilities; the use of information about production possibilities, for example, need not depend on the rate of production. In the second place, there is a fundamental paradox in the determination of demand for information; its value for the purchaser is not known until he has the information, but then he has in effect acquired it without cost. Of course, if the seller can retain property rights in the use of the information, this would be no problem, but given incomplete appropriability, the potential buyer will base his decision to purchase information on less than optimal criteria. He may act, for example, on the average value of information in that class as revealed by past experience. If any particular item of information has differing values for different economic agents, this procedure will lead both to a nonoptimal purchase of information at any given price and also to a nonoptimal allocation of the information purchased.

WELFARE ECONOMICS AND INVENTIVE ACTIVITY

It should be made clear that from the standpoint of efficiently distributing an existing stock of information, the difficulties of appropriation are an advantage, provided there are no costs of transmitting information, since then optimal allocation calls for free distribution. The chief point made here is the difficulty of creating a market for information if one should be desired for any reason.

It follows from the preceding discussion that costs of transmitting information create allocative difficulties which would be absent otherwise. Information should be transmitted at marginal cost, but then the demand difficulties raised above will exist. From the viewpoint of optimal allocation, the purchasing industry will be faced with the problems created by indivisibilities; and we still leave unsolved the problem of the purchaser's inability to judge in advance the value of the information he buys. There is a strong case for centralized decision making under these circumstances.

Invention as the Production of Information

The central economic fact about the processes of invention and research is that they are devoted to the production of information. By the very definition of information, invention must be a risky process, in that the output (information obtained) can never be predicted perfectly from the inputs. We can now apply the discussion of the preceding two sections.

Since it is a risky process, there is bound to be some discrimination against investment in inventive and research activities. In this field, especially, the moral factor will weigh heavily against any kind of insurance or equivalent form of risk bearing. Insurance against failure to develop a desired new product or process would surely very greatly weaken the incentives to succeed. The only way, within the private enterprise system, to minimize this problem is the conduct of research by large corporations with many projects going on, each small in scale compared with the net revenue of the corporation. Then the corporation acts as its own insurance company. But clearly this is only an imperfect solution.

The deeper problems of misallocation arise from the nature of the product. As we have seen, information is a commodity with peculiar attributes, particularly embarrassing for the achievement of optimal allocation. In the first place, any information obtained, say a new method of production, should, from the welfare point of view, be

ALLOCATION OF RESOURCES FOR INVENTION

available free of charge (apart from the cost of transmitting information). This insures optimal utilization of the information but of course provides no incentive for investment in research. In an ideal socialist economy, the reward for invention would be completely separated from any charge to the users of the information.[5] In a free enterprise economy, inventive activity is supported by using the invention to create property rights; precisely to the extent that it is successful, there is an underutilization of the information. The property rights may be in the information itself, through patents and similar legal devices, or in the intangible assets of the firm if the information is retained by the firm and used only to increase its profits.

The first problem, then, is that in a free enterprise economy the profitability of invention requires a nonoptimal allocation of resources. But it may still be asked whether or not the allocation of resources to inventive activity is optimal. The discussion of the preceding section makes it clear that we would not expect this to be so; that, in fact, a downward bias in the amount of resources devoted to inventive activity is very likely. Whatever the price, the demand for information is less than optimal for two reasons: (1) since the price is positive and not at its optimal value of zero, the demand is bound to be below the optimal; (2) as seen before, at any given price, the very nature of information will lead to a lower demand than would be optimal.

As already remarked, the inventor will in any case have considerable difficulty in appropriating the information produced. Patent laws would have to be unimaginably complex and subtle to permit such appropriation on a large scale. Suppose, as the result of elaborate tests, some metal is discovered to have a desirable property, say resistance to high heat. Then of course every use of the metal for which this property is relevant would also use this information, and the user would be made to pay for it. But, even more, if another inventor is stimulated to examine chemically related metals for heat resistance, he is using the information already discovered and should pay for it in some measure; and any beneficiary of his discoveries should also pay. One would have to have elaborate distinctions of partial property rights of all degrees to make the system at all tolerable. In the interests of the possibility of enforcement, actual patent laws sharply restrict the range of appropriable information and thereby reduce the incentives to engage in inventive and research activities.

[5] This separation exists in the Soviet Union, according to N. M. Kaplan and R. H. Moorsteen of The RAND Corporation (verbal communication).

WELFARE ECONOMICS AND INVENTIVE ACTIVITY

These last considerations bring into focus the interdependence of inventive activities, which reinforces the difficulties in achieving an optimal allocation of the results. Information is not only the product of inventive activity, it is also an input—in some sense, the major input apart from the talent of the inventor. The school of thought that emphasizes the determination of invention by the social climate as demonstrated by the simultaneity of inventions in effect emphasizes strongly the productive role of previous information in the creation of new information. While these interrelations do not create any new difficulties in principle, they intensify the previously established ones. To appropriate information for use as a basis for further research is much more difficult than to appropriate it for use in producing commodities; and the value of information for use in developing further information is much more conjectural than the value of its use in production and therefore much more likely to be underestimated. Consequently, if a price is charged for the information, the demand is even more likely to be suboptimal.

Thus basic research, the output of which is only used as an informational input into other inventive activities, is especially unlikely to be rewarded. In fact, it is likely to be of commercial value to the firm undertaking it only if other firms are prevented from using the information obtained. But such restriction on the transmittal of information will reduce the efficiency of inventive activity in general and will therefore reduce its quantity also. We may put the matter in terms of sequential decision making. The a priori probability distribution of the true state of nature is relatively flat to begin with. On the other hand, the successive a posteriori distributions after more and more studies have been conducted are more and more sharply peaked or concentrated in a more limited range, and we therefore have better and better information for deciding what the next step in research shall be. This implies that, at the beginning, the preferences among alternative possible lines of investigation are much less sharply defined than they are apt to be later on and suggests, at least, the importance of having a wide variety of studies to begin with, the less promising being gradually eliminated as information is accumulated.[6] At each stage the decisions about the next step should be based on all available information. This would require an unrestricted flow of informa-

[6] The importance of parallel research developments in the case of uncertainty has been especially stressed by Burton H. Klein; see his, "A Radical Proposal for R. and D.," *Fortune*, May 1958, p. 112 ff.; and Klein and W. H. Meckling, "Application of Operations Research to Development Decisions," *Operations Research*, 1958, pp. 352–363.

ALLOCATION OF RESOURCES FOR INVENTION

tion among different projects which is incompatible with the complete decentralization of an ideal free enterprise system. When the production of information is important, the classic economic case in which the price system replaces the detailed spread of information is no longer completely applicable.

To sum up, we expect a free enterprise economy to underinvest in invention and research (as compared with an ideal) because it is risky, because the product can be appropriated only to a limited extent, and because of increasing returns in use. This underinvestment will be greater for more basic research. Further, to the extent that a firm succeeds in engrossing the economic value of its inventive activity, there will be an underutilization of that information as compared with an ideal allocation.

Competition, Monopoly, and the Incentive to Innovate

It may be useful to remark that an incentive to invent can exist even under perfect competition in the product markets though not, of course, in the "market" for the information contained in the invention. This is especially clear in the case of a cost reducing invention. Provided only that suitable royalty payments can be demanded, an inventor can profit without disturbing the competitive nature of the industry. The situation for a new product invention is not very different; by charging a suitable royalty to a competitive industry, the inventor can receive a return equal to the monopoly profits.

I will examine here the incentives to invent for monopolistic and competitive markets, that is, I will compare the potential profits from an invention with the costs. The difficulty of appropriating the information will be ignored; the remaining problem is that of indivisibility in use, an inherent property of information. A competitive situation here will mean one in which the industry produces under competitive conditions, while the inventor can set an arbitrary royalty for the use of his invention. In the monopolistic situation, it will be assumed that only the monopoly itself can invent. Thus a monopoly is understood here to mean barriers to entry; a situation of temporary monopoly, due perhaps to a previous innovation, which does not prevent the entrance of new firms with innovations of their own, is to be regarded as more nearly competitive than monopolistic for the purpose of this analysis. It will be argued that the incentive to invent is less under monopolistic than under competitive conditions but even in the latter case it will be less than is socially desirable.

WELFARE ECONOMICS AND INVENTIVE ACTIVITY

We will assume constant costs both before and after the invention, the unit costs being c before the invention and $c' < c$ afterward. The competitive price before invention will therefore be c. Let the corresponding demand be x_c. If r is the level of unit royalties, the competitive price after the invention will be $c' + r$, but this cannot of course be higher than c, since firms are always free to produce with the old methods.

It is assumed that both the demand and the marginal revenue curves are decreasing. Let $R(x)$ be the marginal revenue curve. Then the monopoly output before invention, x_m, would be defined by the equation,

$$R(x_m) = c \,.$$

Similarly, the monopoly output after invention is defined by,

$$R(x'_m) = c' \,.$$

Let the monopoly prices corresponding to outputs x_m and x'_m, respectively, be p_m and p'_m. Finally, let P and P' be the monopolist's profits before and after invention, respectively.

What is the optimal royalty level for the inventor in the competitive case? Let us suppose that he calculates p'_m, the optimal monopoly price which would obtain in the postinvention situation. If the cost reduction is sufficiently drastic that $p'_m < c$, then his most profitable policy is to set r so that the competitive price is p'_m, i.e. let,

$$r = p'_m - c' \,.$$

In this case, the inventor's royalties are equal to the profits a monopolist would make under the same conditions, i.e. his incentive to invent will be P'.

Suppose, however, it turns out that $p'_m > c$. Since the sales price cannot exceed c, the inventor will set his royalties at,

$$r = c - c' \,.$$

The competitive price will then be c, and the sales will remain at x_c. The inventor's incentive will then be, $x_c(c - c')$.

The monopolist's incentive, on the other hand, is clearly $P' - P$. In the first of the two cases cited, the monopolist's incentive is obviously less than the inventor's incentive under competition, which is P', not $P' - P$. The preinvention monopoly power acts as a strong disincentive to further innovation.

ALLOCATION OF RESOURCES FOR INVENTION

The analysis is slightly more complicated in the second case. The monopolist's incentive, $P' - P$, is the change in revenue less the change in total cost of production, i.e.,

$$P' - P = \int_{x_m}^{x'_m} R(x)\,dx - c'\,x'_m + c\,x_m\,.$$

Since the marginal revenue $R(x)$ is diminishing, it must always be less than $R(x_m) = c$ as x increases from x_m to x'_m, so that,

$$\int_{x_m}^{x'_m} R(x)\,dx < c\,(x'_m - x_m)\,,$$

and,

$$P' - P < c\,(x'_m - x_m) - c'\,x'_m + c\,x_m = (c - c')\,x'_m\,.$$

In the case being considered, the postinvention monopoly price, p'_m, is greater than c. Hence, with a declining demand curve, $x'_m < x_c$. The above inequality shows that the monopolist's incentive is always less than the cost reduction on the postinvention monopoly output, which in this case is, in turn, less than the competitive output (both before and after invention). Since the inventor's incentive under competition is the cost reduction on the competitive output, it will again always exceed the monopolist's incentive.

It can be shown that, if we consider differing values of c', the difference between the two incentives increases as c' decreases, reaching its maximum of P (preinvention monopoly profits) for c' sufficiently large for the first case to hold. The ratio of the incentive under competition to that under monopoly, on the other hand, though always greater than 1, decreases steadily with c'. For c' very close to c (i.e., very minor inventions), the ratio of the two incentives is approximately x_c/x_m, i.e., the ratio of monopoly to competitive output.[7]

[7] To sketch the proof of these statements quickly, note that, as c' varies, P is a constant. Hence, from the formula for $P' - P$, we see that,

$$d(P' - P)/dc' = dP'/dc' = R(x'_m)\,(dx'_m/dc') - c'(dx'_m/dc') - x'_m = -x'_m\,,$$

since $R(x'_m) = c'$. Let $F(c')$ be the difference between the incentives to invent under competitive and under monopolistic conditions. In the case where $p'_m < c$, this difference is the constant P. Otherwise,

$$F(c') = x_c\,(c - c') - (P' - P),$$

so that

$$dF/dc' = x'_m - x_c\,.$$

For the case considered, we must have $x'_m < x_c$, as seen in the text. Hence, $dF/dc' \leq 0$, so

WELFARE ECONOMICS AND INVENTIVE ACTIVITY

The only ground for arguing that monopoly may create superior incentives to invent is that appropriability may be greater under monopoly than under competition. Whatever differences may exist in this direction must, of course, still be offset against the monopolist's disincentive created by his preinvention monopoly profits.

The incentive to invent in competitive circumstances may also be compared with the social benefit. It is necessary to distinguish between the realized social benefit and the potential social benefit, the latter being the benefit which would accrue under ideal conditions, which, in this case, means the sale of the product at postinvention cost, c'. Clearly, the potential social benefit always exceeds the realized social benefit. I will show that the realized social benefit, in turn, always equals or exceeds the competitive incentive to invent and, a fortiori, the monopolist's incentive.

Consider again the two cases discussed above. If the invention is sufficiently cost reducing so that $p'_m < c$, then there is a consumers' benefit, due to the lowering of price, which has not been appropriated by the inventor. If not, then the price is unchanged, so that the consumers' position is unchanged, and all benefits do go to the inventor. Since by assumption all the producers are making zero profits both before and after the invention, we see that the inventor obtains the entire realized social benefit of moderately cost reducing inventions but not of more radical inventions. Tentatively, this suggests a bias against major inventions, in the sense that an invention, part of whose costs could be paid for by lump-sum payments by consumers without making them worse off than before, may not be profitable at the maximum royalty payments that can be extracted by the inventor.

---

that $F(c')$ increases as c' decreases.

Let $G(c')$ be the ratio of the incentive under competition to that under monopoly. If $p'_m < c$, then,

$$G(c') = P'/(P' - P),$$

which clearly decreases as c' decreases. For $p'_m > c$, we have,

$$G(c') = x_e (c - c')/(P' - P).$$

Then,

$$dG/dc' = [- (P' - P) x_e + x_e (c - c') x'_m] /(P' - P)^2.$$

Because of the upper bound for $P' - P$ established in the text, the numerator must be positive; the ratio decreases as c' decreases.

Finally, if we consider c' very close to c, $G(c')$ will be approximately equal to the ratio of the derivatives of the numerator and denominator (L'Hopital's rule), which is, x_e/x'_m, and which approaches x_e/x_m as c' approaches c.

ALLOCATION OF RESOURCES FOR INVENTION

Alternative Forms of Economic Organization in Invention

The previous discussion leads to the conclusion that for optimal allocation to invention it would be necessary for the government or some other agency not governed by profit-and-loss criteria to finance research and invention. In fact, of course, this has always happened to a certain extent. The bulk of basic research has been carried on outside the industrial system, in universities, in the government, and by private individuals. One must recognize here the importance of nonpecuniary incentives, both on the part of the investigators and on the part of the private individuals and governments that have supported research organizations and universities. In the latter, the complementarity between teaching and research is, from the point of view of the economy, something of a lucky accident. Research in some more applied fields, such as agriculture, medicine, and aeronautics, has consistently been regarded as an appropriate subject for government participation, and its role has been of great importance.

If the government and other nonprofit institutions are to compensate for the underallocation of resources to invention by private enterprise, two problems arise: how shall the amount of resources devoted to invention be determined, and how shall efficiency in their use be encouraged? These problems arise whenever the government finds it necessary to engage in economic activities because indivisibilities prevent the private economy from performing adequately (highways, bridges, reclamation projects, for example), but the determination of the relative magnitudes is even more difficult here. Formally, of course, resources should be devoted to invention until the expected marginal social benefit there equals the marginal social benefit in alternative uses, but in view of the presence of uncertainty, such calculations are even more difficult and tenuous than those for public works. Probably all that could be hoped for is the estimation of future rates of return from those in the past, with investment in invention being increased or decreased accordingly as some average rate of return over the past exceeded or fell short of the general rate of return. The difficulties of even ex post calculation of rates of return are formidable though possibly not insuperable.[8]

The problem of efficiency in the use of funds devoted to research

---

[8] For an encouraging study of this type, see Z. Griliches, "Research Costs and Social Returns: Hybrid Corn and Related Innovations," *Journal of Political Economy*, 1958, pp. 419–431.

WELFARE ECONOMICS AND INVENTIVE ACTIVITY

is one that has been faced internally by firms in dealing with their own research departments. The rapid growth of military research and development has led to a large-scale development of contractual relations between producers and a buyer of invention and research. The problems encountered in assuring efficiency here are the same as those that would be met if the government were to enter upon the financing of invention and research in civilian fields. The form of economic relation is very different from that in the usual markets. Payment is independent of product; it is governed by costs, though the net reward (the fixed fee) is independent of both. This arrangement seems to fly in the face of the principles for encouraging efficiency, and doubtless it does lead to abuses, but closer examination shows both mitigating factors and some explanation of its inevitability. In the first place, the awarding of new contracts will depend in part on past performance, so that incentives for efficiency are not completely lacking. In the second place, the relation between the two parties to the contract is something closer than a purely market relation. It is more like the sale of professional services, where the seller contracts to supply not so much a specific result as his best judgment. (The demand for such services also arises from uncertainty and the value of information.) In the third place, payment by results would involve great risks for the inventor, risks against which, as we have seen, he could hedge only in part.

There is clear need for further study of alternative methods of compensation. For example, some part of the contractual payment might depend on the degree of success in invention. But a more serious problem is the decision as to which contracts to let. One would need to examine the motivation underlying government decision making in this area. Hitch has argued that there are biases in governmental allocation, particularly against risky invention processes, and an excessive centralization, though the latter could be remedied by better policies.[9]

One can go further. There is really no need for the firm to be the fundamental unit of organization in invention; there is plenty of reason to suppose that individual talents count for a good deal more than the firm as an organization. If provision is made for the rental of necessary equipment, a much wider variety of research contracts with individuals as well as firms and with varying modes of payment, including incentives, could be arranged. Still other forms of organiza-

[9] *Op. cit.*

ALLOCATION OF RESOURCES FOR INVENTION

tion, such as research institutes financed by industries, the government, and private philanthropy, could be made to play an even livelier role than they now do.

COMMENT

C. J. HITCH, The RAND Corporation

There is, I think, one important aspect of government policy with respect to research and development that Markham failed to discuss—the government's contracting and management policies in this area. The problems here are related to Arrow's discussion of incentives, particularly his remarks concerning risk bearing and the adverse allocative effects of cost-plus contracts.

Let me illustrate one set of such problems by contrasting the management policies used by the Army Air Corps before World War II in developing new combat aircraft with the policies now used by the Air Force in developing aircraft and missiles.

Before the war the Air Corps would typically announce a competition for a new aircraft type, the desired characteristics of which would be described in general terms. Any aircraft company that wanted to enter the competition would develop and build, with its own funds, the required number of prototypes (usually one to three). The competition consisted in flying and testing, at Dayton, the prototypes entered by the companies. The prize for the winner was a production contract. The losers lost their stake.

Now, typically, the competition occurs at the design stage. The competing companies enter drawings, with their estimates of performance (and time and cost of development). The winner of the design competition is awarded a development contract which, if things go favorably, is transformed later into a production contract. Occasionally, if the program is considered very important, two competing designs may be approved for development or even production (cf. the Atlas and Titan). But usually the development of more than one model is considered too expensive.

In fact, the greatly increased cost of development is the reason given for this change in policy. When the cost of developing a new vehicle is from $0.5 billion to $2.0 billion, it seems evident that no aircraft company can assume the risk, and perhaps also that even the government can not finance multiple developments.

Nevertheless, the new policy appears far from ideal. The aircraft companies risk nothing (even the cost of preparing designs is usually reimbursed). Because of the great uncertainties involved in any major development, it is hard to make a wise selection at the design stage. Companies have a natural tendency to be optimistic in estimating performance, cost, and availability at this stage—sometimes much more so than at other stages as Klein and Marshall and Meckling have shown. And the Air Force has a natural tendency to favor the more optimistic proposals. As a result, the specifications in the development contract are sometimes unrealistic to the point of causing inordinate delay.

Moreover, once the winner has been selected, there is no more competition. The company may put its best team on the development for the sake of patriotism or its own long term reputation, but the powerful incentive of competition is lacking. Partly for this reason the Air Force, locked to a sole source with a cost-plus contract, has to exercise a kind and degree of control during the development process that is inconsistent with management prerogatives as they are understood and practiced in other parts of the free enterprise economy.

I believe the inefficiencies resulting from these policies and procedures are serious, and worthy of much more attention by economists. It does no good simply to inveigh against the iniquities of cost-plus contracting and government risk bearing when we are unable to propose a practical alternative. Perhaps part of the answer lies in some form of risk sharing. What is badly needed here is an economics invention or, more probably, several of them. The government is going to be in the business of supporting research and development on a large scale for a long time, and it is important that it use policies that take advantage of the incentives present in the economy.

[15]

Prometheus, Vol. 9, No. 1, June 1991   5

ADVANCES IN INFORMATION TECHNOLOGY AND THE INNOVATION STRATEGIES OF FIRMS*

Gerhard Rosegger

The ability to appropriate newly-generated technical knowledge is a key to the strategic behaviour of firms. Therefore, institutional and organisational arrangements are eventually challenged and transformed by major new (Schumpeterian) innovations. The effects of recent, revolutionary advances in information technology provide an especially striking illustration of this interplay. Although these tensions have always existed, their current dimensions are new. The seemingly inexorable development of highly-efficient, global information networks is transforming the strategic responses of firms to changing market conditions. Nowhere is this transformation more evident than in the changing role of property rights to firm-specific technical and market knowledge.

Keywords: Information technology, information strategies, firms, knowledge acquisition, monitoring.

INTRODUCTION

In 1516, Franz von Thurn und Taxis was granted a charter to establish the first scheduled, public postal service. In the same year, his relays of mounted messengers began delivering mail between Vienna and Brussels. A few decades later, the service connected most of Europe's political and commercial centres. Even government officials had started to rely on the mail in preference to sending their own couriers. After the Thirty Years War, the monopoly of the house of Thurn und Taxis was broken, and soon a dense network of competing routes, most of them operated by small states and municipalities, covered Europe.[1]

Although the use of relays to transmit urgent messages was not a novelty, the development of regular, long-distance mails represented a genuine breakthrough in communication technology. For the first time, ordinary merchants, bureaucrats, scientists, and other men of affairs could avail themselves of a service that reliably carried letters to their destination at the unprecedented speed of 130 to 150 kilometers per day.

The innovation's characeristics were shaped in good part by existing technical and institutional conditions. Thus, for example, although carriages would have had a clear advantage in capacity, the absence of

* This paper was presented at a seminar at CIRCIT (Centre for International Research on Communication and Information Technologies), Melbourne on 6 February 1991.

6   *Gerhard Rosegger*

decent roads meant that messengers on horseback could move much faster. As Werner Sombart pointed out in a biting commentary, the states had no interest in improving roads, for the slower the progress of carriages through their territory, the greater the earnings of innkeepers and craftsmen.[2] Even in the late 18th century, for example, the roughly 200-kilometer trip by mail coach from Frankfurt to Stuttgart took 40 hours. Of course, the layout of messenger routes was also influenced by the location of inns or other places that could serve as relay stations. And the existence of numerous political units, each with its own commercial interests, produced a hodge-podge of frequently duplicative services that failed to realise the efficiency gains that might have been obtained through what we nowadays call systems integration.

On the other hand, the innovation also helped to transform existing institutions and established ways of doing things. Perhaps its most significant impact was to undermine the power of large merchant houses, whose access to information through their far-flung branches had given them a distinct competitive advantage. Furthermore, major nodes in the postal system soon attracted all kinds of organisations dependent for their business on timely information. Improved communications among these centres also fostered the development of standardised commercial practices.

Equally important was the innovation's effect on the spread of technical knowledge. Historians agree, for example, that without regularly receiving information from abroad, a scholar like Georgius Agricola would have been unable to write his famous *De re metallica,* a classic survey of the state of the art in mining and metallurgy at more European locations than he could possibly have visited in person.

Soon, however, there arose concern that some of this diffusion of knowledge via the postal services might not be quite what the senders had in mind. According to contemporary accounts, messengers were frequently suspected of "using subtle practices to open the letters of learned men and having their contents copied. Then they sold these copies and thus unwittingly contributed to the spread of new ideas."[3] The refinement of such subtle practices obviously was another manifestation of technological progress. In this connection, it is worth mentioning also that the authors of technical and commercial compendia frequently were accused by businessmen of publicising their trade secrets.[4]

My brief account of an early breakthrough in information technology is not meant to imply that its technical feaures, the speed of its diffusion, or its socioeconomic ramifications are comparable to those of late 20th century innovations. Nevertheless, I want to use this historical example to suggest that, although the dimensions of the current revolution in information technology are unprecedented, its contours represent familiar variations on a few persistent themes:

• there is the influence of existing institutions, interests, and practices on the rate and direction of technical progress;

- there is the potential of major innovations to transform, and in many instances to revolutionise, prevailing social and economic arrangements; and
- there is the concern of actors (individuals and organisations) that their ability to appropriate new knowledge, as well as to hold on to old knowledge, may be threatened by innovations in the transmission of information.

In considering how the new information technologies have affected the innovation strategies of firms, the economist's interest is drawn, quite naturally, to the possible conflict between the benefits of improved communication and the perceived risks of losing firm-specific knowledge. In particular, I want to reflect on the implications of those technical advances that have greatly increased the possibiliies for exchanges of information among firms, given the fact that each firm still regards its special body of knowledge as its most important asset.

Evaluations of these possibilities have ranged from exuberantly optimistic to more or less skeptical. Thus, for example, one observer concluded that organisations are "moving inexorably toward electronic interdependence,"[5] and another judged that "the communication and computing networks which serve us are making step-function changes to the manner, *richness of content* (my emphasis), and modes of our interactions."[6] Conversely, Peter Drucker complained some time ago that, despite technological advances, "[t]he communications gap within institutions and between groups in society has been widening steadily."[7] Even Adam Osborne, pioneer and ardent booster of microelectronics development, cautioned that there are activities where computers should not be used for the collection and transmission of information because of the risks of abuse.[8] And, on a more philosophical plane, Jesse Shera commented on the potential of the new technologies to produce information overload and thus to stifle creative ideas, with a poignant, "Data, data everywhere — and not a thought to think![9]

Since my attempt at an assessent focusses on a thin slice of the problem, I must define terms that have come to be used in a confusing variety of meanings. I follow that master of economic semantics, the late Fritz Machlup, in considering information a flow concept, and knowledge a stock concept.[10] Information is transmitted to a recipient (an individual or an organisation) from an external source through communication, adding to the recipient's stock of knowledge; however, I shall suggest below, this stock can also be increased by means having nothing to do with information, in the sense in which I use the word. My only excuse for this narrow definition is that it serves my purposes, and that it permits me to avoid considering those embodiments of information technology that might enhance the execution, though not the conception, of innovation strategies. In other words, the impact of stand-alone computers, CAD/CAM systems, robots, industrial controllers, knowledge-based systems, artificial intelligence, etc., is beyond my purview.

8   *Gerhard Rosegger*

HOW FIRMS ACQUIRE KNOWLEDGE

Most economists accept the notion that firms survive in competition by possessing technical and market knowledge that is in some sense different from the knowledge of their rivals. Therefore, firms' innovation strategies will be aimed primarily at protecting and enhancing such firm-specific knowledge. Their success in doing so will depend, in the first instance, on how and over what period of time they acquired the knowledge.

For the purposes of an economic evaluation, one may usefully distinguish four main determinants of the rate at which a firm acquires technical knowledge; these are not, of course, independent of one another.

The rate at which the firm produces new knowledge internally.

The most obvious examples here are research, development, design, and engineering (R,D,D&E). These are costly and risky activities, and without the prospect of being able to appropriate sufficient returns from the investment, firms would have little incentive to undertake them. In other words, it is essential that a substantial proportion of the newly-generated knowledge not spill over into the firm's environment, especially not to competitors.

Equally significant is knowledge about the technical requirments of their customers, generated by firms as a byproduct of their ongoing marketing effort. The strategic exploitation of this knowledge once again requires that it be internalized. What matters in this connection is not necessarily that the firm acquires objective data that are unavailable to competitors, but that it be able to convert generally accessible data into (subjective) information giving it some sort of competitive advantage.

Another internal source of new technical knowledge is *learning by doing*. By definition, firms accumulate this type of knowledge in the process of pursuing their current activities. Some of the results of learning may be codified, but others consist of the *know-how* acquired by individuals as well as of *organisational routines*.[11] Learning requires some continuity in basic technology and thus may become an impediment to major innovation, causing firms not to utilise information obtained from their environment. This, however, is an issue beyond the purview of my observations.

There is a negative corollary to all of this — *forgetting by not doing*. Individual know-how and organisational routines will atrophy without continuing exercise.[12] In the case of technological innovation, this implies not only a decline in the ability to generate new ideas, but also a concomitant reduction in the ability to absorb and interpret information from outside the firm. In this sense, at least the internal acquisition of new knowledge and the utilisation of 'outside knowledge' are complements rather than substitutes.

The rate at which the firm acquires public goods-type knowledge from its environment.

At any given time, there exists a vast body of knowledge of value to a firm that is in the nature of a public good. By definition, such a good can be 'consumed' by any one economic agent without thereby impairing the consumption of the same good by other agents. In the sphere of technology, channels whereby firms acquire public goods knowledge include, for example, scientific and technical publications, the patent record, databases, free-access information networks, technical meetings, informal exchanges among personnel, study tours, plant visits, and a host of others.

In their chain-linked model of innovation, Kline and Rosenberg refer to the activities involved in obtaining this kind of information as monitoring.[13] Generally, the marginal cost of obtaining information through these channels is so low that monitoring can involve a wide range of possible sources. Efficiency gains are more likely to come from careful organisation and management of the relevant activities than from an *a priori* restriction of their scope.[14] The success of the Japanese in becoming 'fast seconds' in innovation has often been attributed to their highly developed monitoring systems.

There can be little doubt that modern information technology has enabled firms to draw on public goods knowledge to an unprecedented extent. Where at one time hard-copy publications and contacts among people were the firm's main sources, a multiplicity of techniques for the storage and transmission of such information now provides strategists with a seeming surfeit of inputs into their decisions. At the same time, the fact that R&D activities in many sectors still tend to cluster regionally is evidence of the continuing importance of personal interactions in innovation. Although such clustering may have some straightforward economic explanations, one suspects that the often-cited synergy effects also depend on people communicating face-to-face, rather than through electronic media.[15]

The rate at which the firm acquires other firms' proprietary knowledge.

Technical knowledge can be transferred from one firm to another by a variety of formal and informal methods. Among the first, arm's-length and know-how transfer agreements are the most obvious. The second include reverse engineering, the hiring away of people from competitors, and direct exchanges of information among employees.

This last mechanism deserves special mention because it reflects, at the level of individuals, precisely the conflicting forces that are one of the key themes of my observations. Just as firms derive returns from proprietary knowledge, so do members of these organisations. Their personal knowledge helps to define their status role. Therefore, they are often less likely to share such knowledge with fellow employees than with their professional counterparts in other firms, including competitors.

The last decade has seen a rapid growth of bilateral, co-operative arrangements in procurement, production, and marketing. Whether organised as formal joint ventures or in other ways, these arrangements generally have been based on the exploitation of asymmetries in the knowledge of firms. Although institutionalised exchanges of this type often start out quite modest in scope, the realisation of mutual benefits tends to lead to more intensive linkages, through which an increasingly widening range of information is transferred.[16]

The rate at which the firm generates new technical knowledge jointly with other firms.

For reasons having to do with high costs and high risks, as well as with the need to bring complementary bits and pieces of knowledge to bear on the solution of common problems, firms in many industries have increasingly relied on multilateral co-operation for the development of generic (pre-competitive) technical knowledge. In many instances, such co-operation has been stimulated and subsidised by national governments.

Nevertheless, even in this framework the issue of individual participants' interest in appropriating results arose very quickly. Outstanding examples are provided by the American Microelectronics and Computer Technology Corporation (MCC) and the British Alvey Programme. Both were hampered by conflicts about intellectual property rights and soon reached the point where pressures for short-term achievements at the commercial level frequently won out over the intended, longer-term objectives of these programs.[17]

HOW FIRMS ATTEMPT TO APPROPRIATE TECHNICAL KNOWLEDGE

The discussion so far suggests that strategists of a profit-oriented organisation have to do a balancing act between the benefits of relying on their own resources for innovation and the obvious gains of drawing relevant information from the firm's environment. The consensus seems to be that modern information technologies have made the balancing act more difficult, precisely because they have created the potential for electronic interdependence. But whatever the outcome of individual decisions, the goal of turning information into firm-specific knowledge lies at the roots of all strategies.

A recent report of the US Office of Technology Assessment put the problem very succinctly:

> . . . the new information and communications technologies available today are challenging the intellectual property system in ways that may only be resolvable with substantial changes in the system or with new mechanisms to allocate both rights and rewards. Once a relatively slow and ponderous process, technological change is now outpacing the legal structure that governs the system.[18]

In focussing solely on the legal protection of knowledge, however, this statement both over-dramatises and oversimplifies the issue. To be sure, the patent and copyright systems continually have been put to the test of accommodating the results of technological advances, yet these systems are but one of a number of mechanisms for appropriating the returns from innovation.

Nevertheless, at least in some industries and for some new knowledge, seeking patent protection has been the preferred strategy of firms. They have done so from a variety of motives: to prevent duplication in the case of new ideas from which they drew direct commercial benefit; to shelter existing technology against inroads by competitors; to derive returns from licensing the technology to others; and to retain rights to knowledge that may become useful at some time in the future.

Ostensibly, patents grant temporary monopoly rights to knowledge; however, from a dynamic point of view they have limits, as Alfred Marshall pointed out a 100 years ago:

> In many businesses only a small percentage of improvements are patented. They consist of many small steps, which it would not be worth while to patent one at a time. Or their chief point lies in noticing that a certain thing ought to be done; and to patent one way of doing it is only to set other people to work to find other ways of doing it against which the patent cannot guard.[19]

From this observation, Marshall went on to extol the benefits of secrecy as a means for appropriating new technical knowledge. There is little need to belabour the point that efforts to maintain secrecy are often seen as threatened by the advent of new information technologies. Indeed, as many incidents have shown, these technologies provide a host of "subtle practices" for intruding upon the intellectual terrain of others.

Yet another form of protection of technical knowledge is provided by a firm's existing know-how. This implies not only the ability quickly to absorb new information, but even more importantly the ability to organise and manage activities. Wherever firms impose restrictions on the movement of employees to competitors, for example, they presumably try to prevent the outward transfer of know-how.

A fourth strategy is to rely on lead times in innovation and on a quick move down the learning curve to appropriate returns from innovation. Short-lived as such advantages may be, they frequently give innovators a sufficient competitive headstart, especially if they can also rely on established marketing and service networks.

Finally, vertical integration of all relevant operations is a strategy aimed at securing full control over a technology. It is particularly attractive in situations where the alternative would be to share knowledge with suppliers who are also serving a firm's competitors. Control over old and new technical knowledge through integration also has been one of the major motives of multinational corporations in their efforts to adapt to different markets and yet to avoid large spill-overs.[20]

STRATEGIC IMPLICATIONS

Strategies over the technology life cycle

At the outset of the preceding section I addressed the need for strategists to do a balancing act between internally-generated knowledge and external sources of information. Although success or failure depends on a host of highly firm-specific and industry-specific factors, empirical investigations nevertheless suggest certain regularities with respect to the determinants of shifts in the balance.[21] These have to do mainly with the effects of the technology life cycle on firms' strategies.

The features of the life cycle have been elaborated in an extensive literature. For our purposes, a highly stylised version suffices, in which the evolution of a basic technology is characterised by reductions in technical uncertainty, and subsequently in commercial uncertainty, while at the same time there occurs a steady increase in the technology's complexity.

Reductions of technical uncertainty are the results of accumulating knowledge about the workability of an idea. In the early phases of the cycle, the search for such knowledge typically is concerned with an understanding of broad principles and generic problems underlying the successful operation of a new technology. Continuing investment in R&D produces increasingly specific knowledge through bench tests, prototypes, pilot operations, etc.

Up to a point, commercial uncertainty is attenuated through cost studies and market surveys; beyond this point, however, only actual experience will result in further useful knowledge. It seems clear, in any event, that firms accumulate this kind of knowledge through both their own efforts and through information obtained from the observable experience of others.

Increases in complexity are an inevitable accompaniment of the development of successful basic technologies. They have two sources. The first involves a proliferation of technical features that are highly specific to a new device or process; these are mitigated in part by the standardisation of some components. The second has to do with the increasing specificity of the socio-technical systems evolving around an innovation.[22] To say that technology is complex is not the same as saying that it is complicated. Thus, early computers were complicated because they involved large numbers of vacuum tubes, connections, and switches; they became complex only as assemblages of previously-known components were replaced by product-specific components. Similarly, the electronic systems of commercial aircraft are complicated as long as they involve miles of wires and thousands of connections; they become increasingly complex as digital data bus terminals using microprocessors replace traditional methods of signal transmission.[23] Needless to say, innovations that successfully reduce technical uncertainty by increasing complexity tend to take on a public goods character; conversely, innovations that introduce complexity for the sake of product differentation or cost reduction are often highly firm-specific.

Figure 1 illustrates how changes in the three variables — technical uncertainty, commercial uncertainty, and complexity — might influence the strategic balance between stand-alone efforts and reliance on information exchanges with other firms.

FIGURE 1 EXAMPLES OF CHANGING STRATEGIC BALANCE OVER THE TECHNOLOGY LIFE CYCLE.

Life-cycle Phase	Stand-Alone Effort in Technology Dev.	Reliance on Information Exchanges
Dominance of technical uncertainty	Expected appropriability of generic knowledge high (required capacity in place; property rights obtainable; anticipation of first-to market advantages).	Expected appropriability of generic knowledge low (complementary inputs required; information flows assured).
Dominance of commercial uncertainty	Competitive advantage in marketing & distribution; complementarities between existing products and new technology.	Informational asymmetries among firms; advantage of standardisation; government sponsorship.
Dominance of complexity	Enhancement of existing products & processes. Cost reduction; product differentation.	Information gaps (technology slip); economies of scale and scope.

The point of these examples is to emphasise that strategies are guided not by objective facts but by managerial perceptions about the current and likely future states of a technology and therefore about the benefits and costs of going it alone or of relying on exchanges of information with other firms. Clearly, the accuracy of these perceptions hinges on the extent to which credible forecasts of technical developments can be made, a subject on which experts differ.[24] At the same time, however, one must recognise that when certain perceptions become part of an industry's conventional wisdom, they may turn into self-fulfilling prophecies. Thus, if decision-makers in a mature-technology industry believe that the costs, risks, and prospective returns no longer justify stand-alone efforts at major innovation, they will consider joint efforts the only viable alternative.

One of the crucial questions, then, is to what extent the rapid diffusion of new communication and information technologies has influenced strategists' perceptions about the respective merits of the two approaches to acquiring new technical knowledge. Casual evidence would suggest that these technologies have accelerated the trend toward co-operation, albeit with consequences for individual firms' long-run competitive position that are far from clear.[25]

For the student of the economics of technological change a somewhat disconcerting conclusion follows from these speculations about strategic behaviour: observed life-cycle phenomena are the result of a mixture of whatever objective laws may govern the development of technologies and of subjective managerial assessments of opportunities for innovation. While these two influences usually can be disentangled with the wisdom of twenty-twenty hindsight, they make the predicting of industrial growth patterns, based on the logic of technological evolution, a quite hazardous undertaking.[26]

Effects of the Revolution

The main line of my arguments so far has been that, other things equal, firms surely would prefer having strong property rights to their existing knowledge as well as appropriating all new technical knowledge generated through their innovative efforts. It is the nature of technological revolutions, however, that they do not leave other things equal. The recent breakthroughs in communication and information technology did not change the motives of participants in the economic game, but they have begun to transform the rules of the game as well as its institutional setting in ways we are only beginning to understand. Were it not for the persistence of old modes of thought, one would hardly need to state the obvious: the new technologies no more represent just faster means for transmitting data and messages through networks than the automobile represented just a faster substitute for the horse-drawn carriage!

In his 1989 CIRCIT seminar, Bela Gold made an ardent plea for a 'top-down', strategic approach to harnessing the potentials of information technology in the internal operations of firms.[27] His argument, that 'business as usual' will not do, applies with equal force to the development of strategies for interfirm communication. Competitive survival will force firms to adapt to the emerging new environment.

Given the uncertainties of the current situation, it would be tempting to derive guidance from the experience of sectors that are leading in their utilisation, such as banking and finance. While the technical, structural, and institutional transformations wrought there by the electronic revolution have been spectacular,[28] they probably offer little in the way of guidance as to the directions of change in other sectors. Depending on one's perspective, it is encouraging or sobering to realise that a short two decades ago no one would have dared to predict how the world's financial markets would be affected by these technological advances!

Nevertheless, it is clear already that the global transformation of these markets has profoundly affected the allocation of capital and other resources, changing their relative values in the process. One observer concluded rather sweepingly that, ''[T]he communications revolution, in short, is altering the very foundations of modern society and the economic, social, and strategic importance of information.''[29]

When one descends from such a high level of generalisation, the picture very quickly becomes cloudy. Any effort to disentangle the implications of the information revolution for innovation strategies probably should start with a distinction between direct and indirect effects on particular industries. Among the former, I would count all the issues having to do with the difficulties of appropriating the returns from innovation in the information sector itself. The software, direct satellite broadcasting, sound and video recording industries come to mind as prime examples. A detailed consideration of these would go well beyond the scope of my observations.

What I want to speculate about is the indirect, but in a broader sense more profound, effects on the industrial sector in general, including those industries whose own technologies are generally regarded as mature. Here one can discern the revolution's effects in some developments that would have been quite unattractive, and perhaps even impossible, without modern communication and information technologies. Virtually every one of these developments is likely to undermine the foundations of firms' traditional strategies for acquiring and protecting knowledge, as I outlined them in preceding sections. The range of examples is wide, but I restrict myself to a few that I have come across in my work involving manufacturing industries:

(1) While multifirm R&D consortia are not new in themselves, their current scope and intensity are difficult to imagine in the absence of concurrent advances in the participants' ability continuously to exchange information. From the individual firm's point of view, the pervasive trend toward such co-operation in the generation of basic technical knowledge has forced a re-evaluation of the benefits, costs, and risks of stand-alone efforts. One may well venture the guess that, in most industries, the luxury of going it alone in major innovation will be open only to dominant firms. Nevertheless, these firms may then face coalitions offering serious challenges to their positions. The problem, here, is of course not just one of business strategy; rather, the trend toward co-operation has raised serious questions for traditional competition policy, at least in the United States.[30]

(2) The rapid growth of production joint ventures similarly has been made possible by the communications revolution. This is especially true in those cases where manufacturing is carried out in widely dispersed locations and the final product assembled elsewhere. One of the most spectacular examples is provided by the European Airbus venture, with components of each plane produced in several countries. Even more than in mass production, success in this kind of operation hinges on the continuous exchange of information among the participants. From the economist's point of view, the most interesting consequence of these developments is that they have put into question the traditional arguments for economies of scale and of agglomeration. It is only fair to point out, however, that technological progress in transportation has

also played a major role in the establishment of geographically-dispersed production joint ventures.

(3) The growth of permanent subcontracting networks, now widespread in many manufacturing industries, presumably could not have occurred without the communication and data processing facilities developed in the last two decades. Whereas in the past firms tended to maintain an arm's-length relationship with their suppliers, the establishment of long-term ties has now begun to replace short-term and spot transactions. This has affected not only production processes themselves but has spilled over into involvement of suppliers in the R&D, design, and engineering phases of product development by their customers.

(4) A further corollary has been the development of manufacturing services on the basis of new communication technologies. To an ever-increasing degree, manufacturing firms are spinning off to outside companies a number of service functions traditionally performed in-house. Outsiders could not perform these specialised functions, typically related to design, engineering, finance, and marketing, without continuous interchanges of information with their principals.

(5) Effective and efficient communications technologies have also helped to accelerate interfirm co-operation in the distribution of products. Joint wholesale and dealer networks are becoming more common in all those industries dependent on a wide dispersion of sales effort. As a consequence, traditional notions about the minimum efficient size of dealer networks, have had to be revised, and such co-operation has made entry into new markets easier than before. At the same time, firms have had to revise their notions as to the strategic importance of such factors as the exclusiveness of distribution systems.

(6) In many industries, customer involvement and customer feedback during the R&D stage is becoming increasingly important. Therefore, continuous interaction with customers plays an important role in all phases of the process whereby new products are brought to market. Medical technology offers an outstanding example of this development.

Other examples could be added, but I hope the point is made: new information technologies have expanded the range of strategic options available to firms, and they have at the same time forced a reassessment of the goals of innovative activity. Even more important, they have begun to change the assumptions and conceptual foundations of strategy formulation by shifting the traditional boundaries between private and public technology. If the incremental cost of acquiring information is sufficiently low, and if rapid technological advances create no more than transitory advantages for firms possessing unique technical knowledge, then one would expect these firms to place less emphasis on appropriability, and more on co-operatively-generated knowledge.

These observations raise the question whether the resulting increases in the homogeneity of technical knowledge possessed by firms will tend to undermine their respective competitive advances. If it is true that firms survive in competition by being different from their rivals, where will the differences come from? Conventional economic theory would suggest that, when all firms in an industry are 'on' the same production function, only differences in input prices can explain their competitve performance. The empirical evidence does not, however, support such a simple explanation. In fact, the last two decades have seen an increasing interpenetration of markets by firms possessing essentially identical, formal technical knowledge.[31] Furthermore, studies of comparative performance show that accelerated transfers of technical knowledge *per se* have done little to eradicate interfirm differences in organisational capabilites, in the quality of managements, and in the speed and effects of learning. The evidence also suggests that this kind of knowledge is much more difficult to transfer from one setting to another, even if one sets aside questions about the influence of sociocultural factors on industrial performance.

CONCLUDING OBSERVATIONS AND EXTENSIONS

In market economies, neither the recent breakthroughs in communication and information technology nor any of the preceding technical revolutions have changed the basic motive of firms in committing resources to innovation: the prospect of being able to appropriate (at least some of) the returns from the investment. However, such sweeping advances are often preceived as threatening appropriability, and therefore they impinge on the strategic balance among both the methods whereby firms acquire new technical knowledge and the means whereby they protect this knowledge.

Although these effects are just beginning to be understood, one may speculate that they depend in large measure on how firms adapt their strategies in different phases of their basic technologies' life cycles. There can be little doubt that the improved quantity and quality of information flows, as well as their reduced costs, have played an important role in the trend toward interfirm co-operation in technology development. This trend probably has been accelerated by the increasing cost of major R&D projects and by the belief that life cycles in many industries have been shortened, thus reducing the benefits a firm might capture from a stand-alone strategy and emphasising the ostensible benefits of co-operation in the reduction of technical uncertainty.

When all this has been said, however, there remains the fact that competitive survival depends only in part on bold innovation. While the often stunning successes of technological pioneers make for fine case studies, the great majority of businesses succeeds in global competition by capitalising on other strengths, such as established brand names, well-developed marketing networks, and excellence in service. No doubt the information revolution has affected the performance of these firms as profoundly as it has that of technology-driven companies. As Gold[32] has pointed out, technological superiority, although widely regarded as *the* key to market success, is but one of a number of equally important factors.

18   *Gerhard Rosegger*

The matter deserves attention only because the capability-expanding and integrative powers of the new communication and information technologies are so often seen in a high-technology context only. Like all technological revolutions, however, they have spilled over into all sectors of the economy and offered opportunities for efficiency gains even in areas well inside the technological frontier. It is useful, in this connection, to remind oneself of Friedrich v. Hayek's observation that, "[T]o know of and put to use a machine not fully employed, or somebody's skill which could be better utilised, or to be aware of a surplus stock which can be drawn upon during an interruption of supplies, is socially quite as useful as the knowledge of better alternative techniques."[33]

Even after recognising this aspect of the new technologies' impact, however, we are left with issues that transcend the scope of my review. Crucial among them is the question of how, in the longer term, the information revolution will affect the formal and informal institutions supporting the appropriation of technical knowledge. An answer to this question clearly must go beyond the problems raised whenever innovations undermine the existing legal and organisational frameworks, such as in the cases of property to software and data bases. If the formation of global networks is indeed the essence of the revolution, then a greater international co-ordination of laws, regulations, and business practices becomes a necessary first step in the adaptation of the strategic environment. But such adaptation is purely reactive and will do little to deal with the more fundamental transformations brought about by the rapid diffusion of information technologies.

One of these transformations will no doubt have to do with the changing context for government policy. There is, first of all, the sovereign right of states to control information flows across their borders; but the exercise of this right assumes that control be technically possible, surely an unwarranted assumption even at the present stage of development! More seriously, however, the information revolution raises the question as to what end a state would want to control information flows. Setting aside matters of military security, it is becoming increasingly difficult unequivocally to define a set of national interests that might guide policy. As the interests of commercial and industrial organisations become more and more intertwined with but small regard for national boundaries, the formulation of technology policies and industrial policies is bound to run up against the problem of weighing benefits and costs that completely transcend the traditional perspectives of policy-makers.

A final observation about the consequences of these developments requires no great predictive powers: Unless the nations that have regarded themselves as the historical leaders in technology can sustain a rate of innovation that is higher than the rate at which technological knowledge is diffused among economies, the worldwide convergence of technical capabilities becomes a matter of simple arithmetic. The point would hardly be worth making, were it not for the copious writings that bemoan this convergence as a loss of competitiveness. They do so from a point of view that seems largely irrelevant to contemporary assessments of the relative merits of competition and co-operation in innovation. If business decision-makers increasingly regard the globe as their proper playing field, competitiveness defined in purely national terms is bound to lose significance as a guide to policy and strategy. In the end, this may well turn out to be the most important transformation wrought by the information revolution.

NOTES AND REFERENCES

1. For this account I have drawn on K. Gertels, 'Reisen, Boten, Posten, Korrespondenz in Mittelalter und früher Neuzeit', in H. Pohl (ed.), *Die Bedeutung der Kommunikation für Wirtschafts und Gesellschaft*, Stuttgart, Steiner, 1989, pp. 19-36, as well as on L. Darmstaedter (ed.), *Handbuch zur Geschichte der Naturwissenschaften und der Technik*, 2nd edn., Berlin, Springer, 1908, pp. 258, 261.
2. W. Sombart, *Die deutsche Volkswirtschaft im Neunzehnten Jahrhundert*, Berlin, Bondi, 1903, pp. 4-5.
3. Quoted in Gertels, *op. cit.*, p. 32.
4. W. Sachse, "Wirtschaftsliteratur und kommunikation bis 1800," in Pohl, *op. cit.*, p. 206.
5. P.J. Denning, 'Worldnet', *American Scientist*, 77, 5, 1989, pp. 432-4.
6. P.V. Norden, 'Message from the General Chairman', *ORSA/TIMS Bulletin, Program of the 28th Joint National Meeting*, 1989, pp. vi-vii.
7. P. Drucker, 'Information, communications, and understanding', in *Technology, Management and Society*, New York, Harper & Row, 1970, p. 3.
8. A. Osborne, *Running Wild: The Next Industrial Revolution*, Berkeley, CA, Osborne/McGraw-Hill, 1979, ch. 7. Ironically, Osborne cautioned especially against the application of new techonlogy in three areas where it has since progressed very rapidly — voting, funds tranfers among banks, and the operation of stock exchanges.
9. J.H. Shera, 'Librarianship and information science', in F. Machlup and U. Mansfield (eds), *The Study of Information: Interdisciplinary Messages*, New York, Wiley, 1983, pp. 379-88.
10. F. Machlup, 'Semantic quirks in the study of information', in Machlup and Mansfield, *op. cit.*, pp. 641-71.
11. R.R. Nelson and S.G. Winter, *An Evolutionary Theory of Economic Change*, Cambridge, Mass., Belknap Press of Harvard University Press, 1982.
12. Another reason why organisational knowledge may deteriorate is that distortion, noise, and bias may affect its *internal* transmission. Furthermore, as I argue below, it may not always be in the interest of individuals to share their specialised knowledge with other members of the organisation.
13. S.J. Kline and N. Rosenberg, 'An overview of innovation', in R. Landau and N. Rosenberg (eds), *The Positive Sum Strategy: Harnessing Technology for Economic Growth*, Washington, DC, National Academy Press, 1986, pp. 275-305.
14. G. Rosegger, 'Technologie-monitoring: Konzeption und Anwendungen', *Der Wirtschaftsingenieur*, 21, 3, 1989, pp. 24-7.
15. This argument is elaborated in E.J. Malecki, 'The R&D location decision of the firm and "creative" regions', *Technovation*, 6, 3, August 1987, pp. 205-22.
16. An illustration of this tendency is provided in G. Rosegger, "Co-operative research in the automobile industry: a multinational perspective", in A.N. Link and G. Tassey (eds), *Co-operative Research and Development: The Industry-University-Government Relationship*, Boston, Kluwer, 1989, pp. 167-86.

20   Gerhard Rosegger

17. See, for example, Office of Technology Assessment, *Commercialising High-Temperature Superconductivity*, Washington, DC, US Government Printing Office, 1988, esp. p. 135; and B. Oakley and K. Owen, *Alvey: Britain's Strategic Computing Initiative*, Cambridge, Mass., MIT Press, 1989, p. 28 and elsewhere.
18. Congress of the United States, Office of Technology Assessment, *Intellectual Property Rights in an Age of Electronics and Information*, Washington, DC, US Government Printing Office, 1986, p. 3.
19. A. Marshall, *Principles of Economics*, 1890, 8th edn, New York, Macmillan, 1920, p. 281n.
20. The desire to internalise knowledge is, of course, one of the main reasons given for the existence of multinational firms. For implications of interest in the present context, see R.D. Pearce, *The Internationalisation of Research and Development by Multinational Enterprises*, New York, St. Martin's Press, 1989.
21. See for example, G. Rosegger, 'The benefits and costs of international and technical co-operation in mature industries: and US perspective', in Bela Gold (ed.), *On the Increasing Role of Technology in Corporate Policy*, special publication of the *International Journal of Technology Management*, 5, 7-9, 1991, pp. 256-73; and 'Diffusion through interfirm co-operation: a case study', in N. Nakicenovich and A. Grübler (eds), *Rat Race Dynamics and Crazy Companies: The Diffusion of Technologies and Social Behaviour*, Berlin-New York, Springer, in press.
22. K.B. DeGreene, *Sociotechnical Systems: Factors in Analysis, Design and Management*, Englewood Cliffs, NJ, Prentice-Hall, 1973.
23. B.A Cosgrove, 'Aircraft technology development: the need for change', paper presented at the International Conference on Technology Management, University of Miami, 17 February, 1988 (Seattle, WA, Boeing Commercial Airplane Co., 1988).
24. For an extended discussion, see R.U. Ayres, 'Barriers and breakthroughs: an "expanding frontiers" model of the technology-industry life cycle', *Technovation*, 7, 2, May 1988, pp. 87-115.
25. *cf.*, Rosegger, "The benefits and costs . . .", *op. cit.*
26. B. Gold, 'Industry growth patterns: theory and empirical results', *Journal of Industrial Economics*, 13, 1 1964, pp. 53-73.
27. B. Gold, 'Improving managerial approaches to information technology', *Prometheus*, 7, 2, December 1989, pp. 213-24.
28. L.S. Mayne, 'Technological change and competition in American banking', *Technovation*, 4, 1, January 1986, pp. 67-83.
29. R.P. Benko, *Protecting Intellectual Property Rights: Issues and Controversies*, Washington, DC, American Enterprise Institute, 1987, p. 36.
30. W.F. Baxter, "Antitrust law and technological innovation", *Issues in Science and Technology*, Winter 1985, pp. 80-91.
31. See for example, A. Erdilek (ed.), *Multinationals as Mutual Invaders: Intra-Industry Direct Foreign Investment*, London, Croom-Helm, 1985.
32. B. Gold,'Technological and other determinants of the international competitiveness of US industries', *IEEE Transactions on Engineering Management*, EM-30, 2, May 1983, pp. 53-9.
33. F.v. Hayek, 'The use of knowledge in society', *American Economic Reivew*, 35, 4, September 1945, pp. 519-30.

Part V
International Aspects

[16]

International Information Issues

BETH KREVITT ERES
Interdisciplinary Center for Technological
Analysis and Forecasting
Tel-Aviv University

INTRODUCTION

Over the last twenty-five years, the electronic movement of information has become a precondition and necessary part of the physical movement and trade of goods and services. Orders are placed electronically, point-of-sales computers immediately update inventories, and new international information services are constantly being offered. With the growing dependence of the world economy on this information transfer, international information issues have become the focal point in both economic and political decision making.

In the 1970s and early 1980s, the less developed countries (LDCs) showed a growing fear of cultural imperialism, a fear that the developed world was monopolizing and controlling information to such an extent that the national and cultural sovereignty of the LDCs was threatened (HEIM). The concept of the New World Information and Communication Order (NWICO), as presented in the MACBRIDE report and described by SURPRENANT (1985), summarizes the virulent debate that ensued. As a result of this and other issues, the United States withdrew from Unesco (DEMAC; GONZALEZ-MANET; HEIM).

Information as an economic resource and as the underlying basis of international trade has emerged as the major issue of the late 1980s and early 1990s. Thus, CRAWFORD depicts the crucial role of telecommunications in the plans of the EEC (European Economic Community) for the New Common Market, which is to take effect in 1992. Countries are positioning themselves along such lines as economic centralization, protectionism,

Annual Review of Information Science and Technology (ARIST), Volume 24, 1989
Martha E. Williams, Editor
Published for the American Society for Information Science (ASIS)
By Elsevier Science Publishers B.V.

4   BETH KREVITT ERES

employment, competitiveness, and so forth (CRONIN; ROBINSON, 1987).
International political issues relating to trade in services have become impor-
tant global issues with information services as the underlying denominator.
This is not surprising if we recognize that the information industry is already
the third largest in the world economy (U.S. CONGRESS. OFFICE OF
TECHNOLOGY ASSESSMENT, 1986).

FEKETEKUTY & ARONSON show that an information-based economy is
not just an extension of the industrial society but is very different in its basic
concepts. First, time plays a different role in an economy in which the
transfer of the good sold (information) is both instantaneous and of unpredictable value. Second, the cost of transporting physical goods is closely
linked to distance, but the transfer of information is distance independent
and, moreover, exploits time-difference phenomena.

Previous *ARIST* chapters have touched directly or indirectly on international information issues. KEREN & HARMON dealt specifically with
information services in LDCs. ROSENBERG described national information
policies and included a preview of national security issues, which are just now
coming into focus. LAMBERTON (1984) reviewed the economics of information and organization while GRIFFITHS (1982) discussed the value of
information systems, products and services. SURPRENANT (1985) looked
specifically at three global threats to information—radio-frequency allocations, the New World Information and Communication Order (NWICO), and
transborder data flows. In the 1988 *ARIST* volume, RATH & CLEMENT discussed information policies in science and technology, referring to the
international issues of national security and information as an economic
resource.

This chapter focuses on those international issues that revolve around
information as an essential economic commodity in world trade and development. It continues where Surprenant left off in his discussion of transborder
data flows and stresses the international aspect of the views expressed by
Rath and Clement. Thus the time period covered generally ranges from the
mid-1980s to early 1989.

Transborder Data Flow

Transborder data flow (TBDF) has been defined as the "electronic transmission of data across political boundaries for processing and/or storage in
computer files" (SURPRENANT, 1985) and as "the movement across
national boundaries of machine-readable data for processing, storage or
retrieval" (U.N. CENTRE ON TRANSNATIONAL CORPORATIONS, 1982).
The latter definition is somewhat less restrictive than the former and includes
the physical transport of such media as tapes and floppy disks from one
nation to another. In either case, both definitions are inclusive of the three
major classes of flows: marketed data services, international trade-related data
flows, and intracorporate flows (CRONIN).

Objections have been raised that the term transborder data flow is not
representative of the issues at large. ROBINSON (1987), in a very comprehen-

INTERNATIONAL INFORMATION ISSUES 5

sive review of the topic, suggests that "international data services" better reflects the problems since the flow itself, according to him, is not the issue. The Brazilians, on the other hand, have suggested "transborder information resources flow" (U.N. CENTRE ON TRANSNATIONAL CORPORATIONS, 1983). From their perspective, the flow of resources out of their country *is* the crucial issue. To be consistent with most of the literature, we use the term transborder data flow (TBDF) in the rest of this chapter to refer to the transfer of information in any format over national borders.

Even at the national level, TBDF represents a unique problem since it cuts across traditional lines of ministerial responsibilities, with the policies and actions of various bureaus often pulling in different directions (CRONIN; ROBINSON, 1987). The Ministry of Telecommunications, for example, might wish to increase data communications use of international telecommunications lines while the Ministry of Trade might wish to encourage use of domestic information services. At the international level the scene is complicated by a multitude of actors. MOWLANA classifies them into two groups: 1) nation states, that is, intergovernmental organizations such as the International Telecommunications Union (ITU), the International Standards Organization (ISO), and the Intergovernmental Bureau for Informatics (IBI); and 2) nongovernmental organizations such as private communication carriers, data processing service bureaus, multinational corporations, and transnational associations. Mowlana further describes the types of flows that are involved and their direction of movement, each flow being influenced by the regulatory conditions in the transmitting country, the receiving country, the country of processing, the country of storage, and the location of the user.

FEKETEKUTY & ARONSON point out that the picture is further confused, since some of the telecommunications-related services are either owned or highly regulated by the government while others are owned privately. Thus, political-level discussions may be carried out by organizations with different levels of power (e.g., government vs. private industry) and, in these cases, market forces alone cannot deal with these concerns and conditions (ROBINSON, 1987).

It should also be remembered that the goals of each state are different. HEIM explains how France is aiming for technological self-sufficiency while Canada is interested in limiting foreign competition. Japan seeks economic development and progress based on trade in information goods and services, while Brazil is looking to develop its economy by protecting its domestic information industry through the restriction of data communications, data processing, and data access by those outside the country (U.N. CENTRE ON TRANSNATIONAL CORPORATIONS, 1983).

The issues involved in TBDF include national sovereignty, the unrestricted flow of information, personal and corporate privacy protection, the ownership of information, computer crime, national security and law enforcement, protection of home industries and business, high-technology transfer, and guaranteed access to national data. They are discussed below under the headings of technological, legal and sociopolitical, and economic issues.

6   BETH KREVITT ERES

TECHNOLOGICAL ISSUES

The technologies that affect the flow of information are constantly changing and converging. They include the hardware, the software, the communications channels, and the information itself. Some of the major technological
issues relate to:

- The use of telecommunications networks as international free-
  ways;
- The fact that complex technologies require complex policies;
- Competition with countries that have a leading edge;
- The creation of and adherence to international standards; and
- The overcoming of technological nontariff barriers.

For example, one resulting issue related to competition is how a developed
country balances its need to protect industry and maintain a leading technological edge with its responsibilities toward both its trading partners and
LDCs.

Telecommunications networks have become information freeways that
make national and geographic boundaries irrelevant (CRONIN). Packet-
switched networks, microwave and satellite communications, ISDN (integrated
services digital network), and transnational ventures reflect McLuhan's notion
of the global village. According to SURPRENANT (1985), information technologies are becoming so complex and at such a rapid pace that nontechnical
policy-makers are unable to address the problems in a comprehensive fashion.
As the technologies become more complex, so do the policies needed to deal
with them (HEIM). ROBINSON (1987) also suggests that as the traditional
boundaries between industries such as telecommunications, publishing, and
broadcasting become eroded, so do the boundaries between governmental
bodies that make the policy for these industries.

Another problem has been the difficulty of LDCs in entering markets in
which the leading developed countries have an edge. SURPRENANT (1985)
claimed in 1985 that both Japan and the United States had a monopoly on
the technologies that comprise the information grid, making it highly unlikely
that any other nation would be able to compete in this sphere of development. Lubbock, at a meeting on TBDF held by the INTERGOVERNMENTAL
BUREAU FOR INFORMATICS, remarked that the electronic information
industry is such a high-risk sector that only strong organizations with high
entrepreneurial and managerial skills can successfully compete. This concept
is challenged, on the other hand, by FEKETEKUTY & ARONSON who
suggest that the cost of telecommunications is declining in real terms at such
a rate that entry costs will be reduced, resulting in greater competition and
faster industry growth. The international trends toward mergers within the
industry, however, appear to discredit the easy-entry concept.

National and international standards can take the form of rules and regulations or voluntary practices. Moreover, trade can be distorted as a result of
discriminatory technical standards or restrictive procurement practices

(FEKETEKUTY & ARONSON). Examples include Japan's move to limit the use of a leased line to the access of only one computer at the other country's side and the forbidding of the sharing of unused capacity on leased lines.

BUCKLAND & LYNCH show that even when international standards are set with the best intentions, problems of incompatible language can create obstacles to the acceptance of an information technology or service. Areas of difficulty include different alphabets and character sets, different filing rules, and different cataloging codes.

International regulations concerning rates for common carriers, the manner of use of leased lines, the types of equipment that can be attached at the end of a line, and who can sell what type of equipment or service are examples of nontariff barriers affecting the ability of a country to compete or even use the marketplace. FEKETEKUTY & ARONSON detail this in a comprehensive 1984 paper, which, except for discussions of the 1986 Uruguay Round of the General Agreement on Tariffs and Trade (called GATT), is still very much up-to-date.

LEGAL AND SOCIOPOLITICAL ISSUES

It is sometimes difficult to differentiate among legal, social, economic, political, and cultural issues. Therefore, this section focuses on the issues of data protection and privacy, national security, protection of intellectual property, and national sovereignty. Problems in these areas are not readily solved since the remedies sometimes conflict with one another. MOSCO & WASKO have tried to deal with these and similar problems in a thorough collection of articles representing myriad viewpoints on the political aspect of the economics of information.

Data Protection and Privacy

Regulations concerning data protection and privacy differ from nation to nation in varying degrees of breadth and enforcement. In some countries, for example, not only are persons guaranteed the right of privacy protection but so are all legal entities (FEKETEKUTY & ARONSON). In general, however, the principles that are often included in the laws are (MOWLANA):

- Openness (no secret personal data record-keeping systems);
- Individual access (the right to know what data are on record and how they are being used);
- Individual participation (the right to amend or correct personal data about oneself);
- Collection (limits on the types of data that can be collected and the use to which they can be put);
- Use (right to limit the use of one's personal data to the use for which they were collected);

8   BETH KREVITT ERES

- Disclosure (limits on the external disclosure of personal data
  that have been collected by an organization);
- Information management (requirements for the implementation
  of data management policies by record-keeping organizations);
  and
- Accountability (accountability of record-keeping organizations
  for their operations regarding the data).

Difficulties in dealing with the often-conflicting rules and regulations
abound. ROBINSON (1987) describes the case of the Canadian bank held in
contempt by a U.S. court for failing to comply with a grand jury subpoena to
produce records held in its offices in the Bahamas while the Bahamian law
protected the release of those records.

In other cases, organizations have tried to go around laws that "protect"
data. In an extensive article on the legal and social aspects of TBDF, MILLER
points out that some organizations have been known to use TBDF to
"export" data to "data havens" in order to circumvent the laws requiring
data protection. ROBINSON (1988), however, is neither sure that such a
thing as a "data haven" exists nor sure that if it existed, it would pose any
real threat to data protection.

As LAMBERTON (1984; 1988) has shown on more than one occasion,
very little economic theory or quantitative economic analysis exists with
regard to information services. However, JUSSAWALLA & CHEAH have
tried to introduce both an economic model of privacy protection and an
econometric model of regulatory choice.

National Security

In his 1982 *ARIST* chapter ROSENBERG discussed the increasing use of
restrictions on the transmission of information or data as nontariff barriers
to the free flow of information. In general, these laws, rules, regulations, and
procedures have been established to prevent U.S. and large multinational
corporations headquartered in other countries from dominating information
markets. However, Rosenberg adds, these restrictions are being applied increasingly to prevent scientific and technological information from flowing
out of a country. As SURPRENANT (1987b, p. 435) said of the United
States, "We. . .have tended to point the finger at other nations because we
perceive ourselves as champions of the free flow of information concept. Not
any more. We are on the edge of becoming the most information restrictive
nation in the world." The simplest examples of such restrictions involve the
databases of NASA and of the Department of Energy. They are available
online through the vendor DIALOG Information Services but are restricted
(via password control) to use by U.S. citizens and corporations registered in
the United States for the U.S. aspect of their work only.

RATH & CLEMENT, in their 1988 *ARIST* chapter, briefly describe the
chronological sequence in which a new classification scheme for "sensitive

INTERNATIONAL INFORMATION ISSUES   9

but unclassified" information was created as a National Security Decision Directive of the U.S. National Security Agency. The decision was later withdrawn in response to pressure by the public and the information industry. A U.S. DEPARTMENT OF DEFENSE "White Paper" explicitly describes methods used by the Soviets to acquire knowledge of Western technologies. This paper was used as one of the key arguments in favor of the original directive.

In a rather comprehensive paper on the subject, BOLLINGER & ELLINGEN detail this chronology and explain three global trends behind the classification scheme. First, there is a growing awareness of the economic value of scientific and technological information. Second, world social and political patterns are shifting because of satellite communications, multinational data networks, gateways, and international information exchanges. Third, scientific research itself is becoming internationalized. The authors quote a 1984 speech by Harry Collier representing the British information industry in which he speculates on the cause of politicians' fears of the free flow of scientific and technological information as: "the protection of their own information industries; the retention of national sovereignty (i.e., self-sufficiency) in technical information; and safeguarding the national security from enemies and competitors" (p. 522). Bollinger and Ellingen conclude that "attempts to establish political controls over technological advances are usually doomed to failure either by their direct defiance and circumvention, or their own stifling effect over time on the very economies they seek to protect" (p. 527). The primary example of this type of interference by politicians in the conduct of science is the notorious Lysenko affair, in which the Soviet agronomist T. D. Lysenko succeeded, for a time, in rewriting the rules of genetics in the Soviet Union (MEDVEDEV).

To show the level of absurdity to which secrecy rules can be applied, ROBINSON (1987) describes the case of a Norwegian social research worker found guilty of espionage in Norway for publishing findings on the implications of NATO installations. Such information was restricted in Norway, but the documents on which the findings were based were obtained freely online from the United States.

SHATTUCK & SPENCE describe other U.S. policies toward restricting the free flow of information, including restrictions on conference attendance wherein only unclassified papers would be presented and security review would be required before papers were published even though, in some cases, the papers were the result of research not funded by the U.S. government. DEMAC also details policies affecting the media and the reduction in the number of government-produced publications.

The newspaper *USA Today* ran an opinion page concerning the FBI's Library Awareness Program through which the FBI was trying to achieve the cooperation of librarians in determining which foreigners might be obtaining unclassified but potentially sensitive material from libraries. Various individuals presented their views on the freedom of acquiring information. SCHLAFLY, for example, felt that librarians should report to the FBI on

10   BETH KREVITT ERES

users of scientific and technical information while SCHMIDT described the
FBI program as both useless and dangerous.

SCHILLER & SCHILLER detail the long-running conflict between
libraries, on the one side, and private information suppliers and their
advocates in government, on the other. They further describe the general
impact that restrictive government policies have had on the U.S. library
system, asserting that the consequences of the privatization of information
and the restriction of its flow can seriously damage the underpinning of
democratic order. The Office of Technology Assessment has recently produced
a report emphasizing the issue of the private versus the public sector as
providers of public information and the need to maintain equity in public
access (U.S. CONGRESS. OFFICE OF TECHNOLOGY ASSESSMENT,
1988b).

WALLERSTEIN & GOULD prepared a special issue of *Issues in Science
and Technology* on the balance between freedom of scientific communication and national security. Representatives of the United Kingdom, France,
the Federal Republic of Germany, Japan, and the United States presented
their opinions about restrictive scientific communications policies. Representatives of the three European nations expressed concern with recent U.S.
policies affecting the openness of scientific communication and presented
their case for their nation's being more open. The Japanese representative
discussed his country's efforts to increase the exchange of information,
acknowledging the special difficulties which arise in the need to translate to
and from Japanese. The U.S. representative explained how some mistakes
had been made in the name of national security but expressed optimism that
they could be cleared up satisfactorily with proposed revisions to the Export
Administration Act. This act would explicitly couple national security contract controls with export controls before research begins and would allow
"fundamental" research to be made freely available without restrictions.

Intellectual Property Rights

Intellectual property rights can be discussed within the context of international trade. Because "information and information-based products and
services [have] become major trade items and the basis for economic growth,
international trade and economic considerations will be brought to bear on
the resolution of intellectual property issues" (U.S. CONGRESS. OFFICE OF
TECHNOLOGY ASSESSMENT, 1986, p. 213).

The 1986 Office of Technology Assessment (OTA) report just mentioned
contains an extensive study of the impact of new technologies on the international intellectual property rights system. OTA describes the present international system and its agreements and conventions, the stresses caused by
information technologies, and the policy implications at the legal, political,
and cultural levels. The fact that the United States was neither a signatory to
the Berne Convention until 1989 nor a member of Unesco (since the early
1980s) is used as a case in point. (The U.S. has since agreed to join the Berne
Convention).

INTERNATIONAL INFORMATION ISSUES 11

The report describes how, for example, information and communication technologies, such as satellite, cable, photocopying, audio and video recording devices, and electronic information storage, retrieval, and distribution systems, undermine mechanisms for enforcing intellectual property rights. Likewise, the report discusses the emergence of new information-based products and services that do not fit within the traditional intellectual property protection categories or jurisdictions, such as computer software or products developed in space.

In summary, OTA reports the difficulties regarding intellectual property rights as being related to the increased information flow between and among nations, the growing economic importance of information technologies, the increasing cultural and political significance of these new technologies, the increasing difficulties in enforcement of the intellectual property system and the convergence of international property issues with other issues (e.g., trade).

According to HEIM, there does not appear to be a clear public mandate as to who should own information and the rights that accrue to such ownership. She suggests, moreover, that the public is indifferent to what she terms "information theft."

A study of videocassette recorders (VCRs) by GANLEY & GANLEY exemplifies this phenomenon. They detail the use of VCRs as an entertainment medium and as a political tool. They further describe the largely unsuccessful efforts made by some countries to control pirating of copyrighted material. In an informal survey in 30 developing and newly industrialized countries, they were repeatedly told that either the government does not try to enforce relevant intellectual property rights laws such as copyright or it cannot.

In a recent issue of the journal *Economic Impact*, various authors attempted to evaluate the challenges to trade presented by intellectual property issues. According to STALSON, the increased economic losses to U.S. companies that are perceived as being related to foreign infringement of U.S. intellectual property rights were estimated at between $43,000 and $61,000 million a year for 1986 alone. She detailed the possibilities of GATT's setting up a code for intellectual property which would specifically relate to such issues. In the same issue, MANSFIELD explained the importance of intellectual property rights to the process of innovation, and the U.S. CONGRESS. OFFICE OF TECHNOLOGY ASSESSMENT (1988a) presented a summary of the work described above.

A recent article by BRAUNSTEIN compares the economic value to the United States of various international copyright conventions. He suggests that "the choice of which cooperative agreement(s) a nation should join depends on the pattern of demand for imported works in that nation, the volumes of work produced by the members of the agreements, and the size of the potential reduction in any barriers" (p. 16). Between the acceptance of Braunstein's paper (February 1988) and its publication in January 1989, Congress approved the U.S.'s joining the Berne Copyright Convention (*INFORMATION TODAY*).

12   BETH KREVITT ERES

National Sovereignty

The issue of national sovereignty is intensified by fears of social, political, economic, and cultural imperialism (GONZALEZ-MANET). For example, some countries fear that if their data reside outside their boundaries, national regulatory efforts could not reach such data and the country could be held for ransom (BEARMAN; MILLER).

The greatest anxieties concern the fear of cultural dominance or imperialism; the fear of another country's language and culture superseding that of the host. This was the major point of the MACBRIDE Report but is further exacerbated today by the newer technologies, such as VCRs (GANLEY & GANLEY) or direct broadcast satellites which make it easier for the individual consumer to view in his home material produced in another country. Control of what can be seen is difficult when all a consumer need do is spend several hundred dollars on a satellite dish antenna. This so-called cultural contamination refers to television, radio, and databases as well. A suitcase lost enroute to Copenhagen from Tel-Aviv through Zurich is found by means of a central computer in Atlanta, GA. A U.K. advocate who wishes to search British case law must go online to Ohio. Even the United States is concerned; for example, the Spanish International Network is programmed outside the United States and broadcast to over 200 broadcast and cable outlets in the United States (CRONIN).

National sovereignty is also used as a synonym for national security when a country decides, for strategic reasons, that "it needs an indigenous capability to produce certain services or is unwilling to allow data pertaining to strategic issues to leave the country" (LESSER, p. 22). This is described in somewhat more detail in the section of this chapter on national security. The whole issue of nontariff trade barriers (also discussed later) is related to the issues surrounding national sovereignty.

ECONOMICS

Information is a distinctive good whose value is determined by the expected return from its use (GRIFFITHS, 1982). Furthermore, information has high fixed-cost components (i.e., its acquisition and processing) and low variable costs (i.e., its replication and distribution) (BATES). The cost of information "is independent of the scale on which it is used. A given piece of information costs the same to acquire, whether the decision to be based on it is large or small" (Kenneth J. Arrow as quoted in LAMBERTON, 1984, p. 7).

The concept of information as an economic resource, or, as SCHILLER prefers, as an economic commodity, has entered the vocabulary of political scientists, economists, and lawyers. However, as pointed out by LAMBERTON (1984), ROBINSON (1987), and SCHILLER, the implications of this fact have not penetrated economic theory. Debates on international trade, for example, do not take into account the economic role of the transfer of information.

BATES suggests that economists have resisted attempts to define and measure the impact of information as an economic resource. ROBINSON (1987, p. 372) states that "we do not even know what to measure, let alone how to measure it." Efforts have been limited to external indicators of the amount of information at its flow, such as those of POOL ET AL. or gross indicators of aggregate value, such as those of MACHLUP, PORAT, RUBIN, and the ORGANISATION FOR ECONOMIC CO-OPERATION AND DEVELOPMENT (OECD) (1987) for the developed countries and R. L. KATZ (1986a; 1986b; 1987) and JUSSAWALLA ET AL. for the developing countries. Recent works by JUSSAWALLA & CHEAH and BRAUNSTEIN are an exception. These authors respectively suggest an econometric model of regulatory choice with regard to telecommunications, for example, and an economic analysis of the value in the signing of intellectual property treaties.

One complicating factor is the indeterminacy of the value of a piece of information. The value varies according to the customer, the certainty of the information, its immediate or future relevance and applicability, and the structural and political factors surrounding its reception. Thus, the ultimate value of information to the user comes from its expected use at some future point and is influenced by the circumstances of its use (BATES).

Nevertheless, there is little doubt that information technologies and information-based services have a profound effect on the world economy. Information is power, and "power is used to shape the production, distribution and use of information as a commodity. . .A fundamental source of power in capitalist countries is profit from the sale of commodities to the marketplace" (MOSCO, p. 3). Aspects that concern us here include information industry policy and strategy at a national and regional level, the growing internationalization and convergence of the information-based industries, the growing importance and need to govern trade in services, and nontariff barriers set up by nations and supranations to control this trade.

Information Industry Policy and Strategy

In recent years much discussion has arisen over the policies and strategies that need to be established at national and regional levels to meet the challenges of the converging information technologies. ARNOLD & GUY, for example, focus on the "policy paths" of nine countries (United States, Japan, United Kingdom, France, Federal Republic of Germany, Belgium, Canada, the Netherlands, and Switzerland) and on the European Economic Community. They describe the historical developments, current policies and strategies, and the strengths and weaknesses of each. They differentiate between the large producing countries and the small "niche" countries, questioning the path the middle-sized countries should follow.

JOWETT & ROTHWELL (p. 71) indicate that in studying such policies one must always be aware that the:

> major electronics IT [information technology] companies of Japan, the United States, Europe and the United Kingdom, being

14   BETH KREVITT ERES

multinationals with global strategies, are not constrained by
national boundaries, and while they participate in government
programmes, as a means of securing financial assistance, this has
not prevented them from sacrificing the potential success of
these schemes by collaborating or competing with each other.

The U.S. CONGRESS. OFFICE OF TECHNOLOGY ASSESSMENT (1985)
elucidates this with a list of examples of such relationships. MOSCO describes
how a multinational, such as Digital Equipment Corp., builds its computers:
keyboards made in Boston, display monitors made in Taiwan, floppy disk
drives made in Singapore, power supplies made in Arizona, circuit modules
made in Puerto Rico, and so forth. Without doubt an equally international
list could be drawn up for competing multinationals such as IBM or Philips.

ARNOLD & GUY suggest that research of the 1950s could be described
as being based on the slogan "the Russians are coming" while that of the
1980s is based on the notion that "the Japanese are coming." As a result of
the fear of Japanese dominance, both Europe and the United States are in the
throes of trying to establish policy and set strategy to deal with this competition from the Far East. The response has included an outpouring of funds
into related R&D activities as well as trade restrictions on both production
and marketing. MACKINTOSH and JOWETT & ROTHWELL describe
Europe's attempts to revitalize the information technology (IT) industry.
A report by the ORGANISATION FOR ECONOMIC CO-OPERATION AND
DEVELOPMENT (1987) depicts an in-depth study to determine the
economic prospects of IT in Europe. KIMBEL summarizes this report noting
that a 1% reduction in the cost/performance ratio of existing information
technologies can lead to a 30% increase in demand for the IT product. What
appears to be needed are methods of encouraging expansion in the uses of
information technologies and of developing a work force skilled in their use.
CRAWFORD cites the White and Green papers, which outline the plans for
the New Common Market of Europe for 1992 (EC '92); these plans are
based on the strategy of an integrated European market with, for example,
one currency, unrestricted work and travel and joint R&D to increase efficiency and allow for large-scale production.

The U.S. CONGRESS. OFFICE OF TECHNOLOGY ASSESSMENT (1985)
has similarly suggested that in order to maintain U.S. viability in information
technology, particularly in the light of Japanese competition, more attention
should be paid to R&D in information technology. It states that "industry
has generally looked, and still looks, to the academic community to perform
and the Federal Government to fund the long-term basic research that will
underlie future technological advances" (p. 5). It also notes that at this time
nearly 80% of federal funding in information technology originates with the
Department of Defense and that an important issue for consideration is
whether increased funding by nondefense agencies might focus more work on
civilian needs. This is of particular concern in an era wherein it is recognized
that the trade war can equally affect the future of a nation. The report also
makes recommendations concerning the need to find better mechanisms for

INTERNATIONAL INFORMATION ISSUES 15

accessing foreign information while also tightening outflows of technical information for reasons of security.

Internationalization and Convergence of the Information-Based Industry

Because of the value of services in the world's economy and the increasingly large part played by information-based services in particular, it is not surprising that the information services industry itself has been going through a period of what DAVENPORT & CRONIN (1986; 1987) term massification and consolidation. It is a period of buyouts and divestitures and changing market definitions. As a result of the deregulation of national telecommunications monopolies, for example, of AT&T in the United States and British Telecom in the United Kingdom, we see the subsequent entry of the spinoff companies into other information service markets such as videotex or electronic mail. The result is an oligopoly, which is in fact as regulated in its way as the previous monopolies were (CRONIN; DAVENPORT & CRONIN, 1986). Thus, the information services industry is beginning to look like the computer equipment industry, which, HEIM explains, depends on a very small number of large suppliers.

One sees examples of the growing strength of a limited number of major companies in this market (CRONIN; LANDAU). BellSouth, an AT&T spinoff, for example, is setting up a subsidiary in the United Kingdom. We see myriad transnational alliances, such as that of Olivetti of Europe with AT&T of the United States and Fujitsu of Japan with Amdahl of the United States. Large multinational conglomerates, such as TBG (Thyssen-Bornemisza), have made information markets their primary targets and are attempting vertical integration through a very focused acquisition program (CRONIN; DAVENPORT & CRONIN, 1986). We see, for example, the purchase by Robert Maxwell of producers of information (e.g., Pergamon or the Mirror Group), of distributors of information (e.g., the BRS information retrieval service), and of technology facilitators (e.g., SCITEX, the producer of newspaper production technologies relating to high quality graphics). MATTELART & SCHMUCLER describe this strategy of integration "through the acquisition of missing links, from above by information providers and from below by producers, so as to control the whole chain of services from the creation of information to the supply to the user" (p. 125).

The electronic information business is so risk intensive that only the big players can enter. If countries want to encourage companies to enter this business sector, they must also be willing to make seed capital available (CRONIN). It is generally agreed that the United States has an amazing lead in the information business, due to its early start in computerizing databases and its lead in communication and software techniques. The third world bitterly complains about the focus on English-language material which represents U.S. culture even if translated (BEARMAN). Europe, too, exports raw data in paper form to the United States and reimports it in the form of databases (CRONIN). For this reason, many governments see the need to support the increase in databases produced by their country and in their country's language as a way to defend their cultural and national sovereignty.

SCHILLER points out that we err if we judge information services only by their profitability, that we do not yet know how to evaluate the social benefit derived from these services. He implies that this social benefit should be used not just to determine whether the government should establish an information service but also to determine how to support the information industry in its endeavors.

On the other hand, excessive government subsidy of information-based services can be counterproductive. CRONIN uses as one example the increasing ratio of expenditure to income of the German information service DIMDI. Governments, he suggests, should be aware that the answer to such problems of information dependence is neither "an elaborate database creation programme, nor the petulant imposition of tariff or non-tariff restrictions on the offending transborder data flow, but enhanced and selectively funded R&D programmes, bolstered by effective trans-national/trans-sectoral collaboration at the pre-competitive stage" (p. 134). Extreme cases also exist in which governments financially support information services that manage to service only an elite clientele (MENOU, 1983).

Trade in Services

In 1980 the International Monetary Fund estimated the global export of services at $350 billion, equal to 25% of all exports of goods (HAMELINK). Yet, to take one example, the 1987 *Trade and Development Report* of the U.N. CONFERENCE ON TRADE AND DEVELOPMENT does not mention services at all, let alone information-based services.

GATT (General Agreement on Tariffs and Trade) is an organization devoted since its establishment in 1947 to the governance of world trade. HAMELINK describes how the ministers of trade from 92 GATT contracting (member) countries met in Uruguay in 1986 to continue their discussions of the reduction of trade barriers and to take measures against distortion of trade. Considering that the balance of trade in U.S. exports of information services totalled $30 billion in 1984 (FEKETEKUTY & ARONSON), it is not surprising that since 1982 the United States has been pressing to place trade in services on the agenda for the Uruguay Round of negotiations. The third world countries (particularly Brazil and India) felt, however, that they had more to lose by the removal of nontariff barriers, and they opposed the discussion of trade in both goods and services at the same round. Such services include but are not limited to international banking, insurance, telecommunications, data processing, database searching, and news services. By the end of the first conference, it was agreed that a special "Group of Negotiation on Services" would be established to deal with this issue (HAMELINK).

FEKETEKUTY elucidates this conflict in an extensive book prepared for the Uruguay Round of GATT. He explains that most domestic services are purchased by individuals but that most imported services are purchased by businesses. Similarly, most international trade in services is conducted by large corporations. "All international trade in services either requires the application of value-enhancing services to goods, people, money or information that are subsequently moved from one country to another, or requires the application of services that will help move goods, people, money or information from one country to another" (p. 30).

Unfortunately, we are not yet able to clearly define and measure these services. Statisticians have defined a service as any economic activity that does not result in the manufacture of a product, and export of services is the selling of services to residents of another country. They still have difficulty accounting for the transfer of multinational corporation services over national boundaries (FEKETEKUTY).

Information technologies are at the heart of this conflict. FEKETEKUTY depicts three sets of major issues. First, new services have been created that depend on telecommunications and are related to data processing, electronic databases, banking, insurance, and transportation. "Since the competitive position of firms offering these services often hinges on the terms and conditions of access to communications facilities, disputes over communications charges and restrictions placed on the use of the communications facilities have become trade issues" (p. 253). Second, many corporations and industry associations have established their own communications networks for internal management services or distribution of services to their members or clients. This often conflicts directly with the public networks. Third, telecommunications services can now be supplied on a competitive basis, thus engendering disputes over even the most basic ground rules.

Nontariff Trade Barriers

FEKETEKUTY questions whether international trade theory applies to services and describes some of the different nontariff trade barriers that governments use to try to protect their domestic services from competition. Governments have to exercise control over the point of transaction and thus limit or try to limit:

- The purchase of foreign exchange needed to pay for imported services;
- The movement of all people, information, goods, and money across the border;
- The sales of services inside the country by a foreign business;
- The employment of foreign service workers in the importing country; or
- The consumption of services required to meet regulatory requirements (FEKETEKUTY, p. 135).

By setting up trade barriers to information flow, one not only restricts the services themselves but also the means of providing information about trade opportunities in services since the provision of such information is in itself just such a restricted service. Despite this, several nations such as Brazil have proposed or enacted legislation that goes far beyond protecting privacy. This legislation is seen as threatening the essence of international trade and business (MILLER).

Types of nontariff trade barriers that have been used and that affect information technology-based services are: discriminatory taxes, discriminatory fees for services that must be bought from the government, discriminatory access to government agencies, discriminatory delays in required licenses, work permits and similar documents of approval, unfair competition from government-owned enterprises or from government-supported industry, discriminatory pricing, and restrictions on the employment of foreign nationals (FEKETEKUTY). Laws for data protection have the secondary effect of border regulation (HEIM). For example, Canada has used the powers of its Foreign Investment Review Agency to pressure investors to locate data processing facilities in Canada (FEKETEKUTY & ARONSON).

CRAWFORD points out that much conflict exists between nations whose trade policies are based primarily on the principle of strong regulation and those whose policies invoke a laissez faire attitude. Germany, Spain, and Italy as strong regulators, for example, often stand opposed to the United Kingdom, the Netherlands, and France in EEC discussions concerning the regulation of telecommunications.

The motivations of nations are also different. HEIM explains that the United States is looking to maintain its lead as a supplier of high-tech products while at the same time staving off competition from other countries. The other industrialized countries are trying to provide a serious challenge to the United States and thereby increase their market shares. The newly industrialized countries (NICs), on the other hand, are trying to develop their indigenous information industries, while the poorest of the less-developed countries (LDCs) are still crying for a redistribution of technologies. Thus, it is not surprising that the NICs are the biggest opponents to the removal of nontariff barriers (HAMELINK).

Despite these differences, the European countries are trying to band together, and they have already agreed that as part of the New European Common Market (EC'92) they will: 1) allow full liberalization of terminal equipment by 1991 such as the ability to buy and use any modem meeting set standards, 2) open the value-added end of the telecommunications services to competition, 3) separate in each country the regulatory and operational activities of the telecommunications authorities, 4) set telecommunications tariffs according to a common set of principles and related to costs of production, 5) allow the telecommunications authorities to participate in newly competitive areas on an equal footing, and 6) set standards for defining requirements that telecommunications authorities impose on network users. There are, of course, many other areas in which consensus has not yet been reached.

INTERNATIONAL INFORMATION ISSUES 19

Newly Industrialized and Less-Developed Countries

MATTELART & SCHMUCLER have attempted to fill a void in the analyses of new communication and information technologies in relation to less-developed countries (LDCs). They remark that most existing studies either analyze the consequences of one aspect of the dominance of information technologies (e.g., automation of world production) or unrealistically believe that by solving one aspect (e.g., reequilibrium of information flows), all other problems will vanish. They conducted a study involving seven Latin American countries (Mexico, Panama, Venezuela, Colombia, Peru, Chile, and Brazil). As a result of many interviews and analyses of data available, they provide a typology of the specific forms taken by the computerization process in these countries: where information technologies are being used, for what purpose and within what sociopolitical and strategic guidelines.

Not all the third world countries or all LDCs are the same; they are comparatively more heterogeneous than the developed countries (RADA). In some, such as the Latin American countries, communication and information systems have reached high levels of development (MATTELART & SCHMUCLER). In others, such as the centrally controlled (socialist) economies, links with the rest of the world are still weak (U.N. CENTRE ON TRANSNATIONAL CORPORATIONS, 1984).

Many conditions—economic, labor, physioecological, cultural, demographic, social, and political—that inhibited successful information technology transfer in the LDCs in the 1970s (ERES, 1981) have improved for the newly industrialized (or informationized). The poorer LDCs remain the same or poorer. Further, two different countries with similar resources and skills may still perform differently due to differences in management and organization (RADA). R. L. KATZ (1986a; 1986b; 1987) has also shown that there is a structural difference between the less-developed and the industrialized countries. He attributes this difference to several factors. In the developed world the increased size of the information infrastructure—i.e., the degree of informatization of society- appears to be related to industrial growth. In the developing world, Katz hypothesizes, the size of the information infrastructure is first a logical consequence of the expanding role of the state in the economy and only secondly a result of industrial growth. At early levels of development, government expansion in terms of authority and manpower occurs in parallel with an abundant supply of an overeducated work force, which has a positive effect on the size of the information sector. Katz's second major point is that the diffusion of information technologies internationally is related as much to national policies as to market forces.

The newly industrialized countries (NICs) in the 1980s fear cultural dominance less than economic dominance. They particularly fear the loss of jobs due to automation of industrial production in the industrialized countries such that there will be reduced use of LDC and NIC services both in production and in areas such as data entry, computer programming, typesetting and editing (ROBINSON, 1987; U.N. CENTRE ON TRANSNATIONAL CORPORATIONS, 1983). Thus, the previous low-wage advantage held by

20   BETH KREVITT ERES

LDCs is being eroded by higher productivity levels in the rest of the world
(MILLER). Even such activities as database searching abroad means loss of
jobs at home (BEARMAN). In a 1981 study on information activities in
LDCs, it was shown that the purchase of information technologies from
abroad was negatively correlated with a country's ability to produce information itself (ERES, 1985).

The importance of the regulation of information flow (TBDF) has been
particularly important to government and, specifically, to the transnational
corporations conducting business within the country (U.N. CENTRE ON
TRANSNATIONAL CORPORATIONS, 1982; 1983). The LDCs consider
themselves to be "fighting for their economic futures by the attempts to
restrict the control of their fledgling information industries" (HEIM, p. 28).
However, this type of control can backfire. Throughout the world it is recognized that much of the international trade in services occurs within a firm
rather than from one firm to another. As such, the large transnational
corporations often choose to open offices in countries that offer political
stability, economic incentives, and linguistic convenience (HEIM).

Brazil is usually considered an extreme example of a country's efforts to
protect its information industry; the report of the U.N. CENTRE ON
TRANSNATIONAL CORPORATIONS (1983) describes the Brazilian policy
in detail. The Brazilians control access to foreign data sources and monitor
information exchange activities as well as maintain strict import controls on
equipment, software, and data transmission. Although the results of this strict
regime have been questioned, it has certainly provided a model wherein information moved from the status of a secondary support activity to that of a
self-contained high-priority topic (MENOU, 1983).

Many international agencies and nongovernmental organizations have been
established to deal in one way or another with information issues such as
Unesco's General Information Programme or the United Nations-sponsored
Intergovernmental Bureau for Informatics, to name only two. VAGIANOS
notes that such agencies created to further information systems and services
development, particularly in the nonindustrialized world, are not effective
for the following reasons (p. 23):

- Extraordinary duplication of effort;
- Organizational conflict;
- Lack of information on projects and their status. . . ;
- Waste and confusion;
- Conflicting protocols and technical specifications; [and]
- Competition from for-profit enterprise.

He lists 28 national, regional, or international agencies that are involved
in third world information development. MARCULLI-KOENIG confirms that
within the United Nations the generous attitude of the organization to give
freely is somewhat thwarted by the lack of effort in organization and communication.

INTERNATIONAL INFORMATION ISSUES 21

Two recent declarations, however, appear to make some effort to deal with the international questions of information flow and access. The first, the OECD Declaration (quoted in ROBINSON (1987, p. 369–370)) has four major points:

- Promote access to data and information and related services, and avoid the creation of unjustified barriers. . .to the international exchange of data and information;
- Seek transparency in regulations and policies relating to information, computer and communications services affecting transborder data flows;
- Develop common approaches for dealing with issues related to transborder data flows and, when appropriate, develop harmonized solutions; [and]
- Consider possible implications for other countries when dealing with issues related to transborder data flows.

The Glenerin Declaration (available in its entirety in VAGIANOS) is an agreement only among the United States, United Kingdom, and Canada. Its eight recommendations are slightly broader than those of the OECD declaration; in addition to the TBDF issues, it also deals with: 1) the need to understand and measure the influence and impact of information on the world economy, 2) intellectual property law, 3) the need to make the public aware of the usefulness of information and to encourage its use, and 4) the need for governments to assume responsibility for providing information to their citizens.

CONCLUSIONS

The literature on information issues is as diverse as the issues themselves. Thus, we see sociologists, political scientists, lawyers, politicians, information scientists, and telecommunications specialists all writing about the problem from their perspectives. In general, there is a common thread; information is a commodity in international trade. This commodity is essential to trade in goods and services and is itself a commodity that can be traded. Information is unique in that its transfer is instantaneous, thus removing barriers of distance and allowing even the manipulation of time-zone differences. Further, its value can be determined only at a particular time and to a particular set of users at that time. Finally, it is easily transportable and can be transferred almost invisibly over thin optic fibers or through the air on electromagnetic waves.

Those characteristics that distinguish information-related issues also make those issues more difficult to deal with. Countries that fear loss of their national security and sovereignty as well as their economic prosperity some-times enact legislation that appears to hurt rather than help their cause. Such laws, rules, and regulations often take the form of nontariff barriers that implicitly limit the trade in services and sometimes even the trade in goods by limiting information-based activities. The developed countries would, in general, like to see these barriers removed, at least to a great extent, although there is some disagreement between those countries with strong centralized policies and those with a more laissez-faire attitude. Many of the NICs or LDCs are afraid of the impact of the lowering of nontariff barriers. At present, the Uruguay Round of the General Agreement on Tariffs and Trade has agreed to discuss these issues. Although this does not promise that all problems will be immediately solved, it does show that the importance of the issue is being recognized.

BIBLIOGRAPHY

ANTHONY, L. J. 1982. National Information Policy. Aslib Proceedings (U.K.). 1982 June/July; 34(6/7): 310–316. ISSN: 0001-253X; CODEN: ASLPAO.

ARNOLD, ERIK; GUY, KEN. 1986. Parallel Convergence: National Strategies in Information Technology. Westport, CT: Quorum Books/Greenwood Press; 1986. 220p. ISBN: 0-89930-226-2.

AUSTRALIA. DEPARTMENT OF SCIENCE. SCIENTIFIC DEVELOPMENT DIVISION. 1987. Scientific and Technological Information: Its Use and Supply in Australia. Canberra, Australia: Australian Department of Science, Scientific Development Division; 1987 June. Available from: the Division.

BAKER, DALE B. 1987. Chemical Information Flow Across International Borders: Problems and Solutions. Journal of Chemical Information and Computer Sciences. 1987 May; 27(2): 55–59. ISSN: 0095-2338; CODEN: JCIDS8.

BATES, BENJAMIN J. 1988. Information as an Economic Good: Sources of Individual and Social Value. See reference: MOSCO, VINCENT; WASKO, JANET, eds. 76–94.

BEARMAN, TONI CARBO. 1986. National Information Policy: An Insider's View. Library Trends. 1986 Summer; 35(1): 105–118. ISSN: 0024-2594; CODEN: LIBTA3.

BELL, DANIEL. 1987. The World and the United States in 2013. Daedalus. 1987; 116(3): 1–31. ISSN: 0011-5266; CODEN: DAEDAU.

BOLLINGER, W. A.; ELLINGEN, D. C. 1987. Evolving United States' Information Policy and Its Effects on International Access to Online Technical Databases. In: Online Information: Proceedings of the 11th International Online Meeting; 1987 December 8–10; London, England. Oxford England: Learned Information (Europe) Limited; 1987. 519–528. ISBN: 0-317-65173-0.

BORTNICK, JANE. 1985. National and International Information Policy. Journal of the American Society for Information Science. 1985 May; 36(3): 164–168. ISSN: 0002-8231; CODEN: AISJB6.

BRAUNSTEIN, YALE. 1989. Economics of Intellectual Property Rights in the International Arena. Journal of the American Society for Information Science. 1989 January; 40(1): 12–16. ISSN: 0002-8231; CODEN: AISJB6.

INTERNATIONAL INFORMATION ISSUES 23

BUCKLAND, MICHAEL K.; LYNCH, CLIFFORD A. 1988. National and International Implications of the Linked Systems Protocol for Online Bibliographic Systems. In: Carpenter, Michael, ed. National and International Bibliographic Databases: Trends and Prospects. New York, NY: Haworth Press; 1988. 15–33. ISBN: 0-86656-749-6.

BURGER, ROBERT H., ed. 1986. Privacy, Secrecy and National Information Policy. Library Trends. 1986 Summer; 35(1): 3–182. (Special issue). ISSN: 0024-2594.

CARPENTER, MICHAEL, ed. 1988. National and International Bibliographic Databases: Trends and Prospects. New York, NY: Haworth Press; 1988. 276p. (Also published as Cataloging & Classification Quarterly. 1988; 8(3/4)). ISBN: 0-86656-749-6.

CHIHARA, HIDEAKI. 1987. Factors Involved in Japan's Contribution to International Chemical Information Activities: Present Status and Prospect. Journal of Chemical Information and Computer Sciences. 1987 May; 27(2): 59–62. (Paper presented at: American Chemical Society 191st National Meeting; 1986 April 16; New York, NY.) ISSN: 0095-2338; CODEN: JCIDS8.

COMMISSION OF THE EUROPEAN COMMUNITIES. 1987. Draft Guidelines for the Public Sector on the Provision of Information Services. Commission of the European Communities; 1987 March. 18p. (SOAG/14/87). Available from: Commission of the European Communities, DG XIII.

COMPAINE, BENJAMIN M. 1988. Information Technology and Cultural Change: Toward a New Literacy. In: Compaine, Benjamin M., ed. Issues in New Information Technology. Norwood, NJ: Ablex Publishing Company; 1988. 145–178. (Communication and Information Science series. B. Dervin, ed.). ISBN: 0-89391-500-9; ISBN: 0-89391-468-1.

CRAWFORD, MORRIS H. 1988. EC'92: The Making of a Common Market in Telecommunications. Cambridge, MA: Center for Information Policy Research, Harvard University; 1988 July. 28p. (I-88-2). Available from: Harvard University, Center for Information Policy Research, Program on Information Resources Policy.

CRONIN, BLAISE. 1987. Transatlantic Perspectives on Information Policy: The Search for Regulatory Realism. Journal of Information Science: Principles and Practice (United Kingdom). 1987; 13(3): 129–138. ISSN: 0165-5515.

CZERMAK, M. J. 1986. New Trends in Specialised Information Policy within the Federal Republic of Germany. Information Services & Use. (The Netherlands). 1986; 6(1): 27–33. ISSN: 0167-5265.

DAVENPORT, LIZZIE; CRONIN, BLAISE. 1986. Vertical Integration: Corporate Strategy in the Information Industry. Online Review. 1986; 10(4): 237–247. ISSN: 0309-314X.

DAVENPORT, LIZZIE; CRONIN, BLAISE. 1987. Government Policies and the Information Industry—The Balance of Interests. Aslib Proceedings (UK). 1987 May; 39(5): 159–167. ISSN: 0001-253X.

DEMAC, DONNA A. 1988. Hearts and Minds Revisited: The Information Policies of the Reagan Administration. See reference: MOSCO, VINCENT; WASKO, JANET, eds. 125–143.

DEMAC, DONNA A.; PELTON, JOSEPH N., eds. 1986. Telecommunications for Development—Exploring New Strategies: Proceedings of an

International Forum Sponsored by Intelsat, New York University, Department of Interactive Telecommunications, The Economic Development Foundation and the Intergovernmental Bureau of Informatics; 1986 October 28; New York, NY. Washington, DC: Intelsat (International Telecommunications Satellite Organization); 1986. 176p. (6/12/2375).

DORDICK, HERBERT S. 1983. The Emerging World Information Business. Columbia Journal of World Business. 1983 Spring; 18(1): 69–76. ISSN: 0022-5428; CODEN: CJWBAU.

DOSA, MARTA L. 1985. Information Transfer as Technical Assistance for Development. Journal of the American Society for Information Science. 1985 May; 36(3): 146–152. ISSN: 0002-8231; CODEN: AISJB6.

DOSA, MARTA L.; HOLT, DARLA. 1987. Information Counseling and Policies. Reference Librarian. 1987 Spring; (17): 7–21. ISSN: 0276-3877; LISA: 88-3557.

ERES, BETH KREVITT. 1981. Transfer of Information Technology to Less Developed Countries; A Systems Approach. Journal of the American Society for Information Science. 1981 March; 32(2): 97–101. ISSN: 0002-8231; CODEN: AISJB6.

ERES, BETH KREVITT. 1985. Socioeconomic Conditions Related to Information Activity in Less Developed Countries. Journal of the American Society for Information Science. 1985 May; 36(3): 213–218. ISSN: 0002-8231; CODEN: AISJB6.

ERES, BETH KREVITT. 1987. Information Services in Industry: Difficulties in Less Developed and Small or Peripheral Countries. Reference Librarian. 1987 Spring; (17): 199–202. ISSN: 0276-3877; CODEN: RELB06.

ERES, BETH KREVITT; BIVINS NOERR, K. T. 1985. Access to Primary and Secondary Literature from Peripheral or Less Developed Countries. Journal of the American Society for Information Science. 1985 May; 36(3): 184–191. ISSN: 0002-8231; CODEN: AISJB6.

FEKETEKUTY, GEZA. 1988. International Trade in Services: An Overview and Blueprint for Negotiations. Cambridge, MA: Ballinger Publishing Company; 1988. 355p. ISBN: 0-88730-241-6.

FEKETEKUTY, GEZA; ARONSON, JONATHON D. 1984. Meeting the Challenges of the World Information Economy. The World Economy. 1984; 7(1): 63–86. ISSN: 0378-5920.

GANLEY, GLADYS D.; GANLEY, OSWALD H. 1987. Global Political Fallout: The First Decade of the VCR, 1976-1985. Norwood, NJ: Ablex Publishing Corporation; 1987. 166p. (A Harvard University, Center for Information Policy Research, Program on Information Resources Policy publication). ISBN: 0-89391-435-5.

GONZALEZ-MANET, ENRIQUE. 1988. The Hidden War of Information. Alexandre, Laurien, translator. Norwood, N.J.: Ablex Publishing Corporation; 1988. 173p. (Communication and Information Science series. B. Dervin, ed.). ISBN: 0-89391-532-7 (cloth); 0-89391-560-2 (ppk).

GOULD, STEPHEN B. 1986. Secrecy: Its Role in National Scientific and Technical Information Policy. Library Trends. 1986; 35(1): 61–82. ISSN: 0024-2594.

GRIFFITHS, JOSE-MARIE. 1982. The Value of Information and Related Systems, Products and Services. In: Williams, Martha E., ed. Annual

INTERNATIONAL INFORMATION ISSUES 25

Review of Information Science and Technology: Volume 17. White Plains, NY: Knowledge Industry Publications for the American Society for Information Science; 1982. 269–284. ISSN: 0066-4200; CODEN: ARISBC.

HAMELINK, CEES J. 1988. The Technology Gamble; Informatics and Public Policy: A Study of Technology Choice. Norwood, NJ: Ablex Publishing Corporation; 1988. 117p. ISBN: 0-89391-478-9.

HARTLEY, JILL; NOONAN, ARMAND; METCALFE, STAN. 1987. New Electronic Information Services: An Overview of the UK Database Industry in an International Context. United Kingdom: Gower Press; 1987. 147p. ISBN: 0-566-05489-2.

HEIM, KATHLEEN M. 1986. National Information Policy and a Mandate for Oversight by the Information Professions. Government Publications Review. 1986; 13: 21–37. ISSN: 0277-9390.

HERNON, PETER; RELYEA, HAROLD C. 1988. The U.S. Government as a Publisher. In: Williams, Martha E., ed. Annual Review of Information Science and Technology: Volume 23. Amsterdam, The Netherlands: Elsevier Science Publishers for the American Society for Information Science; 1988. 3–33. ISSN: 0066-4200; ISBN: 0-444-70543-0; CODEN: ARISBC.

HINDLEY, BRIAN. 1988a. Service Sector Protection: Considerations for Developing Countries. The World Bank Economic Review. 1988 May; 2(2): 205–224. ISSN: 0258-6770.

HINDLEY, BRIAN. 1988b. Trade in Services: Why Developing Countries Should Liberalize It and How. The World Bank Research News. 1988 June; 8(2): 1–2, 11. ISSN: 0253-3928.

HORTON, FOREST W. 1982. Understanding U.S. Information Policy: The Infostructure Handbook. Washington, DC: Information Industry Association; 1982. 133p. (3 volumes). Available from: The Information Industry Association.

INFORMATION TODAY. 1988. IIA Hails Passage of Berne Copyright Treaty Bill. Information Today. 1988 December; 5(11): 1. ISSN: 8755-6286.

INTERGOVERNMENTAL BUREAU FOR INFORMATICS. 1984. Proceedings of the 2nd World Conference on Transborder Data Flow Policies; 1984 June 26–29; Rome, Italy. Rome, Italy: Intergovernmental Bureau for Informatics (IBI); 1984. 334p. (TDF-260). Available from: IBI.

JACOB, M. E. L.; RINGS, D. L. 1986. National and International Information Policies. Library Trends. 1986 Summer; 35(1): 119–169. ISSN: 0024-2594; CODEN: LIBTA3.

JOHNSTON, ANN; SASSON, ALBERT, eds. 1986. New Technologies and Development. Paris, France: Unesco; 1986. 281p. (Subtitle: Science and Technology as Factors of Change: Impact of Recent and Foreseeable Scientific and Technological Progress on the Evolution of Societies, Especially in the Developing Countries). ISBN: 92-3-102454-X.

JOWETT, PAUL; ROTHWELL, MARGARET. 1986. The Economics of Information Technology. New York, NY: St. Martin's Press; 1986. 108p. ISBN: 0-312-23434-1.

JUSSAWALLA, MEHEROO; CHEAH, CHEE-WAH. 1987. The Calculus of International Communications: A Study in the. Political Economy of

26   BETH KREVITT ERES

Transborder Data Flows. Littleton, CO: Libraries Unlimited, Incorporated; 1987. 159p. ISBN: 0-87287-503-2.

JUSSAWALLA, MEHEROO; LAMBERTON, DONALD M.; KARUNA-
RATNE, NEIL DIAS. 1988. The Cost of Thinking: Information
Economies of Ten Pacific Countries. Norwood, NJ: Ablex Publishing Corporation; 1988. (Communication and Information Science series. B. Dervin, ed.). ISBN: 0-89391-419-3.

KATZ, JAMES E. 1988. Public Policy Origins of Telecommunications
Privacy and the Emerging Issues. Information Age. 1988 July; 10(3):
169-176. ISSN: 0261-4103.

KATZ, RAUL L. 1986a. Explaining Information Sector Growth in Developing Countries. Telecommunications Policy (UK). 1986 September;
10(3): 209-228. ISSN: 0308-5961.

KATZ, RAUL L. 1986b. Measurement and Cross-National Comparisons
of the Information Work Force. The Information Society. 1986;
4(4): 231-277. ISSN: 0197-2243.

KATZ, RAUL L. 1987. The Information Society: An International Perspective. New York, NY: Praeger Publishers; 1987. 168p. ISBN:
0-275-92659-1.

KATZ, RAUL L. 1988. The Road to Information Technology Deregulation in Developing Countries. Prepared for: International Telecommunications Society 7th International Conference; 1988 June 30. 1-27.
(Available from: author, at Booz, Allen & Hamilton, New York, NY).

KATZ, WILLIAM A.; FRALEY, RUTH A. 1987. International Aspects of
Reference and Information Services. New York, NY: Haworth Press,
Incorporated; 1987. 244p. (Also published in: Reference Librarian.
1987 Spring; 17). ISBN: 0-86656-573-6.

KEREN, CARL; HARMON, LARRY. 1980. Information Services Issues
in Less Developed Countries. In: Williams, Martha E., ed. Annual Review of Information Science and Technology: Volume 15. White Plains,
NY: Knowledge Industry Publications, Inc. for the American Society for
Information Science; 1980. 289-313. ISSN: 0066-4200; CODEN:
ARISBC.

KIMBEL, DIETER. 1987. Information Technology: Increasing the Engine
of OECD Economies. OECD Observer. 1987 August/September; 147:
17-20. ISSN: 0029-7054.

LAMBERTON, DONALD M. 1984. The Economics of Information and
Organization. In: Williams, Martha E., ed. Annual Review of Information Science and Technology: Volume 19. White Plains, NY: Knowledge
Industry Publications, Inc. for the American Society for Information
Science; 1984. 3-30. ISSN: 0066-4200; CODEN: ARISBC.

LAMBERTON, DONALD M. 1988. The Regional Economy: Its Measurement and Significance. Prepared for the European Conference on Information, Instituto de Empresa; 1988 May 26-27; Madrid, Spain. 1-20.
(Available from: author at Department of Economics, University of
Queensland, Australia).

LANDAU, HERBERT B. 1988. The Internationalization of the U.S. Information Scene: Examples of Foreign Ownership in the U.S. Information
Industry. Bulletin of the American Society for Information Science.
1988 October/November; 15(1): 12-15. ISSN: 0095-4403; CODEN:
BASICR.

INTERNATIONAL INFORMATION ISSUES 27

LESSER, BARRY. 1988. Information in the Economy: Information Protection Issues in the Information Economy. Bulletin of the American Society for Information Science. 1988 February/March; 14(3): 21-22. ISSN: 0095-4403; CODEN: BASICR.

LINOWES, DAVID F.; BENNETT, COLIN. 1986. Privacy: Its Role in Federal Government Information Policy. Library Trends. 1986 Summer; 35(1): 19-42. ISSN: 0024-2594; CODEN: LIBTA3.

LITTLE, THOMPSON M. 1988. OCLC's International Initiatives of North American Bibliographic Databases. In: Carpenter, Michael, ed. National and International Bibliographic Databases: Trends and Prospects. New York, NY: Haworth Press; 1988. 67-78. ISBN: 0-86656-749-6.

MACBRIDE, SEAN. 1980. Many Voices, One World: Towards a New More Just and Efficient World Information and Communication Order. Paris, France: Unesco; 1980. 312p. (Known as "the MacBride Report").

MACHLUP, FRITZ. 1962. The Production and Distribution of Knowledge in the United States. Princeton, NJ: Princeton University Press; 1962. 416p. ISBN: 0-691-08608-7 (Hardcover); ISBN: 0-691-00356-4 (paperback).

MACKINTOSH, IAN. 1986. Sunrise Europe: The Dynamics of Information Technology. London, England: Basil Blackwell; 1986. 304p. ISBN: 0-631-14406-4.

MAHON, BARRY. 1986. Transborder Data Flow—How it Impinges on the Information Industry. Aslib Proceedings (UK). 1986; 38(8): 257-261. (Presented at: Information for Decision Making: Aslib 58th Annual Conference; 1986 April 23-25; University of Manchester Institute of Science and Technology, Manchester, England.) ISSN: 0001-253X.

MANSFIELD, EDWIN. 1988. Intellectual Property, Technology and Economic Growth. Economic Impact. 1988; 312-317. Available from: U.S. Information Service.

MARCULLI-KOENIG, LUCIANA. 1983. Use of International Documents in Developing Countries. Unesco Journal of Information Science, Librarianship, and Archives Administration (UN). 1983; 5(4): 211-220. ISSN: 0379-122X.

MARMEL, STEVE. 1988. Security and Resolve will Protect Us. USA Today. 1988 May 24; 10A; column 2-4.

MARTYN, JOHN. 1986. Transborder Data Flow: An Introduction. IFLA Journal (GW). 1986; 12(4): 318-321. ISSN: 0340-0352.

MATTELART, ARMAND; SCHMUCLER, HECTOR. 1985. Communication and Information Technologies: Freedom of Choice for Latin America. Norwood, NJ: Ablex Publishing Corporation; 1985. 186p. (Communication and Information Science Series. M.J. Voigt, ed.; Original French Title: L'ordinateur et la Tiers Monde; Translated by D. Buxton). ISBN: 0-89391-214-X.

MCDONALD, FRANCES M. 1986. Technology, Privacy, and Electronic Freedom of Speech. Library Trends. 1986 Summer; 35(1): 83-104. ISSN: 0024-2594; CODEN: LIBTA3.

MEDVEDEV, Z. A. 1969. The Rise and Fall of T.D. Lysenko. New York, NY: Columbia University Press; 1969. 284p. ISBN: 0-231-03183-1. (Out of print; Reprinted version available from: Books on Demand, UMI. ISBN: 0-317-26082-0).

28   BETH KREVITT ERES

MENOU, MICHEL J. 1983. Informational Development: The Third
    Frontier for the Survival of Latin American Countries. In: Conference
    on the Transfer of Scholarly, Scientific and Technical Information
    between North and South America; 1983 April 11–14; Ann Arbor, MI.
    1–8. (Available from: author at 129 av. P. Vaillant-Couturier, 94250
    Gentilly, France).
MENOU, MICHEL J. 1985a. An Information System for Decision Support
    in National Information Policy-Making and Planning. Information
    Processing & Management. 1985; 21(4): 321–361. (Paper presented at:
    9th Cranfield Conference on Mechanised Information Transfer; 1984
    July 24–27; Cranfield, UK). ISSN: 0306-4573.
MENOU, MICHEL J. 1985b. An Overview of Social Measures of Informa-
    tion. Journal of the American Society for Information Science. 1985
    May; 36(3): 169–177. ISSN: 0002-8231; CODEN: AISJB6.
MIDDLETON, R. 1985. The Development of the European Information
    Industry. Electronic Publishing Review (UK). 1985 March; 5(1): 49–
    61. ISSN: 0260-6658.
MILLER, ANTHONY P. 1986. Teleinformatics, Transborder Data Flow
    and the Emerging Struggle for Information: An Introduction to the
    Arrival of the Information Age. Columbia Journal of Law and Social
    Problems. 1986; 20(1): 89–144. ISSN: 0010-1923.
MOSCO, VINCENT. 1988. Introduction: Information in the Pay-per
    Society. See reference: MOSCO, VINCENT; WASKO, JANET, eds.
    3–26.
MOSCO, VINCENT; WASKO, JANET, eds. 1988. The Political Economy
    of Information. Madison, WI: The University of Wisconsin Press; 1988.
    334p. ISBN: 0-299-11570-4 (cloth); ISBN: 0-299-11574-7 (paper).
MOWLANA, HAMID. 1985. International Flow of Information: A Global
    Analysis and Report. Paris, France: Unesco; 1985. 75p. ISBN: 92-3-
    102312-8.
NEELAMEGHAN, A.; TOCATLIAN, J. 1985. International Cooperation
    in Information Systems and Services. Journal of the American Society
    for Information Science. 1985 May; 36(3): 153–163. ISSN: 0002-
    8231; CODEN: AISJB6.
NEUBAUER, K. W. 1985. Online Information Services, Document Delivery
    Systems, and Libraries in the Federal Republic of Germany. Electronic
    Publishing and Bookselling. 1985 March; 3(2): 10–18. ISSN: 0737-
    5336.
NKEREUWEM, E. E. 1985. A Conceptual Framework for the Use of
    Scientific and Technical Information in National Development in Nigeria.
    Information Services and Use (The Netherlands). 1985; 5(6): 323–330.
    ISSN: 0167-5265; LISA: 88-4053.
ORGANISATION FOR ECONOMIC CO-OPERATION AND DEVELOP-
    MENT (OECD). 1981. Guidelines on the Protection of Privacy and
    Transborder Flows of Personal Data. Paris, France: OECD; 1981. 36p.
    ISBN: 92-64-12155•2.
ORGANISATION FOR ECONOMIC CO-OPERATION AND DEVELOP-
    MENT (OECD). 1987. Information Technology and Economic Pros-
    pects. Paris, France: OECD; 1987. 221p. (Information & Computer
    Communications Policy Series; Volume 12). ISBN: 92-64-12927-8.

INTERNATIONAL INFORMATION ISSUES   29

O'LEARY, MICK. 1988. Dun & Bradstreet vs. the Unions: An Old Struggle Enters the Online Arena. Database. 1988 April; 11(2):34–38. ISSN: 0162-4105.

PIPE, G. R. 1987. The Ultimate Bypass (GATT, International Services Trade). Datamation. 1987 August 1; 33(15): 60-1-9. ISSN: 0011-6963.

POOL, ITHIEL DE SOLA. 1983. Technologies of Freedom: On Freedom in an Electronic Age. Cambridge, MA: The Belknap Press of Harvard University Press; 1983. 299p. ISBN: 0-674-87233-9.

POOL, ITHIEL DE SOLA; INOSE, H.; TAKASAKI, N.; HURWITZ, R. 1984. Census of Communications Flows. Amsterdam, The Netherlands: North-Holland Publishing; 1984. 196p. ISBN: 0-444-87521-2.

PORAT, M. U. 1977. The Information Economy. Washington, DC: Department of Commerce, Office of Telecommunications; 1977. Available from: NTIS.

RADA, JUAN. 1985. Information Technology and the Third World. In: Forester, Tom, ed. The Information Technology Revolution. Cambridge, MA: The MIT Press; 1985. 571–589. ISBN: 0-262-06095-7 (hard); ISBN: 0-262-56033-X (paper).

RATH, CHARLA M.; CLEMENT, JOHN R. B. 1988. Information Policy Issues in Science and Technology. In: Williams, Martha E., ed. Annual Review of Information Science and Technology: Volume 23. Amsterdam, The Netherlands: Elsevier Science Publishers for the American Society for Information Science; 1988. 35–57. ISSN: 0066-4200; ISBN: 0-444-70543-0; CODEN: ARISBC.

RELYEA, HAROLD C. 1986. Secrecy and National Commercial Information Policy. Library Trends. 1986 Summer; 35(1): 43–60. ISSN: 0024-2594; CODEN: LIBTA3.

RESEARCH LIBRARIES GROUP, INC. 1987. International Conference on Research Library Cooperation. New York, NY: Haworth Press, Incorporated; 1987. 168p. (Also published as Collection Management. 1987; 9(2/3)). ISBN: 0-86656-596-5.

ROBINSON, PETER. 1987. From TDF to International Data Services. Telecommunications Policy. 1987 December; 11(4): 369–376. ISSN: 0308-5961.

ROBINSON, PETER. 1988. Facing the Technological Challenge. Telecommunications Policy. 1988 September; 12(3): 292–293. (Book review of: Jussawalla, Meheroo & Cheah, Chee-Wah. The Calculus of International Communications: A Study in the Political Economy of Transborder Data Flows). ISSN: 0308-5961.

ROSENBERG, VICTOR. 1982. National Information Policies. In: Williams, Martha E., ed. Annual Review of Information Science and Technology: Volume 17. White Plains, NY: Knowledge Industry Publications, Inc. for the American Society for Information Science; 1982. 3–21. ISSN: 0066-4200; CODEN: ARISBC.

RUBIN, MICHAEL ROGERS. 1986. The Emerging World-Wide Information Economy. Library HiTech. 1986 Winter; 4(4): 79–86. ISSN: 0737-8831. LISA: 87-5046.

SAMAHA, E. K. 1987. Document Delivery: The AGRIS Cooperative Solution. Information Development. 1987 April; 3(2): 102–107. ISSN: 0266-6669. LISA: 88-286.

30   BETH KREVITT ERES

SARACEVIC, TEFKO; BRAGA, GILDA M.; AFOLAYAN, MATTHEW A.
   1985. Issues in Information Science Education in Developing Countries.
   Journal of the American Society for Information Science. 1985 May;
   36(3): 192–199. ISSN: 0002-8231; CODEN: AISJB6.
SCHILLER, DAN. 1988. How to Think about Information. See reference:
   MOSCO, VINCENT; WASCO, JANET, eds. 27–43.
SCHILLER, HERBERT I.; SCHILLER, ANITA R. 1988. Libraries, Public
   Access to Information and Commerce. See reference: MOSCO,
   VINCENT; WASKO, JANET, eds. 146–166.
SCHLAFLY, PHYLLIS. 1988. It's Librarians' Duty to Help Catch Spies.
   USA Today. 1988 May 24; 10A; column 5–6.
SCHMIDT, C. JAMES. 1988. This Program is Useless, Dangerous. USA
   Today. 1988 May 24; 10A; column 2–4.
SHANK, RUSSELL. 1986. Privacy: History, Legal, Social and Ethical
   Aspects. Library Trends. 1986 Summer; 35(1): 7–18. ISSN: 0024-
   2594; CODEN: LIBTA3.
SHATTUCK, JOHN; SPENCE, MURIEL MORISEY. 1988. The Dangers of
   Information Control. Technology Review. 1988 April; 91: 64–73.
   ISSN: 0040-1692; CODEN: TEREAU.
SIMPSON, J. W. 1985. Information Megatrends. In: Online Information:
   Proceedings of the 9th International Online Meeting; 1985 December 3–
   5; London, England. Oxford, England: Learned Information (Europe)
   Limited; 1985. 15–21. ISBN: 0-904933-50-4.
SINGH, INDU B., ed. 1983. Telecommunications in the Year 2000:
   National and International Perspectives. Norwood, NJ: Ablex Publish-
   ing Corporation; 1983. 221p. (Communication and Information
   Science Series. M. J. Voigt, ed.). ISBN: 0-89391-137-2.
SLAMECKA, VLADIMIR. 1985. Information Technology and the Third
   World. Journal of the American Society for Information Science. 1985
   May; 36(3): 178–183. ISSN: 0002-8231; CODEN: AISJB6.
SPERO, JANE EDELMAN. 1982. Information: The Policy Void. Foreign
   Policy. 1982 Fall; 139–156. ISSN: 0015-7228.
STALSON, HELEN. 1988. Intellectual Property Rights and U.S. Competi-
   tiveness. Economic Impact. 1988; 306–311. Available from: U.S.
   Information Service.
STARR, BARBARA; PORT, OTIS; SCHILLER, ZACHARY; CLARK,
   EVERT. 1986. Are Data Bases a Threat to National Security? Business
   Week. 1986 December 1; 39. ISSN: 0007-7135; CODEN: BUWEA3.
SURPRENANT, THOMAS T. 1985. Global Threats to Information. In:
   Williams, Martha E., ed. Annual Review of Information Science and
   Technology: Volume 20. White Plains, NY: Knowledge Industry Publi-
   cations, Inc. for the American Society for Information Science; 1985.
   3–25. ISSN: 0066-4200; CODEN: ARISBC.
SURPRENANT, THOMAS T. 1987a. Problems and Trends in International
   Information and Communication Policies. Information Processing and
   Management. 1987; 23(1): 47–64. ISSN: 0306-4573.
SURPRENANT, THOMAS T. 1987b. The Effects of Transborder Data
   Flow Policies on International Information. In: Williams, Martha E.;
   Hogan, Thomas H., comps. Proceedings of the National Online Meeting;
   1987 May 5–7; New York, NY. Medford, NJ: Learned Information;
   1987. 433–438. ISBN: 0-938734-17-2.

TRAUTH, EILEEN M. 1986. An Integrative Approach to Information Policy Research. Telecommunications Policy. 1986 March; 10(1): 41–50. ISSN: 0308-5961.

U.N. CENTRE ON TRANSNATIONAL CORPORATIONS. 1982. Transnational Corporations and Transborder Data Flows: A Technical Paper. New York, NY: United Nations; 1982. 149p. (ST/CTC/23;E.82.II.A.4).

U.N. CENTRE ON TRANSNATIONAL CORPORATIONS. 1983. Transborder Data Flows and Brazil: Brazilian Case Study. New York, NY: United Nations; 1983 February. 418p. (Prepared by the Presidency of the Republic of Brazil, National Security Council, Special Secretariat of Informatics in Co-operation with the Ministry of Communications of Brazil; ST/CTC/40; 3.83.ii.a.3).

U.N. CENTRE ON TRANSNATIONAL CORPORATIONS. 1984. Transborder Data Flows and Poland: Polish Case Study. A Technical Paper. New York, NY: United Nations; 1984. 75p. (Prepared at the Request of the Government of Poland, Ministry of Trade by the Foreign Trade Centre; ST/CTC/50; E.84.II.A.8).

U.N. CONFERENCE ON TRADE AND DEVELOPMENT (UNCTAD). 1987. Trade and Development Report 1987. New York, NY: United Nations; 1987. 227p. (Prepared by the UNCTAD Secretariat; UNCTAD/TDR/7; E.87.11.D.7). ISSN: 0255-4607; ISBN: 92-1-112233-3.

U.S. CONGRESS. HOUSE OF REPRESENTATIVES. COMMITTEE ON GOVERNMENT OPERATIONS. 1986. Electronic Collection and Dissemination of Information by Federal Agencies: A Policy Overview. Washington, DC: Government Printing Office; 1986. 599p. ERIC: ED 267-752. Available from ERIC at 3700 Wheeler Ave., Alexandria, VA 22304-5110.

U.S. CONGRESS. OFFICE OF TECHNOLOGY ASSESSMENT. 1985. Information Technology R&D: Critical Trends and Issues. Washington, DC: Government Printing Office; 1985 February. 342p. (OTA-CIT-268).

U.S. CONGRESS. OFFICE OF TECHNOLOGY ASSESSMENT. 1986. Intellectual Property Rights in an Age of Electronics and Information. Washington, DC: Government Printing Office; 1986 April. 299p. (OTA-CIT-302). GPO: 052-003-01036-4; NTIS: PB 87-100 301/AS.

U.S. CONGRESS. OFFICE OF TECHNOLOGY ASSESSMENT. 1988a. Disseminating Information: Evolution of a Concept. Economic Impact. 1988; 318–323. Available from: U.S. Information Service.

U.S. CONGRESS. OFFICE OF TECHNOLOGY ASSESSMENT. 1988b. Informing the Nation: Federal Information Dissemination in an Electronic Age. Washington, DC: Government Printing Office; 1988 October. (OTA-CIT-397). GPO: 052-003-01130-1.

U.S. CONGRESS. SENATE. COMMITTEE ON FOREIGN RELATIONS. 1983. International Telecommunications and Information Policy: Selected Issues for the 1980's. Washington, DC: Government Printing Office; 1983. 60p. (Prepared by the Library of Congress Congressional Research Service; Committee Print 98-94).

[U.S. DEPARTMENT OF DEFENSE]. 1985. Soviet Acquisition of Militarily Significant Western Technology: An Update. [Washington, DC: Department of Defense]; 1985 September. 34p.

VAGIANOS, LOUIS. 1988. Information in the Economy: The Third World Perspective. Bulletin of the American Society for Information

Science. 1988 February/March; 14(3): 23–26. ISSN: 0095-4403; CODEN: BASICR.

VAN ROSENDAAL, C. JANSEN. 1984. European Information Policy Situation. Aslib Proceedings (UK). 1984 January; 36(1): 15–23. ISSN: 0001-253X; CODEN: ASLPAO.

WALLERSTEIN, MITCHEL B.; GOULD, STEPHEN B., eds. 1987. A Delicate Balance: Scientific Communication vs. National Security. Issues in Science and Technology. 1987 Fall; 4(1): 42–55. (Special issue). ISSN: 0748-5492.

YANG, CHEN-CHAU. 1985. Application and Design Considerations for CJK Information Interchange Code. Journal of Library and Information Science. 1985; 11(1): 24–32. LISA: 86-4128.

[17]

The technology transfer process in foreign licensing arrangements

Lawrence S. Welch

Introduction

Technology transfer between nations takes place in a variety of forms and through a variety of business arrangements. Very often the technology is transferred in the 'embodied' form of physical goods, or as part of a significantly wider arrangement, for example, as an element of the foreign investment package or a systems sale. While much of the debate surrounding technology transfer, particularly from the advanced to the developing countries, has focused on the appropriateness of the technology for the recipient nation, and the price and conditions of transfer, less attention has been given to the efficiency and effectiveness of the technology transfer process itself.[1] Although it has sometimes been analytically convenient to depict technology as a good, this has led to an oversimplification of the demands of the transfer process.[2] Technology is not simply purchased and transferred in an 'off-the-shelf' manner; frequently a complex process of definition, marketing, negotiation and implantation is involved over an extended period. 'It is much more accurate to view technology transfer as a relationship rather than as an act.'[3] The transfer may be part of a multi-faceted interaction between two organisations over time.

In this chapter the international technology transfer process is examined from the perspective of licensing arrangements. From an aggregate perspective, foreign licensing occurs principally between related organisations. For example, in 1976 the proportion of total US receipts from royalties and management fees which were intra-firm had reached 82 per cent.[4] Other countries appear to be following the US pattern although the intra-company proportion tends to be lower because outward foreign investment activities have not yet developed as strongly. The intra-company proportion of total Australian receipts from the provision of technical know-how to foreign organisations was 45 per cent in 1976-77.[5] Within the foreign investment framework, though, licensing appears as only one element of the overall strategy, and its purpose is often connected with considerations such as control, the transfer of funds, and taxation reduction.[6] Thus, licensing, as a medium of technology transfer, will be examined outside the foreign investment context in this article—as a relationship between independent organisations.

While it has been argued that the marginal cost of transferring new techno-logical information is low once the development costs have been incurred, empirical evidence indicates that transfer costs can be considerable.[7] They may even be such as to act as a real impediment to the effectiveness of the technology transfer process.[8] In fact, transfer costs and a variety of constraints emerge at different stages of the transfer process in licensing, and it is an impor-tant objective of this chapter to assess their nature and significance in deter-mining the effectiveness of the whole process. Technology transfer is taken to refer to the whole range of activities by which licensor and licensee come into contact, negotiate an arrangement and carry through the transfer demands of the arrangement. The object of the exchange will, however, frequently encom-pass more than just technology.

The licensing package

One of the reasons why licensing is often favoured as a means of technology transfer is because it allows a company to purchase the required technology without the implications of foreign ownership. Japan is frequently cited as an example of a nation that has been able to restrict foreign investment but still obtain the technology required for industrialisation by a deliberate policy of licensing. By so doing, Japan has been able to 'unbundle' the foreign investment package and extract the parts which were most appropriate to its own situation. This policy was clearly assisted by Japan's heavy emphasis on technological absorption in its research and development as a means of ensuring the utilisation of the technology transferred.[9] Thus, licensing appears as an attractive, low-cost means of isolating and purchasing the specific technological component required.

Nevertheless, licensing normally implies more than a transfer of 'pure' techno-logical information. While the component parts of the technology transfer in the licensing arrangement are more clearly defined, it is nevertheless true that, like foreign investment, there has been an inevitable building up of a 'package' around the technological core. One important element of this broader package is what Stewart has defined as 'marketing rights':

Technology was defined as knowledge of how to do and make useful things. But in practice examination of the market for technology suggests that in the process of commercialization of this market, the content of technology transfer has become more complex than this. A major element in technology transfer is the acquisition of the right to use certain trademarks and/or access to certain markets and inputs. For shorthand we may describe the acquisition of trademarks, and privileged access gained to markets and/or to inputs as *marketing rights*. These may be highly valuable to individual firms in helping gain markets or inputs . . . the acquisition of marketing rights forms an important element of *costs* and is also a significant aspect of *motivation*. Discussion of the international transfer of technology thus covers both the communication (or sale) of knowledge and the sale of marketing rights.[10]

The gradual evolution of the broadening licensing package represents a response to pressures on both sides of the licensing arrangement. For the user there is a concern to ensure that the technology is translated as rapidly as possible into an efficiently working, and marketable, form. To achieve this, relevant working knowledge, and any associated rights, which can help to assure the outcome of the transfer process, are clearly desired. The line between technological and other forms of knowledge in the transfer process is blurred from the user's perspective: he is seeking all of those interrelated elements which add up to a perceived likelihood of commercial viability.

From the licensor's perspective there is an inevitable concern to wrap the technological information, which may be the basis of a transfer, into a more secure package. By broadening the elements in the package into such areas as marketing and managerial know-how, and marketing rights, the whole is made much stronger from the point of view of protecting the firm's proprietary rights over its industrial property. Not only that, but the marketability of the package is improved and the basis of income generation is extended. The broadened package provides a better basis for assuring returns in the short run and market development in the long run.

The pressures from both ends, therefore, have strengthened the trend towards a broadening of the licensing package, with growing emphasis on commercial know-how and a more complex intertwining generally of the technological and commercial elements. Some indication of the growth in importance of 'commercial technology' and associated rights is given in a recent study of Finnish industrial companies licensing to independent foreign licensees. The proportionate inclusion of the different objects of licensing in licensing arrangements was was follows:[11]

technical know-how	96.1%	marketing know-how	24.7%
patents	48.0%	management know-how	11.7%
trademarks	36.4%	designs	5.2%

As well as a broadening in the objects of licensing contained in the package, licensing arrangements may also be extended in a number of other ways. Licensing is frequently associated with a variety of exports to the licensee, such as plant and equipment, component parts or raw materials. The aggregate value of exports of associated plant and inputs by Finnish companies to independent licensees was more than double the value of licensing income.[12] In a study of Australian companies licensing abroad, just over one-third of respondent firms reported that the arrangement had resulted in sales of associated products.[13] The licensing relationship may also be extended into other areas of co-operation, for example, cross-licensing or joint activity in third markets. Such cases will often emerge as the relationship evolves over time.

Thus, the licensing package, and licensing relationship generally, which has been evolving as a medium of technology transfer, has tended to become broader and more complex around the technological core. This has had the effect of making licensing a more complex exercise, and of increasing the demands on both licensor and licensee in the whole transfer exercise—to identify and assess relevant company knowledge, to undertake the necessary registration of industrial property, to develop the various elements into a cohesive whole, to undertake negotiations across a wider spectrum, to effect the range of transfers required and to develop a more comprehensive interaction between the two organisations as a consequence. In general, a broader 'systems' approach to licensing appears to be demanded.

Patents and know-how

As the above Finnish evidence indicates, patents continue to occupy an important position within the licensing package, although apparently less important than unpatented know-how. Helleiner has argued that: 'the consensus emerging seems to be that unpatentable knowledge with respect to the process of production is of greater significance than patented know-how . . . Knowledge embodied in the patent is, in any case, normally insufficient, by itself, to permit its efficient working.'[14] This pattern was confirmed in an Australian study which indicated that, of a sample of mainly smaller companies licensing overseas, 32.6 per cent had not attempted to file for overseas patents. The overall breakdown showed that patents were responsible for only 20.1 per cent of licensing receipts, compared with a figure of 69.8 per cent for the know-how component.[15] While there was considerable variation on a company-to-company basis, the general impression gained was that unpatented know-how was recognised to be the crucial element in the technology transfer process—by both licensors and licensees. The pre-eminence of unpatented know-how demonstrates that the clearly specified technical information for public registration does not fulfil the demand of effective technology transfer in most situations. The technological know-how which the companies consider of greater importance is of a more intangible, company-specific nature, and requires person-to-person interaction for the transfer to be realised.

Ability of the technology recipient

Ability to use bare, documented technological information is, of course, partly dependent on the technological absorption capacity of the recipient. In general it can be argued that the wider the gap between the technical skills of the transferor and the recipient, and the more complex the technology in question, the greater the demand on the companies to bridge the gap in the transfer situation. At the extreme, the less developed countries, with limited absorption ability, are likely to place even greater reliance on non-patented knowledge to assure effective transfer. Studies by Contractor indicate that less developed countries place greater emphasis on organisational and production management assistance in licensing arrangements than do advanced countries.[16] He notes that, 'technologically advanced firms will frequently obtain bare patent rights and go on to produce on their own, because they have already "internalized" knowledge from past experience with similar products'—although this did not happen in the majority of cases.[17] Absorption ability tends to be related to specific technical skills within the company, though, and the further it has to move away from the skills foundation it possesses, the greater the need for extended transfers of technological information and assistance in the licensing arrangement—even in technically advanced companies.

Importance of patents

In some cases, companies are unprepared to take out patents because they have a poor view of their value. Patents may be considered to provide insufficient protection against direct infringement, or regarded as being too easy to invent around. Nevertheless, they remain the principal public means of establishing proprietary rights to the firm's technology, and, in fact, appear to play a far broader role in the technology transfer process than simply industrial property protection and definition of the firm's core technology.

Patents are an important consideration for the licensee—in providing a degree of protection in the licensee's market as well as perhaps forestalling potential competition. They also provide some measure of the licensor's technological credibility to an uncertain licensee. When the knowledge gap between potential licensor and licensee is large, patents represent one important means of helping to bridge it, and of reducing uncertainty. In an Australian study, it was reported that patents were particularly necessary as a prelude to licensing into the US market: 'many US companies regarded patents as a guarantee or safeguard of the technical respectability of the licensor and would not enter into negotiations without them'.[18] In addition to their individual role, however, patents make a vital contribution to supporting the total licensing package, and making it more marketable. This strengthens the hand of the licensor in negotiations. The same Australian study found that larger companies, and those with greater international licensing experience, tended to have a more positive view of the value of patents.[19] This appeared to be because of a clearer recognition of the marketing value of patents. In one company it was interesting to note that international patenting and licensing activity had been initiated by the marketing manager, despite the scepticism of technically orientated executives, who considered patents to be of little value.

Inventors without a manufacturing base, and without the assurance of a broader licensing package, clearly tend to view patents differently from manufacturers. The patent may be the only source of income-generation. They, therefore, tend to rely heavily on the abilities of the licensee to recognise the value of the technological information and to apply it within a production and marketing context. The exposed position of the inventor weakens his ability to carry through the marketing and negotiation exercise. The problems experienced by inventors in selling and transmitting their unique knowledge give an indication of the limitations of licensing only the bare technological information if the technology transfer process is to operate effectively.

Other package components

The unpatented know-how component of the licensing package is normally the crucial element of effective technology transfer because it is the information which enables the technology to be made to work in practice. For the licensor, possession of such know-how strengthens his bargaining position and makes him less susceptible to patent infringement, because the patent of itself is usually insufficient to demonstrate how the technology operates in practice. Considerable costs have normally been incurred—in the areas of development, manufacturing start-up and commercialisation—in the process of generating the firm's unique know-how. These represent a significant barrier to those companies which merely have patent details as a starting point. From the licensee's standpoint, of course, such costs are one of the reasons why the know-how factor is valued so highly—it allows production to occur without repeating many of the learning costs associated with development. In addition, it allows the licensee to proceed more rapidly to the marketplace. In this latter respect, managerial and marketing know-how may be just as important as technical know-how. Because much of the know-how is intangible in character, and firm-specific, the demands on interaction between the two parties in order to effect the transfer are increased, while the preceding negotiation process becomes more complex and difficult. The value and effectiveness of the know-how are difficult for the licensee to assess in the negotiation situation.

Trademarks, designs and other marketing rights, such as access to certain key inputs, are also valuable related elements of the licensing package. Trademarks particularly have tended to be stressed because of their contribution to marketing penetration. While not in themselves communicating useful knowledge, they may be important in the marketing build-up, and in providing a further element of protection for the licensing package.

Each element of the licensing package, therefore, contributes to the range of knowledge and rights which can potentially assist the licensee in establishing and commercialising the technology in question. The packaging of technology and associated rights under licensing is becoming more complex and the transfers more demanding, but in part this is a reflection of the complexity of the technology transfer process itself.

Exchange demands

The effective transfer of the various elements of the licensing package is a demanding process, involving a variety of transfer mechanisms, flows and types of interaction between organisations and personnel. These activities are reflected in the range of transfer costs. Contrary to the notion that the marginal cost of transferring technology, once developed, will be low, the evidence indicates that transfer costs can be very substantial. For example, in a study of the cost of technology transfer by US multinationals, including both transmission and absorption costs, Teece found that transfer costs were on average 19 per cent of total project costs, ranging from 2 per cent to 59 per cent.[20] Other studies, specifically of licensing, confirm the importance of transfer costs.[21] Oravainen's study included an assessment of the implicit costs associated with foreign licensing, especially that of managerial time. When time costs were included, and valued at the relevant salary level, they resulted in most early licensing agreements of the Finnish companies being unprofitable.[22]

Australian companies interviewed about the costs of establishing foreign licensing agreements invariably reported that the costs were far greater than anticipated. In addition, there was a range of continuing maintenance costs. The cost and time scale associated with establishing a licensing agreement were related to the need for learning regarding the licensing activity, the demands of locating and selecting suitable licensees, the negotiation process and post-agreement transfers. Overall costs of establishing licensing agreements were, on average, 46.6 per cent of total licensing costs, as against 24.8 per cent for the protection of industrial property and 29.0 per cent for maintenance costs. The main establishment costs were (in order):

  communication between the involved parties;
  searching for suitable licensees;
  training personnel for the licensee.[23]

The costs of achieving an acceptable exchange between the two parties to the licensing arrangement are clearly considerable, reflecting the range of activities which must occur in the initial stages of the transfer process.

Communication requirements

The transfer process in licensing emerges as a highly communication-intensive activity, from initial contacts through to long-run interrelationships between the parties. This is related to the nature of the technology market, which requires a high level of communication if the uncertainty and knowledge gap between potential partners is to be bridged and exchange effected. This is especially the case when the 'commodity' being exchanged, knowledge, is of such an intangible character. By the same token, communication intensity means that there is considerable scope for distortion or disturbance of the communication process, which may interfere with transfer possibilities in various ways. For example,

162   *Lawrence S. Welch*

Australian evidence indicates that the cultural factor is one potentially distorting influence in communication activities.[24] Australian companies tended to feel ill at ease in operating within legal systems of a non-British nature. A number of licensing possibilities were passed up because the country in which the licensee was located was regarded as providing insufficient protection for the firm's industrial property.

The exchange framework

The market for technology is a difficult and uncertain one for buyers and sellers seeking to achieve efficient exchange. The impediments to effective exchange when the parties are unrelated and have no knowledge of each other are considerable. It has, in fact, been suggested that the constraints in the exchange process are supportive of a foreign investment strategy instead.[25] There are major problems at the outset in identifying potential licensees or licensors and obtaining adequate information about their operations, and yet the selection decision is critical to long-run success. If the companies are incompatible and do not work together on the transfer objective, the whole operation is likely to fail. Much depends on preceding experience, of course. In some cases, licensing will follow other forms of foreign operations in the foreign market concerned which reveal a prospective partner, perhaps the company's own representative. To begin the exercise from scratch is more difficult. Australian companies tended to allocate more time and care to the selection process as their experience developed, a recognition of the importance of this step. In interviews it was frequently stressed that selection of a good licensee was far more important than a 'tight' legal document.[26]

At the outset there is also uncertainty about what elements of technical and commercial know-how are saleable, where the appropriate markets are located and what is an appropriate price for the technology being offered. The value of the technology is often difficult for both licensor and licensee to determine.[27] Given the frequently intangible nature of the knowledge asset on offer, the negotiation process can be a demanding exercise before an acceptable agreement is established. A constraint often encountered is that although the potential licensee needs adequate information in order to test the worth and performance of the technology, the licensor is concerned that, having provided this information, the potential licensee will be in a position to use it without entering into an agreement. Secrecy agreements represent only a partial solution to this perceived problem. At all stages preceding agreement a difficult decision must be made by the licensor as to just what level of information needs to be provided to potential licensees. Negotiations may be aborted in situations where excessive concern for secrecy on the part of the licensor limits the ability of the potential licensee to form an effective judgement of the technology on offer. Where the licensor has limited industrial property protection, and the technology has not been commercialised, as is commonly the case with individual inventors, such concern tends to be greater still.

Because of the uncertainties and constraints on the licensor's approach to the technology market, it is not surprising that the initiative for sale often comes from technology purchasers. They may have a clearer understanding of the potential for some new technology in their own market, or they may be seeking a specific technological solution to a problem within the company. In a recent British study it was found that most of the licensing agreements for a sample of small to medium-sized firms were initiated by licensees.[28]

The stages leading up to the signing of the licensing agreement, the formal basis of exchange between the parties, can therefore comprise a difficult, tenuous and time-consuming process, with significant cost implications. In the longer run, success in this licensing activity depends heavily on the acquisition of appropriate skills and knowledge, mainly through experience, which can be applied in successive licensing episodes. Lowe and Crawford concluded that small firms 'without such skills or without access to relevant advice frequently experience substantial problems'.[29]

Organisational fit and interaction

For technology transfer to be effective beyond the signing of the licensing agreement, especially when there is a high degree of intangible know-how involved, a significant level of interaction between the two parties will be necessary. Where there is a high level of disparity between the technological and marketing skills of the licensor and licensee, the transfer and interaction demands are generally accentuated—especially in the case of licensing from advanced to developing countries. However, even between companies in the advanced countries, the further the shift from existing technological and marketing skill areas by the licensee, the greater the amount of learning which will be necessary, requiring extensive personal interaction.[30] As Turnbull has noted, 'personal contacts are at the heart of interaction between organizations and serve as a primary medium of communication in both buying and selling'.[31] In fact, effective technology transfer requires interaction between the parties across a number of dimensions and activities, not just of a technological nature (see Figure 13.1). Social exchange, for example, may be an important interconnected component:

> The need for social exchange is especially significant when the decision makers through social exchange can compensate for a portion of the uncertainty . . . there exists an intimate connection between the physical and social exchange, since the former demands the latter and is also a carrier of same.[32]

Given the interaction demands of the licensing relationship for effecting technology transfer, the fit and compatibility of the parties, the preparedness

164   *Lawrence S. Welch*

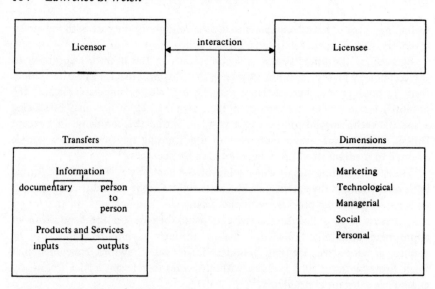

Figure 13.1. An interaction perspective on technology transfer

to commit resources to the relationship by the licensor and the extent of active involvement by both parties in the transfer process are clearly key issues. Technological and market fit has already been noted, but there is a wider perspective of compatibility, covering the total fit of the two organisations. Despite some simple 'rules of thumb' which licensors often employ in determining compatibility with potential licensees, such as the avoidance of competitors in the field, the assessment of this factor is difficult before the relationship is established.[33] It tends to be developed, or not, in the transfer activities of the post-agreement signing phase, and is heavily dependent on the preparedness to react and adapt to the other's requirements in a way which is normally not written down in the agreement itself.

The demands of interaction impose costs on the licensor, which are normally not fully covered by additional payments. These costs impose a limit on the preparedness of the licensor to enter into interaction activities, despite their benefits and the vested interest of the licensor in ensuring successful technology transfer to, and market operations by, the licensee. It is a question of the perceived relative benefit-cost as an ultimate outcome of the relationship. The evidence indicates that licensing is often seen as a marginal exercise, or only used when other more preferred market servicing options are constrained for various reasons.[34] With such a secondary view, it is not surprising that there is sometimes little commitment to the transfer process. In a study of British firms licensing to India, Davies found that:

. . . only a small proportion of the UK collaborators sampled devoted resources to adaptation. The licensors interviewed were concerned solely with the provision of information on the British product or process, leaving their Indian partner to make its own adjustments or establish a facsimile.[35]

This approach appeared to flow from a view about the peripheral nature of the market concerned, which meant that the returns from greater involvement in and commitment to the transfer process were not considered sufficient to justify the effort.

Thus, the transfer demands of the licensing relationship cause costs which are not always recognised on both sides, nor adequately compensated for in the licensing arrangement from the licensor's viewpoint. Consequently, they remain a significant barrier to the effectiveness of the technology transfer process and help to explain why alternative forms of foreign market involvement may be preferred—by widening the basis of returns they justify a deeper transfer commitment. In general, though, the more compatible the licensing partners, and the more positive and committed both are to the licensing relationship, the more likely it is that the technology will be effectively transferred, implanted and commercialised. A further implication of the stress on compatibility and of the demands of interaction is that licensors or licensees are not so much seeking to buy or sell technology, but are rather seeking a partner with whom to establish an exchange process, based on technology transfer.

Technology transfer in the longer term

Licensing is often viewed as a relationship in which, once the agreed elements have been duly transferred, commitment and involvement cease, apart from general policing of the agreement. Technology transfer, however, is not a single act or episode, but a process. To be effective it normally requires some continuing interaction between the parties. Continued adaptations, adjustments, training and updating of know-how are part of 'technological maintenance'. Of total maintenance costs for a sample of Australian licensors, 65 per cent were concerned with back-up services to the licensee.[36] With such a commitment, the licensing agreement is clearly more attractive for the licensee, while the licensor achieves a measure of positive control over continuing operations, and helps to ensure the long-run success of the licensee on which the ultimate success of the licensing venture depends. In the long run a better understanding of the other's requirements and possibilities tends to grow out of the interaction process, thereby creating a better environment for technology transfer. The learning process is important, not just for general transfer ability, but also within a given relationship.

From a recent study of licensing activity by some Swedish companies, it was concluded that the reason for success or failure had little to do with the licensing object itself, but rather depended on the patience of the parties in building a long-term relationship for mutual benefit.[37] An unsuccessful relationship was

166   *Lawrence S. Welch*

seen to be a result of passive involvement. Thus, the effectiveness of technology transfer in licensing has a long-run dimension, which depends on the quality of continuing interaction between the parties. The benefits of continuing inter-action are greater than just the assurance of licensing success. This may lead to associated exports, return flows of technology and other valuable information, as well as wider co-operation possibilities. However, the longer term demands and possibility of licensing tend not to be clearly recognised by companies new to licensing, and this constrains its effectiveness as an instrument of technology transfer.

Policy implication

The less developed countries have expressed considerable concern about the terms and conditions of international technology transfer, their concern being reflected in the effort to develop a Code of Conduct on Technology Transfer.[38] Already, though, a number of countries, especially in Latin America, have introduced a variety of controls on technology transfer arrangements in an effort to remove restrictive practices and reduce the costs to the recipients.[39] While the control policies appear to have gone some way towards achieving their objectives:

> more comprehensive policies are necessary if the promotion of technological developments locally is the main objective: indeed for countries which have the capacity and intention to pursue this as a major objective the cost issue —on which so much attention is currently focussed—becomes of subsidiary importance.[40]

The preceding analysis has shown that exchange or relations efficiency between two organisations is an important determinant of the effectiveness of technology transfer. Clearly controls cannot of themselves ensure good relations between the transfer partners. As a result, if policies for technology transfer are to become more effective, they must include a more positive approach towards the building of strong relations between technology buyers and sellers. For example, assistance may need to be provided in the search for, and assessment of, appropriate technology suppliers.

Conclusion

Technology transfer is a highly demanding exchange process, especially when the companies are unrelated and joined only by a licensing arrangement. To be effective, it requires a high degree of commitment by both parties to exchange activities. In general, the greater the interaction, in the short run and long run, the more likely it is that transfer will be successfully accomplished.

However, there are serious constraints on technology transfer in licensing which frequently limit, or even prevent, achievement of the transfer objective.

Technology transfer and foreign licensing 167

Licensing is often adopted as a secondary international marketing strategy, and this is reflected in a limited commitment to the activity. More important, though, is the nature of the 'arm's-length' relationship which licensing involves, and the intangible character of the product being exchanged. The distance between the parties in all respects increases uncertainty and constrains contact, negotiation and transfer activities. There are difficulties in defining and valuing the transfer object, and in determining an appropriate price. As many of the demands of effective transfer can never be settled in the agreement, much depends on the way the relationship evolves. Thus, there is considerable room for distortion and misunderstanding in. the exchange process, which may seriously interfere with the final outcome. Also all of the stages in effective transfer have considerable cost implications. In many cases, licensors are unprepared to commit adequate resources to the transfer process because the returns are considered to be insufficient to justify the expenditure. Given the trend towards more complex licensing packages, it is likely that the demands and costs of effective transfer will increase.

Notes and references

1. See Helleiner, G. (1975), 'The role of multinational corporations in less developed countries' trade in technology', in Kojima, K. and M. Wionczek (eds), *Technology Transfer in Pacific Economic Development*, Tokyo, Japan Economic Research Centre; Stewart, F. (1979), *International Technology Transfer: Issues and Policy Options*, World Bank Staff Working Paper No. 344, Washington D.C.; Contractor, F. and T. Segafi-Nejad (1981), 'International technology transfer: major issues and policy responses', *Journal of International Business Studies*, 12: 113–35.
2. See Helleiner, op. cit., pp. 84–5.
3. Contractor, F. (1980), 'The composition of licensing fees and arrangements as a function of economic development of technology recipient nations', *Journal of International Business Studies*, 11: 47.
4. Stewart, op. cit., p. 19.
5. Australian Bureau of Statistics (1979), *Research and Experimental Development: Private Enterprises, 1976-77*, Canberra, AGPS.
6. Stopford, J. and L. Wells (1972), *Managing the Multinational Enterprise*, London, Longman, pp. 121-2.
7. Teece, D. (1977), 'Technology transfer by multinational firms: the resource cost of transferring technological know-how', *Economic Journal*, 87: 242–61.
8. Davies, H. (1977), 'Technology transfer through commercial transactions', *Journal of Industrial Economics*, 26: 161–75.
9. Blumenthal, T. (1976), 'Japan's technological strategy', *Journal of Development Economics*, 3: 245–55.
10. Stewart, op. cit., pp. 3–4.
11. Oravainen, N. (1979), *Suomalaisten Yritysten Kansaivaliset Lisenssi—Ja Know-How —Sopimukset (International Licensing and Know-How Agreements of Finnish Companies)*, Helsinki, Helsinki School of Economics, FIBO Publication No. 13, p. 35.
12. Oravainen, op. cit., p. 99.
13. Carstairs, R. and L. Welch (1981), *A Study of Outward Foreign Licensing of Technology by Australian Companies*, report prepared for the Licensing Executives Society and Industrial Property Advisory Committee of Australia, revised edition, p. 48.
14. Helleiner, op. cit., p. 82. See also Pengilley, W. (1977), 'Patents and trade practices—competition policies in conflict', *Australian Business Law Review*, 5: 201.

168   *Lawrence S. Welch*

15. Carstairs and Welch, op. cit., p. 22.
16. Contractor, op. cit., pp. 48–50.
17. Ibid., p. 47.
18. Carstairs and Welch, op. cit., p. 23.
19. Ibid., pp. 22–4.
20. Teece, op. cit., p. 247.
21. Contractor, F. (1981), *International Technology Licensing: Compensation, Costs and Negotiation*, Lexington, Mass., Lexington Books; Oraivanen, op. cit.
22. Oravainen, op. cit., pp. 47–9.
23. Carstairs and Welch, op. cit., pp. 36–9.
24. Ibid., pp. 40–2.
25. Teece, D. (1981), 'The multinational enterprise: market failure and market power considerations', *Sloan Management Review*, 22: 9–10.
26. Carstairs and Welch, op. cit., p. 30.
27. Killing, J. (1980), 'Technology acquisition: licence agreement or joint venture', *Columbia Journal of World Business*, 15: 44.
28. Lowe, J. and N. Crawford (1982), *Technology Licensing and the Small/Medium Sized Firm*, Interim Report, School of Management, University of Bath, p. 19.
29. Ibid., Appendix 3, p. 3.
30. Killing, op. cit., p. 39.
31. Turnbull, P. (1979), 'Roles of personal contact in industrial export marketing', *Organisasjon, Marked og Samfunn*, 16 (5): 335.
32. Håkansson, H. and B. Wootz (1979), 'A framework of industrial buying and selling', *Industrial Marketing Management*, 8: 30–1.
33. Welch, L. and R. Carstairs (1982), 'Some international marketing implications of outward foreign licensing', *Journal of International Marketing*, 1 (3); 177–85.
34. Carstairs, R. and L. Welch (1982), 'Licensing and the internationalisation of smaller companies: some Australian evidence', *Management International Review*, 22 (3): 34–5.
35. Davies, op. cit., p. 173.
36. Carstairs and Welch, op. cit., 1981, p. 38.
37. Wiedersheim-Paul, F. (1982), *Licensing as a Long Run Relation*, Working Paper 1982/2, Centre for International Business Studies, University of Uppsala, Sweden, p. 20.
38. Thompson, D. (1982), 'The UNCTAD code on transfer of technology', *Journal of World Trade Law*, 16: 311–37.
39. Correa, C. (1981), 'Transfer of technology in Latin America: a decade of control', *Journal of World Trade Law*, 15: 388–409.
40. Stewart, op. cit., p. 62.

[18]

Controlling the Flow of High-Technology Information from the United States to the Soviet Union: A Labour of Sisyphus?

STUART MACDONALD

FOR MORE THAN 35 years, the United States has had legislation to control the flow of goods to the Soviet Union and its allies. The Export Control Act of 1949 denied permission for the export of any commodity which would contribute to either the military or the economic power of communist states. Under the conditions of the Cold War, the latter provision produced a virtual embargo on goods. Even so, the Act seems to have had little impact on either the economic growth or the foreign policy of the Soviet Union,[1] and it was replaced by the Export Administration Act of 1969. Though still concerned with prohibiting the export of goods which would increase the military strength of the Soviet Union, that Act was no longer directed towards inflicting damage on the economic capacity of communist countries. Various amendments and other legislation further qualified the trade policy of the United States towards the Soviet Union and its satellites.[2] The Export Administration Act of 1969, while allowing export controls to be used for the ends of foreign policy as well as those of national security, was applied in the era of *détente* in which it was sometimes argued that more liberal policy in trade with the Soviet Union could enmesh the Soviets in a web of interdependence. In fact, the spirit of *détente* was unlikely to have been entirely responsible for the change; the opposite policy had simply not worked, in part because other countries were willing to supply the Soviet Union with commodities American companies were not permitted to supply.[3] The foundations for the more recent return to the stricter policy were laid before the passage of the new Export Administration Act in 1979. That Act is the basis for the present restrictions on the export of high technology from the United States.

---

[1] Bingham, Jonathan and Johnson, Victor, "A Rational Approach to Export Controls", *Foreign Affairs*, LVII (Spring 1979), pp. 894–920.

[2] Branting, Luther, "Reconciliation of Conflicting Goals in the Export Administration Act of 1979: A Delicate Balance", *Law and Policy in International Business*, XII, 2 (1980), pp. 415–460. The Equal Opportunity Act of 1972 permitted export from the United States when items were available from other countries, unless decontrol posed a security threat; committees, with private sector representatives, were formed to advise on the administration of controls; licence applications were to be processed in fewer than 90 days from 1974; and, by 1977, the assumption that all items were controlled unless specifically excluded had been reversed.

[3] Bingham, J. and Johnson, V., *op. cit.*, pp. 896–897.

40   *Stuart Macdonald*

It was probably President Carter, rather than President Reagan, who was responsible for the return to stricter controls, through a variety "characterised by on-again, off-again sanctions and inconsistencies on export denials and approvals".[4] In 1977, the administration of President Carter had been encouraging the sale of oil and gas by the Soviet Union to the West in order to diversify Western sources of energy; by 1978, the United States had imposed export controls on equipment for oil and gas exploration and production in response to various Soviet actions, and in order to exert influence on the Soviet Union. The Soviet Union bought its equipment elsewhere. Despite this dénouement, the same devices were selected to express moral indignation at the invasion of Afghanistan in December 1979, and export licences were suspended for a few months. Exactly a year later, the same restrictive devices were again employed in response to the imposition of martial law in Poland. That move led to the American efforts to persuade governments in Western Europe not to supply equipment for a gas pipeline. A crisis occurred in June 1982 when the United States sought to prevent the supply to the Soviet Union of oil and gas equipment incorporating American technology. The United States was eventually forced to limit its action to the denial of exports to offending companies in countries which resisted attempts by the United States to impose controls beyond its boundaries.[5] In late 1982, unilateral controls were removed and negotiations were started to repair damaged relations with friendly countries.[6]

The value of exports to the American economy is much appreciated in the findings of the Export Administration Act of 1979.[7] This is not consistent with the intention of that legislation to use export controls not only for the purposes of national security, but also those of foreign policy.[8] While the use of export controls for national security is common among Western countries, their employment for the ends of foreign policy is rare.[9] The United States is exceptional among Western countries in not believing that the ends of foreign policy are best pursued through continuation of trade. There has been a great deal of discussion in the United States of the use of controls over the export of high technology, and much of that discussion has obscured the distinction between national security and foreign policy. It has

---

[4] Root, William, "Trade Controls that Work", *Foreign Policy*, LVI (Fall 1984), p. 65.

[5] The governments of Britain, France, Italy and West Germany either ordered or encouraged firms to defy American legislation.

[6] Root, W., *op. cit.*, pp. 65–67. See also Hill, Malcolm, "Western Companies and Trade and Technology Transfer with the East", in Schaffer, M. (ed.), *Technology Transfer and East–West Relations* (London: Croom Helm, forthcoming).

[7] *Export Administration Act of 1979*, Public Law No. 96–72, 93 Stat. 503, Section 2.

[8] "It is the policy of the United States to use its economic resources and trade potential to further the sound growth and stability of its economy as well as to further its national security and foreign policy objectives." The Act also authorises the use of export controls to prevent the depletion of scarce materials, and contains anti-boycott and anti-terrorist provisions. *Ibid.*, Section 3.

[9] Branting. L., *op. cit.*, p. 440.

Controlling the Flow of High-Technology Information   41

become almost impossible to discern such a distinction in the arguments of those who would influence new legislation regarding the control of exports. In the countries allied to the United States, the rapidly growing debate is being thrown into confusion by the failure of the United States to clarify the difference between national security and foreign policy.[10]

The Export Administration Act of 1979 expired in September 1983. Until Congress passed a temporary extension, the United States was in a state of national emergency so that the President could retain his powers to control exports.[11] Emergency powers were invoked again in April 1984.[12] By the end of 1984 there was still no new act, and debate had been protracted, fierce and chaotic between those in Congress who wanted to repair the existing Export Administration Act and those in the Senate, supported by the Department of Defense, both of which wanted much tighter controls.[13]

If the House bill passes, the Department of Defense can give up the effort to try and contain the flow of critical military technology to the Soviet Union. . . . The bill reported out by the House of Representatives, voted by the House, tilts so completely in the direction of accommodating business concerns that it is going to have a devastating effect on national security.[14]

There was no immediate prospect of a compromise.

Since 1949, the export of goods to the Soviet Union and its satellites has been controlled by a multinational Co-ordinating Committee ("CoCom"), of which Japan and the countries of the North Atlantic Treaty Organisation—though not Iceland and Spain—are currently members. The Co-ordinating Committee is a product of international treaties and is not recognised by any domestic legislation. It had a budget of just $500,000 in 1983,[15] and a small permanent secretariat located in an annexe of the United States Embassy in Paris. Its task is to maintain a list of goods which require licences if they are to be exported to the countries adhering to the Warsaw Pact. The status and role of the Co-ordinating Committee were discussed at the Ottawa "summit meeting" in 1981. A meeting of high officials of the

---

[10] Congressional Research Service, *An Assessment of the Afghanistan Sanctions: Implications for Trade and Diplomacy in the 1980's*, report prepared for Subcommittee on Europe and the Middle East of the Committee on Foreign Affairs, House of Representatives (Washington DC: US Government Printing Office, April 1981), p. 130; Office of Technology Assessment, *Technology and East–West Trade: An Update* (Washington DC: US Government Printing Office, May 1983). p. 4.

[11] Roth, Toby, "U.S. Must Throttle Leaks of High Technology to Soviets", *Human Events*, 10 December, 1983.

[12] Bechner, Steven, "Strategic Export Bills Nearing Action", *Washington Times*, 6 April, 1984.

[13] "High-Tech Leaks to Soviet Military Undermine American Defense", *Defense Watch* (March–April 1984), pp. 12–13; "Why the Export Bill is Going Nowhere", *Business Week* (6 August, 1984), p. 95; Glennon, Michael, "Business Wins House Reversal on Easing High-Tech Exports", *Congressional Quarterly* (5 November, 1983), p. 2,313.

[14] Perle, Richard, transcript of "It's Your Business" programme broadcast by Station WJLA-TV, Washington DC, 29 January, 1984.

[15] Beresford, Philip and Hosenball, Mark, "Roms, Rams and Reds", *Sunday Times*, 6 May 1984.

committee followed in January of 1982—the first in 25 years.[16] The issue of licences is the responsibility of national governments, which supply their own versions of the Co-ordinating Committee's list to their industries; the complete list is classified. The Co-ordinating Committee itself deals with exceptions; its rules require unanimous agreement when exceptions are sought. The United States is the guiding force behind the committee; it is also the United States which has submitted most requests for exceptions. During the period of *détente*, the value of goods exported as exceptions to the committee's prohibitions increased substantially, from $19 million in 1969 to $214 million in 1979.[17] This increase is attributable partly to the change in the political climate, and partly to the fact that technological change has occurred more rapidly than revisions of the committee's list. Following the Soviet invasion of Afghanistan in late 1979, there was agreement among the members of the committee to allow no exceptions to the prohibitions. The result was that the official list, out of date though it was, determined what high technology might be exported to the Soviet Union or its allies.

There are other lists of goods which require licences before they may be exported to those countries. The United States Department of Commerce maintains its own "commodity control list", which is rather more extensive than the committee's list. The Department of Defense has its "munitions list" under the Arms Export Control Act. Since 1980, though, that Department has also been amassing a voluminous list of "militarily critical technologies", which was confidential until November 1984; this is constructed on the basis of a new philosophy that key technological knowledge rather than goods should be subject to control. The list of "militarily critical technologies" has, in fact, become a huge catalogue of modern technologies.[18] "The list we have been using on controlled commodities has become almost unmanageable. The concept we are promoting in the new list emphasizes control of the *know-how* essential to manufacturing militarily critical items, and of a limited set of commodities which are keystones to the manufacturing process."[19]

Regular review of the Co-ordinating Committee list has been delayed because of a chain of incidents.[20] The list of 1974 was scheduled for revision in 1978, when the United States wished to tighten restrictions on computers with potential military applications, and to clarify the position of software.

[16] Testimony of Brady, Lawrence (Department of Commerce) to Permanent Subcommittee on Investigations, Committee on Governmental Affairs, Senate Hearings, *Transfer of United States High Technology to the Soviet Union and Soviet Bloc Nations* (Washington, DC: US Government Printing Office, May 1982), p. 265.

[17] Bertsch, Gary, *East–West Strategic Trade, CoCom and the Atlantic Alliance* (Paris: Atlantic Institute for International Affairs, 1983), p. 35.

[18] "Technology Transfer: A Policy Nightmare", *Business Week* (4 April, 1983), pp. 64–70; Norman, Colin, "Administration Grapples with Export Controls", *Science*, CCXX (June 1983), pp. 1,021–1,024.

[19] Olmer, Lionel (Department of Commerce), "America's Challenges in High Technology", paper to National Press Club, 30 March, 1983, p. 3.

[20] See Root, W. *op. cit.*, pp. 61–80.

Negotiations with its allies were proceeding when the United States, prompted by the invasion of Afghanistan, submitted even more restrictive proposals; this effectively terminated the discussions. The discussions were taken up again in 1982 and were nearing completion in September 1983 when the Department of Defense recommended that the United States hold fast to its position of 1978. A new list of the Co-ordinating Committee was not agreed on until late in 1984; until then, the effective list was that fixed some ten years earlier. During that period there had been sufficient change in high technology to render the committee's list, and the national lists derived from it, ineffective. The prohibition of the export of all goods containing micro-processors—including electronic toys—shows how unrealistic the lists had become:

During the past six years, [the] State [Department] has been particularly ineffective in leading negotiations on the most important item on the CoCom agenda: the updating of computer controls. The U.S. position has simply been the Defense Department's position. State accepted Defense's recommendations as policy, even though Commerce did not concur and it was evident that our allies would not accept the Pentagon's views.[21]

The Belief in the Importance of High-Technology Industry

There is no wholly satisfactory definition of high technology, though uncertainty over exactly what it is has not dampened enthusiasm for its promotion. High technology is imagined to be a universal panacea for all the ills afflicting a modern economy during recession.[22] High technology is to create both jobs and wealth, and is apparently capable of doing so even in the most remote places, with scant resources, and with none of the unfortunate costs of traditional industrialisation.[23] Because high technology is independent of ordinary factors in industrial location—it requires no bulky raw materials, no large supply of labour, no local market—the common assumption is that it can be located just about anywhere, in Siberia as easily as Silicon Valley. Schemes abound to turn some of the most desolate corners of the world into Silicon Valleys; in fact, the more the region is in need of development the more it is urged that it needs high-technology industry and the greater the political determination to establish it there.

Because high technology is regarded as the antidote to recession, and because its requirements are so indeterminate, it has become irresistible to politicians and bureaucrats. Despite the association of high-technology industry with private enterprise and minimal governmental intervention, even governments reluctant to interfere with market forces have been ready

---

[21] Root, William, "State's Unwelcome Role", *Foreign Service Journal* (May 1984), pp. 26–29.
[22] See Macdonald, Stuart, "The Lowdown on High Technology Industry in Australia", in Birch, A. (ed.), *Science Research in Australia: Who Benefits?* (Canberra: Centre for Continuing Education, 1983), pp. 155–172.
[23] Macdonald, Stuart, "High Technology Policy and the Silicon Valley Model", *Prometheus*, I (December 1983), pp. 330–349.

44   *Stuart Macdonald*

to regard high technology as something special and have espoused interventionist high-technology policies. So great and so necessary are the benefits from high technology thought to be, and so immediate the results, that a government with no care for promoting its development would nowadays be quite exceptional.

Of course, high technology does not really do all that is expected of it. High technology is not a large employer, and particularly not of those displaced from decaying industries.[24] Nor is high technology a significant generator of wealth, though it has the capacity to make a few individuals very rich and consequently to raise problems over the distribution of wealth. Nor are the concentrations of high-technology industry the paradises so frequently portrayed. The congestion, pollution and social problems of Silicon Valley itself are evidence enough of that.[25] Perhaps the most effective role of high technology is to help to change the basis of developed economies from traditional industries to an information sector. It is widely agreed that this is urgent. What is not recognised is that the transition will be lengthy and difficult, and that it will require a reassessment of the function of manufacturing industry as the basis of a modern economy, and an acceptance of the proposition that wealth can take intangible as well as tangible forms.

President Reagan's sudden conversion to high technology has been dated from the publication, in late 1982, of a paper describing the importance of high technology in the organisation of the American economy.[26] But this view was not accompanied by awareness that policies appropriate to traditional industries producing tangible wealth are not necessarily appropriate to industries using and producing high technology. Export controls have previously been directed towards the restriction of the movement of tangible goods: they are not obviously appropriate to the control of intangible goods in the form of information. Information is vital in high-technology industry.

Information and High-Technology Industry

The innovative process—in every industry—is largely a process of the movement and creation of information.[27] Information is gathered from

[24] See Markusen, Ann, "High Tech Jobs, Markets and Economic Development Prospects: Evidence from California", *Built Environment*, IX (1983), pp. 18–28.

[25] Rogers, Everett and Larsen, Judith, *Silicon Valley Fever* (New York: Basic Books, 1984).

[26] The paper is Cook, James, "The Molting of America", *Forbes* (22 November, 1982), pp. 161–167. On its impact, see Skeleton, George, "Technology Offers Nation New Hope, President Says", *Los Angeles Times*, 26 January, 1983; Sing, Bill and Harris, Kathryn, "Reagan High-Tech Plan Called 'Utopic'", *Los Angeles Times*, 27 January, 1983. See also Keyworth, George, "The Role of Science in a New Era of Competition", *Science*, CCXVII (August 1982), pp. 606–609.

[27] See Macdonald, Stuart, "Technology Beyond Machines", in Macdonald, Stuart, Lamberton, Don and Mandeville, Thomas (eds), *The Trouble with Technology* (London: Frances Pinter, 1983), pp. 26–36.

various sources and occasionally new information is created—most notably through research, but also in the course of other phases of innovation, such as development and marketing. The synthesis of various bits of information into a new pattern is essential to a new product—or process—whether it takes tangible or intangible form. In many mature industries, the marginal content of a new product over its predecessor, with respect to the information which has gone into it, may be small, and the pattern of information may be little changed. Large firms within such industries may find it possible to gather nearly all the information required for this new pattern from within their own organisation. They may find, however, that their own complex, rigid organisational forms interfere with the assembly of new patterns of information. Indeed, large firms, especially in traditional industries, are often castigated for their lack of desire for innovation, although this is usually attributed to insufficient incentive to innovate rather than to their inability to exploit information resources.

High-technology industry is markedly different; one difference is the importance of small, new firms in that industry. It is not that a firm in high-technology industry necessarily requires more information than other firms in order to innovate, but it does require more information relative to other factors. Its activities are "information-intensive"; so much so, in fact, that it cannot rely on internal sources for all the information it needs. A firm in high-technology industry must actively seek information outside itself and it is dependent on the efficiency of its means of obtaining information from the world outside. The characteristics of information make it difficult to negotiate about and difficult to price, so that information is commonly exchanged for other information. The high technology firm must supply information in order to procure information and what it supplies need not be from its own internal stock.

Information moves through institutional arrangements, such as patent specifications, licences, books, articles in journals, trade publications and conferences. Information may also be embodied in the material goods a firm produces and sells. None of these methods, though, guarantees that information transferred will be strictly relevant and comprehensive—or sometimes even intelligible. There are other ways in which information can move which are able to compensate for the inadequacies of the institutional arrangements. The importance of informal personal relationships as a means of gaining and supplying fuller and more specific information has long been recognised.[28] Informal personal contact is not a substitute for more institutional arrangements for the transfer of information, but it is a complement to them.

[28] See Teece, David, *The Multinational Corporation and the Resource Cost of International Technology Transfer* (Cambridge, Mass.: Ballinger, 1976), pp. 23–30; Cetron, Marvin and Davidson, Harold, *Industrial Technology Transfer* (Leiden: Noordhoff, 1977), pp. 257–274; Macdonald, Stuart, "Agricultural Improvement and the Neglected Labourer", *Agricultural History Review*, XXXI (1983), pp. 81–90.

46   *Stuart Macdonald*

High-technology industry in the United States is reliant on informal, personal relationships for the flow of information. Important members of the staffs of firms in high technology have their own networks of relationships through which information which is not clearly proprietary is exchanged for other information. There is much mobility of such persons between firms in the industry; the information they possess moves at the same time.[29] Very often the information which flows in this way is commercial rather than technological because it is essential to the success of high-technology industry that information about the market be joined as early and as thoroughly as possible with technological information. There is now even a substantial high-technology "headhunting" industry in Silicon Valley, which is the result of the growing demand for persons who have acquired information in their previous places of employment which they will bring with them to the new firm. The "headhunters" are frequently commissioned to search for individuals who possess both technological knowledge and related commercial expertise, the latter type of knowledge being rather more rare and precious than the former. Very often the information that is most valued in high-technology industry is that which is acquired through practical experience and generated by imagination, rather than the sort of information acquired in the course of study for a university degree.

The way in which information moves in high-technology industry in the United States is partly cause and partly consequence of the extremely rapid rate of technological change in the industry. Because information can move more voluminously and more rapidly when there are informal personal channels, change is swift. Because change is swift, there is great demand for information. One begets the other. High-technology industry in the United States continually initiates changes and adjusts to changes; even the semiconductor industry—now 30 years old—has not become a traditional, mature industry.[30] Most high-technology firms in most other countries—especially the large firms which receive so much governmental support in those countries—have great trouble keeping pace.[31] The firms in these other countries are so organised that the flow of information along informal personal channels is blocked. Only the Japanese, who have been forced to compensate for the total absence of informal, personal movement of information, have formed a completely different system of organised movement of information and they have overcome this obstacle. Elsewhere, and even in those parts of the United States distant from centres of high technology, there is inadequate recognition of the importance of information to high technology, particularly of the informal personal

[29] See Baram, Michael, "Trade Secrets: What Price Loyalty?", *Harvard Business Review*, XLVI (November–December 1968), pp. 66–74.
[30] Braun, Ernest and Macdonald, Stuart, *Revolution in Miniature, The History and Impact of Semiconductor Electronics* (Cambridge: Cambridge University Press, 1982).
[31] See "Europe's Technology Gap", *Economist*, CCXCIII (24 November, 1984), pp. 99–110.

relationships through which much information must move. Consequently, policy for the promotion of high-technology industry is generally framed in ignorance of the real requirements of the industry for information. There is ample evidence of that in the efforts of some countries to encourage their own high-technology industries simply by creating "technology parks" in the vicinity of universities, on the assumption that those institutions contain all the information that high-technology industry needs and that proximity and pleasant surroundings will be sufficient to promote its transfer.

Policy which is directed to the control of high technology and which deals inadequately with the essential information component of that technology, through disregard for the use of information as the primary resource of the industry—which is, in other words, unaware of the channels through which high-technology information flows—may very well cause serious damage to the industry while failing to control the transfer of its most essential ingredient. A policy which recognises the importance of information to high-technology industry, but which attempts to control information as if it were merely a physical good like any other, is more damaging.

Controlling the Flow of Information

Technology is largely information and high technology is high largely because of its "high information-intensity". The inability of those export controls employed by the government of the United States to cope adequately with information flow is a fundamental weakness. It has both seriously impaired the effectiveness of operations, and also engendered the necessity—and the opportunity—for measures of re-enforcement. Most of these measures seem to have had consequences which are not desired. Legislation for the control of exports has usually been aimed at the control of the export of tangible goods to the Soviet Union and its satellite countries, and recent legislation, although acknowledging the value of technological information in non-tangible form, has been rendered ineffective by this tradition.

Information is, of course, an economic good, but it is a very different sort of good from most others.[32] When information is transferred, not only does it pass to the buyer, but it also remains with the seller. The information must not be fully disclosed to a buyer before purchase, otherwise there will be no need for him to buy it. All 'goods—even the most prosäic—contain an information component; even a ton of coal should be priced to cover the cost of information required to mine, process, transport and organise the good, though little of that information will be apparent from the examination of individual lumps of coal. More complex manufactured items not only

---

[32] See Lamberton, Don (ed.), *Economics of Information and Knowledge* (Harmondsworth: Penguin, 1971); Lamberton, Don, Macdonald, Stuart and Mandeville, Tom, "Information and Technological Change: A Research Program in Retrospect", *Greek Economic Review*, VI (December 1984), pp. 483–495.

require more information to produce, but may also embody some of that information in a form that may subsequently be detached from the physical object in which it is contained. "Reverse engineering" is a systematic process by which information may be detached from physical objects, but less rigorous examination and even mere experience with physical objects will still yield some information. Those who purchase automobiles soon learn what are the weak and strong points of their hardware. High technology hardware, such as a computer, embodies a higher proportion of information than an automobile. In neither case, though, is the purchaser paying mainly for steel and plastic and rubber; he is paying for the information required to form these materials into a useful product.

Much of the information required to make a high-technology product may not be deduced from the material product itself. "Reverse engineering" may betray details of what has been made, but not necessarily the information about how that was made; it will say little, for example, about furnace temperatures or yields or speeds of production. Nor will "reverse engineering" reveal information about commercial, managerial and organisational matters, which are as essential as technological information in making a product. Indeed, it has been argued that much of the information required for successful innovation comes from the market in which the product is used, rather than from the firm or the research laboratory which devised the prototype.[33] Such information, though very much embodied in the product—and in the case of high technology comprising most of its value—cannot be extracted by techniques of "reverse engineering". "Reverse engineering", by itself, is highly unlikely to result in the successful transfer of technological information.

Then, of course, there is disembodied information, technological information that is not at all embodied in a physical object, though nowadays machinery is extremely likely to be used in its collection, storage and processing. It has become difficult for some persons to perceive any information having a use beyond being an input to manufacturing and to see wealth in any other form than tangible wealth. The value of a book lies not in its cover or its pages or its printing, but in the intangible information it contains. In a modern economy—which increasingly means an economy in which information plays a crucial role—much wealth is produced in just this intangible form. Hence the growth in the numbers of information workers,[34] in the demand for information services, and in the adoption of information technology.[35]

If controlling the flow of tangible goods presents problems, controlling

---

[33] Macdonald, S., "Technology Beyond Machines", *op. cit.*

[34] See Organisation for Economic Co-operation and Development, *Information Activities, Electronics and Telecommunications Technologies* (Paris: OECD, 1981).

[35] Mandeville, Thomas, Macdonald, Stuart, Thompson, Beverley and Lamberton, Don, *Technology, Employment and the Queensland Information Economy* (Brisbane: Queensland Department of Employment and Labour Relations, 1983).

Controlling the Flow of High-Technology Information 49

the flow of intangible goods is vastly more difficult. Attempting to exercise this control by established, traditional means has already amply demonstrated their inadequacy. Existing copyright laws are not appropriate for the protection of software; the patent system is not suited to the circumstances of high-technology industry; computer data banks and data transfer by telecommunications have rendered existing legislation inadequate to protect privacy; telecommunications charges are traditionally based on time and distance and not on the amount of information transmitted; customs duties are levied on the medium carrying information and not on information itself. The list could be greatly extended. It is indicative only of the inadequacies of existing legislation and institutions, and of the lingering traditional attitudes towards wealth in an information society.

As long as the efforts of the United States to control the export of high technology were directed mainly towards controlling the export of machinery, they may have been ineffective, but they caused little difficulty. The new determination to apply the controls to technological information has given rise to new difficulties. Technological data are subject to export controls, both in such tangible forms as blueprints or operating manuals, and also in intangible form. Export control regulations contain specific provisions concerning "any release of technical data of U.S. origin in a foreign country", whether by visual inspection by foreign nationals, by oral exchanges of information in the United States or abroad, or by the application to situations abroad of knowledge or technical experience acquired in the United States. The same provisions exist for information originating in the United States and sent from one foreign country to another.[36] Moreover, the licensing system which regulates the control of exports from the United States demands knowledge of the ultimate destination and ultimate use of goods, including information exported from the United States and passed on by word of mouth outside the United States.[37] In fact, technological information has long been subject to control. What has changed is the emphasis on controlling information rather than merely physical objects, and the effort applied to the enforcement of these restrictions on the flow of high-technology information. The difficulties which currently beset the export controls of the United States are almost entirely a consequence of the failure of the regulations to cope with disembodied information, and of inappropriate steps taken to rectify this situation.

Yet, if the export of high technology to the Soviet bloc is to be restricted, it is only reasonable to restrict its main ingredient, which is information. To prohibit the export of a ballistic missile while permitting the export of the

---

[36] Department of Commerce, *Export Administration Regulations* (Washington, DC: US Government Printing Office, 1 October, 1984), Part 379, p. 1.

[37] Fazzone, Patrick, "Business Effects of the Extraterritorial Reach of the U.S. Export Control Laws", *International Trade Law and Practice*, VIII (1982), pp. 596–598.

50   *Stuart Macdonald*

information necessary to make a ballistic missile is clearly nonsensical. The value of the information associated with high technology became glaringly obvious during the 1970s. As computer hardware became cheaper, the information required for its operation—the software—became relatively much more expensive. The policy of concentrating controls on what was cheap and widely available, while neglecting what was obviously much more valuable, became quite impracticable.

Recognition of this situation was expressed in the Bucy report of 1976, a short but very important document produced by the Department of Defense.[38] Fred Bucy, with a background in semiconductors, argued that "a new approach to controlling technology exports is overdue" in that "control of design and manufacturing know-how, is absolutely vital to the maintenance of U.S. technological superiority. Compared to this, all other considerations are secondary".[39]

The key to success in high technology is "know-how"—information at the most practical level, and likely to be transferred through informal personal channels: "there is unanimous agreement that the detail of *how to do things* is the essence of the technologies. This body of detail is hard earned and hard learned. It is not likely to be transferred inadvertently. But it can be taught and learned."[40]

The "body of detail" of how to do things is covered by the Export Administration Regulations, which declare that "U.S. origin technical data does [sic] not lose its U.S. origin when it is redrawn, used, consulted, or otherwise comingled abroad. . . ."[41] There follows a series of answers judged likely to satisfy the questions of those encountering practical problems in this field. The main point of these answers is that technicians, without a licence, may supply customers with no more information than is provided in the manuals and instructions which accompany equipment.[42] The British, in their attempts to control the export of technological information through personal and informal channels, are rather less precise:

The purpose of these restrictions may be defeated if [Eastern bloc countries] are supplied with technological information relating to the goods appearing in the schedule. Great care, therefore, should be taken to prevent this happening—for example, when technicians or students from the proscribed countries are visiting or being trained at British factories.[43]

---

[38] Department of Defense Science Board Task Force on Export of United States Technology, *An Analysis of Export Control of U.S. Technology: A DOD Perspective* (Washington, DC: Office of the Director of Defense Research and Engineering, February 1976).
[39] *Ibid.*, p. iii.
[40] *Ibid.*, p. 3.
[41] *Export Administration Regulations, op. cit.*, Supplement 1 to Part 379, p. 1.
[42] *Ibid.*, pp. 1–6.
[43] "Security Export Control", *British Business*, 1, Supplement (28 March, 1980), p. 1. The responsible department was able to offer no elucidation on what was meant by "great care".

Controlling the Flow of High-Technology Information 51

Of course, Mr Bucy was correct: the sort of information which is called "know-how" is the most valuable part of high technology. Quite wrong, though, is the assumption that the export of this information can be controlled by export controls as easily, and in the same way, as any physical good. That assumption promotes only complication, confusion and ineffectual control—and perhaps those individuals who are determined to take advantage of such a situation.

The Response of American Industry

In addition to the public costs of the control over the export of high technology, there are private costs which must be borne by American high-technology industry. That industry is encouraged to bear these private costs by emphasis on national security rather than on the purposes in foreign policy of the controls, by associated appeals to patriotism, by fines for detected contravention, and—especially—by the threat of obstacles to obtaining export licences. The costs of the paperwork of licence application, of delays and uncertainty, and of lost markets are frequently acknowledged by the United States government and attempts are made to reduce such costs.[44] There are complaints from American high-technology industry, of course,[45] but these are outweighed by testimony to the loyalty and compliance of that industry.[46]

That sketch is incomplete. From the late 1970s, it became suddenly and then increasingly obvious to American industry that it was no longer pre-eminent in all fields of high technology and that other countries, especially Japan, had become internationally competitive. Studies of the Japanese "threat" and of the Japanese "way" abounded, and many concluded that much Japanese success was attributable to the various forms of assistance the Japanese government provided its high-technology industry. Parallels were drawn with the assistance given by European governments, though the failure of those schemes to achieve much international competitiveness was largely ignored. There was concern about what ailed American innovation,[47] about whether there was sufficient venture capital, about the significance of small firms, about whether enough was being spent on research and development—even about whether chips

[44] One example is the time-limits imposed on the processing of applications by the Export Administration Act of 1979.

[45] E.g., "Hamstringing High-Tech", *San Jose Mercury*, 7 February, 1984. New groups have been formed in industry to make protest more effective: Lachica, Eduardo, "U.S. Move to Stiffen Standards on Export of Technology Brings Business Criticism", *Wall Street Journal*, 20 March, 1984, p. 10.

[46] E.g., Mohl, Bruce, "National Security vs. Free Trade", *Boston Globe*, 1 April, 1984.

[47] E.g., Rabinow, Jacob, "Is American Genius Being Stifled?", *U.S. News and World Report*, 23 December, 1974; "The Breakdown of U.S. Innovation", *Business Week* (16 February, 1976), pp. 66–68.

52   *Stuart Macdonald*

produced by the American semiconductor industry were still good enough for the Department of Defense.[48] Given that high technology was regarded as crucial to recovery from recession, it was asserted that it was necessary for the United States government to do something, or at least to be seen to be doing something, for high technology. Yet, paradoxically, high technology was the flagship of the free market system, the pride of capitalism. For a conservative government, sworn to the preservation of the American way of free enterprise, the justification of intervention posed particular problems.[49]

Industry itself, despite the unimpressive record of the United States government's intervention in the semiconductor industry, seems to have been sufficiently panicked by the fear of Japanese competition that changes in strategy, including the acceptance of government intervention, were welcomed by at least some sections of the industry.[50] High-technology firms have been investing heavily in academic research, sometimes collaboratively.[51] Some, following what they take to be the European and Japanese models, have even put their faith in "pre-competitive research" and have joined the Microelectronics and Computer Technology Corporation, directed by Admiral Bobby Guy Inman at Austin.[52] New high-technology industrial associations have been formed to make representations to the government, and these have taken a particular interest in international trade in high technology, and especially the non-tariff barriers to trade maintained by Japan.

Information is the most precious commodity of high-technology industry. No single high-technology firm can generate sufficient information to create new products and processes; each is dependent on the flow of information from other sources, and the major source is competing firms. This information is most commonly procured by information exchange, a process often involving informal, personal contacts. For the individual firm, a delicate balance must be maintained between the giving of information and its receipt. It is possible that the recent period of national alarm about high technology has upset that balance in favour of more stringent efforts to control the movement of information. There has been an increase in the use

---

[48] "Big Pentagon Probe of Microchip Frauds", *San Francisco Chronicle*, 26 December, 1983; "Defense Department Bans Microcircuit Shipments", *Aviation Week and Space Technology*, CXX (9 January, 1984), p. 24.

[49] See Kaus, Robert, "Can Creeping Socialism Cure Creaking Capitalism?", *Harper's* (February 1983), pp. 17–22; Reich, Robert, "Beyond Free Trade", *Foreign Affairs*, XLI (Spring 1983), pp. 773–804.

[50] See Noyce, Robert, "Semiconductor Firms Need Fair Access to Foreign Markets", *Sacramento Bee*, 26 December, 1983.

[51] Norman, Colin, "Electronics Firms Plug into the Universities", *Science*, CCXVII (August 1982), pp. 511–514.

[52] Larsen, Judith, "Cooperative Research in the Semiconductor Industry", paper given to Conference on Industrial Science and Technological Innovation, Raleigh, North Carolina, May 1984.

Controlling the Flow of High-Technology Information 53

of litigation—previously rare—to punish miscreant ex-employees,[53] and the government has shown enthusiasm for the detection and prosecution of high-technology "spies".[54] In late 1983, Soviet diplomats, journalists and industrial managers were officially banned from visiting Silicon Valley.[55] Those who transfer information, despite the importance of their role in the prosperity of high-technology industry, have been prosecuted with as much vigour as those who steal components. There has been a strong international flavour to these prosecutions; what was tolerable behaviour for employees of American high-technology firms is intolerable for employees of foreign concerns. Yet foreign firms have been moving into Silicon Valley since the latter part of the 1970s for the very purpose of joining the information networks of American high-technology industry. When the United States government prosecuted Hitachi in late 1983 for stealing secrets from IBM, the Japanese, who had simply acted in the same way as American firms, were astonished.[56]

Zealous efforts to prevent communists from stealing high-technology information in the United States seem to have confused foreign firms dealing with American high-technology firms over just what kind of acquisition of information remains legal.

You have got to question about the validity of the firm you are dealing with, especially a foreign firm. Go to the FBI, ask questions. The FBI has recently sought to publicize their efforts in this problem in our particular area by putting up billboards similar to the World War II type of thing about the walls having ears.[57]

This confusion may appear to be of some potential advantage to American high-technology firms, but the partial severance of their own channels of information is likely to be extremely costly.

Corporate executives and leaders of the business community must not only be understanding of the need for compliance and be supportive of the government's export control efforts, they must translate this state of mind into effective action by their company staff, managers and supervisors.[58]

[53] Cohen, David, "Labour Mobility and Trade Secrets in Knowledge-Intensive Industries", paper given to TIP Workshop, Department of Economics, Stanford University, 2 June, 1983, pp. 7ff.

[54] See, e.g., Lindsey, Robert, "Some Losers in Silicon Valley Turn to Spying for Wealth", *New York Times*, 23 October, 1983; Dworkin, Peter, "U.S. Warms up War on High-Tech Spies", *San Francisco Chronicle*, 22 June, 1983; "FBI Swoops in the Valley of the Spies", *New Scientist*, C (27 October, 1983), p. 251. See also some extraordinary accounts of preventive measures in Melvern, L., Anning, N., Hebditch, D. and Hosenball, M., *Techno-Bandits: How the Soviets are Stealing America's High Tech Future* (Boston: Houghton Mifflin, 1984).

[55] "Silicon Valley Off-Limits to Soviets", *San Jose Mercury*, 20 November 1983; Magagnini, Steve, "Where Russians Can't Go", *San Francisco Chronicle*, 21 November, 1983.

[56] See Lindsey, Robert, "There are Still Plenty of Bugs in Silicon Valley Security", *New York Times*, 23 October, 1983.

[57] Testimony of Southard, Douglas (Deputy District Attorney, Santa Clara County) in *Transfer of United States High Technology to the Soviet Union and Soviet Bloc Nations*, *op. cit.*, p. 153.

[58] Wu, Theodore (Department of Commerce), "The Citizen Partner: A Key Force in Effective Strategic Export Control", *Signal* (August 1983), pp. 106–108.

Small, highly innovative firms, for example, are being encouraged to take much greater security precautions,[59] yet these are the very firms which have been most active in creating new patterns in the movement of information in American high-technology industry. There is a growing feeling in that industry that the paraphernalia of export controls may stifle their innovative activity.[60]

The association of diminishing competitiveness in American high technology with unfair behaviour by foreigners has done much to muster political support for export controls on high technology by the United States government.[61]

Increasingly in Europe and the U.S. domestic companies are serving as a "Trojan Horse" for Japanese semiconductor and computer suppliers. That is, the Japanese companies such as NEC, Fujitsu, Hitachi have made arrangements to supply top-of-the-line computers and permit the domestic firms to affix their own labels. We view this as a dangerous course in a national security context as well as in a commercial context.[62]

Neither the Soviet Union nor any other communist state poses a commercial threat to American high technology. However, export controls have permitted interference with the flow of high technology from the United States to countries, including Japan, which are serious competitors in some fields of technology.[63] This consequence has certainly not escaped the notice of high-technology firms outside the United States, and it is one which the American government, anxious to assist its own industry, seems unwilling to prevent.[64] Ironically, having disputed with the Japanese for years over Japan's reluctance to open her market to imports of high technology from the United States, the Americans are now themselves restricting the flow of their high technology to Japan.[65] Equally ironically, having striven valiantly for even longer to restrict the flow of high technology to the People's Republic of China, the United States had opened access to this market by 1983.[66] Referring to the political implications of such a move, two authors had remarked in 1979: "a policy of using export controls for the explicit

---

[59] Casey, William (director of CIA). "The Challenge of American Intelligence", speech to Commonwealth Club of California, Palo Alto, 3 April, 1984, p. 7.
[60] McLucas, John, "Technology Transfer Scare Hurts Innovation", *Aerospace America,* XXII (June 1984), p. 6.
[61] See Handleman, Howard, "The Great Technology Robbery", *Pacific Defence Reporter* (February 1984), p. 65.
[62] Casey, W., *op. cit.*, p. 9.
[63] See Norris, William, "Limiting Japan's Access to our Research", *New York Times,* 24 July, 1983.
[64] See Cullison, A. E., "Soviets Take Fast Path to High-Tech Advances", *Journal of Commerce* (17 July, 1984), p. 4.
[65] Auerbach, Stuart, "U.S., Japan Clash on High-Tech Trade", *International Herald Tribune,* 14 January, 1984; "Japanese Bank's Proposal for Venture Capital Business is Turned Down by Americans", *Japan Economic Journal* (20 December, 1984), pp. 4–5; "Japan is Target of U.S. Policy to Stem Outflow of New Technology", *ibid.,* (13 December, 1984), p. 4.
[66] Mann, Paul, "U.S. Relaxes Rules on Exports to China", *Aviation Week and Space Technology,* CXIX (5 December, 1983), p. 167.

Controlling the Flow of High-Technology Information   55

purpose of building up China at the expense of the Soviet Union would be dangerous."[67] The political results of such policy may give cause for concern, but the commercial consequences of export controls for purposes of foreign policy, and justified in terms of national security, should also give some cause for concern.

The Academic Reaction

As long as the main emphasis of export controls by the United States rested firmly on curtailing the export of tangible goods to the Soviet Union and its allies, American universities were little affected by them. Universities are "information factories"; in their research activity they collect bits of information—and occasionally create new bits—in order to assemble those bits into new patterns which will be transmitted to the world at large. A major difference between academic research and research in industry is that the latter is much more concerned with development and is not intended to be published. Yet, the more information-intensive an industry, the more its research is likely to resemble that carried out in universities. Certainly the means by which information moves in high-technology industry are reminiscent of the academic tradition of the eager exchange of ideas for common benefit, and the importance of informal personal contacts is evident in both cases.[68] As controls became increasingly aimed at restricting the export of technological information rather than merely goods, it was inevitable that their operation would bring them into conflict with the universities. Restricting the flow of information from high-technology industry was pointless when much of the same information was available from universities only too eager to promote its diffusion.

There have been incidents in which the Department of Defense has requested—with intimated threats—the withdrawal of conference papers, and attendance at conferences has been refused to those who are not American citizens.[9] The Department has also requested that universities limit the movements of foreign visitors and research workers lest they obtain controlled information. While that approach has prompted condemnation from some universities, it is consistent with parallel attempts to prevent the flow of controlled information from commercial centres of research in high technology. It is also consistent with the early arguments of both the Central Intelligence Agency and the Department of Defense that few of the students

[67] Bingham, J. and Johnson, V. *op. cit.*, p. 919.

[68] See Macdonald, Stuart, "Personal Communication in Research and Development", in Callebaut, W., *et al.* (eds), *Theory of Knowledge and Science Policy* (Ghent: University of Ghent, 1980), pp. 255–271.

[69] "Science and the Citizen", *Scientific American*, CCLI (July 1984), p. 66; "Restrictions on Technical Papers Raise Concerns". *Aviation Week and Space Technology*, CXVIII (17 January, 1983), pp. 22–23; "Pentagon Blocks Papers at Scientific Meeting", *Chemical and Engineering News*, LX (13 September, 1982), p. 6.

from the Soviet Union and its allies studying in the United States were, in fact, genuine students.

These so-called exchange students run around 35 years old, on the average, and they are always skilled in highly technical areas—electronics, physics, that sort of thing . . . [American exchange students] average 22 years of age and they are studying Russian history, the history of the icon, that sort of junk.[70]

The Department of Defense has provided examples of "academic spies",[71] and though these have been denied by academic scientists,[72] the notion that foreigners in the United States are either potential or actual "technology spies" is still forcefully argued. If this is accepted, it becomes difficult to believe that foreigners located outside the United States can be any more reliable.

Whatever benefits the United States gains from controlling the flow of information from universities must be set against the possible cost of injury to their research.[73] The quality and timeliness of research are likely to be very much related to the ease with which scientists can procure information. The direct effects of measures to help export controls may be small: indirect effects in terms of, e.g., papers withheld from conference organisers, and the risks avoided by not communicating research results may impose more serious costs. Nor can the effects of restrictions on the flow of information be easily confined to those disciplines most obviously relevant to high technology; for example, the voluntary restraints which have been established in cryptography have begun to be expected from other disciplines.[74] Similarly, clauses demanding review prior to publication can now appear even in government contracts for unclassified research. For example:

The contractor shall not disclose any confidential information obtained in the performance of this contract. Any presentation of any statistical or analytical material or reports based on information obtained from studies covered by this contract will be subject to review by the Government's Project Officer before publication or dissemination for accuracy of factual data and interpretation.[75]

It is hard to know what information to control before the information is produced, and harder still to control that information after it has been

[70] Robert Gast as reported in Raess, John, "Silicon Valley: A Tempting Espionage Target", *Peninsula Times Tribune*, 12 May, 1983.
[71] "Scientific Exchanges and U.S. National Security", *Science*, CCXV (January 1982), pp. 139–141.
[72] Letters from Lappin, Joseph and Zimmer, Gyorgy, *Science*, CCXVI (April, 1982), pp. 124, 126.
[73] See Unger, Stephen, "The Growing Threat of Government Secrecy", *Technology Review*, LXXXV (1982), pp. 30–39, 84–85.
[74] See Nelkin, Dorothy, "Intellectual Property: The Control of Scientific Information", *Science*, CCXVI (April 1982), pp. 704–708.
[75] Office of Government, Community and Public Affairs, Harvard University, *Federal Restrictions on the Free Flow of Academic Information and Ideas* (Harvard: October 1984), p. 11; reprinted in "Secrecy and Freedom of Communication in American Science", Reports and Documents, *Minerva*, XXII (Autumn–Winter 1984), pp. 421–436.

Controlling the Flow of High-Technology Information 57

produced. Conceivably a wide range of information emanating from, and relevant to, universities might be affected by new attitudes towards the control of information. Academics working in nuclear research have found that information hitherto unclassified has suddenly become classified.[76] Restrictions on the flow of information arising from the Export Administration Act have been accompanied by other legislation intended to have complementary effect. For example, Executive Order 12356 of April 1982, according to some critics, imposed a system of security classification which disregards notions of public interest, weighs heavily in favour of stricter classification, and allows information arising from research to be classified at any stage of the research project and for as long as government officials deem prudent.[77] In the same vein, the Freedom of Information Act and statements of environmental impact are frequently claimed to be exploited by communist countries:[78]

In 1979, Soviet embassy personnel copied information from an Environmental Impact Statement on a weapons manufacturing plant in Tennessee. The statement had been placed in a public library for review. A Defense Intelligence Agency investigation revealed that it contained enough technical data to reconstruct the entire manufacturing process.[79]

Some academics have been strong in their objections.[80] Members of the academic community were particularly aroused in January 1982 by a speech from Admiral Inman, then deputy director of the Central Intelligence Agency, to the United States National Academy of Sciences, in which he said that there had been a "haemorrhage" of American high technology information to the advantage of the Soviet Union and its associates.[81] The National Academy organised a committee to investigate the issues raised.[82] That committee, having been cleared to receive classified information from the Department of Defense, determined that the government would often have to be involved in decisions to publish in the grey areas between classified and unclassified academic research.[83] The committee seems to have accepted the premise that some control of information from

---

[76] Norman, Colin, "Universities Denounce DOE's Secrecy Rules", *Science*, CCXXI (September 1983), pp. 932–933; Holden, Constance, "Historians Deplore Classification Rules", *ibid.*, CCXXII (December 1983), pp. 1,215, 1,218.

[77] Office of Government, Community and Public Affairs, Harvard University, *op. cit.*, pp. 13–17; Rosenbaum, R., *et al.*, "Academic Freedom and the Classified Information System", *Science*, CCXIX (January 1983), pp. 257–259.

[78] E.g., Fry, Glenn, "Technology Transfer: a Perspective from the Congressional Side", *Signal* (August 1983), pp. 109–111.

[79] Guida, Richard, "Protecting America's Military Technology", *U.S. Naval Institute Proceedings* (January 1984), pp. 35–40.

[80] See Gelbspan, Ross, "Academe Protests U.S. Censorship", *Boston Globe*, 14 May, 1982.

[81] See "Smothered, by a Security Blanket", *New York Times*, 12 April, 1982.

[82] The Corson Committee's Report is National Academy of Sciences, *Scientific Communication and National Security* (Washington, DC: NAS Press, 1982).

[83] "An Ominous Shift to Secrecy", *Business Week* (18 October, 1982), pp. 138–142.

universities was obviously in the national interest; its conclusion was consistent with the premise.[84]

Implications of American Export Controls for Western Industrial Countries and Japan

If it is argued that export controls deprive American high-technology firms of markets overseas, it follows that those same controls present potential new markets to firms from other Western industrial countries and Japan. The loss to the United States might be someone else's gain and there are few other suppliers of high technology. Yet, there is no evidence that non-American firms see the situation in this light. Indeed, there is strong suspicion that American high-technology firms are able to manipulate the export regulations to their own advantage and so increase their trade with the Soviet Union and other communist countries, and especially with China, at the expense of the high-technology firms of other countries.[85] While the allies of the United States concede that export controls determined by multilateral agreement are necessary, they bridle at controls imposed unilaterally by the United States. There is also strong objection in the United States to unilateral controls, on the grounds that other countries can supply similar high technology and will, in fact, fill the gap left by American firms. To prevent this happening, the United States has attempted to enforce its own unilateral controls over alternative suppliers of high technology to the Soviet Union and its allies. It is to the imposition of American law outside the United States that other countries have made the most vociferous objections. As Her Majesty's Secretary of State for Trade and Industry said recently: "We can't impose our laws in the United States, and frankly they can't impose their laws within Britain."[86]

While opinion in the United States seems sensitive to the offence which its allies must take to the principle of extraterritoriality, the practice has been a common part of American legislation. The issue of extraterritoriality has irritated its allies; the United States has attempted to assuage that irritation, but not necessarily by ceasing attempts to enforce American law outside the boundaries of the United States. The issue poses small, practical difficulties in the United States: among its allies the matter is one of principle.

Whether the United States can or should exert extraterritorial jurisdiction is clearly a matter of importance, but it is marginal to the central issue of the control of the exportation of high technology. Extraterritoriality has distracted attention from whether export controls, either agreed

[84] Chalk, Rosemary, "Commentary on the NAS Report", *Science, Technology and Human Values*, VIII (1983), pp. 21–24. The National Academy of Sciences is about to start a further study of export controls; this will deal with their impact on American industry and with how other countries regulate exports. *Aviation Week and Space Technology*, CXXI (19 November, 1984), p. 15.

[85] *Hansard*, House of Commons (13 April, 1984), cols 697–705.

[86] Tebbit, Norman, transcript of "Today" programme, BBC radio, 20 January, 1984.

Controlling the Flow of High-Technology Information 59

multilaterally or imposed unilaterally by the United States, do produce costs to its allies in excess of benefits. If the United States succeeds in restricting the flow of information on high technology, the damage to its own high-technology industries may be more severe than that felt by the communist countries.[87] Western European high technology is openly dependent upon information from American sources,[88] and is especially reliant on formal channels for its transfer, although the inadequacy of these channels has stimulated resort to less formal means of the movement of information in recent years. European and Japanese high-technology firms have, for example, been anxious to locate some of their activities close to those in the United States in order to draw on their stock of information. The formal insitutional transfer of information is less flexible than informal transfer and it is difficult to compensate for the disruption of one source of information by increasing the flow through other channels. In contrast, in the acquisition of high-technology information the Soviet Union and its allies take advantage of whatever sources of information, legal and illegal, are available. The Soviet bloc is therefore able to cope with American export controls in a way that the allies of the United States are not.[89] Although penalising allied firms is not the ostensible intention of the Export Administration Act, there are firms in American high-technology industry which would welcome any impediment to the competitiveness of the Japanese.

European governments seem only vaguely aware of this situation, though recognition may grow as the European Economic Community deliberates on the implications of export controls for its member states.[90] Concentration on the issue of extraterritoriality is only partly responsible. Western European firms trade much more extensively with the communist countries than does the United States, and the obvious threat to valued markets for their exports is taken seriously, expecially as the United States views those countries participating most actively in Soviet bloc trade as the most

[87] Of the pipeline dispute, the Office of Technology Assessment commented, "It would appear in this case that the United States has used its foreign policy controls on exports to the USSR as much to inconvenience and modify the policies of its allies as to inconvenience or exact concessions from the Soviet Union." Office of Technology Assessment, *op. cit.*, p. 68.

[88] A recent survey of over 200 chief executives of large European firms found little confidence in Europe's technological competitiveness and admitted general technological dependence on the United States and Japan. European Panel of Chief Executives, *The Management of Technology* (Brussels: Wall Street Journal (Europe)/Booz Allen Hamilton, February 1984). See also Speiser, A. P., "European Technology between Two Poles: The United States and Japan", Reports and Documents, *Minerva*, XXIII (Winter 1985), pp. 508–520.

[89] Office of Technology Assessment, *op. cit.*, p. 70.

[90] EEC Memo 104/804 (Brussels: 16 October, 1984). See also Lowe, A. V., "Public International Law and the Conflict of Laws: The European Response to the United States Export Administration Regulations", *International and Comparative Law Quarterly*, XXXIII (July 1984), pp. 515–530; Tagliabue, John, "US Trade Stance Irks Europeans", *New York Times*, 11 August, 1984; Cheesewright, Paul, "EEC Counts Cost of US Curbs on Technology Transfer", *Financial Times*, 17 October, 1984.

unreliable.[91] Japan is among those countries.[92] So too is Austria, where major legislative changes were made recently to oblige the Americans,[93] and especially the Department of Defense, which acquired the responsibility for reviewing high-technology exports to unreliable countries in March 1984.[94] More recently, the Department set a precedent by partly compensating a Belgian firm for the loss of a Russian order for a high-technology lathe,[95] a contrivance described in a newspaper article as a tired old machine,[96] harmless as far as defence is concerned.[97]

It might be that disruption to the flow of high-technology information from the United States to its allies might spur the industries of those countries to greater independence in their attempts to innovate. Such a consequence would accord with current industrial policy in many of these countries, but it could well be an expensive and uncertain course to independence in high technology and one which would take a long time to be effective. Indeed, the Soviet Union has demonstrated that innovation in high technology is possible despite partial isolation from foreign high-technology industry, but also how costly such an independent course can be for the rest of the economy. It would be strange if European governments in particular were to welcome American export controls as abetting their domestic industrial policies.[98]

American controls on high-technology exports increase the level of uncertainty for the high-technology industries of American allies and thus impose a major cost.[99] It is just not possible for individual firms, especially small firms, to be quite sure that their intended exports are not proscribed by the full list of the Co-ordinating Committee or by the various lists in the United States. Inconsistencies in decisions taken by United States government agencies are probably fostered by export control legislation, which expressly excludes provisions for judicial review of those decisions. Even the sanctions imposed in retribution on firms by those agencies are largely beyond review.[100] Uncertainty is aggravated by the delay inherent in

[91] Kempe, Frederick, "Austria Ignores Efforts by the U.S. to Curtail Technology Shipments", *Wall Street Journal*, 25 July, 1984.

[92] Anderson, Jack, "Japan is Sieve for High-Tech Leaks to Soviets", *Washington Post*, 26 May, 1984.

[93] Kempe, Frederick, "Austria Moves to Stop Transfers of Technology, Appease U.S.", *Wall Street Journal*, 30 November, 1984.

[94] Schrage, Michael, "Reagan Gives Pentagon Right to Review Exports of High Technology", *International Herald Tribune*, 26 March, 1984.

[95] "U.S. Pays Belgians not to Sell to Soviets", *Washington Post*, 10 August, 1984.

[96] Dryden, Steven, "U.S. Clashes with Allies on Exports", *Philadelphia Inquirer*, 13 August, 1984.

[97] Yerkey, Gary, "Reagan Keeps High-Tech from Soviets—at a Price", *Christian Science Monitor*, 13 August, 1984.

[98] See Gee, Jack and Cahill, Kevin, "France Goes it Alone after US Cray Ban", *Computer Weekly* (3 February, 1983), p. 1.

[99] See Feazel, Michael, "U.S. Curbs on Technology Said to Hinder NATO Unity", *Aviation Week and Space Technology*, CXIX (17 October, 1983), p. 100.

[100] Fazzone, Patrick, "Business Effects of the Extraterritorial Reach of the U.S. Export Control Laws", *International Trade Law and Practice*, VIII (1982), p. 594.

Controlling the Flow of High-Technology Information   61

the licensing procedure, especially when firms of countries allied to the United States must seek licences from both their own government and that of the United States.[101] Uncertainty also arises in trying to import high-technology goods and information from the United States. American firms may themselves be delayed in their exports to the firms of Western European countries, or they may choose to avoid the risk of transgressing the law by playing safe and simply refusing to export their products. Penalties imposed on some American firms which have unwittingly infringed the law have been considerable.[102] Penalties exacted on Western European firms are much less certain. The United States can hardly impose fines or other penalties on firms overseas, but it can most certainly deny exports to foreign firms alleged to have infringed American law. The official "denial list" contains only 154 firms located outside the United States,[103] but there seem to be other lists compiled by departments with a responsibility to review licence applications. The Central Intelligence Agency, for example, has identified 300 firms in more than 30 countries, engaged in diverting American high technology to communist countries[104] and the Office of Export Administration has, for some time, been using its own methods, described as "outstanding in identifying firms engaged in diverting critical technology to the Soviet Union".[105]

Being placed on a blacklist can have serious consequences for firms. The following is an extract from a letter sent by solicitors representing General Instrument Microelectronics Limited to a British firm on the official "denial list":

There has been brought to our clients' attention an order of the U.S. Department of Commerce [International Trade Administration] dated 18th February 1984 temporarily denying export privileges to you personally and to Contel Equipment, amongst others. The order specifically denies all privileges of participating directly or indirectly in any manner or capacity in any transaction involving commodities or technical data imported from the United States in whole or in part to be exported. In the light of that order, our clients have no alternative but to terminate, with immediate effect, the above arrangement and the purpose of this letter is to give you notice to that effect.[106]

---

[101] Mann, Paul, "Export Control Shift Worries Europeans", *Aviation Week and Space Technology*, CXX (30 April 1984), p. 59.

[102] Digital Equipment Corporation (DEC) paid a reduced fine of $1.1 million in 1984 and agreed to a substantial "good-behaviour bond" in order to retain its distribution licence. Taylor, Paul, "Digital Fined $1.5m over Computer Exports", *Financial Times*, 6 September, 1984.

[103] Many of these are clearly duplicates. No fewer than 63 firms are located in Austria, Switzerland, South Africa and Sweden. *Export Administration Regulations, op. cit.*, Supplements 1 and 2 to Part 388.

[104] Casey, William, "The Challenge of American Intelligence", speech to Commonwealth Club of California, Palo Alto, 3 April, 1984, p. 7. See also Beresford, Philip, "CIA Admits Spying on British Firms", *Sunday Times*, 29 April, 1984.

[105] Testimony of Brady, Lawrence (Department of Commerce) in *Transfer of United States High Technology to the Soviet Union and Soviet Bloc Nations, op. cit.*, p. 266.

[106] Maclay, Murray & Spens to Moller-Butcher, A., 9 October, 1984.

The firm's complaint to the responsible British minister is sufficiently eloquent to illustrate the problems likely to be faced not just by the small number of firms on the "denial list", but by those firms which have no means of knowing whether they have offended and whether they are suffering the consequences.

I am a small trader in the U.K. engaged in the sale and brokerage of Used Semiconductor Process Equipment.

I have received from Maclay, Murray & Spens, acting on behalf of General Instruments Microelectronics Ltd., the enclosed letter, which in effect breaches an agreed contract, the reason given being the U.S. Commerce Department's Denial List.

In addition G.I. Microelectronics' staff have endeavoured to persuade my customers Bafak AB, not to place a service/repair contract for the goods under discussion (Used-Disposable Wafer Manufacture Equipment), despite previous settled arrangements.

I have also been denied surplus equipment from Texas Instrument, Macro Marketing, and also recently had my service contract with Rank Zerox, to service the Rank Zerox Copying Machine cancelled. (We changed the machine for a Japanese.)

I do not need to remind you that the USA Denial List has no standing with the U.K., you yourself have personally criticised the Export Administration Act which gives rise to the Denial List. Having brought to your attention my personal case of Breach of Contract by the U.S. subsidiary, G.I. Glenrothes, acting on instructions obviously from within the U.S., I now ask your department to help my situation and enforce British Law within the U.K.[107]

The degree of uncertainty over export controls prevailing in Western European firms can perhaps best be illustrated by an internal working document from one large European firm. It speaks of "growing technological imperialism by the United States" and declares that:

The U.S. will assert control over an end product, such as a computer built in the U.K., if such an end product contains a controlled U.S. origin component and the end product, had it been built in the United States, would have been subject to control. This means that, in theory, a large British-built computer containing components costing say, 1% of the total would, nevertheless, be subject to U.S. re-export controls.

A U.S. licence is required for the oral disclosure of U.S. origin technical data by a non-U.S. citizen to a Communist end user which occurs outside the United States. Such a situation could arise, for example, where a non-U.S. technical expert acquired controlled U.S. origin technical data as part of training in the U.S. or work on a joint venture with a U.S. company anywhere in the world. Such U.S. control is asserted even where U.S. origin technical data is "comingled" with non-U.S. data.[108]

If large firms interpret the implications of export controls in this way, smaller concerns can be forgiven their confusion and their dismay at some of the anomalous consequences of those controls.[109] For example, computers

---

[107] Butcher, B. A. to Tebbit, Norman, 12 October, 1984.

[108] Strachan, Jeremy, "US Trade Law: The Triple Threat. The Stifling of High Technology Business", ICL internal working paper (London: 1983).

[109] E.g., Lamb, John, "West Counts the Cost of Computer Ban", *New Scientist*, CI (23 February, 1984), pp. 12–13.

Controlling the Flow of High-Technology Information   63

have recently been removed from the duty free shop at Heathrow airport, an action defended by the British Minister for Trade:

The facts are that all computers require a licence before they can be exported. It is clearly impossible for HM Customs to enforce an export control when the goods in question are on the "air side" of Customs control: and Customs asked the company to move. I understand that they were quite content to do so and are in fact doing substantial business from their new location. As will be clear from what I said in the House on 13 April we do not agree that it is necessary to control the export of a number of lower powered computers, some of which are no doubt available at Heathrow. But the present position is—and this will remain the position until there is agreement to change it—that the export of these computers is controlled not only by agreement among our CoCom partners but also as a matter of UK law. I am sure that you would agree that the law must be properly enforced.[110]

Small high-technology firms outside the United States are likely to suffer more than large firms; they lack both the lobbying power of large firms and staff and procedures capable of dealing with a myriad of export control regulations. The advice received from American firms operating overseas does nothing to dispel their anxiety. A letter to British leasing companies from IBM United Kingdom Limited contains the following passage:

Some recent Press reports about the effect of US Export Regulations on computer equipment have tended to be concerned with exports from the United Kingdom. As you are aware, transactions *within* the United Kingdom involving "Advanced Systems" are also subject to the obtaining of US export licence approval. Such transactions include not only the initial installation of a new machine with a user, but also any subsequent dealings or transfers in such machines (at least while they remain an "Advanced System").[111]

While the publication of this letter created a furore at the time,[112] official reaction has been expressed in a more subdued tone: "The Secretary of State has said that for the moment companies who own or lease IBM computers should proceed with some caution. It appears that the arrangement set out in the IBM letter has been going for some time without creating major practical problems."[113]

The Bucy report, which is fundamental to the new approach towards export controls taken by the United States, was forthright about what enforcement action should be taken. It argued that penalties should be imposed on whole countries rather than firms; this is logical, assuming that internal flows of technology in foreign countries cannot be totally controlled by the United States. "The U.S. should release to neutral countries only the technologies we would be willing to transfer directly to Communist

[110] Channon, Paul to Ashdown, Paddy, 9 May, 1984.
[111] Correspondence from branch manager, Computer Related Industries Branch, IBM United Kingdom Limited, 22 December, 1983.
[112] On this matter see *Hansard*, House of Commons (17 February, 1984), cols 498-9; "Trade Department to Question IBM on Computer Warning", *Financial Times*, 10 January, 1984; Tyler, Christopher, "Tebbit to Pursue U.K. Computer Licence Row", *Financial Times*, 16 January, 1984.
[113] Butcher, John (Parliamentary Under Secretary of State for Industry) to Stott, Roger (Opposition Spokesman on Information Technology), 9 February, 1984.

countries . . . any CoCom nation that allows [key] technology to be passed on to any Communist country should be prohibited from receiving further strategic know-how."[114]

European political reaction to the American actions has generally been restrained, despite the occasional untethered outburst. It seems to be assumed that the main threat is to sovereignty rather than to high-technology industry, that a new Export Administration Act will remove most difficulties, and that diplomacy is therefore the obvious and best course to follow.[115] It would, though, be possible for the British to apply the provisions of the Protection of Trading Interests Act 1980, which was used to deal with American blacklisting of firms during the pipeline crisis, and for other countries to introduce similar legislation.[116] Indeed, in a statement issued upon the expiration of the Export Administration Act of 1979, the British government used the threat of such legislation in what was probably a futile attempt to influence the content of the new act.[117] At present there is no indication that the new and much delayed Export Administration Act will take a position of compromise, and it is possible that Western European governments might take retaliatory legislative action. In any case, as concurrence with the Co-ordination Committee agreement is in each case ultimately left to each individual country,[118] only unilateral export controls effectively enforced by the United States can provide the total assurance it is currently seeking.

Trade in High Technology

The most striking feature of American trade with communist countries in high technology is how little there is of it. Concentration on issues of high technology alone can lead to the belief that it dominates the imports to communist countries from the West.[119] It does not (Table I). There has been a gradual decline, since 1970, in the proportion of exports from the West to the Soviet Union and its allies that can be classified as high

[114] Bucy report, *op. cit.*, pp. xiv–xv. Similar arguments have been made more recently by an influential private group. See "Staunching the Technology Flow to Moscow", *Backgrounder* (Boston: Heritage Foundation, 23 September, 1983).

[115] See *Hansard*, House of Commons (13 April, 1984), col. 704; Gray, Frank, "Britain and U.S. to Consult Before Using Trade Powers", *Financial Times*, 24 November, 1984.

[116] The Protection of Trading Interests Act 1980 was originally introduced to counter the effects in Great Britain of United States anti-trust legislation. It empowers the British government to force firms to fulfil their contracts. West Germany has threatened similar legislative action: Getler, Warren, "Bonn Says It Will Ignore U.S. Technology Curbs", *International Herald Tribune*, 9 August, 1984; Tagliabue, John, "U.S., Europeans Split on Sale of High Technology", *ibid.*, 13 August, 1984, p. 9.

[117] "U.S. Export Administration Act: HMG statement", *British Business*, XII (28 October, 1984), p. 436.

[118] Office of Export Administration, Department of Commerce, *Export Administration Annual Report FY 1982* (Washington DC: US Government Printing Office, 1983), p. 24.

[119] Much of the data presented in this section is from Martens, John, *Quantification of Western Exports of High-Technology Products to Communist Countries* (Washington DC: International Trade Administration, Department of Commerce, February 1983, draft).

Controlling the Flow of High-Technology Information 65

TABLE I

Western Exports of High Technology to the Soviet Union and its Allies

	1970	1979	1980	1981
Millions of US dollars	816.9	4,731.4	4,524.5	3,456.8
Percent of all Western exports to Soviet Union and its allies	13.6	13.0	11.5	9.3

SOURCE: Martens, John, *Quantification of Western Exports of High Technology Products to Communist Countries* (Washington DC: International Trade Administration, Department of Commerce, February 1983, draft), p. 7.

TABLE II

Western Sources of High-Technology Exports to the Soviet Union (Other Communist Countries not Included)

	Percentage of Total	
	1970	1981
West Germany	23.0	28.9
Japan	10.8	21.1
France	14.5	11.8
Italy	17.3	9.0
Finland	1.6	7.0
United Kingdom	13.9	5.4
Switzerland	5.9	4.6
Sweden	5.5	4.5
United States	3.1	3.3
Other Western Countries	4.4	4.4
	100.0	100.0

SOURCE: Martens, John, *Quantification of Western Exports*, *op. cit.*, p. 13.

technology, while there has been a great increase in the volume of all exports since that date, including those of high technology. Japan, the Federal Republic of Germany and other European countries are the overwhelming source of high-technology exports from the West to the Soviet Union (Table II). The United States was responsible for only 3.3 per cent of that trade in 1981. An extension of this observation is that third countries are the major source of illegal shipments of high technology from the United States to controlled destinations.[120] Officials in the United States Department of Defense emphasise this point:

. . . the volume of high-technology trade with the Eastern Bloc, which is what we're principally concerned about is insignificant, both to American industry and to the

[120] Testimony of Brady, Lawrence (Department of Commerce) in *Transfer of United States High Technology to the Soviet Union and Soviet Bloc Nations*, *op. cit.*, p. 264.

66   *Stuart Macdonald*

future growth of American industry . . . The illegal acquisitions by the Soviet Union arrive in the Soviet Union mostly by way of friendly allied countries which receive those exports legally from the United States.[121]

Only Hungary and Czechoslovakia appear to be moderate recipients of high-technology exports from the United States, and even these countries are less reliant on high technology from the United States than is the world as a whole (Table III). Only about 2.3 per cent of all United States exports of high technology go directly to countries of the Soviet bloc.

TABLE III

High Technology Exports to the Soviet Union and its Allies: 1981

	Percentage of Total
Bulgaria	2.5
Czechoslovakia	11.7
German Democratic Republic	0.9
Hungary	13.7
Poland	2.3
Romania	3.4
USSR	2.4
World	16.0

SOURCE: Martens, John, *Quantification of Western Exports, op. cit.*, p. 15.

Of course, it should be acknowledged that the United States is very likely to be the original source of much more high technology than is suggested by the bare trade figures. Other Western countries are dependent on American high technology for their own industries. Thus, most export of American high technology to the Soviet bloc is indirect and probably impossible to assess quantitatively. That being so, the practicability of unilateral American export controls to restrict the flow of American high technology to the Soviet bloc is questionable. If the flow is to be reduced or halted, then it is clearly important to deal with that part which emanates from other Western countries. This obviously requires multilateral agreement and raises questions of American emphasis on unilateral controls. Indeed, this is recognised in the United States, though in a way that can afford no comfort to its allies: "Of greatest concern is the demonstrated capability of the USSR to exploit the dependency on its markets by Western firms and industrial sectors. In effect, the USSR has created a veritable 'Soviet Lobby' in Western business and government circles that can facilitate the implementation of its objectives."[122]

[121] Perle, Richard, transcript of "It's Your Business" television programme, Washington DC, Station WJLA-TV, 29 January, 1984.
[122] Brady, Lawrence (Assistant Secretary of Commerce for Trade Administration), "New Directions in U.S. Trade Policy", speech to International Trade Committee, National Association of Manufacturers, San Francisco, 13 January, 1982, p. 9.

Controlling the Flow of High-Technology Information   67

Although the United States is not a major direct source of high technology generally, it might still be an important source of crucial high technology to the Soviet Union. There is, however, no means of ascertaining whether American exports of high technology to the Soviet bloc are qualitatively different from those of other countries. Using figures for Export Administration licences is scarcely satisfactory because most licences granted in the past have not actually been used.[123] Moreover, the statistics of licences are confused by items that are not high technology; for instance, agricultural commodities also require licences. Nevertheless, it is worthwhile looking at patterns of licensing over the last few years in certain important high-technology categories (Table IV). It is evident that exports have declined in all five areas, but that the precipitous decline in exports of integrated circuits and semiconductor manufacturing equipment is quite exceptional.

TABLE IV

Value of Applications Approved for United States Exports to the Soviet Union and Its Allies, by Selected Category

	Fiscal Year			
	1980	1981	1982	1983
	Thousands of US Dollars			
Communications equipment	9,120	3,561	1,597	2,603
Electronic computing equipment	117,814	86,996	110,677	66,384
Electronic test equipment	33,196	26,205	27,228	17,876
Integrated circuits	6,965	918	263	54
Semiconductor manufacturing equipment	11,983	163	10	150

SOURCE: Derived from US Department of Commerce, *Export Administration Annual Report* (Washington, DC: US Government Printing Office, 1981–84).

Internecine Struggles

Those who believe that the United States and the Soviet Union are destined to remain implacable enemies, that military conflict is probably inevitable, and/or that it is primarily the threat of retaliatory force which restrains Soviet aggression are likely to judge that the benefits of US policies have outweighed the costs. Those who believe that the United States can and must learn to live with a strong Soviet Union, and that the USSR is best restrained by being drawn into normal relations with the Western world are more likely to look askance at the utility of trade sanctions in moderating Soviet behaviour.[124]

There has been great dispute amongst those responsible for export controls. The American system of government is not monolithic and senior

[123] Martens, J., *op. cit.*, p. 20.
[124] Office of Technology Assessment, *op. cit.*, p. 72.

administrators wrangle over policy as vigorously and as publicly as politicians. A contentious issue like export controls, with its marked focus on national security, has given rise to an internecine struggle in which departments are strengthened or weakened and careers made or ruined.

The Department of Commerce, despite a few dissidents, is on one side, and the Department of Defense, with the Treasury, which is responsible for the Customs Service, is on the other.[125] The administration of export controls has been largely the responsibility of the Department of Commerce, a responsibility, which—according to the Department of Defense—is quite incompatible with the more general duty of the Department of Commerce to encourage trade. The latter has been steadily losing ground to the Department of Defense. For example, in the hearings held by the Senate in 1982, the Department of Commerce had nothing with which to counter accusations that the enforcement of the entire American grain embargo had been left to a single officer, that prosecutions for infringement of export controls had been rare, and that penalties had been derisory:[126] "less than you would get for taking a deer out of season in Maine."[127] Even a senior official of the Department of Commerce described his department's previous performance in issuing licences for the export of high technology as "a shambles".[128]

It was the Department of Defense which instigated the Bucy report, which forthrightly declared that: "While Defense does not have the primary responsibility for control of technology export, . . . the initiative for developing policy objectives and strategies for controlling specific technologies are their responsibility."[129] The Department of Defense has accepted this responsibility, and has increasingly influenced what items should be controlled and how it should be done. Not only has it produced its own exhaustive "Militarily Critical Technologies List"[130] and restricted publication of some of the academic research done with its financial support, but it has also generally increased its influence through offering advice about application for licences to other parts of the government. In March 1984, President Reagan granted the Department of Defense the power to review export licences for high technology to non-communist countries.[131] In 1983 the Department of Defense contributed $30 million of the $31 million required for "Operation Exodus", the programme of the Customs Service

[125] See McDonald, Greg, "U.S. Officials Face off over Hi-Tech Exports", *Atlanta Constitution*, 4 April, 1984; Madison, Christopher, "Commerce Department Feels the Heat over Diversion of High-Tech Exports", *National Journal* (10 March, 1984), pp. 465–468.
[126] *Transfer of United States High Technology to the Soviet Union and Soviet Bloc Nations*, *op. cit.*, pp. 90–131.
[127] *Ibid.*, p. 131.
[128] *Ibid.*, p. 263.
[129] Bucy report, *op. cit.*, p. iii.
[130] See Office of Technology Assessment, *op. cit.*, p. 92.
[131] Auerbach, Stuart, "Reagan Scored on Export Controls", *Washington Post*, 27 March, 1984; Farnsworth, Clyde "Pentagon's Wider Role on Exports", *New York Times*, 21 March, 1984.

to reduce infringements of export controls.[132] As the Commissioner of Customs said recently:

The Defense Department has the experts on what items have military applications. That Department is a great supporter of the Customs Service and I'm a great supporter of the Defense Department. Therefore, the more involvement that the Defense Department has in the decisions to license high-technology exports, the happier I am.[133]

To strengthen its case dramatically, the Defense Department has repeatedly referred to certain examples of outright theft of American technology by communist countries. In one case, customs agents entered an aeroplane on the verge of departure to prevent Richard Mueller from sending a DEC VAX 11-782 computer to the Soviet Union via South Africa, Germany and Sweden; the retrieved goods were triumphantly exhibited in a large hangar at Andrews Air Force Base. The evidence permitted the conclusion that the Soviet Union had planned to assemble an entire factory for integrated circuits,[134] although computer professionals have rejected that conclusion.[135] Similarly, the Department of Defense has asserted that the Soviet An-76 cargo aeroplane was developed from stolen American C-141 technology; this has been rejected out of hand in technical journals.[136] Again, in arguing that small computers should be subject to export control, Mr Richard Perle, assistant secretary of defense for international security policy, has stated: "We are now using Apple II computers to target nuclear weapons, Apple II computers with the standard software."[137] That such a modest computer should be employed for this purpose, and that it is even possible, has astonished some computer experts.[138] The Department of Defense argued—successfully, until late in 1984—that all items containing microprocessors, including personal computers and electronic toys, should be subject to export controls, regardless of the foreign availability or the strategic significance of these objects.[139] The Department of Defense was most enthusiastic about the

---

[132] Transcript of "Videocom '84" interview with Perle, Richard (23 March, 1984), p. 9. Project Rampart, to install electronic "bugs" in computers so that they may be traced, is apparently now being considered by Customs. Williams, M., "How not to Capture the Export Trade", *Fortune* (6 August, 1984), p. 69.

[133] Rees, John, "William von Raab", *Review of the News* (25 January, 1984), pp. 39–43, 45–48.

[134] Kelly, Orr, "High-Tech Hemorrhage from U.S. to Soviet Union", *U.S. News and World Report* (7 May, 1984), pp. 47–48. See also Black, George, "Soviet-Bound VAX was 'War Material'", *Computer Weekly* (5 January, 1984), p. 1.

[135] See Conrad, Geoff, "The Clowns Are on at the U.S. Exports Circus", *Datalink* (30 July, 1984).

[136] Gregory, William, "When to Transfer Technology", *Aviation Week and Space Technology*, CXVIII (13 June, 1983), p. 11.

[137] Transcript Perle, Richard, *op. cit.*, p. 12.

[138] E.g., Gregory, William, "The Technology Transfer Mess", *Aviation Week and Space Technology*, CXX (14 May, 1984), p. 13.

[139] Office of Technology Assessment, *op. cit.*, p. 95; "The Electronic Tide", *Economist*, CCXC (21 January, 1984), pp. 14–15.

70   *Stuart Macdonald*

recommendation of the Bucy report that export controls should concentrate on information rather than products. Assistant secretary Richard Perle expressed the same view:

> On the whole, the best way to prevent the Soviet Union from acquiring Western technology is by concentrating on protecting manufacturing know-how rather than products. By focusing on basic know-how, we can'hope to slow the pace at which the Soviets are able to field new weapons. It needs to be emphasized that it should be the state-of-the-art in the Eastern Bloc, not in the West, that serves as a guideline for what may or may not be transferred.[140]

Disagreements within departments are expressed in public.[141] At least one critic of the dominant position has resigned his office.[142] When Mr William Root resigned as director of the Office of East–West Trade in the State Department, he declared: "The arrogance of the United States Government is rapidly eroding the effectiveness of controls on the export of strategic equipment and technology. Those who proclaim the loudest the need to strengthen these controls are doing the most to weaken them."[143] Not surprisingly, some of those who have in the past been sympathetic to the views of the Department of Defense in these matters now find that events have passed them by, and that they can no longer agree with the policies they once helped to formulate.[144] When extremes succeed, they do so in both senses.

Implications for the Soviet Union

Recent studies suggest that basic organisational obstacles to innovation in the Soviet Union have resulted in the maintenance of an undiminished technology gap between it and the West.[145] Moreover, the time required in the Soviet Union to move from research and development to production continues to be very large, and there is little evidence of successful diffusion from imported technology.[146] This being the case, it is possible that the

[140] Perle, Richard, "The Eastward Technology Flow: A Plan of Common Action", *Strategic Review* (Spring 1984), pp. 24–32.
[141] Mann, Paul, "Dispute Persists over Export Licensing", *Aviation Week and Space Technology*, CXX (28 May, 1984), pp. 26–27. See also Root, William, "Trade Policy: The U.S. Needs to Listen to its Allies . . ." and Brady, Lawrence, ". . . But Should Beware of Helping the Soviet Union", *Business Week* (21 November, 1983), pp. 22, 23.
[142] See Harford, James, 'DOD Position no Perle of Wisdom", *Aerospace America* (July 1984), p. 15; Mann, Paul, "Export Policy Triggers Dispute", *Aviation Week and Space Technology*, CXIX (19 December, 1983), pp. 18–20.
[143] Root, William, "Open Letter to the President and to the Congress", 24 September, 1983.
[144] Inman and Corson are quoted in Clark, Evert and Hall, Alan, "The Administration vs. the Scientists: A Dangerous Rift over Locking up Sensitive Data", *Business Week* (4 June, 1984), p. 79.
[145] E.g., Amann, R., Cooper, J. and Davies, R., *The Technological Level of Soviet Industry* (New Haven: Yale University Press, 1977).
[146] Holliday, George, "Western Technology Transfer to the Soviet Union: Problems of Assimilation and Impact on Soviet Exports", in Joint Economic Committee, US Congress, *Soviet Economy in the 1980s: Problems and Prospects* (Washington, DC: US Government Printing Office, 1982), Part I, pp. 522–523.

Soviet Union has decided to procure very specific parts of high technology instead of attempting expensive importation over the whole range of high technology, which probably could not advantageously be incorporated into economic production.

The Soviet Union, rather than its satellites around the world, is the chief target of United States controls over the export of high technology. The argument is quite straightforward: the Soviet Union is regarded as the main adversary of the United States, and therefore neither the United States nor its allies should export to the Soviet Union or to the communist countries those things which contribute to its military strength. Armaments clearly fall into this category and so too does high technology, though the latter relationship is more complicated. Part of this complexity is a consequence of the fact that most high technology has both military and civilian application;[147] part of the complication is the fact that any trade, by its very nature, is likely to benefit the Soviet economy and thus create resources which can be allocated to the military sector.[148]

It has never been unanimously agreed that export controls on high technology would work to the disadvantage of the Soviet Union. Some have argued that policy for more trade in high technology rather than less is appropriate in that it would help bind the Soviet economy into the international capitalist web; others argue that the expansion of trade in high technology would make the Soviet Union more dependent on the United States, and therefore less likely to act against it. Another argument for more exportation of high technology is that the diffusion of information technology in the Soviet Union might possibly weaken the highly centralised organisation of a communist state.[149] Still another argument for the export of American high technology to the Soviet Union is that restriction would stimulate the Soviet Union to devote more effort to research and development and might make it more innovative.[150]

Any assessment of exportation of high technology from the West to the Soviet Union must take into account that the Soviet economy is much less dynamic and much more self-reliant than those of most Western countries. The Soviet Union is "Neither a major importer of technology nor a major exporter of high-technology manufactured goods . . . the Soviet Union is a relatively small-time player in the international game of high-technology

---

[147] "Nearly all new technological developments have direct or indirect military application": Schneider, William, "Export Control of High Technology", *State Department Bulletin* (June 1983), pp. 71–74.

[148] The argument could become circular in view of the considerable production of civilian goods from Soviet defence plants. Cooper, Julian, "The Civilian Production of the Soviet Defence Industry", paper delivered to the Symposium on Soviet Science and Technology, Birmingham, September 1984.

[149] Rickman, Sheldon, "Let Them Have the Computers", *St. Louis Post-Dispatch*, 10 June, 1984; Malik, Rex, "Communism vs. the Computer: Can the USSR Survive the Information Age?", *Computerworld* (9 July, 1984), pp. 1D/35–1D/48.

[150] See Cahill, Kevin, "Europe Loses out as Russia Builds its Own", *Computer News* (8 November, 1984), p. 8.

trade".[151] The high-technology trade of the United States with the Soviet Union is so small that its curtailment could hardly be expected to have much generalised effect on that country. High-technology exports from the Western European allies of the United States are much greater, but even their total stoppage would hardly bring such a huge economy to its knees. In any case, a total cessation of all exports of high technology by all countries is very unlikely to occur.

The Soviet Union and its allies have long exploited less regular means of acquiring information in matters of high technology. Export controls are likely to increase the use of such irregular and informal channels. For example, the protracted nature of negotiations about high technology between the Soviet Union and Western firms means that Soviet specialists have much more opportunity to absorb information on high technology from Western suppliers than do their Western counterparts.[152] Such negotiations are likely to become even more protracted, and they may increase the acquisition by the Soviet Union of high-technology information through informal personal contact.

Almost all high technology has military applications—hence the possession of knowledge of it by the Soviet Union is regarded by the United States government as a danger to its military strength. The export of American high technology to the Soviet Union is regarded as heightening that danger.

What has been forgotten in the squabbles over who should control what and how it should be done, and how vital to national security that control is, is just what is being controlled. High technology has become a fetish in the concern for national security. The struggle is engaged in for a multiplicity of motives: there are those who would advance the fortunes of their departments, or their own fortunes; those who would improve the standing of their political parties, or their own political prospects; those who fervently believe in American ideals, or their own ideals.

Export controls would be as incidental to high technology, as high technology essentially is to export controls, were it not for the change of emphasis in those controls advocated by the Bucy report. In seeking to control the flow of information, export controls touch the very heart of high technology, or, more accurately, its circulation system. They operate with all the finesse and subtlety that might be expected from an apprentice butcher, and high technology is likely to bear not only the scars of such inept intervention, but also to suffer long-term damage from the obstacles which

[151] Holliday, G., *op. cit.*, p. 516.
[152] Hill, Malcolm, *East–West Trade, Industrial Co-operation and Technology Transfer* (Aldershot: Gower, 1983), pp. 69–71.

Controlling the Flow of High-Technology Information   73

are being proposed or actually being erected against the free circulation of information. Among those who are preoccupied with national security with high technology, there appears to be little appreciation of precisely how information is important in a highly information-intensive industry.

Part VI
Information Policy

[19]

Developing information policy

Donald A. Dunn

The author first considers some of the policy issues that arise in connection with the creation of new information, primarily scientific and technical information. He then discusses specific policy problems stemming from communications and information storage and retrieval systems and their use. A broader integrative view of this field could help develop a national information policy for the future. Such integrative work remains to be done, and suggestions for future studies in this area are given.

Keywords: Information processing; Data communications; Policy formulation

The author is Professor of Engineering-Economic Systems, Stanford University, Stanford, CA 94305, USA. Tel 415-497 3930.

This article is a revised version of a paper presented in the National Science Foundation Report to the President and Members of Congress, The Five-Year Outlook on Science and Technology, Vol II, May 1980, pp 493–507.

[1]ie 'very large scale integration'.
[2]Edwin B. Parker, 'Information services and economic growth', The Information Society, Vol 1, 1981, pp 71–78.
[3]Anthony G. Oettinger, 'Information resources: knowledge and power in the 21st century', Science, Vol 209, 4 July 1980, pp 191–198.

It is only in the past twenty years that the possibility of a coherent national information policy has been discussed and its importance recognized.[1] Although we now have a National Telecommunications and Information Administration in the USA, we do not yet have a national information policy. The people and institutions concerned with the creation, distribution, and use of information can be regarded as making up the national information infrastructure.[2] To take an example, US investment in the exploration of space has yielded two things: a set of data, reports, and facts that relate to space and space technology; and a set of people and facilities in universities, private firms, and NASA spaceflight centres who are capable of applying space technology to new problems. This combination of people, facilities, know-how, and retrievable facts makes up the national information infrastructure in the space technology area. The retrievable facts represent one of the tools that the people working in this area make use of in designing new systems. These facts also can be valuable to people in other fields. It should be emphasized, however, that these facts and the information storage and retrieval systems in which they are stored represent only a small fraction of the total information and capability that is available in this field.

Viewed as a national resource, the information infrastructure is the most valuable resource a nation has.[3] Information policy is concerned primarily with the management of this resource at the local, state, and national levels. National objectives with respect to this resource would include (at least) the efficient provision of high quality, diverse information services to business and consumers, some measure of freedom of access to these services by both providers and users, and the protection of individuals against invasions of privacy and the misuse of information about them.

Information policy, like information systems and services, can be thought of in relation to four levels of information and activities: (1) creation; (2) distribution/communication; (3) storage and retrieval; and (4) use/application. I will, in this article, discuss information policy in relation to this four-level structure. Different government agencies and policy instruments have been used in each of these areas to promote the national interest, and technological change has had very different impacts at each of these levels.

One of the most important changes that is taking place in the information industry today is the restructuring of firms that formerly specialized in information services at only one of these levels, into multilevel vertically integrated firms. In addition, firms that formerly specialized in a particular distribution medium are now acquiring the capability to distribute services in several media. For example, newspaper firms are now often owners of broadcast stations and cable television systems. Cable television system operators, like broadcasters, also now provide some of the content for their programmes. Videodiscs and videocassettes offer competitive forms of distribution, but these systems too are likely to be owned by the same firms that own other distribution systems. AT&T is, to a limited extent, already providing information content, as well as its traditional message service.

At first glance, this trend towards multilevel, multimedia service appears to ensure a more competitive market than we have had in the past. To some extent this is true, especially in the entertainment field in which a number of competitors to broadcasting now exist. However, it is not yet clear that increased diversity in programming will result. A cable television system that provides 50 channels of news and entertainment may limit its offerings in critical areas to a single source, one it shares ownership with. And it is quite likely to be the only cable system in any given city, at least for a number of years into the future. Thus, while it is clear that the large information service firms are becoming more diversified and their markets are becoming less subject to displacement or loss due to technological change, it is not clear that this trend will result in a form of competition that will solve any of the traditional information policy problems. In fact, the tendency to combine the provision of distribution service, which is often a local monopoly, with the provision of content, may reduce the competitiveness of the market for content.

One of the driving forces for change in information technology has been the evolutionary, steady reduction in cost in the computer and communication industries. As the cost of computation has dropped new information products, such as the pocket calculator, have come into being and have become almost universal tools in business and home. Although we are now reaching some fundamental physical limitations in such fields as VLSI (very large scale integration), cost reductions are expected to continue.

Information systems based on computer-communication technology include EFT (electronic funds transfer), EMS (electronic message systems), POS (point-of-sale funds transfer and inventory control systems), and office automation. Systems tailored to the home market are also evolving. Home computers are now widely available at prices below $1000, and devices to permit these computers to link with each other and with larger computers and with larger computers through the telephone network (as business computers have done for many years) are available at prices below $200. Video recording technology, cable television systems with viewer signalling capability, scrambler systems for pay-by-programme television, and several new forms of information storage and retrieval systems that will use the television set as a display terminal are available today at modest cost.

New 'stand-alone' systems, such as the pocket calculator, raise few policy issues. The markets that supply these systems are unregulation and competitive. Information systems combining computer power with communication offer a variety of services that stand-alone systems cannot provide. One category of such systems is person-to-person communication systems that transmit messages, store them in a computer-controlled storage medium, and offer random access to any message from a list of messages arranged and displayed by sender name or some other indexing arrangement. Such electronic message systems can transmit messages through the telephone network or a data network. Input terminals can be conventional computer terminals with alphanumeric keyboards or communicating word processing typewriters. Voice message systems of this type that provide a displayed list of messages and random access to any message on the list will probably soon be available. In the long term, the world's telephone networks are evolving into electronic message systems that will handle both voice and character-based messages and that will provide computer-controlled message storage, indexing, and retrieval, in addition to the directly connected person-to-person service they now provide. In addition to person-to-person message systems, information systems, such as Videotex, that provide access to large databases will utilize either cable-television systems or the telephone network for delivery of character-based information to homes and offices.

These network-based systems raise policy issues in two areas: (1) with respect to the network itself, which has been provided in a market in which entry and prices have been governmentally controlled; and (2) with respect to the content of the information provided through the network. I will discuss the content-related issues first, in the next section on the creation of new information. The network-related issues will be discussed in the following section on communications and distribution. Content issues also, of course, arise in connection with stand-alone systems, which, in fact, do not really stand alone, but form the terminals of distribution systems that relay on physical delivery of print materials, magnetic storage media, videodiscs, and other storage media. And content issues also are closely linked to the storage and retrieval technologies that are used in electronic publishing.

The creation of new information content

Policy options regarding the creation of new information are discussed here in relation to: patents and copyrights; public investments in artistic activities, basic research, and applied research and development; encouragement of industrial investment in these activities through tax incentives and other approaches; and consumer interests in the rate and direction of research and development. While a wide variety of cultural factors affect a society's orientation toward art, science, and technological change, economic factors play a central role in determining the rate and direction of change. The following discussion considers only economic factors, emphasizing change in science and technology.

Many information policy issues arise out of the peculiar nature of information, when it is viewed as an economic good. Information has many of the properties of a 'public good', ie a good that one user can consume without diminishing its availability or usefulness to another user. Information products or services typically involve a high fixed cost of creation and a low marginal cost to make the service available to each additional user. Because it is possible to copy information at a much lower cost than to create it, investors who might hope to profit from the sale of information will tend to underinvest in this type of activity, relative to their investment in other activities not subject to copying. It is this economic argument that underlies patent and copyright policy. Patents and copyrights create property rights in information and ideas with the objective of making investments in the creation of intellectual property more attractive, relative to investment in goods not subject to copying. Patents and copyrights not only protect the creator'of new information from 'piracy' by others seeking to make copies, but also create transferable pieces of property that can be sold in the market, thus enhancing the value of new information by making it more like other goods.

The same property rights in new information that provide incentives to create it also operate to encourage the wide distribution of this information. Owners of information products seeking to maximize their profits will obviously attempt to sell their products widely. There is an apparent tension between the policy objectives of obtaining a high national level of creativity and the policy objective of obtaining rapid dissemination of the results of the creative process. The policy instruments, such as copyright laws, that have been used to encourage creativity do so by creating barriers to copying and apparently act as obstacles to rapid dissemination. However, the tension is primarily a tension between short-term and long-term objectives. In the short term, an innovation can perhaps be most rapidly disseminated by allowing free access to it. But in the long term, it is necessary to be concerned not only with dissemination of known ideas, but also with the continued creation of new ideas, so there will continue to be something to disseminate. Patents and copyrights encourage both innovation and the disclosure of innovation. The alternative, allowing free dissemination, can result in secrecy about innovation, which obviously does not promote dissemination. Even under a property right system many innovations are not protected, and innovators often go to considerable lengths to keep their ideas secret.[4]

The effects of patent laws on the operation of a modern, competitive industrial market can be rather different from the effects on individual inventors. In modern industry, the invention process has been commercialized. Inventors are hired and organized to create new ideas that will be most beneficial to the firms that employ them. In some markets the innovation process has been accelerated to a very high pace. The computer industry, for example, has a rapid development cycle, typically less than five years for a major innovation. A rapid obscolescence of products naturally accompanies this rigid introduction of new products.

An important distinction needs to be made between the invention process that may be involved in creating a new product and the innovation process that is concerned with selecting the specific characteristics and technology of the new product and bringing it to the marketplace. Many innovations are not patentable, but innovation is protected by trade secret law and by the length of time it takes to copy a new product. In a high-technology field, the time to copy may be more than a year. A firm that is a year or two behind its competitors may find that its competitors have written off the costs of creation by the time its product reaches the market, so it does not gain a price advantage through copying. Copying would thus not be a successful strategy in such a market. The role of patents in such a market is unclear. Patents on basic inventions that will be used in several cycles of innovation have long-term value. Patents on obsolete products are obviously not of value. The usual argument that firms will underinvest in innovation does not seem to apply to rapidly changing, high-technology markets. Firms in these markets must innovate in order to survive. The economics of invention and innovation in markets with rapidly changing technology appears to be an important field for research.[5] Neither the operation of such markets

[4]Susan H. Nycum, 'Legal protection for computer pograms', *Computer Law Journal*, Vol 1, 1978, pp 1–83; Deborah Shapley, 'Electronics industry, takes to "potting" its products for market', *Science*, Vol 202, 24 November 1978, pp 848–849.
[5]Almarin Phillips, 'Patents, potential competition and technical progress', *American Economic Review*, Vol 56, May 1966, pp 301–310.

without government intervention nor the effects of patents and cross-licensing agreements in such a market is now well understood.

Firms can effectively nullify the effects of patents by entering into cross-licensing agreements. Firms, in effect, give up the potential rewards from occasional basic patents to avoid the risk of competitors' inventions blocking their access to the market. There is a risk that cross-licensing and patent pools can violate the antitrust laws,[6] but if all new entrants to an industry can join the licensing agreements, the effects are not necessarily anticompetitive.

Public investment

As an alternative to creating property rights in new information through patents and copyrights, direct public investment can be made in the creation of new information and works of art. In areas in which the government has a mission responsibility, as in defence and space, it can be expected to support the research that it believes will be most beneficial to its missions in the long term. In areas in which the private sector is responsible for providing products and services to consumers, there is also a potential role for government-supported research, especially basic research. The economic argument that firms will underinvest in research that leads to inventions subject to copying is even more applicable to basic research aimed at understanding nature, because patents do not cover theories or laws of nature. Thus, the discoveries that come from basic research will benefit a firm's competitors as much as the firm itself (except for public relations benefits), so the amount of basic research done in the private sector will tend to be less than is socially optimal.[7] Some form of governmental intervention in the market to create increased incentives for carrying out basic research is therefore appropriate, and direct government funding is a straightforward way to support basic research.

Once government funding of research is adopted as national policy, a question arises with respect to the ownership of patents and copyrights on innovations made in this research. Presumably, the national interest is best served by a government patent policy that will maximize innovation. Government ownership of patents results in disclosure, but it does not create incentives for firms to make the necessary investments to bring these patented innovations to the market. Granting exclusive rights to firms that do make such investments would enhance the incentives to develop these innovations, much as homestead rights have been used to encourage the development of government land.

Another important policy issue in this area is that of the allocation of funds. What areas of research should receive funding, and at what levels? A balance of many diverse interests is somehow achieved in the present system. However, there may be opportunities for improving the present system: for example, by creating more independent sources of research funding likely to support research leading in new directions. Both industry and mission-oriented agencies could strengthen their positions in the long term by supporting basic research projects of special interest to them, rather than relying on others to provide this support.

Industrial investment

Industrial investment in research can be increased through tax incentives. However, there is the risk that the amount of new research may be small

[6]Donald F. Turner, 'Patents, antitrust, and innovation', *University of Pittsburgh Law Review*, Vol 28, 1966, pp 151–160.
[7]William D. Nordhaus, *Invention, Growth, and Welfare: A Theoretical Treatment of Technology Change*, Cambridge, MA, 1969; Edwin Mansfield, 'Research and development, productivity change, and public policy', *NSF Colloquim on R&D and Productivity*, Washington, DC, November 1977.

in relation to the amount of tax subsidy, because firms have an incentive to reclassify existing activities to qualify for favourable tax treatment as well as to initiate new research.

Also important is the possibility of more industry-sponsored research on an industry-wide basis, in universities, industrial research laboratories, or research institutes. There are likely to be more cases like VLSI arising in the future, in which it is important for an entire industry to develop a new set of techniques that will be used throughout the industry in the future. Projects to develop these techniques could appropriately be funded and managed by the concerned industries themselves, without governmental intervention. Industry cooperation in such research programmes could, however, have antitrust implications, and it is possible that new legislation would be helpful in encouraging this type of industry-wide research activity. Most of the precedents for industry-wide research occur in regulated industries, and even then the precedents are mixed. For example, Bell Laboratories serves the operating companies of the Bell System, but it does not directly serve independent telephone companies. The Electric Power Research Institute (EPRI) is an industry-wide organization in the electric utility industry. Until recently, the electricity utilities relied primarily on General Electric and Westinghouse to do the research and development in electric power, with only a small industry-wide research programme. Now EPRI receives 1% of the revenues of the electric utilities to use for research.

The most important feature of industry sponsorship of research, in my opinion, is that industry would inject its own ideas and interests into research that it sponsors. Development and design engineers from industry have a significant contribution to make to the direction of basic research that could most effectively be expressed in an organizational context in which industry is paying the bill.

Consumer interests

The principal consumer interest in research and development is selection of projects that will lead to products and services of the greatest value to the consumer. When the market is functioning properly, no special attention to this problem is required. But the market often fails to function properly, as a result of governmental intervention or some other cause. In such cases, research and development can come to emphasize the interests of producers rather than consumers. Examples can be found in nuclear energy, military hardware, and medical technology, all of which rely on non-market forces to determine project selection.

Two approaches to this distortion of the market are possible. First, an attempt can be made to increase competition and to allow producers a wider latitude in their choices of the approach to be taken in meeting consumer needs. Second, increased participation of consumers in the project selection process can be encouraged. For example, consumers can influence future project selection by evaluation of the results of previous projects or existing services. To be effective in representing consumer interests, an evaluation would have to be carried out entirely under consumer control.[8]

Current moves towards deregulation in many industries offer significant opportunities for benefits to consumers from the more rapid introduction of new products and services. Regulation often has had the effect of slowing technological change, sometimes with the intention of benefiting consumers through reduced prices. But by keeping prices low, regula-

⁸E. Scott Maynes *et al*, 'The local consumer information system: an institution to be?', *Journal of Consumer Affairs*, Vol 11, Summer 1977, pp 17–33; Donald A. Dunn and Michael L. Ray, *Local Consumer Information Services*, Report No 16, Program in Information Policy, Engineering-Economic Systems Department, Stanford University, Stanford, CA, April 1979.

Developing information policy

tors have limited the rate at which new technologies could be introduced. The telephone industry provides a good example of this effect. The rate of introduction of new technology into the local exchange portion of the US telephone plant has been slow.[9] It is not clear that the consumer benefits more from this policy than would be the case if prices today were higher and the newer technology were made available sooner. Similar effects have been caused by restrictions on entry into regulated markets by firms that would force a more rapid pace of technological change.[10] Again, the telephone industry provides a good example. Since 1968, the interconnection of customer-provided terminals, PBXs, and on-premises wiring to the telephone network has been allowed under FCC and state rules.[11] The pace of innovation in this market has dramatically increased since this policy was fully implemented in 1976, and American business now has a much wider range of options for telephone service open to it than could reasonably have been expected if pre-1968 policy had been continued. Many of the innovations in this field have been introduced by the new, unregulated interconnect industry, but many innovations are a result of telephone company response to competition.

Consumers benefit from diversity of content in information services, and it is clear that a competitive market provides more diversity than a monopoly. It is therefore in consumers' interests for all providers of information services to have freedom of access to whatever distribution systems exist. Freedom of access exists to a large extent in books and magazines, but not in newspapers or television. Wherever the owner of the distribution system also has provided the content, there has been a tendency to exclude independent producers of content. As videotex and teletext services become widely available in the next few years, a similar situation could arise. The UK Prestel system provider deliberately chose to stay out of the content business, and it therefore a favourable model for future systems, from the consumer's viewpoint.[12]

In summary, the creation of new information content is costly and will not be undertaken, if the creators do not have an economic incentive to create. Property rights in information content provide imperfect protection against copying by individuals for their own use but provide fairly adequate protection against copying for profit. Therefore, property rights offer a reasonably satisfactory policy approach to the incentive problem in this field. However, this incentive to create will be partially lost, if providers of distribution media do not provide freedom of access to their distribution systems to independent content providers. Two policy options that responds to this problem are: a policy that guarantees access at a reasonable price; or a policy that separates the ownership of the distribution system from the provision of content.

Communication and information distribution services

Traditionally, in most countries, the telephone and broadcasting systems are provided by government monopolies. Newspapers, while less often government controlled, rarely experience competition from more than one rival in any local market. Monopoly in these distribution systems has often been justified on the basis of the cost structure of these industries, which involve large fixed costs. However, there are policy options for dealing with such industries other than the imposition of a government monopoly. The US broadcast industry provides an example of a system

[9]US House Subcommittee on Telecommunications, Consumer Protection, and Finance, 'Telecommunications in transition: the status of competition in the telecommunications industry', 3 November 1981.
[10]Richard A. Posner, 'Taxation by regulation', *Bell Journal of Economics and Management Science*, Vol 2, Spring 1971, pp 22–50; William M. Capron, ed, *Technological Change in Regulated Industries*, Brookings Institution, Washington DC, 1971.
[11]US FCC, Use of the Carterfone Device in Message Toll Telephone Service, 13 FCC 2d 420 (1968), Reconsid, 21 FCC 2d 153 (1970).
[12]Alex Reid, 'Flying fast but safe', *Intermedia*, International Institute of Communications, London, May 1979, pp 22–25.

Developing information policy

with free entry into a market with a deliberately limited number of stations per city. The US telephone system now has limited competition in the interexchange market and interconnection in some form to all local exchanges is assured for the competing interexchange carriers. Legislation that would expand and continue this policy has been passed by the US Senate, and similar legislation will probably soon be before the House.[13] Competition in newspapers could be encouraged, if existing papers were required to deliver competitors' inserts on the same terms now offered to advertisers.

New technologies and new services offer further opportunities for less monopolistic policy options in the distribution of information services. For example, the possibility of competition in the local exchange portion of the telephone plant now makes economic sense using radio communication. Proposals to use portions of the FM radio band and portions of the band near 10 GHz for digital radio transmission are now being considered in the USA.[14] Bands in the 2 to 3 GHz region have already been allocated to Multipoint Distribution Service (MDS) that could be used for local distribution of digital radio signals in competition with the local telephone plant. Current trends in US communication policy favour the introduction of competition and will probably result in a growing number of choices for users, both among technologies for local and interexchange service and among firms capable of providing basic communication services.

Electronic message service (EMS) is an example of a new communication service being offered in a competitive market. Any company offering time-shared computing service usually offers its customers EMS. Packet-switched data networks, such as Tymnet and GTE-Telenet, also offer EMS on a network-wide basis to all of their customers. EMS is a form of message service in which a user types a message on his terminal, edits it, and transmits it to one or more addressees. The message is then stored in a computer. When an addressee is ready to receive messages, he indicates this to the computer and a list of messages waiting for him is provided. The texts of individual messages may be requested, read, and filed if desired for future reference. Users have found that being able to send each other short, typed messages is a valuable adjunct to the telephone and regular mail service. It now seems likely that this type of service will grow rapidly in the next few years and that businesses that are not otherwise computer users will use it widely. Studies of offices suggest that the most important opportunities in office automation lie in improving executive communication through such techniques as EMS.[15]

The policy issues raised by EMS in the US stem from the form of the 1934 Communications Act and its interpretation to the effect that communication services must be regulated, while non-communication services must not be regulated.[16] Thus, the issue arises whether EMS is a communications service within the meaning of the act or whether it is some form of data processing. If it is a communication service, all providers of this type of service must be regulated and existing carriers will be able to offer it. This result is not desirable, because it requires regulation of services for which the usual justifications for regulation are missing. This issue has been resolved in a sensible way by the recent FCC Computer Inquiry II which is currently before the courts for review. In this decision, computer 'enhanced' services such as EMS are not regulated, even if they are communication services. The FCC has re-interpreted the 1934 Act to mean that communication services that are

[13]Telecommunications Competition and Deregulation Act of 1981, S 898, Bill introduced by Mr Packwood, Mr Goldwater, Mr Schmitt, and Mr Stevens, 97th Congress, 7 April 1981.
[14]US FCC, Digital Termination Systems, 86 FCC 2d 360 (1981).
[15]J.H. Bair, 'Communication in the office of the future: where the real payoff may be', Proceedings 4th Intl Conf on Computer Communication, Kyoto, 26–29 September 1978, pp 733–739.
[16]Donald A. Dunn, 'Limitations on the growth of computer communication services', *Telecommunications Policy*, Vol 2, June 1978, pp 106–116, US FCC, Amendment of Section 64.702 of the Commission's Rules and Regulations, Docket 20828, Notice of Inquiry, 61 FCC 2d 103, 1976.

provided in competitive markets are adequately regulated by the market and require only occasional FCC review.[17]

EMS, EPT, POS, and facsimile together provide a capability to transact much of the world's business electronically, on a terminal-to-terminal basis, without the need for the use of any hand-carried mail. For some years to come it will be more economical to use hand-carried mail for transmitting long documents rather than facsimile. But it is evident that over the next decade or two we will see a shift from the use of hand-carried mail to electronic mail for a large fraction of mail carrying short, transaction-oriented messages. The need for a postal service, as we now know it, will undoubtedly diminish. However, as has been the case with many other new media, the coming of electronic mail will undoubtedly only partially replace hand-carried mail. Some hand-carried mail will also be originated as electronic mail. Mail can be sent by electronic means to the post office nearest the recipient and hand-delivered from that office to recipients that do not have appropriate electronic mail terminals. Mailgram is an existing service of this type in the USA, provided by Western Union in cooperation with the US Postal Service.

This shift from hand-carried to electronic mail will strongly affect the future of the US Postal Service.[18] The private express statutes give the postal service a monopoly over some kinds of mail service, but presumably not electronic mail. Clearly the postal service is free to use electronic mail internally. It is also able to offer various forms of hybrid service, analogous to Mailgram, in which messages are transmitted to the postal service electronically or in the form of computer tape and converted to hand-delivered letters. The first version that it plans to offer, ECOM, is very similar to Mailgram and will compete with Mailgram. It was difficult for the US Postal Service to get authorization for ECOM from the Postal Rate Commission, because the electronic mail industry objected to Postal Service provision of the electronic portion of the service, both in the Postal Rate Commission and Congress.[19]

Future policy issues in this area will undoubtedly be similar to those that have already arisen as competition has been introduced into the US telephone industry. With private industry and the postal service competing in the electronic mail business, problems of interconnection and cross-subsidies of postal service EMS from other revenues are almost certain to arise. The long-term issue is really whether or not the US Postal Service will be able to successfully provide the new technologies and new services appropriate to the information markets of the future. Its principal present resource is its existing delivery system, protected by the private express statutes. A major initiative will be required for it to enter these new markets, other than as a contractor for private sector services that it resells.

Subsidies in distribution

Cross subsidies from one user class to another are almost inevitable in telephone service. An important element of information distribution policy is pricing policy, or rate structure policy, which determines these subsidies.

In the US, most local telephone service is available at a flat rate per month, without regard to the number of calls made or the duration of those calls. Such a pricing policy clearly subsidizes heavy users of the telephone at the expense of light users, unless the flat rate is extremely high, which it is not. Such a pricing policy only makes sense, if the cost of

[17]US FCC, Second Computer Inquiry, 77 FCC 2d 384 (1980).
[18]US Commission on the Postal Service, Report of the Commission on the Postal Service, The Commission, Washington, DC, April 1977.
[19]Philip S. Nyborg, 'Regulatory inhibitions on the development of electronic message systems in the USA', *Telecommunications Policy*, Vol 2, December 1978, pp 316–326.

determining the number and duration of calls and of billing for them, is high, which it is not. Many US telephone companies are now starting to move to usage-sensitive pricing, which will correct this inequity and also give users more accurate price signals on which to base their telephone usage decisions.

One type of cross-subsidy in communication services can be beneficial to most users. This subsidy is one from heavy users to light users of the service. It is beneficial to all users to have as many users on the system as possible, in order to increase the number of users with whom communication is possible. In order to induce marginal users to join the system, the fixed cost of joining may appropriately be set somewhat below cost and the difference made up by charging higher prices per unit of usage. This policy helps to achieve universal service, often stated as an objective of the US telephone industry.[20] This pricing policy can be advantageous to providers of service, when the new marginal subscribers use additional optional services, such as long-distance service, and make a net positive contribution to costs. Countries that set the price of obtaining service initially at a price higher than cost are losing this benefit.

In the US, there is also a large subsidy of local calls by long distance calls, which are priced at several times their cost. Such a subsidy has several effects that are probably unwanted. It raises the cost of national, interstate business and reduces the cost of local business. It gives potential entrants to the telephone industry false price signals, inducing entry into the long-haul market and discouraging entry into local markets. It also distorts the incentives for innovation, favouring innovation in the long-haul market and discouraging innovation in the local market. AT&T's innovations in the last 30 years have followed this set of incentives. A continuing sequence of innovations in long-haul service has not been matched by innovation in local exchange service.[9] Similarly, rural (local) telephone service has received subsidies not only from long distance revenues, but also from below-market load subsidies. The rural telephone market is also notable for its relative lack of innovations in the last 30 years. Subsidies that lowered its price to users have made it an unprofitable market in which to innovate.

A related subsidy is the subsidy of low traffic density long-haul routes in the US by high traffic density routes. This subsidy is the result of a rate structure that is based on mileage, but not on the locations of the city pairs that are served. AT&T proposed a two-level rate structure, the Hi-Lo tarriff, that would have corrected this situation to a considerable extent, but this proposal was never implemented.[21]

Generally speaking, consumers and most business interests benefit most from a differentiated rate structure that reflects costs reasonably wel.[22] Uniform rate structures are less desirable, not only because they subsidize some classes of users at the expense of others, but also because they transmit false price signals to potential entrants and to potential innovators.

[20]Richard R. Hough, 'The uncommon commonplace', *Telephony*, 8 October 1979, pp 82–94.
[21]Gerald W. Brock, *The Telecommunications Industry*, Harvard University Press, Cambridge, MA, 1981.
[22]Donald A. Dunn, 'National and international policy issues in computer communications', Proceedings 4th Intl Conf on Computer Communication, Kyoto, 26–29 September 1978, pp 209–214.

Interconnection policy

Although common carriers are supposed to provide non-discriminatory access to their service to all users, they resist providing service to competitors that intend to interconnect a competing network to the carrier network. For example, the *Carterfone* case involved the connection of the Carterfone mobile radio network to the AT&T network, using an ordinary telephone. AT&T imposed conditions on its users that blocked

Developing information policy

uses of this type. The FCC in 1968 held that such conditions were unlawful.[11] This same type of situation also arose when MCI sought to interconnect its long-haul network to AT&T's network. Again the FCC required interconnection on at least the same terms as other AT&T customers.[23] MCI has sought interconnection on the same terms as AT&T's Long Lines Department, but that request has not yet been resolved.[21]

Interconnection of networks enhances the value of service for users on both networks, so the consumer's interest is ordinarily enhanced by interconnection. At first glance, it appears that interconnection also would benefit network providers, who would be able to extract some of the benefits of interconnection in the form of competition in which each hopes to become the dominant provider. In such cases, providers will resist interconnection. Providers who are already dominant use refusal to interconnect as a weapon against new entrants. Historical studies of the evolution of the US telephone network provide examples of both types of behaviour.[24]

Within the next few years the interconnection issue can be expected to arise with respect to EMS. It will be in the users' interest to have a basic capability to send messages to users in any EMS network from any other EMS network. It may be possible to provide a minimum form of interconnection that will allow this capability while allowing each provider of service to offer special features that add to the basic capability. New small EMS providers will undoubtedly favour interconnection, and large EMS providers seeking to achieve a dominant market position will probably resist it.

Thus, interconnection policy is very likely to lead to conflicts between user interests and the interests of dominant firms. Interconnection, from the user's standpoint should be provided on a non-discriminatory basis to all users. Such a policy will favour competition, a cost-based rate structure, innovation, and diversity of service offerings. In cases in which a carrier offers interconnection to any other user (such as its own subsidiary) on favourable terms, interconnection on the same terms would be available to all users, including competitors. This policy is not quite firmly established in the USA, but it appears likely that it will be adopted. If there is any one policy in the communication/distribution portion of information policy that is of the greatest importance to users, it is, in my opinion, interconnection on a non-discriminatory basis.

Information storage and retrieval

Some information can be expressed in print form; other information requires photographs, motion video, audio, or the physical presence of a particular person. If information can be expressed in a medium subject to storage and retrieval, it can be made accessible to users at times and places of their own choosing.

A reduction in the cost of videorecording technology has made television into a medium, similar to books, that can be used on demand. Although the cost of professional television programming is so high that a programme must be shared widely in order to reduce the cost per user to an acceptable level, this sharing need not take place through broadcasting, now that videorecording is available. A shift from broadcast viewing to individual viewing on demand, and various intermediate forms of 'narrowcasting', is now beginning.

[23]US FCC, Restrictions on interconnection of private line service, 60 FCC 2d 939, 1976.
[24]Richard Gabel, 'The early competitive era in telephone communication', *Law and Contemporary Problems*, Vol 34, Spring 1969, pp 340–359; US v AT&T, Plaintiff's statement of contentions and proof, Civil Action 74–1698, D Ct DC (1978), pp 118–178.

In the print media, the use of copying machines to produce copies of books and journals on demand has or may soon become sufficiently low in cost to permit a new approach to libraries. Rather than being a source of items to be loaned, a library is likely to become a source of items to be copied. Various storage media, such as microfilm and the optical disc, are adaptable to the automated production of low-cost copies. Once the cost of production of a single copy of a book or article on demand becomes sufficiently low, it will be more efficient to use the library as a storage and production centre rather than as a storage and loan centre. When this occurs, a reorganization of the publishing industry can be expected, especially in connection with the publication of low circulation items such as professional journals. From the standpoint of the user, such a change is likely to result in greatly enhanced access to the print media, increased use of the literature, and substantially increased expenditure on printed media and library services. Particularly interesting is that the critical cost at which it will become economically efficient to produce documents at the library is not just the library's cost of doing so. Rather, it is the user's cost: ie the sum of the price charged by the library plus the user's time cost. Obviously, the user will be willing to pay something to get a copy of a document immediately rather than later. Therefore, the library's price for producing a copy on demand can be substantially higher than the price that could be charged for future delivery from a publisher's stock of mass-produced copies that might cost less per copy to produce.

Perhaps, the most significant changes are taking place as a result of reduction in the cost of computer memory. Computer memory costs are being reduced both (a) in very rapid access time systems that use magnetic and semiconductor memory and are suitable for heavily used files; and (b) in longer access time systems that are much less costly and will use the random access optical disc for less often used information. The optical disc appears to be the technology that this field has been looking for for many years.[25]

The storage and retrieval of information from computerized databases is now one of the most pervasive forms of computer usage. For many purposes, it is extremely useful to have a single, continuously updated, master file of information. This file need not be located in a single location. Pieces of it can be distributed among a number of locations, but it is essential that the combined set of pieces of information form a single database. This type of system is widely used in two rather different applications: (a) files of information on transactions that typically include data on individual users, such as the amounts of their purchases, their bank balances, etc; (b) files of less heavily used information on subject matters of importance, such as company correspondence.

Libraries of the future

Once information has been put into a medium subject to storage and retrieval, it can be stored in some form of library, and bibliographic entries that describe it in terms of its author and subject matter can be entered into one of the computer-based bibliographic search systems now widely available. The library of the future probably will include: (a) a single bibliographic search system that can be used to search nearly the entire collection of the world's literature; (b) immediate access to the full text of all heavily used references on the same computer system that is used to store bibliographic data; (c) access within less than an hour, by facsimile, to the full text of most other references that are indexed in the

[25]George C. Kenney *et al*, 'An optical disc replaces 25 mag tapes', *IEEE Spectrum*, 16 February 1979, pp 33–38.

bibliographic database. Certainly a user would appreciate these features. The technology for such systems is available now, but full text systems are still expensive. The major cost component of bibliographic search systems is the cost of manual indexing and database maintenance, not the cost of hardware or software.

The consumer stands to benefit from moves toward standardization, both of the format used for entries and of the software used to gain access to computer-based library systems.[26] There is a real possibility that a standardized system could be developed that would allow supplementary features to be added by specialized service providers, but that could be used without these features for general searches. Such a system would permit growth and improvement to take place, while maintaining simplified access to the bulk of the world's literature.

It is, of course, evident that once a library system of this type becomes available, it will reduce the incentive for individuals to have subscriptions to journals. At this point, the present system of publication of scientific papers may become obsolete. Users will prefer a system that allows them to seek out specific papers on specific topics of interest rather than browsing through journals, which mostly contain papers of little immediate interest. Of course, computer-based systems also will allow users to browse through the most recent papers in any specified field of interest when this is desired.

The mechanism for financing the library of the future is built into its structure. Computer-based bibliographic search obviously can be charged for in proportion to the cost of locating the document and of providing a copy. Presumably there will be a national or international network of libraries that store documents and offer document retrieval service.

This type of library is protected against copying and reselling of both its full text documents and its bibliographic search file on a large scale by copyright law. Small-scale copying and sharing cannot reasonably be prevented. But such sharing will not be worth the trouble in most cases, because few users (other than students) will want copies of documents that their friends have at the same time as their friends. In the long term, the cost per document will probably be too low to make sharing worthwhile.

In addition to these core services, most occasional library users will want personalized librarian service to provide assistance in using the computerized bibliographic search service. And a few users will want access to persons with specialized knowledge of the field being searched. A good library should be able to provide these additional services to users willing to pay their costs.

Prestel

The library of the future will come into being more rapidly, if a large number of users have terminals that give them access to information storage and retrieval services. A large market will mean cost sharing on a large scale and hence lower cost per user. The importance of Prestel and other similar videotex and teletext systems being planned in the USA, Japan and Europe lies in their potentially very rapid growth and high ultimate market penetration. Because they are based on the use of the television set and either the television broadcasting network or the telephone network, they can be made available in most homes and businesses in the USA at very modest cost, and consequently in a relatively short time. Systems like Prestel that use the telephone network

[26]Helen F. Schierer, 'Bibliographic standards', in C. Cudra, A.W. Luke and J.L. Harris, eds, *Annual Review of Information Science and Technology*, Vol 10, American Society for Information Science, 1975, pp 105–138.

will be able to offer a very large number of different pages of information to their users. Prestel plans to offer 170000 pages.[28] Broadcast systems like Ceefax, also a UK system, are limited to a much smaller number of pages, such as 100. Experiments using the broadcast network are in various stages of development in the USA in Salt Lake City, St Louis, and Philadelphia. The US Department of Agriculture is sponsoring an experiment in Kentucky that will provide farmers access to weather, crop, and market information.

The crucial question in all of these systems is the extent to which people will want these services and be willing to pay for them. Only fairly large-scale market trials that allow times for producers to adapt to user interests will give reliable answers. The most interesting feature of Prestel is its adaptive, open market approach to the question of what information should be included. Instead of trying to decide this question by administrative decision, it is left to suppliers of information, who pay so much a page to have their information stored. Suppliers receive payment on a per page per use basis, and can set their own price per use, but they must pay the Prestel system a minimum price per page per use.

Policy issues

There is a basic national interest in having high quality information storage and retrieval services available. Governments can contribute to the achievement of this objective either through direct government action or through policies that encourage the operation of the market. For example, government actions that might lead to standardization of bibliographic search systems would improve the operation of the market in bibliographic search services. The government directly affects this market by its approach to the funding and operation of libraries and similar institutions. Libraries are not like research. There is no intrinsic difficulty in charging users for library services, so the private sector will not underinvest in library services, and private sector underinvestment is therefore not a reason for governments to subsidize or operate libraries. However, historically governments have been the principal funding sources and operators of libraries, partly on equity grounds and partly because libraries, like schools, have been seen as providing beneficial externalities (ie beneficial effects received by members of the community other than library or school users as a result of the use of the library or schools).

The main difficulty with government operation of libraries is the pricing policy that has usually been adopted. Users pay nothing for service, and both users and non-users pay for the libraries through taxation. Users are thus subsidized by non-users, but going with this subsidy is the inability of users to influence the services they receive, either by refusing to pay or by otherwise expressing their preferences. When legislatures make grants to libraries or schools, the libraries and schools naturally seek to satisfy the legislatures rather than the users. When the consumer pays directly, assuming there is no governmentally induced monopoly, the consumer can exercise a choice and patronize the library or school that offers the best service. In response to the concern that some low-income users may receive no service under a user-pay system of libraries, low-income users could be given the subsidies rather than giving the subsidy to the libraries. Users could be given aid in the form of 'library stamps' or scholarships.[27] The advantage of this form of

[27]Milton Friedman, *Capitalism and Freedom*, University of Chicago Press, Chicago, IL, 1962.

subsidy is that it allows users to express their preferences, just as in an unsubsidized market.

A further difficulty with tax-supported libraries is that they drive most private-sector library services out of the market, because the price to users is zero. Only private library services offering quite different services can co-exist with a public library offering zero-price service. The scientific and technical user, as well as most other users, probably would be best served by libraries that charged prices to users proportional to cost. Government policies that provide payments to libraries through users and that encourage the operation of a market in library services would be beneficial to users, because a greater diversity of service offerings would be expected. Experimental programmes designed to test these ideas could be implemented at very low cost.

Privacy

Many of the most significant information policy issues arise in connection with databases that contain information on specific individuals. The principal dangers in this area involve misuse of data on an individual either by an individual or by an organization that is either not authorized to have access to the data or that may have a right of access to the data for one purpose but uses the data for another purpose.

Various legal safeguards are already in existence in many countries to protect individuals' files from unauthorized access by others and to provide individuals access to data concerning themselves.[28] A number of governments have passed privacy legislation concerned with databases containing personal data on a nation's citizens that may be located in a foreign country.[29] To comply with these laws, international data service providers may find it necessary to maintain databases in each country where they have customers. It is by no means clear that the result of such legislation will be increased privacy for the customers, since their own governments will have easier access to their files.

Service providers have not yet offered many innovative services intended to increase privacy. However, as more financial services are automated, the market can be expected to present a range of privacy options to its users. The principal obstacle to the offering of privacy in the market will probably be governmental regulations, some of which probably will have been enacted to protect consumers' privacy. An important policy issue will soon arise as to the right of an individual to conduct his or her financial affairs in secret. A related issue will be the right of an individual to communicate by means of encrypted data flows. The issue will not be acute, as between individuals, but rather as between an individual and the government. The way this issue can be expected to arise became clear in connection with discussions concerning the adoption of a US data encryption standard recently.[30] The proposed standard is believed to yield encrypted data that can be decoded with a computer that would cost in the tens of millions of dollars in 1980 and that would be readily available only to very large organizations. If system providers ignore this standard and offer encryption that cannot be decoded with even the largest computers available today, users will be able to achieve more privacy than some governments may wish. Similar secure database services will also probably soon be available. Thus, this policy issue may soon be whether or not the market in privacy will be allowed to function.

A somewhat different privacy issue arises in relation to advertisers who wish to use various information media to reach potential customers.

[28] *Personal Privacy in an Information Society*, Report of the Privacy Protection Study Commission, US Government Printing Office, Washington, DC, July 1977.
[29] J.G. Maisonrouge, 'Regulation of international information flows', *The Information Society*, Vol 1, 1981, pp 17–30.
[30] W. Duffie and M.E. Hellman, 'Exhaustive cryptanalysis of the NBS data encryption standard', *Computer*, Vol 10, No 6, June 1977, pp 74–84.

Some users of these media may wish to use the capability of the media to reject all advertisements. For example, the post office could offer a service to customers that wished it to dispose of all junk mail rather than delivering it. Similar services could be made available to users of electronic mail services of the future. The most critical area today for consumers is the telephone, because its use for advertising is potentially so much more intrusive and disturbing than the use of mail systems or even television. Telephone users in the USA would now almost certainly be subjected to electronically automated advertising messages on a large scale, if it were not for the intervention before federal and state utility commissions of a few consumer-oriented individuals. Even though the issue is unresolved, a number of firms are already transmitting automated messages to homes.[31] The policy issue presented by automated telephone advertising is whether or not users have a right to choose whether they will receive such advertisements or not.

Privacy policy can be viewed as a piece-by-piece building up of the definition of an individual's property rights in his or her own personal data, communications, and connections to the national communication networks. A continuing examination of this set of issues will be required, as the new media become more widespread.

Access

The other side of the privacy issue is access. Under what conditions shall the government, a corporation, or an individual have the right to unauthorized access to stored information about another person, corporation, or governmental activity? This issue is quite clearly delineated when it arises within the purview of a court, as a part of a legal proceeding. For example, the rights of the parties in an antitrust suit to gain access to each other's internal memos and other private documents have been litigated many times and are fairly well defined. Similarly, the government's right to access to private information when it obtains a search warrant is fairly clear. However, when the government collects information without a warrant and without notice to the individual, such as the telephone numbers called from a particular telephone or the names of payees and the amounts of cheques written by an individual, the issue is less clear.[32]

A rather different kind of access issue arises in connection with access to new information created through investments in research and development. Such information may, of course, be classified in a military sense, but assuming it is not, should restrictions be put on access to such information by foreign nationals? In the USA, the transfer of some unclassified defence-oriented technology and information is made more difficult through the operation of the Trading with the Enemy Act. However, if information does not fall within the scope of this Act and is unclassified, should it be made available to foreign competitors on the same basis that it is made available to one's own national industry? Should information only be made available to nations that adopt reciprocal policies?

Three alternative policies could be followed in this area: (a) attempt to impede the flow of new information in science and technology to foreign nationals while not impeding the flow of information to one's own national industry; (b) seek to give industry special help in making use of new information of this type, wherever it originates; or (c) make no distinctions between users on the basis of their citizenship or their home country.

[31]Stan Crock, 'If the phone rings and it's Zsa Zsa, don't be surprised', *Wall Street Journal*, 15 August 1979, p 1.
[32]Reporters Committee for Freedom of the Press v AT&T, 593 F 2d 1030 (DC Cir 1978), Cert Den 99 S Ct 1431 (1979).

Developing information policy

The first option is likely to work poorly in preventing determined seekers of information from getting access to whatever is available. Most high-technology industry is now highly internationalized, and it is difficult to distinguish, in many cases, between national companies and foreign companies. The first option will almost certainly impede the flow of information to one's own national industry, even though it would be intended to avoid this result. The costs associated with this option could turn out to be greater than the benefits.

The second option is worth exploring, and there may be some practical actions that could be taken. As noted, however, often the special skills and know-how of industrial groups are more valuable than the facts filed in libraries. Recognizing this fact, foreign firms have acquired blocks of stock in US high-technology firms in recent years, at least partly in order to increase their access to this more subtle type of information.[33] Specific proposals to enhance the quality of science- and technology-related information services have been proposed in the USA.[34]

In summary, the transfer and exchange of science and technology information on an international basis is a subject that requires a national choice. Further research and analysis of these issues would be helpful in arriving at a national policy.

Commercial law

As we move away from the use of cheques and other pieces of 'commercial paper' and move towards electronically maintained financial records, a whole new set of legal rules will have to be adopted with respect to the responsibility of the parties for losses incurred in a transaction.[35] An important element of computer databases is that all parties to a transaction will be able to gain access to the same data at the same time. Transactions will be completed without any waiting period during which pieces of paper are moved physically from place to place.

A wide range of new business opportunities will be created when users in most homes and offices have the ability to commit funds from terminals located in the home or office. Many transactions that are now simply too cumbersome will become feasible. In particular, the possibility of a great many more auction sales will exist. Some new opportunities for the sale of perishable commodities will arise. For example, hotels with empty rooms may be willing to rent some of them at greatly reduced prices, and auctions of rooms at hotels throughout the world may be held on a continuous basis.

The policy issues in this area will not be greatly different from those in other areas of business law, but it will be necessary to adopt new rules to deal with the new ways transactions will be made.

National information policy

The scope of national information policy has been suggested by the topics treated above, but many related topics also could have been included. The proper scope of national information policy has not yet been delineated. However, there are good reasons for drawing the boundaries around at least the topics treated here. The creation of new information is closely connected with the use of existing information and the ways that existing information is stored and retrieved. And storage and retrieval are closely connected with business transactions and personal communication, because much of the same hardware and software is used by the

[33]Gene Amdahl, Testimony concerning financing of Amdahl Corp by means of Japanese venture capital. Field Hearings, Senate Committee on Commerce, Science and Transportation, San Francisco, CA, 30 October 1978; 'A.G. Siemens completes formation of microcomputer company with Advanced Micro Devices, Inc, purchases 400000 shares of Advanced Micro Devices for $18 million', *Wall Street Journal*, 20 January 1978, p 17; 'A.G. Siemens, owner of 80 percent of common stock of Litronix, Inc, plans to offer $8 million for remaining shares', *Wall Street Journal*, 8 November 1978, p 36; 'Northern Telecom, Inc, US subsidiary of Northern Telecom, Ltd, Canada, plans to boost its stake in Intersil, Inc to 20 percent from current 11 percent', *Wall Street Journal*, 31 May 1977, p 36.

[34]The National Technology Innovation Act of 1979, S. 1250, Bill introduced by Mr Stevenson, Mr Hollings, Mr Inouye, Mr Ford, Mr Riegle, Mr Moynihan and Mr Schmitt, 95th Congress, 24 May 1979.

[35]William F. Baxter, Paul H. Cootner, and Kenneth E. Scott, *Retail Banking in the Electronic Age: The Law and Economics of Electronic Funds Transfer*, Allanheld Osmun & Co, Montclair, 1977.

same people in all of these types of service. Once the field has been defined to include these areas, we see that we have included what we know as a people, what we are doing to learn more, and the tools that we use to conduct individual transactions and to communicate on a person-to-person basis.

There is a value in bringing together the ideas and issues involved in this set of national activities, because doing so calls to our attention the interrelatedness and importance in our lives. There are opportunities for improving the operation of the systems that provide information services in ways that will lower prices and increase the number of users served, the quality of service, and the privacy and security offered to users. Many of these opportunities will be enhanced by taking an integrated view of this area.

The perspective that has been emphasized here has been economic. The policy option that has been suggested in most situations is to limit governmental action to the definition of property rights designed to encourage the operation of the market. This same approach has been suggested in patent and copyright, privacy, interconnection, and the management of communication systems generally. Certain situations in which government regulation or government provision of services traditionally have been operative offer opportunities for improved service to consumers through deregulation or the adoption of user-pay pricing policies. In some cases, the optimum policy is unclear, and research is needed to formulate a new policy. I hope that the possibilities suggested here will be of assistance in that formulation.

[20]

Information distortions in social systems: the underground economy and other observer–subject–policymaker feedbacks

ROBERT R. ALFORD and EDGAR L. FEIGE

Social indicators are historically important as part of the general effort to quantify information into data usable for the social sciences. This development has fundamentally changed the character of every such field of inquiry. The earlier qualitative and philosophical approach to the study of human behavior has given way to quantitative and formal attempts to mimic the natural sciences by emphasizing statistical inference and experimental design. Specialization grew dramatically not only between disciplines but also within them. Political economy became political science and economics. Economics split into macro- and micro-specialties.

Although major gains have resulted from the tendency to quantify and specialize, there have also been major costs, and every discipline debates the relative costs and benefits of these developments.[1] In those social sciences concerned with the relations between institutions and individual behavior, the problem is not limited to the scientific issues of the validity of experiments and the appropriate objects of statistical hypotheses. Enormously complex social phenomena have been telescoped into aggregate measures usable as an input into public policy. A vast array of information about economic activity, political behavior, and social trends are summarized into quantitative symbols, sometimes a single number such as the gross national product (GNP). Because of their apparent objectivity, simplicity, and universality, these measures are used as a basis for both scientific investigations and public policy. In complex social systems, social indicators have become crucial informational inputs for both private and public decision making.

---

[1] Psychologists have come closest to replicating the natural sciences, but even psychology is embroiled in a fundamental debate between "authenticity" and a holistic approach vs. "accuracy" and a scientific approach. See Gibbs (1979). The dominant issue in the debate is how, and whether, discoveries based on experimental data can be useful in real-world situations.

ROBERT R. ALFORD AND EDGAR L. FEIGE

This development has raised a new set of issues about the reliability of the indicators, which have typically been dealt with from the narrower methodological perspective of the problem of measurement error (Morgenstern, 1963). Our concern is with the more complex interaction between the "subject" reporting data, the "observer" collecting and aggregating those reports into social indicators, and the "policymaker" who utilizes the indicators in the decision-making process.[2] Recent research on the unobserved economy provides an important exemplar of the complex interactive system we shall call "observer–subject–policymaker feedback." We believe that this phenomenon has critical implications for both social science and public policy.

The importance of social indicators

The social indicators – national census, surveys of public opinion, national income data, voting records, crime statistics, time series data for all kinds of social records and archives – are a product of the age of industrialization par excellence. It has been argued that the expansion of a centralized state apparatus made systematic data gathering both necessary and possible. Both socialist and capitalist economies require data for planning the allocation and distribution of society's resources. Increasingly, the basic economic data necessary for both economic and political decisions are gathered by the state. Data gathering and aggregation have become professionalized. The specialized social sciences are both based upon and help generate certain types of data: demography based on the census; macro- and microeconomics use national income accounts and surveys; political science and sociology use voting statistics and public opinion surveys.

The reliability and validity of social measurements are important. Accurate data provide the empirical foundation for developing social policy, informing public opinion, and conducting social research. In the case of highly policy-oriented disciplines such as economics, the policy, opinion, and research functions of social indicators merge.

---

[2] See Feige (1982b). Our thesis is an extension of the important argument of Kenneth Boulding, who has repeatedly asserted that knowledge of the social system is an integral part of the system's dynamic behavior. See Boulding (1971). More specifically, Campbell (1974) cited several instances of what he calls "the corrupting effects of quantitative indicators" in the context of evaluation research. The implications of their important ideas have not yet been incorporated into the corpus of social science inquiry nor have they been adequately recognized by policymakers. See also Campbell et al. (1965).

Information distortions in social systems

Recent indicators of system "crisis"

An alarming coincidence of signals from various indicators suggest that fundamental changes have occurred during the past decade. Disciplinary specialization has allowed certain trends to be observed, but there has been all too little interdisciplinary concern with what they may mean from a societal perspective.

Sociologists have drawn attention to a classic theme in their discipline, "social organization," which conventionally includes indicators of divorce, crime, and industrial strife. Divorce rates in both the United States and Europe have shown dramatic increase, almost doubling between 1965 and 1975 in the United States and more than tripling in countries such as the United Kingdom and the Netherlands during the same period. A recent study of crime in the United States revealed that it "has grown at a rapid rate in all U.S. cities regardless of their size, location, minority populations or whether they are gaining or losing population."[3] Crime statistics in European countries reveal similar trends, nearly doubling during the decade of the 1970's. The first half of the 1970's also "saw a general increase of labor disputes everywhere... across the whole of Europe" (Flora, 1981, p. 379).

Political scientists have independently expressed a growing concern with the problem of society's "ungovernability" and the emergence of new forms of political participation. Indices of "trust in government" have plummeted over the past fifteen years. As Table 2.1 indicates, survey response indexes reflecting trust in the U.S. federal government fell from a value of 55 in 1964 to a value of −39 in 1978.[4] Similarly, indicators representing the perception of citizens' perception of honesty in government declined dramatically, while there was a growing perception that the government was run by "big interests" rather than for the benefit of the public as a whole.

European indicators tell a similar story. Governing majorities in most European democracies dwindled steadily during the 1970's. From 1949 to 1972, the average share of parliamentary seats held by the governing coalition in twelve European countries was 59 percent and never fell below 55 percent. Yet from 1972 to 1976, the average share fell just below 50 percent (Flora, 1981).

---

[3] A report in the *International Herald Tribune* (March 3, 1982) of a study by Herbert Jacob and Robert L. Lineberry of Northwestern University. Ten cities were studied in depth, and 396 cities over 50,000 were studied for selected variables.

[4] *American National Election Studies Sourcebook 1952–78*, University of Michigan Survey Research Center: Ann Arbor, Michigan.

ROBERT R. ALFORD AND EDGAR L. FEIGE

Table 2.1. *Trust in federal government index*

Year	PDI[a]
1958	50
1964	55
1966	34
1968	25
1970	9
1972	8
1974	−26
1976	−30
1978	−39

[a] PDI refers to the proportion answering "always or most of the time" minus the proportion answering "some or none of the time" to the question relating to trust in the federal government.
Source: American National Election Studies Data Sourcebook, 1952–78 (University of Michigan Survey Research Center), p. 257. For a detailed review of many surveys reporting the same general trend, see Lipset and Schneider (1983).

Similar patterns of widespread malaise in Western democracies have been reflected in economic indicators: slowed growth rates in real income, declining trends in productivity, substantially higher levels of unemployment, and inexplicably high rates of inflation. These signals have encouraged a general concern with an "economic crisis." Simultaneously, and we believe not unrelated, there is evidence of declining compliance with existing tax regulations, a growth in what has been described as the "underground," or "unobserved," economy (Feige, 1980) and the associated development of alternative forms of economic organization.

Each of the disciplines has separately voiced apprehension about the apparent disintegration of the institutions it monitors, as indicated by the trends just summarized. Do these signals represent evidence of some more fundamental underlying process? Are they perhaps evidence of the manner in which economic events affect political and social behaviors and vice versa? Are we observing an explosive social system, which violates our usual assumptions of equilibrium and homeostasis? If the indicators are not objective measures of the social activities under study but are rather themselves outcomes of the system, the process that generates the indicators requires description.

Information distortions in social systems

Models of social systems and the role of information flows

Social systems are inherently so complex that any attempt to model them requires a high degree of simplification and abstraction. Disciplinary specialization has resulted in the development of models of separate components of the social system's building blocks. Thus, economists have constructed sub-system models that purport to explain economic outcomes such as income growth, inflation, and unemployment. Political scientists have modeled voting behaviors and bureaucratic decision making. Only recently have serious efforts been made to capture the critical linkages between the economy and the policy. A typical schema for a simplified political–economic system model is presented in Figure 2.1. Almost every casual arrow or feedback loop in such models assumes accurate information, whether coming to or from voters, economic policymakers, other government officials, or firms (Hibbs and Fassbinder, 1981).

Systems of the type displayed in Figure 2.1 are equilibrium models incorporating the fundamental notion of homeostasis, namely, the maintenance of critical variables within a tolerable range of limits. In such models, external shocks to the system activate either economic or political responses that return the system to an equilibrium state. Such models therefore require various control mechanisms that receive, interpret, and respond to information signals. The information signals are typically conveyed by the symbols of social indicators. Thus, in the model described in the preceding, information concerning the economy is conveyed through the indicator system of national income accounts and price and unemployment indices. These signals, insofar as they affect mass political support, will be transformed into other information signals representing voter preferences that are again captured in the symbols of social indicators that influence the decisions and policies of government.[5]

Virtually all policy implementation assumes that the signals from the information network operate effectively, providing social indicators that contain approximately correct information. Our contention is that this latter assumption is likely to be incorrect under a wide range of circumstances. Indeed, we wish to argue that the information content of social indicators is likely to become distorted by the very operation of

[5] In some instances, economic indicators immediately trigger policy reactions, as in the case of "automatic stabilizers." Here, pre-existing rules short cut the discretionary government decision network in order to eliminate the lagged response of the political process. Indexation of wages and salaries to price indexes, nominal tax schedules, unemployment benefits, and indexed social payments are obvious examples.

ROBERT R. ALFORD AND EDGAR L. FEIGE

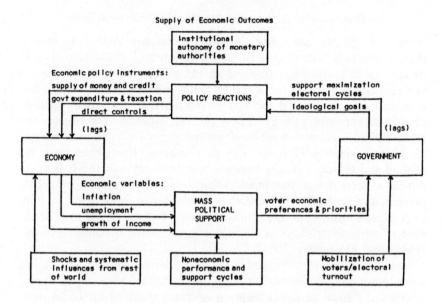

Figure 2.1. Typical model of political–economic system. (*Source:* Hibbs and Fassbinder, 1981, p. 4.)

the economic, social, and political institutions they seek to describe. We shall argue that the more important a social indicator becomes as a signaling device for public policy responses, the more likely it is that the indicator itself will degenerate as a descriptive measure of the behavior of the social system. Moreover if this degeneration of information content is not perceived by decision makers, or if they are unable to do anything about it, the social system itself may become highly unstable.[6]

Observer–subject–policymaker feedback

In order to gain insight into the nature of an information system that relies on social indicators, we must first examine the institutional requirements for the production of social indicators. First, there is the primary information source, the subject. A subject is typically an individual, firm, or government agency furnishing information in the form of records, or responses to questionnaires or through self-reporting.

[6] See McGee and Feige (1982). See also Feige (1981). See Gordon (1981) for a critique of one important social indicator as unreliable but for different reasons.

Information distortions in social systems

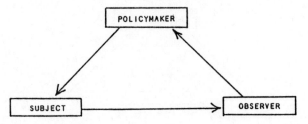

Figure 2.2. Simple information system.

Second, an institutional entity collects and aggregates the basic data reported by (or the behavior exhibited by) the subject. We call this actor the observer. Third, some institutional entity, or the policymaker, must exist to interpret and apply the data to some social policies that are relevant to specific interests.

Informational integrity of a system assumes that each of the three actors' interests and perceptions have a significant degree of autonomy such that informational transfers between the actors in the system will be relatively accurate and unbiased. This assumption justifies the dual claim of social indicators to objectivity and of public policy to rationality. Direct unbiased information flows can thus be represented by the diagram displayed in Figure 2.2.

What types of informational disturbances can induce dysfunction of such a control system? At the most trivial level, there may be a changed relationship between the underlying social phenomenon we wish to measure and the measurement instrument, which generate continual adjustments and redefinitions of social indicators such as GNP, price indices, unemployment statistics, and various survey indices. Such "improvements" in measurement often take the form of changing the domain of observation and thus change the meanings attached to former values of the indicators. If it becomes difficult to distinguish between changes in the indicators due to changes in measurement techniques and changes in the actual phenomenon being measured, appropriate interpretation and "recalibration" can become a severe problem. In developing economies, for example, improvements in the economic reporting mechanism that increase the domain of economic observation can easily be misinterpreted as representing a period of unusual growth, or takeoff.

In Figure 2.3 we represent various types of possible feedbacks between the subject, the observer, and the policymaker that are, we believe, a more accurate representation of the actual workings of the

63

ROBERT R. ALFORD AND EDGAR L. FEIGE

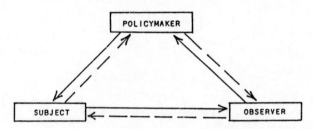

Figure 2.3. Information system with feedback loops.

information system, including the significant probability of systematic information distortion.

First, the very fact of being observed and the potential use of that information by policymakers may change both the reporting and the actual behavior of the subject. Consider, for example, the interaction between the subject and the observer. In social systems where the subject is a human being, the presence of an observer can have a major effect on both the reporting of the subject and the subject's actual behavior.[7]

The subject, the observer, and the policymaker interact in diverse ways, with multiple feedbacks of various kinds and intensities. Figure 2.3 represents a simple taxonomy of feedback possibilities. Different social indicators may be quite differently affected depending upon the source, motivation, and intensity of the feedback effect. Each feedback loop is complicated by different economic, bureaucratic, or political interests that create varying intensities of feedbacks. The degree of the feedback will be intensified where each actor has special interests in the indicator and a stake in the continuation of the feedback system itself.

Various observer–subject–policymaker feedbacks take place in different contexts. The first type of feedback takes place in a context in which the observer and policymaker are perceived by the subject as being closely interrelated. The most obvious example is reporting on tax information, where the subjects readily understand that their self-reported activities will have immediate and predictable consequences

---

[7] Such effects have been recognized in particular disciplines, and research techniques have been developed to reduce specific impacts of such feedbacks. Medical experiments consider the "placebo effect," and the important contributions of the evaluation research literature attempt to design measurement systems that minimize the corruption of the measurement instrument (Campbell, 1974). Sociology and psychology concern themselves with "unobtrusive measures" designed to minimize the effect of the observer on the subject.

Information distortions in social systems

for them. Underreporting of income, even though subject to penalties, also holds the possibility of reduced tax liabilities.

The second type of feedback arises when the roles of the subject and observer fuse, as in the case of bureaucratic performance. Here the policymaker attempts to derive information on the subject–observer with the intent of measuring performance standards. When such measures are perceived by the bureaucracy being studied as inputs to policy decisions affecting the bureaucracy itself, strong incentives arise for the falsification or non-reporting of critical information. The stronger the perceived negative consequences of accurately and completely reporting various types of information, the more likely is the possibility of false and misleading information being produced.

Relatively little attention has been directed to the implication of these feedback effects on the specification and operation of social information systems. The problem of feedback of social indicators on the system itself arises because of the simultaneous increase in both the necessity and the capacity to measure social, economic, and political behavior by economic and political institutions. Recent dramatic feedback effects may be due to the rapid development of the information system coupled with a growing awareness on the part of subjects of the consequences of their own reporting activities. Information is disseminated so rapidly and acted upon so directly that subjects, observers, and policymakers perceive their own interests are directly affected not simply by the quality of the information transmitted but by the nature of the information itself. As policymakers exercise greater control over both subjects and observers, the informational inputs required for that control are increasingly likely to be contaminated.

System effects: the unobserved economy

Although separate examples of policy feedback have been noticed in each discipline, their full social implications have not been realized, partly because of disciplinary specialization itself, partly because of the absence of a significant exemplar. Our concern is to show the pervasive character of information and policy feedbacks using the example of the growth of the unobserved economy as a way of justifying a call for interdisciplinary methodological and theoretical work.

Economists in the 1960's believed that they could control the economy with automatic stabilizers and "fine tuning," but the turbulent decade of the 1970's witnessed the failure of central predictions of macroeconomic models. The growing disparity between the theoretical predictions of economics and actual macroeconomic trends constitute a

ROBERT R. ALFORD AND EDGAR L. FEIGE

series of anomalies the theoretical models of economics cannot adequately explain. Ad hoc explanations range from "supply shocks" (Peruvian anchovy harvest failures and the formation of the OPEC oil cartel) to the failure of central banks to implement the policies of monetarists. It is ironic that at the time when information systems may have become most vulnerable to distortion, economic theorists have explained away the impotence of government policies with "rational expectations" hypotheses.

Statistics used to measure and explain these trends are informational inputs for both discretionary government policies and the "thermostatic" controls for the fiscal systems linked to policy. They require accuracy, yet reflect only the activities in the observed sector of the economy: income, consumption, investment and savings, prices, and unemployment. Any systematic discrepancy between the social indicators and the economic activity they purport to measure will generate serious errors of policy. Recent research suggests that systematic biases associated with a large and growing sector of unrecorded economy activity have been introduced into the system of social indicators.[8] The unobserved sector escapes the social measurement apparatus because of accounting conventions, non-reporting, or underreporting. It includes both market and non-market exchanges that utilize money and also barter in both legal and illegal economic activities.

The observer–subject–policymaker feedback mechanism can be illustrated in the context of the unobserved economy by regarding government data collection as the *observer* and individuals and firms as the *subjects* who volunteer information through the vehicles of surveys, or self-reporting. Subjects perceive the observer as an agent of a government that taxes, regulates, subsidizes, and transfers resources, thereby creating both disincentives to report honestly and incentives to underreport incomes, expenditures, and employment. Potential exposure or detection is reduced by "skimming," false invoicing, and going off the books. Subjects are also likely to shift from taxed and regulated activities toward non-market and "do-it-yourself" activities, enhancing eligibility for subsidies and transfer payments.

The policy consequences may be drastic. Consider an economy whose total economic activity grows at some normal rate, whatever that might be, but whose unobserved sector grows faster than the observed sector due to shifts from the latter to the former. The causes for such shifts may

---

[8] For example, the Bureau of Economic Analysis (Parker, 1984) has recently incorporated an improved adjustment for tax source misreporting in 1977 amounting to $81.5 billion for charges against GNP and a $69.3 billion adjustment for personal income.

Information distortions in social systems

be increased tax burdens, increased costs of regulatory compliance, or simply a general erosion of trust in government. As the observed sector activity becomes a smaller fraction of total economic activity, income statistics will display a reduced growth, falsely signalling the onset of a recession. This impression will be reinforced as unemployment figures are bloated by workers who shift to off-the-books activities but claim unemployment insurance benefits. At the same time, consumer price indices will *overstate* the true price level. Price statistics are gathered exclusively from the observed sector. They do not reflect the lower prices potentially available in the unobserved sector.

Lower growth, higher unemployment, and lower productivity induce both direct and indirect governmental actions that stimulate expenditures and transfers. Higher price indices via indexation induce higher wages, social security benefits, and retirement pay. They also stimulate inflationary expectations that themselves bring on real inflation. Thus, traditional economic theory and common sense tell us that what may begin as a statistical illusion is soon transformed into an unpleasant reality. Nor does the story end here. Higher prices push people into higher marginal tax brackets, thereby increasing real tax burdens. This in turn will induce further shifts into the unobserved sector, and the cycle begins anew. When the tax base shrinks at the very time that government expenditures increase, government deficits grow, requiring higher interest rates to attract funds to finance the deficit and to compensate lenders for higher expected inflation. In market economies, exchange rates will be affected as well as the balance of payments. As citizens begin to perceive that governmental actions are exacerbating the economic disturbances, trust in government declines and compliance is further reduced. This feedback process has no invisible hand to wave it back to stability because the corrective mechanisms are flawed.

This picture is one of a growing economy that exhibits symptoms of stagflation solely as a result of a statistical artifact. The economic patient is healthy, but the social thermometer has gone awry.

This analysis is supported by empirical evidence that there is, in fact, a substantial and growing unobserved sector. Studies of the United States, Canada, Italy, Germany, and the United Kingdom suggest that the monetary unobserved economy ranges between 5 and 25 percent of the observed income.

As illustrated by Figure 2.4, the unobserved sector in the United States and United Kingdom has grown dramatically during the 1970's, a growth corresponding to the onset of major perceived economic difficulties.

The usefulness of the unobserved economy exemplar is that it con-

ROBERT R. ALFORD AND EDGAR L. FEIGE

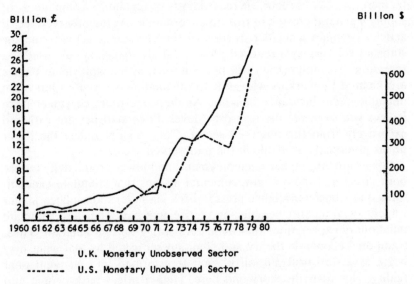

Figure 2.4. Estimates of the U.K. and U.S. unobserved monetary sector, 1960–79.
(*Source:* Adapted from Feige, 1981.)

ceptually illustrates the various types of information feedbacks displayed in Figure 2.3. Conventional models of the political–economic
process allow for one set of important interactions between the political
and economic systems, but such models are incorrectly predicated on
the assumption that information flows are unaffected by these interactions. The unobserved economy example illustrates how the *information
system* itself can become contaminated in such a way as to produce
misleading social indicators and, consequently, misguided actions on the
part of citizens and policymakers alike.

Political implications of the unobserved income hypothesis

The hypothesis that there exists a large and growing unobserved economy partially explains some of the paradoxical anomalies that confront
the economics profession. It might equally serve to shed light on some
of the empirical anomalies in the political science literature. Citing
the Michigan Survey Research Center findings, McCracken (1973) has
noted: The striking feature of responses, however, is the extent to which
there is substantially more optimism reflected in people's view generally
about their own economic situation than in their views about the economic and political environment. If individual participation in unob-

Information distortions in social systems

served economic activities is not reflected in broad social indicators of economic activity, this presents a possible explanation for the discrepancy between the perception of the general economic situation and the individual's personal economic situation. What is particularly paradoxical, however, is that aggregate economic indicators appear to affect political popularity to a much greater extent than individuals' perceptions of their own economic situation. Fiorina reveals that "previous micro level research has found weak and inconsistent effects of personally experienced economic conditions" (1981). Whereas Frey claims that "actual data on economic conditions as collected and published by statistical offices perform very well in popularity functions...Among perceived economic indicators, those referring to general economic conditions perform better than those referring to the respondent's own economic conditions" (Frey and Schneider, 1981).

The empirical findings suggest that individuals evaluate their own economic conditions more optimistically than they do general economic conditions but rely on economic indicators rather than their personal experiences in their voting decisions. But the publicity given to economic indicators may override individually perceived economic conditions as a factor influencing political responses.[9] This possibility suggests not only that social indicators produce wrong signals but more ominously that citizens use false information in their political and economic decision making. This hypothesis would help to explain the decline in trust in government and unduly pessimistic economic expectations. If political and economic behaviors are shaped not by individual life cycle experience (Wilensky, 1981) but more importantly by social indicators signalling information at odds with individual experience, then we must seriously reassess the foundations of "rational" decision making in both the economic and political domains.[10]

The observer: professional and bureaucratic performance

The simple information model assumes that both the observer and the policymaker are separate and disinterested actors. In fact, both are

[9] Lipset and Schneider (1983) summarize recent research that found "people's assessment of their own personal well-being remains high, even while their confidence in institutions and their optimism about the country as a whole is deteriorating" (p. 402). Lipset and Schneider, however, accept the basic validity of economic indicators of unemployment, inflation, and productivity, using them to interpret survey data on the steady loss of popular confidence in American institutions (p. 407).

[10] The standard economics view is expressed well by Arrow (1951), who assumes that "individual values are taken as data and are not capable of being altered by the nature of the decision process itself." He asserts that this is a "standard view" in economic theory. Clearly, that assumption must be questioned.

ROBERT R. ALFORD AND EDGAR L. FEIGE

diverse and have interests of their own that affect the measurement of social indicators and their translation into public policy. For example, attempts by observers (professional bureaucrats, social scientists, and government agencies responsible for gathering and aggregating data,) to measure bureaucratic performance may distort the behavior of the subject. Attempts to gather information at the "top" of an organization about the performance of subordinate officials changes the behavior and activities of those below. Subordinates try to evade observation and to shift behavior toward creditable and rewarded activities. Similarly, bureaucratic units either shift their behavior toward measurable activities that create the appearance of serving organizational goals or face immediate sanctions: budget and personnel cuts, denial of necessary resources, reorganization, or even termination.

Moreover, "hard" indicators of performance (dollars spent, buildings built, employees hired) may only be imperfectly related to the legitimate goal of the agency. This behavior is reinforced by value-added measures of government production that assume dollars spent is an indication of contribution to social welfare by the state.[11]

Another instance of feedback in measures of bureaucratic performance is the innovation of plea bargaining in courts. This was an organizational adaptation by police departments to the bureaucratic and political requirement of increasing their ratio of solved to unsolved crimes: the "clearance rate." This measure provided an incentive to change the behavior of subjects – criminals and the police. Criminals who confessed to more crimes got leverage with the police to recommend a lower sentence. As a result, the clearance rates were themselves affected. Public policy dealing with the causes of crime and the management of the courts could be affected by the fictitious inflation of the proportion of "solved" crimes, resulting from the creation of a performance indicator (Skolnick, 1966, Chapter 8).

None of these examples question the integrity of bureaucratic officials. On the contrary, our argument rests on the assumption that officials are professionals who act neutrally to further organizational goals, among which is the valid purpose of protecting the jurisdictions set up by legitimate legislative decisions. Public programs and agencies are given organizational autonomy in order to allow accountability, in-

---

[11] A pertinent discussion of the problem of "contaminated" data in the reports of bureaucratic agencies, particular data likely to be used in assessing performance in budgetary review, appears in Hood and Dunsire (1981, pp. 28–36). Although they do not let the ambiguities of the data interfere with systematic empirical analysis, one of their main points is that there is almost no way in which even to define a "department" because information on staffing, budgets, jurisdictions, programs, and legal authority are almost impossible to discover and correlate with each other.

70

Information distortions in social systems

cluding the capacity to measure effective performance. If officials were given less autonomy, measurable indicators of performance would be even more difficult to devise because the organizational boundaries of accountable behavior could not be defined clearly, either for legal or political surveillance. This is an intrinsic dilemma in the development of social indicators of organizational performance. The basic point is that the internal incentives within bureaucracies are not likely to lead to a search for the best economic indicators.

Many of the features of the actor we have called the observer are analyzed in the literature called "evaluation research." Crime statistics and plea bargaining are only two examples of topics upon which evaluation research has been conducted. Whereas many works of this type have real value, they are still subject to the distortions inherent in disciplinary specialization and dependence upon quantitative indicators. For example, with the shift in educational resources toward the hard sciences and away from the social sciences and humanities, social scientists increasingly feel the need to publish articles that have some kind of quantitative data and statistical techniques of analysis. Looking too deeply into the presuppositions underlying the generation of the data will result in delay at best or at worst in failure to be able to publish at all.[12] Considerable incentives are created to accept readily available "databank" sources of information and to analyze them in a manner that generates statistically significant results (Feige, 1975).

The policymaker: elite responses to political participation

Analogous processes of observer–subject–policymaker feedback in both political institutions and public bureaucracies exacerbate the difficulties of dealing with the consequences of a large and growing unobserved economy. The incentives governing the behavior of bureaucrats and legislators make it difficult for them to discover and to act upon the deficiencies of core economic indicators. The conventional indicators used by policymakers to assess public opinion and preferences tend to be either surveys or elections results. Both are likely to be afflicted with the equivalent of non-response and sampling biases, which reduce both

---

[12] A recent example from some of the best and most careful work in political science shows that the assumption that the basic data on national income, employment, and the size of the public sector are basically accurate is simply taken for granted and does not even require discussion. If the bias introduced by observer–subject–policymaker feedback varies systematically with some of the dependent and independent variables, the conclusions may be seriously affected, but it is beyond our scope to speculate on how. See Cameron (1978, pp. 1243–61).

ROBERT R. ALFORD AND EDGAR L. FEIGE

the adequacy of the data and the potential capacity for recognizing the biases.[13]

The assumption of the simple information model is that policymakers want objective data from the bureaucracy, want objective feedback, and have no interests of their own except to register public preferences and produce effective public policy that will maintain social order and further economic growth. But here, again, the simple element we have labeled the policymaker is in fact a complex coalition of political and administrative elites with their own electoral and career interests. In some cases political elites do not want accurate data. Having direct and documented access to the "facts" closes the escape hatch of "plausible deniability" so popular in the Nixon administration and with corporate executives who did not want to know, for example, about the bribery of officials in foreign countries.

Similarly, the process of establishing a program or agency by a legislature or other policymaking body is not a disinterested act. Frequently, politicians create programs and their bureaucracies as a symbolic response to public pressure but do not give those programs enough resources and authority to do their mandated job. They can argue in the electoral arena that they have been responsive and responsible by creating a program and deserve to be rewarded in the next election. By establishing the bureaucracy, politicians have simultaneously escaped responsibility, since inefficiencies can be blamed on an agency outside their control, but they have earned political credit as responsible policymakers.

The relevant point here is that neither professional politicians nor bureaucrats have a stake in accurate social indicators. The multiple feedbacks that generate the consequences we have outlined are a system problem. No individual and no political or governmental institution is in a position to correct them because of *their* own structural interests.

The non-response problem

Political elites normally assume that the non-respondents to surveys are not significant. Interested citizens will respond, and a lack of response is tantamount to satisfaction or to an inability or unwillingness to act. In either case there is no political threat.

[13] A pioneer sociological essay defending the possibility of rational social policy based on valid "social indicators" (Bell, 1973) contains absolutely no discussion of the validity of the data or the possibility of contamination and distortion of the fundamental information by observer–subject feedback. Yet the entire argument assumes without any question the possibility of gathering valid data about social and economic trends.

Information distortions in social systems

The problem is analogous both for elites and for social science estimates of the probable attitudes and behavior of non-respondents. In many economic surveys in the United States and in Europe, the non-response rate is 25–40 percent on survey questions. Typically, the way this is handled is to assume that the responses of non-respondents would have been the same as those of respondents with the same demographic characteristics.

In more refined work, respondents' demographic characteristics are compared to known population values in order to assign more informed values to the imputations required for non-respondents. However, this solution is insufficient when there is reason to believe that non-respondents with typical demographic characteristics nevertheless engage in fundamentally different behavior than respondents. In the case of illegal or quasi-legal activity, this presumption seems highly plausible. To date, there is no solution to this problem, but recognizing its existence explains in part the discrepancy between estimates of unobserved activities based on survey methods as opposed to indirect macromethods since the survey suffers more from the non-response bias.

However, if the non-response is not an accident but a volitional act, then any particular non-respondent is likely to be someone who has something at stake, necessarily disqualifying them as "uninterested" citizens. Traditional methods of dealing with omitted information of this type are flawed. They are incapable of accounting for the self-selection of non-respondents, nor can they assess the degree of bias in the answers of respondents.[14]

Similar problems plague the construction of other economic indicators, most notably national accounts, which rely on survey data for estimates of income and expenditures.[15] In each case, non-respondence is at least partly a result of observer–subject–policymaker feedback. Non-response and underreporting of incomes and expenditures represent biases introduced into social indicators as a direct result of actions by subjects motivated by their perception that observers and policymakers can regulate, tax, or otherwise influence their behavior as a consequence of reporting requirements.

[14] The problem of non-response has become one of the major issues in recent econometric literature, and some important new techniques are being developed to deal with the problem. See Heckman (1979). The issue is important not only for voting behavior, but is perhaps even more salient for research being undertaken to measure the size of the unobserved economy by survey methods. In general, survey techniques yield estimates of unobserved economic activity well below those derived from indirect macromethods.

[15] For example, in the current population survey data base, family non-response rates on questions pertaining to income increased from 14 percent in 1970 to 26 percent by 1976. See Feige (1980, p. 35).

ROBERT R. ALFORD AND EDGAR L. FEIGE

Information–behavior feedback

In political science it is recognized that public opinion polls change opinion both at the point of reporting opinion and after the feedback to the public about what "most people think." People tend to give what they think will be the most effective or the most legitimate response. In the case of political party support, if a party is rising in the polls, it will attract more support because it is perceived as a potential winner. If it is seen as losing (other things being equal, of course), the process of decline will be accelerated. Thus, the observation and reporting of public opinion feeds back on public opinion itself. The reporting of public opinion on whether a party is likely to win or a program is popular also affects decisions of political leaders concerning strategy, media reporting, and policy. In turn, their actions either reinforce or undermine the actions of key opinion-making elites. This phenomenon has assumed greater importance with the highly visible actions of political leaders and the practically instant feedback of public opinion measures back to the public itself.[16]

However, political institutions function as if public opinion is a valid measure of what people want and how they are likely to behave in elections. Institutional arrangements only allow public opinion to be expressed and responded to in certain ways. Expressions of preferences and political demands are channeled through interest groups and parties. In a political context in which parties have become weakened both because of loss of a solid base in party identification and because of the increasing power of interest groups to maintain direct access to policy-makers, quicker feedback of opinion via the media may reduce the capacity of public opinion to discipline political leaders *if* it is seen by leaders as subject to manipulation.[17] However, regardless of the direction of causality, if public opinion is shaped by erroneous economic

---

[16] In partial response to this problem, France allows no polling one week prior to the election.

[17] Key, a political scientist, in his seminal study of American public opinion (1961), discussed "linkages" and "feedback" but did not consider the possibility of observer–subject feedback. Basically, his concept of feedback consisted of the idea of the mutual influence of political leaders attempting to "mold public opinion toward support of (government) programs and politics" (p. 422) and of the "flow of influence to as well as from the government" by public preferences (p. 423). Key's subtle analysis of the multiple and interrelated impacts of government decisions upon public opinion is an elaborate version of a mechanical control model of information. He says, for example, that "the opinion context...may be regarded as a negative factor; it fixes the limitations within which action may be taken but does not assure that action will be taken" (p. 424).

74

Information distortions in social systems

indicators, whatever impact it has upon governmental decision making will be distorted.

"Unobserved politics": social movements

Another example is a political analog to the economy. Political elites, similar to economic elites, "measure" political activity by yardsticks drawn from conventional institutionalized procedures. Just as economic activity is reported by surveys and various direct measures of economic activity, so political activity is "reported" via voting and related legitimate mechanisms of political participation. Policy is based on the assumption that the entire electorate is "counted" in the composition and policies of the coalition constituting the government at any given time. Just as the measure of GNP assumes that all significant economic activity has been measured, so reports of voting behavior assume that all significant political opinion and activity is ultimately registered in the ballot box.

The formation of an effective governing coalition fails if the main reason for a large amount of non-voting is alienation, not satisfaction, and if non-voters have a capacity and a readiness to re-enter the political system in non-institutionalized forms of social movements that are not "registered" except as illegal and disruptive behavior.

The political analog to the unobserved economy is therefore the development of unobserved politics, the unhinging of individual political participation from the traditional apparatus of democratic representation: elections, parties, and legislatures. Temporary one-issue movements, social movements around new issues – recently feminism, environmentalism, anti-abortion, the nuclear freeze – become the expression of political consciousness. Such movements are based upon fluid political identities and do not rely upon traditional political symbolism to generate support. Traditional symbols of party loyalty (i.e., Democrat and Republican) no longer tie an individual to a party or even to a government identified with a stable political ideology and policy commitments. The prevalence of incremental policies attempting to remove the ideological, Left–Right dimension from politics has reduced the proportion of the electorate identifying with a party viewed as representing their interests.

The greater interdependence of economic and political institutions is not matched by an integration of the bulk of the population into those institutions. On the contrary, just as an increasing fraction of economic activity is not accurately measured by the indicators that shape policy, an increasing fraction of political activity is not taken into account by the

ROBERT R. ALFORD AND EDGAR L. FEIGE

institutionalized measures of participation. Whether some of this non-institutionalized political behavior is a response to the perceived "costs" of conventional reported behavior is an important question, as is the issue of the extent to which the general loss of trust in social and political institutions leads to unobserved political movements. Or, political behavior that is not "measured" by established political institutions may simply make it more difficult for policymakers to deal with the consequences of the unobserved economy.

Failure of disciplinary specialization and institutional interdependence

The consequences of observer–subject–policymaker feedback are further exacerbated by the difficulty of an integrated theoretical and empirical attack upon the problem. Specialization in the social sciences is based upon the assumption that there are relatively autonomous clusters of causes and consequences conventionally labeled the "economy," the "political system," the "social structure," or the "culture." The fundamental assumption about the nature of modernizing societies within which these disciplines developed and that justified the specialization in the first place is that institutions become differentiated to serve specialized functions. It is assumed that causal sub-systems define a scientific object (a "field") and become the focus for disciplines studying the economic, political, or social factors, behaviors, and institutions.[18]

Such overall differentiation was historically seen as a positive and progressive trend linked to economic growth, individual freedom, increasing education, and social mobility, increasing political participation. "Dysfunctions" were indeed recognized – the decline of traditional bases of social solidarity and the loss of older forms of social control over behavior – but these dysfunctions were seen as temporary, as lags, as problems to be solved, partly with the aid of the specialized social sciences. If they were confined within a given institutional realm, they could be compensated for, either by further differentiation to mute the structural strains or by one institution "stepping in" to restore equilibrium resulting from the malfunctioning of another.

"Slack" in the total system was seen as allowing a considerable

---

[18] Conventional work both in political science and in Marxist political economy take the rational capacity of the state to make policy, and specifically its capacity to gather accurate economic data, simply for granted. A critique of this literature from a philosophic standpoint is Connolly (1981), who argues that both Marxist economists and mainstream political scientists "underplay...the extent to which citizens... quietly obstruct the performance of the political economy." (p. 136).

Information distortions in social systems

amount of "error" in any one institution or sub-system. Public opinion would act as a corrective mechanism, disciplining political leaders. The economy could function with minimum regulation. The state would mainly protect the institutions of markets and production and mediate social conflicts. Communities and families would be subject to the impact of economic growth and decline, but the state would step in if necessary to provide basic welfare subsistence. Each social science field assumed that the institutions in the intellectual jurisdiction of the *other* fields functioned normally and did not have to be considered in their own specialized analyses.

The consequences of information distortion

Even in some theoretical monographs that consider feedback as a system problem, the consequences for the accuracy of data are not considered.[19] The examples we have given are separate illustrations of observer–subject–policymaker feedback in economic activity, public opinion, and bureaucratic performances. Their combined effects are impossible to understand within any single disciplinary perspective.

This point must be stressed. Each institution involved with the social measurement of economic activity, public opinion, and bureaucratic performance must rely upon, must assume, and is even a *product* of social measurement. These institutions are based upon the premise that there are (within reasonable ranges of error) objective ways of measuring how much income people earn, whether they are working, and what they want from government. If multiple feedbacks exist, then the problem of valid social measurement and the search for an analytic framework that can comprehend them is compounded.

Observer–subject–policymaker feedback in the realms of public opinion, organizational performance, and economic activity are closely related. Analyses of them cannot assume that they are independent. If social indicators of public opinion, the performance capacity of state agencies, and GNP are simultaneously distorted in ways that are connected, obviously some serious problems exist. These problems are hardly even recognized by social science analysts and policymakers alike because they are perceived within specialized disciplinary frameworks and not captured by the established machinery of social measurement.

Some might argue that the unobserved economy constitutes a safety

---

[19] Despite the importance of the concept of feedback in the pioneering work by Deutsch (1966), he does not consider the possibility of systematic contamination of the basic data by the processes we have defined as observer–subject–policymaker feedback.

ROBERT R. ALFORD AND EDGAR L. FEIGE

valve. People can opt out of the observed economy to find employment in the unobserved one, and this provides flexibility and increased options. But this view takes no account of the cumulative social psychology of this behavior. If people begin to act in ways that are contrary to law or are no longer subject to social constraints, even if the economic implications in the short run are healthy, in the longer run the bases of social order may be eroded. Although the sheer burden of taxes and regulation may partly explain the growth of the unobserved economy, as most economists would argue, the erosion of "trust in government" is also important (Feige, 1980). Political and social alienation is becoming apparent with the decline of party identification and the erosion of governing majorities. When political alienation interacts with economic incentives, threshold tolerances of social cohesion may be reached.

State policymakers are under multiple pressures from powerful interests groups, from the general need to keep the economy productive, and from the need to legitimize the system by democratic procedures that allow mass participation. One important manifestation of breakdown may be an inability to develop internally rational procedures for gathering accurate social measurements.

Conclusions

Because part of our argument is based upon data derived from social indicators and another part is a critique of their validity, we have to be especially clear about what is real and what is not. Not all of the social indicators that have exploded in the 1970's are illusory fictions. On the contrary, the expansion of the unobserved economy may indeed be linked to larger political problems of "social disorganization" and "political ungovernability" as conventionally described. The indicators behind those labels refer to real trends. Crime and divorce rates have climbed in Western societies. Identification with major parties has indeed dropped, as has the stability of ruling political coalitions. The trends are real, although their meaning, causes, and consequences remain obscure. The reality of these trends may be linked to the growth of the unobserved economy. The conceptual elaboration of the problem of observer–subject–policymaker feedback is intended to point toward a general hypothesis about the apparent anomalies in the key empirical indicators central to the social sciences.

One result of observer–subject–policymaker feedback is to distort the social indicators and instead signal the onset of economic crisis. What is ominous about this possibility is that the empirical evidence

Information distortions in social systems

from political science appears to support the view that the distorted social indicators also influence political decision making. If true, an initial statistical illusion will become actual political and economic malaise. *Rational individuals* are basing decisions on *irrational information*. Thus, the evidence of economic, social, and political "crises" may well reflect in part a flaw in the information system, which itself is structurally generated.

The introduction of quantitative data and the statistical techniques has given rise to cliometrics, sociometrics, and econometrics. The *T*-statistics, regression analyses, and path analyses replaced literary and qualitative descriptions of social behavior and institutions, embodied in the quantitatively unsupported theories of Marx, Adam Smith, Weber, and de Tocqueville. It is time to ask new questions about the quality of our quantitative evidence as opposed to simply further manipulating the same kind of evidence. In economics, this means making inquiries into the implications of rational behavior based on "irrational" information. The question can be extended to the other specialized social science disciplines with particular ramifications for both public policy and research design, especially evaluation research.

What is required is a reevaluation of our fundamental data bases in the light of an assumption of observer–subject–policymaker feedback. The concept of a society as a whole composed of sub-systems with feedbacks would broaden the scope of theoretical conceptions of problems and the relevant data. We wish to restore the role of the generalist as legitimate and thus the importance of multiple types of legitimate information and evidence without denying the role of the specialist. In fact, the immediate and dramatic exemplar of the unobserved economy suggests the possibility that specialists in different areas may resolve to pursue these issues in their own disciplines and develop interdisciplinary strategies to understand them. Our rough effort to put together pieces of an interdisciplinary puzzle has relied upon the insights and the data developed by the specialized disciplines. Separately, these pieces are necessary but not sufficient to analyze the increasingly complex social system in which rapid changes are generating forms of economic, social, and political behaviors that escape traditional modes of measurement. Information is central to an understanding of complex social systems. With equal force, we must come to recognize that knowledge of the social system is required for the understanding of our own information base.

79

References

Arrow, K. J. 1951. *Social Choice and Individual Value*. Wiley, New York.

Bell, D. 1973. *The Coming of Post Industrial Society*. Basic Books, New York.

Boulding, K. E. 1971. *Collected Papers* (F. Glahe, Ed.). Colorado Associated University Press, Boulder.

Cameron, D. R. 1978. "The Expansion of the Public Economy: A Comparative Analysis." *American Political Science Review* 72: 1243–61.

Campbell, D. T. 1974. "Assessing the Impact of Planned Social Change." Dartmouth/OECD Seminar on Social Research Public Policies, September.

Campbell, D. T., et al. 1965. *Unobtrusive Measures*. Rand McNally, Chicago.

Connolly, W. 1981. *Appearance and Reality in Politics*. Cambridge University Press, Cambridge.

Deutsch, K. W. 1966. *The Nerves of Government, Model of Political Communication and Control*. Free Press, New York.

Feige, E. L. 1975. "The Consequences of Journal Editorial Policies and a Suggestion for Revision." *Journal of Political Economy*. (December): 1291–5.

   1980. "A New Perspective on Macroeconomic Phenomena. The Theory and Measurement of the Unobserved Sector of the United States Economy: Causes, Consequences, and Implications." Paper presented at the 1980 meetings of the American Economic Association, pp. 1–63.

   1981. "The U.K.'s Unobserved Economy: A Preliminary Assessment." *Journal of Economic Affairs* 1: 205–12.

   1982b. *Observer-Subject Feedback: The Dynamics of the Unobserved Economy*. E. J. Brill, Leiden.

Fiorina, M. 1981. "Short- and Long-term Effects of Economic Conditions on Individual Voting Decision." *Contemporary Political Economy*. (D. A. Hibbs and H. Fassbinder, Eds.). North-Holland, Amsterdam.

Flora, P. 1981. "Solution or Source of Crises? The Welfare State in Historical Perspective." *The Emergence of the Welfare State in Great Britain and Germany* (W. Mommsen, Ed.). Croom Helm, London, p. 379.

Frey, B. S. and F. Schneider, 1981. "Recent Research on Empirical Politico-economic Models." *Contemporary Political Economy* (D. A. Hibbs and F. Fassbinder, Eds.). North-Holland, Amsterdam.

Gibbs, J. C. 1979. "The Meaning of Ecologically Oriented Inquiry in Contemporary Psychology." *American Psychologist* 34(2): 127–40.

Gordon, R. J. 1981. "The Consumer Price Index: Measuring Inflation and Causing It." *The Public Interest*, No. 63, Spring.

Heckmann, J. J. 1979. "Sample Selection Bias as a Specification Error." *Econometrica* 47: 153–69.

Hibbs, D. A. and H. Fassbinder (Eds.). 1981. *Contemporary Political Economy*. North-Holland, Amsterdam.

Hood, C. and A. Dunsire. 1982. *Bureaumetrics. The Quantitative Comparison of British Central Government Agencies*. Gower, London, pp. 28–36. *International Herald Tribune*, March 3, 1982.

Key, V. O., Jr. 1961. *Public Opinion and American Democracy*. Knopf, New York.

Lipset, S. M. and W. Schneider. 1983. *The Confidence Gap*. Free Press, New York, pp. 402, 407.

McCracken, P. W. 1973. "The Practice of Political Economy." *The American Economic Review*, May, 168–171.

McGee, R. and E. L. Feige 1982a. "Policy Illusion, Macroeconomic Instability and the Unobserved Economy.' Netherlands Institute for Advanced Study, April 1982. See also Chapter 3, this volume.

Morgenstern, O. 1963. *On the Accuracy of Economic Observations*, 2nd ed. Princeton University Press, Princeton, NJ.

Parker, R. P., 1984. "Improved Adjustments for Misreporting of Tax Return Information Used to Estimate the National Income and Product Accounts, 1977." *Survey of Current Business*, 64(6): 17–25, United States Department of Commerce, Bureau of Economic Analysis.

Skolnick, J. H. 1966. *Justice without Trial: Law Enforcement in Democratic Society*. Wiley, New York, Chapter 8.

Wilensky, H. L. 1981. "Family Life Cycle, Work, and the Quality of Life: Reflections on the Roots of Happiness, Despair and Indifference in Modern Society." *Working Life: A Social Science Contribution to Work Reform* (B. Gardell and G. Johansson, Eds.), Wiley, London.

[21]

32

The Patent System

by Aubrey Silberston

TODAY, the value of invention and innovation is seldom questioned. This is a change from pre-war days. When Sir Arnold Plant wrote his classic article on patents in 1934[1], he expressed the suspicion that the patent system might be encouraging "too much invention of the wrong kind" and contributing to an "increasingly rapid rate of obsolescence of industrial equipment"—although even then, it must be admitted, Sir Arnold's views were not universally held.

Whatever may have happened to other growth-rates in recent years, that of "research and development" has been high. Investigations are made into the proportion of the national income devoted to such activities in the leading industrial countries, and both countries and individual industries are criticized for not carrying out sufficient research. A prosperous future for Britain, it is commonly said, is dependent on our keeping in the forefront of technological advance, and we now have a Ministry of Technology to set an official stamp of approval on this view. The academic study of research and development is expanding also and, in a number of universities, special units are being set up to examine the economic and social problems of research. It seems, therefore, an appropriate moment to take another look at the ancient patent system: the system under which monopoly privileges are granted to those who succeed in making technical progress of a special kind in particular fields.

This is, of course, a very big subject and in a short article it is not possible to do more than skim the surface. At the University's Department of Applied Economics in Cambridge we have been carrying out research into the patent system for a number of years, with the help of a grant from the Nuffield Foundation. The first

The author is a University Lecturer in Economics and a Fellow of St. John's College, Cambridge. He is grateful to J. Field, C. Freeman, K. D. George, G. C. Harcourt, R. C. O. Matthews, W. B. Reddaway and S. I. Levy for helpful comments on a first draft of this article.
    [1] "The Economic Theory Concerning Patents for Inventions," *Economica*, February, 1934.

33

fruits of this will be a volume on the administration of the British patent system, now in the press.[1] Work is proceeding on a further volume, devoted to an economic assessment of the system, with particular reference to this country; and a number of industrial case studies, together with a statistical investigation, are being carried out in connection with this. A good deal of further research still needs to be done, however, and for this reason the views expressed in this article on the economic effects of the patent system may well need to be revised at some future date.

THE ECONOMIC THEORY OF PATENTS

Patents embody information. Once information is produced it is what economists call a "free good"; the use of it does not diminish the stock and it cannot be appropriated by individuals. If it were sold on the open market it would at once become freely available because it can be reproduced at little or no cost. Because the cost of transmitting information is so low, the economic theory of the "optimal allocation" of resources suggests that information should be transmitted freely and without limit.

It is true that information can be kept secret, at least up to a point, but, given the fact that information is a free good, secrecy clearly leads to an inefficient allocation of resources. However, if information about inventions were made freely available as soon as it was discovered, this might give no incentive for anyone to incur the risks involved in undertaking research in order to make inventions, or to spend money on developing them. If resources are to be devoted to research, therefore, a reward for invention seems necessary. Patents are a device for ensuring that such a reward is made possible, but the higher the reward that ensues, the further we are from an optimal allocation of resources. This is why it has been said that "in an ideal socialist economy, the reward for invention would be completely separated from any charge to the users of the information.[2]" In such an economy, however, the relationship between the reward for invention and the incentive to invent would need careful consideration.

We have, therefore, a fundamental dilemma. Information is of its nature a free good, yet if a means cannot be found of rewarding

---

[1] *The British Patent System. I. Administration.* By Klaus Boehm, in collaboration with Aubrey Silberston, to be published by the Cambridge University Press in 1967.

[2] K. J. Arrow, "Welfare Economics and Inventive Activity", in *The Rate and Direction of Inventive Activity*, National Bureau of Economic Research (Princeton, 1962), p. 617. Arrow's article contains a helpful discussion of these theoretical problems.

34

those who produce information there may not be any new information to distribute. There is, clearly, a conflict here between the best allocation of resources under static conditions and the desire for improvement and growth. The patent system has been evolved in free-enterprise economies to encourage the production of new information, but the form that it has taken has been greatly influenced by a wish to make information as freely available as is compatible with the fundamental aim: to provide an incentive for invention. Proposals to abolish or to modify the patent system are nearly always motivated by a desire to produce a better balance between these conflicting aims than we have yet been able to achieve.

OUTLINE OF BRITISH PATENT SYSTEM

All major countries have patent systems, including the Soviet Union, although in the communist countries patents are mainly employed when dealing with foreigners. The British patent system differs a good deal in detail from those of other countries (although it is closely paralleled in a number of Commonwealth countries) but its main principles are universal.

Any inventor or his agent can apply for a patent to the Patent Office in London. There the claimed invention is subjected to a detailed examination by one of five hundred or so patent examiners, all men with technical qualifications. If the invention is patentable, and if it has not been anticipated in the United Kingdom in a previous patent or in a prior publication, a patent will be granted for it. The relevant legal provisions are contained in the 1949 Patents Act, where an invention is defined as "any manner of new manufacture" or "any new method or process of testing applicable to the improvement or control of manufacture" (Section 101). This definition clearly excludes basic scientific principles from the category of patentable inventions, and it has been held in the past to exclude many inventions relating to agriculture. However, as a result of the 1962 Swift case (concerned with a method of injecting animals before slaughter in order to make their meat more tender), a wider range of inventions than in the past is now coming to be regarded as being within the scope of patentable inventions as defined in the legislation.

When a patent is accepted by the Patent Office it is published within a few weeks. At this stage, therefore, the secret of the invention is disclosed to the world. However, the various processes involved in getting the patent to this stage, after it has been filed, will probably have taken an average of two to three *years*. If, on the

35

other hand, the inventor had sought patent protection in countries where no real examination is conducted—Belgium or South Africa, for example—his invention would have been published very soon after he had filed his application for patent protection. For this reason, patent specifications tend to be published earlier in Belgium than elsewhere, and the scrutiny of Belgian patents by individuals and companies, in order to gain the earliest possible knowledge of new inventions, is a thriving activity.

*　　*　　*

About 33,000 patents are now granted annually in Britain. Of all patent applications, only about 30 per cent. are made by United Kingdom residents, and the proportion (but not the absolute number) has been falling steadily for some years. Patents run for sixteen years from the date when the complete specification is filed. It is possible to file an earlier provisional specification; this affects priority but not the date from which the patent runs.

Patents lapse after their fourth year if renewal fees (which rise from £6 in the fifth year to £30 in the sixteenth year) are not paid. Most patents are not, in fact, renewed for their full sixteen years. In 1965, for example, renewal fees were paid for 11,554 patents in their tenth year, as compared with the 19,900 patents sealed in 1956, and for only 3,126 patents in their sixteenth year, as compared with the 13,500 patents sealed in 1950. The total number of patents in force on December 31st, 1965, was approximately 188,000.

*　　*　　*

The grant of a patent can be opposed by an interested party, who can also institute proceedings for revocation of a patent which has already been granted. In certain cases, the grant of a patent can be contested right up to the Court of Appeal and the House of Lords.

Once a patent has been granted, a patentee can obtain an injunction from the courts against anyone using the invention without his permission. A patentee may, if he wishes, allow others to use his invention by granting them a licence on terms mutually negotiated. The Patents Act forbids clauses in such licensing agreements which require the acquisition of articles, or prohibit the use of articles or processes, other than the patented ones. Apart from these limitations, however, licence agreements may, and often do, contain a number of restrictions: for example, on markets to be supplied, on prices to be charged, and so on.

*　　*　　*

36

Two interesting provisions of the British patents legislation, which are not found in the United States legislation, relate to compulsory licences.[1] After three years have passed from the sealing of a patent, anyone may apply for a compulsory licence if he can show that one of a number of conditions is fulfilled: for example, that the patent is not being commercially worked in the United Kingdom, or that demand for the patented article has not been met on reasonable terms, or that an export market has not been supplied (Section 37). Where inventions relating to food and medicine are concerned, anyone may apply for a compulsory licence at any time, and the Comptroller-General must grant a licence "on such terms as he thinks fit, unless it appears to him that there are good reasons for refusing the application" (Section 41). There has never been much activity under Section 37 (perhaps the threat of an application for a compulsory licence induces the granting of a voluntary licence), but in recent years the number of applications under Section 41 has been growing rapidly.

Another provision in the Patents Act which has recently attracted attention is Section 46. This lays down that any government department may use any patented invention for the services of the Crown at any time. This section was invoked in 1961 to enable the Ministry of Health to import tetracycline at low prices from Italy (where there are no patents on pharmaceuticals) for use in National Health Service hospitals. The upsurge of applications, many of them from importers, for compulsory licences under Section 41 (food and medicine) has been connected with a desire to sell drugs like tetracycline cheaply to chemists and other private purchasers without infringing the relevant British patents.

Where compulsory licences are granted, or where the government makes use of a patent for the services of the Crown, reasonable remuneration has to be paid to the patentee. It is a fair inference that this payment (which, in the last resort, may have to be settled by the courts) is likely to be less than that which the patentee would have exacted under a voluntary licence agreement.

EFFECTS OF THE PATENT SYSTEM

From one point of view, the patent system is the safeguard of the small inventor: it gives him some hope of financial gain from his invention. On the other hand, the patent system is biased against the

---

[1] Compulsory licence provisions of some sort are, however, found in the majority of countries.

37

small man, because its successful use may involve the expenditure of large sums of money. Such expenditure includes the fees to file specifications (£10 for a complete specification), to renew patents after their fourth year, and to engage patent agents (whose services are usually necessary). Above all, money may be needed to defend patents in the courts. It has been said that a patent is a "licence to sue", i.e. it gives grounds for an infringement action. But such an action is not likely to be started by a small inventor with slim financial resources.

The position of the small man under the patent system has been strengthened in recent years by the creation of such bodies as the National Research Development Corporation, set up in 1949 by the government and financed from government sources. Nevertheless, the patent system is becoming less and less concerned with inventions made by the small man. It has been estimated that, in the United States, the proportion of patents issued to corporations has risen from 18 per cent. of the total at the beginning of the century to over 60 per cent. today. In some fields—for example, chemical and electrical—the proportion of patents issued to corporations is now much higher than this. In engineering, however, the proportion of patents issued to corporations is below the average. Similarly, in the United Kingdom, patent applications from companies have risen from an estimated 15 per cent. of the total in 1913 to some 70 per cent. now. Again, applications from companies are a very high proportion of the total in the electrical and chemical fields.

It seems clear from these figures (which admittedly are impressionistic, because of the difficulties of estimation) that any assessment of the patent system today must be concerned primarily with its impact on companies rather than on individuals and, particularly, as studies of research and development expenditure have shown, with its impact on large industrial companies and other organizations which spend heavily on research. This is not, of course, to deny that the impact of the patent system on the small inventor is a matter of considerable importance, especially from the point of view of equity.

What effect, then, does the existence of the patent system have on the activities of large industrial firms and other bodies and what are the consequences, both for them and for the economy as a whole? The answer to this question can, perhaps, best be discussed under three headings: invention; development and innovation; monopolistic practices.

38

Invention

By "invention" I mean the creation of a new idea. Put more concretely, it is, under our present institutional arrangements, that stage in the development of a new process or product which may culminate in an application for a patent.

It obviously cannot be argued that, if there were no patent system, large industrial companies and other organizations such as government research establishments would not try to make inventions. A large number of industries are now subject to rapid technical change. If firms in these industries wish to be successful, obviously they must participate in this change. It is inconceivable, whether or not there is a patent system, that the leading firms in such industries would abandon the attempt to make inventions. Indeed, much research is now done by firms which seldom take out patents, preferring to rely on trade secrets or simply on being first in the field. Government and government-sponsored research would also be little affected.

In the absence of a patent system there might, of course, be some change in the *distribution* of firms carrying out research. Some of the firms which now do research, in the hope of obtaining patents, might be content to sit back and rely on others if they thought that they could get the benefits of their research activities without payment.

In the absence of patents, there might also be a change in the *direction* of research activity by big firms. Promising lines of research would be pursued, as now. However, at present much research is defensive, that is, it is directed to making an advance before competitors do, because it would be financially disastrous to allow them to take out all the patents in a particular field. Similarly, some research today is devoted to designing around other people's patents. Presumably, in the absence of a patent system, there would be less of these two types of research activity. It may well be, therefore, that a good deal of duplication in research would be avoided.

On the other hand, the absence of a patent system would undoubtedly lead to greater secrecy than at present. A process invention, which now might be patented, could possibly be kept secret for a very long time, although in these circumstances industrial espionage may well be stepped up. Product inventions could not be kept secret in this way, but presumably secrecy would be carefully maintained up to the stage at which the new product was launched, in the hope that rapid imitation would not occur. It may be that there would be an attempt to develop new products designed in such a way that they could not be imitated very quickly.

Greater secrecy would be likely to lead not only to a lack of publication of new technical specifications, but also to less publication of general technical information than now occurs. It might also be that firms would be more reluctant than now to sell "know-how" to other firms, since difficulties would perhaps be more likely to occur than under the present system, where "know-how" agreements are very often linked to patent licensing agreements.

*   *   *

On balance, the absence of patent protection would be likely to prevent some of the present duplication in research but, because of its encouragement to secrecy, it might well hinder the rapid spread of technical knowledge. The quality of invention might also be adversely affected because of this. Even the absence of designing around other people's patents might not be a pure gain, since this activity might, on occasion, lead to progress in unexpected directions. Duplication is not necessarily bad.

It might be argued that State rewards for inventors, as in the Soviet Union, would enable the advantages of the patent system to be retained, both as regards the encouragement of invention and the spread of knowledge, while avoiding its monopoly features. There is clearly something in this. But rewards of this sort are very difficult to assess, because of all the uncertainties involved. Also, if the rewards were at all substantial, they would encourage something like the present "race to the Patent Office" and would not, therefore, avoid duplication in research. They might, however, reduce research devoted to designing around others' patents and also defensive research.

Development and Innovation

The "development" stage comes between the making of an invention and its development to the point where commercial production is possible. It includes pilot-plant production. "Innovation" is the action of bringing an invention into commercial production, and normally involves investment in new equipment.

It is usually said that development is far more expensive than invention. An average cost ratio of ten to one has been quoted for this country and of six to one for the United States but, obviously, in any individual case the ratio may be very different from this.

40

A system of authors' certificates, which would simply reward inventors for their inventions but give them no monopoly of their exploitation, would clearly offer no incentive for the expenditure of large sums of money on development or—*a fortiori*—on innovation. There is no doubt that, in the absence of a patent system, firms would continue to pursue development and innovation in "certainties". However, it seems probable that they would be less likely than at present to take risks with inventions whose commercial possibilities were doubtful. Under the present system, patent protection ensures that expensive and risky development will carry with it monopoly advantages if it is successful. In the absence of patent protection, firms might well avoid risky development since, even if success were achieved, the fruits might have to be shared with other firms which were capable of speedy imitation.

In spite of the doubts on this score expressed by Sir Arnold Plant, it seems to me that the protection given to the development and innovation of expensive and risky inventions is one of the main economic justifications for the patent system. It could, of course, be argued that risks are an inherent part of business life, and that there is no need to give a special bonus to risks of the sort that we have been discussing. Even so, given all the uncertainties, the long gestation period of many inventions—for example, the hovercraft—and the great potential benefits that may result from them, there is clearly much to be said for providing some special encouragement for this type of activity.

It does not follow that the only way in which special encouragement can be given is through our present system. A system of authors' certificates could be compatible with the protection of development and innovation if the State, after rewarding the inventor, granted the right to exploit his invention either to a small number of firms or to one of them. Such a system, however, would bear a considerable resemblance to our present system, as it would confer monopoly privileges on those firms which were given the right to exploit the invention.

Monopolistic practices

Much of the discontent that has been expressed with the present system is bound up with allegations that the monopoly privileges that it grants have been abused. It is undoubtedly true that many practices of a restrictive character have grown up in connection with the patent system. Most of these practices are legal and in this country do not run foul of our present laws concerning

41

monopoly and restrictive practices. Nevertheless, they undoubtedly strengthen the monopolistic character of the patent system.

These practices have been investigated more fully in the United States than in this country. Corwin Edwards, for example, discussed them in his book *Maintaining Competition*, and the U.S. Congress has recently carried out extensive studies through the Sub-Committee on Patents, Trademarks and Copyrights of the Senate Committee on the Judiciary. Corwin Edwards' view is that "the patent system has become a device through which the verbal facility and negotiating skill of lawyers may be rewarded by grants of monopoly running appreciably further than would be necessary to recognize the contributions of inventors" (p. 222). He cites the way in which one concern may gain control over a large number of patents, and then attempt to acquire others in order to dominate an industry, excluding competitors from the field by preventing them from using alternative processes. Even if some of these patents are weak—if, that is, they could be readily overthrown should they be challenged in courts—licensing agreements may insist on the acceptance of the validity of weak patents as a condition for the receipt of licences on strong ones. Another means whereby large firms may gain control through patents is to acquire licences on the patents of weaker firms by threatening to oppose the grant of their patents or even to petition for their revocation in the courts. The expense of such an action is often beyond the means of small firms, which feel compelled to grant the licences concerned.

Other devices with monopolistic consequences are the accumulation of patents through time—in such a way as to perpetuate the exclusive position of a company even after the original important patents have expired—and the granting of licences which impose restrictive conditions. It is also asserted, by Corwin Edwards among others, that one of the consequences of the patent system is that good inventions are kept out of use by monopolists who do not wish their existing facilities to become obsolescent.

From one point of view, the monopolistic power of patentees is reduced by the practice of patent pooling (such as occurs in the British computer industry). Such practices, however, can be made restrictive on outsiders, and in these cases the group involved in patent pooling may in effect act as a dominant monopolist.

* * *

There is, at the moment, comparatively little information available about the monopolistic effect of patent practices in the

42

United Kingdom. This is one of the areas in which we hope to carry out further research. But there can be little doubt that many of the practices found in the United States also exist in this country. Indeed, in one respect—the restrictive conditions attached to the grant of licences—the situation may be worse than in America. There, the use of licences to restrict the territories in which a good may be sold, or to impose a minimum price on the sale of goods, may, in certain circumstances, be judged illegal under the anti-trust laws. Because of this, such conditions in licences granted in the United States carry more risk than they do in this country, where there is exemption from the 1956 Restrictive Trade Practices Act (Section 8 (4)) for this kind of licence agreement.

More knowledge about exclusionary patent practices in this country is clearly desirable. One certainly cannot feel happy about our present ignorance in this sphere, or about the comparative lack of provision for investigation into possible abuses. It might perhaps be added, however, that one accusation at least—that patents may be accumulated in order that good inventions may be suppressed— does not appear to be supported by what evidence exists at present. This is not to deny, of course, that the speed with which different inventions are developed is something which varies a great deal according to competitive and other circumstances.

PROPOSALS FOR CHANGE

In the nineteenth century there was very considerable pressure for the complete abolition of the patent system. Today, this force has virtually disappeared. The patent system in its broad outlines is generally accepted and proposals for its reform are all, to some extent, peripheral. Even Professor Machlup, a trenchant critic of the patent system, concludes his study for the Sub-Committee on Patents, Trade-marks and Copyrights,[1] with the following words:

   . . . since we have had a patent system for a long time, it would be irresponsible, on the basis of our present knowledge, to recommend abolishing it. This last statement refers to a country such as the United States of America—not to a small country and not a predominantly non-industrial country, where a different weight of argument might well suggest another conclusion.

   While the student of the economics of the patent system must, pro-visionally, disqualify himself on the question of the effects of the system *as a whole* on a large industrial economy, he need not disqualify himself as a judge of proposed *changes* in the existing system. While economic analysis does not yet provide a basis for choosing between "all or nothing",

---

[1] Sub-Committee on Patents, Trade-marks and Copyrights of the Committee on the Judiciary, United States Senate, 85th Congress, Second Session, *An Ecohomic Review of the Patent System*, Study No. 15 (Washington, 1958), p. 80.

43

> it does provide a sufficiently firm basis for decisions about "a little more or a little less" of various ingredients of the patent system. Factual data of various kinds may be needed even before some of these decisions can be made with confidence. But a team of well-trained economic researchers and analysts should be able to obtain enough information to reach competent conclusions on questions of patent reform.

Would that everyone shared Professor Machlup's faith in the wisdom of well-trained economic researchers and analysts!

No doubt, one of the reasons why the attitude that the patent system ought not to be fundamentally changed is so widely held is that it is recognized that no one country could easily do away with its patent system while others retain theirs. Quite apart from the adverse effects that might follow for research and development in the country concerned, there would undoubtedly be a great deal of international unpleasantness if firms in a particular country freely borrowed inventions made overseas (as Italian drug firms do now, with acrimonious consequences). There would also be considerable difficulties in export markets if goods were exported which were based on patents held in overseas countries. In practice, international pressure is now in the direction of strengthening the patent system, rather than anything else. Ever since the late nineteenth century there has been an International Patent Convention, enabling applicants for patents in any convention country to obtain protection in any other convention country if the application is made within 12 months of the first application. There are proposals now for a European patent which would impose uniform standards of patentability on all those participating in it. Such a system, in which the United Kingdom may well take part, may differ substantially from our present system, and might possibly include a more rigorous examination than we now have.

Quite apart from anything else, the growth in the number of patent applications throughout the world is increasing the pressure for some form of international simplification. The British Comptroller-General of Patents comments, in his 1965 report, as follows:

> In the international field the general picture is one of mounting concern at the problems with which the continued increase in patent applications is facing patent offices and a growing feeling that the international nature of patents necessitates much greater co-operation and harmonisation of laws and practice in the interest of both the offices and of industry. For the moment this has not got much further than discussion but it seems likely that more concrete results will follow over the next few years, as indeed they must if the patent system is not to get into serious difficulty.

*   *   *

44

In addition to proposals for greater international co-operation, the main proposals for change that merit discussion are perhaps those for reform of licensing provisions. As an example, the British pharmaceutical industry feels that its ability to recoup heavy research expenditure from the prices charged for new drugs has been threatened in a number of ways in recent years. First, there was the use in 1961 of Section 46 of the Patents Act to import drugs from Italy for National Health Service hospitals; and then there was the upsurge of applications for compulsory licences under Section 41 (food and medicine). Many in the pharmaceutical industry would like to see Section 41 of the Patents Act repealed, leaving pharmaceuticals subject only to the ordinary compulsory licence provisions.

As opposed to this, it has been suggested that the licence provisions of the Patents Act should be altered so as to make them even more liberal and to reduce their monopolistic consequences. One possible step would be to compel all licence agreements to be registered with the Patents Office and opened to public inspection; at present the Office maintains a licence register, but it is far from complete. Another suggestion is that the difficulties placed by the Act in the way of those desiring compulsory licences under Section 37 should be removed, so that anybody wanting a licence could be readily granted one at any time on reasonable terms. Both these suggestions raise very considerable problems. If the publication of licence agreements were insisted upon, licensing agreements would be likely to become narrower in scope, and other agreements would be made to cover matters which it is desired to keep confidential. Or if, following the other suggestion, compulsory licences were made freely available, it might be very difficult to induce firms which now develop their own inventions or are granted exclusive licences to enter upon heavy capital expenditure for development.

All these questions clearly need careful thought, as do proposals for the greater application to patent matters of the laws relating to monopoly and restrictive practices. We hope that when our research at Cambridge is further advanced we shall be in a better position to throw light on this range of problems.

January, 1967   Aubrey Silberston

"The simplistic, but dangerous approach
advocated by the NCLIS Task Force
should not stop us from fully confronting the issues..."

Information Justice

A review of the NCLIS Task Force Report:
Public/Private Sector Interaction
in Providing Information Services

By Patricia Glass Schuman

GUTENBERG spent five years setting type for the Bible. Today its entire contents can be transmitted by satellite in less than one second. Whirlwind I—a pioneering computer of the 1950's—cost $5 million. A microcomputer with comparable features can be bought now for under $2000. New technologies offer unparalled opportunities for information production, management, and dissemination.

Patricia Glass Schuman, President of Neal-Schuman Publishers, Inc., has worked as a librarian in school, public, and academic libraries

Close to half the U.S. labor force is involved in some kind of information transfer. More than $50 billion is spent annually for information—telephone services, postal services, television, radio, satellite transmission, computers, books, newspapers, magazines, libraries, etc. The federal government paid over $6 million for data processing alone in 1981. Some 50 percent of the gross national product relates to the production, processing, and distribution of information; the information industries are growing more than twice as fast as the GNP.

"Information Age," "Knowledge Society," "Post-industrial Society"—the terms describing the U.S. economy's shift from a manufacturing base to an information base began to sound like tired clichés. The very real societal transformation they describe, though, is causing heightened tensions, increased debate, and some realignment between social goals and private interests. Recommendations and decisions are being made which will have far-reaching effects not only on information services, but on the quality of our lives and the future of American democracy.

The need for information, and its value to society, is not new. But the amount of information an individual requires to negotiate through complex social and economic structures—and the power of that information to determine who will do well and who will do poorly—in our society is unprecedented. Theoretically, we are surrounded by an abundance of information, but the channels for obtaining specific information are complex and confusing: television, radio, newspapers, magazines, government agencies, social service agencies, libraries, data base services, information brokers, telephone services, publishers, etc. Methods of information production and delivery often cross the line between the public and the private sectors, and the conflict between the seemingly divergent philosophies of free access and free markets is escalating.

Although technology is rapidly reducing the costs of storing, producing, and processing information, the costs of the intellectual labor to create it are rapidly rising. Some segments of society are already receiving more benefits from new technologies and information because they have both the sophistication to use them and the money to pay for them. Our information society raises constitutional, social, political, and economic issues which may force us to seek new answers to some of the old questions: Is access to information a right of every individual? If it is, how will that right be upheld? Who will bear the cost? Does the First Amendment apply to all forms of information? When do issues like privacy, confidentiality, or ownership take precedence over rights of access? What are appropriate mechanisms for which kinds of information distribution, for whom, and under what circumstances? When should—or do—the laws of the marketplace apply? Though it may be a truism that an informed citizenry is a prerequisite for a functioning democratic society, the argument about citizen rights of access to information is being intensified both by the capital investment necessary to produce it and the decline in government support of public services.

The policy problem

Merging social and economic priorities has long been a subject of debate. The question of *who* should invest *how much* in *what* information, *when* and for *whom* becomes critical in a society in which information becomes the major force. We may be very close to the reality of the technology necessary for a true information society, but as a nation we do not have an appropriate societal framework with which to handle the complexities. There have been numerous attempts to tackle elements of national information policy. The latest emanates from the National Commission on Libraries and Information Services. In 1979, it appointed a Task Force on Public/Private Sector Interaction in Providing Information Services. Its charge was to:

Identify and illustrate the types of library and information service functions that should be carried out by government or by the private sector; define and illustrate the criteria used to determine what information services should be supported by tax funds or by the marketplace; identify activities within government and the private sector which now contradict the Task Force views; and identify means and actions to be taken to correct the balance, and identify the parties, including NCLIS, that should take them.

This charge mandated a Herculean undertaking by any standard. Early on, Task Force members concluded that it was inconsistent with "the actual problems of concern" and that the assignment of functions was not the way "to guide interaction" between the sectors, since no function was the "exclusive province" of one or the other. Instead, they focused "almost solely" on federal government involvement, especially in distribution of information—directly or through the private sector. Issues relating to "private copyright, to conflicts between different private information activities, and to conflicts between the providers of information services and purchasers" were not considered, unless they involved "the government as a party in those conflicts." Issues related to technology or international data flow were not considered either. Rather than identifying current areas of conflict, the Task Force concluded that the only way it could make progress was to "limit its consideration to activities that might arise in the future," leaving the question of existing situations to be "considered on an 'ad hoc' basis."

The Task Force

The 20 members of the Task Force, according to NCLIS, were "carefully chosen to be as representative as possible of several constituencies involved." Seven members came from the private sector (a newspaper, and six information industry companies); one from a not-for-profit organization with a data base product; five people represented various government sectors; and two were former government employees. The five library community members included two library school deans (one a past ALA President, the other a well known consultant to the information industry), a library school educator, a state librarian, and the director of a private research library.

Task Force members were able to agree that "information resources, products, and services" are "vital components of our society, of our economic productivity, of our individual growth and well-being . . . Government policy should be designed to foster the development and use of information resources and to eliminate impediments to such development and use." There were, however, basic differences concerning the "proper role" of government as creator and provider of information resources and products. Much of the text of the NCLIS report focuses on this debate.

The debate

One side argued that government entry into the marketplace has a "chilling effect" on private sector investment in information services. They favored severely restricting the role of government, and instead placing total reliance on competitive market forces to provide a wide choice of information services needed by society. Members who disagreed with such restrictions pointed to the need "to ensure equitable, open access by the public in general" to information supported with public funds. They argued that information needs not met by the marketplace must be met by the government; that democratic government needs informed and aware citizens, regardless of their ability to pay.

A "simplified" table summarizing "Schematic Contexts for Conflict Concerning the Role of the Federal Government in Providing Information Resources, Products, and Services" was developed. Essentially, it says that when a federal agency determines that an information service is needed, the likelihood of conflict is high if the information is extensively marketed and intended to influence policy. "There would be little, if any conflict when a function is Constitutionally defined (support of National Defense, for example)." The more specific the audience and the more able the audience is to pay, the more likely the conflict if the federal government provides an information service. "Information of high economic value is information that the private sector wants to repackage, to market, to distribute."

On the other hand, it asserts that information of high value to society as a whole—disaster information and medical data, for example—is "unlikely to be controversial." The sensitivity of the contexts escalate with the amount of "user specificity," "value added," and "form of availability." If government information services include tailoring data specifically to user needs, doing additional processing, or providing sophisticated means for access, then the likelihood of conflict increases. Among the most serious causes of conflict the report says, are governmental services which directly compete with private sector activities.

Philosophical differences among the Task Force members are abundantly clear within their report, totalling almost 100 pages. Yet, after two years of meetings, they agreed "almost unanimously" on seven principles and 27 recommendations to "guide the information policies" of the government. (See "Principles & Recommendations" in box.)

Of these seven principles, the first four deal specifically with the extent and nature of Government's role in providing information. The Task Force "does not feel that a 'national information policy' is the answer." Instead, the federal government should limit itself to "leadership," encouraging private sector information services and products, and providing incentives to industry. Government should not engage

"in commerce" unless there are "compelling reasons" to do so, and the property rights of the private sector should be protected at all times. The remaining three principles represent an attempt to satisfy the concern that "information distributable by the Government should be openly and readily available." But the prices and means for gaining access to that information should be such "that the private sector will be encouraged to create new products and services."

The leadership role specified for government is intended to preclude government management of information, which the Task Force says is "counter to the political philosophy of the country." They consider the private sector the most efficient means for information diversity because the criteria for distribution are then "economic forces, rather than political, with profit as a means of rewarding individual entre-

Principles & Recommendations

Listed below are the seven Principles and 27 Recommendations included in *Public/Private Sector Interaction in Providing Information Services*, the report of the Public/Private Sector Task Force of the National Commission on Libraries and Information Science:

Principle 1. The Federal government should take a leadership role in creating a framework that would facilitate the development and foster the use of information products and services.

Recommendation #1. Provide an environment that will enhance the competitive forces of the private sector, so that the market mechanisms can be effective in allocating resources in the use of information and in directing innovation into market determined areas.

Recommendation #2. Affirm the applicability of the First Amendment to information products and services.

Recommendation #3. Encourage Congress to be consistent in the language used and in the application of principles relating to information products and services, such as those identified in this Report, when it formulates legislation and when it exercises its oversight role.

Recommendation #4. Encourage government agencies to utilize the most efficient (information) technologies.

Recommendation #5. Encourage the setting and use of voluntary standards that will not inhibit the further development of innovative information products and services.

Recommendation #6. Encourage and support educational programs that provide the professional skills needed to further the development and use of information as an economic and social resource.

Recommendation #7. Encourage and support both basic and applied research in library and information science.

Recommendation #8. Encourage and support statistical programs and related research to provide the data needed to deal with information policy issues.

Principle 2. The Federal government should establish and enforce policies and procedures that encourage, and do not discourage, investment by the private sector in the development and use of information products and services.

Recommendation #13. Identify and eliminate legal and regulatory barriers to the introduction of new information products and services.

preneurs." Many of the 27 recommendations focus on reducing the uncertainties and risks the private sector may face when it invests in information resources, and what the Task Force considers necessary steps the government should take before it engages "in commerce." Libraries, particularly public libraries, are the "safety valve" proposed to provide a means for distribution ". . . on a less active basis than the entrepreneur" and ensure that "ability to pay" does not prevent access to government information.

While the principles and recommendations obviously represent compromise, the Task Force report emphasizes a view of information as a "commodity, a tool—of substantial value in the marketplace . . . "a product that can . . ." lead entrepreneurs to the development of products and services for sale. Information is a "capital resource."

Though lip-service is paid to the societal value of information, clearly and definitively, the report favors a free market system, with as little government intervention as possible. While this conclusion is not particularly radical, given our current political climate, its underlying assumptions require careful scrutiny. Taxpayer dollars which have already paid for the initial gathering of the information that industry is so anxious to resell (if there's a profitable market) are largely ignored.

The Information Industry Association goal "To promote the development of private enterprise in the field of information, and to gain recognition for information as a commercial product" certainly receives strong support from this NCLIS report. But, as Anita and Herb Schiller point out in their recent *Nation* article: "Commonplace and benign as that (goal) may

---

Recommendation #14. Encourage private enterprise to "add value" to government information (i.e., to repackage it, provide further processing services, and otherwise enhance the information so that it can be sold at a profit).

Recommendation #15. Provide incentives to existing organizations, such as libraries and bookstores, that will encourage them to expand their activities in dissemination of governmentally distributable information.

Recommendation #16. Establish procedures which will create a realistic opportunity for private sector involvement in the planning process for government information activities.

Recommendation #17. Involve the private sector in the process of formulating standards relating to Federal information activities.

Recommendation #18. Create or improve mechanisms for ensuring that the actions of government agencies, in developing information resources, products, and services, are consistent with the policies, goals, and long range plans that are announced.

Principle 3. The Federal government should not provide information products and services in commerce except when there are compelling reasons to do so, and then only when it protects the private sector's every opportunity to assume the function(s) commercially.

Recommendation #19. Announce intentions sufficiently ahead of time to provide an opportunity for private sector involvement when a government agency, for reasons it regards as compelling, should plan to develop and/or to market an information product or service.

Recommendation #20. Review and approve, before implementation, any plans for the government to develop and/ or market an information product or service, the review to be carried out by an agency appropriate to the branch of government (such as OMB, GAO, CBO).

Recommendation #21. Include an "information impact and cost analysis" as part of the process of review, evaluation, and approval of any plans for the government to develop and/or to market an information product or service, the analysis to cover economic and social effects, effects on existing products and services, effects on potential private sector products and services, and benefits to the public.

Recommendation #22. Review periodically to evaluate the desirability of continuation of any information product or service as a governmental activity.

Recommendation #23. Do not arbitrarily restrict the Federal government from enhancement of information products and services, even if solely to meet the needs of constituencies outside the government itself.

Recommendation #9. Conduct a periodic economic assessment of the impact of Federal government information products and services.

Principle 4. The Federal government, when it uses, reproduces, or distributes information available from the private sector as part of an information resource, product, or service, must assure that the property rights of the private sector sources are adequately protected.

Principle 5. The Federal government should make governmentally distributable information openly available in readily reproducible form, without any constraints on subsequent use.

Principle 6. The Federal government should set pricing policies for distributing information products or services that reflect the true cost of access and/or reproduction, any specific prices to be subject to review by an independent authority.

Principle 7. The Federal government should actively use existing mechanisms, such as the libraries of the country, as primary channels for making governmentally distributable information available to the public.

Recommendation #10. Encourage Federal agencies to regard the dissemination of information, especially through the mechanisms of the private sector (both for profit and not for profit), as a high priority responsibility.

Recommendation #11. Identify and evaluate alternatives to existing federal information dissemination mechanisms.

Recommendation #12. Develop and support the use of libraries as active means for access to governmental information by the public.

Recommendation #24. Announce the availability of governmentally distributable information and maintain one or more registers to help the public determine what governmentally distributable information is available.

Recommendation #25. Deposit governmentally distributable information, in whatever form it may be available, at national and regional centers, including regional depository libraries, where it may be examined at no charge.

Recommendation #26. Do not assert any Federal government copyrights on information the Federal government makes domestically available.

Recommendation #27. Use the nation's libraries and nongovernmental information centers as means for distribution of governmentally distributable information instead of creating new governmental units or expanding existing ones.

appear, it represents a reversal of a national commitment to the ideal of public knowledgeability and the informed citizen."

With this report, NCLIS fundamentally departs from what has long been accepted by many—in the information and library community at least—as conventional wisdom. "Serious problems" are now seen in the prospect of a national information policy if that implies any kind of "management" of information by government. Cooperation between the public and private sectors may be highly controversial, because ". . . cooperation with government carries with it commitments to support and participate with the government, to some extent yielding the independence of action so vital for a free press."

A rather subtle, but definite, semantic switch occurs concerning the question of access within the report. Numerous previous documents, including a White House Conference on Library and Information Services resolution, call for guarantees of "full and equal access" to information, yet the report says that the public library's view is ". . . that there should be equity *if not equality* for all users." Despite some ten pages devoted to definitions of terms, the words access, equity, and equality are not defined, though a distinction between "open availability" and "free availability" is defined, since the latter term could be interpreted as meaning "without cost." A rather revealing interpretation of access is buried within the discussion presented for Principle 5:

> The term access was discussed, and interpreted as including retrieval of prespecified (not user-specified) packages of information. It would include an ability to communicate online, but with only limited interaction with the user. Access would include availability at identified national and regional centers and depository librarians. Access by user-specified retrieval would be provided only if specifically authorized.

In other words, libraries can provide access, as long as it's not too useful to the user.

Confusing and questionable terminology abounds throughout the report. Libraries are variously included within either the public sector, the private sector—or separated out entirely. Overwritten and poorly organized, over 70 percent of the text is devoted to a rehash of broad and general discussions; the reader is offered few specifics. An appendix, designed to illustrate cases the principles apply to, presents almost meaningless examples like:

> The NTIS, as the agency principally responsible for the distribution and governmental information, provides the largest single example of governmental service to which principles and policies could be applied.

There is no further explanation; there is a hidden agenda. Those familiar with the controversy know that the information industry would prefer that NTIS disband to allow similar services to be sold by entrepreneurs.

The Task Force makes *no* concrete recommendations about increasing financial support for libraries. Their reasoning is revealing: "In fact, there would have been significant differences in views within the Task Force concerning the value and appropriateness of any of them."

Market solutions

Obviously, the perspective advocated by the Task Force must be read in the context of our current political and economic climate. Many of its explicit and implicit assumptions are part of a larger national debate about economic productivity and social justice. Foremost among these is what economist Robert Lekachman calls an "American fixation on market solutions to public problems." Do we indeed have a free, competitive market situation with respect to information services that will—if left to its own devices—produce efficiency, innovation, and equity? The NCLIS Task Force thinks so. "The kind of things the private sector can do most effectively are those which respond most directly and immediately to the needs of the marketplace *and thus to the consumer*." Demand, they say, is measured by "voluntary payment of a price. . . . The decision is made in terms of "individual decisions—by the entrepreneur and the purchaser . . . the cumulative decisions lead to the optimum allocation of resources to produce the products and services that the purchaser wants, not those that a Government agency determines they need."

Maybe, sometimes, but, as Martha Williams succinctly pointed out at the recent National Online Meeting:

> If the Government hadn't succeeded in some of its information ventures, no one would be concerned—nor are private sector information industry proponents concerned about those activities that have not and don't appear to be able to attract a sizable paying clientele. There are a very few successful activities but one must remember that they didn't start out that way and that if the government hadn't carried out or sponsored much of the pioneering work in the development of databases and online systems, the information industry—both U.S. and worldwide—would not have reached the stage of development it enjoys today. . . .
> . . . The government did more than develop technologies; it also created markets for the new technologies and it didn't happen overnight nor did it occur in competition with industry. The government filled a gap that at the time was not perceived by the private sector as being able to produce profits in the near term. Such investments by the government have paid dividends for the private sector, and no doubt this pattern will repeat itself. . . .

NCLIS, in accepting the report of this Task Force, runs the risk of adopting a very simplistic perspective on the "free marketplace" for information.

The government itself is not only a major compiler of statistical, bibliographic, scientific, and other information, but is also a major consumer and subsidizer of information resources. Government funding for educational and library services has long provided major markets for the publishing/information industry. Government regulation (copyright, fair use) and subsidy (special postal rates for libraries and books) are an established tradition. Agencies like the Department of Defense and of Education, and the National Science Foundation, have underwritten the production of information on a massive scale.

What happens in either sector has an impact on the price and type of services available in the other. The Reagan Administration is making concerted attempts to undercut many traditional government supports and subsidies for information. Government Printing Office reductions, cutbacks in education and library programs, the National Archives, and NTIS are only a few examples. Nevertheless, the increased budget proposed for national defense research, if adopted, will increase the government's power as a creator and consumer of information.

Another harsh reality is the increasing number of interlocking multiconglomerates (well represented within the Information Industry Association) which own both hardware and software—publishers, computer companies, data processing services, telephone services, television networks, newspapers, and the like. Some of these cross national boundaries and owe no particular allegiance to any nation. For example, Elsevier North Holland counts among its holdings *Excerpta Medica*, Congressional Information Service, and Greenwood Press. Information Handling Services, which recently acquired both BRS and Predicasts, is a subsidiary of Indian Head, which in turn is owned by Thyssen Bornemisza of The Netherlands. Time, Inc. owns five magazines, 17 weekly newspapers, five publishing houses, a television station, a cable system, a record firm, the Book of the Month Club, and more. ITT, in addition to its numerous communications, data processing, and computer subsidiaries, also publishes books under the labels of Bobbs-Merrill, Sams, Audel, G. K. Hall, Gregg, and Twayne.

Public goods

Another problem with the pure free market approach, as Marc Uri Porat graphically illustrates in his classic study of *The Information Economy*, is that the private information infrastructure:

. . . operates under a mixed regime of protective monopoly (telephone), regulated competition (the specialized common carriers) and unregulated competition (computer and other equipment manufacturers). And that the major users of information technology are also subject to a multitude of Federal and State regulations (e.g., finance, USPS). And that even the competitive sectors are characterized by allegations of oligopolistic leadership. Even if our best sentiments are in favor of market solutions, the stark realities of existing market structure defy a laissez-faire approach. . . .

The popular theory underlying the Reagan economic

program holds that the only legitimate functions of government are the provision of public goods and the correction of market failures. Unfortunately, the realities of implementing these functions are dependent on political judgments. This is made abundantly clear by the 1982 Economic Report of the President. National defense is described as a "true" public good, while education is a good that "could be private." On the topic of safety regulation, the budget report states: ". . . the best solution would probably be to rely on market judgments about the value of safety."

A recent contretemps between the White House staff and the Department of Labor reported by the *New York Times* underlines the possible consequences of this skewed emphasis on market forces. The argument centered around a regulation requiring that toxic chemical hazards, symptoms, and hazard-preventing measures be listed on product containers. Labor estimated that 4000 cancer deaths annually could be prevented by this measure. The Office of Management and Budget disagreed: their estimate was only 400 cancer deaths: ". . . workers' 'right to know' about chemical dangers in the workplace should not be considered a 'right' in isolation from the cost considerations of the employers and manufacturers who would have to supply the information." Fortunately for those affected, OMB was finally overruled by the Task Force on Regulatory Relief.

Not a commodity

The view of information as a commodity that can and should be bought and sold represents yet another kind of problem with an unregulated free market approach. The perception of the value of information is not new. There has always been a price. Traditional ways of absorbing costs have varied from tax funds to support library services on one end of the spectrum to direct user purchase on the other. As information increases in quantity, and as information products reach new levels of sophistication, questions of value become more complex, but treating information strictly as a commodity is problematic. Edwin Parker, of the Institute for Communications Research at Stanford, summarizes the dilemma:

Information as such is not a commodity that can be readily bought and sold. There are no satisfactory units for measuring quantities of information, or for establishing a price per unit. Physical commodities have the property that when one person gives or sells them to another, the original owner gives up possession. This is not true for information, because the seller or giver of information retains the information after he has transmitted it to someone else. Sometimes the value of the information to the original possessor is increased after it is widely disseminated. . . . According to neoclassical economic theory and conventional wisdom in economic policy, the production and distribution of physical commodities can best be handled within a competitive economic system. When all the assumptions of the economic theory are met, unrestricted competition should lead to optimal total investment (even if the distribution of benefits from that investment offends our social consciences). One of the key assumptions, however, of the economic theory leading to that conclusion is the assumption of standardized products about which consumers have perfect information. This leads to impossible contradictions in the case of information treated as a commodity. If the buyer has perfect information about the information he is considering buying, he has no need to buy it. In addition, the seller cannot relinquish possession of the information because he still has it after the transaction.

Even if we were able to treat information as a pure economic commodity, would society really benefit by leaving the fate of information creation, production, and dissemination—and therefore policy—to the whimsy of the marketplace? Is quality and need determined only when people are *aware* of their need, as well as able and willing to pay the price? Products which can be bought and sold will certainly be bought and sold, but who will finally decide that a product is salable and therefore should be produced? Should information be held hostage to this year's bottom-line considerations alone, to what the sellers perceive we want and are willing to pay for? Suppose the marketing experts guess wrong?

This NCLIS Task Force report should be carefully examined by all interested parties, as should the activities of NCLIS itself. If the commission is truly committed to the goal it stated in 1975 to: ". . . eventually provide every individual in the United States with equal opportunity of access" to information regardless of his or her "social or physical condition or level of achievement," it will have to involve many more people in this particular discussion. The current Task Force membership is skewed. It represents neither the end users of information, traditional publishers, or librarians working in different types of libraries.

A weak compromise

NCLIS as a whole, as of this writing, has not yet acted on this report. It was released in February for "review and reaction." The full text, and the reasoning behind the principles and recommendations, must be read carefully to understand their full impact. All concerned with information policy should do so and react. Neither the public nor private sectors are well served by isolation. The principles and recommendations promulgated in this report represent an attempt to compromise, to gloss over the very real differences of motives and goals which exist in various sectors. The potential economic and social consequences of information policy are too crucial to settle for such a compromise.

The danger of narrowly focusing on only internal parts of the problem and coming up with short sighted "vertical" policies are aptly underscored by Porat:

Hardly a word was breathed in the 1890's about the potentially destructive effects of transportation on the environment, on inner cities, on social adjustments. Hen-

ry Ford sold cars and trucks; the suburb, the collapse of the inner city, environmental pollution, energy shortages and a stream of property damage and broken bodies emerged much later.

After the inventors work their miracles and entrepreneurs push ideas into material realities, we are left with the untidy portion of the problem: the externalities. Enter the academic economists and sociologists, who are brought in *after* economic and social realities are upon us, to measure the rate at which the horse left the barn. Then, as now, few with power paused to reflect on the implications of the new technology.

Satisfactorily merging questions of information access and social justice with economic profit and progress is not a simple task. We cannot unwittingly commit our future by allowing information policy to become a bread and butter issue of big business, or any other special interests, at the expense of the national interest. Equal access to information is a natural extension of democratic principles. If information is a public good, and an informed individual contributes to the benefit of society as a whole, then access to information must be guaranteed—not only in principle, but in fact. People with a competitive edge in life are those who are best informed.

Information justice

Guaranteeing a just distribution of information will require continuing debate among the various stakeholders, including the present and potential users of all manners of information products and services. Such a debate requires a much more active stance than the passivity reflected in this report, a more active stance for government, the library community, and the citizens of our nation. The simplistic, but dangerous, approach advocated by the NCLIS Task Force should not stop us from fully confronting the issues. What we desperately need is a forum which will both encourage argument on all sides and creatively channel the tensions, the conflicts, and the healthy controversies towards the achievement of long-term benefits for all—rather than short-term profits for a few.

BIBLIOGRAPHY:

National Commission on Libraries and Information Services. *Public Sector/Private Sector Interaction in Providing Information Services.* Report to NCLIS from the Public/Private Sector Task Force. Stock number: 052-003-00866-1. GPO February 1982. $5.50.
Parker, Edwin B. "Social Implications of Computer/Telecoms Systems," *Telecommunications Policy,* December 1976, p. 3–20.
Porat, Marc Uri. *The Information Economy. Definition and Measurement.* U.S. Dept. of Commerce, Office of Telecommunications. GPO, 1977.
Schiller, Anita R. & Herbert I. Schiller. "Who Can Own What America Knows?," *The Nation,* April 17, 1982, p. 461–63.
Williams, M. E. & Thomas Hogan. *National Online Meeting Proceedings, 1982.* Medford, N.J., Learned Information, Inc., 1982.

Part VII
Selected Classics

[23]

RICHARD T. ELY LECTURE

THE ECONOMICS OF KNOWLEDGE AND
THE KNOWLEDGE OF ECONOMICS

By KENNETH E. BOULDING
University of Michigan

What might be called, perhaps somewhat grandiloquently, the Epistemological Question has received rather scant attention at the hands of economists.[1] There are, of course, a number of epistemological questions, some of which lie more in the province of the philosopher than they do the economist or the social scientist. The one with which I am particularly concerned here is that of the role of knowledge in social systems, both as a product of the past and as a determinant of the future. There is a little terminological problem here, that the word "knowledge" in English has some tendency to approach the meaning of "truth." We really have no convenient word to describe the content of the human mind without regard to the question as to whether this content corresponds to anything outside it. For this reason I have in the past used the term "image" to mean this cognitive content of the human mind.[2] But this term also is subject to misunderstanding, so for the purposes of this paper I will revert to the term "knowledge," with a warning, however, that I make no assumptions about the content of people's minds being true. We may recall the classic *bon mot* attributed to Will Rogers, that "the trouble isn't what people don't know; it's what they do know that isn't so." So little accustomed are we to analyzing this problem that there is even an ambiguity in the word "ignorance." It may mean that people have no image at all about something where an image is possible, or it may mean that they have images which are false or untrue. The pursuit of the question as to what we mean by truth or untruth, however, leads us into a philosophical morass from which, as David Hume suggested, the only escape is to climb out, clean oneself off, and go home and have a good dinner and forget all about philosophy. Otherwise we may be swallowed up in a paralyzing skepticism, and become, like Hamlet, "sicklied o'er with the pale cast of thought."

[1] Naming names is always a little invidious, but I must give honorable mention to F. A. Hayek, Fritz Machlup, T. E. Schultz, and Fred Harbison, as members of the little band who have taken this problem seriously.

[2] K. E. Boulding, *The Image: Knowledge in Life and Society* (Univ. of Michigan Press, 1956 and 1961).

1

I shall become very pragmatic at this point and consign the philosophical problems to my esteemed colleagues who make this their specialty, and I shall assume simply that knowledge, that is, images, exist; they can be observed or at least deduced through the instrument of language, combined with introspection; and that some images get us into more trouble than others; and that we tend to revise those images which get us into trouble. A decent, orderly, and at the same time imaginative and systematic revision of images that get us into trouble is a process which edges us, one hopes constantly, towards truth. This proposition, I must confess, is an act of faith. At its most sophisticated and orderly, this is the method of science. The same method, however, also produces images which approximate the truth in both what I would call folk knowledge, which is the knowledge gained in the ordinary living of daily life, and literary knowledge, which is folk knowledge chewed over, reflected upon, digested, and expanded by intakes from the written word.

I must resist the temptation to be philosophical, however, and come back to business; that is, economics. The question of what is economics can be almost as troublesome as what is knowledge? Here again I will be fairly ruthless and define economics as the study of the "econosphere" with a view of gaining knowledge about it, and I will go on to define the econosphere as that subset of the sociosphere, or the sphere of all human activity, relationships, and institutions, which is particularly characterized by the phenomenon of exchange. One might limit it further and consider only that part of the sphere of exchange which is subject, in A. C. Pigou's great phrase, to "the measuring rod of money." As I am a great believer in making boundaries of all kinds insignificant enough to be taken off the human agenda, in both the international system and in the republic of letters, I am not going to bother very much about where the boundary lies.

As it is exchange or potentiality of exchange or relevance to exchange that makes things commodities, one would think that economists would be interested in knowledge itself as a commodity. It is certainly something which is bought and sold. It is a little hard to put a price on it because of the difficulties of measuring the quantity of the commodity itself. We can put prices on the printed page, the hour's lecture, the newspaper, the tip sheet, or the newsletter and even perhaps on the golf course or the cocktail hour. The absence of any unit of knowledge itself, however, and perhaps the intrinsic heterogeneity of its substance, makes it very difficult to think of a price of knowledge as such, and indeed has probably contributed to a certain resistance which we feel to thinking of knowledge as a commodity. One longs, indeed, for a unit of knowledge, which perhaps might be called a "wit," analogous to the "bit" as used in information theory; but up to now at any rate no such practical unit has emerged. It is certainly tempting to think of knowledge as a capital stock of information, knowledge being to information what capital is to income, and to use the bit itself in the form of a stock as the measure of knowledge. Certainly the improbability of a structure, which is what the bit really measures, is highly related to the knowledge concept. The bit, however, abstracts completely from the content of either information or knowledge, and while it is enormously useful for telephone engineers, who have no interest in what is being said over their telephones, for purposes of the social system theorist we need a measure which takes account of significance and which would weight, for instance, the gossip of a teenager rather low and the communications over the hot line between Moscow and Washington rather high. Up to now we seem to have no way of doing this, short of a kind of qualitative guesswork, though even this will be better than nothing.

Another difficulty is that only things which are clearly capable of being appropriated are subject to being exchanged, and if a thing cannot be property, it obviously cannot be a commodity. While knowledge has many of the aspects of property, its capacity for reproduction in many minds and its accessibility in the form of the published word make it a very peculiar form of property. Thus as Major John Wesley Powell said to a congressional committee in 1886: "Possession of property is exclusive; possession of knowledge is not exclusive, for the knowledge which one man has may also be the possession of another."[3] In spite of Major Powell's dictum, some knowledge, of course, is exclusive, such as trade secrets and patents, and thereby becomes property. What is perhaps even more important, knowledge which has the capacity of generating more knowledge in a single head is also exclusive and becomes property to the individual possessing it.

These difficulties may have led to a certain neglect of the commodity aspects of knowledge, even in economic theory itself. One notices this in at least three areas of economic thought: in the theory of the market, in the theory of development, and in the theory of decision making, both public and private. In the theory of the competitive market, there is usually made an explicit assumption about "perfect knowledge." What this means in effect is that the acquisition of knowledge of prices or exchange opportunities in a perfect market is costless, so that knowledge is, as it were, a free good. This assumption might be plausible if there were only a few buyers and sellers. However, the perfect market also assumes large numbers of buyers and sellers, and pre-

[3] Quoted in Don K. Price, *The Scientific Estate*, p. 284, footnote 36 (Belknap-Harvard. 1965).

sumably large numbers of prices, and the more prices there are, the more transactions there are, clearly the less plausible becomes the assumption that knowledge is costless. We can perhaps wriggle our way out of this dilemma by supposing that the knowledge problem in perfect markets is taken care of by specialized arbitrageurs, who by devoting themselves full time to the problem of knowing what prices there are in different parts of the market and by taking advantage themselves of the price differentials thereby revealed, reduce these price differentials to so small a quantity that all the rest of the people in the market are justified in assuming that the price which they happen to observe at one point is characteristic of all transactions all over the market. From a social point of view, the income of the arbitrageurs might be regarded as the cost of acquiring the knowledge which is necessary to operate the market, and the other people in the market are evidently willing to pay this rather than become arbitrageurs themselves.

We can then think of the development of imperfect markets as a result of the fact that when commodities become extremely diverse and complicated, when we have to know not only their price but also their quality, arbitrage in effect breaks down, because the cost of acquiring the relevant knowledge is more than the market is willing to support. Hence we get imperfect markets facing both buyers and sellers, in which they face not merely a price at which they can buy and sell as much as they wish but a function relating the amount that can be bought or sold to the price at which it can be bought or sold. Once we have imperfect markets, however, the epistemological problem for the marketers themselves increases enormously. If prices are advertised in a perfect market, or "cried," every seller knows his sales function and every buyer knows his purchase function immediately. If, however, we have an imperfect market, the problem of knowing what are the sales or purchase functions becomes not only acute but almost insoluble, simply because in order to know a function we must have experience with a system beyond its present point. It is this failure to understand the epistemological problem involved which has vitiated much of the otherwise laudable attempt to expand the theory of perfect competition into imperfect markets. This attempt which began so hopefully in the 1930's now seems to have petered out in an epistemological swamp.

When it comes to the theory of economic development, the failure to recognize explicitly the essentially epistemological nature of the problem has led to a proliferation of mechanical models of very doubtful value, and, one fears, the giving of a large amount of bad advice. The theory of economic development is part of the general problem of evolutionary change, and its poor condition reflects the general poverty of the theory of dynamic systems. Throughout the sciences, physical, biological, and social, we are still really more at home with equilibrium systems than we are with dynamic systems.

The plain fact is that knowledge or something equivalent to it in the form of improbable structures is the only thing that can grow or evolve, and the concept is quite crucial in any evolutionary theory. As far as matter and energy are concerned, we are subject to inexorable laws of conservation. Here we are faced with simple exchange: what one system acquires, another system must give up. In the case of available energy, there is not even conservation; the second law of thermodynamics informs us there is constant degradation and decay. From the point of view of energy alone, the universe is clearly running down into a very thin brown soup, and all processes in time are seen merely as the exhaustion of preexisting potential, a kind of squandering of available energy capital. It is only information and knowledge processes which in any sense get out from under the iron laws of conservation and decay, though they only do this, as it were, by operating at another level. Two processes may be distinguished here. The first might be called printing, in which a structure is able to reproduce itself by making a copy of itself out of the incoherent matter around it. The gene evidently operates in this way; the mass production of commodities is largely three-dimensional printing; and even the transmission of a good deal of knowledge by rote learning in the educational process falls into this category. Printing by itself, however, would never organize an evolutionary or developmental process. It would merely fill the whole universe with copies of an initial structure. There must therefore be a second process to which we might give the name of organizing. This is the kind of process, for instance, by which the coded information contained in the gene is able to organize a phenotype such as a man. This is the way in which a blueprint organizes the construction of a building. This is the way in which an idea creates an organization, or an image of the future governs an individual life.

We then see any developmental process, whether this is the development of a fertilized egg into a human being, the development of an idea into an organization by an entrepreneur, the development of a religion out of a "sacred history," or even the process of economic development itself, as essentially a combination of printing and organizing, the one developing rote knowledge, the other new knowledge. Thus we can think of capital essentially as knowledge imposed on the material world, in the first place by an organizing process which creates a producing organization and in the second case by a process akin to three-dimensional printing. In this view, consumption is essentially consumption of knowledge-structures, either human knowledge through death or decay, or of the bodily structure through metabolic processes, or through wear and tear of material structures, or even through the disorganizing processes which afflict organizations. Production is then seen essentially as a process of increasing structure, repairing the decay and depreciation of consumption, replacing the knowledge lost by death, and so on. We could further think of production as having two functions: one a replacement function, which is necessary to restore an existing knowledge and capital structure; the other a developmental function which expands, improves, and reorganizes the structure of knowledge in general into new forms. If consumption is so great that all production has to be used for maintenance, there will, of course, be no development. We also get certain consumption processes which can be remedied by no known input, such as aging. Fortunately in society we have solved this problem by having babies, and in organizations we solve it by having competition, bankruptcy, and various forms of organizational death. Birth and death, indeed, are the price that we pay for aging, so that we can have a population that does not age, even though the individuals do.

The recognition that development, even economic development, is essentially a knowledge process has been slowly penetrating the minds of economists, but we are still too much obsessed by mechanical models, capital-income ratios, and even input-output tables, to the neglect of the study of the learning process which is the real key to development. It is true, of course, that what might be called the "human resources school" of Theodore Schultz and Fred Harbison has laid very proper stress on education as the mainspring of the developmental process. Even here, however, there has perhaps not been sufficient attention paid to the problem of learning as a whole, outside as well as inside the institutions of formal education; and there has been a considerable neglect of the role of the price system as a teacher.

It is always depressing to go back to Adam Smith, especially on economic development, as one realizes how little we have learned in nearly two hundred years. It is, however, perhaps worthy of notice that our father Adam saw very clearly that the learning process was the key to development, for if we examine his causes of the increase in the productive powers of labor, which is what we mean by economic development, we see that they all involve the knowledge process. The first of these, the development of skill and dexterity through the division of labor, is a learning process mainly in the lower nervous system. The second, the gains due to constant application at a single task and the elimination of "sauntering," involve the problem of forgetting and relearning as we take up tasks intermittently; and the third, and by far the most important, is the development of machines (frozen knowledge, as I would call them) as a result of the work not only of specialists in the production of such things, but also as the result of the work of "philosophers" who augment knowledge in general. Thus even before 1776 Adam Smith had perceived the enormous importance of what today we would call research and development in the processes by which everybody gets richer.

The third area of interest to economists where the epistemological problem is overwhelmingly important is in the area of decision making itself, in the private sector, in households and businesses, and in government; for the problem of government policy is just as much a problem in decision making as is the problem of the behavior of private persons and organizations. In my book, *The Image,* I have sketched what might be called an epistemological theory of behavior, pointing out that a decision is always a choice among alternative perceived images of the future. The study of decision, therefore, must concentrate on how these images of the future are derived from the information inputs of the past, as this is the only place from which they can come. That is, we have to think of our images of the future as essentially learned out of our inputs from the past, and the nature of this learning process is therefore of overwhelming importance. Similarly, the utility or welfare function, which we impose over these images of the future, is likewise learned, though economists have been surprisingly unwilling to recognize this fact, perhaps because it was called to their attention in such strident tones by Veblen, who argued most convincingly, to my mind, that if we wanted to have a dynamic economics, we could not simply take preferences for granted but had to regard them as essentially learned. The process by which we learn our preferences, however, is mysterious indeed. A substantial monkey wrench is thrown into dynamic economics by the fact that the price system itself may operate as a teacher, and preferences may change in response to the price structure just as the price structure changes in response to preferences. We have, for instance, what might be called the "sour grapes" principle—that what we cannot get we decide we do not like. There is also a counterprinciple that might be called the "Mount Everest" principle, that if something is hard to get, we want it, just because it is hard to get. Furthermore, if we know somebody else has paid a different price from what we have paid, our satisfaction may be correspondingly increased or diminished.

The epistemological theory of decision making is, of course, pretty empty unless we can specify ways in which the inputs of the past determine the present images of the future. Unfortunately, the observations of economists on this question are for the most part simple-minded to the point of embarrassment. The concept of elasticity of expectations, for instance, would only be interesting if there were any evidence at all that as a parameter it had some stability, or even that its rate of change had some stability. There may be some stability in expectations when there is nothing to expect, that is, in a poor, stable environment, but outside of this the evidence for any simple relationship between present rates of change and future is not well supported. Perhaps the most plausible theory is that people tend to interpret the present in terms of the traumatic experiences of their youth. Thus a generation that was traumatized by inflation will have different images from one traumatized by depression. It is clear we are on the borderline here between economics and psychology, and it is to the interstitial discipline of economic psychology that we must look for answers. The trouble is, of course, that even psychology knows very little about the human learning process, mainly because it takes place over such a long period and is almost certainly subject to phenomena such as "imprinting" in which inputs at certain moments of "readiness" in the development of the person produce effects which far outweigh their intrinsic importance.

Another profitable line of study lies in economic sociology, in the analysis of the way in which organizational structure affects the flow of information, hence affects the information input into the decision-maker, hence affects his image of the future and his decisions, even perhaps his value function. There is a great deal of evidence that almost all organizational structures tend to produce false images in the decision-maker, and that the larger and more authoritarian the organization, the better the chance that its top decision-makers will be operating in purely imaginary worlds. This perhaps is the most fundamental reason for supposing that there are ultimately diminishing returns to scale. In the most extreme form of this view, we can suppose that the role structure and communication network of an organization determine the inputs to each role so completely that there is virtually no freedom of decision at all, and that no matter who is the role occupant, the decisions will be much the same. The inference of this theory, of course, is that fools in high places will make just the same decisions as wise men, and though there is something comforting in this, one certainly hesitates to believe it too wholeheartedly.

Let me now focus my attention even more narrowly on the problem of the contribution of economic knowledge itself, that is, what economists know, to the processes of operation of the economic system. We have here a certain epistemological paradox, that where knowledge is an essential part of the system, knowledge about the system changes the system itself. This is a kind of generalized Heisenberg Principle, which is particularly troublesome in the social sciences. What this means, of course, is not that knowledge is unattainable, but that we must regard it as part of a total dynamic system. That is to say, we are not simply acquiring knowledge about a static system which stays put, but acquiring knowledge about a whole dynamic process in which the acquisition of the knowledge itself is a part of the process. It is quite legitimate, therefore, to ask ourselves what is the impact of economic knowledge, that is, of the image of the economic system or econosphere, in the minds of professional economists, on the dynamic processes of the econosphere itself. The only point at which knowledge can affect a social system is through its impact on decisions. This impact can be small or large, depending on the relevance of the knowledge in question. Thus in the case of the operations of a market and the behavior involved in buying and selling, it is doubtful whether the knowledge of economics as such makes very much difference. Economists, for instance, have not been noted for their success in market speculation, with two notable exceptions of Ricardo and J. M. Keynes, and even in their cases, they made their major contributions to economics after, not before, they made fortunes in speculative markets. There are certainly few marketers who have been assisted in their operations by knowledge of the Walrasian Equations, just as few tennis players are much assisted by knowledge of the mathematics of moving balls.

At some points, however, economic knowledge is showing some danger of being useful. Economists can take a good deal of credit for the stabilization policies which have been followed in most Western countries since 1945 with considerable success. It is easy to generate a euphoric and self-congratulatory mood when one compares the twenty years after the first World War, 1919-39, with the twenty years after the second, 1945-65. The first twenty years were a total failure; the second twenty years, at least as far as economic policy is concerned, have been a modest success. We have not had any great depression; we have not had any serious financial collapse; and on the whole we have had much higher rates of development in most parts of the world than we had in the 1920's and 1930's, even though there are some conspicuous failures. Whether the unprecedented rates of economic growth of the last twenty years, for instance in Japan and Western Europe, can be attributed to economics, or whether they represent a combination of good luck in political decision making with the expanding impact of the natural and biological sciences on the economy, is something we might argue. I am inclined to attribute a good deal to good luck and noneconomic forces, but not all of it, and even if economics only contributed 10 percent, this would amount to a very handsome rate of return indeed, considering the very small amount of resources we have really put into economics.

Another point where the knowledge of economics has had some payoffs in the social system has been through the development of operations research and management science, with the aid of computer technology. Here again it is not altogether clear how much economics itself has contributed to this, as the basic ideas, for instance of maximizing something under constraints, are so obvious that it is almost embarrassing to credit economics with them, and it is the technology that has really made the difference. However, I suppose it can be argued that if economics had not beaten out the marginal analysis with an intellectual sledge hammer over a couple of generations, the computer boys might have had to spend a few minutes in thinking about what they were doing. Some of us, perhaps, still have to learn that arithmetic is a complement to, not a substitute for, thought, and that what my spy in IBM calls the "gigo principle" (that is, garbage in, garbage out) is a sound approach even to the most elegantly computerized simulation. I confess I am a little worried about one aspect of this movement, fruitful as it undoubtedly is. The very power of the computer to simulate complex systems by very high-speed arithmetic may prevent search for those simplified formulations which are the essence of progress in theory. I have an uneasy feeling, for instance, that if the computer had been around at the time of Copernicus, nobody would have ever bothered with him, because the computers could have handled the Ptolemaic epicycles with perfect ease.

The general movement towards the rationalization of decision-making processes in both private and public life through the use of optimizing procedures applied to complex masses of information may have some other costs lurking among the benefits, particularly in regard to political decision making. For one thing, these elaborate procedures may easily produce a sense of subjective certainty, which is quite unwarranted by the uncertainties of the actual system. One worries about this particularly in the international system, where the principle that "he who hesitates is saved" is usually very sound, and an illusion of certainty can be quite disastrous. The use of political war games and of computer simulation in the Department of Defense is a genuine cause for alarm on this score, and one would very much like to see some studies of the effect of gaming, for instance, on business behavior. It could easily be that the euphoria produced by these exercises resulted in some disastrous decisions, though I have not been able to document this hypothesis. The great danger of rationality is of course suboptimization; that is, finding and choosing the best position of part of the system which is not the best for the whole. Too many people, indeed, and especially too many experts, devote their lives to finding the best way of doing something that should not be done at all. Decision making by instinct, gossip, visceral feeling, and political savvy may stand pretty low on the scale of total rationality, but it may have the virtue of being able to take in very large systems in a crude and vague way, whereas the rationalized processes can only take subsystems in their more exact fashion, and being rational about subsystems may be worse than being not very rational about the system as a whole. I would not argue, of course, that rationality about the system as a whole is impossible. On the other hand, the economist has a certain mind-set in favor of his own skills, and it is easy for him to leave out essential variables with which he is not familiar. Here, indeed, a little learning may be a dangerous thing, or even a little rationality.

One area where economists have a good deal to be humble about is in the field of economic development of the poor countries. In the rich countries we have done fairly well; in the poor countries our record is distinctly spotty. This is almost certainly because we are dealing in this case with a total social process, and the economic abstractions are simply not sufficient to deal with the problem. Here what we need is clearly economic anthropology, and this science, unfortunately, hardly exists. Our great gift to the world is national income statistics and the percentage rate of growth of GNP. In fact, as every economist knows, calculations of GNP, especially in the poor countries, are largely exercises in the statistical imagination, and even if they were accurate, the GNP itself can be a very poor measure of welfare. The GNP can rise because of arms races, because of stupid dam-building, or even through the building of presidential palaces. It can be rising because a small proportion of a population is getting better off while the vast majority remain in stagnant misery. Valuable as the GNP is, therefore, as a rough overall measure of economic success, it can easily become a fetish and a quite misleading statistic. Economists certainly should be the first to issue warnings against its misuse.

Let me conclude with some brief notes on the state of economic knowledge in the United States. At the moment I get the impression that economists in this country are bathed in a warm glow of self-congratulation, rising out of the long Kennedy-Johnson upswing and the successful tax cut, and they are all climbing onto the bandwagon of the Great Society, waving flags and tooting horns. That we have some causes for self-congratulation I would not deny, and I hate to seem like a skeleton at the feast. There is real danger, however, that our current euphoria will prevent us from seeing the immensity of our unsolved problems and the enormous intellectual task that still awaits us. It is not much to the credit of the economics profession, for instance, that it took an engineer, Seymour Melman,[4] to call our attention to the fact that our obsession with being a great power and our neurotic masculine compulsions about military strength are seriously depleting the technical resource base in the civilian sectors of the economy. The nonsense which is talked about cyberculture and the hooting and hollering about automation at a time when substantial segments of the economy are technologically stagnant or even deteriorating is another tribute to a major intellectual default on the part of the economics profession. The plain fact is that economists have neglected the study of technical change at the structural and micro level to the point where we are quite incapable of answering many of the most important questions of our day. We have been obsessed with macroeconomics, with piddling refinements in mathematical models, and with the monumentally unsuccessful exercise in welfare economics which has preoccupied a whole generation with a dead end, to the almost total neglect of some of the major problems of our day. Almost the only group of economists who have much sense of realism are the agricultural economists, and these are dealing with a vanishing sector that is now only 5 percent of the total economy. The whole economics profession, indeed, is an example of that monumental misallocation of intellectual resources which is one of the most striking phenomena of our times. It would be an interesting exercise to compare the distribution of economists specializing in different sectors of the economy with the contribution of these sectors to the GNP. I would not be surprised to find 75 percent of the economists are concentrated in 10 percent of the GNP. Where, for instance, are the economists who are really studying the service trades and the tertiary industries? Where are the economists who are really studying the 10 percent of the economy devoted to the space-military complex? Where are the economists even who are really studying the impact of automation? And the answer is, practically nowhere. Far from being in a mood of self-congratulation, we should be in a mood of repentance.

A mood of repentance, however, implies a hope of salvation. It is on this note that I would like to conclude. In almost every generation, the oldsters mourn that things are not what they were in their young days. I remember Hicks once telling me that he heard Foxwell's last lectures at London School of Economics, in which he commiserated with the young men of the 1920's that they lived in a dull age of economics, and that they could never hope to recapture the enormous thrills of the bimetallism controversy. One is tempted to sing the same song today, in describing the Keynesian raptures of the 1930's. "Bliss was it in that dawn to be alive, but to be young was very heaven," as the aging

[4] Seymour Melman, *Our Depleted Society* (Holt, Rinehart, and Winston, 1965).

Wordsworth wrote about the French Revolution. Little indeed did Foxwell know. It is tempting to say, "Those were the days," and leave it at that. But these are the days too. It may be, of course, that the intellectual fervor which in the 1930's we devoted to the problem of unemployment must now be devoted to the graver problem of human survival in an international system which has clearly broken down. It may be that intellectual excitement has shifted from economics towards political science or towards social psychology. Let us not think, however, that all our problems have been solved. An enormous intellectual task still awaits the economist. We are a very long way from writing finis to this chapter of the human enterprise. We still cannot handle some of the most elementary problems regarding economic development, economic dynamics, the function of the price system, the relative merits of centrally planned as against market economies, the economics of distribution, the development of the "grants economy," the behavior of economic organizations of all types, from the corporation to the foundation, the role of the price system in the developmental and learning process, the learning process itself by which we acquire our images of our economic environment. We are still, like Isaac Newton, only a boy playing on the seashore, and the great ocean of Truth still lies all undiscovered before us. That undiscovered ocean is Man himself. What we discover about him, I hope, will be for his healing. I did not become an economist for anybody's applause; I became an economist because I thought there was an intellectual task ahead, of desperate importance for the welfare and even the survival of mankind. A mere thirty-five years have not been long enough to change my motivation. Something has been accomplished; a great deal more remains to be done. To this unfinished task I commend us all.

[24]

RICHARD T. ELY LECTURE
ECONOMICS OF INQUIRING, COMMUNICATING, DECIDING*

By Jacob Marschak
University of California, Berkeley

We hear much of today's "informational revolution." We are also told of the rapid growth of the "knowledge industry." Informational revolution is exemplified by TV pictures of the moon surface and also by robotized stock market transactions and, hopefully, by computerized professors. Fritz Machlup defined the knowledge industry to include education and research as well as publishing and broadcasting. He estimated its share in the gross national product of 1958 at 23 percent to 29 percent, and its growth rate at about 10 percent, or twice that of the GNP. Projecting to the present, the share of the knowledge industry would then appear to straddle the 40 percent mark!

There is a suspicious overlap between these activities and those which Adam Smith and Karl Marx called "unproductive" and which include the work of kings and professors, none of whom add to the vendible and visible stocks of the nation. To be sure, recent analysis—for example, by T. W. Schultz and Carl v. Weizsaecker—found it both convenient and feasible to define human capital and thus to consider education as investment. But the notable fact remains that professors and kings or the modern equivalent of kings—managers, both public and private—are strongly involved in those trends: informational revolution and growing knowledge industry.

Professors and managers, but also computers and TV sets, are involved in still another trend relevant to my talk. A growing proportion of both manhours and machine-hours is not employed for using large amounts of energy (muscular or otherwise) to transform or transport matter. Instead, so-called "brains" (human or otherwise) are employed to manipulate symbols. A sequence or network of such symbol manipulators uses up a minute amount of energy to eventually release, trigger-like, large amounts of energy through the more brutal medium of generators, muscles, and machine tools. In a modern assembly or disassembly plant (sawmill, meat packing), a growing majority of people,

* Supported by a grant from the Ford Foundation to the Graduate School of Business Administration, University of California at Berkeley, and administered through the Center for Research in Management Science. Facilities of the Western Management Science Institute, Univ. of California at Los Angeles (supported by grants or contracts of the National Science and the Ford Foundations and of the Office of Naval Research) were used in preparing the present revised version.

wearing white collars, or blue denims as well, do the brain work of in-specting, deciding, reporting—shunting, pushing buttons—and not the muscular work of shaping or carrying material masses; and a growing proportion of machines, called control mechanisms, are also busy with inspecting, reporting, deciding, and not with transforming or transport-ing matter and energy.

My topic is the economics of what I shall call the services of inquiring, communicating, deciding. Data are gathered. They are communicated to the decision-maker. He, on the basis of the message received, decides upon the action to be taken. A higher-order decision must have been made previously. Someone representing the interests of the economic unit considered—its head, leader, organizer—must have chosen a par-ticular combination of these three services from all those available in their respective markets. The maker of this higher-order decision (the "meta-decider," sometimes called "the organizer") may happen to be the same person who will decide upon acting. Or more generally, the organizer will hire the services of the decision-maker—who, in appro-priate cases, may be just a robot.

I might also call my topic the economics of the instruments, or de-vices, human or otherwise, for inquiring, communicating, and deciding. For it is not relevant, for my purposes, to distinguish between purchased instruments and hired services, provided the length of the hire contract is specified. In any case, I shall be concerned with symbol manipulators, human or otherwise, rather than with processors or transporters of matter or energy.

Here is what I plan to do. I shall present, in turn, from the user's point of view, the successive links in the sequence of symbol-manipu-lating services: inquiry, or data gathering; communication of messages; and deciding upon actions on the basis of messages received. It will turn out, in fact, that the link called "communication" must be broken into two distinct services: on the one hand, the service of "encoding and de-coding" which, at the present state of arts and in the most numerous and socially most important cases, is best supplied by men; and on the other hand, the service of "transmission" which is best supplied by inanimate equipment. As to the supply conditions of services of inquiry, or data production, and of decision making, I shall be able to submit nothing but crude illustrations, I am afraid. As to the demand side, economists will not be surprised that to make an economical—that is, optimal, efficient —choice the user must choose those links, or components, simultane-ously (just as a manufacturer cannot choose between rail and road as means of bringing him fuel without making up his mind, at the same time, whether the fuel should be coal or oil). Hence, the jointness of de-mand for services of inquiry, communication, and decision.

To be sure, current engineering science finds it convenient to isolate a pure theory of communication—a theory of efficient coding and transmission alone, essentially created by Claude Shannon and streamlined by Jack Wolfowitz. At the other extreme, statistical decision theory culminating in the work of David Blackwell leaves out the communication component and only analyzes, from the point of view of a perfect decision-maker, the optimal choice of inquiry, or data producing, services, also called "experiments." I shall later state the implicit tacit assumptions made in each case. If they are not satisfied, the user guided by those subtheories will have suboptimized. This is not to say that we ought not to break up a complex problem into subproblems, assuming them independent as a provisional first approximation. Given our human limitations, this may even be the optimal research strategy. It just happens that the economist is aware of interdependencies: he calls them complementarity and substitutability of goods. He is also traditionally permitted—as is the philosopher—to attack complexities with ridiculously simple examples in order to get directly to the general and fundamental.

Let me, then, go ahead with a simple example. I must decide this Thursday night whether to fly West next Saturday morning. Visibility and winds along the airplane's route the day after tomorrow will determine whether, if I do fly, I shall arrive in time for an important appointment or shall be killed in a crash. If I don't fly, I miss the appointment. But I cannot know what the weather will be. Instead, I may look tonight at the hotel barometer; or I may rely on the radio reports of other, more numerous and accurate barometer readings; or I may rely on the *Farmer's Almanac*. If the cost of these various services were equal, I would choose the one which gives data most closely reflecting (in some sense) the actual event I am interested in: the weather on Saturday. But perfection is costly, and I shall choose a service that is known not to mislead too grossly or too frequently, yet will be relatively cheap.

Take another example. A store's profit will be influenced by its inventory policy, given the actual future demand for its merchandise. Lacking the knowledge of this demand, the firm will have to choose between various services of market forecasters differing in precision and accuracy but also in the fees charged.

So much about services that inquire; i.e., produce data. These data are not identical with, yet do reflect in some sense the events that are relevant to, the result of a decision. Now, the decision-maker may or may not be able to obtain such data directly. Another service called "communication" will bring to him, not those data, but a message, possibly delayed or distorted, about those data. He must decide on the basis of such a message, which is now twice removed, in a sense, from the actual, result-relevant event: weather on Saturday, demand next month, and so on.

The inventory example illustrates also the nature of decision services.

4   AMERICAN ECONOMIC ASSOCIATION

Inventory policy is a rule stating whether and how much to reorder when the stock at hand is at a given level and you have some—usually imperfect—knowledge related to the prospective demand of your customers. One policy is similar to the one you use when you decide whether to refill your car's oil tank up to a certain upper level (this you will do whenever oil is below a certain lower level) or to leave it alone. Except that in the inventory case the two critical levels themselves are not fixed but should depend on what the store has learned—however imperfectly— about future demand; that is, on the message it has received about the data produced by a market forecast. Such a decision rule or strategy—a rule of how to respond to the message—may require the sophisticated services of a specialist or a computer. Contrast with this a simple routine rule: to refill the inventory every Monday to a constant level. This can be handled by an unskilled clerk or a cheap robot. The more sophisticated, flexible, nonroutine rule would be preferable if it were not for its higher cost.

To state more precisely the problem facing the user of the data producing, communication, and decision services, it is convenient to represent each service as a transformer of inputs into outputs. (Transformer, transformation, and function mean essentially the same thing.) A data producing service such as a barometer is a transformer whose input is the result-relevant event (weather next Saturday) and whose output is an observed value, a datum (the barometer reading tonight). We say that the data service is both precise and reliable if to each result-relevant event corresponds one observation or datum, and conversely. But this perfection is almost never attained. Generally, each event may be reflected in various alternative observed values, with some alternatives more likely than others. We have here the case of an "unreliable" (probabilistic, stochastic, noisy) transformer. For example, suppose that if Saturday's weather is going to be good, the chance that the barometer shows high pressure tonight is 80 percent. We say that the likelihood of the observation "high pressure," given the event "good weather," is 80 percent. Suppose the likelihood of low pressure if the weather is going to be dangerous is also 80 percent. Suppose that on a second barometer both these likelihoods are lower: 60 percent and 60 percent, say. If you have access to both barometers at the same cost or effort, you will prefer to be guided by the first one. For, in an obvious sense it is more reliable (more informative, in Blackwell's terminology). Indeed, in the case of perfect reliability the two likelihoods would be 100 percent and 100 percent; and clearly our first barometer (with 80 percent, 80 percent) comes closer to this perfection than the second (with 60 percent, 60 percent). In fact, the second comes closer than the first to the other extreme: likelihoods 50 percent, 50 percent, in which case the barometer would be useless.

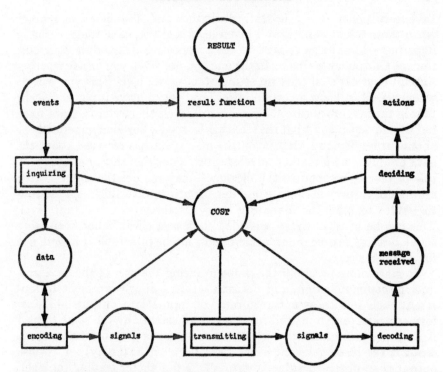

○ Circles = variables (generally random).
□ Boxes = transformers (noisy if double-framed). User maximizes average result minus cost (assuming additive utilities).

NOTE: In statistical theory, the lower row encoding→ · · · →decoding is omitted so that messages received = data. In communication theory, data = events; actions = messages received; and result = "bad" or "good" according as message received is or is not identical with datum.

Or consider a consumer survey conducted by a government agency. The success of the government decision to undertake one or another administrative action depends on the attitudes of all consumers. But only a certain number are sampled. The larger the sample the more reliable is the estimate of people's attitude. But also the more expensive. It is not different with research into the laws of physics or biology. What I called "result-relevant events" the statisticians call "hypotheses." The data producing service (e.g., a sampling) they call "experiment," and the data are called "observations."

Unfortunately, it is not always possible to compare two data producing services on the basis of the likelihoods only. How does our first barometer, with the 80 percent likelihood of high pressure given good weather, and 80 percent likelihood of low pressure given dangerous weather compare with the following one: if the weather is going to be good, the barometer will show high pressure for sure, i.e., with likelihood

100 percent; but given dangerous weather, it will show high or low pressure, not with 80:20 but with 50:50 chances. Thus, whenever the new barometer shows low pressure, it gives you absolute certainty that the weather cannot be good. But when it shows low pressure you are left guessing, and you might be better off with the original barometer. Which barometer should guide you?

Here I must remind you that, just as economists are Keynesians or non-Keynesians, the statisticians are Bayesians or non-Bayesians. The Bayesians, having given serious thought to our problem, tell me to consult two further items: (1) the approximate, so-called "prior," probabilities that I would assign to dangerous versus good weather for next Saturday—in the absence of any barometer, e.g., on the basis of my previous experience with December weather; (2) the utilities that I assign to various results of my actions and whose actuarial value I would like to be as high as possible. In our case, the best result is: surviving and making the appointment. The second best is: surviving but missing the appointment. The worst is death. What matters is the ratio of the disadvantage of missing the appointment (but staying alive) to the disadvantage of death. Now, unless a barometer is useless, I would fly if it shows high pressure and not fly otherwise (or vice versa). The probabilities of these pressure readings depend on my prior probability of the two states of weather and on the likelihoods characterizing each of the two barometers. Therefore, those pressures will be read on the two barometers with different probabilities. Hence the average utility of the results of actions dictated by each barometer and weighted by the probabilities of its readings will differ as between the two barometers. I prefer the one whose dictation will yield, on the average, the higher utility.

Suppose, then, the prior probability of bad (i.e., deadly dangerous) weather is, in my judgment, about 10 percent. Should I use the "old" barometer (whose likelihoods are 80 percent and 80 percent) or the "new" barometer (whose likelihoods are 100 percent and 50 percent), still assuming that the costs are equal. It turns out that I should stick to the old barometer as long as I judge the disadvantage of missing the appointment (while staying alive) to be less than one-seventh of the disadvantage of death. This is surely my case!

I believe this business of assigning prior probabilities to events and of utilities to results is a headache familiar to cost-benefit analysts, certainly present in this very room! It surely requires some soul-searching to appraise and reappraise the subjective probabilities ("beliefs") and utilities ("goals," "values," "tastes") of your government agency. You will presumably try out various plausible assumptions and see whether your boss likes the decisions derived from them; and whether under repeated trials of this kind his choices reveal a consistency of his beliefs and of his tastes. Or perhaps such trials will gradually train him toward consistency—toward learning what he wants and believes.

So far, we have seen how the consistent user should choose between available inquiry services when their costs are equal. This has required, for some though not all pairs of such services, to take account of the user's utilities and prior probabilities in order to compute the average utility attainable on the basis of an inquiry. If costs are not equal, the knowledge of prior probabilities and utilities becomes necessary in all cases. For simplicity, a tacit assumption is made. One assumes, in terms of our example, that it is possible to represent the utility of, say, "having made the appointment and having my wealth diminished by the dollar cost of a particular inquiry" as a sum of two utilities. In other words, utility is assumed to be additive and to be commensurable with dollars. Under this assumption, one may call the average utility of results of actions guided by an inquiry simply its dollar value to the user, his demand price. He compares it with the dollar cost, which is the supply price. The additivity assumption is implicitly made by statisticians. They assume in effect that the disutility of a result of action based on a sampling survey is measured by the size of the error of an estimate, and then vaguely compare its average with the dollar cost of the sampling survey. Engineers indulge in similar practices, as we shall see. Not so the economists. Sophisticated in matters of substitution, income elasticity, and risk aversion—all of which question the assumption of additive utility—they raise a warning finger. They do so at least when they talk theory and are not themselves engaged in the practical pursuits variously called "management science," "operations research," "system analysis," "cost-benefit analysis."

My barometer case—with just two alternative events, two possible observations, and two actions—is probably the simplest nontrivial problem in statistical decision theory. As I said before, this theory neglects the communication link. Result-relevant events, each having some prior probability, are transformed into data by a transformer called an "inquiry," or an "experiment" (like a barometer, or a sampling survey). Data flow directly into the transformer called "decision-maker," who applies a decision rule (e.g., "fly if barometric pressure high") and puts out actions. Finally, events and decisions are joint inputs of a transformer which may be called "result function": its output is a result. Assuming additive utility, a dollar amount can be attached to each result. And the probability of each result is determined by the prior probability of each event, by the array (characteristic of the data producing service) of the likelihoods of the data, given each event, and by the decision rule (characteristic of the given decision service) transforming data into actions. The probabilities of the results thus derived serve as weights to obtain the average of their utilities. This average may be called the "gross value," to a given user, of the given pair of data producing and decision-making services. It is the maximum demand price offered by their user. Their combined cost asked by the suppliers is the minimum supply price. The difference may be called "the net combined value of these two services to the user." He will choose the combination with highest net value.

This net value depends, then, on the one hand, on the choice of services made by their user. On the other hand, it depends on conditions outside of his control: viz., his utilities and prior probabilities and the costs of available services. His problem is to maximize the net value of the data producing and decision-making services, given those noncontrolled conditions.

Those familiar with what has been called "information theory" in the last two decades will have noticed that, so far, we have not used the concept of amount of information, measured in units called "bits." My uncertainty about a set of alternative events is the same as the amount of information that I would receive if that uncertainty were completely removed; that is, if I would know exactly which particular event does happen. Roughly speaking, this uncertainty is measured by the smallest average number of successive yes-and-no answers needed to completely remove uncertainty. This number depends roughly on the prior probabilities of events. Suppose, for example, that the following four events have equal probabilities (one-quarter each): the bride at the neighborhood church next Saturday will or won't wear a mini-dress, and her dress will or won't be white. To learn the color of the dress I need one yes-or-no question; so my uncertainty about color measures one bit. For the same reason, my uncertainty about both color and style is two bits since I need two yes-and-no answers to answer it. Thus the uncertainty, measured in bits, about those two mutually independent sets of events is the sum $(1+1=2)$ of the uncertainties about each of them. The number of bits is, in this sense, additive: a property that we require of every genuine measure, such as that of time, distance, volume, energy, dollar income, and dollar wealth.

If the four bridal events were not equally probable—for example, if the odds for a maxi-dress were not 1:1 but 9:1 (while a dress of each style were still as likely as not to be white)—the average necessary number of yes-and-no questions and thus the number of information bits would be smaller in the long run, i.e., over a long sequence of such events: for we can then profitably identify the more probable sequences (i.e., those mostly consisting of maxi-dresses) by asking a few questions only—as any skilled player of the "20 questions game" knows. As before, the count of bits agrees remarkably with the intuitive use of the

English word uncertainty: for when the odds are 9:1 I am almost certain, and with odds 1:1, I am fully ignorant, am I not?

Now suppose you have the choice between learning both the style and the color of the bride's dress and learning, with equal speed and for the same fee, the future price of your stocks. Suppose the price is as likely to rise as to fall. Depending on your selling or purchasing now, you may lose or double your fortune. A service that will tell you correctly whether the stock price will rise or fall conveys only one bit of information; whereas the service telling you correctly both the style and the color of the dress provides two bits. Yet you will prefer to learn about the stocks, not about the dress. There is, thus, no relation between the number of bits conveyed and the gross value of the data producing service. Nor does there seem to be a relation between the number of bits and the cost of a data producing service. For example, the cost of a sampling survey depends on its size, and this is not clearly related to the number of bits involved.

On the other hand, the number of yes-and-no symbols involved is clearly relevant to the performance and the cost of the transmission service regardless of whether these symbols refer to the length of the bridal skirt or to the trend of prices of your stock. To the economist, the contrast between production and transmission of data is strikingly analogous to the contrast between production and transportation of goods. A gallon of whiskey is more valuable than a gallon of gasoline: their costs to the producer and their values to the buyer are quite different. Yet to transport one gallon over one mile costs about the same for any liquid.

When, some twenty years ago, those elusive things labeled by the vague English words "uncertainty" and its negative, "information," were harnessed, subjected to genuine measurements (as was energy some hundred years ago, and mass and force much earlier), it was easy to understand the enthusiasm of people in elusive fields such as psychology. But also, to some extent, in statistics and in mathematics, where it was partly due to deep and beautiful theorems developed in this context. It is remarkable that C. Shannon who first proposed these theorems clearly limited their application to communications.

Statistical decision theory deals only with the choice of experiments and of decision rules; that is, with the choice of data producing and of deciding services. It omits the lower row of the chart reproduced above: encoding of data into signals, transmitting signals through a "communication channel," and decoding them back into messages that the decider would understand. In other words, for the statistician the decision is taken on the basis of a message which is simply the same thing as the data produced by the inquiry or experiment.

Not so with the communication engineer. His responsibility is to construct channels for the fast and reliable transmission of signals. (It all started in the telephone industry!) He is therefore also interested in devising appropriate codes which translate ordinary English into signals and signals back into English. But, to concentrate his mind on pure communication economics he makes, in effect, the following simplifying assumptions: First, events and data are identical, for he is not interested in the imperfections of the data producing service. Second, deciding is the same thing as decoding; so that action is simply the same thing as the message received. Third, as we have observed for the case of non-equiprobable events (which is, of course the usual case), the count of bits presupposes, in general, long sequences of events; and, as we shall see, such long sequences are also essential to make the crucial concept of "channel capacity" useful. Fourth, in most though not all[1] of their work, communication engineers assume an extremely simple result function. There are only two results: bad (say, minus one), when the decoded, received message is not identical with the datum sent; good (say, zero), when the two are identical. That is, all errors are equally important, have the same disutility, whether an inch is taken for a mile or merely a colon is taken for a semicolon. Finally, utility is assumed to be additive; i.e., it is conceived as the sum of certain measurable advantages and disadvantages, appropriately converted into dollars. We have seen that statisticans make the same assumption when they compare the sampling error with the dollar cost of the sample. The economist who detects and warns against this assumption is somewhat of a purist. The assumption is surely convenient for practical purposes and its removal is perhaps not that urgent.

Indeed this last assumption permits the engineer to ask the following economic question on behalf of the user of transmission channels and of coding services. Given the dollar costs of available channels, what is the best combination of the following evils: the probability of error (any error); the cost of the channel; the average time delay, which depends both on the length of signal sequences transmitted at a time and on the size of the code's vocabulary. That is, disutility is thought of, in effect, as a sum of dollars that buy a given channel; plus the dollar-equivalent of an error (any error); plus the dollar-equivalent, to a given user, of each time delay arising in the coding and transmission of a given datum. The user's problem is to choose that combination of channel and code which will minimize the sum of the averages of these amounts, weighted by appropriate probabilities. What do these probabilities depend on? On the uncertainty about data (= events); on the likelihood array characterizing the channel's reliability (the array of conditional probabilities

---

[1] Not, in particular, in Claude E. Shannon's work on a "fidelity criterion," which does correspond to a general result function.

of output symbols given an input symbol); and on the coding and de-coding procedures.

Clearly, an appropriately redundant code can almost overcome the lack of reliability of the channel; that is, it can almost eliminate the occurrence of errors. For example, the encoder just lets every "yes" or "no" to be repeated many times, and the decoder takes "no" for the answer if he has received more "no"'s than "yes"'s. "Don't!—repeat, don't!—repeat, don't shoot!" If I have heard two don'ts and only one do, I shan't shoot. However, we may need great redundancy of the code if the channel is very unreliable; and this will cause long delays if the channel is slow. But a channel that is fast and reliable is expensive.

If the user can afford to wait for a long sequence of data to flow in before they are encoded, the problem of choosing between channels is simplified, for their variety is reduced as follows. Instead of a whole array of likelihoods (of channel output symbols, given each input symbol) it becomes sufficient to use a single reliability measure (in bits per input symbol) which, multiplied by the channel's speed of transmission (in input symbols per time unit), gives the channel's "capacity," in bits per time unit.[2] Provided this capacity is larger than the number of bits per time unit that characterizes the uncertainty and speed of the flow of data, it has been shown that the user can achieve any desired probability of errors, however small, by using an appropriate, though redundant, code. Assuming that such codes have indeed been constructed (quite a difficult problem, solved only to a small part), it would be for the user to weigh against each other the disadvantages of errors, of time delays and of the high costs of high-capacity channels.

To avoid errors in our mutual understanding, let me be redundant, mindful of my low transmitting capacity and of your limited memory. I said a short time ago that engineers have isolated the pure communication problem by not concerning themselves with the services that produce data and that decide on acting; and also by usually refusing to distinguish between important and unimportant errors. I also pleaded, a longer time ago, on behalf of economists who emphasize that the demand for all services, all the transformers on my chart, is a joint one. Indeed, the user can improve the reliability of messages on which decisions are based by improving the communication service, but also by improving the data producing service which he is free to choose. Similarly, the user (the "meta-decider") is free to choose the deciding service; for example, he may prefer not to burden the unskilled but inexpensive decider with messages written in a vocabulary that is too rich and fine.

---

[2] For example, two channels with equal transmission speeds and each characterized by the same array of likelihoods as, respectively, the old and the new barometer of our previous illustration have approximately equal capacities, in bits per second.

Moreover, depending on the user's result function, he may fear some errors of communication but be indifferent to others. He may be indifferent to the music of the voice at the other end of the telephone; so he does not really need a high-fidelity telephone.

On the other hand, statisticians have isolated their problem, also essentially an economic one, by omitting the communication components. As I said before, this may be a good research strategy. I am told that in the early space vehicles rectangular pieces of equipment were used although the vehicles had circular cross-section. That is, the problem of building a good battery (say) was solved separately from, not jointly with, the problem of building a fast vehicle. Our problem-solving (decision-making) capacity is limited to only a few good solutions per manhour. To take up all problems at once is desirable but not cheap and perhaps not feasible. However, as time goes on the joint approach should be tried. Hence this economist's appeal to both statisticians and engineers.

I have just said that the limitation of the research capacity of all of us explains and possibly justifies the fact that engineers and statisticians have broken up the economics of symbol manipulation into separate sections, neglecting the essential complementarity of the several services from the point of view of the demand by the user.

However, this separation seems to be partly justified also by the economics of the services themselves; viz., by the supply side. I mean in particular the conditions for the production, and therefore for the supply, of inanimate transmission channels, such as telephones, the broadcasting apparatus, perhaps even the products of the old-fashioned printing press.

To be sure, you may not be anxious to learn about the bridal dress and be very much interested in the stock market. Yet your morning newspaper will bring you both a society page (which you will throw away) and a stock market page. Any page costs as much to print as any other page. The cost depends on the number of symbols on the page, and this corresponds to the number of bits transmitted by the printed messages. And the cost per bit turns out to be smaller if every subscriber receives both the social page and the stock market report and the sports page and the political news, regardless of his special tastes. Similarly, I am forced to subscribe to a high-fidelity telephone service although I am not interested in the music of the other person's voice. I suppose this is due to the economies of mass production. It is cheaper to produce instruments that will minimize the probability of transmission error—any error, however unimportant to me personally—than to custom-make instruments which would suit people's individual preferences. Remember that, in this country at least, with its large total demand for clothing and for food, consumers do find it advantageous to buy ready-made suits and standardized groceries. To go to a Bond Street tailor or to buy fancy foods is slightly more satisfactory but so much more expensive!

The problem is familiar to operations researchers as that of optimal assortment. It is also known to social and economic statisticians, editors of census volumes, and makers of production indices. They call it "optimal aggregation." What indeed is the most economical way to break down a collection of items into groups, each to be treated as if it were homogeneous, when every detail suppressed involves some sacrifice, yet also saves cost?

Thus, it is just possible that, for the purposes of large markets (but not, I would think, for the purpose of building a particular satellite!) the isolated theory of transmission channels that minimize the probability of error—any error—is exactly what one needs. Yet, to be sure of this, we ought to have at least an approximate idea as to whether the services immediately complementing the transmission, that is, the services of coding, also exhibit advantages of mass production; and that the imperfections of available data producing and decision-making services are indeed negligible as to their economic effects.

Inanimate transmission channels do display the advantages of mass production. This makes it useful, when studying their supply conditions, to apply the pure theory of communication and to derive economically significant results from measuring information in bits. But what about other symbol-manipulating services: inquiry, coding, deciding? What can we say, in particular, about those supplied not by machines but by humans?

Before commenting on this most fascinating question, let us remind ourselves of the principles of the analysis of demand, supply, and the markets, and apply them, in particular, to the markets of symbol-manipulating services.

The demands of individual users are aggregated into the total demands for various data-providing services: total demands for weather forecasters and market prophets; for the output of research laboratories, for services of spies and detectives—given the prices of each of these services. Similarly with the total demands for various communication services—television, telephones, post office, newspapers, but also schools! —given, again, the prices of each. And so also with the demand for deciders—inventory clerks and vice-presidents for finance, and humble robots. Some of these services are substitutes for one another: for example, TV, radio and newspapers; telephone and mail. Some are mutual complements: the demand for weather data and for radio sets boosts each other.

Now, to explain the "given prices" in the markets and the kind and volume of transactions that actually come about, we need to know also the supply conditions. What does it cost to produce a market survey; to print a mass-circulation paper or a professional periodical; or to run a school? And to rear and train a vice-president or to build an automatic pilot? Again, the supply conditions are interrelated, although perhaps not as closely as the demand conditions. An automatic pilot combines the services of inquiring and of deciding, and it might be more costly to produce these services separately.

At any rate, the supply of a given service or a bundle of services—at given prices!—will depend on the costs of producing various kinds and amounts of them. Under competition the price will, then, equate demand and supply.

Is this not classroom economics? Yes indeed. But it should include the more advanced parts of it which allow for oligopoly, uncertainty, and other such things, mildly called "imperfections." Particularly important are the facts of indivisibility, or more precisely, the lack of homogeneity, of standardization of many of the symbol manipulators. There exist almost unique, irreplaceable research workers, teachers, administrators; just as there exist unique choice locations for plants and harbors. The problem of unique or imperfectly standardized goods is not peculiar to the economics of inquiring, communicating, and deciding. But it has been indeed neglected in the textbooks.

Let us return to the comparison of services supplied by men and by machines. The subject has seriously worried the most creatively imaginative pessimists of science fiction—from Karel Čapek to Ray Bradbury. It has also fascinated, and has led to some serious work of, psychologists and computer scientists. The results of this work, however tentative, are of great interest to us economists.

To begin with, humans are very poor transmission channels. "Indeed," says George Miller, a leading psycholinguist, "it is an act of charity to call a man a channel at all. Compared to telephone or television channels, man is better characterized as a bottleneck. Under optimal conditions it is possible for a skilled typist or piano player to transmit 25 bits per second. . . . We shall have to regard 25 bits per second as near the upper limit." More usually, the transmission capacity of an average person in our culture is only 10 bits or less, that is, we are unable to identify a stimulus without error when the stimulus is selected from more than 2^{10}, i.e., about a thousand equiprobable alternatives (that is, when the identification logically requires at least ten yes-or-no questions). As to the so-called "short memory," an important accessory of many transmission instruments, George Miller says that "no self-respecting photographic plate would even bother to sneer at us."

But what about the other symbol-manipulating services? Take coding. The lady who is typing the almost illegible manuscript of this lecture has an uncanny gift of recognizing the intended meaning of letters and words. I think she does this mostly by looking at the context of a whole sentence, or even of the whole paper itself. This we can interpret either by saying that she has the ability of encoding almost without errors the data presented in longhand into the symbols of the typewriter alphabet; or that she decodes the longhand symbols given to her, into messages, and these into actions; viz., into pressing the keys, mostly in such a way that no error occurs. As you know, the computer industry has just begun to construct machines that may one day match the human ability to recognize simple visual patterns such as hand-written individual letters (not whole sentences!). But some people believe it will take a very long time (generations or centuries, Y. Bar-Hillel thinks) until a machine can conduct "intelligent conversation" with a man or with another machine. The key words are "heuristics" and "intuition." They are as vague as "pattern recognition," "Gestalt," and "context," and all these words are perhaps intended to have the same meaning. It is remarkable, in fact, in this very context, that you and I vaguely understand each other as to what the word "context" is intended to mean. We understand each other not letter by letter, not even word by word, but by grouping symbols into large chunks—letters (or, rather, phonemes) into words, and words into sentences, and even into larger entities, each including all sentences with the same so-called "meaning." The chunks forming the vocabulary of a human coder or decoder are of course much less numerous than the ensemble of all possible combinations of a given number of letters, say. The use of chunks diminishes therefore the flow of signals through the channel; it is more efficient, more economical. Consider the three letters C, O, W. They can be combined in six possible ways. But only one of the six combinations occurs in your vocabulary: cow. And, remarkably, it invokes not just the few properties listed by taxonomists who define a cow, but a whole image of shapes and sounds and colors and the tail waving the flies away. A most efficient, economical code—the living human language!

Most important, when you, a man, talk to a fellow human you adjust your code to the receptor, and keep readjusting it, sensitive to his feedback responses. Is this not what characterizes a good teacher? James Boswell, young and smug, wrote in his diary:

> Health, youth, and gold sufficient I possess;
> Where one has more, five hundred sure have less.

He could as well have said: my wealth is at the uppermost half percentile. This would be economical if you would address income statisticians: you would utilize a "subroutine" that has been educated into them! But when you address other people, better recite a poem.

Even the talking to computers is better done by men, at least today. The encoding, or programming, of a difficult problem for a computer is said to be an art, not a science. People who say this probably mean precisely this: the activity of programming cannot be delegated by men to machines, at least not in serious cases and not in the present state of technology. Hence the very large proportion (one-half, I understand) that the human activity of programming contributes to the value added by computing organizations.

To turn from coding to inquiring services. A biochemist (J. Lederberg) and a computer scientist (E. Feigenbaum) have told a computer how to generate the graphs of all imaginable organic compounds of a certain class, and also how to match them with certain empirically observed spectra. This was essentially a job of mathematical routine. But now comes the heuristics! The biochemist had accumulated enough experience and a flair to eliminate as unrealistic all but a few patterns from the thousands that the computer had omitted. Yet the human being, a Nobel laureate, was not able to articulate his flair, although he did learn in this direction from the cooperation with the computer. Given the abilities and the technologies, there is some optimal way of allocating the tasks between men and machines—as economists have known long ago. And we must not be too hard on the computer: its hardware is certainly much less complex than the man's genetic endowment, and the computer's short babyhood is not rich in experience.

Finally, the service of decision making or problem solving. How to allocate tasks of this nature among executives and machines? A delicate problem! It involves all echelons of a corporation, up to, but of course not including, the president, who cannot fire himself. I had better skirt this subject!

But let me remind you of the distinction I have made earlier, between decision making and the higher-order activity of choosing who or what should provide a given service of decision making or of inquiring or of coding or transmitting. The man in charge was called the "leader" or 'organizer." It is his judgment of prior probabilities and utilities, his "beliefs" and his "tastes" (or "values," in other words), that are used among the "givens" of the organizer's problem. He cannot delegate them, either to men or machines.

His problem may be, in fact, much, much larger than my chart suggests at first glance. The economic problem of organization is that of allocating numerous kinds of tasks, symbol manipulating as well as physical, to numerous transformers, arranged in a complex yet efficient network. And further complications, of a different kind, arise when a single organizer is replaced by several. Their beliefs and utilities are not the same. They engage in a nonconstant sum game. The economist's problem is then shifted from the search for optimality to the search for stability: he tries to explain, as does the biologist or anthropologist, why certain arrangements, certain allocations of tasks and incentives (rewards) have a greater chance to survive over a given period than other arrangements, and under what conditions.

The criterion of survival, viability, stability guides the social scientist who describes, and tries to explain, the existing institutions. Yet not everything that is stable is desirable. Some wicked dictatorships have been quite stable. Along with the stability criterion, the economist uses a weak collective optimality criterion, a modest common denominator on which people might agree in spite of their divergent utilities and beliefs: an arrangement of tasks and incentives is optimal in this modest sense if there is no feasible arrangement that would be better or at least not worse for all members of the organization.

What, then, if we consider the whole society as an organization? How should incentives and tasks be allocated in a way that is stable or is collectively optimal, or, if possible, both? Further, some of us cannot help but smuggle in our own values, in particular a high valuation of liberty and equity. I suppose "public policy," "public good," in our tradition, mean somehow to reconcile the criteria of stability and of collective optimality with those of liberty and equity. Though the economic theorist prefers to hide behind the technical term "welfare economics," he means not just Secretary Gardner's Department of Health, Education and Welfare, but much more, the whole public policy. Nor is our special concern only education, even if taken in the broad sense of the communication of what my chart calls "data," to the whole or some parts of the public. For research, inquiry has been also our concern here. Public policy problems in the field of symbol manipulation are crudely exemplified by questions such as, "When, if at all, should the government subsidize or protect research and teaching and the dissemination of news?"

As far as I know, welfare economics of symbol manipulation is at its beginning. Special problems, such as the theory of patents and of public versus private broadcasting and, most importantly, of the economics of education, have been studied and the names of Silberston, Coase, Gary Becker come to mind.

On the more abstract level, a basic distinction exists between the information about external facts and the information conveyed to a member of society about the doings of others. A preliminary analysis of economic policy of information about external facts has been made by my colleague Hirshleifer. If correct, his conclusions on teaching and re-

18 AMERICAN ECONOMIC ASSOCIATION

search are quite relevant to the California battle of tuition fees, although Hirshleifer's analysis had to be based on some extreme, simplifying assumptions. To analyze the economics of information of people about other people is even harder. Game theorists have provided some building blocks. Ożga has worked on "imperfect markets through lack of knowledge" and Stigler on the information in the labor market. It is just one year ago that Leijonhufvud told this Association that Keynesian unemployment may be mostly due to lack of information. We know very little about the technology of such information; for example, about the optimal language. Indeed, many believe that the run on gold is dammed, not by verbal announcements in English or even in French, but by actually selling gold to all comers. And Radner has penetratingly pointed to the setup cost of information which makes for increasing returns to scale and makes it difficult to apply the classical theory of free markets, which reconciles optimality and stability.

All this discussion, mostly by young members of our Association, is very recent, very exciting, and, I believe, very important. The informational revolution is upon us, and the manipulation of symbols dominates our lives more and more. I do hope we shall soon understand how to harness and benefit from those trends in our culture.

[25]

THE PRETENCE OF KNOWLEDGE*

Friedrich August von Hayek

Salzburg, Austria

The particular occasion of this lecture, combined with the chief practical problem which economists have to face today, have made the choice of its topic almost inevitable. On the one hand the still recent establishment of the Nobel Memorial Prize in Economic Science marks a significant step in the process by which, in the opinion of the general public, economics has been conceded some of the dignity and prestige of the physical sciences. On the other hand, the economists are at this moment called upon to say how to extricate the free world from the serious threat of accelerating inflation which, it must be admitted, has been brought about by policies which the majority of economists recommended and even urged governments to pursue. We have indeed at the moment little cause for pride: as a profession we have made a mess of things.

It seems to me that this failure of the economists to guide policy more successfully is closely connected with their propensity to imitate as closely as possible the procedures of the brilliantly successful physical sciences—an attempt which in our field may lead to outright error. It is an approach which has come to be described as the "scientistic" attitude—an attitude which, as I defined it some thirty years ago, "is decidedly unscientific in the true sense of the word, since it involves a mechanical and uncritical application of habits of thought to fields different from those in which they have been formed".[1] I want today to begin by explaining how some of the gravest errors of recent economic policy are a direct consequence of this scientistic error.

The theory which has been guiding monetary and financial policy during the last thirty years, and which I contend is largely the product of such a mistaken conception of the proper scientific procedure, consists in the assertion that there exists a simple positive correlation between total employment and the size of the aggregate demand for goods and services; it leads to the belief that we can permanently assure full employment by maintaining total money expenditure at an appropriate level. Among the various theories advanced to account for extensive unemployment, this is probably the only one in support of

* Nobel Memorial Lecture held December 11, 1974. © The Nobel Foundation, 1975.
[1] "Scientism and the Study of Society", *Economica*, vol. IX, no. 35, August 1942, reprinted in *The Counter-Revolution of Science*, Glencoe, Ill., 1952, p. 15 of this reprint.

which strong quantitative evidence can be adduced. I nevertheless regard it as fundamentally false, and to act upon it, as we now experience, as very harmful.

This brings me to the crucial issue. Unlike the position that exists in the physical sciences, in economics and other disciplines that deal with essentially complex phenomena, the aspects of the events to be accounted for about which we can get quantitative data are necessarily limited and may not include the important ones. While in the physical sciences it is generally assumed, probably with good reason, that any important factor which determines the observed events will itself be directly observable and measurable, in the study of such complex phenomena as the market, which depend on the actions of many individuals, all the circumstances which will determine the outcome of a process, for reasons which I shall explain later, will hardly ever be fully known or measurable. And while in the physical sciences the investigator will be able to measure what, on the basis of a *prima facie* theory, he thinks important, in the social sciences often that is treated as important which happens to be accessible to measurement. This is sometimes carried to the point where it is demanded that our theories must be formulated in such terms that they refer only to measurable magnitudes.

It can hardly be denied that such a demand quite arbitrarily limits the facts which are to be admitted as possible causes of the events which occur in the real world. This view, which is often quite naively accepted as required by scientific procedure, has some rather paradoxical consequences. We know, of course, with regard to the market and similar social structures, a great many facts which we cannot measure and on which indeed we have only some very imprecise and general information. And because the effects of these facts in any particular instance cannot be confirmed by quantitative evidence, they are simply disregarded by those sworn to admit only what they regard as scientific evidence: they thereupon happily proceed on the fiction that the factors which they can measure are the only ones that are relevant.

The correlation between aggregate demand and total employment, for instance, may only be approximate, but as it is the *only* one on which we have quantitative data, it is accepted as the only causal connection that counts. On this standard there may thus well exist better "scientific" evidence for a false theory, which will be accepted because it is more "scientific", than for a valid explanation, which is rejected because there is no sufficient quantitative evidence for it.

Let me illustrate this by a brief sketch of what I regard as the chief actual cause of extensive unemployment—an account which will also explain why such unemployment cannot be lastingly cured by the inflationary policies recommended by the now fashionable theory. This correct explanation appears to me to be the existence of discrepancies between the distribution of demand among the different goods and services and the allocation of labour and other resources among the production of those outputs. We possess a fairly good "qualitative" knowledge of the forces by which a correspondence between demand and supply in the different sectors of the economic system is brought about, of the conditions under which it will be achieved, and of the factors likely to prevent such an adjustment. The separate steps in the account of this process rely on facts of everyday experience, and few who take the trouble to follow the argument will question the validity of the factual assumptions, or the logical correctness of the conclusions drawn from them. We have indeed good reason to believe that unemployment indicates that the structure of relative prices and wages has been distorted (usually by monopolistic or governmental price fixing), and that to restore equality between the demand and the supply of labour in all sectors changes of relative prices and some transfers of labour will be necessary.

But when we are asked for quantitative evidence for the particular structure of prices and wages that would be required in order to assure a smooth continuous sale of the products and services offered, we must admit that we have no such information. We know, in other words, the general conditions in which what we call, somewhat misleadingly, an equilibrium will establish itself: but we never know what the particular prices or wages are which would exist if the market were to bring about such an equilibrium. We can merely say what the conditions are in which we can expect the market to establish prices and wages at which demand will equal supply. But we can never produce statistical information which would show how much the prevailing prices and wages *deviate* from those which would secure a continuous sale of the current supply of labour. Though this account of the causes of unemployment is an empirical theory, in the sense that it might be proved false, e.g. if, with a constant money supply, a general increase of wages did not lead to unemployment, it is certainly not the kind of theory which we could use to obtain specific numerical predictions concerning the rates of wages, or the distribution of labour, to be expected.

Why should we, however, in economics, have to plead ignorance of the sort of facts on which, in the case of a physical theory, a scientist would certainly be expected to give precise information? It is probably not surprising that those impressed by the example of the physical sciences should find this position very unsatisfactory and should insist on the standards of proof which they find there. The reason for this state of affairs is the fact, to which I have already briefly referred, that the social sciences, like much of biology but unlike most fields of the physical sciences, have to deal with structures of *essential* complexity, i.e. with structures whose characteristic properties can be exhibited only by models made up of relatively large numbers of variables. Competition, for instance, is a process which will produce certain results only if it proceeds among a fairly large number of acting persons.

In some fields, particularly where problems of a similar kind arise in the

436   *F. A. von Hayek*

physical sciences, the difficulties can be overcome by using, instead of specific information about the individual elements, data about the relative frequency, or the probability, of the occurrence of the various distinctive properties of the elements. But this is true only where we have to deal with what has been called by Dr Warren Weaver (formerly of the Rockefeller Foundation), with a distinction which ought to be much more widely understood, "phenomena of unorganized complexity", in contrast to those "phenomena of organized complexity" with which we have to deal in the social sciences.[1] Organized complexity here means that the character of the structures showing it depends not only on the properties of the individual elements of which they are composed, and the relative frequency with which they occur, but also on the manner in which the individual elements are connected with each other. In the explanation of the working of such structures we can for this reason not replace the information about the individual elements by statistical information, but require full information about each element if from our theory we are to derive specific predictions about individual events. Without such specific information about the individual elements we shall be confined to what on another occasion I have called mere pattern predictions—predictions of some of the general attributes of the structures that will form themselves, but not containing specific statements about the individual elements of which the structures will be made up.[2]

This is particularly true of our theories accounting for the determination of the systems of relative prices and wages that will form themselves on a well-functioning market. Into the determination of these prices and wages there will enter the effects of particular information possessed by every one of the participants in the market process—a sum of facts which in their totality cannot be known to the scientific observer, or to any other single brain. It is indeed the source of the superiority of the market order, and the reason why, when it is not suppressed by the powers of government, it regularly displaces other types of order, that in the resulting allocation of resources more of the knowledge of particular facts will be utilized which exists only dispersed among uncounted persons, than any one person can possess. But because we, the observing scientists, can thus never know all the determinants of such an order, and in consequence also cannot know at which particular structure of prices and wages demand would everywhere equal supply, we also cannot measure the deviations from that order; nor can we statistically test our theory that it is the deviations from that "equilibrium" system of prices and wages

---

[1] Warren Weaver, "A Quarter Century in the Natural Sciences", *The Rockefeller Foundation Annual Report 1958*, chapter I, "Science and Complexity".
[2] See my essay "The Theory of Complex Phenomena" in *The Critical Approach to Science and Philosophy. Essays in Honor of K. R. Popper*, ed. M. Bunge, New York 1964, and reprinted (with additions) in my *Studies in Philosophy, Politics and Economics*, London and Chicago 1967.

which make it impossible to sell some of the products and services at the prices at which they are offered.

Before I continue with my immediate concern, the effects of all this on the employment policies currently pursued, allow me to define more specifically the inherent limitations of our numerical knowledge which are so often over-looked. I want to do this to avoid giving the impression that I generally reject the mathematical method in economics. I regard it in fact as the great advantage of the mathematical technique that it allows us to describe, by means of algebraic equations, the general character of a pattern even where we are ignorant of the numerical values which will determine its particular manifestation. We could scarcely have achieved that comprehensive picture of the mutual interdependencies of the different events in a market without this algebraic technique. It has led to the illusion, however, that we can use this technique for the determination and prediction of the numerical values of those magnitudes; and this has led to a vain search for quantitative or numerical constants. This happened in spite of the fact that the modern founders of mathematical economics had no such illusions. It is true that their systems of equations describing the pattern of a market equilibrium are so framed that *if* we were able to fill in the blanks of the abstract formulae, i.e. *if* we knew all the parameters of these equations, we could calculate the prices and quantities of all commodities and services sold. But, as Vilfredo Pareto, one of the founders of this theory, clearly stated, its purpose cannot be "to arrive at a numerical calculation of prices", because, as he said, it would be "absurd" to assume that we could ascertain all the data.[1] Indeed, the cief point was already seen by those remarkable anticipators of modern economics, the Spanish schoolmen of the sixteenth century, who emphasized that what they called *pretium mathematicum*, the mathematical price, depended on so many particular circumstances that it could never be known to man but was known only to God.[2] I sometimes wish that our mathematical economists would take this to heart. I must confess that I still doubt whether their search for measurable magnitudes has made significant contributions to our *theoretical* understanding of economic phenomena—as distinct from their value as a description of particular situations. Nor am I prepared to accept the excuse that this branch of research is still very young: Sir William Petty, the founder of econometrics, was after all a somewhat senior colleague of Sir Isaac Newton in the Royal Society!

There may be few instances in which the superstition that only measurable magnitudes can be important has done positive harm in the economic field: but the present inflation and employment problems are a very serious one. Its

[1] V. Pareto, *Manuel d'économie politique*, 2nd ed., Paris 1927, pp. 223–4.
[2] See, e.g., Luis Molina, *De iustitia et iure*, Cologne 1596–1600, tom. II, disp. 347, no. 3, and particularly Johannes de Lugo, *Disputationum de iustitia et iure tomus secundus*, Lyon 1642, disp. 26, sect. 4, no. 40.

effect has been that what is probably the true cause of extensive unemployment has been disregarded by the scientistically minded majority of economists, because its operation could not be confirmed by directly observable relations between measurable magnitudes, and that an almost exclusive concentration on quantitatively measurable surface phenomena has produced a policy which has made matters worse.

It has, of course, to be readily admitted that the kind of theory which I regard as the true explanation of unemployment is a theory of somewhat limited content because it allows us to make only very general predictions of the *kind* of events which we must expect in a given situation. But the effects on policy of the more ambitious constructions have not been very fortunate and I confess that I prefer true but imperfect knowledge, even if it leaves much indetermined and unpredictable, to a pretence of exact knowledge that is likely to be false. The credit which the apparent conformity with recognized scientific standards can gain for seemingly simple but false theories may, as the present instance shows, have grave consequences.

In fact, in the case discussed, the very measures which the dominant "macroeconomic" theory has recommended as a remedy for unemployment, namely the increase of aggregate demand, have become a cause of a very extensive misallocation of resources which is likely to make later large-scale unemployment inevitable. The continuous injection of additional amounts of money at points of the economic system where it creates a temporary demand which must cease when the increase of the quantity of money stops or slows down, together with the expectation of a continuing rise of prices, draws labour and other resources into employments which can last only so long as the increase of the quantity of money continues at the same rate—or perhaps even only so long as it continues to accelerate at a given rate. What this policy has produced is not so much a level of employment that could not have been brought about in other ways, as a distribution of employment which cannot be indefinitely maintained and which after some time can be maintained only by a rate of inflation which would rapidly lead to a disorganisation of all economic activity. The fact is that by a mistaken theoretical view we have been led into a precarious position in which we cannot prevent substantial unemployment from re-appearing; not because, as this view is sometimes misrepresented, this unemployment is deliberately brought about as a means to combat inflation, but because it is now bound to occur as a deeply regrettable but inescapable consequence of the mistaken policies of the past as soon as inflation ceases to accelerate.

I must, however, now leave these problems of immediate practical importance which I have introduced chiefly as an illustration of the momentous consequences that may follow from errors concerning abstract problems of the philosophy of science. There is as much reason to be apprehensive about the long run dangers created in a much wider field by the uncritical acceptance of assertions which have the *appearance* of being scientific as there is with regard to the problems I have just discussed. What I mainly wanted to bring out by the topical illustration is that certainly in my field, but I believe also generally in the sciences of man, what looks superficially like the most scientific procedure is often the most unscientific, and, beyond this, that in these fields there are definite limits to what we can expect science to achieve. This means that to entrust to science—or to deliberate control according to scientific principles—more than scientific method can achieve may have deplorable effects. The progress of the natural sciences in modern times has of course so much exceeded all expectations that any suggestion that there may be some limits to it is bound to arouse suspicion. Especially all those will resist such an insight who have hoped that our increasing power of prediction and control, generally regarded as the characteristic result of scientific advance, applied to the process of society, would soon enable us to mould society entirely to our liking. It is indeed true that, in contrast to the exhilaration which the discoveries of the physical sciences tend to produce, the insights which we gain from the study of society more often have a dampening effect on our aspirations; and it is perhaps not surprising that the more impetuous younger members of our profession are not always prepared to accept this. Yet the confidence in the unlimited power of science is only too often based on a false belief that the scientific method consists in the application of a ready-made technique, or in imitating the form rather than the substance of scientific procedure, as if one needed only to follow some cooking recipes to solve all social problems. It sometimes almost seems as if the techniques of science were more easily learnt than the thinking that shows us what the problems are and how to approach them.

The conflict between what in its present mood the public expects science to achieve in satisfaction of popular hopes and what is really in its power is a serious matter because, even if the true scientists should all recognize the limitations of what they can do in the field of human affairs, so long as the public expects more there will always be some who will pretend, and perhaps honestly believe, that they can do more to meet popular demands than is really in their power. It is often difficult enough for the expert, and certainly in many instances impossible for the layman, to distinguish between legitimate and illegitimate claims advanced in the name of science. The enormous publicity recently given by the media to a report pronouncing in the name of science on *The Limits to Growth*, and the silence of the same media about the devastating criticism this report has received from the competent experts,[1] must make one feel somewhat apprehensive about the use to which the prestige

---

[1] See *The Limits to Growth: A Report of the Club of Rome's Project on the Predicament of Mankind*, New York 1972; for a systematic examination of this by a competent economist cf. Wilfred Beckerman, *In Defence of Economic Growth*, London 1974, and, for a list of earlier criticisms by experts, Gottfried Haberler, *Economic Growth and Stability*, Los Angeles 1974, who rightly calls their effect "devastating".

of science can be put. But it is by no means only in the field of economics that far-reaching claims are made on behalf of a more scientific direction of all human activities and the desirability of replacing spontaneous processes by "conscious human control". If I am not mistaken, psychology, psychiatry and some branches of sociology, not to speak about the so-called philosophy of history, are even more affected by what I have called the scientistic prejudice, and by specious claims of what science can achieve.[1]

If we are to safeguard the reputation of science, and to prevent the arrogation of knowledge based on a superficial similarity of procedure with that of the physical sciences, much effort will have to be directed toward debunking such arrogations, some of which have by now become the vested interests of established university departments. We cannot be grateful enough to such modern philosophers of science as Sir Karl Popper for giving us a test by which we can distinguish between what we may accept as scientific and what not—a test which I am sure some doctrines now widely accepted as scientific would not pass. There are some special problems, however, in connection with those essentially complex phenomena of which social structures are so important an instance, which make me wish to restate in conclusion in more general terms the reasons why in these fields not only are there absolute obstacles to the prediction of specific events, but why to act as if we possessed scientific knowledge enabling us to transcend them may itself become a serious obstacle to the advance of the human intellect.

The chief point we must remember is that the great and rapid advance of the physical sciences took place in fields where it proved that explanation and prediction could be based on laws which accounted for the observed phenomena as functions of comparatively few variables—either particular facts or relative frequencies of events. This may even be the ultimate reason why we single out these realms as "physical" in contrast to those more highly organized structures which I have here called essentially complex phenomena. There is no reason why the position must be the same in the latter as in the former fields. The difficulties which we encounter in the latter are not, as one might at first suspect, difficulties about formulating theories for the explanation of the observed events—although they cause also special difficulties about testing proposed explanations and therefore about eliminating bad theories. They are due to the chief problem which arises when we apply our theories to any particular situation in the real world. A theory of essentially complex phenomena must refer to a large number of particular facts; and to derive a prediction from it, or to test it, we have to ascertain all these particular facts. Once we succeeded in this there should be no particular difficulty

---

[1] I have given some illustrations of these tendencies in other fields in my inaugural lecture as Visiting Professor at the University of Salzburg, *Die Irrtümer des Konstruktivismus und die Grundlagen legitimer Kritik gesellschaftlicher Gebilde*, Munich 1970, now re-issued for the Walter Eucken Institute, at Freiburg i.Brg. by J. C. B. Mohr, Tübingen 1975.

about deriving testable predictions—with the help of modern computers it should be easy enough to insert these data into the appropriate blanks of the theoretical formulae and to derive a prediction. The real difficulty, to the solution of which science has little to contribute, and which is sometimes indeed insoluble, consists in the ascertainment of the particular facts.

A simple example will show the nature of this difficulty. Consider some ball game played by a few people of approximately equal skill. If we knew a few particular facts in addition to our general knowledge of the ability of the individual players, such as their state of attention, their perceptions and the state of their hearts, lungs, muscles etc. at each moment of the game, we could probably predict the outcome. Indeed, if we were familiar both with the game and the teams we should probably have a fairly shrewd idea on what the outcome will depend. But we shall of course not be able to ascertain those facts and in consequence the result of the game will be outside the range of the scientifically predictable, however well we may know what effects particular events would have on the result of the game. This does not mean that we can make no predictions at all about the course of such a game. If we know the rules of the different games we shall, in watching one, very soon know which game is being played and what kinds of actions we can expect and what kind not. But our capacity to predict will be confined to such general characteristics of the events to be expected and not include the capacity of predicting particular individual events.

This corresponds to what I have called earlier the mere pattern predictions to which we are increasingly confined as we penetrate from the realm in which relatively simple laws prevail into the range of phenomena where organized complexity rules. As we advance we find more and more frequently that we can in fact ascertain only some but not all the particular circumstances which determine the outcome of a given process; and in consequence we are able to predict only some but not all the properties of the result we have to expect. Often all that we shall be able to predict will be some abstract characteristic of the pattern that will appear—relations between kinds of elements about which individually we know very little. Yet, as I am anxious to repeat, we will still achieve predictions which can be falsified and which therefore are of empirical significance.

Of course, compared with the precise predictions we have learnt to expect in the physical sciences, this sort of mere pattern predictions is a second best with which one does not like to have to be content. Yet the danger of which I want to warn is precisely the belief that in order to have a claim to be accepted as scientific it is necessary to achieve more. This way lies charlatanism and worse. To act on the belief that we possess the knowledge and the power which enable us to shape the processes of society entirely to our liking, knowledge which in fact we do *not* possess, is likely to make us do much harm. In the physical sciences there may be little objection to trying to do the impossible; one might even feel that one ought not to discourage the over-confident because their experiments may after all produce some new insights. But in the social field the erroneous belief that the exercise of some power would have beneficial consequences is likely to lead to a new power to coerce other men being confered on some authority. Even if such power is not in itself bad, its exercise is likely to impede the functioning of those spontaneous ordering forces by which, without understanding them, man is in fact so largely assisted in the pursuit of his aims. We are only beginning to understand on how subtle a communication system the functioning of an advanced industrial society is based—a communications system which we call the market and which turns out to be a more efficient mechanism for digesting dispersed information than any that man has deliberately designed.

If man is not to do more harm than good in his efforts to improve the social order, he will have to learn that in this, as in all other fields where essential complexity of an organized kind prevails, he cannot acquire the full knowledge which would make mastery of the events possible. He will therefore have to use what knowledge he can achieve, not to shape the results as the craftsman shapes his handiwork, but rather to cultivate a growth by providing the appropriate environment, in the manner in which the gardener does this for his plants. There is danger in the exuberant feeling of ever growing power which the advance of the physical sciences has engendered and which tempts man to try, "dizzy with success", to use a characteristic phrase of early communism, to subject not only our natural but also our human environment to the control of a human will. The recognition of the insuperable limits to his knowledge ought indeed to teach the student of society a lesson of humility which should guard him against becoming an accomplice in men's fatal striving to control society—a striving which makes him not only a tyrant over his fellows, but which may well make him the destroyer of a civilization which no brain has designed but which has grown from the free efforts of millions of individuals.

Part VIII
New Directions

[26]

Informational Structure of the Firm

By KENNETH J. ARROW*

The modern firm is typically not only large but complex. It has an internal structure, and its parts have to communicate and coordinate with each other. This is hardly a new observation. If you will forgive my use of the English platitude, "it's all in Marshall," let me quote, "the development of the organism, whether social or physical, involves an increasing subdivision of functions between its separate parts on the one hand, and on the other a more intimate connection between them" (Marshall, 1948, p. 241).

The complexity of the firm has of course scarcely gone unnoticed in more recent literature. Alfred Chandler (1979) has given a first-rate account of the evolution of the firm's internal structure in response to changing economic needs. Oliver Williamson and others in the bounded rationality tradition stemming from Herbert Simon have sought to create a theory which will accommodate the observed structures of industry. But the history of economic thought suggests that these theories will only find analytic usefulness when they are founded on more directly neoclassical lines, that is, in terms of individual optimization and equilibrium. I do not regard this point of view as some kind of absolute methodological imperative. I merely argue that it has typically been found most convenient to use whether for theory or as a basis for empirical work, and it is worth while to pursue the viewpoint of optimization to see where it will lead.

Nor will I try to give here a full-scale neoclassical theory of internal structure based on specialization and coordination. Rather my aim is to indicate some serious problems in formulating the interchange of information among the component parts of a firm or, indeed, other organization.

I take as the basic model the theory of teams (see Jacob Marschak, 1953, 1954; Marschak and Roy Radner, 1972). Although this theory is now more than thirty years old, its development has been sporadic. It has had as much influence among control theorists as among economists.

The elements of a firm, in team theory, are *agents* among whom both decision making and knowledge are dispersed. The problem, at least as usually formulated, is that of *design*. It is to determine an allocation of information and a set of decision rules for the individual agents so as to optimize some given payoff function for the firm. The payoff depends on the actions taken by all the agents in the firm and on some environmental factors (such as prices or technological conditions) not known at the time the team is designed. These environmental factors are usually referred to as the *state of the world*. The concept of information for an agent is defined as usual in statistical decision theory or communication theory. Each agent observes a random variable, sometimes termed a *signal*. There is a joint distribution of the state of the world and the signals to all agents, which defines a conditional distribution of the state of the world and of other agents' signals given the signal to any one agent.

Each agent has a set of actions from which choice is to be made. Since the agent observes only the appropriate signal, his or her decision rule is a function mapping the agent's signal to that agent's action space. The design problem properly speaking is then both to choose a signal for each agent and a decision rule mapping that signal into actions. We may call the assignment of signals to agents the *information structure* and the choice of decision rules the *decision structure*.

The choice of information structures must be subject to some limits, otherwise, of course, each agent would simply observe the entire state of the world. There are costs of

*Stanford University, Stanford, CA 94305.

information, and it is an important and incompletely explored part of decision theory in general to formulate reasonable cost functions for information structures. Indeed, most of the theory of teams to date has concentrated on choosing optimal decision structures for a given information structure, rather than optimizing on information structures, thereby avoiding explicit consideration of cost functions.

Up to this point, the model has assumed an initial distribution of information followed by decisions. In the vast literature on economic planning, emphasis is put on communication. Before action is taken, there is an exchange of information, which may take place many times, infinitely often in fact in the analysis of convergent optimization processes. These can be assimilated to team theory. At each stage, the message for each agent to each other agent is a function of the information available to that agent, which now includes the agent's original signal plus all messages received by that agent in previous rounds. What has only now begun to be recognized is that one has to add to an agent's information all the inferences that can be made from the signal and subsequent messages.

The team model does abstract from one very important aspect of organization much stressed in recent literature, that of incentives. It is assumed that the firm as such has organizational objectives which are adhered to by each member. I certainly do not wish to minimize the importance of incentives to perform. There are two reasons why I accept this abstraction here: 1) I want to emphasize the choice of the information structure, which is still of great importance in models with incentives and has been neglected; these models invariably take the structure as given. 2) The present incentive models take a very limited view of the information structure. In fact, within a firm there are many forms of information gathering ("monitoring," in the usual terminology of principal-agent theory) beyond those in our current models. It may be a good abstraction to regard monitoring within the management structure of a firm as sufficiently complete that shirking is not an issue. It is noteworthy that bonuses are to a

large extent discretionary (i.e., tied to observations that cannot easily be quantified) rather than defined functions of measurable performance variables.

With this lengthy background, let me take up some specific problems in characterizing information and communication in firms. First, I will study Martin Weitzmann's (1974) paper on prices vs. quantities as a team problem, to illustrate the analysis in a simple case. I will also use this example for some reflections on the counterintuitive implications of the much-used quadratic payoff functions. Then I want to consider alternative possible assumptions on the cost of information, including the well-known Radner-Stiglitz (1984) theorem suggesting a nonconcavity in the production of information. Finally, I will conclude by resuming some recent developments which illustrate some economies in information transfer when the law of large numbers can be used.

Weitzmann proposed the following simple model of decentralization. There are n productive units, each of which can produce the same product. The cost function of unit i is

$$C_i(q_i) = t_i q_i + (c/2) q_i^2.$$

Here, q_i is the output of unit i; t_i is a signal observed by the unit but not by any other agent. Let q be total output, so that $q = q_i$. Let the benefits from a total output of q be $B(q) = aq - (b/2)q^2$.

The random variables t_i are assumed independently and identically distributed. Without any real loss of generality, it can be assumed that they each have mean zero. Let S be the common variance of the parameters t_i. Weitzmann compares two coordination policies. One is to set an output price; each agent maximizes profits given its cost function. The price is chosen to maximize expected benefits minus expected losses. The other policy is that an output quota be set for each firm. Since the prior information is the same for all units, the quota is the same for all units. Unlike the price policy, there is no feedback from the actual signals at all.

Let P_p and P_q be the expected payoffs under the price and quantity policies. Then

Weitzmann shows that

$$P_q = na^2/2(nb+c),$$

$$P_p = P_q + \left[n(c-b)S/2c^2 \right].$$

The team theory solution is to choose the *optimal* decision rule relating q_i to t_i, instead of confining attention to two kinds of rules, that derived from assuming a price and that derived by assuming no dependence of q_i on t_i. Because the problem is quadratic, it can be seen that the optimal decision rules are linear. The optimal rule can be found easily (it is in fact a special case of a very general result in Marschak and Radner, pp. 167–69). It can be shown that the expected payoff to the optimal team policy is $P_t = P_q + nS/ [2(b+c)]$.

As is obvious from its derivation as an optimal policy and as can be calculated directly, P_t is greater than either P_p or P_q. The optimal team policy always lies between the unit outputs derived from the price and quantity policies. Hence, the Weitzmann problem of choosing between the two extremes seems unnecessarily limited.

When examined closely, there are some peculiar aspects to the variation of the optimal payoff with respect to the number of agents, n, and the variance S of the cost parameter. The payoff P_t increases linearly in n when there is some variance, and so approaches infinity with the number of firms. The same is true of the expected return to the price policy if $c > b$. (If $c < b$, the expected return to the price policy approaches negative infinity, even more surprisingly.) It is also true that the expected return under the optimal team policy increases with the variance, though possibly this is less paradoxical. The possibilities of gains from trade increase with the diversity of the units.

In fact, all these counterintuitive consequences spring from the quadratic payoff functions together with the failure to observe nonnegativity constraints on the output variables. I take this result to be a warning about trusting quadratic functions too strongly. The quadratic hypothesis has been common in control theory, as well as the economics of

uncertainty, for its analytic convenience. But for some purposes at least it can be very misleading.

This example has taken the information structure as given. If we want to analyze the choice among information structures, it is necessary to include in the analysis measures of their costs. I will give two examples, with applications, before turning to the general question of concavity of the cost function. The first is the Shannon measure of information. Suppose X is a random variable with a discrete distribution, with $p(x)$ as the probability that X takes on the value x. Suppose we have the following procedure for identifying the true value of X: at each stage, the remaining possible values of X can be divided in any desired way into two parts, and it is possible to identify in which part the true value lies. Then a well-known theorem of information theory tells us that the minimum expected number of stages needed to find the true value of X lies between $H(X)$ and $H(X)+1$, where $H(X) = -\sum p(x)\log_2 p(x)$, the Shannon measure interpreted as a cost. This technology for determining the true value is not entirely convincing, but at least it is a consistent story. As it stands, it is a measure of the cost of going from a probability distribution to certainty. It may be generalized to yield a cost of going from a distribution to a conditional distribution. Let S be a signal. If S takes on a particular value, say s, let $H(X|s)$ be the Shannon measure for the conditional distribution of X given $S = s$. Then the average reduction in the Shannon measure of uncertainty is, $H(X) - E_s[H(X|S)] = R(X, S)$, defined as the *rate of transmission*. This suggests that the cost of a signal S be taken as proportional to the rate of transmission with respect to the state of the world, X.

For an application of this measure, I draw upon some earlier work (1971). Suppose an investor can buy a portfolio of *elementary* securities, that is, each security pays off in exactly one state of the world, x. Let each security have a price of one dollar per unit, and let r_x be the payment to a unit security for state x. The investor has A dollars to invest. The investor's utility function for terminal wealth is taken to be the (natural) logarithm. The action is the choice of amounts a_x to be invested in security x. Terminal wealth then is $a_x r_x$. Hence, the chosen portfolio is that which maximizes $E(\ln a_x r_x)$ subject to the condition, $\Sigma a_x = A$. Straightforward calculation shows that the optimal portfolio is the choice, $a_x = Ap(x)$.

Now suppose the investor has the option of buying any signal S at a price proportional to the rate of transmission, that is, $cR(X, S)$ for some constant c. Assume that the signal must be purchased prior to observation of the outcome, so that the purchase price must be subtracted from initial assets before investment. It is easy to see that if a signal with transmission rate $R(X, S) = R$ is purchased, then the optimal decision rule is to set $a_x(s) = (A - cR) \, p(x|s)$, where s is the observed value of S and $p(x|s)$ the conditional probability that $X = x$ given that $S = s$. The expected payoff with the optimal policy is,

$$E(\ln r_x) + \ln(A - cR) - H(X) + R.$$

Note that this is a concave function of R. It is maximized with respect to R by setting $R = (A - c)/c$ if $c < A$, $= 0$ otherwise.

Consider an alternative model for suggesting a cost function for information, namely Bayesian normal sampling. The cost of the information obtained from a sample is taken to be proportional to the size of the sample. For a normal distribution, it is reasonable to take the amount of information to be the reciprocal of its variance, called the *precision*. Let X be normally distributed with precision h_x. Consider a sequence of signals, S_i, whose distributions conditional on X are normal, independent, and identical. Let the conditional precision of any one be h_s. The agent has to choose an action a, with loss $(X - a)$.

The agent can observe the first n signals before performing the action. The value of n is also subject to choice. If n is chosen, the precision of the conditional distribution of X given $S_1, \ldots, S_n$ can easily be calculated to be $h = h_x + nh_s$. Since the cost of sampling is proportional to n, it can also be seen to be linear in h. If we assume that the cost of sampling is added to the loss due to the

action, it can be seen that the agent wants to choose h to minimize $h^{-1} + ch$, again a concave function. The optimal value of h is $c^{-1/2}$.

Radner and Stiglitz have proved the following remarkable theorem:

Let $S(t)$ be a one-dimensional family of signals defined for $t \geq 0$. The conditional density of $S(t)$ given X is $p_t(s|x)$, assumed differentiable in t at $t = 0$. Further assume that $p_0(s|x)$ is independent of x, that is, $S(0)$ yields no information about X. Let $a(s, t)$ be the action taken if the signal $S(t)$ has been chosen and takes on the value s. Let $w(a, x)$ be the outcome in money terms if action a is taken, and the state of the world is x, and let $c(t)$ be the cost of having the signal $S(t)$; assume that $c'(0) > 0$. Finally, let $V(w - c)$ be the utility function for income. Then the expected utility gain by changing the signal from $S(0)$ to $S(t)$ is always negative for t sufficiently small.

Alexander Pope told us, "a little learning is a dangerous thing." Radner and Stiglitz, a little more circumspectly, tell us that a little information is never worth the cost. This conclusion implies that the value of information is not concave, at least not in the neighborhood of the origin, which corresponds to an uninformative signal. But in our two examples, both certainly reasonable, the value of information was concave in a properly chosen measure. The Radner-Stiglitz theorem is correct mathematically, so that we can be sure that one of its hypotheses does not hold in the two examples. The hypothesis that fails is the seemingly innocuous condition that the likelihood function $p_t(s|x)$ is differentiable in t at $t = 0$. If we parametrize the signals in our two examples by R or h, respectively, then $p_t(s|x)$ has an infinite derivative with respect to t at $t = 0$.

I conclude by discussing a different kind of subtlety in the use of information. Team theory differs from the classical work on the economics of socialism in several ways, but one is the use of a priori information in guiding the communication and coordination processes. One particular kind of argument that has been developed is to take advantage of the law of large numbers when the agents form a well-defined statistical universe. In a resource allocation problem, when the center's action is the allocation of some scarce resource among units, the optimal action will in general depend on the productivities of all the units. However, if these productivities can themselves be considered as a random sample from a known distribution and if there are many units, then effectively the distribution in the sample can be regarded as known. Therefore, some information need not be collected, or, more precisely, its value goes to zero as the number of agents approaches infinity. A model of this kind has been studied by myself and Radner (1979), and similar reasoning has been used independently by J. K. Leenstra et al. (forthcoming), though more for the purposes of approximating the solution of nonconcave problems.

These remarks are just a few of the many possibilities which can be invoked in theory to analyze the optimal informational structure of firms. They suggest that the solutions in different circumstances may look very different, even though based on the same maximizing principles.

REFERENCES

Arrow, Kenneth J., "The Value of and Demand for Information," in C. B. McGuire and R. Radner, eds., *Decision and Organization*, Amsterdam: North-Holland, 1971, 131–39.

_____ and Radner, Roy, "Allocation of Resources in Large Teams," *Econometrica*, March 1979, *47*, 361–85.

Chandler, Alfred, Jr., *The Visible Hand*, Cambridge: Belknap Press, 1979.

Leenstra et al., J. K., "A Framework for the Probabilistic Analysis of Hierarchical Planning Systems," *Annals of Operations Research*, forthcoming.

Marschak, Jacob, "Équipes et Organisatons en Régime d'Incertitude," in Centre National de la Recherche Scientifique, *Économetrie*, Paris, 1953, 202–11.

_____, "Towards an Economic Theory of Organization and Information," in R. M. Thrall et al., eds., *Decision Theory*, New York: Wiley & Sons, 1954.

_____ and Radner, Roy, *Economic Theory of Teams*, New Haven: Yale University Press, 1972.

Marshall, Alfred, *Principles of Economics*, 8th ed., New York: Macmillan, 1948.

Radner, Roy, and Joseph Stiglitz, "Nonconcavity in the Value of Information," in M. Boyer and R. E. Kihlstrom, eds., *Bayesian Models in Economic Theory*, Amsterdam: Elsevier, 1984.

Weitzman, Martin L., "Prices *vs.* Quantities," *Review of Economic Studies*, October 1974, *41*, 477–92.

[27]

International Journal of Policy Analysis and Information Systems, Vol. 4, No. 1, 1980

The Best Use of "Information Budgets" in Purposive Organizations: A Finite Approach

T. A. Marschak[1]

Received July 23, 1979

A new approach is proposed to assess the benefits and costs of alternative organizational schemes. An organization has to choose new actions in response to a changing, incompletely observed environment. The scheme used to generate new actions is modelled as a collection of finite-state machines whose inputs are environmental observations and messages (from other machines) and whose outputs are messages and actions. A scheme's cost is assumed to be an increasing function of the sizes of the finite sets defining the machines. For a given payoff function (defined on action and environment), a given probability distribution of environments, and a given "budget," the question becomes: what scheme not exceeding the budget achieves highest expected payoff? An algorithm for answering the question in simple cases is sketched.

KEY WORDS: Information processing; organizations; finite-state machines; teams.

1. INTRODUCTION

In this paper we consider a new approach to the comparison of organizational schemes—schemes for resource-allocating economies or multibranch firms, for multi-unit agencies (bureaucracies) confronting agencywide as well as "local" choices, and for other purposive organizations. In the new approach one commits oneself to a certain modeling of the organizational schemes *and of the information technology which they use.* Specifically, the scheme is a collection of finite-state sequential machines which communicate with each other and, taken together, assign organizational actions to values of the organization's environment. *The technology is such that the sizes of the finite input, output, and memory sets in these machines determine the cost of operating the scheme.* Having accepted this modeling, one can then study the following typical question: Given the information costs of a

---

[1]School of Business Administration, University of California, Berkeley, California.

scheme—the information "budget" required to operate it—*does there exist another scheme for the organization which requires no larger budget and achieves at least as good a performance (as measured by average payoff streams over time)?*

2. AN EXAMPLE: ONE-STEP SCHEMES FOR A THREE-PERSON ORGANIZATION

Consider an organization composed of three "units" or "persons"— two "local" persons (called "1" and "2") and a "center." The organization confronts an environment, takes an action, and collects a payoff which depends on action and environment. The environment is a vector $e = (e_1, e_2)$ in a set $\mathcal{E} = \mathcal{E}_1 \times \mathcal{E}_2$; e_1 is the *local environment* of 1 and e_2 is the local environment of 2. The organizational action is a vector $a = (a_1, a_2)$ in a set $\mathcal{A} = \mathcal{A}_1 \times \mathcal{A}_2$; a_1 is 1's *action* and a_2 is 2's *action*. The environment changes at the start of each *day*. Each local unit then observes "its" environment with a fineness which *we, as designers of the scheme the organization is to use, select*. This local unit then sends a *report*, based on its observations, to the center, and at the same time stores in its memory information about its observation. The center receives reports and computes and sends an *instruction* to each local unit. The local unit uses the instruction and the information stored in its memory to compute an *action*. The actions to be used by i out of the set $\mathcal{A}_i$—the *fineness of implementation* for i—are again a matter of choice for the designer. The *rules* which prescribe the stored information, the instructions, the reports, and the actions are also elements of the designer's choice. After actions have been taken each local memory is cleared and the same procedure is repeated the next day, following the next day's new environment. The scheme is called a *one-step* scheme, since there is only one interchange between local units and the center; no further "dialogue" takes place during the day.

Formally, we use the general concept of a machine as a quintuple of three finite sets and two functions:

(memory set, input set, output set, next-state function, output function)

Both functions are *from* the product of the memory set and the input set; the next-state function is *to* the memory set, and the output function is *to* the output set.

Then local unit i, $i = 1, 2$, is machine

$$M_i = (S_i, E_i \times I_i, R_i \times A_i, \lambda_i, \mu_i)$$

where S_i is the memory set; E_i is the *observation set*, the set of values taken by some finite-valued function on $\mathcal{E}_i$; I_i is the *instruction set*; R_i is the *report set*; A_i, a finite subset of $\mathscr{A}_i$, is the *action set*; and λ_i and μ_i are the next-state and the output functions, respectively. The machine M_i, then, has observations and instructions as inputs, reports and actions as outputs. The center is a machine

$$M_i = (\,\cdot\,, R_1 \times R_2, I_1 \times I_2, \,\cdot\,, \bar{\mu})$$

The center needs no memory (which we express by writing a dot as the first and fourth elements of the quintuple), since it responds to reports with instructions in the same day. The center has reports as inputs and instructions as outputs; its output function is $\bar{\mu}$. Figure 1 portrays the situation.

Now let there be given (1) a *payoff function* θ, from $\mathscr{A} \times \mathscr{E}$ to the reals, which ranks action–environment pairs; (2) a probability measure on $\mathscr{E}$; and (3) an *information cost function* δ on the set of ten-tuples

$$x_{M_1 M_2 \bar{M}} \equiv \{\nu_{S_1}, \nu_{S_2}, \nu_{E_1}, \nu_{E_2}, \nu_{R_1}, \nu_{R_2}, \nu_{I_1}, \nu_{I_2}, \nu_{A_1}, \nu_{A_2}\}$$

where ν_H denotes the number of elements in the set H. The function δ is increasing in each of its arguments. The problem of optimal design for the three-person one-step scheme is as follows:

> Given an *information budget B*, choose a scheme $(M_1, M_2, \bar{M})$ so that expected value of $\theta(a, e)$ is a maximum subject to the constraint
>
> $$\delta(x_{M_1 M_2 \bar{M}}) \leq B$$

Whether it is reasonable to let set sizes determine cost is an empirical question. We assume, for example, that it is more costly if a local unit has to stand ready to distinguish four local environments than if it has to stand ready to distinguish only three. The fact that some environments are more

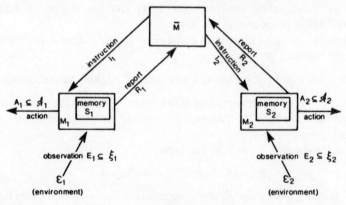

Fig. 1

probable than others is not taken into account by the function δ. If the probabilities are close to equal, the omission is not serious. *Only* experience with modeling of the observing, storing, communicating, computing, and implementing tasks in real organizations can reveal the appropriateness of the assumption that cost depends on set sizes.

3. GENERALIZATIONS

Generalization of the problem can proceed in several ways. (1) One can permit the center to observe its own part of the total environment, with the value of the center's environment entering the payoff function. (2) One can consider multistep schemes; in a two-step scheme, for example, a local unit may request more information about the other's observations, the request depending on what the local unit receives from others in the first step. (3) One can study resource-allocating adjustment processes involving "managers" and a "price setter." Such a process can be written as a machine triple [or $(n+1)$-tuple if there are n "managers"], with the number of steps used equaling the number of iterations the process is operated following a new environment. The classic processes are temporally homogeneous, i.e., each machine engages in the same operations (defined by next-state and output functions) in each step. One could compute the information budget from such a process, could hold constant the number of iterations, and could ask whether another temporally homogeneous process requiring no higher budget could achieve better actions when it terminates. (4) One could permit "interaction" between successive "days," so that a day's payoff depends on a state variable which is a function of today's environment, today's action, and yesterday's value of the state variable.

4. "RESOURCES FOR COORDINATION VERSUS RESOURCES FOR LOCAL EXPERTISE" RATHER THAN "CENTRALIZATION VERSUS DECENTRALIZATION"

The simple three-person example suggests a new approach to the centralization–decentralization issue.

Abandon both terms and instead group the tasks performed in the "daily" operation of the scheme into two suggestive families: tasks of *local expertise* and tasks of *coordination*. The former are observing, remembering, and action-taking; the latter are reporting and instructing. Now suppose the function δ can be decomposed as follows:

$$\delta\{x_{M_1 M_2 \bar{M}}\} = \tilde{\delta}[\delta^{\text{coord}}\{\nu_{R_1}, \nu_{R_2}, \nu_{I_1}, \nu_{I_2}\},$$
$$\delta^{\text{exp}}\{\nu_{E_1}, \nu_{E_2}, \nu_{S_1}, \nu_{S_2}, \nu_{A_1}, \nu_{A_2}\}]$$

where $\tilde{\delta}$ is increasing in both its arguments and δ^{coord}, δ^{exp} are each increasing in *their* arguments. Then the "centralization–decentralization" question is replaced by the question, "*What is a good allocation of a given information budget between local expertise on the one hand and coordination on the other?*" A related question, of particular interest, is: What is the path traced out by the highest attainable expected payoff as one keeps constant the budget B while increasing δ^{exp} and decreasing δ^{coord} (so that $\tilde{\delta}$ remains no larger than B)? To trace out this path one studies alternative pairs (δ^{coord}, δ^{exp}) and for each such pair finds a machine triple ($M_1, M_2, \bar{M}$) which yields that pair and gives rise to an expected payoff not lower than that given rise to by any other triple which yields that pair. (A simple function $\tilde{\delta}$ is, of course, $\tilde{\delta} = \delta^{coord} + \delta^{exp}$). Are there any payoff functions and environmental probability distributions for which the path so traced out first rises and then falls, so that there is, in fact, one *best* division of each information budget between expertise and coordination? If so, that would be a valuable finding, because such "single-peakedness" would simplify the search for a good scheme. If, for example, one were to examine three schemes—say, X, Y, and Z—with X more coordinated than Y and Y more coordinated than Z, and if Y is found to yield higher expected payoff than both X and Z, then one must search among schemes more coordinated than Y but less so than X, or among schemes less coordinated than Y but more so than Z. If payoff improves as one moves from Y to a scheme slightly more coordinated, then the former search is proper; if payoff declines, then the latter search is proper.

More generally, such a finding would give some meaning to the elusive search for a "good balance between centralization and decentralization." Earlier attempts to be precise about such a balance ran into the extreme difficulty of defining "more decentralized than" in an acceptable way. For a specific choice of the functions δ^{coord}, δ^{exp}—a choice to be justified empirically—the question of a good balance, in our new sense, is clear. It seems likely, moreover, that if one wanted to reconcile the term "more coordinated" (less of the budget devoted to local expertise and more to coordination) with various earlier definitions of "more centralized," one could do so, for a variety of models of the organization. If, for example, "more decentralized" means, in an appropriate sense, "more scope for local decisions," then this might well coincide with "less coordinated," since if more resources are available for local expertise and less for coordination, then local units take a wider range of actions, based more closely on local observation and constrained relatively weakly by the "coarse" instructions received from the center (which is deprived of the resources needed for "fine" instructions).

5. AN ALGORITHM FOR THE STUDY OF THREE-PERSON ONE-STEP SCHEMES

To gain insight into these matters it seems essential to start with simple numerical examples. The difficulty is, however, that the number of schemes (machine triples in the three-person case) to be compared quickly becomes large. Thus, for example, in the three-person one-step case, let the information budget—call it $\bar{B}$—be large enough so that the sets $E_i, S_i, R_i, I_i, A_i, i = 1, 2$, can each contain three elements. Then there are close to a billion distinct triples $(M_1, M_2, \bar{M})$ for which the sets have three elements, and many additional triples for which the sets are of different sizes but which also do not require a budget higher than $\bar{B}$. In brief the advantage of a finite modeling of information technology is that it gives one something precise to count in measuring costs; the disadvantage is that there may be very many alternatives to compare.

But other combinatorial problems, involving, in principle, a large number of comparisons, have been dealt with. This leads one to construct an algorithm which will engage in an "intelligent" search through the tree of possibilities so that, in the typical application, a great many of the possible alternatives need not be examined.

Suppose that in the three-person one-step case, $\mathscr{E}_i$ and $\mathscr{A}_i, i = 1, 2$, are sets with three elements each; $\mathscr{E}_i$ contains the elements e_i^1, e_i^2, e_i^3. A matrix $\{(U_{ae})\}$ is given, where U_{ae} equals the organization's payoff when (a, e) is the action–environment pair *multiplied by* the probability of e. Suppose we require that

$$\nu_{E_1} = \nu_{E_2} = \nu_{S_1} = \nu_{S_2} = \nu_{R_1} = \nu_{R_2} = \nu_{I_1} = \nu_{I_2} = \nu_{A_1} = \nu_{A_2} = 2$$

This means that the "day's" action for a local unit is to be chosen from two of the three available actions and is to be based on (1) a two-element memory, which permits a twofold partitioning of i's environment, and (2) on a twofold instruction from the center which is based, in turn, on a twofold report from the other unit. The problem which is associated with the sextuple $(2, 2, 2, 2, 2, 2)$ and which we may denote as $\mathscr{P}_{222222}$ is, then, to find

1. a twofold partitioning, for unit 1, of E_1 and also of E_2;
2. a twofold partitioning, for unit 2, of E_1 and also of E_2;
3. an assignment of one or the other out of two actions in $\mathscr{A}_1$ to 1's fourfold information about $E_1 \times E_2$, information obtained from the partitioning in item 1 above;
4. an assignment of one or the other out of two actions in $\mathscr{A}_2$ to 2's fourfold information about $E_1 \times E_2$, information obtained from the partitioning in item 2 above.

The choice of (1–4) is to be best, i.e., if $a(e)$ denotes the action which the choice of (1–4) implies for the environment e, then no other choice of (1–4) must yield a higher value of $\sum_{e \in E} U_{a(e)e}$.

The algorithm explores the possible choices of 1, 2, 3, and 4 (there are 46,656 possible choices) in a "branch-and-bound" manner. This requires procedures for computing upper and lower bounds to payoff (to $\sum_e U_{a(e)e}$) at various points in the tree of possibilities. The algorithm first asks whether or not e_1^1 and e_1^2 are in the same equivalence class in 1's partitioning of E_1. In connection with this question an upper and a lower bound are obtained as follows.

An upper bound. Consider the following linear programming problem, with the indices i, j, r, s denoting elements of E_1, E_2, A_1, A_2, respectively (thus, e.g., if $i = k$, 1's environment is e_1^k); $U_{rsij} \equiv U_{ae}$, where $a = (r, s)$ and $e = (i, j)$.

Choose $\{p_{ijrs}\}, \{X_r\}, \{Y_s\}$, all nonnegative, so as to maximize $\sum_{ijrs} p_{ijrs} U_{rsij}$ subject to

$$\sum_{r,s} p_{ijrs} = 1, \quad \text{all } i, j \tag{1}$$

$$\sum_{ijs} p_{ijrs} \leq X_r, \quad \text{all } r \tag{2}$$

$$\sum_{ijs} p_{ijrs} \leq Y_s, \quad \text{all } s \tag{3}$$

$$\begin{cases} X_r \leq 2, & \text{all } r \\ Y_s \leq 2, & \text{all } s \end{cases} \tag{4}$$

$$p_{1jrs} = p_{2jrs}, \quad \text{all } j, r, s \tag{5}$$

The variable p_{ijrs} may be interpreted as the probability that, when the environment is $e = (e_1, e_2) = (i, j)$, then the action taken by the organization is $a = (a_1, a_2) = (r, s)$. Constraints (2), (3), and (4) ensure that not more than two of 1's actions and not more than two of 2's actions are used. Constraint (5) expresses the fact that whether or not a particular action (r, s) is used depends on whether 1's environment is or is not e_1^3; but, if it is not, then the use or nonuse of (r, s) does not depend on whether 1's environment is e_1^1 or e_1^2. Solutions to the programming problem clearly include solutions in which every p_{ijrs} is one or zero. If, moreover, we had a solution to the problem $\mathcal{P}_{222222}$ in which e_1^1 and e_1^2 were in the same equivalence class with respect to 1's partitioning of E_1, then we would have a solution to the linear programming problem. The reverse is not true, since a solution in which an X_r or a Y_s were nonintegral would not assign one organizational action to each environment, and since there is no constraint expressing the required twofold partitioning of E_2 for unit 1 and of E_1 and E_2 for unit 2. The payoff in the solution to the linear programming problem (i.e., $\sum_{ijrs} p_{ijrs} U_{rsij}$) is then an upper bound.

A lower bound. A lower bound to $\sum_e U_{a(e)e}$, given that 1's partitioning of E_1 combines e_1^1 and e_1^2, is obtained as follows:

1. To the environments (e_1^1, e_2^1) and (e_1^2, e_2^1) assign the action a which yields the highest value of $\max[U_{a,(e_1^1,e_2^1)}, U_{a,(e_1^2,e_2^1)}]$. Let ρ_1 denote the sum of the U_{ae}'s so identified.
2. To the environments (e_1^1, e_2^2), (e_1^2, e_2^2) make the analogous assignment; call the analogous payoff sum ρ_2.
3. To the environments (e_1^1, e_2^3), (e_1^2, e_2^3) assign the better (with respect to the sum of the corresponding U_{ae}'s) of the two actions identified in steps 1 and 2. Let ρ_3 denote the associated sum of U_{ae}'s.
4. To the environments (e_1^3, e_2^1), (e_1^3, e_2^2), (e_1^3, e_2^3) assign one action, namely, the action with the highest U_{ae} for these three environments. Let ρ_4 denote the sum of the U_{ae}'s so identified.

Then a lower bound is $\rho_1 + \rho_2 + \rho_3 + \rho_4$, since that payoff can always be achieved while meeting the constraints of ρ_{222222}.

The algorithm next asks whether 1's twofold partitioning of E_1 combines e_1^2 and e_1^3 and finds, in the manner just shown, the lower and upper bounds associated with that possibility. If the upper bound when e_1^2 and e_1^3 are combined is less than the lower bound when e_1^1 and e_1^2 are combined (or vice versa), then one of these two possibilities (and the entire "subtree" of possibilities associated with it) can be discarded. Similar computations are made for the combining of e_1^1 and e_1^3. For each of the undiscarded possibilities, the algorithm then explores in an analogous manner the possibilities for 2's twofold partitioning of E_2, then 1's partitioning of E_2, and then 2's partitioning of E_1. In "favorable" problems, only a few possibilities for the choice of steps 1–4 in $\mathscr{P}_{222222}$ will remain after a reasonable number of steps.

The same algorithm deals with problems in which the defining subscript sextuple is different. Only experience can show how large the sets $\mathscr{E}_1$, $\mathscr{E}_2$, $\mathscr{A}_1$, $\mathscr{A}_2$ can be if the "favorable" case is to be the typical one.

The algorithm can be combined with a routine for arranging the sextuples according to the values of $\tilde{\delta}$, of δ^{coord}, and of δ^{exp} which they imply *for the case in which δ, δ^{coord}, and δ^{exp} are linear in set sizes.* That is to say, a "price" for the size of each set is specified and the best expected payoff for a given budget and a given division of the budget between coordination and expertise is found, by exploring all the sextuples consistent with that budget and that division of the budget.

6. APPLICATIONS OF THE ALGORITHM

To illustrate the application of the algorithm, consider the organization studied by Groves and Radner.[1] In a simplified version there are n

enterprises and a resource manager. Each enterprise i's output y_i depends on the amount (L_i) it chooses to use of a "local" resource ("labor") and on the amount (k_i) allocated to it of a "central" resource ("capital"); the dependence is expressed by a quadratic production function $y_i = k_i^2 + L_i^2 + q_i k_i L_i - \bar{e}_i k_i - \bar{\bar{e}}_i L_i$, where q_i is a constant and i's changing local environment is $e_i = (\bar{e}_i, \bar{\bar{e}}_i)$, $\bar{e}_i > 0$, $\bar{\bar{e}}_i > 0$. The resource manager's local environment is k, the availability of the central resource; he must choose the k_i so that $\sum_i k_i \leq k$. The organization's payoff is the sum of enterprise outputs, $y = \sum_i y_i$.

A "one-step-Lange–Lerner" scheme is investigated. In this scheme a price for the central resource is announced to enterprises, and each enterprise responds with a "profit-maximizing demand" for the central resource. One then finds the best rules for assigning to each enterprise's information (its current e_i and the announced "price") a value of its action (the amount of the local resource which it employs), and for assigning to the center's information (the current availability of the central resource and the enterprises' "demands") an allocation of the central resource among enterprises. The rule determines payoff, and one can then compare the (best attainable) expected payoff under the one-step-Lange–Lerner scheme with the best possible expected payoff (obtainable under a complete exchange of information).

The shortcoming of this approach is that it leaves one in the dark about the *costs* of the one-step-Lange–Lerner scheme (as compared, for example, to the costs of full information); and to defend the interest of the result, one must fall back on the classical view that the Lange–Lerner scheme is "decentralized" and is therefore, in some unspecified sense, appealing.

Using the algorithm one can hope, to some extent, to remedy this shortcoming. A start could be made with the case of two enterprises and a resource manager, with the availability of the central resource *remaining constant* (but at least one of the local linear production coefficients $\bar{e}_i$, $\bar{\bar{e}}_i$ changing). The two local quadratic production functions would be discretely approximated by, say, a tenfold "grid." The one-step scheme would then be expressed as a machine triple $(M_1, M_2, \bar{M})$, and the information budget which it uses—for a function δ linear in set sizes—would be computed. Probabilities would be specified for the finite number of environments. The critical question would then become: *Given the information budget required by the one-step-Lange–Lerner scheme, can one find another machine triple (scheme) which does not exceed the budget and which achieves a higher expected payoff, or a scheme which achieves the same expected payoff but requires a smaller budget?* The question can be explored for a variety of environmental probabilities and set-size "prices" (i.e., linear functions δ), to determine the robustness of the answer against changes in these parameters.

The path traced out by the expected payoff as more of a budget is devoted to local expertise and less to coordination can also be studied.

These questions can be explored again for the case in which the center also makes observations—the availability (k) of the central resource is random, and the center observes it. Then, in the machine triple $(M_1, M_2, \bar{M})$, the input set for $\bar{M}$ is the product of the report sets of 1 and 2 and of an observation set for $\bar{M}$; the size of the latter set—the fineness of the center's observations—can be chosen and enters the cost function, which is a revised version of the function δ. This more general problem would require either an expansion of the original algorithm or a special-purpose algorithm designed solely for study of the Groves–Radner organization.

In the same spirit other applications of the algorithm could deal with simple examples of economies and of one-step schemes which achieve optimality in these economies. One example is a two-person two-commodity trade economy in which a center computes and announces those prices for which utility-maximizing trade responses achieve optimality. One computes the information budget the scheme requires and then asks, "Are there other machine triples which also achieve optimality but do so with a lower budget?" The question is, in a sense, a simple discrete analogue of the "continuum" investigation by Mount and Reiter[2] into the "size" of message spaces required by the competitive mechanism, except that the (finite) approach permits assessment not only of communication costs but also of observation and implementation costs.

REFERENCES

1. T. Groves and R. Radner, "Allocation of resources in a team," *J. Economic Theory* 3:415–441 (1972).
2. K. Mount and S. Reiter, "The informational size of message spaces," *J. Economic Theory* 8(2):161–192 (1973).

[28]

The Economics of Modern Manufacturing: Technology, Strategy, and Organization

By Paul Milgrom and John Roberts*

Manufacturing is undergoing a revolution. The mass production model is being replaced by a vision of a flexible multiproduct firm that emphasizes quality and speedy response to market conditions while utilizing technologically advanced equipment and new forms of organization. Our optimizing model of the firm generates many of the observed patterns that mark modern manufacturing. Central to our results is a method of handling optimization and comparative statics problems that requires neither differentiability nor convexity. (JEL 022)

In the early twentieth century, Henry Ford revolutionized manufacturing with the introduction of his "transfer line" technology for mass production, in which basic inputs are processed in a fixed sequence of steps using equipment specifically designed to produce a single standardized product in extremely large quantities for extended periods of time. Although the specialization of Ford's factories was extreme—the plants had to be shut down and redesigned when production of the Model T was ended—the transfer line approach influenced generations of industrialists and changed the face of manufacturing (see David A. Hounshell, 1984).

In the late twentieth century, the face of manufacturing is changing again.[1] First, the specialized, single-purpose equipment for mass production which had characterized Ford's factories is being replaced by flexible machine tools and programmable, multitask production equipment. Because these new machines can be quickly and cheaply switched from one task to another, their use permits the firm to produce a variety of outputs efficiently in very small batches,[2] especially in comparison to the usual image of mass production (Nicholas Valery, 1987). Kenneth Wright and David Bourne (1988) report that in a recent survey of aerospace and other high precision industries 8.2 percent of all batches were of size one and 38 percent were sixteen or less. An Allen-Bradley Company plant making electric controls is reported to be able to switch production among its 725 products and variations with an average changeover time for resetting equipment of six seconds, enabling it to schedule batches of size one with relative efficiency (Tracy O'Rourke, 1988). Even in the automobile industry, flexible equipment has become much more common. Recently,

*Professor of Economics, Department of Economics. Stanford University, Stanford, CA. 94305-6072 and Jonathan B. Lovelace, Professor of Economics, Graduate School of Business, Stanford University, CA. 94305-5015.
The research reported here was supported by the National Science Foundation and the Center for Economic Policy Research of Stanford University. We are grateful to Tim Bresnahan, Morris Cohen, Xavier de Groote, Victor Fuchs, John McMillan, Roger Noll, Mike Riordan, Nate Rosenberg, Ed Steinmueller, Hal Varian, Steve Wheelwright, and two anonymous referees for helpful discussions, comments, and suggestions.

[1] Probably no single firm is involved in all the changes we will describe. Nevertheless, there is a definite, discernable pattern of change in technology, manufacturing, marketing, and organizational strategy that characterizes successful "modern manufacturing." For a description of the technologies involved, see U.S. Congress Office of Technology Assessment, 1984.

[2] Optimal batch size can be determined via a standard Economic Order Quantity model, in which the setup costs of switching from making one product to making another are traded off against the costs of holding the larger average inventories of finished goods that go with longer runs and less frequent changeovers. Optimal batch size is a decreasing function of setup costs and so batch sizes optimally decrease as more flexible machines are introduced.

General Motors' engineers were able, for the first time in company history, to use a regular, producing facility to make pilots of the next year's model cars. The engineers set the equipment to make 1989 models after workers left the factory on Friday afternoon, ran the equipment to manufacture the new models over the weekend, and then reset the equipment to produce 1988 model cars so that regular production could be resumed on Monday morning (Thomas Moore, 1988). In contrast, with the older, less flexible technologies that have been the norm in the industry, changing over to produce the new year's models typically involved shutting down production for weeks.

Flexible equipment and small batch sizes have been accompanied by other changes. Smaller batch sizes are directly associated with a shortening of production cycles and with reductions in work-in-process and finished goods inventories. Shorter product cycles in turn support speedier responses to demand fluctuations and lead to lower back orders. Indeed, a general strategic emphasis on speeding up all aspects of the firm's operations is becoming common (Brian Dumaine, 1989). This is manifested in shorter product-development times, quicker order-processing, and speedier delivery, as well as in producing products faster. Examples abound. General Electric has reduced the design and production time it takes to fill an order for a circuit-breaker box from three weeks to three days, in the process reducing back orders from sixty days to two (Dumaine). The Allen-Bradley plant mentioned above fills orders the day after they are received, then ships them that same day by air express (O'Rourke). Building on early development by Toyota, many manufacturers now plan production jointly with their suppliers and maintain constant communication with them. This allows the downstream firms to replace inventories of components and supplies with "just-in-time" deliveries of needed inputs (James Abegglen and George Stalk, Jr., 1985; Nicholas Valery, 1987). Combining flexible production and low finished goods inventories with reliance on electronic data communications, Benetton maintains inventories of undyed clothing

(shirts, scarves, pullovers) and uses nightly sales data gathered at its automated distribution center from terminals in individual stores to determine the colors it should make and where to ship its output (Tom Peters, 1987). Strategies like this one require not only flexible equipment to produce the right products, but short production cycles so that products are available at the right time. The extreme of this line of development is production of previously mass-produced items on a make-to-order basis: Moore reports a widespread rumor that the GM Saturn project will involve cars being custom-built within days of receipt of customers' computer-transmitted individual orders.

The manufacturing firms that adopt these new technologies and methods appear to differ from traditional firms in their product strategies as well. Many firms are broadening product lines, and there is a widespread increased emphasis on quality, both through frequent product improvements and new product introductions, and through reductions in defects in manufacturing. Caterpillar Corporation's $1.2 billion "Plant with a Future" modernization program has been accompanied by a doubling of the size of its product line (Ronald Henkoff, 1988). Rubbermaid insists that 30 percent of its sales should come from the products introduced in the preceding five years, and 3M Company has a similar 25 percent rule for each of its 42 divisions, with 32 percent of its $10.6 billion in 1988 sales actually coming from products less than five years old (Russell Mitchell, 1989). Meanwhile, reports of order-of-magnitude reductions in percentage defects are becoming commonplace.

New organizational strategies and workforce management policies are also part of this complex of changes. Ford has adopted a parallel, team (rather than sequential) approach to design and manufacturing engineering that, in conjunction with CAD/CAM (*Computer Aided Design/Computer Aided Manufacturing*) techniques, has cut development time on new models by one third (Alex Taylor, III, 1988). AT&T successfully used a similar, multidepartmental team approach in developing its new 4200 cordless phone (Dumaine), as did NCR with its recently introduced 2760 electronic cash register (Otis Port, 1989b). Lockheed Corp.'s Aeronautical Systems Group has managed to reduce the time for designing and manufacturing sheet-metal parts by 96 percent, from 52 days to 2; the project manager credits organizational changes (including the arrangement of workstations, redefinition of worker responsibilities, and adoption of team approaches) with 80 percent of the productivity gain (Port, 1989a, p. 143; Warren Hausman, 1988). Motorola's adoption of a pay scheme based on the skills employees acquire (rather than on their job assignments), its elimination of segmented pay categories among production workers, and its giving workers multiple responsibilities (including having production workers do quality inspections) is credited with major improvements in quality (Norm Alster, 1989). A further auto industry example comes from GM's massive investments in new technology, which have gone hand-in-hand with new supplier relations and more flexible work arrangements, as well as a broadened product line (General Motors Corporation, 1988).

More generally, Michael J. Piore (1986) provides survey evidence from firms around Route 128 in Boston of wider product lines, shorter product life cycles, greater emphasis on product quality, increased reliance on independent suppliers and subcontractors, and a more flexible organization of work that is supported by new compensation policies. Banri Asanuma, (1988a), has found similar trends among Japanese firms, Valery provides more anecdotal evidence drawn from a wide variety of industries internationally, and earlier Piore and Charles F. Sabel (1984) described related developments among small businesses in Italy and Austria.

A striking feature of the discussions of flexible manufacturing found in the business press is the frequency with which it is asserted that successful moves toward "the factory of the future" are not a matter of small adjustments made independently at each of several margins, but rather have involved substantial and closely coordinated changes in a whole range of the firm's activities. Even though these changes are implemented over time, perhaps beginning with

"islands of automation," the full benefits are achieved only by an ultimately radical restructuring. Henkoff (p. 74) noted that one of the lessons of Caterpillar's program was: "Don't just change selected parts of your factory, as many manufacturers have done. To truly boost efficiency...it's necessary to change the layout of the entire plant." The first lesson that Dumaine drew from studying successful adoption of speed-based strategies was to "start from scratch." In discussing the adoption of "computer integrated manufacturing" (CIM), Valery (p. 15) stated that "nothing short of a total overhaul of the company's strategy has first to be undertaken." And in a parallel fashion, Walter Kiechel III (1988, p. 42) noted: "To get these benefits (of more timely operations), you probably have to totally redesign the way you do business, changing everything from procurement to quality control."

This paper seeks to provide a coherent framework within which to understand the changes that are occurring in modern manufacturing. We ask, Why are these changes taking place? Is it mere coincidence that these various changes appear to be grouped together, or is there instead some necessary interconnection between them and common driving force behind them? What are the implications of the changes in manufacturing technology for inventory policy, product market strategy, and supplier and customer relations? What are the implications for the "make or buy" and vertical integration decisions and for the structure of business organization more generally?

Our approach to these questions is a price-theoretic, supply-side one involving three elements: exogenous input price changes, complementarities among the elements of the firm's strategy, and non-convexities. The first element is the effect of technological change in reducing a set of costs. The particular ones on which we focus include: the costs of collecting, organizing, and communicating data, which have been reduced over time by the development of computer networks and electronic data transmission systems; the cost of product design and development, which have fallen with the emergence of computer-aided design; and the costs of flexible manufacturing, which have declined with the introduction of robots and other programmable production equipment. We take these relative price reductions, whose existence is well documented, to be exogenous.

The direct effect of any of these price changes individually would be to increase use of the corresponding factor: for example, the emergence (i.e., falling cost) of CAD/ CAM encourages its adoption, and the reduced cost of designing and beginning production of new products directly increases the attractiveness of expanded product lines and frequent product improvements. However, with several relative prices falling, there are multiple interactions, both among the corresponding technological factors and between them and marketing and organizational variables. These interactions give rise to indirect effects that might in principle be as large as the direct effects, and opposite in sign. Here, the second element of our analysis appears: These indirect effects tend, in the main, to reinforce the direct effects because the corresponding relationships are ones of "complementarity." Here, we use the term "complements" not only in its traditional sense of a relation between *pairs of inputs*, but also in a broader sense as a relation among *groups of activities*. The defining characteristic of these groups of complements is that if the levels of any subset of the activities are increased, then the marginal return to increases in any or all of the remaining activities rises. It then follows that if the marginal costs associated with some activities fall, it will be optimal to increase the level of all of the activities in the grouping.

As an illustration, let us trace some of the indirect effects of a fall in the cost of computer-aided design (CAD) equipment and software that leads to the equipment being purchased. Some CAD programs prepare actual coded instructions that can be used by programmable manufacturing equipment, so one effect of the adoption of CAD may be to reduce the cost of adopting and using programmable manufacturing equipment. Since the prices of that equipment are also falling, the effects of the two price changes on the

adoption of that equipment are mutually reinforcing. Of course, CAD also makes it cheaper for the firm to adopt a broader product line and to update its products more frequently. If the firm does so, than an indirect effect is to make it more profitable to switch to more flexible manufacturing equipment that is cheaper to change over. So, this indirect effect reinforces the direct effects of the changing input prices. With short production runs, the firm can economize on inventory costs (such as interest, storage, and obsolescence) by scheduling production in a way that is quickly responsive to customer demand. Such a scheduling strategy increases the profitability of technologies that enable quicker and more accurate order processing, such as modern data communications technologies. So, another indirect effect of falling CAD prices coincides with the falling price of data communication equipment. Thus, CAD equipment, flexible manufacturing technologies, shorter production runs, lower inventories, increased data communications, and more frequent product redesigns are complementary. However, the complementarities do not stop at the level of manufacturing, but extend to marketing, engineering, and organization.

The marketing side of the analysis involves two additional elements besides those already mentioned. First, more frequent setups lower the inventory necessary to support a unit of sales and thus also the marginal cost of output. This encourages lower prices. The second element arises because buyers value fast delivery. If most customers have good alternative sources of supply and only a few are "locked in," then the resulting relationship between delivery time and demand is convex. In that case, reducing or eliminating production delays makes it profitable to reduce other sources of delay as well. Then, computerized order processing and a fast means of delivery are complementary to the quick responsiveness of the modern factory to new orders.

On the engineering side, as product life cycles become much shorter than the life of the production equipment, it becomes increasingly important to account for the characteristics of existing equipment in designing new products. At the same time, the emergence of computer-aided design has made it less costly to modify initial designs, to estimate the cost of producing various designs with existing equipment, and to evaluate a broader range of potential designs. These changes have contributed to the growing popularity among U.S. firms of "design for manufacturability," in which products are developed by teams composed of designers, process engineers, and manufacturing managers (Robert Hayes, Steven Wheelwright, and Kim Clark, 1988), and the corresponding practice among Japanese automakers of providing preliminary specifications to suppliers who comment on the proposed design and supply drawings of parts (Asanuma, 1988b)—innovations in engineering organization that contribute to a more efficient use of existing production equipment and manufacturing know-how. Moreover, taking account of the limits and capabilities of production equipment in the design phase makes it easier to ensure that quality standards can be met, and so is complementary to a marketing strategy based on high quality.

The firm's problem in deciding whether to adopt any or all of these changes is marked by important *non-convexities*. These are first of the familiar sorts associated with indivisibilities: product line sizes are naturally integer-valued. A form of increasing returns also figures in the model, because the marginal impact of increasing the speed with which customers are served increases the service speed. Beyond these, however, the complementarities noted above can be a further source of non-convexities that are associated with the need to coordinate choices among several decision variables. For example, purchase of CAD/CAM technology makes it less costly for a firm to increase its frequency of product improvements, and more frequent product introductions raise the return to investments in CAD/CAM technology. Thus, it may be unprofitable for a firm to purchase a flexible CAD/CAM system without changing its marketing strategy, or to alter its marketing approach without adopting a flexible manufacturing system, and yet it may be highly profitable to do both together. (In contrast, if the value of a smooth

concave function at some point in the interior of its domain cannot be increased by a small change in the value of any single variable, then the function achieves a global maximum at that point.) These non-convexities then explain why the successful adoption of modern manufacturing methods may not be a marginal decision.

It is natural to expect the characteristics of the modern manufacturing firm to be reflected in the way the firm is managed and the way it structures its relations with customers, employees, and suppliers. Exploiting such an extensive system of complementarities requires coordinated action between the traditionally separate functions of design, engineering, manufacturing, and marketing. Also, according to transaction costs theories, the increasing use of flexible, general purpose equipment in place of specialized, single purpose equipment ought to improve the investment incentives of independent suppliers (Oliver Williamson, 1986; Benjamin Klein, Robert Crawford, and Armen Alchian, 1978; Jean Tirole, 1986) and to reduce cost of the negotiating short-term contracts (Milgrom and Roberts, 1987) and so to favor short-term contracting with independent suppliers over alternatives like vertical integration or long-term contracting. The supplier relations that mark modern manufacturing firms—involving close coordination between the firm and its independently owned contractors and suppliers—appear to be consistent with these theories, and inconsistent with theories in which joint planning can only take place in integrated firms.

In this essay, we develop a theoretical model of the firm that allows us to explore many of the complementarities in modern manufacturing firms. The non-convexities inherent in our problem makes it inappropriate to use differential techniques to study the effects of changing parameters. Instead, we utilize purely algebraic (lattice-theoretic) methods first introduced by Donald M. Topkis (1978), which provide an exact formalization of the idea of groups of complementary activities. In problems with complementarities among the choice variables this approach easily handles both indivisibilities and non-concave maximands while allowing sharp comparative statics results. In particular, we give conditions under which the set of maximizers moves monotonically with changes in a (possibly multidimensional) parameter. Because these methods are quite straightforward and would seem to be of broad applicability in economics, but are not well known among economists, we describe them in some detail in Section I.

Our model and its basic analysis are provided in Section II. The firm in our model choices its price; the length of the product life cycle or frequency of product improvements (a surrogate for quality); its order-receipt, processing, and delivery technologies; various characteristics of its manufacturing and design technologies as reflected in its marginal cost of production and its costs of setups and new product development; its manufacturing plan, including the length of the production cycle (and, implicitly, its inventory and back-order levels); and aspects of its quality control policy, all with the aim of maximizing its expected profits. Using reasonable assumptions about the nature and equipment costs, we find that the complementarities in the system are pervasive. We use the firm's optimizing response to assumed trends in input prices (the falling costs of communication, computer-aided design, and flexible manufacturing) in the presence of these complementarities to explain both the clustering of characteristics and the trends in manufacturing.

In Section III, we turn our attention to the organizational problems associated with the new technologies. We summarize and review the predictions of the model in the concluding Section IV.

I. The Mathematics of Complementarities

Here we review some basic definitions and results in the mathematics of complementarities. The results permit us to make definite statements about the nature of the optimal solution to the firm's problem and how it depends on various parameters, even though the domain of the objective function may be non-convex (for example, some variables may be integer-valued) and the objective function itself may be non-concave, non-differentiable, and even discontinuous at some points.

For additional developments and missing proofs, see Topkis.

We first introduce our notation. Let $x, x' \in \mathbf{R}^n$. We say that $x \geq x'$ if $x_i \geq x_i'$ for all i. Define $\max(x, x')$ to be the point in $\mathbf{R}^n$ whose ith component is $\max(x_i, x_i')$, and $\min(x, x')$ to be the point whose ith component is $\min(x_i, x_i')$. This notation is used below to define the two key notions of the theory. The first notion is that of a supermodular function, which is a function that exhibits complementarities among its arguments. The second is that of a sublattice of $\mathbf{R}^n$, a subset of $\mathbf{R}^n$ that is closed under the max and min operations and whose structure lets us characterize the set of optima of a supermodular function.

Definition 1: A function $f: \mathbf{R}^n \to \mathbf{R}$ is *supermodular* if for all $x, x' \in \mathbf{R}^n$,

$$(1) \quad f(x) + f(x') \leq f(\min(x, x')) + f(\max(x, x')).$$

The function f is *submodular* is $-f$ is supermodular.

Inequality (1) is clearly equivalent to

$$[f(x) - f(\min(x, x'))] + [f(x') - f(\min(x, x'))] \leq f(\max(x, x')) - f(\min(x, x')):$$

the sum of the changes in the function when several arguments are increased separately is less than the change resulting from increasing all the arguments together. The inequality is also equivalent to

$$f(\max(x, x')) - f(x') \geq f(x) - f(\min(x, x')):$$

increasing one or more variables raises the return to increasing other variables. These reformulations of the defining inequality make clear the sense in which the supermodularity of a function corresponds to complementarity among its arguments.

Note that any function of a single variable is trivially supermodular. This observation serves to resolve various questions about possible relationships between supermodularity and other concepts. However, even in a multidimensional context, supermodularity is distinct from, but related to, a number of more familiar notions. First, supermodularity has no necessary relation to the concavity or convexity of the function: consider $f(x_1, x_2) = x_1^a + x_2^b$, which is supermodular for all values of a and b but may be either concave or convex (or both or neither). Nor, in the context of production functions, does supermodularity carry implications for returns to scale. For example, the Cobb-Douglas functions $f(x_1, x_2) = x_1^a x_2^b$ may show increasing or decreasing returns to scale but are supermodular for all positive values of a and b. This is most easily checked using Theorem 2, below, which states that a smooth function f is supermodular if and only if $\partial^2 f / \partial x_i \partial x_j \geq 0$ for $i \neq j$. Thus, if f is supermodular and smooth, then the smooth supermodular function $-f$ shows weak cost complementarities as defined by William Baumol, John Panzar, and Robert Willig (1982, pp. 74–75). Even without smoothness, it is easily shown that a submodular function that is zero at the origin shows economies of scope as defined by Baumol et al. More generally, submodularity is related to, but distinct from, the notion of subadditivity that figures centrally in the study of cost functions.[3] For example, any function of a single variable is submodular, but obviously not all such functions are subadditive. Meanwhile, the functions on $[0,1] \times [0,1]$ given by $f(x_1, x_2) = 1 + x_1 + x_2 + \varepsilon x_1 x_2$ are submodular for $\varepsilon > 0$, supermodular for $\varepsilon \geq 0$, and subadditive for all ε sufficiently close to zero in absolute value.

Six theorems about supermodular functions are provided here. The first four together provide a relatively easy way to check whether a given function is supermodular. Theorem 5 indicates how, in a parameterized maximization problem, the maximizer changes with changing parameters, while Theorem 6 characterizes the set of maximizers of a supermodular function. It is Theorem 5 that makes our comparative statics exercises possible.

Let $x_{\setminus i}$ denote the vector x with the ith component removed and let $x_{\setminus ij}$ denote x

---

[3]A function f is subadditive if $f(x) + f(y) \geq f(x + y)$ for all x and y.

with the ith and jth components removed. Let subscripts on f denote partial derivatives, for example, $f_i = \partial f / \partial x_i$, $f_{ij} = \partial^2 f / \partial x_i \partial x_j$.

THEOREM 1: *Suppose $f: \mathbf{R}^n \to \mathbf{R}$. If for all i, j, and $x_{\setminus ij}$, $f(x_i, x_j, x_{\setminus ij})$ is supermodular when regarded as a function of the arguments (x_i, x_j) only, then f is supermodular.*

THEOREM 2: *Let $I = [a_1, b_1] \times \cdots \times [a_n, b_n]$ be an interval in $\mathbf{R}^n$ with nonempty interior and suppose that $f: I \to \mathbf{R}$ is continuous and twice continuously differentiable on the interior of I. Then f is supermodular on I if and only if for all $i \neq j$, $f_{ij} \geq 0$.*

Theorem 2 is stated above in the form given in Topkis. For our application, we will need a slightly stronger theorem in which the condition that f is twice continuously differentiable is weakened to the condition that it can be written as an indefinite double integral with a nonnegative integrand. The precise extension is stated and proved in the Appendix.

THEOREM 3: *Suppose that $f, g: \mathbf{R}^n \to \mathbf{R}$ are supermodular functions. Then $f + g$ is supermodular. If, in addition, f and g are nonnegative and nondecreasing, then fg is supermodular.*

THEOREM 4: *Suppose that $f: \mathbf{R}^{1+n} \to \mathbf{R}$ is supermodular and continuous in its first argument. Then for all a, $b \in \mathbf{R}$, the function $g: \mathbf{R}^n \to \mathbf{R}$ defined by $g(x) = \max_{y \in [a,b]} f(y, x)$ is supermodular.*

PROOF:

Since f is continuous in its first argument, the function g is well defined. For all x and x', there exist y and y' with $g(x) = f(y, x)$ and $g(x') = f(y', x')$. Then,

$$g(x) + g(x') = f(y, x) + f(y', x')$$
$$\leq f(\max(y, y'), \max(x, x'))$$
$$+ f(\min(y, y'), \min(x, x'))$$
$$\leq g(\max(x, x'))$$
$$+ g(\min(x, x')). \qquad \square$$

In what follows we will be particularly concerned with constrained optimization of supermodular functions, and our results will depend on the constraint set having the right structure or shape, namely, that of a sublattice of R^n.

Definition 2: A set T is a *sublattice* of R^n if for all $x, x' \in T$, $\min(x, x') \in T$ and $\max(x, x') \in T$.

In our application, the definition of a sublattice represents the idea that if it is possible to engage in high (respectively, low) levels of each of several activities separately, then it is possible to engage in equally high (resp., low) levels of all of the activities simultaneously. Thus, for example, if $S_1, \ldots, S_n$ are arbitrary subsets of R, then $S_1 \times \cdots \times S_n$ is a sublattice of R^n. However, the product sets are not the only sublattices. The sublattice structure also permits the possibility that some activities can be engaged in at a high level *only if* the others are also carried out at a high level. For example, if $x \geq x'$, then $\{x, x'\}$ is a sublattice.

Definition 3: Given two sets $S, S' \subset R^n$, we say that S is *higher than* S' and write $S \geq S'$ if for all $x \in S$ and $x' \in S'$, $\max(x, x') \in S$ and $\min(x, x') \in S'$.

THEOREM 5: *Suppose* $f: R^{n+k} \to R$ *is supermodular and suppose* $T(y)$ *and* $T(y')$ *are sublattices of* R^n. *Let* $S(y) \equiv \operatorname{argmax}\{f(z, y) | z \in T(y)\}$, *and define* $S(y')$ *analogously. Then* $y \geq y'$ *and* $T(y) \geq T(y')$ *imply that* $S(y) \geq S(y')$.

PROOF:

Let $x \in S(y)$ and $x' \in S(y')$ and $y \geq y'$ so that $y = \max(y, y')$ and $y' = \min(y, y')$. Since $T(y) \geq T(y')$, $\max(x, x') \in T(y)$ and $\min(x, x') \in T(y')$. From the definitions, $f(x, y') \geq f(\max(x, x'), y)$ and $f(x', y') \geq f(\min(x, x'), y')$, but since f is supermodular, $f(x, y) + f(x', y') \leq f(\max(x, x'), y) + f(\min(x, x'), y')$ from which the conclusion is immediate. □

THEOREM 6: *Suppose* $f: R^n \to R$ *is supermodular and suppose* T *is a sublattice of* R^n. *Then the set of maximizers of* f *over* T *is also a sublattice.*

PROOF:
Apply Theorem 5 with $y = y'$. □

Theorem 5 is particularly important for our application. When its conclusion holds, we shall say that the set of optimizers "rises" as the parameter values increases. What justifies this language? The theorem implies, for example, that if $x^*(y)$ and $x^*(y')$ are the unique maximizers given their respective parameter vectors y and y' and if $y \geq y'$, then $x^*(y) \geq x^*(y')$. (For uniqueness implies that $x^*(y) = \max(x^*(y), x^*(y'))$, from which $x^*(y) \geq x^*(y')$ follows.) Alternatively, suppose we assume that f is a *continuous* supermodular function that T is *compact* sublattice, so that the set of maximizers corresponding to any parameter vector y is compact. Then, by Theorem 5, there are greatest and least elements $\bar{x}(y)$ and $\underline{x}(y)$ in the set of maximizers S. One can show that both $\bar{x}(y)$ and $\underline{x}(y)$ are nondecreasing functions of y. (Using Theorem 6 and the definitions, $\bar{x}(y') \leq \max(\bar{x}(y), \bar{x}(y')) \leq \bar{x}(y)$ and similarly $\underline{x}(y) \geq \min(\underline{x}(y), \underline{x}(y')) \geq \underline{x}(y')$.)

II. Complementarities in Production

We study a model of a multiproduct firm facing a downward sloping demand curve. The firm may be a monopoly or monopolistic competitor. Alternatively, our model may be viewed as a building block for a model of oligopolistic markets.

In the formal model, the firm chooses the levels of the following decision variables:

Variable	Interpretation
p	Price of each product
q	(Expected) number of improvements per product per period
a	Order receipt and processing time
b	Delivery time
c	Direct marginal costs of production
d	Design cost per product improvement
e	Extra set-up costs on newly changed products

m	Number of setups per period
r	Probability of a defective batch
s	Direct cost of a setup
w	Wastage costs per setup

In addition, we denote the number of products by n.

The functional relationships and parameters that complete the model include the demand specification, the specification of the capital costs of different levels of the technological variables, the functional relation linking the average delay between receipt of an order and its being filled to the number of products and of setups, the marginal cost of production, the marginal cost of reworking defectives, the cost of holding inventories, and a time parameter that will proxy for the state of technology and demand. More specifically, we have

Parameter	Interpretation
ρ	Marginal cost of reworking a defective unit
τ	Calendar time
ι	Cost of holding inventory per unit
κ	Capital costs $(\kappa = \kappa(a,b,c,d,e,r,s,w,\tau))$
μ	Base demand per product $(\mu = \mu(p,q,n,\tau))$
δ	Demand shrinkage with delay time $(\delta = \delta(t,\tau))$
ω	Expected wait for a processed order to be filled $(\omega = \omega(m,r,n))$

The total expected wait for an order to be received, processed, filled, and shipped, which determines the value of the shrinkage factor (δ) on demand, is $t = a + \omega + b$, and realized demand is then $\mu(p,q,n,\tau)\delta(a + \omega + b,\tau)$. Thus, the firm's payoff function Π is

$$\Pi(p,q,m,a,b,c,d,e,r,s,w,\tau)$$
$$= (p - c - r\rho - \iota/m)n\mu(p,q,n,\tau)$$
$$\times \delta(a + \omega(m,r,n) + b,\tau)$$
$$- m(s + w) - nq(d + e)$$
$$- \kappa(a,b,c,d,e,r,s,w,\tau).$$

The total profit Π is the operating profit minus the fixed costs associated with machine setups, product redesign, and the purchase of capital equipment.

The first term $(p - c - r\rho - \iota/m)n\mu\delta$ is the operating profit. For each unit sold, the firm receives the price p and pays direct production costs, expected rework costs, and inventory holding and handling costs. In line with the Economic Order Quantity models commonly used for inventory analysis, we treat the average levels of work-in-process and finished goods inventories as being directly proportional to demand and inversely proportional to the number of setups. Similarly, back orders are directly proportional to demand and decreasing in the number of setups. We have used the function δ, which we take to be uniform across products, to model the cost of back orders; this takes the form of lost demand when delivery is delayed. We have also modeled the firm as setting a uniform price (p) across the product line, which is reasonable given the symmetry of the products in the model.

The second term $m(s + w)$ is the cost of the setups, which, as suggested above, consists of the number of setups times the sum of the direct costs plus wastage per setup. The term $nq(d + e)$ is the cost of redesign over the period, including the extra setup costs on newly altered products. In this term, nq is the total number of redesigns or improvements.

The last term is κ, which is the capital cost of selecting the various technological variables, a, b, c, d, e, r, s, and w, at any date τ. Among these technology variables, the order receipt and processing time (a) is determined by the technology used for communicating orders (mail, express courier, FAX, electronic data communications networks, etc.) and by the means used to handle orders once received (manual entry, computerized order entry systems). Whichever choices are made, there are capital costs involved in setting up the corresponding systems. Similarly, different options exist that determine the speed of delivery (b) from inventory, and these too have differing capital costs.

Our model allows us to represent many aspects and tradeoffs in the firm's choice of manufacturing strategy. For example, the flexibility of design technology is modeled by the variable d. The introduction of computer aided design (CAD) lowers these marginal costs of redesigning and improving products, but it also involves significant capital expenditures on training, hardware, and software. Both of these effects are captured in our profit function.

Flexibility of manufacturing equipment has a number of aspects, several of which are represented in our model. First, flexibility is often associated with low costs of routinely changing over from producing one good to another. Here, this effect is represented first through the variable s: more flexible equipment means lower setup costs in terms of the downtime and direct labor costs involved in resetting the machines, switching dies, etc. Also, more flexible equipment might involve less wastage (lower w) per setup. This wastage might be in the form of extra inspection, scrap, rework, and repair costs that are necessary when a changeover is made. The precision of computer aided equipment, "design for manufacturability" (facilitated by CAD-CAM), and similar investments lower these costs. Finally, flexibility might involve costs of changing machinery over to produce new or redesigned products (low values of e).

The technological quality variable (r) captures a somewhat different feature of modern manufacturing methods. Improving quality on this dimension may involve investing in more precisely controlled machinery which may even constantly monitor and adjust itself. It may also improve more prosaic but possibly more significant efforts aimed at changing attitudes toward quality, such as giving workers the ability to stop the production line when a problem arises.

Although we do not explicitly model labor force decisions here, an element of the flexibility of modern manufacturing is associated with broadly trained workers and with work rules that facilitate frequent changes in activities. In this context we may interpret investments in flexibility in terms of worker education and industrial relations efforts, as well as the purchase of physical capital. Certainly, flexibility in the labor force and in the capital equipment are mutually complementary.

Finally, the choice of c, the marginal costs of production, has capital cost implications, if only through investing in learning how to control costs.

Even before we make any assumptions about the form of the unspecified functions κ, μ, δ, and ω, certain complementarities are evident in the model. For example, with more frequent changeovers (higher q), the returns to more efficient technologies for redesigning products and changing over equipment (higher values of $-d$ and $-e$) will naturally rise and, conversely, more efficient changeover and redesign technologies raise the marginal returns to increasing q. Similarly, an increase in the number of setups per period (m) and the concomitant reduction in inventories and back orders is complementary with a reduction in the components of set-up costs (increases in $-s$ and $-w$). Technologically, one expects that reduced set-up and changeover costs are bundled together in the new equipment. However, conclusions such as that one require that we make an assumption about the properties of the unspecified function κ. To make further statements, we need to make assumptions about properties of all the unspecified functions.

Our assumption about the form of δ is the following:

ASSUMPTION A1: δ is twice continuously differentiable, nonnegative, decreasing and convex in t, nondecreasing in τ and submodular in (t, τ).

The assumption that δ is decreasing in t simply means that increased delay reduces sales, while convexity says that the larger is the delay, the smaller is the marginal impact of additional delay. Inclusion of τ allows for a time trend in demand through δ. This trend must be nonnegative for our results, but it could be trivial. The submodularity assumption means that, as time passes, δ_t becomes weakly more negative or, equivalently, the returns to reducing waiting time, $-t$, increase weakly. This might come about because the adoption of more modern manufacturing methods by the firm's customers raises the importance of speedy service to them.

An immediate implication of the convexity assumption in Assumption A1 is that activities that reduce the several components of delay time ($a, b,$ and ω) are mutually complementary, as can be easily verified by checking that the corresponding mixed partial derivatives of the profit function are positive. These complementarities may seem surprising, since the three components of waiting time are perfect substitutes for one another in determining the total delay. However, as our analysis shows, the possibility of substituting these elements to achieve a fixed time delay is irrelevant to their assessment as potential complements within the corporate strategy.

To complete our evaluation of the complementarities associated with speed, we must take an assumption about the ω function. Generally, we would expect ω to be increasing in the probability of a batch requiring reworking (r) and decreasing in the number of setups (m). The one nonobvious element in Assumption A2 below is that r and m are complements in determining ω: an increase in the number of setups (or decrease in batch size) is assumed to raise the impact on delay time of an increase in the probability of a batch being defective. This complementarity may be caused by the more frequent changeovers in the rework facility being required by more frequent changeovers in the main facility. Otherwise, it seems natural to expect the effect to be zero, which is also consistent with our assumption.

ASSUMPTION A2: $\omega = \omega(m, r, n)$ *is twice continuously differentiable, decreasing in m, increasing in r and supermodular in m and r, given n. That is, $\omega_m \le 0$, $\omega_r \ge 0$, and $\omega_{mr} \ge 0$.*

As a consequence of (A1) and (A2), $-a$, $-b$, m and $-r$ are mutually complementary in increasing demand.

To complete our analysis of the marketing aspects of strategy, the form of the demand function μ must be restricted. We make two assumptions. The first is a standard one:

ASSUMPTION A3: μ *is twice continuously differentiable, increasing in q, and decreasing in p, while operating profits, defined by $(p -$*

$c - r\rho - \iota/m)n\mu(p, q, n, \tau)\delta(a + \omega + b, \tau)$, *are a strictly quasi-concave function of p.*

The first part asserts innocuously that consumers prefer lower prices and higher quality. Since we will hold n fixed, we need make no assumptions on its effect, although it would be natural to assume that $n\mu$ is increasing in n. The assumption that demand is quasi-concave in prices is standard. The nonstandard part of our assumption about demand is contained in Assumption A4:

ASSUMPTION A4: $\mu(p, q, n, \tau)$ *is nondecreasing in τ and supermodular when regarded as a function of $-p$, q and τ, for given n.*

A4 is a complicated assumption. It would be satisfied, for example, by a multiplicatively separable specification of demand, $\mu = A(p)B(q)C(\tau)$, as well as by additively separable demand $A(p) + B(q) + C(\tau)$, and $A' < 0$, $B' \ge 0$, and $C' \ge 0$ in both cases. It asserts that the quantity demanded becomes (weakly) more sensitive to price and quality with passing time, and that at higher quality levels the quantity demanded is more sensitive to price changes. Again, we emphasize that we allow demand to be independent of τ, but if a dependence exists, it should not be such as to offset the supply-side effects of technological progress embodied in the effect of τ in the κ function.

Our final assumption is the following one, on the κ function. It is key because it embodies the presumed technological changes in the capital goods industries supplying the firm that are the basis for our arguments.

ASSUMPTION A5: $\kappa(-a, -b, -c, -d, -e, -r, -s, -w, \tau)$ *is submodular.*

This assumption is stated in terms of the negatives of the natural decision variables because a and b decrease with improved communication systems, better data transmission, entry, storage, manipulation, and retrieval systems, and speedier delivery methods, and the other choice variables decrease with improved design, manufacturing, quality, and cost-control technologies, that is, with increases in τ.

Conceptually, A5 has two parts. The first is our assumption about the time path of exogenous technological change: the incremental capital costs of modern technologies for communication, delivery, design, and flexible production are falling over time. Assuming differentiability of κ, so that Theorem 2 applies, these trends are captured in the inequalities $\partial^2\kappa/\partial x\,\partial\tau \le 0$, $x = -a$, $-b, -c, -d, -e, -r, -s, -w$: technological change among capital equipment suppliers lowers the costs over time of the firm's increasing delivery speeds, using more flexible manufacturing methods, reducing the probability of defects, reducing costs of redesign and controlling production costs. Notice that we require no assumptions about the relative rates at which these prices are falling, because all these price changes will turn out to have mutually reinforcing effects.

The second part of A5 concerns the interrelationships among investments in the new technologies. For example, assuming that the mixed partial derivative of κ with respect to $-d$ and $-e$ is positive means that the level of investment in flexible equipment necessary to reduce extra set-up costs by a given amount is reduced by investments in flexible design equipment. Of course, if the technologies were completely separable, the condition would be met but, as we argued in the introduction, separability is not a realistic assumption. The cost of instituting both computer-aided design and flexible machining systems (FMS) to achieve given levels of design and set-up costs is generally less than the sum of the costs of instituting the two separately because the CAD equipment may provide set-up instructions readable by the FMS machinery, eliminating the costly step of encoding (possibly with error) the design instructions into a form readable by the flexible machine. Other complementarities in the physical equipment are similarly represented in κ. Thus, CAD makes it less costly to reduce defects by making it much cheaper to design products that are easily manufactured, while a computerized order-entry system can eliminate the need to transcribe order information into a form readable by the manufacturing computers, saving costs and reducing errors.

Other interactions, based on substitute uses of resources, could work against our complementary assumptions. For example, if the firm faces a fixed capital budget or a rising cost of capital with increased levels of investment, or if there are constraints on space or personnel and computer based systems for communication and design compete for these resources, then an investment in lowering a would raise the cost of investments to lower d. The second part of A5 is the hypothesis that the technological complementarities we have identified are larger than the effects of any constraints on the resources that the systems must share.

Note that throughout the analysis, we are holding the rework cost parameter ρ and the inventory holding cost parameter ι fixed.

The problem of maximizing Π is not amenable to standard, calculus-based techniques. First, although demand is assumed to be a quasi-concave in price, we have made no other concavity assumptions. Indeed, the assumed convexity of δ means that profit, exclusive of capital costs, is actually *convex* in the total delay between placing an order and receiving shipment, and since A5 places no restrictions on the concavity or convexity of κ, Π may well be convex in $-a$, $-b$, m and $-r$ over some ranges. In this case, satisfaction of a first-order condition identifies a (local) minimum with respect to the variable in question. Moreover, it is natural to take m to be integer-valued of the form, nk, where k is the number of production cycles per period and n is the number of products. However, the methods developed in the previous section are applicable here, once we have the necessary complementarities. In this, A5 plays a major role.

We are now ready to state and prove our main results. The idea is to use Theorem 2 to show that the firm's objective function is supermodular in the firm's (sign-adjusted) decision variables and that consequently, by Theorems 5 and 6, the set of optimizers forms a sublattice that moves up over time. However, it is not true that Π is a supermodular function of all its arguments, because the mixed partial derivatives of that function in price and the determinants of waiting time have the wrong sign when the

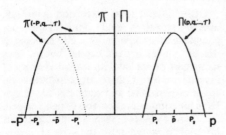

FIGURE 1. OBTAINING π FROM Π

NOTE THAT

$$\max_{p \geq P_1} \Pi = \Pi(\bar{p}, \dots, \tau) = \pi(-\bar{p}, \dots, \tau)$$
$$\text{WHILE } \max_{p \geq P_2} \Pi(p, \dots, \tau) = \Pi(P_2, \dots, \tau)$$
$$= \pi(-P_2, \dots, \tau)$$

price is set too low. To get around that difficulty, we consider the optimized value of profit with respect to price where the price is restricted by a lower bound P. (See Figure 1.) Letting this bound replace the price as the choice variable in our problem, it is apparent that this change of variables leaves the optimal values of the non-price variables unchanged. By A3, for any fixed values of the other decision variables and parameters, the corresponding optimal value of p is unique, and the *highest* optimal value of P equals the optimal price p.[4] Moreover, as we now show, the new function is super-modular in the sign-adjusted decision variables.

THEOREM 7: *Assume A1 through A5. Then the function*

$$\pi(-P, q, m, -a, -b, -c, -d, -e, -r,$$

$$-s, -w, \tau)$$

$$\equiv \max_{p \geq P} \Pi(p, q, m, a, b,$$

$$c, d, e, r, s, w, \tau)$$

is supermodular on the sublattice of $\mathbf{R}^n$ defined by the restrictions that all the decision variables be nonnegative.

---

[4]This construct also ensures that the price at which demand is calculated will always weakly exceed marginal cost, $c + rp + \iota/m$.

PROOF:

By Theorem 3 and A5, it is enough that the function $\pi + \kappa$ be supermodular. If $\pi + \kappa$ were twice continuously differentiable everywhere, then by Theorem 2 it would be sufficient to check that all the cross-partials of $\pi + \kappa$ are nonnegative. The verification is routine, except that $\pi + \kappa$ may have no second derivatives on the set of points in the domain where $\partial(\Pi + \kappa)/\partial p = 0$. However, it is straightforward to verify that the slightly weaker assumptions of Theorem 2* in the Appendix are satisfied, so $\pi + \kappa$ is supermodular, as we had required.   □

THEOREM 8: *Assume A1 through A5 and that κ is continuous. Let the individual decision variables each be constrained to lie in a compact set consistent with the nonnegativity requirement, so that together they lie in a compact set that is a sublattice. Then the set of maximizers of π is a compact sublattice which rises with τ.*

PROOF:

Apply Theorems 6 and 7. Note that this result allows us to restrict the decision variables to be integer-valued and to limit the number of available technologies to some finite set. The supermodularity of the functional form $\pi + \kappa$ is verified by investigating its derivatives on continuous intervals, and the restriction to a compact sublattice is imposed later in a way that permits a restriction to discrete choices.

The key conclusion is that the sign-adjusted decision variables all rise over time. Thus, as time passes, one expects to see a pattern of the following sort linking changes in a wide range of variables:

- Lower Prices,
- Lower Marginal Costs,
- More Frequent Product Redesigns and Improvements,
- Higher Quality in Production, Marked by Fewer Defects,
- Speedier Communication with Customers and Processing of Orders,
- More Frequent Setups and Smaller Batch Sizes, with Correspondingly Lower Levels of Finished-Goods and Work-In-Process

Inventories and of Back Orders per Unit Demand,
- Speedier Delivery from Inventory,
- Lower Setup, Wastage, and Changeover Costs,
- Lower Marginal Costs of Product Redesign.

The conclusion in Theorem 6 that the set of optimizers forms a sublattice implies that if at any time there are multiple solutions to the optimization problem, then there is a highest and a lowest optimal solution in the vector inequality sense. Further, comparing any two firm's choices, if these differ, then the choice of selecting the higher, "more modern" level for each decision variable is also optimal, as is the vector made up of the term-by-term minimal values of the two firm's choices. More typically, however, we might expect a unique solution.

In any case, the chosen levels move up together over time in response to the falling costs of faster communications, more flexible production, and more frequent redesign.

The model we have presented is a static one, but it is nevertheless suggestive about the nature of the path to the modern manufacturing strategy. Specifically, it suggests that even if the changes that take place in the environment—especially the falling cost of the equipment used under the modern manufacturing strategy—happen gradually, the adoption process may be much more erratic, for two reasons. First, there are nonconvexities, which mean that the optimum may shift discontinuously, with the profit-maximizing levels of the whole complex of variables moving sharply upward. This makes it relatively unprofitable to be stuck with a mixture of highly flexible and highly specialized production equipment. One does not necessarily expect to find that the adoption of the new equipment is sudden; it may still be desirable to iron out the wrinkles in the new technology with an initial small scale adoption. What the theory suggests we should not see is an extended period of time during which there are substantial volumes of both highly flexible and highly specialized equipment being used side-by-side. Then, once the adoption is well underway, it should

proceed rapidly, with increasing momentum.

Second, there are the complementarities, which make it relatively unprofitable to adopt only one part of the modern manufacturing strategy. The theory suggests that we should not see an extended period of time during which one component of the strategy is in place and the other components have barely begun to be put into place. For example, we should not see flexible equipment used for a long period with unchanging product lines.

The conclusion of Theorem 8 that firms will increase quality in the sense of reducing the probability r of a defective batch is worth further comment. Many observers have noted a focus on increased quality of output among modern manufacturing firms. One would expect that design for manufacturability would result directly in lower defect rates. However, the complementarities displayed in the model provide a second, less obvious incentive for increased quality. Decreases in the probability of defects are strictly complementary with increases in m through the effect on operating profit: demand grows with increases in m, and this increases the return to lowering costs by reducing the probability of reworking.[5]

Recall that we have held n, the number of products, fixed throughout this analysis. Inspection of the profit function in light of the arguments in Theorem 7 should make the necessity of doing this clear: neither n nor its negative are naturally complementary with the other decision variables. This shows up most clearly in the cost of redesign term, $-nq(d+e)$, where increases in n make decreases in d and e more attractive but increases in q less attractive. There are further potential complications through the demand term, and so without very special assumptions we cannot include n in the cluster of complements.

That we cannot include the number of products is somewhat surprising: surely broader product lines would seem to be

---

[5] Note too that decreases in r are also strictly complementary with increases in the other quality variable, q, as well as with decreases in the delay in communicating with customers and processing their orders (a) and in the time to deliver the inventory (b).

complementary with reduced set-up costs, and this intuition has in fact been verified in simpler models (see Xavier de Groote, 1988). However, the ambiguity surrounding n in richer models appear to reflect something real. On the one side, there are numerous examples of firms massively broadening their product lines with the adoption of modern manufacturing methods, and some of these were cited above. On the other, anecdotal evidence (for example, James B. Treece, 1989) as well as both the discussions of the "focused factory" found in the literature on manufacturing strategy (for example, David A. Garvin, 1988, especially Ch. 8) and some formal statistical analysis (Mikhel Tombak and Arnoud De Meyer, 1988) point to firms having reason to narrow their product lines when shifting to more modern manufacturing patterns and of their acting to do so.

III. Manufacturing and Organization

How is a manufacturing firm most efficiently organized and managed? Several of the trends analyzed in Section II have a direct bearing on this question. First, consider the complementarities that exist between the various functions in the firm: marketing, order-processing, shipping, engineering, and manufacturing. If the firm's problem were smooth and concave (despite the complementarities) and its environment were stationary and if the optimum is not on the boundary of the feasible set, the complementarities would not pose a serious organizational problem: if none of the managers controlling the individual functions can find a small change that raises the firm's expected profits, then there is no coordinated change —large or small—that can raise profits. However, in our non-concave problem, it is possible that only coordinated changes among all the variables will allow the firm to achieve its optimum. Non-convexities and significant complementarities provide a reason for explicit coordination between functions such as marketing and production.[6]

[6]A similar point is made by de Groote, who investigates a different model of complementarities between marketing and manufacturing.

(Extension of the methods in this paper to a game-theoretic context can be used to model this coordination problem and the role of the central coordinator: see Milgrom and Roberts, 1989.)

Even without non-convexities, significant complementarities in a rapidly changing environment provide another reason for close coordination between functions. Think of the managerial planning process as an algorithm to seek the maximum of the profit function. Successful performance in the face of rapid environmental change requires the use of fast algorithms (for example, Newton's method), and these require a coordinated choice of the decision variables that recognizes the interactions among these variables in the profit function.

Second, suppose that the organization being modeled is one where sales are made through several different stores. If the optimal speed of order-processing (a) jumps down, it may be desirable that all the stores install computerized systems linked to the manufacturing facility to track orders and sales. If there are fixed costs or other economies of scale in the computer system, then it is important that all, or nearly all, of the stores participate. However, unless all the costs and benefits of the change accrue to one agent, there arises a standard public goods, free-rider problem. Eliciting efficient cooperation from the store owners could be expensive and may provide a reason for vertical ownership of the distribution channel.

Third, Oliver Williamson and Klein, Crawford, and Alchian (1978) have argued that the advantages of increased vertical governance grow as assets become increasingly specialized. This occurs, it is argued, because the returns from specialized investments are vulnerable to appropriation. Then, as Williamson and Jean Tirole (1986) have argued, fear of appropriation causes insufficient investment to be made or, as we have argued (Milgrom and Roberts, 1987), it encourages the parties to waste resources by investing in bargaining position. Following this line of argument, let us equate "specialization" of assets with inflexibility of retooling to produce different products, so that it may be measured by e. The net costs of governance, bargaining, and deterred or distorted incentives are $\gamma(-v, -e)$, where v is a vector measure of the extent or complexity of vertical governance. We formalize a version of the hypothesis that increased flexibility of assets reduces the marginal value of governance activities with:

ASSUMPTION A6: *The function $\gamma(-v, -e)$ is sub-modular.*

THEOREM 9: *Assume that A1–A6 hold and consider the profit function:*

$$\pi(-p, m, q, -a, -b, -c, -d, -e, -r,$$

$$-s, -w, \tau) - \gamma(-v, -e).$$

Let each decision variable be constrained as in Theorem 8. Then the set of optimizers of $\pi - \gamma$ is a sublattice and rises with τ.

PROOF:
A direct consequence of Theorems 3, 5, 6, and 7, and A6. □

Thus, given Assumptions A1–A6 another predicted attribute in the characteristic cluster for flexible manufacturing companies is low vertical governance, for example, the extensive use of independently owned suppliers and subcontractors. This characteristic is an especially interesting one, given the usual conception of the difference between internal and market organization. Although uncertainty is not formally part of our model,[7] running this sort of "tight," low inventory operation with frequent redesigning of products in a world of uncertainties would surely require close coordination and communications with suppliers.[8] Yet according to our theory, the modern firm—despite its close relationships with suppliers and customers—will have little formal vertical governance.

Economists sometimes emphasize the need for close communication in the presence of supply or demand uncertainty as a reason for vertical integration (for example, Kenneth Arrow, 1975). If we were to formulate this alternative hypothesis using a submodular governance cost function $\lambda(m, v)$, we would arrive at the conclusion that v increases over time and that more extensive vertical governance is part of the cluster of characteristics of a modern manufacturing firm. The anecdotal evidence contained in press reports suggests to us that this conclusion is wrong, and that the former hypothesis A6 is the better one.

IV. Conclusion

The cluster of characteristics that are often found in manufacturing firms that are technologically advanced encompasses marketing, production, engineering, and organization variables. On the marketing side, these firms hold down prices while emphasizing high quality supported by frequent product improvements. Customers orders are filled increasingly quickly, with back-order levels being systematically reduced. In terms of technology, modern manufacturing firms exploit rapid mass data communications, production equipment with low setup, wastage, and retooling costs, flexible design technologies, product designs that use common inputs, very low levels of inventories (of both work in process and finished goods), and short production cycle times. They also seem to push differentially to increase manufacturing quality and. simultaneously, to control variable production costs. At the engineering and organizational levels, there is an integration of the product and process engineering functions and an extensive use of independently owned suppliers linked with the buying firm by close communications and joint planning.

We have argued in this paper that this clustering is no accident. Rather, it is a result of the adoption by profit-maximizing firms of a coherent business strategy that exploits complementarities, and the trend to adopt

---

[7]However, introducing uncertainty would cause no difficulties because the expectation of a supermodular function is supermodular. See Milgrom and Roberts, 1989.

[8]For a model of some aspects of this issue, see Milgrom and Roberts, 1988. In that model, inventories play a buffering role whose importance is reduced when communication is increased.

this strategy is the result of identifiable changes in technology and demand. Our formal model includes eleven decision variables from the claimed cluster of complements plus a parameter to account for the passage of time. There are thus 66 potential cross effects among the twelve variables, and all of these are nonnegative: there are extensive complementarities in marketing, manufacturing, engineering, design, and organization that make it profitable for a firm that adopts some of these characteristics to adopt more. We have also argued that the non-convexities in the problem mitigate against any smooth distribution of these characteristics among firms. For this reason, we are hopeful that empirical work will provide evidence of distinctly separated clusters of firm characteristics as support for our theory. Given our assumptions about time trends in prices, we also expect to find an increasing proportion of manufacturing firms adopting the modern manufacturing strategic cluster that we have described.

APPENDIX

THEOREM 2*: *Let* $I = [a_1, b_1] \times \cdots \times [a_n, b_n]$ *be an interval in* $\mathbb{R}^n$ *with nonempty interior and let* $f: I \to \mathbb{R}$. *Suppose that for every pair of arguments* ij, *there exists a function* $f_{ij}: I \to \mathbb{R}$ *such that f is the indefinite integral of* f_{ij}. *That is, for fixed* $x_{\setminus ij}$ *and for* $x'_i > x_i$ *and* $x'_j > x_j$,

$$f(x'_i, x'_j, x_{\setminus ij}) + f(x_i, x_j, x_{\setminus ij})$$

$$- f(x'_i, x_j, x_{\setminus ij}) - f(x_i, x'_j, x_{\setminus ij})$$

$$= \int_{x_i}^{x'_i} \int_{x_j}^{x'_j} f_{ij}(s, t, x_{\setminus ij}) \, ds \, dt$$

If each f_{ij} *is nonnegative, then f is supermodular on* I.

Remark 1: In our application, f is continuous on I *and twice continuously differentiable on a set* S *with* $\partial^2 f / \partial x_i \partial x_j \geq 0$ *on* S. *Moreover, for all* $\bar{x}_{\setminus ij}$ *the set* $(I - S) \cap \{x | x_{\setminus ij} = \bar{x}_{\setminus ij}\}$ *is a curve. So, taking* $f_{ij} = \partial^2 f / \partial x_i \partial x_j$ *where defined and* $f_{ij} = 0$ *elsewhere, Theorem 2* implies that f is supermodular.*

PROOF:
In view of Theorem 1, it suffices to establish the conclusion for the case $n = 2$. Given any two unordered points x and x' with, say, $x_1 > x'_1$ and $x'_2 > x_2$,

$$f(\max(x, x')) + f(\min(x, x')) - f(x) - f(x')$$

$$= \int_{x'_1}^{x_1} \int_{x_2}^{x'_2} f_{12}(s, t) \, ds \, dt \geq 0,$$

from which it follows that $f(x) + f(x') \leq f(\max(x, x')) + f(\min(x, x'))$. □

REFERENCES

Abegglen, James and Stalk, George, Jr., *Kaisha*: *The Japanese Corporation*, New York: Basic Books, 1985.

Alster, Norm, "What Flexible Workers Can Do," *Fortune*, February 13, 1989, 62–66.

Arrow, Kenneth, "Vertical Integration and Communication," *Bell Journal of Economics*, Spring 1985, *6*, 173–83.

Asanuma, Banri, (1988a) "Manufacturer-Supplier Relationships in Japan and the Concept of Relation-Specific Skill," Kyoto University Economics Working Paper No. 2, 1988 (Forthcoming in the *Journal of the Japanese and International Economies*.)

——, (1988b) "Japanese Manufacturer-Supplier Relationships in International Perspective," Kyoto University Economics Working Paper No. 8, September 1988.

Baumol, William J., Panzar, John C. and Willig, Robert D., *Contestable Markets and the Theory of Industry Structure*, New York: Harcourt Brace Jovanovich, 1982.

de Groote, Xavier, "The Strategic Choice of Production Processes," unpublished doctoral dissertation, Stanford University, 1988.

Dumaine, Brian, "How Managers Can Succeed Through Speed," *Fortune*, February 13, 1989, 54–59.

Garvin, David A., *Managing Quality*: *The Strategic and Competitive Edge*, New York: Free Press, 1988.

Hayes, Robert H., Wheelwright, Steven C. and Clark, Kim B., *Dynamic Manufacturing*: *Creating the Learning Organization*, New York: Free Press, 1988.

Hausman, Warren, "Computer-Integrated Manufacturing: Lessons from Ten Plant Visits," Seminar presented at the Graduate School of Business, Stanford University, Stanford, CA, November 1988.

Henkoff, Ronald, "This Cat Is Acting Like a Tiger," *Fortune*, December 19, 1988, 69–76.

Hounshell, David A, *From the American System to Mass Production: 1800–1932*, Baltimore: Johns Hopkins University Press, 1984.

Kiechel, Walter III, "Corporate Strategy for the 1990s," *Fortune*, February 29, 1988, 34–42.

Klein, Benjamin, Crawford, Robert and Alchian, Armen, "Vertical Integration, Appropriable Rents, and the Competitive Contracting Process," *Journal of Law and Economics*, October 1978, *26*, 297–326.

Milgrom, Paul and Roberts, John, "Bargaining and Influence Costs and the Organization of Economic Activity," Discussion Paper, Graduate School of Business, Stanford University, 1987. (Forthcoming in J. Alt and K. Shepsle, eds., *Positive Perspectives on Political Economy*, Cambridge: Cambridge University Press.)

_____ and _____, "Communication and Inventories as Substitutes in Organizing Production," *Scandinavian Journal of Economics*, 1988, *90*, no. 3, 275–289.

_____ and _____, "Rationalizability, Learning and Equilibrium in Games with Strategic Complementarities," Discussion Paper, Graduate School of Business, Stanford University, 1989.

Mitchell, Russell, "Masters of Innovation: How 3M Keeps Its New Products Coming," *Business Week*, April 10, 1989, 58–63.

Moore, Thomas, "Make or Break Time for General Motors," *Fortune*, February 15, 1988, 32–50.

O'Rourke, Tracy, "A Case for CIM," Lecture delivered at the Conference on Manufacturing, Stanford University, Stanford, CA, May 1988.

Peters, Tom, "Hats Off to Benetton's Apparel Network," *Palo Alto Times-Tribune*, November 18, 1987, p. E1.

Piore, Michael J., "Corporate Reform in American Manufacturing and the Challenge to Economic Theory," mimeo., Massachusetts Institute of Technology, 1986.

_____ and Sabel, Charles F., *The Second Industrial Divide*: *Prospects for Prosperity*, New York: Basic Books, 1984.

Port, Otis, (1989a) "Smart Factories: America's Turn?" *Business Week*, May 8, 1989, 142–48.

_____, (1989b) "The Best-Engineered Part Is No Part at All," *Business Week*, May 8, 1989, 150.

Taylor, Alex III, "Why Fords Sell Like Big Macs," *Fortune*, November 21, 1988, 122–28.

Tirole, Jean, "Procurement and Renegotiation," *Journal of Political Economy*, April 1986, *94*, 235–59.

Tombak, Mikhel and De Meyer, Arnoud, "Flexibility and FMS: An Empirical Appraisal," *IEEE Transactions on Engineering Management*, May 1988, *35*, 101–107.

Topkis, Donald M., "Minimizing a Submodular Function on a Lattice," *Operations Research*, March-April 1978, *26*, 305–21.

Treece, James B., "GM's Bumpy Ride on the Long Road Back,"*Business Week*, February 13, 1989, 74–78.

Valery, Nicholas, "Factory of the Future: Survey," *The Economist*, May 30, 1987, 3–18.

Williamson, Oliver, *Economic Institutions of Capitalism*, New York: Free Press, 1986.

Wright, Kenneth and Bourn, David, *Manufacturing Intelligence*, Reading, MA: Addison Wesley, 1988.

General Motors Corporation, "First a Vision, Now the Payoff," *General Motors Public Interest Report 1988*, Detroit, 1988, 2–15.

U.S. Congress, Office of Technology Assessment, *Computerized Manufacturing Automation*: *Employment, Education and the Workplace*, Washington, 1984.

[29]

The Economic Journal, 100 (*December* 1990), 1147–1158
Printed in Great Britain

INVESTMENT IN GENERAL TRAINING: THE ROLE
OF INFORMATION AND LABOUR MOBILITY*

Eliakim Katz and Adrian Ziderman

Following the seminal work of Becker (1964), it is widely accepted in the literature that firms will be unwilling to finance training which workers may use in other firms. This paper takes issue with this prediction and suggests that firms will frequently share in the cost of such general training.[1]

Becker argues that a firm which pays for the training of workers in skills of potential use to other firms will lose these workers: since other firms bear none of the costs of general training, they can attract a worker with such training by outbidding the firm which trained him. Recognising this absence of property rights over an investment in general training, firms will refuse to provide it. Hence, if general training is to take place, the trainee will have to pay for it. If potential trainees are unwilling or unable to pay, general training will not take place. A shortage in general training is likely to emerge; this may be especially pronounced in developing countries.[2] In contrast, the outlook for *specific* training (training that is of value only in the firm providing it) is less pessimistic, since firms are willing to finance such training. Indeed, it is likely that specific training will be a shared investment between worker and employer. There is a broad literature on various aspects of sharing specific training investments.[3] Yet apart from an early insight by Eckaus (1963), the possibility of shared worker-employer investments in general training has received but scant attention in the literature.[4]

Implicit in Becker's result is the view that a poached worker can immediately and painlessly start working, and yield full value, in a job commensurate with his training. Obviously, this approach implies negligible transactions costs. In particular, Becker's theory seems to suggest that a potential recruiting firm has full information regarding training carried out by other firms. No costs related to the absence of information are admitted.

The major premise of this paper is that potential recruiters do not possess much information on the extent and type of workers' on-the-job training. Workers taken for trained might turn out to possess no, or very little, general

---

* The views expressed in the paper are the authors'; they are not necessarily those of the organisations with which they are affiliated.

[1] An earlier presentation of our ideas was given in Katz and Ziderman (1989).

[2] Poverty, low liquidity and badly functioning capital markets militate against the possibility of significant worker-financed general training. Becker's result, therefore, implies a dismal outlook for general training in developing countries.

[3] See Parsons (1972), Donaldson and Eaton (1976), Hashimoto (1980), Hashimoto and Yu (1981).

[4] Notable exceptions are a series of papers on firm-sponsored education (Glick and Feuer, 1984; and Feuer et al. 1987) and the model of Bishop and Kang (1984). Unlike our approach, which relates to general training alone, these are mixed training models, which show that firm-financed general training may take place in the presence of specific training.

training. Also, a worker recruited for a given job may possess the wrong type of general training. All this imposes substantial information-based costs on firms that recruit rather than train. These costs include opportunity costs, actual expenses and increased exposure to risk. As a result, a recruiting firm will place a lower value on a recruited worker with general training than the firm that trained him. The wages paid to such a worker will reflect this lower value.

The informational asymmetry between a training and a recruiting firm therefore reduces the net benefits that a worker with general training can obtain by moving to another firm. We shall argue that this implies that a firm may find it feasible to finance part, or all, of a worker's general training. Indeed, under certain circumstances, *only* firms will be prepared to invest in general training: informational asymmetry considerations may reverse the predictions of Becker's model.

Section I considers the value of a worker with general training to the firm that trained him. The information about the value of such a worker that a recruiting firm is likely to possess is then examined. The cost implications of informational asymmetry between a training and a recruiting firm are discussed in Section II. Section III brings together the main strands of the argument to show that firms may finance part or all of its workers' general training. Extensions and some welfare and policy implications are offered in Section IV.

I THE VALUE AND INFORMATIONAL ASYMMETRY OF GENERAL TRAINING

Traditionally, the benefits of an investment are measured by the net present value of the income that the investment is expected to generate in its intended use. Recently, it has become recognised that the benefits of an investment include the options it provides in the face of random shocks and changes. Hence, the value, V, of an investment in general training is made up of two components: Z, the net present value of the training for the intended employment; and OV, the options value of the training. Z is a familiar source of value. The concept of the options value of general training, however, is likely to be less familiar. A brief description of OV is, therefore, in order.

The option value of general training may have several components.[5] For example, if the need arises, a worker's general training may be used as a basis for advanced training. Also, training for one job imparts related skills that enable the firm to employ the workers at other tasks. Perhaps most important, a given general training can enhance a worker's ability to deal with certain types of new technologies.[6]

Thus, workers with general training provide their training firm with the ability to respond efficiently and swiftly to various potential shocks and changes. Shifts in tastes, changes in technology, the sudden departure or

---

[5] See Weisbrod (1962), for a discussion of some of the option components in the return to education.

[6] In order to tap these options, firms will, in general, have to make a further, minor investment in training (akin to the exercise price of a financial option). This further required investment will, however, be relatively low and the options will materialise quickly.

absence of key workers are but a few typical shocks which general training options might accommodate. The value of these options is likely to be considerable. Indeed, one simulated result has generated option values (for capital investment) that exceed 100 % of the cost of the investment (see Majd and Pindyck, 1987.)[7]

In the following section, we suggest that the value of a worker to a firm is an increasing function of the information it has about the worker's general training. A worker with general training achieves his full value only in a firm that possesses full training information about him. Hence, in order to determine the value of a worker with general training to different firms, it is necessary to consider the information available to such firms. Specifically, the difference between the information about a worker's training that is available to a training firm and to potential recruiting firms plays a crucial role in our results.[8]

The above emphasis on the distinction between Z and OV can now be seen in terms of the main aim of this paper. The difficulty of discerning a worker's Z will differ from the difficulty of determining his OV. The loss of value due to absence of information will, therefore, vary with the relative weights of Z and OV in a worker's general training.

General training is typically provided on-the-job: it is heterogeneous, informal, and frequently tailored for individual workers. This non-stan-dardisation implies that, even for Z, certification of training is unlikely. Nonetheless, a non-training firm may, though at significant costs, obtain information regarding a worker's Z. With time and careful observation this information will unfold.

However, general training will also contain many nuances and options, of which even trainees may not be fully aware. Another firm will find it extremely difficult to determine the full extent of this, more subtle, component of general training. The option value of a worker's training can, at best, be partially discovered. Since the primary aim of poaching a worker is to employ him at his intended tasks, his general training options will not, in general, be observed. Indeed, a firm which is unsure about some aspects of a worker's training may be loath to call upon him to carry out certain tasks. His skills at such tasks may, therefore, never be revealed. Also, even if a firm does wish to discover a worker's training options, it may be forced (by the observation time required, for example), to limit itself to a small subset of the (possible) options imbedded in his training.

Informational asymmetry, then, is particularly pronounced and intractable for the option values of training. Hence, the informational asymmetry between the training firm and other firms will tend to be an increasing function of the options component in general training. Even if the options component is small,

---

[7] One particular feature of an option is that its value is an increasing function of the randomness underlying its use. In view of the large amount of randomness that firms in developing countries typically face, the option components of V in developing countries will be particularly high.

[8] Of course, this information gap is unlikely to have much significance if the worker's new employer can quickly and cheaply determine a worker's Z and OV. In this case the recruiting firm incurs negligible information-based costs and therefore puts the same effective value on a worker as the firm that trained him. Under these unlikely circumstances, Becker's result would hold.

however, there will still be a major information gap between the firm that provides the training and other firms.

II THE VALUE OF A RECRUITED WORKER

This section examines the information-based costs incurred by a recruiting firm. Given these costs, the net present value of a generally trained worker to a recruiting firm, V_N, is smaller than his value, V_T, to his training firm. Let i denote the number of periods since a worker has been recruited. Define V_T^i and V_N^i as the value in period i of a worker with general training, to the training and recruiting firms, respectively. In the event of full discovery over time, Z_N^i would increase with i. Nonetheless, given the intractability of discovering full information about OV_N, V_N^i will fall short of V_T^i, no matter how large i becomes.

The matrix in Table 1 illustrates the loss in a worker's value due to the information asymmetry, for the simple case of one type of non-option general training and one type of job requiring training. The value of a worker to the recruiting firm in a time unit during the discovery period,[9] depends on the job in which he is placed (requiring or not requiring training), and on whether or not the worker has received general training.[10] In Table 1, K will be the largest payoff and Q the smallest. Q might well be negative: placing an untrained worker in a position requiring training may be directly wasteful and destructive. Also, if the values of workers are interdependent, as in a production line, an untrained worker can impose negative externalities on other workers, potentially causing substantial losses.

Table 1
Z Values of Worker

Worker	Job	
	Requires training	Does not require training
Trained	K	R
Untrained	Q	S

If the recruiting firm has no prior knowledge of the probability that a recruit has been suitably trained, it is likely to adopt a maximin strategy. Since Q is smaller than both R and S, this implies that the firm will employ all recruited workers at jobs that do not require training. The Z_N^i of a worker with general training is $(R - M - A)_i$, where M is the cost of monitoring the worker and A is the cost of the risk-averse firm's exposure to risk. In this two-way case, the

[9] Clearly, it is only the discovery period that matters. After this period, when the recruiting firm knows the worker's product, the recruiting firm and the training firm have the same information about Z (though still not about the worker's option values).

[10] As mentioned in footnote 6, a further investment is usually needed to activate training options. Thus, no option values will be revealed in Table 1.

recruiting firm will know after only one period whether the worker is trained as it observes outcome R or outcome S. It can then place the worker in an appropriate position. However, it seems very possible that S and R are equal so that information can only be obtained by employing the worker on a job requiring training; given the possibility of Q, this may be an unacceptable risk to the firm. Hence, information might never surface and recruiting will be effectively blocked.

For several reasons, however, the discovery process will be considerably longer and more complex. A firm is likely to need workers with different types of general training. The information value of trying a worker out in a given job, and finding him untrained for that job, may be very low. Consider, for example, a firm with one job that requires no training and l jobs all requiring different types of general training. Then, if a worker is not successful at job 1, say, he might be untrained, or trained in one of the $l-1$ other jobs. Hence, even if the recruiting firm is, in principle, prepared to take the risk of employing an unknown worker in a job requiring training, the probability of failure to discover much information is likely to cause it to desist.[11]

Many jobs involve complex tasks, the fulfillment of which is difficult to measure, and a worker's Z^t might not be directly observable. Also, many jobs are carried out by teams rather than individuals, and the contribution made by a given worker is hard to discern. Furthermore, even if a worker performs a complete job by himself, his product will depend on the effort and training of other workers and inputs, about whom there may also be an absence of information. These considerations make it likely that a worker will have to be observed for several periods to determine his Z. Alternatively, discovery may take only one period, but this period will be long.[12]

The values in Table 1 are free of random components. This assumption makes discovery appear to be easier than is the case. In reality, the value of a worker at a given job in any one period is a random variable. This value is, in general, a drawing from a distribution whose parameters are a function of the worker's training and of the job requirements. The randomness of values renders the recruiting firm's search for information concerning a worker's general training more difficult, since it implies that the firm must extract information about a worker's training by sampling. The discovery process will be lengthy and costly, further reducing the Z_N of a recruited, trained worker.[13]

In addition, the randomness of the individual's Z^t is more likely to act as a total barrier on recruiting trained workers. Recall that to block recruiting in the deterministic case, the values of trained and untrained workers in tasks not

[11] For each type of general training, there is likely to be a corresponding, but different, specific training required. Thus, trying out a worker in one of the $l-1$ other jobs will entail additional investments in specific training, again adding to the costs of discovery.

[12] In a private communication, Jacob Mincer points out that a trained worker has an incentive to convey information about his training to the recruiting firm, which could be verified after a relatively short period. The central question, however, is whether the trained worker would be believed, given that untrained workers may attempt to obtain a free ride by posing as trained.

[13] A discussion of the technical aspects of such sampling, accompanied by some numerical examples, is available in an appendix to a mimeo version of this paper in Katz and Ziderman (1990).

requiring training, had to be equal. In the random case, recruiting may be blocked even if these values are not identical. Where $E(R)$ and $E(S)$ are not too far apart, a recruiting firm gains little information from each period of employing an unknown worker in an untrained capacity. To be effective, the sampling period may need to extend over years. But, the longer the required discovery period, the greater will be the loss incurred by a trained worker. Workers may, therefore, refuse jobs which do not require their training. To expedite the process of obtaining information about workers, the firm can try out the worker in a job that requires training. As suggested above, however, an untrained worker may have a negative (expected) value in such a job. Hence, if the potential damage is large, and the firm is not convinced that he is appropriately trained, the firm may refuse to employ an unknown worker in a job requiring training.

In sum, the firm might not offer an unknown worker a job requiring training, and the worker, in turn, may reject jobs which do require training. This blocks the inter-firm movement of workers with general training. It therefore ensures firms will be prepared to finance some, or all, of a worker's general training.

Thus far it has been assumed that a potential recruiter is ignorant of the probability that a worker from a training firm has the appropriate general training. The recruiter may, however, have some idea about the proportion of such workers in the training firm's workforce. When this probability, p, equals unity, there is no asymmetric information regarding Z (though uncertainty regarding OV remains). Of course, this is unlikely, especially given the need to identify not just a worker with general training, but the particular general training that a trained worker possesses.

Since knowledge of p constitutes information, such knowledge may reduce the informational asymmetry and its consequential costs. If p is large and known outside the training firm, both the cost of each stage in the discovery process and the expected length of this process may be significantly reduced. If, however, p is small, knowledge of p outside the firm will be of little value to potential recruiters. Hence, if information on a firm's training programme (but not information on individual trainees) is likely to be available to other firms, general training may be constrained. The proportions of workers trained in particular forms of Z-enhancing training, might have to be sub-optimal, in order to protect the firm's investment in training. Given that most firms are likely to require workers with various types of general training, however, such sub-optimality is unlikely to be needed.

Even if the recruiting firm does eventually discover a worker's Z^t, it will not know his options value. Observation of the worker in a given task may be an effective, though slow and expensive, means of determining a worker's general training for intended employment. The options component of training is unlikely to be revealed in this way. The options implicit in a worker's training cannot be determined by observing the worker in his intended job. Furthermore, a job rotation strategy means that a worker would be doing jobs for which he is not currently needed. Also, the discovery process for each option will be similar in nature and in length to the process of determining a worker's Z. Information on a worker's OV will remain broadly unknown to a recruiting firm. Over and above losses in Z^t, a worker moving to another firm effectively loses all of his OV.

III PAYING FOR GENERAL TRAINING

The above discussion shows that asymmetry in information will cause the value of a trained worker with general training to be highest in his training firm. On moving to other firms, a worker's value declines by L, where $L = V_T - V_N$. This section examines the relation between the symmetry of training information, the workers' loss of value, and the financing of general training.

Let T be the cost of a worker's general training.[14] Then, if $T > L = V_T - V_N > 0$, a training firm will be willing to pay up to $V_T + L - T$ towards a worker's general training. The worker will therefore have to contribute no less than $T - L$ for the training. If the worker were to move to another firm he would gain $V_T - L$ in income but forfeit his training investment, $T - L$. Hence, in a competitive setting, where $V_T = T$, the worker's net gain from moving is zero. The firm's share in the cost of training would be no more than L/V_T and poaching would not take place.

The worker must be able to contribute $V - L$ for his general training for the general training to take place. Even if he is able to contribute more than $V - L$, however, he will not do so. On the presumption that the training firm will only pay him his transfer price, his return to investing in general training will not exceed $V - L$. Hence, the minimal proportion of the cost of general training that a worker will expect his employer to finance is L/V_T. If $V_T - L > 0$, therefore, the ratio $(V_T - L)/L$ constitutes the only feasible sharing scheme between worker and employer.

If L is no less than V_T, the worker's move to another firm is blocked. In this case, the asymmetry of training information reduces the value of a worker's general training in potential recruiting firms, to zero. His wage is, therefore, no higher than that of an untrained worker. The implication is that the training firm will be prepared to pay for the full cost of the worker's general training and capture the full return on the training investment. While this is an extreme situation, it is indicative of the efficacy of asymmetric information in reducing poaching and resurrecting property rights in general training investments.

The foregoing analysis is captured in diagrammatic form in Fig. 1. Informational asymmetry, Y, (standardised to the $[0, 1]$ interval), is depicted on the horizontal axis. V_T and V_N are measured along the vertical axis. The functions plotted in Fig. 1 relate to increments in value over that of untrained workers. V_T, representing both the costs and the benefits of training to the training firm, is invariant with respect to the informational asymmetry. $V_N(Y)$, which depicts the relation between Y and the value of a recruited trained worker, shows a steep decline for low values of informational asymmetry

---

[14] It is assumed here that neither T nor V are affected by the number of workers trained.

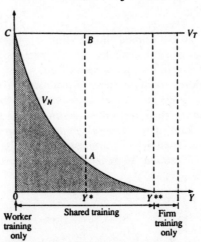

Fig. 1. ▨, Worker finance of general training.

(reflecting the almost inevitable loss of option values). As Y increases, V_N declines more gradually, reaching its lowest level when $Y = 1$.[15]

The firm will be prepared to invest up to L, the vertical distance between V_T and V_N, in the general training of a worker. For example, at Y^*, the training firm is prepared to participate in a worker's general training by AB, requiring that the worker pays AY^*. An increase in the symmetry of training information between training firms and other firms will raise the required share of the worker in the training investment. If this information is fully and freely available to other firms (as Y and L tend to zero), the worker will have to finance all his training (OC). This is equivalent to the case described by Becker, which is seen to coincide with the special case of perfectly symmetric information. Finally, if $Y > Y^{**}$, the value of a trained worker in a recruiting firm will not exceed the value of an untrained worker. The worker will not invest in any general training, whilst the training firm will be prepared to finance it fully.

In sum, for $0 < Y < Y^{**}$, training investment is shared by the worker and the firm. The worker's contribution towards this training for a given Y, is given by the distance between the horizontal axis and the V_N curve. For $Y > Y^{**}$, general training is totally firm-financed. The special case of Becker, with a worker required to fully finance the programme of general training, occurs at $Y = 0$.

IV WELFARE AND POLICY IMPLICATIONS

In this section applications of the model to liquidity constraints, to minimum wages legislation and to certification are discussed.

---

[15] For the purposes of this illustration it is assumed that as the information asymmetry increases, Z_N tends to zero.

Liquidity Constraints

An important and much quoted implication of Becker's model is that potentially profitable general training investments might not take place. Because of their inability to prevent workers from transferring to other firms, firms will not be prepared to finance general training. Workers, however, may not possess sufficient funds nor be able, reasonably, to obtain funds from intermediaries to finance their training investment. Hence, general training may not take place. Also, if the general training programme is divisible, a worker may be able to finance and purchase a part of it. In either case, non-investment or under-investment in general training is predicted.

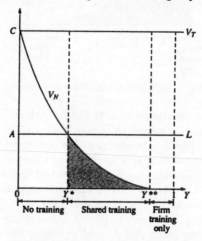

Fig. 2. ▨, Worker finance of general training.

The information-based costs imposed on a recruiting firm may mitigate or resolve this potential problem. This is illustrated in Fig. 2. The worker's liquidity constraint (AL) is parallel to the horizontal axis, intersecting with the V_N curve where informational asymmetry is Y^*. In the case of symmetric information, the worker is able to finance only OA of his potential training investment OC: no training will take place if the training programme is indivisible. Informational considerations alter this result. As before, no training will take place if $Y < Y^*$. However, for $Y^* \leq Y$, the worker's liquidity exceeds the V_N curve. For this range, the worker (while still unable to pay the full cost, OC, of general training) can finance his required share of training, $V_T - L$, without encountering a liquidity constraint. Asymmetric information thus enables workers to participate in financing their general training, despite a shortage of capital or liquidity.

Minimum Wages

An additional source of a shortfall in general training may be the institution of legal minimum wages. If set above a certain level, minimum wages will prevent the worker's wage from falling low enough during training to enable the firm to recover its training costs during the training period (Leighton and Mincer 1979); the result will be an insufficient supply of general training skills available to the economy.

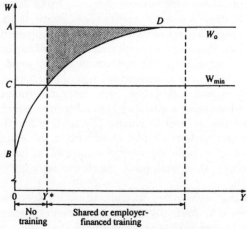

Fig. 3. ▨, Worker finance of general training.

The presence of asymmetric information may mitigate this effect. Consider Fig. 3, in which information asymmetry, Y, is again represented on the horizontal axis and various financial quantities, relating to the training period, are plotted on the vertical axis. W_0 is the trainee worker's opportunity wage during his training period and AB represents the cost of his training. The curve BD (which is the obverse of V_N in Figs. 1 and 2), traces out the wage received by the worker during training, for increasing levels of Y. The vertical distance between BD and AW_0 measures the (diminishing) required amount of worker finance, for increasing levels of Y.

The Becker (symmetric information) case is located on the vertical axis. For the case drawn, the firm cannot both recover its training costs AB during the training period while paying a wage greater than OB. With a minimum wage set at W_{min}, say, no general training will take place. The full cost of training (AB) must be borne by the worker; the imposition of a minimum wage (W_{min}) at a level greater than OB, has brought about a legal obstruction to general training.

Upon introducing asymmetric information, it is clear that, assuming the training programme is indivisible, the minimum wage prevents general training investment from taking place only for $Y < Y^*$. Where $Y > Y^*$, the firm will be prepared to finance an amount of the general training such that the worker can pay the rest via a lower wage, without contravening the minimum wage laws.

Certification

Finally, we consider the implications that our model holds for educational certification. It is widely believed that an extended and more comprehensive system of educational and training certification is to be welcomed, in that it leads to freer mobility of workers and an improved, more effective, use of human capital resources. Such considerations underscore the national systems of compatible qualifications such as those currently being developed in Britain, and the well-established system of certification which is in place in West Germany. Yet, the arguments presented in this paper suggest that certification may lead to less rather than more general training, an effect that policy makers might wish to set against the better known advantages of certification. The case of West Germany may appear to constitute an anomaly here. Certification via in-service training is well-established, yet enterprise-financed training is prevalent. But, institutional constraints on inter-firm poaching of trained workers are noteworthy in West Germany (Dougherty and Tan, 1990). The Chambers of Commerce, which exert considerable influence over member firms, strongly and effectively discourage competition for trained workers (Soskice, forthcoming), thus facilitating enterprise investment in on-the-job training.

We have noted that asymmetry in training information between training and recruiting firms may lead to tensions between the interests of firms and their trainees. The trainee prefers training that is visible and which generally identifies him outside the firm as a trained worker. He will wish to enrol in training that is capable of yielding these signals, which are well achieved by certificates of attainment. The firm, on the other hand, will wish to minimise the amount of information generated about worker's training: this it may do by avoiding training that is highly visible and which may lead to formal certification on completion.[16]

By reducing the extent of asymmetric information concerning workers' training, widespread certification will result in diminished scope for firms to share in the financing of the general training of their workers. Certification, by awarding workers property rights over their general training, limits company financed training, and places a heavier financing burden on workers.

York University, Canada

Bar-Ilan University, Israel and the World Bank

Date of receipt of final typescript: June 1990

REFERENCES

Becker, G. (1964). *Human Capital*. New York: National Bureau of Economic Research.
Bishop, J. and Kang, S. (1984). *On the Job Training/Sorting: Theory and Evidence*. National Centre for Research in Vocational Education, Ohio State University.

[16] This line of reasoning suggests firms would also try to reduce training visibility by refraining from writing references for employees wishing to move to another firm. Indeed, a recent survey has shown that 40% of companies surveyed in the United States have a formal, *written* policy not to provide outside references – a finding in conformity with the predictions of our model (NACPR, 1989). Fear of lawsuits from disgruntled former employees who are turned down for a new job may also help to explain employers' reticence in this matter.

Donaldson, D. and Eaton, B. C. (1976). 'Firm-specific capital: a shared investment or optimal entrapment?' *Canadian Journal of Economics*, vol. 9, Autumn, pp. 462–72.

Dougherty, C. and Tan, J.-P. (1990). *Financing Training: Issues and Options*. Population and Human Resources Department, Washington, DC: The World Bank.

Eckaus, R. S. (1963). 'Investment in human beings: a comment.' *Journal of Political Economy*, vol. 71, October, pp. 501–4.

Feuer, M., Glick, H. and Desai, A. (1987). 'Is firm-sponsored education viable?' *Journal of Economic Behaviour and Organization*, vol. 8, pp. 121–36.

Glick, H. and Feuer, M. (1984). 'Employer sponsored training and the governance of specific human capital investments.' *Quarterly Review of Economics and Business*, vol. 24, Summer, pp. 91–103.

Hashimoto, M. (1981). 'Firm-specific human capital as a shared investment.' *American Economic Review*, vol. 71, March, pp. 475–82.

Hashimoto, M. and Yu, B. (1980). 'Specific capital, employment contracts and wage rigidity.' *Bell Journal of Economics*, vol. 11, Autumn, pp. 536–49.

Katz, E. and Ziderman, A. (1989). *General Training Under Asymmetric Information*. PPR Working Paper No. 170, Washington, DC: The World Bank, April.

—— (1990). 'Shared investment in general training: the role of information.' PRE working papers, Washington, D.C.: The World Bank.

Leighton, L. and Mincer, J. (1981). 'The effect of minimum wages on human capital formation,' in (S. Rothenberg, ed.), *The Economics of Legal Minimum Wages*. Washington D.C.: American Enterprise Institute for Public Policy Research.

Majd, S. and Pindyck, R. S. (1987). 'Time to build, option value and investment decisions.' *Journal of Financial Economics*, vol. 18, March, pp. 7–27.

National Association of Corporate and Professional Recruiters, Inc. (1989). *Fourth Annual Membership Survey Results*. Louisville, KY.

Parsons, D. O. (1972). 'Specific human capital: an application to quit rates and layoff rates.' *Journal of Political Economy*, vol. 80, November–December, pp. 1120–43.

Soskice, D. (1990). 'Reinterpreting corporatism and explaining unemployment: coordinated and uncoordinated economies.' In (R. Brunetta and C. della Ringer, eds.), *Labor Relations and Economic Performance*. New York: NY United Press (forthcoming).

Weisbrod, B. (1962). 'Education and investment in human capital. *Journal of Political Economy* (supplement), vol. 70, pp. 106–23.

[30]

Externalities, Information Costs, and Social Benefit-Cost Analysis for Economic Development: An Example from Telecommunications*

Nathaniel H. Leff
Columbia University

Introduction

The analytics of achieving a socially optimal allocation of investment resources has been a continuing problem in the field of economic development. Early work on this subject focused on externalities and on the need to include in the analysis a project's "indirect" promotional effects.[1] Later research in what came to be called social benefit-cost analysis (SBCA) has added an emphasis on shadow prices, on uncertainty, and, increasingly, on income distribution effects.[2] In principle, these diverse concerns of social benefit-cost analysis are complementary rather than competitive. In the conditions of a less developed country (LDC), an investment project's side effects on income creation can be very significant.[3] Similarly, an investment project's indirect impact on income distribution may also be substantial. Consequently, an analysis incorporating externalities is necessary to take indirect social benefits and costs into account. In practice, however, the more recent concerns of SBCA have sometimes been accompanied by diminished interest in externalities.[4]

This paper presents an example that illustrates the importance of including externalities in considering both the efficiency and the equity consequences of investment choice. Our example analyzes the welfare effects of investment in telecommunications (primarily telephone) facilities in developing countries.[5] Investments that make available additional telephones in LDCs are often viewed as having welfare effects similar to increased availability of consumer durables like color television or air conditioning. Those goods are primarily an added convenience for the upper classes, and their availability enlarges further the gulf between the living standard of the upper classes and that of the vast majority of the population. As we shall see, however, depending on how the additional telephone facilities are allocated, the welfare consequences can in fact be very different. If the incremental telephones are allocated primarily to business users in the public and private sectors (rather than primarily to residential users), and if public as well as private phones are provided, telephone expansion can be equalizing in its distributional impact. Similarly, telephone expansion under those conditions can also have important positive effects on production and economic efficiency. The analysis that leads to these conclusions involves taking account of externalities and of some results from the economics of information.[6]

Our analysis of the welfare effects of telecommunications investment in LDCs is primarily conceptual. Elaboration of an analytical framework is essential to aid empirical work and measurement efforts in this area. The overall perspective we will follow is that of social benefit-cost analysis. Thus we will consider such standard questions as the effects of ex ante uncertainty of investment choice and the impact of telecommunications expansion on the distribution of welfare. Further, because telecommunications service is rarely supplied on purely commercial terms in the LDCs, market profitability gives little indication of the social returns to such investments. Accordingly, our analysis begins by considering the external economies that telecommunications generates.[7]

External Economies
One externality provided by telecommunications expansion in developing countries is straightforward and has been widely noted. Telecommunications technology often entails declining average costs over a wide range. Hence, expanding the system leads to a fall in the social costs of supplying service to earlier subscribers. Another externality relates to the benefit rather than to the cost side and has also been noted in the literature.[8] Consider a new telecommunications project that permits additional subscribers to be connected to the system. The benefits this specific project provides exceed the gains that accrue to the people who are now provided with equipment. A special property of telecommunications investments is that each subscriber's welfare rises with the number of other people who have access to the network and with whom communications can therefore be made. This feature means that the benefits of telecommunications investment increase exponentially as expansion permits new participants to join the system.[9]

This condition is especially pertinent in the context of the developing countries. In most LDCs, only a small fraction of the population are now subscribers.[10] Hence, the possibilities for utilizing the system to communicate are severely limited. Moreover, unlike the case in the more developed countries where telephone density is much greater, telecommunications congestion for individual receivers in the LDCs is likely to be remote. Under these conditions, both on the cost and on the benefit sides, telecommunications expansion leads to a net social gain greater than that which accrues to those who already have the equipment. These external economies also apply intertemporally. That is, future (as well as earlier) subscribers benefit because of a current project that extends the system and increases the number of people with whom telecommunication is possible.

More important, in the conditions of an LDC, increased availability of telecommunications provides external economies that accrue to many other sectors. Once mentioned, these externalities are obvious. Indeed many of them are taken for granted in the economically advanced countries, where telecommunications density is already high and low-cost communication is pervasive. The externalities present in this case are in fact extremely important, for they involve the efficiency with which markets and organizational structures function. These effects are apparent if we consider what it is that modern telecommunications actually does.

Telecommunications is of course a means of transmitting information. Specifically, modern telecommunications sharply reduces the costs of transmitting information over space and time.[11] In both ways, telecommunications expansion facilitates the flow of information that is current and hence useful for economic and organizational decisions. Such conditions that lower the cost of acquiring information are of particular importance in the less developed countries. In the words of Harvey Leibenstein, these are often "obstructed, incomplete and 'relatively dark' economic systems."[12] Or as Clifford Geertz, a social scientist with intensive field experience in LDCs, describes the situation: "information is poor, scarce, maldistributed, inefficiently communicated, and intensely valued."[13] As Geertz suggests, this situation is partly due to the inefficiency with which information is communicated using premodern modes. In addition, other conditions also make for a situation in which both the quantity and the quality of available information are frequently deficient in LDCs. The distortions that characterize many LDC factor and product markets make these markets poor providers of information. Further, the LDCs generally lack a large stock of knowledge about their economies that is available to economic agents as a public good. Finally, instability and rapid structural change may render obsolete much earlier information that was available. All of these conditions lead to a situation in which considerable uncertainty surrounds many economic and administrative decisions.

In many cases, the antidote for uncertainty is additional information. However, the situation described above is often exacerbated because much of the information that does exist in the LDC is not widely available. Once information has been produced, its marginal cost is zero. But to be used information must be sent. And in countries with premodern communications facilities, the costs of transmitting information over space and time are relatively high. Unless the demand for information is totally inelastic with respect to price, the high costs of transmitting information in LDCs limit its use. In such a context, a reduction in the cost (and price) of sending information has multiple effects. First, a movement down the demand curve for transmitting information will increase the amount of information that is sent (both by present users and by new users). Further, enlargement in the size of the market for transmitting information shifts outward the demand curves which face the activities that produce information in LDCs. Thus high transmission costs reduce the quantity of information that is produced in developing countries. And similar effects apply to the quality (timeliness, completeness, and reliability) of the information produced. That is, premodern transmittal facilities limit the number and the range of potential users of information; and small markets lower the returns to investing in the production of information. The prevalence of this situation in which high transmission costs reduce the information generated varies within individual LDCs. The problem is probably most serious in rural-to-urban and rural-to-rural communications. However, the situation also exists in interurban and in intraurban contexts.

More generally, the amount of information used in economic and administrative decision making should satisfy the standard marginal conditions. Consequently, by lowering information costs telecommunications expansion makes it rational for economic agents to acquire additional intelligence that is pertinent to their decisions. Such additions are especially important for decision makers in the conditions of the LDCs. As Geertz has described the situation: "the primary problem facing . . . participants . . . is not balancing options, but finding out what they are."[14] Note further that lower communication costs lead to acquiring more information not only about the mean values of prices and of other economic phenomena but also about their probability distribution. Hence the new information permits the transformation of uncertainty into risk.[15] As a result, probabilistic decision techniques can be applied (if only implicitly), and the scope for more rational decision making is extended.

In some instances, more information may make decision makers aware of contingencies of which they had previously been ignorant. Coming in conjunction with their earlier knowledge, this new intelligence may increase decision makers' uncertainty. Nevertheless, additional intelligence still permits more rational decisions, for what you

Nathaniel H. Leff   259

don't know *can* hurt you. Consequently, even in instances of increased uncertainty, additional information enables people to act in ways that cope more effectively with alternative states of nature.

Still another externality stems from a special feature of telecommunications' role in transmitting new information. New information may be either complementary or competitive with the information that economic agents already possess. What is special is that in either case new information generally increases the demand for communications. These are needed to transfer more messages, regardless of whether the new information supplants or enhances earlier knowledge.[16] In addition, the demand for telecommunications may increase in order to implement decisions that have become rational on the basis of the newly available information. This complementary-competitive feature helps explain why even experienced forecasters have tended to underestimate the growth of demand for telecommunications in developing countries.[17]

Increased availability of modern telecommunications can also lead to benefits in improved organizational performance. Harvey Leibenstein has analyzed the efficiency losses that occur when information does not flow freely within an organization.[18] As we have already noted, modern telecommunications lowers the cost of transmitting and receiving messages. Consequently, telecommunications expansion increases the likelihood that intraorganization information flows will not be prematurely blocked. Thus information whose content and analysis can affect the organization's productivity is more likely to continue flowing until it reaches all the people who can use it. These considerations apply both to messages that originate within the organization and to news that comes from the organization's external environment. The need to avoid premature information blockages is likely to be especially great in the LDCs. In the economically more advanced countries, decision makers may sometimes suffer from "information overload." But our earlier discussion of the conditions making for pervasive uncertainty and information scarcity in LDCs suggests that the situation confronting decision makers in those countries is likely to be very different. In the LDCs, decision makers are often still on the increasing returns segment of the function that relates information and productivity.[19]

Organizational performance may also improve because of the impact of modern telecommunications on the *time* required for information to flow. Not only is the number of messages available to managers increased, but they are also made more current. Consequently, the risks of taking decisions that are poor because they are based on obsolete information diminish. In addition, the fall in the time costs of transmitting information can enhance administrative performance in another way. Effective decision making sometimes requires interactive communication with people—that is, negotiation. In instances where distance separates the participants, the possibilities that telecommunications offer for "on line" negotiation can increase the effectiveness of the decision-making process. Finally, by reducing the costs of two-way information flows, telecommunications expansion also facilitates the effective operation of larger organizations. Such changes are important in cases where economies of scale accrue to production technology but where net economic gains cannot be achieved if organizational effectiveness deteriorates markedly with larger size.[20]

The effects of telecommunications expansion in reducing the costs of information flows over time, over space, and within individual organizations are not limited to one class of organization. Increased availability of telecommunications can improve managerial performance in public-sector agencies as well as in private firms. Similarly, gains to more effective decision making accrue both in interorganizational and in intraorganizational negotiations. And telecommunications' effects in facilitating decision making are relevant both in centralized and in decentralized administrative structures. The benefits we have discussed involve important gains to telephone expansion in LDC conditions. The social gains are of course likely to be greater to the extent that incremental telephone facilities are allocated primarily to business and government users rather than to private residential subscribers.

Information Costs, Decision Making, and Economic Development
The gains we have noted include much more than the time of the administrators involved. First, capital, labor, and land are often strict complements to managers as inputs in production. Consequently, conditions that slow the pace at which decisions are made reduce the social returns to other resources. Similarly, sharp declines in social returns can occur when investment projects are delayed in reaching their rated capacity.[21] Conversely, conditions that enhance the speed and efficiency of the decision-making process also raise the productivity of complementary inputs.

Even more important, as Albert Hirschman has emphasized, the capacity to take (and implement) decisions is itself a key input to the development process.[22] Because of this promotional role, more effective decision making in the public and private sectors can have a far-reaching impact on a country's economic development. Lower-cost information flows and faster communications are not sufficient conditions for a generalized improvement in organizational performance. But it would be surprising if the increased availability of telecommunications did not generate this benefit in at least some firms and government agencies. And as this discussion suggests, the gains include both allocative and x-efficiency. In addition, by providing increased infor-

Nathaniel H. Leff   261

mation, telecommunications expansion can be a partial substitute for increased entrepreneurship in developing countries. Improved information flows may raise the effectiveness of a country's existing stock of entrepreneurial talent.[23]

By lowering communications costs, telecommunications expansion also improves the efficiency with which LDC product and factor markets operate. A standard result of search theory is that as the cost of search falls, the amount of search that is privately and socially optimal rises.[24] Hence, as the expansion of modern telecommunications lowers the cost of acquiring new information, the quantity and quality of information demanded and utilized are likely to increase. A growth in information flows, in turn, can be expected to promote increased arbitrage and enhance market efficiency. These are socially desirable developments, for well-functioning markets themselves provide useful information concerning the prices, quantities, and qualities of goods and factors. Again, there is no necessary private-sector bias here. The information that more efficient markets generate can aid decision makers in the public as well as in the private sector.

The impact of increased information on the functioning of markets is more far-reaching than might initially be assumed. Research in the economics of information has noted that the very existence of markets in many activities cannot be taken for granted.[25] That is, markets—with their pervasive allocational and promotional effects—are themselves a special institution whose emergence depends, inter alia, on relative prices. Two of the key prices that determine whether or not markets emerge in specific activities are the costs of acquiring information and the costs of negotiating transactions.[26] These are precisely the costs that modern telecommunications reduces. Hence it seems clear that telecommunications expansion promotes the spread of markets.

Note, moreover, that two distinct cost phenomena are involved here. Lower costs for acquiring information reduce the fixed-cost hurdle that must be overcome if a market for a given product or input is to emerge at all.[27] In addition, better communications and lower transactions costs reduce the variable costs of market participation and operation. The latter condition, in turn, facilitates the incorporation of more participants—both geographically and over a larger range of activities with diverse opportunity costs. As a result, market prices are likely to become informationally more efficient, reducing resource misallocation and quasi rents.

Our discussion of this subject has thus far been in a priori terms. Empirical verification of these hypotheses requires a consideration of economic history, for the changes we have discussed are by their nature structural and medium-term. One historical study available has considered the impact that construction of the transatlantic telegraph had on international financial markets during the nineteenth century.[28]

Economic Development and Cultural Change

The advent of improved communications did in fact lead to a narrowing in price variance and to increased market efficiency. Similarly, within the United States during the nineteenth century, the rapid spread of telegraphy was due largely to business demand.[29] Important conditions underlying this demand were "certainty in the transmission of intelligence" and the "enormous benefits of instantaneous communications." A major source of demand for telegraphic messages was the transmission of information concerning prices. These changes reduced the uncertainties that surrounded economic decision making in the nineteenth-century United States. In addition, the fall in the cost of transmitting price information facilitated arbitrage between markets. Markets were also enlarged by the linking of economic agents who had previously been isolated. As a result, price differentials diminished, and the economy's capacity to respond to new conditions increased. These consequences of the fall in information costs come as no surprise after our earlier discussion.

Further Discussion
In contemporary less developed countries, the emergence of markets and their improved functioning are likely to have important welfare effects. A reduction in the dispersion of actual prices as well as in the uncertainty concerning expected prices can be expected to promote higher output levels.[30] Moreover, with the larger output evoked by greater ex ante certainty concerning prices, both consumers and producers benefit. Such non-zero-sum-game effects, in which one party's gain is not another party's loss, are rarely available to policymakers. They are at a special premium in the economic development process, which is often full of conflict.

The gains from improved market efficiency may be greatest in LDC agriculture. That sector's development has in recent years been accorded a high priority in many LDCs. For historical reasons, however, the domestic agricultural sector in many developing countries has suffered from an especially inadequate stock of telecommunications facilities. As a result, information flows and market efficiency in domestic agriculture have also been poor, to the point where the pace of rural development may often have suffered. Under these conditions, investments in urban-rural and rural-rural telecommunications can increase the capacity of the domestic agricultural sector to achieve national development objectives. Similarly, the availability of more (and more timely) information can be expected to improve the functioning of factor and product markets in the urban sector of many LDCs. The scarcity of publicly accessible communication and information flows has sometimes exacerbated imperfect market conditions in the industrial sector.[31]

By reducing transmission costs, telecommunications expansion has multiple effects on the availability of information in the LDCs. As noted earlier, greater flows of information that is current and relevant for production, investment, and trading decisions enhance the efficiency of markets. But a two-step process is also at work. For markets (when they exist) are themselves an important mechanism for providing price signals and other information that can aid in the mobilization and rational allocation of resources. Further, as noted above, lower transmission costs enlarge the size of the market for information and thus increase the incentives for producing information in LDCs. With growth in the size of the market, optimal scale and specialization will be more closely approached in the activities that supply information. The changes we have discussed are likely to generate an increase both in the quantity and in the quality of the information produced in developing countries.

A sharp reduction in the cost of transmitting information is not a panacea for all the problems facing LDCs. An increased flow of information, and the destruction of earlier informational monopolies will not alleviate market distortions that derive from other causes. Similarly, lower transmission costs will not loosen intraorganizational information blockages that arise for other reasons. For example, opportunistic behavior may lead individuals or subunits purposely to impede the flow of information within their organizations.[32] And government decision making will not improve in cases where its previous performance reflected not the poor quality of its information and administrative processes but a lack of "political will." In such cases, increased information flows and a reduction in transaction costs are a necessary but not a sufficient condition for better results.

Notwithstanding these limitations, the social gains that can follow from lower information and transactions costs should not be discounted. Indeed, some of the externalities we have noted are sufficiently widespread that they qualify as public goods. That description certainly applies to the improved functioning of product markets and of factor markets. An enhanced organizational capacity to take and implement development decisions may also be a public good. Further, Richard Posner has suggested that many of the special institutional arrangements prevalent in underdeveloped countries stem from the pervasive uncertainty and the high transactions costs that characterize those societies.[33] This observation suggests that a fall in information costs may help facilitate some of the institutional changes that facilitate long-term economic development. More generally, the social gains we have discussed are part of what Charles P. Kindleberger epitomized as "transformation": a society's capacity to respond quickly and effectively to new problems and opportunities.[34] That capacity is a public good par excellence.

The financial (private) returns to telecommunications investment in developing countries seem to be relatively high. Thus, the internal financial rates of return in a sample of recent World Bank projects in telecommunications ranged between 13% and 35%, with an average of 18%.[35] The relevant concern from the viewpoint of public investment choice, however, is SBCA rates of return. Those were estimated approximately 50% higher than the financial (private) returns for the projects in question.[36] The estimates just cited are apparently based largely on efficiency criteria and may not include the externalities and the public-good benefits we have just discussed. Consequently, those estimates may understate the projects' social returns. At the same time as telecommunications investment provides those benefits, however, it also affects inequality and the distribution of income in developing countries. Social benefit-cost analysis urges the necessity of considering such effects, and we discuss them in the next section.

Effects on Inequality and the Distribution of Income

Telecommunications projects raise two separate distributional issues: the impact on the distribution of income, and the impact on equality in access to information and communications. As regards equality of access, few generalizations can be advanced, for much depends on the specifics of how the new facilities are allocated. In addition, one must be clear about the alternative situation with which one is (perhaps implicitly) comparing the equality of access that prevails following telecommunications expansion. Under premodern conditions, access to information and communications in LDCs is usually very unequal. Hence there is no basis for assuming that the previous distribution was in any sense equitable or socially optimal. In such a context, the opening of new communications modes and the extension of the telecommunications network may in fact have equalizing effects. Such changes usually permit people outside of the upper classes to gain access to what had earlier been the exclusive preserve of upper-class groups. Thus telecommunications expansion may in fact permit more equal access to information and communication in developing countries.

Social benefit-cost analysis also emphasizes the need to incorporate *income* distribution considerations in investment evaluation.[37] The SBCA literature focuses on two distinct issues of income distribution. The first involves the interpersonal distribution of income. SBCA proposes the use of distributional weights to favor projects that benefit LDCs' poorer people. The second concern deals with the intertemporal distribution of income. SBCA urges procedures that would give a high priority to investments that generate a future flow of investable resources to the country's government. This condition is assumed to permit higher capital formation and socially more optimal rates of income growth.

Nathaniel H. Leff   265

A standard text on SBCA offers the following comments concerning the sectoral effects of applying this income-distributional approach in LDCs.[38]

> It is not possible to draw more precise conclusions about the sectoral allocation of investment that would result from the systematic use of such weights [reflecting the inter-personal and inter-temporal distribution of income]; but generalizations of the following kind can be made: projects that make heavy demand on scarce public funds (such as most infrastructure projects) will be justified only if they charge high prices or other user charges (thereby replenishing the government's coffers), or if they benefit the poor either through employment or price reductions.

This approach has clear implications concerning the impact of telecommunications projects on the intertemporal distribution of income. In LDCs, telecommunications service is usually provided either by the government or by a state economic corporation. Because of relative transactions and metering costs, user charges are more easily levied on telecommunications than on many other infrastructure services. Consequently, from the viewpoint of generating a continuing flow of investment resources for the government, telecommunications investments appear relatively attractive. (More realistically, these conditions may mean that projects in telecommunications do not impose as large a drain on government resources as do projects in many other infrastructure sectors.) The focus on user charges raises immediate questions concerning pricing policy. But within an SBCA perspective, socially optimal pricing and investment policies are in any case interdependent.[39] Intelligent allocation decisions are aided if decisions concerning user changes are faced explicitly at the outset.

The impact of telecommunications investment on the interpersonal distribution of income is more complex. The quotation just cited mentions two major channels through which investment allocations may lead to a more equal distribution of income: employment creation, and (relative) price changes that favor the poor. Telecommunications investment can have both of these effects. Expanded communications and increased equality in access of information generally intensify competition and improve the functioning of markets. These developments imply a reduction in the monopoly power that penalizes low-income people in LDCs.[40] In addition, depending on the sectors to which the new facilities are allocated, telecommunications expansion may also have other equalizing price effects. As noted earlier, in many LDCs, the stock of telecommunications facilities is especially inadequate in the domestic agricultural sector. Hence telecommunications expansion can have a disproportionately large impact on information flows and development in LDC agriculture.[41] In particular, increased availability of telecommunications is likely to accelerate the rate at which new and more productive techniques are diffused among agricultural producers.[42]

Such changes are pertinent here, for poor people in LDCs spend a relatively large share of their incomes on food. Consequently, even if the farm operators are mainly middle- or upper-income people, telecommunications projects can benefit the LDCs' poor. This is because a more rapid diffusion of improved production technology lowers the relative price of food, with its large weight in low-income budgets. Another process engendered by telecommunications expansion can reinforce this outcome. Marketing of agricultural products in LDCs is often both relatively inefficient and imperfectly competitive. The opening of new communications channels, however, facilitates the emergence of more efficient and more competitive networks in agricultural marketing. Again, low-income people benefit more than other people; for a reduction in the costs and distortions present in the distribution system will also lower the relative price of food.

Telecommunications projects can also help reduce the variance in income distribution that stems from geographical disparities. Once such regional inequalities emerge in LDCs, they show a strong tendency to persist. By lowering the costs of transmitting messages over space, however, telecommunications expansion facilitates administrative and economic decentralization. Centralized management control requires good communications. But for this very reason, more effective communications also permit functional and/or administrative decentralization. Better telecommunications on a national scale may thus help make possible a pattern of development that is geographically more dispersed, and in which the comparative advantage of diverse regions is given greater scope. The availability of such investments that can help check the agglomeration of geographical inequalities may be especially welcome to LDC policymakers.

Telecommunications expansion may also increase equality of access to other goods (see below). This is because telecommunications investment can make available to low-income people certain goods that upper-income people in the LDCs take for granted, but which, with premodern transmission modes, are too costly for the poor. In particular, allocation policies that emphasize *public* telephone facilities can have important welfare effects in the LDCs. A survey of the use that villagers made of public pay telephones installed in rural Costa Rica presents some results that are pertinent in this context.[43] The survey showed that by far the major reason for which calls were made was "personal"—to maintain contact with family and friends who had emigrated from their native villages. Such personal communications may increase the efficiency of migration and marketing decisions, and thus have economic effects, too. But the wider availability of modern telecommunications also facilitates the continuation of ties among people whose poverty would otherwise have precluded maintaining social links over long distances. Social benefit-cost analysts may not be able to obtain prices for valuing the maintenance of personal and social ties. Nevertheless, the private (and social) value of such links in contemporary developing countries may be great. LDCs are often characterized by rapid rural-to-urban migration and social fragmentation.

Finally, telecommunications expansion can also be expected to increase employment in LDCs. The high capital-labor coefficients typical of telecommunications projects mean that relatively few people are directly employed in such projects. As noted earlier, however, in the LDCs, greater availability of telecommunications improves the performance of product and factor markets. Output and investment are likely to increase in response to new opportunities and diminished uncertainties. In the conditions prevalent in the developing countries, in turn, higher output and capital formation usually generate higher employment.[44] Improved information flows and decision-making processes that raise factor productivity will shift outward the marginal productivity of labor curve in the modern sector and raise employment there. In addition, better information and communications may also stimulate additional supplies of capital. As is well known, capital market imperfections in the LDCs often separate potential savers from investors. Consequently, increased availability of information that opens new investment opportunities to individuals, corporations, and state entities are likely to increase rates of saving and investment. The distributional implications of this discussion are straightforward. A major cause of the unequal distribution of income in the LDCs is the low income of the people who are either underemployed or unemployed. Hence the higher employment that comes with increased investment and output can be expected to improve the relative position of an LDC's poorer people.

This discussion of the consequences of telecommunications investment for equality and income distribution in LDCs can be summarized briefly. Telecommunications expansion may well increase equality in access of information and communications. Telecommunications may also have an equalizing effect on the distribution of income. The conclusion follows from our consideration of the relative-price and employment effects, and of the possibilities for levying user charges. One further observation is pertinent. The distributional effects we have discussed are no less important for being indirect. In an SBCA perspective, these consequences are pertinent even if they occur as "side effects"; indeed, even if the individuals who benefit from telecommunications expansion do not themselves use the newly installed equipment. This point is obvious in a discussion that necessarily includes externalities. I mention it only because some perspectives on telecommunications' distributional impact have identified the beneficiaries exclusively as the narrow stratum of people who are the sub-scribers to a new project's facilities.[45]

Uncertainty

The preceding discussion suggests that, from an SBCA viewpoint, tele-communications expansion in developing countries has some attractive features. This conclusion is reinforced if, following SBCA's conceptual framework, we consider ex ante uncertainty concerning a project's future benefits and costs.[46] Because of the instability and random shocks to which the LDCs are often subject, such an assessment is of particular importance for project selection in the developing countries.

Those shocks stem from different sources: economic changes that originate from abroad; internal political or policy shifts; and/or unex-pected weather conditions in economies whose production and con-sumption depend heavily on agriculture. Whatever their source, such random shocks can rarely be avoided. However, the instability they impart adds special uncertainty to the returns that can be expected from investments in developing countries. The difficulties that confront investment planners in the LDCs are further aggravated because the ratio of pure uncertainty to risk is probably greater than in the econom-ically advanced countries. Consequently, standard decision techniques that utilize probability analysis for ex ante investment assessment are less helpful in the LDCs. In addition, the impact of uncertainty on ex post investment results in developing countries is to some extent asym-metrical. The gains from unexpectedly favorable shifts in demand are limited by sectoral capacity constraints. In addition, rigidities in do-mestic demand constrain the windfalls that might otherwise accrue from unexpectedly favorable supply shifts in specific markets. By con-trast, the social losses inflicted by unexpectedly unfavorable changes in supply or in demand are not so easily bounded.

Such cases involve, for example, the port facilities built to serve an export boom that failed to materialize. Or if domestic income and demand do not grow at the pace originally anticipated, factories in-stalled to supply the domestic market with specific products may oper-ate with low utilization rates. By the same token, if the supply of imported intermediate goods should unexpectedly slacken, invest-ments in the activities that use those inputs will show low ex post social rates of return. These examples point to two features of the problem that ex ante uncertainty poses for investment choice in developing countries. First, the instability that affects future benefits and costs may be either systemic or sectoral. Also, the problem is not instability per se; but rather instability combined with a high degree of specificity in interindustry supply and demand patterns. These two conditions put a special premium on investments in activities whose output is rela-tively flexible and/or general in its use. What is relevant in the present context is that telecommunications offers special advantages on both scores.

Compared with many other investments in LDCs, telecommunications projects have a high degree of generality in the sectors they supply. Equipment is not highly specific to demand from individual client sectors. Thus if random shocks favor activity B at the expense of activity A, the telecommunications facilities may be almost as well suited to supply B as A. This property means that the social returns of telecommunications projects are relatively insensitive to random shocks. Although such projects have high fixed costs, these costs are not sunk in any particular activity.[47] Should unexpected contingencies arise, the assets are salvageable in other lines. Because much of the equipment installed to provide service for one activity may ex post transmit messages for very different activities, the losses imposed by sectoral uncertainty are much reduced in the case of telecommunications investment. Further, the demand for telecommunications is relatively unaffected either by systemic shocks or by upward or downward movements within individual sectors. This is because of a special feature in the relation between "news" and decision making. Many production, trading, and investment decisions require the transmission of information concerning new developments regardless of whether the new developments are favorable or unfavorable. It may be as economical to transfer fresh information concerning adverse market shifts as it is to send messages with favorable news.[48] Consequently, the impact of systemic instability and sectoral shocks on the demand for telecommunications (and on the ex post returns to investment projects) is also reduced in the case of this sector. Thus, if we attempt to take into account the special problems that uncertainty poses for investment choice in developing countries, telecommunications also appears relatively attractive.

Some Negatives
Telecommunications expansion in LDCs may also have some negative social consequences. The possibility of conveying messages more cheaply may increase the amount of false information transmitted, with socially pernicious effects. Thus some observers have suggested that radio and television have facilitated the transmission of messages that mislead LDC peasants into thinking that all is well in the city. Such misinformation may help stimulate excessive rural-urban migration. As a result, aggregate social welfare may be reduced rather than increased.

This possibility of increased misinformation applies more to one-way communication media (like radio and television) than to the two-way media (like telephones) on which this paper has focused. Thus in the example given, telephone calls to (or from) potential migrants can dispel the false impressions that one-way media may have created. As this case indicates, the misinformation problem may sometimes be self-correcting. Opening new channels of communication facilitates a flow of additional information that can correct earlier inaccuracies. And again, one must specify accurately the alternative situation with which one is comparing the supply of misinformation following the expansion of modern telecommunications. Premodern communications channels convey false messages, too. Further, it is difficult to see why the absolute sum of the supply and demand price elasticities should be higher for false than for true messages. Hence there seems to be no a priori basis for presuming that modern telecommunications reduce the ratio of true to false messages. In addition, as noted earlier, telecommunications expansion generally involves the opening of additional (and competitive) channels of information. This feature may indeed lead to an increase in the ratio of accurate to false information that is accepted.

Another potential cost of modern telecommunications must also be considered. Our discussion thus far has focused on the effects of telecommunications in lowering the relative price of information, with information treated as a composite good. We have abstracted from the fact that the expansion of modern telecommunications also alters the relative price of different types of information. The price of information that permits easy imitation probably falls more than does the price of information that requires sustained thought and analysis.[49] As with any alteration in relative prices, these changes affect the opportunity set, the mix of goods produced and consumed, and the techniques used to produce them. This internal relative-price change occurs, however, in the midst of a general decline in information costs. Hence it seems unlikely that the net welfare change of the overall shift is negative.

By their nature, the conditions noted in this section do not lend themselves to a conclusive treatment. My own assessment is that they do not outweigh the positive effects discussed earlier.

Conclusions

This paper has discussed some of the welfare consequences of telecommunications investment projects in developing countries. Following the conceptual framework of social benefit-cost analysis, we have considered telecommunications investment in terms of ex ante uncertainty, income distribution effects, and external economies.

Our discussion has focused on an aspect of LDCs that is not always emphasized: their high information and transactions costs. In that context, the impact of modern communications technology in lowering the costs of transmitting information over time and over space is of special importance. By reducing transaction and information costs,

Nathaniel H. Leff   271

telecommunications expansion can have far-reaching effects on economic development. In particular, lower transaction costs and reduced uncertainty can increase the efficiency both of markets and of administrative organizations. The prospect of improved performance in these two sets of institutions should not be taken lightly. They are the two major mechanisms for resource mobilization and factor allocation in economic development. Indeed, the welfare consequences of telecommunications expansion include public-good effects, notably in enhancing a country's capacity for responding to new problems and opportunities. A fall in the costs of obtaining accurate and timely knowledge is particularly important in LDCs, for uncertainty is often pervasive in those economies. And as noted earlier, both the quantity and the quality of the information produced in the LDCs has probably been reduced by the high cost of premodern transmission modes.

Much of our discussion has involved the application of familiar concepts from the economics of information to a field where these ideas have not yet penetrated widely—the economics of development. The fact that the rapidly growing body of research in the economics of information has not yet had much impact in development economics reflects the often-remarked compartmentalization that has occurred within economics. As such, this experience highlights the need for intellectual arbitrage between various subdisciplines within economics. The need for such arbitrage is especially great in a field like development, which necessarily includes many subareas within its purview.

This paper also has implications concerning recent work on social benefit-cost analysis for investment choice in developing countries. One conclusion seems clear from our overall discussion. As we have seen, in an LDC context, telecommunications projects can provide significant external economies. Partly because of these interactivity effects, the telecommunications sector appears to be a relatively attractive candidate for expansion in many LDCs. It may therefore come as a surprise to learn that public investment decisions in many LDCs have followed a very different pattern of resource allocation. In fact, telecommunications investment seems to have proceeded at socially suboptimal rates in numerous developing countries.[50]

This allocation pattern is partly a result of the intellectual shift that has occurred in the field of social benefit-cost analysis for investment choice in LDCs. As noted at the beginning of this paper, in recent decades, formal and informal SBCA have moved away from the early emphasis on externalities. The case we have discussed suggests that this intellectual change has important consequences for investment choice in developing countries. If investment allocations do not take cognizance of external economies, they will accord a low priority to projects whose income-creation and income-distribution effects accrue largely as externalities. The present case illustrates this result. In a perspective of SBCA without externalities, telecommunications has typically been viewed as a consumer rather than a producer good, and one with unequalizing rather than equalizing distributional effects.[51]

There is no necessary reason for the newer concerns of social benefit-cost analysis to "crowd out" the older ones. Full SBCA, including externalities, is presumably the technique that should be used for investment choice in developing countries. Applying that technique may require further work to make the concept of externalities operational. The question of how full SBCA has been implemented by international agencies that are committed to its use is of obvious relevance in this context.[52]

Notes

* My interest in this general area was first stimulated in work for ITT. I am grateful to the Faculty Research Program of the Columbia Business School for financial support. I also thank Yair Aharoni, John Donaldson, Eli Noam, Rita Cruise O'Brien, Hugh Schwartz, William Silber, Hans Singer, N. Usmen, Raymond Vernon, and an anonymous referee of this journal for helpful comments on an earlier draft. I bear sole responsibility for any deficiencies in this paper.

1. Paul N. Rosenstein-Rodan, "Problems of Industrialization of East and Southeastern Europe," *Economic Journal* 53 (June 1943): 202–11; Albert O. Hirschman, *The Strategy of Economic Development* (New Haven, Conn.: Yale University Press, 1958), chaps. 5–6.

2. See, e.g., I. M. D. Little and J. Mirrlees, *Manual of Industrial Project Analysis in Developing Countries* (Paris: OECD, 1968), vol. 2; UNIDO (P. Dasgupta, A. K. Sen, and S. Marglin), *Guidelines for Project Evaluation* (New York: United Nations, 1972); Arnold C. Harberger, *Project Evaluation* (Chicago: Markham Publishing Co., 1973); S. Reutlinger, *Techniques for Project Appraisal under Uncertainty* (Baltimore: Johns Hopkins University Press, 1970; 3d printing, 1976); L. Squire and H. van der Tak, *Economic Analysis of Projects* (Baltimore: John Hopkins University Press, 1975; 4th printing, 1981); F. L. C. H. Helmers, *Project Planning and Income Distribution* (Boston: Martinus Nijhoff, 1979).

3. On this point, see Albert Hirschman's discussion in chap. 5 of his *Development Projects Observed* (Washington, D.C.; Brookings Institution, 1967). The chapter is appropriately entitled "The Centrality of Side Effects."

4. This shift has also been noted by János Kornai in his critique of recent work in SBCA. See his "Appraisal of Project Appraisal" in *Economics and Human Welfare: Essays in Honor of Tibor Scitovsky*, ed. Michael Boskin (New York: Academic Press, 1979), p. 86.

5. I focus on telephones rather than on other forms of telecommunications (e.g., radio or teleprinters) because telephones clearly dominate those alternatives for the uses considered in this paper (see below). For example, telephone users, unlike the users of teleprinters, need not be literate. This feature confers a substantial advantage in many developing countries. Further, unlike radios, telephones permit interactive (rather than one-way) communication. The advantages in terms of the turn-around time for information used in decision making, negotiation, and feedback processes are considerable.

Nathaniel H. Leff   273

6. The literature in that field has been surveyed in J. Hirschleifer and John G. Riley, "The Analytics of Uncertainty and Information: An Expository Survey," *Journal of Economic Literature* 17 (December 1979): 1375–1421.

7. This paper focuses on the domestic effects of telecommunications expansion in developing countries. The international consequences of telecommunications expansion raise a different set of issues. For a perspective on those issues, see Rita Cruise O'Brien and G. K. Helleiner, "The Political Economy of Information in a Changing International Economic Order," *International Organization* 34 (Autumn 1980): 445–70.

8. Arthur Hazlewood, "Optimum Pricing as Applied to Telephone Service," *Review of Economic Studies*, vol. 18 (September 1950), as reprinted in Ralph Turvey (ed.), *Public Enterprise: Selected Readings* (Hammondsworth: Penguin Books, 1968), esp. pp. 254–55 there. See also Lyn Squire, "Some Aspects of Optimal Pricing for Telecommunications," *Bell Journal of Economics and Management Science* 4 (Autumn 1973): 515–25.

9. On possible congestion problems, see the next paragraph. The discussion here also assumes that expansion programs take into account the complementarities between access equipment and circuits.

10. The United States, Sweden, Switzerland, Canada, and New Zealand all have more than 50 telephones per 100 population. By contrast, LDCs generally have fewer than 5 telephones per 100 population. This information is from Robert J. Saunders, "Telecommunications in Developing Countries: Constraints on Development," in *Communication Economics and Development*, ed. M. Jussawalla and D. M. Lamberton (New York: Pergamon Press, 1982), p. 190.

11. These two effects can be integrated in one concept. But for analytical purposes, it is useful to distinguish between the time costs and the other costs that are saved in transmitting information via modern telecommunications.

12. Harvey Leibenstein, "Entrepreneurship and Development," *American Economic Review* 58 (May 1968): 72–83, 77.

13. Clifford Geertz, "The Bazaar Economy: Information and Search in Peasant Marketing," *American Economic Review* 68 (May 1978): 29. Geertz indicates that he considers these features as general and prototypical of many less developed economies (he describes these as economies which are neither "primitive" nor "industrial"). In addition, Geertz makes it clear that the conditions cited are not limited either to bazaars or to peasant marketing.

14. Ibid., p. 30.

15. I use these terms in the sense explicated by Frank H. Knight, *Risk, Uncertainty, and Profit* (Boston: Houghton Mifflin Co., 1921).

16. Thomas C. Schelling has noted also aspects of this phenomenon, albeit in different terms. See his *Micromotives and Microbehavior* (New York: W. W. Norton, 1978), p. 47. In a discussion of "telephoning," he observes, "One call leads to another. It may lead to a return call; or somebody learns something worth passing on; or a call initiates some business."

17. World Bank, *Fourth Annual Review of Project Performance Audit Results* (Washington, D.C., November, 1978), p. 43.

18. See Harvey Leibenstein, *General X-Efficiency Theory and Economic Development* (New York: Oxford University Press, 1978), esp. pp. 37–38, for a general theoretical perspective on the conditions discussed below.

19. This discussion does not imply that it is economically rational to transmit information in an unlimited manner. On the "attention costs" involved in having managers attend to additional information, see Herbert A. Simon, "Rationality as Process and as a Product of Thought," *American Economic Review* 68 (May 1978): 13.

274   *Economic Development and Cultural Change*

20. After an earlier draft of this paper was written, I learned that some of the ideas presented in these paragraphs have also been discussed in Andrew P. Hardy, "The Role of the Telephone in Economic Development," *Telecommunications Policy* (December 1980), pp. 279, 283. See also B. Wellenius, "Telecommunications in Developing Countries," *Telecommunications Policy* (September 1977).

21. R. C. Repetto, *Time in India's Development Programmes* (Cambridge, Mass.: Harvard University Press, 1971), esp. chaps. 1–2.

22. Hirschman, *The Strategy of Economic Development*, pp. 24–28.

23. On complementarity and substitution possibilities that reduce the entrepreneurship requirements per unit of output growth in LDCs, see Nathaniel H. Leff, "Entrepreneurship and Economic Development: The Problem Revisited," *Journal of Economic Literature* 27 (March 1979): 46–64, 47–48.

24. S. A. Lippman and J. J. McCall, "The Economics of Job Search," *Economic Inquiry* 14 (September 1976): 347–68.

25. See, e.g., George Akerlof, "The Market for 'Lemons': Quality Uncertainty and the Market Mechanism," *Quarterly Journal of Economics* 84 (August 1970): 488–500; and Jack Hirschleifer, "Exchange Theory: The Missing Chapter," *Western Economic Journal* 11 (June 1973): 330–35.

26. R. W. Clower, ed., *Monetary Theory* (Hammondsworth: Penguin Books, 1969), "Introduction," pp. 8–14. Similarly, but from a different perspective, see Y. Ben-Porath, "The F-Connection: Families, Friends and Firms and the Organization of Exchange," *Population and Development Review* 6 (March 1980): 1–30.

27. Thus Albert Hischman has noted that following the expansion of the long-distance telephone network in Ethiopia, a credit market for the coffee trade emerged in that country. See his *Development Projects Observed*, pp. 131–32.

28. K. D. Garbade and William L. Silber, "Technology, Communication, and the Performance of Financial Markets, 1840–1975," *Journal of Finance* 33 (June 1978): 819–32.

29. On what follows in this paragraph, see R. B. DuBoff, "Business Demand and the Development of the Telegraph in the United States, 1844–1860," *Business History Review* 54 (Winter 1980): 461–77.

30. For a general discussion of the economic impact of information on market performance, see Michael Rothschild, "Models of Market Organization with Imperfect Information: A Survey," *Journal of Political Economy* 81 (November 1973): 1283–1308.

31. Nathaniel H. Leff, "Industrial Organization and Entrepreneurship in the Developing Countries: The Economic Groups," *Economic Development and Cultural Change* 26 (July 1978): 661–75.

32. See, e.g., Anthony Downs, *Inside Bureaucracy* (Boston: Little, Brown & Co., 1967), on such phenomena which lead to "control loss."

33. For a careful elaboration of this point, see Richard A. Posner, "A Theory of Primitive Society with Special Reference to Law," *Journal of Law and Economics*, vol. 23 (April 1980).

34. Charles P. Kindleberger, *Economic Development* (New York: McGraw-Hill Book Co., 1965), chap. 10.

35. These figures are from Saunders, "Telecommunications in Developing Countries," p. 191. They refer to recent projects in which the World Bank was involved, often as lender of last resort.

36. Ibid. The reasons for the divergence between private (financial) returns and SBCA returns to telecommunications projects in developing coun-

Nathaniel H. Leff   275

tries are discussed in Nathaniel H. Leff, "Social Benefit-Cost Analysis and Telecommunications Investment in Developing Countries," in *Information Economics and Policy* (forthcoming).

37. See, e.g., Squire and Tak, *Economic Analysis of Projects*, pp. 50 ff.

38. Ibid., p. 75.

39. See, e.g., W. G. Shepherd, "Residential Telephone Service in Britain," *Journal of Industrial Economics*, vol. 14 (June 1966). More generally, operating policies during a project's lifetime affect the magnitude of future benefits and costs. Consequently, (implicit) decisions concerning operating policies cannot in practice be avoided in ex ante social benefit-cost analysis. On this point, see I. Heggie, "Practical Problems of Implementing Accounting Prices," in *Using Shadow Prices*, ed. I. M. D. Little and M. Scott (London: Heinemann Educational, 1976).

40. On these effects, see Nathaniel H. Leff, " 'Monopoly Capitalism' and Public Policy in the Developing Countries," *Kyklos* 32 (Autumn 1979): 718–38. Incomplete information flows are of course only one factor in the formation and persistence of such patterns of market power in the developing countries.

41. Emile McAnany, ed., *Communications: The Rural Third World* (New York: Praeger Publishers, 1979).

42. Everett M. Rogers and Lynne Svenning, *Modernization among Peasants: The Impact of Communication* (New York, 1969). In some instances, a two-step process may be involved. Social interaction facilitated by the telephone may make farm operators aware of the successful performance of more productive agricultural techniques. But other means of communications may be required to obtain instruction in the new techniques.

43. Robert J. Saunders and Jeremy Warford, "Telecommunications Pricing and Investment in Developing Countries" (Atlanta: Telecommunication Exposition, 1977), p. 2.

44. William R. Cline, "Distribution and Development: A Survey," *Journal of Development Economics*, vol. 1 (December 1975), esp. pp. 387–90. Cline demonstrates that even with capital-labor substitution, higher output can be expected to generate higher employment in LDCs. In addition, higher output leads to accelerator pressures and increased capital formation. In LDC conditions, a larger capital stock is likely to promote higher employment. See R. S. Eckaus, "The Factor Proportions Problem in Under-Developed Areas," *American Economic Review* 45 (September 1955): 539–65.

45. Despite its inaccuracy, the perspective cited in the text seems to have influenced allocation decisions within developing countries. Cf. the following statement by an experienced observer attempting to explain why national planning authorities in LDCs often give low priority to investment in telecommunications: "Among the more serious reasons for the . . . low rate of investment in the sector . . . [is a] perception that telecommunications investments, while profitable in a financial sense, confer direct benefits only upon a relatively narrow—and privileged—portion of the population in a developing country." This quotation is from Saunders, "Telecommunications in Developing Countries," pp. 195–96. Dr. Saunders heads the division within the World Bank which deals with telecommunications projects. However, his paper is preceded by a disclaimer stating that the paper does not necessarily reflect the views of the World Bank.

46. See, e.g., Reutlinger, *Techniques for Project Appraisal under Uncertainty*.

47. On this distinction between "fixed" and "sunk" costs, see B. Klein and K. B. Leffler, "The Role of Market Forces in Assuring Contractual Performance," *Journal of Political Economy* 89 (August 1981): 615–41, 619.

48. Thus, following the onset of the Great Depression in the United States, the number of telephone calls rose sharply. It was not until 1931 that the income effect led to a reduction in the total number of calls made. See John Brooks, *Telephone* (New York: Harper & Row, 1976), pp. 187–88.

49. This was first pointed out to me by Raymond Vernon.

50. This point is discussed in Saunders, "Telecommunications in Developing Countries," pp. 190–201.

51. See, e.g., n. 45 above.

52. Leff, "Social Benefit-Cost Analysis and Telecommunications Investment."

[31]

ECONOMICS OF LANGUAGE*

(1965)

Jacob Marschak

I. AN OPTIMAL COMMUNICATION SYSTEM

A group of engineers were designing the communication system of a small fighter plane. They were told to keep the communication equipment as light as possible so as not to impair the plane's speed and maneuverability, or the load of fuel and ammunition it can carry. Every pound saved on communication hardware would improve the plane's performance. The different messages that the pilot may have to exchange with his gunner or with other planes or with the ground, and that provide for all the contingencies of navigation and fighting, are not numerous. No need for verbal messages, a telephone. A small set of dials and off-on signals would do.

A psychologist was called in to study the available records of communications in actual combat, and to perform mock-combat tests. The group's final recommendation: restore the telephone. Men in mortal danger, or approaching or escaping it, need to hear and talk to other men, with plenty of redundancy, and not even always confining the talk to the task in hand. Without the relief of verbal, voiced exchange, tension might become intolerable, sometimes to the point of nervous breakdown, and would in any case lead to diminished performance during the same or the next mission. A reminiscence, some banter, a cheer, perhaps a whistled tune, any effective sharing of experience could help. But this requires a richer, a more habitual language than the primitive and exotic dictionary of buttons and dials. Jokes coded in advance are notoriously un-funny.

Thus, nervous relief for the plane's crew is 'worth' a couple of pounds of communication equipment. 'Worth' is an economic term. This does not mean that "worth" is measured in money. Nor can we subtract pounds from, say, microwatt-seconds of nervous exertion. What we do measure is the probability of success of the plane's mission. Adding to a given communication vocabulary tends to decrease this probability (by adding to the plane's load), but also to increase it (by improving the crew's mental

184   INFORMATION AND ORGANIZATION

state). When the advantages and disadvantages are so balanced that the probability of success of the mission is the highest achievable, we say that the system is optimal, or (equivalently) is efficient, or economical.

The present writer does not know whether the recommendation of the psychologist and his colleagues was accepted, and telephones were kept in those fighter plane designs. But he is an economist, and the story impressed him as a problem in the Economics of Language. He apologizes to those of his fellow economists who might prefer to define their field more narrowly, and who would object to this (not at all unusual) identification of economics with the search for optimality in fields extending beyond, though including, the production and distribution of marketable goods. Being ignorant of linguistics, he apologizes even more humbly to those linguists who would scorn the designation of a simple dial-and-buttons system as a language. He does think, however, that his story deals with the essential stuff of economics, in particular the economics of uncertainty that characterizes problems of human information, communication, and organization. See, for example, Marschak (1954, 1959, 1964).

At the same time, the author suspects that these problems are indeed not without pertinence to the phenomenon of language, or at least put them in a perspective worth exploring. With all the reluctance befitting a curious layman he submits this sketch of an article as a question to linguists. He asks them whether their work to date contains building materials for any future economics of the most developed and most fully studied system of communications within human organizations: the language, spoken or written.

II. EFFICIENCY AND VIABILITY

The story of the fighter plane illustrates, however, only one, the *normative* (or *policy*, or *efficiency*) branch of communication economics, namely, the search for communication systems best suited to a given goal; or, more generally, best suited to a given scale of values ('utilities' is the economist's term). It searches for a system that would maximize the average achieved value; it being understood that the average is weighted by the probabilities of the various contingencies. This policy rule goes back to the eighteenth century's idea of maximizing the 'moral value of wealth'

(Daniel Bernoulli, 1738). It was shown more recently that this rule is logically implied by a few plausible axioms of consistency so that it can be regarded, in the words of F. P. Ramsey (1926), as 'an extension of logic'. Still more recent developments, in the theory of games, of statistics, and 'operations research', have brought about a rich literature on the logic of the 'average utility rule', e.g., L. J. Savage (1954).

In the simple case when the value scale has only two points, of which one ('goal attained') is preferable to the other ('goal failed'), maximizing average utility is identical with maximizing the probability of achieving the preferable result (i.e., of attaining the goal), as in our fighter case.

Another branch of communication economics would be the *explanatory* one. It asks: Why are the known languages of the present and the past what they are or were? This is equivalent to asking: Why has any observed trait, or set of traits, of a communication system survived for as long a time as it has, in fact, survived? It will be seen that this is, in turn, equivalent to the following question: Given the environment, what determines the probability that a set of traits will remain in existence for a given length of time? Logically, surviving is a special case of 'attaining a goal'. Viability is thus a special case of efficiency. This goes for language as well as for other aspects of human organization (and thus, of 'culture' if I may use the word). Therefore, explanatory economics of language (as of 'culture' in general) can be regarded, formally, as a special case of the normative, or policy, study: as if the scale of values of a (fictitious) policy-maker consisted in preferring long to short durations of survival of a set of characteristics. To be sure, the historical records of survivals and extinctions of linguistic forms reflect also the efforts of actual, non-fictitious policy-makers, whose scale of values may or may not have been the conservative one.

To exemplify the distinction between a normative and explanatory approach in another branch of anthropology, Kluckhohn and Leighton (1946, pp. 176–177) pointed out that witch-killing seems to benefit a tribe's cohesion; but Michael Polanyi (1965) using his, or our, scale of values could not help expressing his disgust at such a statement. According to Darwin (1872), Goethe, in 1794–5, "pointedly remarked ... that the future question for naturalists will be how, for instance, cattle got their horns, and not for what they are used": an explanatory, nonnormative approach, we would say.

186   INFORMATION AND ORGANIZATION

III. POLICY

When the *Académie Française* debates its Dictionary, it is engaged in policy-making. A word, a rule is accepted, rejected on the basis of some scale of values. I have not followed the debates but imagine something like the following criteria might be used. One of them may be logical consistency: try to avoid too many exceptions to a rule, ban illogical sentences. Another criterion may be the aesthetics of sounds and cadences, as well as of some meanings: avoid vulgar associations. Perhaps more important is the goal of preserving national unity: defend tradition, yet adapt judicially to the new needs, and the changing degrees of influence of various portions of the people, possibly caused by some identifiable change in the environment. Any such criteria need not be, but sometimes are, mutually inconsistent. Then the decision finally made will reflect – and a set of such decisions will indeed define – the relative power of the contestants, as studied, for example, by Harsanyi (1962a, b) in this journal. In this, the *Académie* is presumably not unlike any other legislative body.

In the United States, there is no language legislation. Several dictionaries compete with each other in the market, and they also compete with show business, the schools, the press, the political orators, and the pulpit. There exists nonetheless a public debate on language policy, and it is possible to identify the underlying criteria: see, for example, Sledd and Ebbit (1962) on *Webster's Third* (controversial) *Edition*. As a non-native, therefore self-conscious, user of English, and a reader of both British and American publications and manuscripts (including students' essays), I offer one class of cases that may illustrate further the possible value scales of competing language policies. It seems that, *pace* Dickens, the adjectives 'mutual' and 'common' are treated as interchangeable except possibly in legal and scientific literature. Interchangeable – in the U.S.A. but I think not in England – are also 'present' and 'current'. Some critics of the new *Webster* have pointed out that it equates 'uninterested' with 'disinterested' (which latter should properly mean 'impartial'), thus making "*two words do the work of one.*" For a scientist or lawyer such many-to-one correspondence between words and concepts is surely un-economical for it may leave some concepts wordless. It is vital for the economist that the reader of the expression "national income of 1933 in dollars of current purchasing power" should unequivocally understand "purchasing power of 1933," not of 1965. Also, superfluous words are apt to create pseudoconcepts empty of content and repugnant to the realist. Precisely in this context, Lotka (1924), the scientist, quotes Goethe, the sage: "*Gewoehnlich glaubt der Mensch, wenn er nur Worte hoert,/Es muesse sich dabei auch etwas denken lassen.*" [1]

Yet, to have some 'two words do the work of one' is not uneconomical for people whose tasks and needs do not ordinarily call for distinguishing between the particular concepts in question. Such people may include teen-agers, and lazy reporters. But poets and orators, too, may indulge in, yes be in vital need of, a hoard of synonyms.

Another type of what is sometimes called economy of language may also be actually noneconomical, with respect to some scale of values. The short sentence of some ancients – '*Eo rus* !' '*I*' – is aesthetically appealing as are the sparse brush strokes of an early Chinese drawing. But surely, as we have noted, the aesthetic criterion is not the only one admitted in language policy. Nor is it true that thriftiness is the only criterion in arts, poetry, or literary style – or even in economics (in the narrower sense). Schopenhauer stated his aversion to brevity of style as explicitly as Keynes deplored the public dangers of private thrift. (When the economist Veblen advocated austerity – using, by the way, rather luxuriant language – his criterion was still another one: the moral criterion.) It is possible, to be sure, that economy of effort was operating in the process of language evolution. If so, economy of effort would define just one of the language characteristics that satisfy the survival criterion. We shall return to this in the next section.

Surely the present article does not contain any new linguistic facts. So far its purpose has been to present language as an object of choice, of policy, in exactly the same sense in which the communication system of the fighter plane had to be chosen. "To govern is to choose" (Kennedy, 1963). This presupposes the existence of the chooser's scale of values, the consistency of his 'tastes'. In the case of the fighter plane, the 'tastes' are defined by its mission. The maker of language policies may have to spend some effort to arrive at a consistent scale of values. With the future environment uncertain he must also arrive at consistent 'beliefs' about its probabilities. The actual policy-making, outside of engineering, possibly medicine and some business and administrative, notably military, activities, is certainly far from the ideal concept of consistent policy-making. As Ramsey (1926) remarked, people do not always follows logical rules unless they make an effort ('stop to think'). Indeed, logic is not psychology! The data available to linguistic politicians in particular (or, to *épater* them in another way: linguistic engineers), for checking and rechecking their tastes and beliefs, are, I fear, quite rough. Yet the present attempt to sketch a relation between their task and the logic of policies in general may help to understand the debates and debaters of dictionaries and grammars.

IV. EVOLUTION

If, in a given environment E, a trait X has survived longer than has trait Y, we usually infer: it is probable that 'X is better adapted to E than is Y'. The expression in quotation marks again involves probabilities since it usually means something like the following: 'Given E and given any time length T (in years, say), X is not less likely, and for some values of T is more likely, to survive beyond T years, than is Y'. The double use of probabilities is made necessary, at the first step, by the fewness of available observations ('sampling error'), and, at the second step, by the inherent uncertainty of the phenomenon, presumably due to individually insignificant but numerous, unidentifiable factors. Note also that environment itself must be usually defined, not as a constant, but, instead, as a variable obeying a fixed probability distribution. For example, 'a country is exposed to invasions' or 'to unpredictable weather' means that the probability of invasion, or the variance of temperature, is and remains high.

In brief, what has survived had probably a higher probability of survival than what has not. Like all mathematical statements this is a tautology. Like some of them, it is useful in guiding empirical research – in our case, the search for factors that have, in fact, endowed various traits with higher or lower survival probabilities in given environments.

We have called this section 'Evolution', but only in the sense of the survival of traits best fitted to an environment; not at all in the sense of any progress or improvement or rising complexity. For, as pointed out by Darwin (1859, Ch. IV),

...natural selection, or the survival of the fittest, does not necessarily include progressive development – it only takes advantage of such variations as arise and are beneficial to each creature under its complex relations of life. And it may be asked what advantage, as far as we can see, would it be to an infusorian animalcule – to an intestinal worm – or even to an earthworm, to be highly organized. If it were no advantage, these forms ... might remain for indefinite ages in their present lowly condition.

Whether, or in what environments, there is a change towards a richer or a poorer, a more or a less logical, a more or a less complex language – whatever these general categories may mean – cannot be deduced from the above tautology alone. But empirical research tells whether, or under what conditions, certain directions of change under those general categories have in fact prevailed. A step has then been made toward an explanation, and therefore a prediction, of the form: "such and such an environment will, will not, favor the survival of such and such general property of language." For example, if greater complexity of language means its ability to express a greater variety of situations, and the environment tends to fluctuate strongly and frequently, a complex (or shall we say *flexible?*) language will have a higher chance of survival.

The reader will have noticed that, in our terminology, evolution, in the sense of survival of the fittest characteristics, is the object of 'explanatory economics'. It compares the various alternative traits with respect to their optimality in the sense of maximum survival chance, not in the sense of any other scale of values. It is a question of fact, and depends on the properties of the environment, whether the surviving traits have been also optimal with respect to some other scale such as the degrees of complexity. One will also expect, in particular, that the language reflects the scale of values of the socially dominant group so that, for example, the multiplicity of forms of address would be about coeval with an aristocratic society, etc. I am sure anthropologists and sociologists of culture have their card files full of such observations. Thus W.S. Laughlin (1963, pp. 640–641) compares arctic tribes of different longevity:

... people who lived in the more harsh arctic environments died earlier... the greater overlap between generations associated with greater longevity provides more time for transfer of information. The experience of older people is stored in accessible form for a longer period in more 'storage cells'... artistic expression and the larger number of public ceremonies and myths are among the correlative benefits of greater longevity and greater population.

One would like to know how these differences are reflected in the language.

An exciting study in explanatory economics of language is furnished by 'Zipf's Law' (Zipf, 1949), a class of statistical distributions of words according to the frequencies of their occurrences. The economist recognizes in 'Zipf's Law' the 'Pareto Law', of doubtful empirical validity, of the distribution of incomes by size, and is tempted to transfer his doubts from the one to the other. To my knowledge, neither model has been submitted to appropriate statistical tests, which would compare its 'goodness of fit' with that of other proposed classes of skew distributions. But it is not the empirical validity that we are going to discuss here. G. K. Zipf has intuitively (but vaguely) related this empirical regularity to a 'principle of least effort'. Mandelbrot (1953) has shown that the observed regularity does indeed follow from the assumption of minimum average 'cost' of communication, given the (appropriately defined) rate of information flow, and assuming that a word's 'cost' increases when a letter is added. Mandelbrot's model, described also in Colin Cherry's (1957) well-known book, is wider than Zipf's: it allows (as we shall presently see) one characteristic of the word-distribution to vary from language to language.

Considerations of 'effort' or 'cost' give Mandelbrot's analysis an economic flavor. But this is not all. To understand its evolutionary meaning we note, first, that replacing 'automobile' by 'car' does indeed save one's breath! This is not trivial. If very many such replacements occur, correspondingly more energy or time is left for other uses that are important for the maintenance of the individual's life or of the social fabric in his generation and beyond. Moreover, communication delays make decisions obsolete in the face of quickly changing situations; the brevity of the great leaders' commands has had not only aesthetic value. A language does not survive if its carrier, the society, disintegrates.

Second, the information rate measures, roughly speaking, the variety of potential messages, the degree of precision, of conceptual discrimination. Certain properties of the evironment – technological, forensic, cultic, – may be such that the benefit of greater precision achieved by frequent use of some long words outweighs the disadvantages of effort and delay. These benefits and disadvantages are ultimately measured, not in units of time or energy or in information bits (we must not subtract eggs from apples) but as additions to, and subtractions from, the probability of survival of a given language structure. For remember that Mandelbrot minimizes average 'cost', *keeping the information rate fixed*. The information rate – the degree of variety, precision, discrimination – appears therefore as a parameter of Zipf's distribution (in fact, a slope of a certain line on his diagram). This parameter can itself vary, adapting to the environment. That is, the probability of survival in a given environment is maximized simultaneously (1) over the set of classes of word-distributions (Mandelbrot's is one such class), and (2) over the set of possible information rates (each rate defining one member of Mandelbrot's class).

Viewed in this way, the Zipf-Mandelbrot model, whether empirically valid or not, illustrates our methodological point: to explain why a language is what it is one must show why its properties are, on the balance, conductive to its survival.

NOTES

* A contribution to *Orbis Scriptus: Dmitry Tschiżewskij zum 70. Geburtstag* (W. Weintraub *et al.* (eds.), Eidos Verlag, Munchen), revised for this journal with the permission of the volume's publisher. It is a part of a research project on Individual and Organized Decision Making, carried out at the Western Management Science Institute, University of California at Los Angeles, and supported in part by the Office of Naval Research (Contract No. 233-75) and the Ford Foundation. The author was greatly stimulated by discussions at the Conference on Speech, Language, and Communication sponsored in November, 1963 by the Brain Research Institute, U.C.L.A., and the U.S. Air Force Office of Scientific Research. He owes much to the contributions of P. Garvin, H. Hoijer, S. M. Lamb, and F. A. Lounsbury.

1 Freely translated, "One hears mere words but believes each has a meaning." This goes also for sentences. "*Und so erscheint uns die Evidenz dieses Satzes in ihrer ganzen Notwendigkeit*": a young German philosopher had this in the tentative outline of his proposed Oxford thesis, some 30 years ago. In an effort to translate it into English, the sentence had to be successively pruned to its shorter equivalents, and ultimately to nothing. *Added in 1973.* He was the late Th. Adorno.

BIBLIOGRAPHY

Bernoulli, D., *Specimen Theoriae Novae de Mensura Sortis.* 1738. English translation by Louise Sommer, *Econometrica,* **22** (1954) 23–36. See especially, on page 33, a letter of Gabriel Cramer written in 1724.

Cherry, C., *On Human Communication,* Wiley, New York, 1957.

Darwin, C. (1), *The Origin of Species,* 1859. (2) 'An Historical Sketch of the Progress of Opinion on the Origin of Species', *The Origin of Species* (6th ed.), Preface. 1872. Both reprinted as a Mentor Book, 1958.

Harsanyi, J. C., 'Measurement of Social Power, Opportunity Costs, and the Theory of Two-Person Bargaining Games', *Behav. Sci.* **7** (1962) 67–80. (a)

Harsanyi, J. C., 'Measurement of Social Power in *n*-Person Reciprocal Power Situations', *Behav. Sci.* **7** (1962) 81–91. (b)

Kennedy, J. F., 'Speech at the United Nations', August, 1963.

Kluckhohn, C. and Leighton, Dorothea, *The Navaho*, Harvard Univ. Press, Cambridge, 1946.

Laughlin, W. S., 'Eskimos and Aleuts: Their Origins and Evolution', *Science* **142** (1963) 633–645.

Lotka, A. J., *Elements of Physical Biology*, 1924. Reprinted as *Elements of Mathematical Biology*, Dover Publications, New York, 1956.

Mandelbrot, B., An Information Theory of the Structure of Language Based upon... Statistical Matching of Messages and Coding, in W. Jackson (ed.), *Proceedings of Symposium on Applications of Communication Theory*, Butterworth Scientific Publications, London, 1953.

Marschak, J., 'Towards an Economic Theory of Information and Organization', 1954, *Selected Essays*, 20.

Marschak, J., 'Efficient and Viable Organizational Forms', 1959, *Selected Essays*, 22.

Marschak, J., 'Problems in Information Economics', 1964, *Selected Essays*, 25.

Polanyi, M., 'On the Modern Mind', *Encounter* **24** (1965), 5, 12–20.

Ramsey, F. P., *Truth and Probability*, 1926. Reprinted in H. E. Kyburg and H. Smokler (eds.), *Studies in Subjective probability*, Wiley, New York, 1964.

Savage, L. J., *The Foundations of Statistics*, Wiley, New York, 1954. Revised: Dover, 1972.

Sledd, J. and Ebbit, Wilma, *Dictionaries and that Dictionary*, Scott, Foresman, Chicago, 1962.

Zipf, G. K., *Human Behavior and the Principle of Least Effort*, Addison-Wesley, Cambridge, Mass. 1949.

Part IX
Bibliography

Bibliography

Akerlof, G.A. (1984), *An Economic Theorist's Book of Tales: Essays that Entertain the Consequences of New Assumptions in Economic Theory*, Cambridge: Cambridge University Press.

Akerlof, G.A. and J.L. Yellen (1987), 'Rational Models of Irrational Behavior', *American Economic Review*, **77**, 137–42.

Aldrich, H. and S. Mueller (1982), 'The Evolution of Organizational Forms: Technology, Coordination, and Control', *Research in Organizational Behavior*, **4**, 33–87.

Allen, B. (1991), 'Choosing R&D Projects: An Informational Approach', *American Economic Review*, **81**, 257–61.

Allen, F. (1990), 'The Market for Information and the Origin of Financial Intermediation', *Journal of Financial Intermediation*, **1**, 3–30.

Alogoskoufis, G.S. (1990), 'Monetary Policy and the Informational Implications of the Phillips Curve', *Economica*, **57**, 107–17.

Anderla, G. (1973), *Information in 1985: A Forecasting Study of Information Needs and Resources*, Paris: OECD.

Anton, J.J. and D.A. Yao (1994), 'Expropriations and Inventions: Appropriable Rents in the Absence of Property Rights', *American Economic Review*, **84**, 190–209.

Antonelli, C. (1991), *The Diffusion of Advanced Telecommunications in Developing Countries*, Paris: OECD.

Antonelli, C. (ed.) (1988), *New Information Technology and Industrial Change: The Italian Case*, Dordrecht: Kluwer Academic Publishers.

Antonelli, C. (ed.) (1992), *The Economics of Information Networks*, Amsterdam: North-Holland.

Aoki, M. (1988), *Information, Incentives, and Bargaining in the Japanese Economy*, Cambridge: Cambridge University Press.

Arrow, K.J. (1974), *The Limits of Organization*, New York: Norton.

Arrow, K.J. (1975), *Economic Development: The Present State of the Art*, Honolulu: East-West Center.

Arrow, K.J. (1979), 'The Economics of Information' in M.L. Dertouzos and Joel Moses (eds), *The Computer Age: A Twenty-Year View*, Cambridge, MA: MIT Press.

Arrow, K.J. (1984), *Collected Papers of Kenneth J. Arrow*, Volume 4, *The Economics of Information*, Oxford: Blackwell.

Arrow, K.J. (1987), 'Oral History I: An Interview' in G.R. Feiwel (ed.), *Arrow and the Ascent of Modern Economic Theory*, London: Macmillan, 191–242.

Arrow, K.J. and S. Honkapoha (eds) (1985), *Frontiers of Economics*, Oxford: Blackwell.

Arthur, W.B. (1990), 'Positive Feedbacks in the Economy', *Scientific American*, **262**, February, 80–85.

Babe, R.E. (ed.) (1994), *Information and Communication in Economics*, Dordrecht: Kluwer Academic Publishers.

Badaracco, Jr, J.L. (1991), *The Knowledge Link: How Firms Compete Through Strategic Alliances*, Boston: Harvard Business School Press.

Bamberg, G. and K. Spremann (eds) (1989), *Agency Theory, Information, and Incentives*, Berlin: Springer-Verlag.

Barney, J.B. and W.G. Ouchi (eds) (1986), *Organizational Economics*, San Francisco: Jossey-Bass Publishers.

Barry, J.F. (1981), 'The Economics of Outside Information and Rule 10b–5', *University of Pennsylvania Law Review*, **129**, 1307–91.

Beale, H., R. Craswell and S.C. Salop (1981), 'The Efficient Regulation of Consumer Information', *Journal of Law and Economics*, **24**, 491–544.

Benabou, R. and G. Laroque (1992), 'Using Privileged Information to Manipulate Markets: Insiders, Gurus, and Credibility', *Quarterly Journal of Economics*, **107**, 921–58.

Beniger, J.R. (1986), *The Control Revolution: Technological and Economic Origins of the Information Society*, Cambridge MA: Harvard University Press.

Benito, G.R.G., C.A. Solberg and L.S. Welch (1991), *An Exploration of the Information Behaviour of Norwegian Exporters*, Working Paper No. 38, Sandvika: Norwegian School of Management.

Besanko, D. and D.E.M. Sappington (1987), *Designing Regulatory Policy with Limited Information*, New York: Harwood Academic Publishers.

Besen, S.M. and L.J. Raskind (1991), 'An Introduction to the Law and Economics of Intellectual Property', *Journal of Economic Perspectives*, **5**, 3–27.

Bianchi, M. and H. Moulin (1991), 'Strategic Interactions in Economics: The Game Theory Alternative' in N. De Marchi and M. Blaug (eds), *Appraising Economic Theories: Studies in the Methodology of Research Programmes*, Aldershot: Edward Elgar, 179–96.

Bikchandani, S., D. Hirshleifer and I. Welch (1992), 'A Theory of Fads, Fashion, Custom, and Cultural Change as Informational Cascades', *Journal of Political Economy*, **100**, 992–1026.

Blackorby, C. and D. Donaldson (1994), 'Information and Intergroup Transfers', *American Economic Review*, **84**, 440–47.

Blaug, M. (1994), 'Why I am not a Constructivist: Confessions of an Unrepentant Popperian' in R.E. Backhouse (ed.), *New Directions in Economic Methodology*, London: Routledge, 109–36.

Bourdieu, P. (1977), 'The Economics of Linguistic Exchanges', *Social Sciences Information*, **16**, 645–68.

Bourdieu, P. (1980), 'The Production of Belief: Contribution to an Economy of Symbolic Goods', *Media, Culture and Society*, **2**, 261–93.

Bowles, S. (1986), 'The Production Process in a Competitive Economy: Reply', *American Economic Review*, **76**, 1203–4.

Boyle, James (1992), 'A Theory of Law and Information: Copyright, Spleens, Blackmail, and Insider Training', *California Law Review*, **80**, December, 1413–540.

Bradburd, R.M. and A. Mead Over, Jr. (1982), 'Organizational Costs, "Sticky Equilibria", and Critical Levels of Concentration', *Review of Economics and Statistics*, **64**, 50–58.

Braman, S. (1990), 'Trade and Information Policy', *Media, Culture and Society*, **12**, 361–85.

Braunstein, Y.M. (1985), 'Information as a Factor of Production: Substitutability and Productivity', *The Information Society*, **3**, 261–73.

Bud-Frierman, L. (ed.) (1994), *Information Acumen: The Understanding and Use of Knowledge in Modern Business*, London: Routledge.

Calvert, R.L. (1986), *Models of Imperfect Information in Politics*, New York: Harwood Academic Publishers.

Caminal, R. (1990), 'A Dynamic Duopoly Model with Asymmetric Information', *Journal of Industrial Economics*, **38**, 315–33.

Card, D. (1990), 'Strikes and Wages: A Test of an Asymmetric Information Model', *Quarterly Journal of Economics*, **105**, 625–59.

Carter, C.F. and J.L. Ford (eds) (1972), *Uncertainty and Expectations in Economics: Essays in Honour of G.L.S. Shackle*, Oxford: Blackwell.

Carter, M.J. (1995), 'Information and the Division of Labour: Implications for the Firm's Choice of Organization', *Economic Journal*, **105**, 385–97.

Castells, M. (1989), *The Informational City: Information Technology, Economic Restructuring, and the Urban-Regional Process*, Oxford: Blackwell.

Cawkell, A.E. (1987), *Evolution of an Information Society*, London: Aslib.

Chandler, A.D. (1992), 'Organizational Capabilities and the Economic History of the Industrial Enterprise', *Journal of Economic Perspectives*, **6**, 79–100.

Cherniak, C. (1986), *Minimal Rationality*, Cambridge MA: MIT Press.

Ciborra, C.U. (1993), *Teams, Markets and Systems: Business Innovation and Information Technology*, Cambridge: Cambridge University Press.

Cleveland, H. (1987), 'The Twilight of Hierarchy: Speculations on the Global Information Society', *International Journal of Technology Management*, **2**, 45–66.

Cohen, W.M. and D.A. Levinthal (1989), 'Innovation and Learning: The Two Faces of R&D', *Economic Journal*, **99**, 569–96.

Colander, D.C. and A.W. Coats (eds) (1989), *The Spread of Economic Ideas*, Cambridge: Cambridge University Press.

Compaine, B.M. (1981), 'Shifting Boundaries in the Information Marketplace', *Journal of Communication*, **31**, 132–42.

Computer Science and Telecommunications Board, National Research Council (1994), *Realizing the Information Future: The Internet and Beyond*, Washington DC: National Academy Press.

Cott, J. (1974), *Stockhausen: Conversations with the Composer*, London: Picador.

Cremer, J. and Khalil, F. (1992), 'Gathering Information Before Signing a Contract', *American Economic Review*, **82**, 566–78.

Cronholm, M. and R. Sandell (1981), 'Scientific Information: A Review of Research', *Journal of Communication*, **31**, 85–96.

Daly, G. and T. Mayor (1980), 'Estimating the Value of a Missing Market: The Economics of Directory Assistance', *Journal of Law and Economics*, **23**, 147–66.

Dasgupta, Partha and Paul A. David (1987), 'Information Disclosure and the Economics of Science and Technology' in G.R. Feiwel (ed.), *Arrow and the Ascent of Modern Economic Theory*, London: Macmillan, 519–42.

Dedijer, S. and N. Jéquier (1987), *Intelligence for Economic Development: An Inquiry into the Role of the Knowledge Industry*, Oxford: Berg.

Dervin, B. (1994), 'Information – Democracy', *Journal of the American Society for Information Science*, **45**, 369–85.

Dervin, B. and M. Nilan (1986), 'Information Needs and Uses', *Annual Review of Information Science and Technology (ARIST)*, **21**, 3–33.

Devlin, K. (1991), *Logic and Information*, New York: Cambridge University Press.

Diamond, P. and M. Rothschild (eds) (1978), *Uncertainty in Economics: Readings and Exercises*, New York: Academic Press.

Doessel, D.P. (1992), *The Economics of Medical Diagnosis: Technological Change and Health Expenditure*, Aldershot: Avebury.

Dosi, G. and M. Egidi (1991), 'Substantive and Procedural Uncertainty', *Journal of Evolutionary Economics*, **1**, 145–68.

Dretske, F. (1981), *Knowledge and the Flow of Information*, Cambridge, MA: MIT Press.

Drucker, P.F. (1993), 'The Rise of the Knowledge Society', *Dialogue*, **104**, 13–18.

Earl, P. (1983), *The Economic Imagination: Towards a Behavioural Analysis of Choice*, Armonk NY: M.E. Sharpe.

Earl, P.E. (1988), 'Introduction' in Peter E. Earl (ed.), *Behavioural Economics, Volume I*, Aldershot: Edward Elgar.

Earl, P.E. (1990), 'Economics and Psychology: A Survey', *Economic Journal*, **100**, 718–55.

Earl, P.E. (1994), *The Corporate Imagination: How Big Companies Make Mistakes*, Armonk NY: M.E. Sharpe.

Easterbrook, W.T. (1960), 'Problems in the Relationship of Communication and Economic History', *Journal of Economic History*, **20**, 559–65.

Eaton, J. and G.M. Grossman (1986), 'The Provision of Information as Marketing Strategy', *Oxford Economic Papers*, NS. 80, 166–84.

Eatwell, J., M. Milgate and P. Newman (eds) (1989), *Allocation, Information and Markets*, London: Macmillan.

Eliasson, G., S. Folster, T. Lindberg, T. Pousette and E. Taymaz (1990), *The Knowledge Based Information Economy*, Stockholm: Industrial Institute for Economic and Social Research.

Engelbrecht, H.-J. (1985), 'An Exposition of the Information Sector Approach with Special Reference to Australia', *Prometheus*, **3**, 370–86.

Engels, F., 'Letter to Bloch', quoted by V. Venable (1966), *Human Nature: The Marxian View*, Meridian Books.

Enos, J.L. (1989), 'Transfer of Technology', *Asian-Pacific Economic Literature*, **3**, 3–37.

Enos, J. (1991), *The Creation of Technological Capability in Developing Countries*, London: Pinter Publishers.

Feltham, G.A., A.H. Amershi and W.T. Ziemba (eds), *Economic Analysis of Information and Contracts: Essays in Honor of J.E. Butterworth*, Boston: Kluwer Academic Publishers.

Forester, T. (1992), 'Megatrends or Megamistakes? What Ever Happened to the Information Society?', *The Information Society*, **8**, 133–46.

Forges, F. (1990), 'Equilibria with Communication in a Job Market Example', *Quarterly Journal of Economics*, **105**, 375–98.

Foster, J. (1993), 'Economics and the Self-Organisation Approach: Alfred Marshall Revisited', *Economic Journal*, **103**, 975–91.

Friedman, D.D., W.M. Landes and R.A. Posner (1991), 'Some Economics of Trade Secret Law', *Journal of Economic Perspectives*, **5**, 61–72.

Fulk, J. and C. Steinfeld (eds), *Organizations and Communication Technology*, London: Sage Publications.

Galatin, M. and R.D. Leiter (eds) (1981), *Economics of Information*, Boston: Martinus Nijhoff Publishing.

Gerrard, B. (1994), 'Beyond Rational Expectations: A Constructive Interpretation of Keynes's Analysis of Behaviour Under Uncertainty', *Economic Journal*, **104**, 327–37.

Gold, B. (1991), 'Towards the Increasing Integration of Management Functions: Needs and Illustrative Advances' in B. Gold (ed.), *On the Increasing Role of Technology in Corporate Policy*, Special Publication of *International Journal of Technology Management*, Geneva: Interscience Enterprises.

Goodhart, C.A.E. (1975), *Money, Information and Uncertainty*, London: Macmillan.

Gort, M., H. Grabowski and R. McGuckin (1985), 'Organizational Capital and the Choice between Specialization and Diversification', *Managerial and Decision Economics*, **6**, 2–10.

Gradstein, M. (1992), 'Time Dynamics and Incomplete Information in the Private Provision of Public Goods', *Journal of Political Economy*, **100**, 581–97.

Green, J. (1985), 'Differential Information, the Market and Incentive Compatibility' in K.J. Arrow and S. Honkapohja (eds), *Frontiers of Economics*, Oxford: Blackwell, 178–99.

Greenwood, J. and R.P. McAfee (1991), 'Externalities and Asymmetric Information', *Quarterly Journal of Economics*, **106**, 103–21.

Griliches, Z. (1980), 'Hybrid Corn Revisited: A Reply', *Econometrica*, **48**, 1463–5.

Griliches, Z. (1990), 'Patent Statistics as Economic Indicators: A Survey', *Journal of Economic Literature*, **28**, 1661–707.

Grinols, E.L. (1987), *Uncertainty and the Theory of International Trade*, New York: Harwood Academic Publishers.

Grossman, G.M. and H. Horn (1988), 'Infant-Industry Protection Reconsidered: The Case of Informational Barriers to Entry', *Quarterly Journal of Economics*, **103**, 767–87.

Grossman, S. (1989), *The Informational Role of Prices*, Cambridge MA: MIT Press.

Gudeman, S. (1986), *Economics as Culture: Models and Metaphors of Livelihood*, London: Routledge & Kegan Paul.

Haas, E.B. (1990), *When Knowledge is Power: Three Models of Change in International Organizations*, Berkeley: University of California Press.

Habermas, J. (1984), *The Theory of Communicative Action, Vol. One: Reason and the Rationalization of Society* (translated by T. McCarthy), Boston: Beacon Press.

Hahn, F. (ed.) (1989), *The Economics of Missing Markets, Information, and Games*, Oxford: Clarendon Press.

Harris, J. (1986), 'Spies Who Sparked the Industrial Revolution', *New Scientist*, 22 May, 42–3, 46–7.

Hayes, R.M. (ed.) (1985), *Libraries and the Information Economy of California*, Los Angeles: GSLIS/University of California Los Angeles.

Heiner, R.A. (1983), 'The Origin of Predictable Behavior', *American Economic Review*, **83**, 560–95.

Heller, W.P., R.M. Starr and D.A. Starrett (eds) (1986), *Uncertainty, Information and Communication: Essays in Honor of Kenneth J. Arrow*, Cambridge: Cambridge University Press.

Hendricks, K. and R.H. Porter (1988), 'An Empirical Study of an Auction with Asymmetric Information', *American Economic Review*, **78**, 865–83.

Hepworth, M. and K. Ducatel (1992), *Transport in the Information Age: Wheels and Wires*, London: Belhaven Press.

Hey, J.D. and P.J. Lambert (eds) (1987), *Surveys in the Economics of Uncertainty*, Oxford: Blackwell.

Hicks, J.R. (1939), *Value and Capital*, Oxford: Oxford University Press.

Himmelstrand, U. (ed.) (1992), *Interfaces in Economic and Social Analysis*, London: Routledge.

Hirschman, A.O. (1984), 'Against Parsimony: Three Easy Ways of Complicating Some Categories of Economic Discourse', *American Economic Review*, **74**, 89–90.

Hirshleifer, J. (1989), *Time, Uncertainty, and Information*, Oxford: Blackwell.

Hirshleifer, J. and J.G. Riley (1992), *The Analytics of Uncertainty and Information*, Cambridge: Cambridge University Press.

Hogarth, R.M. and M.W. Reder (eds) (1987), *Rational Choice: The Contrast Between Economics and Psychology*, Chicago: University of Chicago Press.

Holland, J.H. and J.H. Miller (1991), 'Artificial Adaptive Agents in Economic Theory', *American Economic Review*, **81**, 365–70.

Huber, G.P. (1984), 'The Nature and Design of Post-Industrial Organizations', *Management Science*, **30**, 928–51.

Hutchison, T.W. (1977), *Knowledge and Ignorance in Economics*, Chicago: University of Chicago Press.

Information Infrastructure Task Force (1993), *The National Information Infrastructure: Agenda for Action*, Washington DC: NTIA, US Department of Commerce.

Ippolito, R.A. (1989), 'Efficiency with Costly Information: A Study of Mutual Fund Performance, 1965–1984', *Quarterly Journal of Economics*, **104**, 1–23.

Isard, W. (1989), 'Learning, Problem Solving, and Information Research and Development' in *Arms Races, Arms Control, and Conflict Analysis*, New York: Cambridge University Press.

Itami, H. (1987), *Mobilizing Invisible Assets*, Cambridge MA: Harvard University Press.

Johansson, J.K. and A. Goldman (1979), 'Income, Search, and the Economics of Information Theory: An Empirical Analysis', *Applied Economics*, **11**, 435–49.

Jonscher, C. (1983), 'Information Resources and Economic Productivity', *Information Economics and Policy*, **1**, 13–35.

Jussawalla, M. (1992), *The Economics of Intellectual Property in a World Without Frontiers: A Study of Computer Software*, New York: Greenwood Press.

Jussawalla, M. (ed.) (1992), *Global Telecommunications Policies: The Challenge of Change*, London: Greenwood Press.

Jussawalla, M. and D.M. Lamberton (eds) (1982), *Communication Economics and Development*, New York: Pergamon Press.

Jussawalla, M., D.M. Lamberton and N.D. Karunaratne (eds) (1988), *The Cost of Thinking: Information Economies of Ten Pacific Countries*, Norwood NJ: Ablex.

Katz, M. (1986), 'The Role of the Legal System in Technological Innovation and Economic Growth' in R. Landau and N. Rosenberg (eds), *The Positive Sum Strategy: Harnessing Technology for Economic Growth*, Washington DC: National Academy Press, 168–89.

Kennan, J. and R.B. Wilson (1993), 'Bargaining with Private Information', *Journal of Economic Literature*, **31**, 45–104.

King, D.W., N.K. Roderer and H.A. Olsen (eds) (1982), *Key Papers in the Economics of Information*, White Plains NY: Knowledge Industry Publications for American Society for Information Science.

Kitch, E.W. (1977), 'The Nature and Function of the Patent System', *Journal of Law and Economics*, **20**, 265–90.

Knight, F.H. (1921), *Risk, Uncertainty, and Profit*, New York: Houghton Mifflin.

Kochen, M. (1980), 'Coping with Complexity', *Omega*, **8**, 11–20.

Kochen, M. (ed.) (1975), *Information for Action: From Knowledge to Wisdom*, New York: Academic Press.

Kochen, M. and J.C. Donohue (eds) (1976), *Information for the Community*, Chicago: American Library Association.

Kornai, J. (1990), 'The Affinity Between Ownership Forms and Coordination Mechanisms: The Common Experience of Reform in Socialist Countries', *Journal of Economic Perspectives*, **4**, 131–47.

Laffont, J.J. (1989), _The Economics of Uncertainty and Information_, Cambridge MA: MIT Press.

Lamberton, D.M. (1965), _The Theory of Profit_, Oxford: Blackwell.

Lamberton, D.M. (1976), 'National Policy for Economic Information', _International Social Science Journal_, **28**, 449–65.

Lamberton, D.M. (1978), 'The Economics of Communication' in S.A. Rahim, D.M. Lamberton, D. Wedemeyer, J. Holmstrom, J. Middeleton and B. Hudson, _Planning Methods, Models, and Organization: A Review Study for Communication Policy Making and Planning_, Honolulu: East-West Center, 21–97.

Lamberton, D.M. (1991), 'The Information and Communication Industries' Globalization and Regionalization: The Current Trends and Future Prospects', _Proceedings of KISDI Conference on Globalization, Regionalization and Informatization_, Seoul: Korea Information Society Development Institute.

Lamberton, D.M. (1991), 'Information Policy: A National Imperative?' in M. Costa and M. Easson (eds), _Australian Industry: What Policy?_, Sydney: Pluto Press, 207–18.

Lamberton, D.M. (1992), 'Information Economics: "Threatened Wreckage" or New Paradigm?' in U. Himmelstrand (ed.), _Interfaces in Economic and Social Analysis_, London: Routledge, 113–23.

Lamberton, D.M. (1992), 'Information, Exploratory Behaviour and the Design of Organizations', _Human Systems Management_, **11**, 61–5.

Lamberton, D.M. (1993), 'The Information Economy Revisited' in R.E. Babe (ed.), _Information and Communication in Economics_, Dordrecht: Kluwer Academic Publishers, 1–33.

Lamberton, D.M. (1994), 'Information and Organization: Questions and Clues' in M. Feeney and M. Grieves (eds), _Changing Information Technologies: Research Challenges in the Economics of Information_, London: Bowker Saur, 293–302.

Lamberton, D.M. (1994), 'Intellectual Property and Innovation' in M. Dodgson and R. Rothwell (eds), _Handbook of Industrial Innovation_, Aldershot: Edward Elgar, 301–10.

Lamberton, D.M. (1994), 'The Information Revolution in the Asian-Pacific Region', _Asian-Pacific Economic Literature_, **8**, 31–57.

Lamberton, D.M. (1995), 'Organizational Capital: An Information-Theoretic Approach', _International Journal of New Ideas_, **4**, 33–8.

Lamberton, D.M. (1995), 'The Impact of Regions on the Future of Emerging Markets in IT and Trade' in M. Jussawalla (ed.), _Telecommunications: Bridge to the 21st Century_, Amsterdam: Elsevier Science Publishers, 39–61.

Lamberton, D.M. (forthcoming), 'Infrastructure: A Nebulous and Overworked Construct?', _International Journal of Technology Management_.

Lamberton, D.M. (forthcoming), 'Telecommunications and Economic Growth: The Direction of Causality' in P. Droege (ed.), _Intelligent Environments_, Amsterdam: Elsevier Science Publishers.

Lamberton, D.M. (ed.) (1971), _Economics of Information and Knowledge_, Harmondsworth: Penguin Books.

Lamberton, D.M. (ed.) (1974), _The Information Revolution_, Philadelphia: The Annals of the American Academy of Political and Social Science, Volume 412.

Lamberton, D.M. (ed.) (1995), _Beyond Competition: The Future of Telecommunications_, Amsterdam: Elsevier Science Publishers.

Landes, D.S. (1983), _Revolution in Time: Clocks and the Making of the Modern World_, Cambridge MA: Harvard University Press.

Langlois, R.N. (1982), 'Systems Theory and the Meaning of Information', _Journal of the American Society for Information Science_, **33**, 396–406.

Langlois, R.N. (ed.) (1986), _Economics as a Process: Essays in the New Institutional Economics_, Cambridge: Cambridge University Press.

Langlois, R.N. (1988), 'Economic Change and the Boundaries of the Firm', _Journal of Institutional and Theoretical Economics_, **144**, 635–57.

Lee, C.S. and E.D. Gomez (1992), 'The Contribution of the Information Sector to the Industrial Growth of Korea', _Media Asia_, **19**, 156–64.

Leijonhufvud, A. (1981), _Information and Coordination: Essays in Macroeconomic Theory_, Oxford: Oxford University Press.

Lewis, T.R. and D.E.M. Sappington (1991), 'Technological Change and the Boundaries of the Firm', *American Economic Review*, **81**, 887–900.

Loasby, B.J. (1976), *Choice, Complexity and Ignorance: An Inquiry into Economic Theory and the Practice of Decision-Making*, Cambridge: Cambridge University Press.

Loasby, B.J. (1986), 'Competition and Imperfect Knowledge: The Contribution of G.B. Richardson', *Scottish Journal of Political Economy*, **33**, 145–58.

Luostarinen, R. and L. Welch (1990), *International Business Operations*, Helsinki: Helsinki School of Economics.

McCabe, K.A., A.J. Rassenti and V.L. Smith (1992), 'Designing Call Auction Institutions: Is Double Dutch the Best?', *Economic Journal*, **102**, 24–36.

McCain, R.A. (1981), 'Tradition and Innovation: Some Economics of the Creative Arts, Science, Scholarship, and Technical Development' in M. Galatin and R.D. Leiter (eds), *Economics of Information*, 173–204.

McConnell, S. (1989), 'Strikes, Wages, and Private Information', *American Economic Review*, **79**, 801–15.

Macdonald, S. (1990), *Technology and the Tyranny of Export Controls: Whisper Who Dares*, London: Macmillan.

Macdonald, S. (1995), 'Learning to Change: An Information Perspective on Learning in the Organization', *Organization Science*, **6**, 557–68.

Macdonald, S. (forthcoming), *The Information Perspective*, Oxford: Oxford University Press.

Macdonald, S., D.M. Lamberton and T.D. Mandeville (eds) (1983), *The Trouble with Technology: Explorations in the Process of Technological Change*, London: Frances Pinter.

McKenna, C.J. (1986) *The Economics of Uncertainty*, Brighton: Wheatsheaf Books.

McNulty, P.J. (1984), 'On the Nature and Theory of Economic Organization: The Role of the Firm Reconsidered', *History of Political Economy*, **16**, 233–53.

Machina, M.J. (1987), 'Choice Under Uncertainty: Problems Solved and Unsolved', *Journal of Economic Perspectives*, **1**, 121–54.

Machlup, F. (1962), *The Production and Distribution of Knowledge in the United States*, Princeton, NJ: Princeton University Press.

Machlup, Fritz (1979), 'An Economist's Reflections on an Institute for the Advanced Study of Information Science', *Journal of the American Society for Information Science*, **30** (2), March, 111–13.

Machlup, Fritz (1982), 'Optimum Utilization of Knowledge', *Society, Knowledge, Information, and Decisions*, **20** (1), November/December, 8–10.

Machlup, Fritz (1984), *Knowledge: Its Creation, Distribution and Economic Significance, Vol. III: The Economics of Information and Human Capital*, Princeton NJ: Princeton University Press.

Machlup, Fritz and Una Mansfield (eds) (1983), *The Study of Information: Interdisciplinary Messages*, New York: Wiley.

Magat, W.A. and W.K. Viscusi (1992), *Informational Approaches to Regulation*, Cambridge MA: MIT Press.

Maggi, R. (1989), 'Towards an Economic Theory of Barriers to Communication', *Papers of the Regional Science Association*, **66**, 131–41.

Malerba, F. (1992), 'Learning by Firms and Incremental Technical Change', *Economic Journal*, **102**, 845–59.

Malone, T.W. and J.F. Rockart (1991), 'Computers, Networks and the Corporation', *Scientific American*, **265**, 92–9.

Marschak, T. (1967), 'The Microeconomic Study of Development' in T. Marschak, T.K. Glennan, Jr. and R. Summers, *Strategy for R&D*, Berlin: Springer-Verlag, 1–12.

Marschak, J. (1974), *Economic Information, Decision and Prediction: Selected Essays, Volume II*, Boston: Reidel.

Marshall, A. (1925), *Principles of Economics*, 8th edition, London: Macmillan.

Masuda, Y. (1975), 'The Conceptual Framework of Information Economics', *IEEE Transactions on Communications*, COM–23, 1028–39.

Masuda, Y. (1990), *Managing in the Information Society: Releasing Synergy Japanese Style*, Oxford: Blackwell.

Mauro, M.J. (1982), 'Strikes as a Result of Imperfect Information', *Industrial and Labour Relations Review*, **35**, 522–38.

Meier, R.L. (1960), 'Information, Resource Use, and Economic Growth' in J.J. Spengler (ed.), *Natural Resources and Economic Growth*, Ann Arbor: Johns Hopkins University Press, 98–119.

Menou, Michel J. (ed.) (1993), *Measuring the Impact of Information on Development*, Ottawa: IDRC Books.

Miles, I. and contributors (1990), *Mapping and Measuring the Information Economy*, London: British Library Board.

Milgrom, P. (1989), 'Auctions and Bidding: A Primer', *Journal of Economic Perspectives*, **3**, 3–22.

Milgrom, P. and N. Stokey (1982), 'Information, Trade and Common Knowledge', *Journal of Economic Theory*, **26**, 17–27.

Monk, P. (1989), *Technological Change in the Information Economy*, London: Pinter Publishers.

Monk, P. (1992), 'Economic Aspects of Requirements Analysis', *Journal of Strategic Information Systems*, **1**, 84–92.

Monk, P. (1993), 'The Economic Significance of Infrastructural IT Systems', *Journal of Information Technology*, **8**, 14–21.

Moore, W.E. and M.W. Tumin (1949), 'Some Social Functions of Ignorance', *American Sociological Review*, **14**, 787–95.

Morduch, J. (1993), 'Book Review', *Journal of Economic Literature*, **31**, 931–3.

Mowshowitz, A. (1991), *On the Market Value of Information Commodities: I The Nature of Information and Information Commodities; II Supply Price; III Demand Price*, Management Report Series Nos. 90–92, Rotterdam: Rotterdam School of Management.

Mueller, D.C. (1976), 'Information, Mobility and Profit', *Kyklos*, **29**, 419–48.

Narula, U. and W.B. Pearce (1986), *Development as Communication: A Perspective on India*, Carbondale IL: Southern Illinois University Press.

Nelkin, D. (1982), 'The Control of Scientific Information', *Science*, **216**, 14 May, 704–8.

Nelson, R.R. (1980), 'Production Sets, Technological Knowledge, and R&D: Fragile and Overworked Constructs for Analysis of Productivity Growth?', *American Economic Review*, **70**, 62–7.

New York Times (1989), 31 December, 10E.

Noll, R.G. (1993), 'The Economics of Information: A User's Guide' in *The Knowledge Economy: The Nature of Information in the 21st Century*, Nashville, TN: Institute for Information Studies, 25–52.

Nora, S. and A. Minc (1980), *The Computerization of Society*, Cambridge MA: MIT Press.

O'Brien, D.P. and D. Swann (1968), *Information Agreements, Competition and Efficiency*, London: Macmillan.

O'Brien, R.C. (ed.) (1983), *Information, Economics and Power: The North-South Dimension*, Boulder CO: Westview Press.

OECD (1981), *Information Activities, Electronics and Telecommunications Technologies: Impact on Employment, Growth and Trade, Volume I*, Paris: OECD.

OECD (1986), *Trends in the Information Economy*, Paris: OECD.

OECD (1992), *Information Networks and New Technologies: Opportunities and Policy Implications for the 1990s*, Paris: OECD.

Olsen, H.A. (1971), *The Economics of Information: Bibliography and Commentary on the Literature*, Washington DC: American Society for Information Sciences.

Ordover, J.A. (1991), 'A Patent System for Both Diffusion and Exclusion', *Journal of Economic Perspectives*, **5**, 43–60.

Osberg, L., E.N. Wolff and W.J. Baumol (1989), *The Information Economy: The Implications of Unbalanced Growth*, Halifax, Nova Scotia: Institute for Research on Public Policy.

Ozga, S.A. (1965), *Expectations in Economic Theory*, London: Weidenfeld and Nicolson.

Parker, M.M., R.J. Benson and H.D. Trainor (1988), *Information Economics: Linking Business Performance to Information Technology*, London: Prentice-Hall.

Penniman, W.D. (1989), 'New Developments and Future Prospects for Electronic Databases', *Bulletin of the American Society for Information Science*, **15** (6), August/September, 16.

Penrose, E.T. (1980), *The Theory of Growth of the Firm*, 2nd edition, Oxford: Blackwell.

Perelman, M. (1991), *Information, Social Relations and the Economics of High Technology*, London: Macmillan.

Perritt, Jr, H.H. (1989), 'Government Information Goes On-Line', *Technology Review*, **92**, 60–68.

Phelps, C.E. (1992), 'Diffusion of Information in Medical Care', *Journal of Economic Perspectives*, **3**, 23–42.

Phlips, L. (1988), *The Economics of Imperfect Information*, Cambridge: Cambridge University Press.

Prendergast, C. (1993), 'A Theory of "Yes Men"', *American Economic Review*, **83**, 757–70.

Prodrick, G. (1980), 'The Peculiar and Complex Economic Properties of Information', *Canadian Journal of Information Science*, **5**, 89–92.

Radner, R. (1992), 'Hierarchy: The Economics of Managing', *Journal of Economic Literature*, **30**, 1382–415.

Rescher, N. (1989), *Cognitive Economy: The Economic Dimension of the Theory of Knowledge*, Pittsburgh: University of Pittsburgh Press.

Richardson, G.B. (1960), *Information and Investment: A Study in the Working of the Competitive Economy*, Oxford: Oxford University Press.

Robbins, Lord (1968), *The Theory of Economic Development in the History of Economic Thought*, London: Macmillan.

Romer, P. (1993), 'Ideas and Things', *The Economist*, **328**, 11 September, 64, 67–8.

Romer, P. (1994), 'New Goods, Old Theory, and the Welfare Costs of Trade Restrictions', *Journal of Development Economics*, **43**, 5–38.

Rosenberg, N. (1994), 'Telecommunications: Complex, Uncertain, and Path-Dependent' in *Exploring the Black Box: Technology, Economics, and History*, Cambridge: Cambridge University Press.

Rosing, J. (1970), 'The Formation of Groups for Cooperative Decision Making Under Uncertainty', *Econometrica*, **38**, 430–48.

Rubin, M.R. (1983), *Information Economics and Policy in the United States*, Littleton CO: Libraries Unlimited.

Rubin, M.R. and M.T. Huber (1986), *The Knowledge Industry in the United States, 1960–1980*, Princeton NJ: Princeton University Press.

Rubinstein, A. (1990), 'Introduction' in A. Rubinstein (ed.), *Game Theory in Economics*, Aldershot: Edward Elgar.

Sah, R.K. and J.E. Stiglitz (1985), 'Human Fallibility and Economic Organization', *American Economic Review*, **75**, 292–7.

Sauer, C. (1993), *Why Information Systems Fail: A Case Study Approach*, Henley-on-Thames: Alfred Waller.

Schement, J.R. (1990), 'The Origins of the Information Society in the United States: Competing Visions' in J. Salvaggio (ed.), *The Information Society*, New York: Lawrence Erhlbaum, 29–50.

Schumpeter, J.A. (1953), *History of Economic Analysis*, New York: Oxford University Press.

Scotchmer, S. (1991), 'Standing on the Shoulders of Giants: Cumulative Research and the Patent Law', *Journal of Economic Perspectives*, **5**, 29–41.

Sertel, M.R. and A. Steinherr (1984), 'Information, Incentives, and the Design of Efficient Institutions', *Journal of Institutional and Theoretical Economics*, **140**, 233–46.

Shackle, G.L.S. (1967), *The Years of High Theory: Invention and Tradition in Thought 1926–1939*, Cambridge: Cambridge University Press.

Shin, H.S. (1989), 'Book Review', *Economic Journal*, **99**, 864–5.

Shubik, M. (1967), 'Information, Rationality and Free Choice in a Future Democratic Society', *Daedalus*, **96**, 771–8; reprinted in D.M. Lamberton (ed.) (1971), *Economics of Information and Knowledge*.

Shubik, M. (1985), *A Game-Theoretic Approach to Political Economy*, Cambridge MA: MIT Press.

Shurmer, M. (1993), 'An Investigation into Sources of Network Externalities in the Packaged PC Software Market', *Information Economics and Policy*, **5**, 231–51.

Silverstone, R. and E. Hirsch (1992), *Consuming Technologies: Media and Information in Domestic Spaces*, London: Routledge.

Simon, H.A. (1991), 'Organizations and Markets', *Journal of Economic Perspectives*, **5**, 25–44.

Slack, J.D. and F. Fejes (eds) (1987), *The Ideology of the Information Age*, Norwood NJ: Ablex Publishing.

Smythe, D.W. (1977), 'Communications: Blindspot of Western Marxism', *Canadian Journal of Political and Social Theory*, **1**, Fall, 1–27.

Snell, A. (1989), 'Information, Rational Expectations and Macroeconomic Modelling', *Journal of Economic Surveys*, **3**, 179–98.

Sowell, T. (1980), *Knowledge and Decisions*, New York: Basic Books.

Spence, A.M. (1974), 'An Economist's View of Information', *Annual Review of Information Science and Technology (ARIST)*, **9**, 57–78.

Spence, A.M. (1974), *Market Signalling: Informational Transfer in Hiring and Related Screening Processes*, Cambridge MA: Harvard University Press.

Spero, J.E. (1982), 'Information: The Policy Void', *Foreign Policy*, **48**, Fall, 139–56.

Stigler, G.J. (1961), 'The Economics of Information', *Journal of Political Economy*, **69**, 213–25, reprinted in D.M. Lamberton (ed.) (1971), *Economics of Information and Knowledge*.

Stiglitz, J.E. (1985), 'Information and Economic Analysis: A Perspective', *Economic Journal*, Supplement to Vol. 95, 21–41.

Stinchcombe, A.L. (1990), *Information and Organizations*, Berkeley: University of California Press.

Strassman, P.A. (1990), *The Business Value of Computers: An Executive's Guide*, New Canaan CT: Information Economics Press.

Swann, P. (1993), *New Technologies and the Firm: Innovation and Competition*, London: Routledge.

Taylor, L.D. (1994), *Telecommunications Demand in Theory and Practice*, Dordrecht: Kluwer Academic Publishers.

Teece, D.J., R. Rumelt, G. Dosi and S. Winter (1994), 'Understanding Corporate Coherence: Theory and Evidence', *Journal of Economic Behavior and Organization*, **52**, 1085–116.

Thomsen, E.F. (1992), *Prices and Knowledge: A Market-Process Perspective*, London: Routledge.

Tinbergen, J. (1978), 'Alternative Forms of International Co-operation: Comparing Their Efficiency', *International Social Science Journal*, **30**, 223–37.

Tomasini, L.M. (1974), 'The Economics of Information: A Survey', *Economie Appliquée*, **27**, 319–27.

Tomer, J.F. (1987), *Organizational Capital*, New York: Praeger.

Torr, C. (1988), *Equilibrium, Expectations and Information*, Oxford: Blackwell.

Vaillancourt, F. (1982), *The Economics of Language and Language Planning*, Cahier 8222, Department de Sciences Economiques, Université de Montréal.

Vernon, R. (1970), 'Organization as a Scale Factor in the Growth of Firms' in J.W. Markham and G.F. Papanek (eds), *Industrial Organization and Economic Development*, New York: Houghton Mifflin.

Vines, D. and A. Stevenson (eds) (1991), *Information, Strategy and Public Policy*, Oxford: Blackwell.

Wallich, P. (1994), 'Trends in Communications: Wire Pirates', *Scientific American*, **270**, 72–80.

Weizsäcker, C.C. von (1984), 'The Costs of Substitution', *Econometrica*, **52**, 1085–116.

Welch, R.L. (1980), 'Vertical and Horizontal Communication in Economic Processes', *Review of Economic Studies*, **47**, 733–46.

Westin, A.F. (ed.) (1971), *Information Technology in a Democracy*, Cambridge MA: Harvard University Press.

Williamson, O.E. (ed.) (1990), *Organization Theory: From Chester Barnard to the Present and Beyond*, New York: Oxford University Press.

Wolfe, A.W. (1977), 'The Supranational Organization of Production: An Evolutionary Perspective', *Current Anthropology*, **18**, 615–35.

Wright, K. (1990), 'Trends in Communication: The Road to the Global Village', *Scientific American*, **262**, 57–66.

Name Index

The International Library of Critical Writings in Economics

1. Multinational Corporations
   Mark Casson

2. The Economics of Innovation
   Christopher Freeman

3. Entrepreneurship
   Mark Casson

4. International Investment
   Peter J. Buckley

5. Game Theory in Economics
   Ariel Rubinstein

6. The History of Economic Thought
   Mark Blaug

7. Monetary Theory
   Thomas Mayer

8. Joint Production of Commodities
   Neri Salvadori and Ian Steedman

9. Industrial Organization
   Oliver E. Williamson

10. Growth Theory (Volumes I, II and III)
    R. Becker and E. Burmeister

11. Microeconomics: Theoretical and Applied (Volumes I, II and III)
    Robert E. Kuenne

12. The Economics of Health (Volumes I and II)
    A.J. Culyer

13. Recent Developments in Macroeconomics (Volumes I, II and III)
    Edmund S. Phelps

14. Urban and Regional Economics
    Paul C. Cheshire and Alan W. Evans

15. Modern Public Finance (Volumes I and II)
    A.B. Atkinson

16. Exchange Rate Economics (Volumes I and II)
    Ronald MacDonald and Mark P. Taylor

The Economics of Increasing Returns
Geoffrey Heal

The Balance of Payments
Michael J. Artis

Cost-Benefit Analysis
Arnold Harberger and Glenn P. Jenkins

The Economics of Unemployment
P.N. Junankar

Mathematical Economics
Graciela Chichilnisky

Economic Growth in the Long Run
Bart van Ark

Gender in Economic and Social History
K.J. Humphries and J. Lewis

The Economics of Local Finance and Fiscal Federalism
Wallace Oates

Privatization in Developing and Transitional Economies
Colin Kirkpatrick and Paul Cook

Input-Output Analysis
Heinz Kurz and Christian Lager

The Economics of Global Warming
Tom Tietenberg

Political Business Cycles
Bruno Frey

The Economics of the Arts
Ruth Towse

The Economics of Energy
Paul Stevens

The Economics of Intellectual Property
Ruth Towse

Ecological Economics
Robert Costanza, Charles Perrings and Cutler Cleveland

The Economics of Tourism
Clem Tisdell

The Economics of Productivity
Edward Wolff

The Economics of Organization and Bureaucracy
Peter Jackson

Independent Central Banks and Economic Performance
Sylvester Eijffinger

The Economics of the Commodity Markets
David Greenaway and Wyn Morgan

Realism and Economics: Studies in Ontology
Tony Lawson

Women in the Labor Market
Marianne A. Ferber

New Developments in Game Theory
Eric S. Maskin

Economic Demography
T. Paul Schultz